The Anthropology of Isla

"This is a remarkable work that contains some of the classic and contemporary essays representing the ethnographic and conceptual issues within the anthropology of Islam arena. This fine collection will undoubtedly become the standard work for both research and teaching purposes. The volume provides an accessible sophisticated treatment of the field that will engage students and scholars who want to develop a more nuanced perspective and understanding of the Islamic world."

Raymond Scupin, *Lindenwood University, USA*

"This is without a doubt the finest collection of essays on the anthropology of Islam available today. Kreinath has brought together a set of path breaking theoretical texts with some of the richest ethnographic accounts of Muslim societies produced by anthropologists. The result is the strongest demonstration to date of anthropology's unique contribution to our understanding of this religious tradition."

Charles Hirschkind, *University of California, Berkeley, USA*

The Anthropology of Islam Reader brings together a rich variety of ethnographic work, offering an insight into various forms of Islam as practiced in different geographic, social, and cultural contexts. Topics explored include Ramadān and the *hajj*, the Feast of Sacrifice, and the representation of Islam. An extensive introduction and bibliography helps students develop their understanding of the variety of methodological and theoretical approaches involved in the anthropological study of Islam. In his selections, Jens Kreinath highlights the diversity of practices and themes that were formative for this field of study, making this essential reading for students of Islam at undergraduate and graduate level.

Jens Kreinath is an Assistant Professor in the Department of Anthropology at Wichita State University, USA.

The Anthropology of Islam Reader

Edited by Jens Kreinath

Routledge
Taylor & Francis Group
LONDON AND NEW YORK

First published in 2012
by Routledge
2 Park Square, Milton Park, Abingdon, Oxon OX14 4RN

Simultaneously published in the USA and Canada
by Routledge
711 Third Avenue, New York, NY 10017

Routledge is an imprint of the Taylor & Francis Group, an informa business

British Library Cataloguing in Publication Data
A catalogue record for this book is available from the British Library

Library of Congress Cataloging in Publication Data
The anthropology of Islam reader / edited by Jens Kreinath.
p. cm.
Includes bibliographical references and index.
1. Islam–Study and teaching. 2. Anthropology of religion–Islamic countries. 3. Islamic sociology. 4. Anthropology–Methodology.
I. Kreinath, Jens, 1967–
BP42.A58 2011
306.6′97–dc23 2011023681

ISBN: 978-0-415-78024-7 (hbk)
ISBN: 978-0-415-78025-4 (pbk)

Typeset in Baskerville by
HWA Text and Data Management, London

MIX
Paper from
responsible sources
FSC
www.fsc.org
FSC® C004839

Printed and bound in Great Britain by
CPI Antony Rowe, Chippenham, Wiltshire

For Rana Kreinath

Contents

Fasting during the month of Ramadān

Pilgrimage to Mecca

Feast of sacrifice

Almsgiving

Situating anthropology

Representing Islam

Acknowledgments

Every effort has been made to trace copyright holders and obtain permission to reproduce material. Any errors or omissions brought to the attention of the publisher will be remedied in future editions.

Ahmed, Akbar S., *Toward Islamic Anthropology: Definition, Dogma and Directions*, © Herndon: International Institute of Islāmic Thought, 1988.

Asad, Talal, *The Idea of an Anthropology of Islam*, © Washington, DC: Georgetown University, Center for Contemporary Arab Studies, 1986.

Benthall, Jonathan, "Financial Worship: The Quranic Injunction to Almsgiving," © *Journal of the Royal Anthropological Institute*, 5 (1999): 27–42.

Bowen, John R., "On Scriptural Essentialism and Ritual Variation: Muslim Sacrifice in Sumatra and Morocco," © *American Ethnologist*, 19 (1992): 656–671.

Cooper, Barbara M., "The Strength in the Song: Muslim Personhood, Audible Capital, and Hausa Women's Performance of the Hajj," © *Social Text*, 17 (1999): 87–109.

el-Zein, Abdul Hamid, "Beyond Ideology and Theology: The Search for the Anthropology of Islam," © *Annual Review of Anthropology*, 6 (1977): 227–254.

Frankl, P.J.L., "The Observance of Ramadān in Swahili-land,", © *Journal of Religion in Africa*, 26 (1996): 416–434.

Geertz, Clifford, *Islam Observed: Religious Development in Morocco and Indonesia*, © New Haven: Yale University Press, 1968: v–viii, 1–19, 95–117.

Gilsenan, Michael, *Recognizing Islam. An Anthropologists Introduction*, © London: Croom Helm, 1982: 9–22.

Henkel, Heiko, "'Between Belief and Unbelief Lies the Performance of Salat': Meaning and Efficacy of a Muslim Ritual,"© *Journal of the Royal Anthropological Institute*, 11 (2005): 487–507.

Mahmood, Saba, "Rehearsed Spontaneity and the Conventionality of Ritual: Disciplines of *Salāt*," © *American Ethnologist*, 28 (2001): 827–853.

Said, Edward W., *Covering Islam: How the Media and the Experts Determine how we see the Rest of the World*, © New York: Vintage Books, 1997: 135–173.

Schielke, Samuli "Being Good in Ramadān: Ambivalence, Fragmentation, and the Moral Self in the Lives of Young Egyptians," © *Journal of the Royal Anthropological Institute*, 15 (2009): S24–S40.

Scupin, Raymond, "The Social Significance of the *Hajj* for Thai Muslims," © *Muslim World*, 72 (1982): 25–33.

Tapper, Richard, "'Islamic Anthropology' and the 'Anthropology of Islam'", © *Anthropological Quarterly*, 68 (1995): 185–193.

Varisco, Daniel M., *Islam Obscured: The Rhetoric of Anthropological Representation*, © New York: Palgrave Macmillan, 2005: 135–162.

Weiss, Holger, "Reforming Social Welfare among Muslims: Islamic Voluntarism and other Forms of Communal Support in Northern Ghana," © *Journal of Religion in Africa*, 32 (2002): 83–109.

Werbner, Pnina, "'Sealing' the Koran: Offering and Sacrifice among Pakistani Labour Migrants," © *Cultural Dynamics*, 1 (1988): 77–97.

Preface

As usual, new ideas do not come overnight or appear as ready-made brainwaves in a heightened moment of mindful presence, but rather are planted, ripen and harvested over considerable time. Even though I got the idea for this reader and committed myself to it some while ago, it has been brought about by the efforts of many who supported this project and contributed to its realization. I would like to take this opportunity to extend my thanks and express my gratitude to those who were so kind to help me to give birth to this book and some of its ideas. Although I may not be able to acknowledge all who aided and assisted me, I want to express my gratitude to those who left their marks on its journey. First, I would like to mention Peer Moore-Jansen for generously giving me, for the first time, the chance to develop and offer a course on the anthropology of Islam at Wichita State University in Spring 2007 and 2008. I also would like to thank Faruk Birtek who invited me to teach versions of this course in the summer school sessions at Boğaziçi University from 2007 through 2009. I am thankful to William Sax for giving me the chance to teach the Anthropologie des Islam course, as well as to Frederike Faust for enthusiastically proposing my course proposal to the student commission at the University of Heidelberg.

These opportunities not only helped me to rethink and refine my syllabus, but also gave me the rewarding experience to engage with students at universities in different religious, social, and cultural contexts, and to witness their different forms of engagement, adventurousness, and excitement in learning about Islam, and the ways in which they contextualize and conceptualize it anthropologically. I thus want to thank my students, who engaged in often intense and intimate discussions and challenged me to rethink my approach to and ideas on the anthropology of Islam. In particular, I would like to mention those students who took my classes and who I recognize as having a significant impact on the development of my ideas: Randy D. Fortman, Kristen K. Waymire, Jennifer Williams, and Katherine Witsman at Wichita State University; Abdullah Ahmet, Tulin Bilgin, Deniz Duruiz, G. Burcu Ege, Sümeyye Kavuncu, Ülker Sözen, Enes Tüzgen, Dilân Yıldırım at Boğaziçi University; as well as Carolin Bralic, Davina Eggers, Frederike Faust, Arne Heise, Hans Hommens, Anna Sunik, Lisa Zuefle at the University of Heidelberg.

I am grateful to Lesley Riddle, the senior editor at Routledge, and her editorial assistants who patiently waited and repeatedly encouraged me to realize the project of this reader in the best way possible. I am further grateful for the fruitful conversations with Ivan Strenski and Daniel Varisco who helped me at different stages to conceptualize my ideas further. I also would like to thank the contributors who gave permission and generously allowed reprinting of the pieces of their academic work in this reader, as well as the anonymous reviewers of my proposal and book manuscript for their often critical, but always insightful, comments. Once the final time line for publication was established, some of my students committed considerable and invaluable time to this reader. I am grateful to Jonathan Burrow-Branine, M. Bilal Kenasari, and James Simmerman for participating in a reading group and giving valuable comments on the outline of this reader while going through my first edits. Moreover, I would like to thank Eva Bernal and Heidi Page for proofreading major parts of the main manuscript, as well as Teresa Click who not only participated in our reading group but also helped finalize this reader by assisting me on copyright clearances, formatting the manuscript, and checking bibliographic references. I would like to extend my thanks to my research assistant William Silcott for his always generous help, as well as to my colleagues and friends Mara Alagic, Deborah Ballard-Reisch, Dorothy Billings, Deborah Gordon, and Glyn Rimmington for their critical comments on my introduction. I am grateful that Jack Dettenwanger and Amy R. Leiker took the time to read through and comment upon the introductory essay. For their work on the glossary, I want to mention Teresa Click and William Silcott for assisting me in working on the Glossary of Anthropological Terms, as well as Maher Musleh, and Dan M. Varisco in their invaluable help in working on the Glossary of Islamic Terms. I also would like to thank Elizabeth Lonning for assisting me on the last edits of the galley proofs and the index.

I am thankful to everyone involved in other stages of the production of this Reader. Last, but not least, I would like to thank Refika Sarıönder who accompanied me through all stages of the Reader and passionately worked with me, and continues to give inspiring and critical comments in my endeavor to work on what can be called the anthropology of Islam.

Toward the anthropology of Islam

An introductory essay

Jens Kreinath

It is not easy to answer the question "What is the anthropology of Islam?", without becoming too simplistic.[1] However, it might be useful to outline some tentative margins for this field of study by starting with what it is not. The anthropology of Islam is not studying Islam as a world religion, the Qur'ān, or the Prophet Muhammad's life and teachings for their own sakes. It is not studying Islam as a system of beliefs and practices or its teachings of primary doctrines and pillars of faith. Nor is it about describing the essence of Islam, answering fundamental theological questions about justice, faith, and the afterlife, or outlining in the most general terms who or what, including foundational beliefs and rules of conduct, defines Muslims.

The anthropology of Islam instead aims to examine the ways in which religious, ethical, and theological teachings are instituted and work within the social world. For example, how these teachings are negotiated by Muslims within networks of social relationships and how these negotiations affect the peculiarities of everyday life and vice versa. In order to provide a better grasp of the relevance of anthropology for the study of Islam, it is prudent to first gain a thorough understanding of the methods and concepts utilized in social and cultural anthropology.

Therefore, this introductory essay outlines the theoretical and disciplinary foundations for the anthropology of Islam by exploring the following questions: What is distinctive about anthropological research? What can anthropology contribute to the study of Islam? How can the reading of anthropological texts enhance the understanding of Islam? How can reading ethnographic accounts help refine the methods of anthropological fieldwork? This essay acts as a conceptual framework allowing an outline of this Reader's design and explaining how its contributions are arranged.

What is distinctive about anthropological research?

To lay the foundation for the study of Islam from an anthropological perspective, this section will:

1. introduce fieldwork methods as the main basis for approaches to cultural anthropology;
2. account for the contributions of participant observation to anthropological study;
3. discuss the role of interviews and conversations in gaining an insider's perspective;
4. make relevant distinctions between ethnography and ethnology as different perspectives to study people; and
5. attempt to present the ways in which these distinctions can provide a conceptual and methodological venue to overcome forms of ethnocentrism using the notion of cultural relativism.

To clarify what is distinctive about the anthropological study of Islam, it is worth noting the foundations of anthropological research—specifically, how anthropology derives its body of information from the encounter of researchers with the people they study, a sub-discipline typically called social and cultural anthropology.[2] Anthropological research of this kind usually takes place over an extended time period during which the anthropologist lives with the people studied, a method called *fieldwork*.[3] In this manner, anthropologists research the human condition by looking at its economic modalities, political conditions, and cultural expressions using an appraisal of the social and religious diversity within which people practice and contest their ways of life.[4] Anthropologists, in other words, consider different aspects of social and cultural life from an inclusive perspective while acknowledging local and regional features.[5] This principle of inclusiveness is fundamental to all fieldwork-based anthropological research. In accordance with this perspective, anthropology locates its own field of research and outlines the contours of a distinct approach grounded in fieldwork prioritizing the description of unique events over the explanation of timeless structures, living people over written texts, and actual practices and discourses over idealized worldviews and normative doctrines.

As an academic discipline, anthropology is committed to studying the experiences of individuals and groups as *human agents* by focusing on how people live their lives and cope with their everyday concerns.[6] Anthropologists are interested in how social relationships unfold through kinship, affinity, and friendship as well as distinction, exclusion, and conflict in local communities.[7] They also study how acts and habits arise around religious ethics and cultural values which people adopt, adjust, and embody through their daily practices.[8] Therefore, anthropologists ask what individuals *do* and how they *decide* what they do (or intend to do) in light of social commitments, economic constraints, moral codes, and religious obligations.[9] In other terms, anthropology aims to understand the ways in which people value and reinforce their unique ways of life which materialize through words, actions, and performances.[10]

Taking a non-doctrinal but critical, empathetic stance is a necessary precondition for anthropologists in their commitment to a holistic perspective. Holism is an *essential* component to the fieldwork methods employed by anthropologists.[11] It accounts for the interconnectedness of all aspects of human life and culture, necessary to arrive upon by the basic demands of the study of human diversity in the anthropologists' attempts to overcome preconceived notions of religion and culture.[12] The aim of anthropological research is to account for how people communicate through their cultures and embody social relationships, cultural traditions, and religious practices.[13] Thus, in principle, there are no limits (other than ethical, social, or political) placed upon how anthropologists can study the ways in which people, past and present, of different cultures and religions think, act, and believe.[14]

Due to the principle of inclusiveness, anthropological research adds numerous layers to the study and understanding of human cultures and religions. Using a comprehensive point of view and resources from numerous sites, ethnographic fieldwork ultimately enhances the anthropologist's ability to integrate and correlate different, seemingly unrelated facets of social and cultural life.[15] In this regard, the advantage of an anthropological perspective is its pursuit of a holistic understanding of the people and culture under study, including the people studied, and their practices and discourses discovered through first-hand encounters.

Anthropologists become involved with the people they study through what Bronislaw Malinowski, the founder of modern British social anthropology, called "*participant observation*"; which is integral in all fieldwork methods employed in anthropology (Malinowski 1922).[16] *Observation*, as the important means of ethnographic fieldwork, often remains limited to what an anthropologist can see—bound to the distanced and theoretical gaze of the inquirer toward the people studied, even though it provides evidence of actual events or actions in real time and space.[17] *Participation*, as another key concept in anthropological research, in contrast, goes further by bringing the anthropologist into more tangible contact with the people under study and involves the senses and all aspects of body techniques, such as movement and posture, as well as taste, smell, and sound.[18] As a fieldwork method, participation involves the active role and involvement of an anthropologist in social networks. It is thus inherently pragmatic insofar as participation would require anthropologists to directly interact with people they work with by joining in their everyday activities and festivities.[19]

In both participation and observation, anthropological research requires the bodily presence of the researcher in the culture and community studied; fieldwork can thus only be conceived as "being there" (Geertz 1988).[20] The presence of the anthropologist in the field engaged in participant observation establishes a particular relationship in which unpredictable outcomes derive from their encounters with local people.[21] This also implies the emotional impact of the fieldwork experiences upon the researcher, as for example the experience of culture shock.[22] Bodily presence allows anthropologists to experience and then account for the senses in fieldwork before being able to enter the cultural level of symbolic representation through discourse.[23] Anthropologists can participate in the lives of the people by adapting local forms of perception, emotion, and cognition, by studying and speaking the local language, and by learning local styles of discourse through interviews and conversations and the analysis of linguistic ideologies.[24]

Although based on the physical presence of the anthropologist, other ethnographic methods such as *face-to-face interviews* and *conversations* reach beyond the "here and now" by entering the realms of history, discourse, and symbolic representation.[25] Due to the different bodily senses involved, anthropologists commonly distinguish between observation and participation in their research methods, on the one hand, and between conversation and interview, on the other hand, as modes through which professional relationships are established with the people being studied. Through their contact with numerous individuals in the field, anthropologists and the people under study mutually contribute to this endeavor through their differing capacities and relationships.[26]

As described above, anthropology follows the paradigms of social scientific methods and empirical research with specific focus on fieldwork methods and sites, and it operates through an integration of multiple perspectives and sensory experiences in order to achieve a holistic and comprehensive view of a people and culture. Data collected through the interpretation of different forms of sensory perception reveals the multiplicity of perspectives involved in fieldwork, allowing for singular events to be examined from a number of viewpoints.[27] Since fieldwork allows for multiple interpretations, experiences, and observations through concrete case studies, it is the possibility of multiple interpretations that leads to the questioning of universals and abstract concepts.[28]

As indicated, anthropologists collect information and data first-hand through participant observation by working with key informants as well as using conversation and different forms of interviewing techniques. In taking field notes, keeping journals or diaries, and utilizing other means of documentation including voice recording, filming or photography, anthropologists build their body of knowledge with comprehensive evidence.[29] These qualitative research methods allow anthropologists to account for the complexity and diversity of perspectives, which they—to differing degrees—seek to combine in their ethnographies using a variety of techniques of ethnographic representation, thus creating a holistic view.[30] The rhetoric of ethnographic writing can enable anthropologists to account for cultural differences by simply documenting the diversity of viewpoints without further commentary, or—by employing a different theoretical angle and epistemological framework—to unite, integrate, or blend differing viewpoints into a single point or multiple points of view in an attempt to recognize and value unique and mutually exclusive perspectives.[31] This leads anthropologists to recognize and embrace the diversity within and between these perspectives and allows recognition of the reflexive and dialogical nature of anthropological fieldwork.[32]

In this regard, anthropologists generally distinguish between two approaches in studying culture and its practices and discourses: ethnography and ethnology. *Ethnography* is the descriptive and detailed account of a culture which considers all aspects of everyday social life in specified times and places with certain individuals. Ethnographies are usually reported in written form,[33] but may also be expressed using photographs, recorded films.[34] Likewise, *ethnology* is the comparative and more theoretical study of societies and cultures through the reading and analyses of ethnographies and implementation of a conceptual framework to determine the respective points of comparison by focusing on the theoretical framework and analyzing the methodological parameters or by accounting for thematic fields and theorizing through conceptual paradigms.[35] Using grids of predominantly Western academic terminology, anthropologists try to determine not only the similarities and differences between societies and cultures within a broader framework of conceptual analysis, but they also aim to uncover their varying degrees of generality and specificity.[36] Through the methodological intersections between ethnography and ethnology, the different levels of abstraction and angles from which anthropologists study societies and cultures in varying degrees of generality and specificity mutually enhance, reinforce, and complement one another. This allows for an account of different methodological approaches, their conceptual design, and the ways in which they interact in relation to ethnographic data.[37]

In addition to various methodological approaches employed within the field through ethnography and ethnology, anthropologists further distinguish between *emic* (the insider's) and *etic* (the outsider's) perspectives, marking the researcher as a relative outsider and the informant as a relative insider with respect to local knowledge.[38] An *emic* perspective attempts to provide local information, accounts, and interpretations from the position of an insider who lives in and is intimately familiar with the community.[39] An *etic* perspective provides the insights of the researcher through the position of outsider, who learns about a society and culture through comparison, analysis, and conceptualization.[40] The aim of anthropology is finally to integrate both these perspectives in a holistic view, even though anthropological approaches may always place the emphasis differently.[41]

In ethnographic fieldwork, the anthropologist strives toward an understanding of the *emic* perspective as the viewpoint of the culture and society; the researcher attempts to uncover this perspective through the study of, and participation in, discourses and practices of local people.[42] Here, it is important to note that there is not just one *emic* perspective but multiple, often contested—if not contradictory—*emic* perspectives within a community which require documentation by the anthropologist.[43] On the other hand, in ethnological work, the anthropologist takes the *etic* perspective, reflecting on local discourses and practices from the perspective of an outsider.[44] However, it is worth noting that the *etic* perspective is not of a higher logical or categorical order,[45] but is itself the *emic* perspective of the anthropologist based on the classifications of the anthropologist's (academic) culture.[46] The terminological conjunction of participation and observation as indicated above includes the integration of these perspectives as well as the descriptive and comparative dimensions of anthropological research employed in ethnography and ethnology.[47]

Beyond the more methodological questions of the accuracy of anthropological research, it is important to note that cultures of interest to anthropologists may have fundamentally different values and belief systems from those of the researchers. The principles and premises anthropologists apply in coping with such cultural differences are crucial in overcoming *ethnocentrism*, which is the biased attempt to judge another culture based on one's own cultural values.[48] In order to gain a comprehensive understanding of the people they study, anthropologists aim to abstain from any kind of value judgments of other cultures. Commonly labeled *cultural relativism*, the anthropological attempt is to overcome cultural biases and, instead, view other cultures based only on their own value systems and, if possible, using an insider's perspective.[49] Conceptual tensions between ethnocentrism and cultural relativism become most obvious in the discourse on the universality of human rights and the exceptionality of cultural rights.[50] In cases, such as female genital mutilation[51] or when the focus is on the role of Islam, it might be difficult to abstain from their own cultural values regarding the rights of Muslim men and women.[52]

Based on first-hand information obtained through observation and direct encounter with the people studied, anthropologists question forms of knowledge and classification, as well as commonly accepted concepts and definitions, by asking what their sources of information are and how they came to know what they know. For these reasons, ethnographic fieldwork reveals sources of local knowledge and symbolic representations that go beyond what can be already known through conceptualization in anthropology and other fields of research, as, for example, in the definitions of ritual.[53] Examining the formation of anthropological theory, fieldwork, description, and comparison allows anthropologists to scrutinize commonly accepted paradigms of research and classification.[54]

Having established some theoretical and methodological foundations of anthropology as a field of research, the following section continues to describe the contributions anthropology can make to the study of Islam.

What can anthropology contribute to the study of Islam?

To specify what distinctive contributions anthropology can make to the study of Islam on the basis of its methods of ethnographic fieldwork and cross-cultural comparison, this section will:

1 account for the historical and political conditions of the study of Islam from a Western perspective;
2 question the prevalent notions of Islam in the public sphere as being identified with, or located in, the Orient and Middle East;
3 discuss the role of the distinction between Great and Little Traditions in an attempt to overcome essentialist notions of Orientalism using ethnographic research in studying Islam;
4 consider the conditions of colonialism and postcolonialism and their relevance to paradigm shifts in the anthropological study of Islam; and
5 outline the discursive formation of the theoretical and methodological foundations of the anthropology of Islam.

Since the inception of social and cultural anthropology as an academic discipline in Europe and North America, fieldwork as an empirical research method has been, and continues to be, key to radically calling into question the foundations of general, but often empirically unfounded, assumptions about the universals of humankind by grounding the formation of anthropological knowledge in the local political and historical contexts of the discipline of anthropology itself.[55] In contrast to ethnographic research carried out in other parts of the world among predominantly illiterate people[56] with fewer economic interests and political implications, anthropological approaches to Islam were still, with unique exceptions, often connected and identified with area studies, such as the anthropology of the Middle East.[57] One of the primary differences between these approaches is how explicitly they address the role of Islam from the outset.[58]

From the Western perspective, scholars in different disciplines working on the Middle East tended (and still tend) to identify Islam with the *Orient* and, by contrast, confine Christianity with the *Occident*.[59] This tendency can be seen most clearly in earlier descriptions of Muslims represented through travel reports and the first anthropological accounts. Oversimplifying the complexities of historical dynamics, scholars of colonial times writing on North Africa and the Middle East often perpetuated Oriental paradigms and focused on the most "primitive," "exotic," and often heterodox forms of Islam either through their detailed accounts of the Arabic peninsula in travel reports[60] or through earlier anthropological studies of Muslims in North Africa and the Middle East.[61]

In carrying out ethnographic fieldwork among Muslims under colonial premises and paradigms, anthropologists, even in later times, were led to reinforce Western notions of Orientalism for quite some time.[62] The use of distinctions, such as those between Great and Little Traditions, allowed anthropologists to investigate societies and cultures with widespread and highly diversified religious beliefs and practices.[63] This particular distinction utilized a theoretical approach in the study of so-called 'world religions,' providing anthropologists with conceptual tools to account for the study of regional variance and local interpretation and became particularly fruitful for the study of Islam in local contexts.[64] This distinction helped anthropologists to distinguish Islam as a monotheistic religion with a worldwide community of believers from the embeddedness of Muslim traditions in local cultures and among individual believers.[65]

With this analytical framework, anthropologists were able to study how people practiced varying forms of Islam and adapted the religion to local cultures while introducing and instilling their own traditions. This framework set the agenda for the earlier anthropological study of local forms of Islam, in particular of Sufi orders or other forms of social organization among Muslims in North Africa and the Middle East.[66] However, it should be noted that the interest in these local forms of Islam certainly shifted the focus to the study of Sufi traditions, which particularly appealed to Western scholars.[67]

Dominant paradigms of ethnographic research employed by British social anthropology in North Africa and the Middle East, namely *functionalism* and *structural functionalism*,[68] brought attention to the study of subsistence strategies, modes of production, and related forms of political organization in Muslim societies.[69] Studying the many ways Muslims practice Islam and adapt to local environments, it became a common feature of anthropological research to focus on small-scale societies and write mainly on the social life in villages and communities,[70] or other modes of subsistence, like nomadism.[71] To varying degrees, these theoretical paradigms viewed the roles of cultural and religious institutions as either fostering social solidarity and political leadership or contesting traditional authority and requiring political change.[72]

As the focus on political and economic features of Muslim societies dominated early ethnographic research on Muslim communities in the Middle East and North Africa, anthropologists too easily overlooked the importance of addressing the role of Islam in African societies.[73] Restrained by the boundaries of their disciplinary framework, anthropologists often preferred to consider the margins of Islam where local Muslim cultures blended into heterodox forms and traditions of Islam worth studying either in terms of syncretism or hybridity.[74] They marginally accounted for the orthodox forms of Islam as a major cultural and religious factor in shaping the everyday lives of these societies.[75] It is worth noting that the study of spirit possession as one of the key themes in anthropological research also received major attention in the anthropological study of Muslim culture.[76]

The rise of *critical anthropology* since the late 1960s paired with the inception of *structuralism* and *symbolic anthropology* at the fall of colonial regimes led to a blur in the study of cultural systems of classification.[77] As emerging paradigms of ethnographic research, anthropologists advanced the understanding of, and focus on, religious symbols and shifted their research interests toward the experiences of individual agents.[78] During this time period, Muslim communities themselves underwent radical social and political changes due to the formation of nation states throughout Africa, Asia, and the Middle East, leading, despite a continuing Western hegemony, to their formal political independence from colonial powers.[79] Anthropologists came to realize the impact of religious and social movements and forms of human agency spanning from ritual resistance and religious revival to political protest, as well as recognizing the importance of cultural transformations throughout the Muslim world.[80]

The emergence of the discourse on *colonialism* and *postcolonialism* led to a further questioning of theoretical frameworks and disciplinary boundaries legitimizing Western hegemony and domination.[81] The insights of the postcolonial critique into the formations of anthropological knowledge allowed the fieldworker to focus more explicitly on the interaction of different orthodox *and* heterodox traditions within Islam, which is nowadays a more prominent feature in anthropological research.[82] In particular, anthropologists started collaborating with their informants, giving their voices more explicit space in the records of ethnographic writing and accounting for the agency of women in the religious and cultural transformations.[83]

As a consequence of the feminist critique of established paradigms of anthropological research, the ethnographic inquiry into social roles of Muslim women and their religious practices came to the forefront.[84] Anthropologists began to pay attention to culturally ascribed gender roles,[85] social and religious dynamics of women's gatherings,[86] and women's participation in saint venerations and prayer groups.[87]

Ethnographic studies on the ascribed role of Muslim women—often carried out by female anthropologists—were not only dedicated to the study of women's obligations within the family and the public sphere,[88] their roles and responsibilities in weddings[89] and death rituals,[90] but also delved into the study of marriage patterns.[91] Numerous studies addressed the restrictions surrounding their participation in religious and economic activities and their access to the public sphere and, in particular, focused on gender inequalities among Muslims in the legal and political fields.[92]

To the same degree anthropologists studied the role of women in the transformation of the Muslim public sphere, well-documented by ethnographic studies on women who participated in the Islamic movement or objected to an Islamic agenda.[93] This particularly applied to the recognition and study of unique forms of Islamic feminism, which had a significant impact on Islamic movements throughout the Middle East and South Asia, specifically human rights and the equal access to political processes and the public sphere for women.[94] This new role of women in the Muslim public sphere and their visible impact are most significantly embodied in their wearing of headscarves.[95] Although the transformative impact of women's seclusion was of main interest in colonial times, anthropological research underwent a dramatic turn in studying women's veiling and its social and political implications, particularly in conjunction with notions of secularism and modernity.[96]

The transformation of the world on a global scale not only implied the emergence of labor migration to Western countries but also led to the shift in anthropological research to its new focus on the study of Muslims in Europe and North America.[97] This new presence of Muslims in Europe and North America opened up new fields of anthropological research focusing on forms of Islamic practice in a multicultural society as well as on the formation of transnational networks.[98] Anthropologists working in these fields often borrowed methods and concepts also used in sociology and political science addressing notions of secularism and citizenship.[99] The anthropological study of Muslim communities in the Western hemisphere further broadened the issues to be addressed in ethnographic research in other parts of the world, including the contestation of the assumption that the notion of modernity is restricted to the West and is opposed to Islam,[100] even though the notion of modernity itself is negotiated and contested among Muslims.[101] It should be clear that transformations on this scale are notable due to irreversible processes of globalization which sustainably affected Muslims.[102]

As previously indicated, anthropology directs questions not only toward the understanding of local cultures but also toward a critique of different forms of knowledge—an attempt often called postmodern.[103] To return to the formerly posed question: How do anthropologists and other scholars come to know, or the limits of what they *can* know, about a particular object of study, like Islam?[104] The anthropology of Islam is obviously about the people, their lives, and their works and includes the localities and the diverse practices of communities who identify themselves as Muslims.[105] However, anthropologists became aware of the fact that even foundational questions regarding the object of research—for example, who or what a Muslim is and does—are answered by the people themselves before anthropologists enter the field.[106]

This recognition of reflexivity in ethnographic fieldwork is not a limitation, but rather allows anthropologists to give a more precise, empirical account of the context and local embeddedness of the anthropological encounter.[107] In light of this shift in ethnographic writing, anthropologists can answer questions by accounting for the ongoing discourses and practices of a local community through participant observation and qualitative interviews and by observing how people negotiate and contest the issues.[108] In response to questions such as "Who is a Muslim?" the people at the local level engage in discourses anthropologists can witness and record, including questions of Muslim identity often addressed through various forms of verbal (and nonverbal) communication and embedded in practices related to religious education,[109] institutional and legal discourse,[110] or economic commodities.[111]

As anthropologists generally insist, answers to such questions as given by the informants are always situational, relational, and open for revision and interpretation,[112] as Muslims themselves in various contexts and communities agree, to varying degrees, on what makes a person Muslim.[113] Therefore, anthropologists would usually reject any attempt to provide definitive or abstract understandings of Muslims and local versions of Islam from an outsider's perspective without providing a particular context or insight into the discourses and practices that surround such definitions.[114] Instead, anthropologists attempt to understand Muslims from within their local cultures, social relationships, and political economies; from these, practices and discourses emerge.[115] Anthropologists are interested in what the people studied are doing or saying in the context of everyday life, which leads to these understandings and interpretations. Insights into these issues and answers to these questions can only be found by living among Muslims and by realizing the position an anthropologist takes upon entering the field of study.[116]

Due to the different locations, settings, and designs of their ethnographic fieldwork, anthropologists adopt perspectives that presuppose the notion of cultural difference. This approach offers insights into formerly unknown life-worlds and modes of existence crucial to gaining an appreciation for and understanding of the subtleties and ambiguities of everyday and religious life.[117] Due to the particularities of local contexts, anthropologists of Islam learn what it means to be Muslim and how to participate in practices of being Muslim in a certain place and time. By describing and analyzing the discourses and practices of Muslims in the constraints of everyday life, the anthropology of Islam can address how Muslims live, allowing for valuable contributions to the understanding of practiced Islam in its complexity.[118]

This does not necessitate that anthropologists observe Islam as believers do in order to understand; it does, however, mean anthropologists observe people and participate with Muslims in their practices and discourses to such a degree that they are able to grasp the insider's perspective.[119] On the other hand, this does not exclude anthropologists from inquiring about the ways in which Muslims encounter, reinforce, and contest specific practices, or the ways Muslims' understandings of Islam affect their practices in the wider fields of society and culture.[120]

The holistic and inclusive study of Muslims using an anthropological approach demands anthropologists to study the connectedness of themes found in the classical approaches to their discipline, such as economic activity,[121] social organization and political participation,[122] and education[123] as well as art and poetry[124] and friendship.[125] Ethnographic studies are not simply about Muslims, but also focus on how they organize their lives and perceive and practice Islam in the dynamics and complexities of the contemporary world.[126]

The study of Muslim practices using an anthropological perspective may include the establishment of print culture,[127] and the introduction of new media,[128] including the use of television,[129] broadcast media,[130] cassette recordings,[131] and the internet.[132] Among the many effects of the introduction of these media in the transformation of knowledge and power relations in Muslim communities, the introduction of new media also persistently contributed to the transformation in the perception and practice of religious obligations and duties as witnessed by the commercialization and formation of distinctive consumption patterns during Ramadān[133] and the establishment of an Islamic fashion industry, followed by the emergence of a respective consumer culture.[134]

Even though all of these ethnographic accounts are academically, historically, and regionally unique, for students of the anthropology of Islam, they serve as a point of departure to understand the ways in which Muslims conceptualize and negotiate the diverse and ever changing forms of their religious practices. After some major themes and issues specific to the formation of the anthropology of Islam have been established in this section, the practice of reading anthropological texts may be approached.

How can reading anthropological texts enhance the understanding of Islam?

To gain better insight into what the reading of anthropological texts can offer to the understanding of Islam, this section will:

1. review the role of the reader in the understanding of anthropological texts;
2. discuss the impact of social and cultural conditions and conceptual frameworks in the process of understanding; and
3. address the importance of recognizing and voicing underlying prejudices.

The main question here is: What insights into Islam can be identified through the study of Muslim practices? As outlined above, one way anthropologists can advance the understanding of Muslims is by carrying out ethnographic research and disseminating results in scholarly publications. Certainly, another venue consists of reading ethnographic studies of Islam as practiced among Muslims, such as those presented in this *Anthropology of Islam Reader*. The latter approach would include not only the primary involvement of written accounts of participant observation and interviews made by the anthropologists who conducted fieldwork on site, but would also involve the interpretations made by those studying and analyzing these ethnographic works. Reading ethnographic accounts of anthropologists, however, follows rules other than those of participant observation and fieldwork interviewing in the formation of anthropological knowledge and is thus far removed from the first-hand experiences that anthropologists encounter working with people in the field.[135]

Two potential pitfalls may arise in reading such ethnographic accounts. First, because reading directly enters the realm of language as a system of symbolic representations, it primarily involves deciphering messages encoded through the linguistic and textual strategies used by the author. Therefore, the reader plays a decisive role in the process of understanding the ethnographic findings presented in textual forms,[136] which the process of reading brings to the understanding of anthropological texts filtered through systems of cultural classifications leading to new interpretations differing from those made (or intended) by the researcher.[137] Second, the reader needs to be aware of the author's role in the production of knowledge and to employ caution and criticism before accepting tacit assumptions or tenuous conclusions commonly made by the author.[138] By not taking for granted every assumption and conclusion or assuming that findings are inherently accurate, readers of anthropological texts should be cognizant of the ways in which they conceptualize the findings presented and understand how they obtain knowledge through the processes of research and reading encoded through discourse and writing.[139] A reader of anthropological texts should know about the processes and products of knowledge formation since there are no raw data or empirical facts which have not already entered the realm of language; all were filtered through systems of classification and became subject to interpretation.[140]

One first step in this critical process of reading and evaluating ethnographic texts is to gain better understanding of the conditions and conceptual frameworks informing the formation of anthropological knowledge through description and comparison. In *Method and Theory*, the German philosopher Hans Georg Gadamer illuminated the relevance of these processes of understanding and interpretation (1975). As scholars from other fields, like sociology or literary criticism, discovered, researchers usually study issues that are of interest to them, and this interest guides the possible outcome of their findings.[141] Additionally, in their practices of research and reading, researchers bring with them past experiences, present preferences, and future expectations to the site of inquiry, be it the field of study or the text under scrutiny.[142] It is, thus, critically important to realize that perceptions and understandings, for readers and writers alike, both limit and create the conditions of imaginative horizons upon which knowledge is built, underlying, in this case, anthropologists' understandings of "what Islam is."[143]

As readers (and authors) of anthropological works, anthropologists must analyze, compare, and review the results presented in ethnographic accounts and question the assumptions and methods employed before drawing further conclusions so they may realize how ethnographies are constructed and discursive strategies used.[144] Even those approaches in anthropology that claim they give comprehensive ethnographic accounts by providing a thorough body of evidence and presenting thorough representations of social reality in textual form follow the academic principles of scholarly research and use techniques of writing to appropriate their data according to the standards of their discipline.[145] In this regard, the conditions of academic frameworks that set the stage for shaping the interpretation of ethnographic data play a crucial role in the formation of anthropological knowledge and authority.[146] To account for the multiplicity of perspectives involved in the texts and contexts studied, Gadamer recommends scholars working with products of human culture should, in the process of reading and writing, work on clearly articulating their tacit assumptions and unacknowledged prejudices in a preferably dialogical form. By articulating such prejudices and biases in a thoroughly reflexive way, scholars in the field of anthropology could benefit from having sincere confidence in those processes the answers to their questions may lead to and, likewise, could learn to conduct their subsequent research in a way even more suitable and understandable for the people and cultures studied.[147]

In Gadamer's sense, this articulation of prejudices begins by asking open questions either when encountering people in the field of the "here and now" or when reading the written accounts of these first-hand encounters. In his view, everyone embedded in a context has a somewhat unique perspective, and by sharing diverse views, researchers and those studied (through interaction and conversation), as well as readers and authors (through reading and writing), can achieve what Gadamer called the "fusion of horizons." With this conceptual metaphor, he referred to a moment of insightful understanding when the reader grasps and understands the intention of an author by reading his or her work from the author's perspective (1975); this can, with respective refinements, be applied to the fieldwork situation as well as the writing of ethnographic findings. Only by encountering people with different perspectives can anthropologists extend and go beyond the limitations of their initial points of view. However, this also happens when students read and write anthropological texts since the process of understanding is principally open-ended and non-conclusive. According to Gadamer, people with different backgrounds and convictions can reach a mutual understanding as long as those involved are willing to question their provisional presumptions and revise their tentative conclusions.

For example, if people in Europe or North America were to believe that Islam is oppressive to women or that women have no equal political and legal rights in Islam, and if they further believe that women are being "forced" to wear a headscarf as a symbol of repression, they engage in commonly accepted stereotypes and persisting prejudices presented and maintained in Western mainstream mass media, which likely will influence the perception and analysis of the veiling practice in a community of interest. If, on the other hand, non-Muslims are made aware of their tacit biases and see the need to assess their preconceptions by (for instance) reading investigative or scholarly work on such issues and engaging in discourses with women who wear headscarves, they may come to realize those meanings this symbol may hold for the Muslim women they have encountered.[148] Such interaction may lead to the affirmation, rejection, or modification of initial assumptions and prejudices held all along.

While most people certainly may not know how or when they arrived at habitual prejudices or enduring preconceptions, the moment they begin to question their views is the moment they open up to understanding different perspectives and create the potential, in Gadamer's sense, for a "fusion of horizons." By recognizing and respecting the differences of perspectives, thus emerge new levels of mutual understanding which go beyond factual knowledge and require thinking and reflection rather than mere data collection and memorization.[149] After the role of the reader is established, it is worth asking how the reading of anthropological texts can facilitate the refinement of anthropological research methods.

How can reading ethnographies help refine methods of anthropological fieldwork?

After establishing the role of reader and enhancing the understanding of Islam through reading ethnographies, this section aims to:

1 analyze the differences in conceptualizing the meaning of Islamic practices in the anthropology of Islam as a consequence of different forms of knowledge; and
2 elaborate the implications of the position of anthropologists in the relationship between theory and practice as well as between knowledge and power.

One of the main consequences of reading ethnographies in conjunction with conducting ethnographic fieldwork is that professional anthropologists and students of anthropology come to realize people do not always act according to concepts or systems of symbolic representation, even if these are part of their own culture.[150] The dynamics of social and religious life, even if one specifically focuses on ritual practice, go far beyond such concepts and are much more complex than anyone may expect or anticipate.[151] Anthropologists cannot definitively say what, for example, the prayer (*salāt*) is and what it means when they write and read anthropological texts. To continue, can anthropologists say they have a sufficient understanding of prayer if they engage in the ritual practice of only one person, area, or group, or if they engage in only one theoretical approach? Although anthropologists could describe the *salāt* based on what they read, learned, observed, or heard before or during their fieldwork, they could only conceptualize this practice to a certain degree if they want to account for its social and cultural context in a local community. It is therefore possible to argue that the Islamic prayer cannot exist as a universal concept like Islam.

When observing the performance of the ritual prayer *salāt* during fieldwork among Muslims, anthropologists can witness the voiced recitations and the flow of movements only at particular moments on a singular occasion.[152] While they cannot say what the meaning and essence of the *salāt* is, they can at least describe what they observe in written accounts ranging from field notes to ethnographic accounts. The problem remains that a Muslim has instructed the anthropologist about the *salāt* even before he or she attempted to describe it. How, then, can anthropologists give a more appropriate account of the *salāt*? Anthropologists address these forms of theoretical and practical knowledge as knowing *what* and knowing *how*.[153] Although the anthropology of Islam, as an academic discipline, engages in theoretical questions regarding *what* Islam is, it goes beyond technical knowledge to gain a practical sense of *how* to understand Islam.[154]

In light of 'knowing what' and 'knowing how,' it is important to reflect upon the perspective and position of interpretation taken by anthropologists in their research with respect to observation and participation or to ethnography and ethnology; indeed, any anthropological research is impossible without seriously accounting for these issues of method and theory.[155] Two different approaches to anthropological research—one focusing on ethnography and the other on ethnology—provide good examples of how to engage in this endeavor.

In any case, it is important to reflect upon the position taken by the researcher and reader and the limitations their perspectives may have for understanding other perspectives. Some anthropologists argue in their own ways that it is possible to avoid privileging the anthropologist's position in ethnographic research by categorically distinguishing between the subject and object of interpretation while elevating both parties to equal status in an overall structural relationship.[156] In contrast, others assert that anthropological research presents a fundamental epistemological problem: Anthropologists studying human subjects cannot avoid taking positions or having relationships with the people they study and work with because (they argue) without interest and relationship, knowledge would be impossible.[157]

This is not to say an anthropological perspective would itself produce a unified body of knowledge about Muslims or a homogeneous way of conceptualizing Islam by classifying or comparing its diverse practices and discourses.[158] Rather, anthropology inherently aims to present a multiplicity of perspectives through its different methods of description and comparison. The anthropology of Islam is more likely to use the term "Islam," therefore, more as a heuristic tool for comparison based on "family resemblances" (Needham 1975) and to set up a conceptual field and framework of research that allows the investigator to bring to the fore a diversified body of knowledge about Muslim practices and discourses.[159] Employing the principle of inclusiveness and cultural relativism, this framework allows anthropologists to give detailed insights into the different perspectives and perceptions of Muslims as individual agents of change by maintaining the diversity and dynamics within the field without reducing their findings to some timeless structures.[160]

As Michel Foucault (1972) noted, even if researchers choose to take a detached stance in comparing different forms or practices of Islam or claim to favor a neutral stance of truth and objectivity, they still establish a relationship with the object of study, through which they express the desire for truth and objectivity.[161] In this respect, it is important to understand the relationship between knowledge and power in the anthropological study of Islam as well as the relationship of the researcher to the people studied; ethnographic fieldwork considers both relationships in its description of contexts and relational situations.[162]

At the same time, the writing of an ethnography adds another layer of relationships subsequent to the fieldwork situation as the process of writing opens up the findings to the academic audience and enters the discourse of writing and reading (with other scholars as readers). To address this problem in general terms, anthropologists, and social theorists alike, aim to find the ground between theory and practice as well as between concepts and reality by employing concepts such as "mimesis," "agency," or "habitus."[163] This does not presume that tentative representations, comparisons, or conceptualizations are not theoretically or practically possible without such concepts.[164]

After all, anthropology is not merely confined to ethnographic accounts, but also requires comparing data, conceptualizing issues, and theorizing accounts.[165] However, the limited and highly specified focus required for ethnographic fieldwork can provide anthropologists working with Muslims the unique possibility to compare a multiplicity of perspectives on local specificities, which would otherwise be unlikely or silenced by shortcut conceptualizations not grounded in ethnographic findings. This would allow the possibility to give a thorough reading of concise ethnographic accounts of Islam, backed up by the anthropologists' written accounts of real events. In the end, anthropologists only encounter people at the specific occasions when they collect their findings and not in broad generalizations. These, rather, are made by way of conceptual analysis and theorizing starting within, but usually completed far away from, the field by reading and re-reading ethnographic accounts.[166]

How can a set of readings outline the contours of the anthropology of Islam?

The *Anthropology of Islam Reader* aims to offer an overview of some major approaches to the anthropological study of Muslims in different socio-political and cultural contexts. Bringing together some of the most prominent theoretical perspectives, along with in-depth ethnographic accounts of Muslim practices, the contributions to this volume examine some common features formative for Muslims and explore how these features organize their religious practices and discourses. The ethnographic depictions demonstrate unique anthropological encounters with local communities and cultures. As part of the anthropological endeavor, these are quite different from mass media encounters and common-sense perceptions in the public sphere, which can easily lead to the reproduction and circulation of commonly held stereotypes.[167]

The aim of this Reader is to go beyond information given in introductory textbooks on Islam and reflect upon the adventure of anthropological research, its consequences for the researcher, and, most importantly, for the understanding of the lives of those upon which the ethnographic section of this volume is centered. The insights of these ethnographies also reflect upon the different methods of anthropological inquiry, which may further the study of Muslims and the ways they observe Islam. In accordance with the above-stated aim, the *Anthropology of Islam Reader* is comprised of three parts.

The first part, *Theoretical approaches to Islam*, presents programmatic pieces to the anthropological study of Islam. It is subdivided into two sections: the first subsection, *Conceptualizing Islam*, contributes how anthropologists carry out fieldwork and reflect on Islam, and the second subsection, *Approaching Islam*, presents the most prominent theoretical proposals toward the anthropology of Islam and facilitates methods for studying Muslim communities.

The second part, *Religious practices of Islam*, explores with significant detail in ethnographic description how Muslims perform their main obligatory rituals. The set of ten articles is distributed according to five key rituals, examining those rituals in different local contexts explored through ethnographic fieldwork. These articles are arranged in pairs to allow cross-cultural comparison of the respective practices: *Daily prayer* provides studies on discourses and practices of ritual prayer in Egypt and Turkey, *Fasting during the month of Ramadān* contains contributions on how fasting is embedded in social networks in Kenya and Egypt, *Pilgrimage to Mecca* offers an account of the impact of pilgrimage on local Muslim communities of Thailand and Nigeria, *Feast of sacrifice* analyzes the social implications of sacrifice for Muslims in Indonesia and Pakistani migrants in the United Kingdom, and *Almsgiving* puts forward inquiries on the institution of social welfare in Ghana, Jordan, and Palestine.

The third part, *Methodological reflections on the anthropology of Islam*, concludes the Reader and allows for the examination of the relationship between ethnographic accounts of religious practice and their implications for the anthropology of Islam. The first subsection, *Situating anthropology*, addresses the role of the methodological differences between the insider's and outsider's perspectives in studying Islam anthropologically, whereas the second subsection, *Representing Islam*, reflects upon the differences in rhetorical strategies employed by anthropological and non-anthropological writings on Islam.

To add another layer to the composition outlined above, a brief introduction to each contribution is given to indicate its relevance to the *Anthropology of Islam Reader*. The part on *Theoretical approaches to Islam* opens with the subsection *Conceptualizing Islam* and presents classical anthropological works in this field, raising questions about the importance of ethnographic and ethnological approaches. Excerpts from Michael Gilsenan's *Recognizing Islam* (1982) allow for an exploration of the practice of Islam in Yemen and Egypt, which demonstrates the various practices of Islam and shows how the author's own understandings of Islam changed with key experiences during his fieldwork. In selected excerpts of *Islam Observed: Religious Development in Morocco and Indonesia* (1968), Clifford Geertz demonstrates the ways in which the unique history of two regions and their political environments inform the practice of Islam by discussing the varying ways Muslims observe Islam. Both authors give valuable information about the diversity of Islamic practices as well as demonstrating the wide array of theoretical paradigms within the anthropological study of Islam. Reading these pieces while considering the specific time and place when they were written allows the discovery of the authors' different theoretical perspectives and provides an opportunity to consider the different ways in which these anthropologists conceptualize Islam.

In *Approaching Islam*, two complementary proposals to the anthropology of Islam exemplify how theoretical premises lead to the formation of significantly different research agendas. Abdul Hamid el-Zein questions in his review "Beyond Ideology and Theology: The Search for the Anthropology of Islam" (1977) the universal notion of Islam. In discussing the works of Clifford Geertz (1968) and Michael Gilsenan (1973) as well as those of Vincent Crapanzano (1973), Abdulla S. Bujra (1971), and Dale F. Eickelman (1976), el-Zein contests the theoretical assumptions of their anthropological accounts by comparing their work with theological positions of Muslim scholars, showing how similar these approaches are and how important it is to overcome a concept of Islam that precludes cultural and religious diversity. In his programmatic lecture *The Idea of an Anthropology of Islam* (1986), Talal Asad dwells on the scholarship in the field of anthropology and the study of Muslims, yet he provides an alternative and challenging perspective for anthropological analysis. In search of concepts for the anthropological study of Islam, he conceives of Islam as a "discursive tradition" and proposes that anthropologists should start with the Qur'ān and Islamic traditions, as would Muslims. Considering the ways in which the contextual factors of interest and conviction influence the outcome of anthropological research, Asad exemplifies the study of Islam from a reflexive position and calls for considerable changes within this field of study. In concert, both approaches illustrate how assumptions impact methodological considerations in fieldwork and cross-cultural comparison, which allow for the development of important programs for the prospective formation of the anthropological study of Islam.

The second part on *Religious Practices* takes up these insights by exploring some of the most significant aspects of Islam through which Muslims identify themselves. In accordance with the main aim of this Reader, chapters in this second part include those religious obligations most widely accepted among Muslims, in particular the daily prayer (*salāt*), fasting (*sawm*) during the month of Ramadān, pilgrimage (*hajj*) to Mecca, the feast of sacrifice (*id al-adha*), and almsgiving (*zakāt*).[168] Taking the frequency and duration of these practices into consideration,[169] the prayer is performed on a daily basis at specific times, whereas the other practices follow a (more or less specified) time line of the lunar calendar and go along with a particular temporal order. According to the lunar calendar, Muslims fast during the ninth month, which is Ramadān. The subsequent pilgrimage to Mecca is scheduled between the eighth and thirteenth of Dhū al-Hijja, the twelfth and last month of the Muslim year. Being itself an integral part of the pilgrimage to Mecca and celebrated among Muslims worldwide, the feast of sacrifice takes place on the tenth of Dhū al-Hijja and is performed in memory of Ibrahim's (Abraham's) attempt to sacrifice his son Ismail (Ismael) at God's request. Although almsgiving can be viewed as a voluntary obligation throughout the year, it becomes most significant in the distribution of sacrificed meat at the end of the Muslim year. From the perspective of Muslim religious practice, ritual prayer is a recurring duty patterning the routine of everyday life, and almsgiving is a general religious obligation varying according to time and occasion throughout the year; whereas fasting and sacrifice are performed by Muslims at prescribed time periods once a year, and the pilgrimage to Mecca is required only once in a lifetime as part of religious obligations.[170]

The part on *Religious practices of Islam* starts with ethnographic accounts of the five daily prayers (*salāt*), addressing the way Muslims incorporate prayer into the routines of their daily lives. In "Rehearsed Spontaneity and the Conventionality of Ritual: Disciplines of Salāt" (2001b), Saba Mahmood argues for a new conceptualization of ritual practice by emphasizing ethics, bodily discipline, and female agency, giving an in-depth account of the religious discourses of Muslim women involved in the Mosque movement in Cairo. In a similar way, Heiko Henkel argues in "Between Belief and Unbelief Lies the Performance of Salāt: Meaning and Efficacy of a Muslim Ritual" (2005) for a new account of the formal order of ritual practice in Turkey by providing a detailed analysis of how Muslims perform the ritual prayer in Istanbul. Although both contributions use similar methods of anthropological research, they formulate different theoretical positions of how to conceptualize the daily prayer as ritual practice.

The second set of readings on ritual fasting (*sawm*) during the month of Ramadān give different methodological accounts of the experiences and effects of fasting on social relationships among people of Africa. P.J.L. Frankl develops in "The Observance of Ramadān in Swahili-Land" (1996) a detailed ethnographic account which stresses the usage of linguistic categories through the consideration of historical documents and provides lucid descriptions of social and religious events orchestrated during the month of Ramadān. Samuli Schielke stresses in "Being Good in Ramadān: Ambivalence, Fragmentation, and the Moral Self in the Lives of Young Egyptians" (2009) the way youth in Cairo incorporate soccer as a means of disciplining their temptations in the long and exhausting evening hours after a day of fasting. Both readings show how people in different social contexts not only observe the practice of fasting according to their local cultures, but also how individuals employ different strategies to support the solidarity of their community.

With regard to the pilgrimage (*hajj*) to Mecca, different methodological approaches are employed to account for modern transformations in the pilgrimage and how pilgrims returning from Mecca impact their local community due to their acknowledged change in social status. Raymond Scupin uses in his work, "The Social Significance of the Hajj for Thai Muslims" (1982), statistical data to address the establishment of prestige systems associated with certain Islamic practices by stressing how the pilgrimage to Mecca supports local reform movements. Barbara M. Cooper provides in "The Strength in the Song: Muslim Personhood, Audible Capital, and Hausa Women's Performance of the Hajj" (1999) insightful glimpses into the complexity of the modern practice of the women's pilgrimage to Mecca by analyzing the song performances of an elderly woman who went to Mecca on her own and received, as a pilgrim, a new social status within her community. Both authors use different methodological accounts to gather their data and analyze their findings by stressing the transformative dimensions of the pilgrimage to Mecca on a local and global scale.

The essays on the feast of sacrifice (*id al-adha*) reveal the ways in which people sacrifice and utilize this event to establish social relationships. John R. Bowen compares in "On Scriptural Essentialism and Ritual Variation: Muslim Sacrifice in Sumatra and Morocco" (1992) the practices of two local communities that view sacrifices in Morocco as an index of patriarchal structures within Muslim societies, while formulating a critique of essentializing academic discourses and presenting an alternative point of view by presenting his ethnographic insights into the feast of sacrifice in Sumatra. In "'Sealing the Koran': Offering and Sacrifice among Pakistani Labour Migrants" (1988), Pnina Werbner shows the ways in which Pakistani labor migrants living under socially and culturally different conditions in Manchester "naturalize" the sacrifice and "ritualize" their religious and ethnic community through the process of social assimilation and adjustment. Although both readings use similar methods of ethnographic fieldwork representing similar schools of anthropological discourse, their modes of representation not only differ in terms of their emphasis on ethnographic detail and ethnological theory, but also with regard to the contextualization of theory and conceptualization of their data.

The feast of sacrifice is integrally connected with the practice of almsgiving (*zakāt*). The readings in this subsection explore almsgiving as institutionalized practice by addressing the benefits and social drawbacks of such practices for local communities. Holger Weiss in "Reforming Social Welfare among Muslims: Islamic Voluntarism and other Forms of Communal Support in Northern Ghana" (2002) stresses the local dimension of systems of almsgiving and the way they are organized by discussing different institutions and practices of social welfare in Ghana. Jonathan Benthall, in "Financial Worship: The Quranic Injunction to Almsgiving" (1999), dwells on his findings during ethnographic fieldwork in Jordan and Palestine and proposes a theoretical perspective of the local practices and their institutional forms by exploring the broader social and political framework of almsgiving and its implications for social solidarity. Both readings show how the same religious command of almsgiving is differently situated and organized by different social and political contexts, inviting for different modes of analysis and conceptualization.

In the third part, *Methodological reflections*, the Reader closes by taking up meta-theoretical considerations that are crucial to the anthropology of Islam. The excerpts in this section finally allow reflection on the findings presented in the second section on religious practices in methodological terms and relate these insights to the anthropological approaches in the first section. The first set of readings in *Situating anthropology* start with excerpts from the programmatic booklet *Toward Islamic Anthropology: Definition, Dogma and Directions* by Akbar S. Ahmed (1986). In proposing an anthropological approach based on Islamic principles, Ahmed questions the ideological implications of a predominantly Western anthropology, reviewing the colonial heritage and conceptual biases of anthropological research in Islam. Subsequently, Richard Tapper (1995) offers in "'Islamic Anthropology' and the 'Anthropology of Islam'" a timely response to this approach, presenting a distinctive account of the conceptual differences between two contrary approaches to the study of Islam. By carefully reviewing the theoretical assumptions of an Islamic anthropology and elaborating upon the critical approach toward the anthropology of Islam, the readings offer a venue to address underlying assumptions and biases in the anthropological study of Islam, both theoretically and methodologically challenging despite their diametrically opposed stances.

In its concluding part, this volume provides a section on the epistemology and rhetoric of anthropological research entitled *Representing Islam.* The section starts with excerpts from Edward Said's *Covering Islam: How the Media and the Experts Determine How We See the Rest of the World* (1981), articulating a critique of the ways in which Western media and scholars utilize Islam for political purposes while addressing more general questions on the relationship between power and the production of knowledge. Daniel M. Varisco, by way of conclusion, provides in *Islam Obscured: The Rhetoric of Anthropological Representation* (2005) a tempered voice on the study of Islam from an anthropological perspective by discussing the main insights anthropology can offer for the study of Islam while giving numerous examples of how anthropologists can delve into a more subtle understanding of Muslims. These readings allow direction toward more general questions scholars should ask and lead finally into a review of the multitude of sources and perspectives of the anthropology of Islam as an emerging academic field, which students can use to further their understanding of Muslims in a critical and reflexive manner.

The ambition of the collection of essays presented in this Reader is to give original glimpses of the diversity of Islam through different anthropological accounts by showing how studying existing discourses and practices can contribute to a refined understanding of Muslims, their religion, and their practice. Through these studies, students of anthropology as well as Islam can explore the ways in which Muslims adjust their practices to the challenges of modern life and support or question each other by accounting for the diversity of traditions practiced by Muslims. As outlined above, the themes selected for the ethnographic accounts center on religious practices based on some of the main tenets of Islam. The selected set is considerably broad in its diversity and is intended to inform about variation even in common forms of Islamic practice by directing attention to the multiplicity of perspectives involved in the study of local forms of Islam.

In addition, the broad selection of contributions to this volume from different geographic areas allows students to highlight how scholars and anthropologists coming from different traditions of academic training conceptualize the roles of religious beliefs and practices. In reviewing these excerpts with their different ethnological and ethnographic approaches, it becomes clear that, to differing degrees, anthropologists emphasize the relevance and importance of fieldwork and comparison of theory and method. While considering the positions presented in this Reader, the comparison of the contributions may help to configure a conceptual framework through which ethnographic studies, with their empirical focus, can be analyzed and to see how these approaches have an impact on the way anthropologists carry out fieldwork on Islam. As such, this volume aims to offer a foundation of the ongoing debates already in play within the conceptual refinements and contested boundaries of what can be called the anthropology of Islam.

Notes

1 There exists, of course, more than one anthropology of Islam, but for the purpose of this book, I limit the introductory essay to my perceptions and conceptualizations of an emerging field of research.
2 Subsequently the term "anthropology" is used as an abbreviation to refer to "social and cultural anthropology" since no other field of anthropology is addressed in this volume.
3 For early anthropological accounts employing fieldwork as research method, see also Malinowski 1922; Radcliffe-Brown 1922; Evans-Pritchard 1937.
4 For early accounts of the so-called Manchester school in social anthropology, see also Gluckman 1955; Turner 1957; Cohen 1972.
5 For the school of historical particularism, see also the work of Boas 1925; Mead 1928.
6 For earlier accounts of informants as human agents, see also Crapanzano 1980; Abu-Lughod 1990b, 1993b; Stoller and Olkes 1987.
7 On friendship and forms of social relatedness, see also Barth 1969; Boissevain 1974; Desai and Killick 2010.
8 On body techniques and embodiment, see Mauss 1973; Bourdieu 1977; Csordas 1990.
9 On the notions of action and decision, see also Bourdieu 1998; Van der Elst and Bohannan 1999.
10 On anthropological accounts on performance, see also Bauman 1986; Kapferer 1983.
11 For earlier holistic accounts, see also Malinowski 1922; Firth 1936.
12 For a recent discussion on holism in anthropology, see also Parkin and Ulijaszek 2007; Otto and Bubandt 2010.
13 See also Gluckman and Forde 1963; Werbner and Basu 1998.
14 For the ethics of anthropological research, see also Rynkiewich and Spradley 1976; Caplan 2003; Meskell and Pels 2005; Faubion 2009.
15 On multi-sited ethnography, see also Marcus 1995; Weisskoppel 2005; Candea 2007.
16 On Malinowski's account of participant observation, see also Buckley 1994.
17 On the notion of observation in anthropological field research, see also Stocking 1983; Crary 1990; Grimshaw 2001.

18 For the role of participation in ethnographic research, see also Stoller 1989b; Schieffelin 2006.
19 See also Tedlock 1991; Johnson, Avenarius, and Weatherford 2006.
20 For a discussion of the paradigm of anthropological research of "being there," see also Bradburd 1998; Borneman and Hammoudi 2009.
21 For recent accounts of the unpredictable outcomes of ethnographic fieldwork, see also Geros 2008; Borneman 2009.
22 For anthropological accounts of emotion in fieldwork, see Rosaldo 1989; Lutz and Abu-Lughod 1990; Beatty 2005; Davies and Spencer 2010.
23 For accounts on the 'ethnography of speaking,' see Hymes 1962; Bauman and Sherzer 1974.
24 For the anthropological study of linguistic ideologies, see Bauman and Briggs 1990; Woolard and Schieffelin 1994.
25 For anthropological interviewing techniques, see Spradley 1979; Briggs 1986. For the conceptualization of ethnographic representations, see Tedlock 1983; Urban 1996; Bohannan and Van der Elst 1998.
26 For the importance of the relationship and interaction between anthropologists and their informants to the outcome of the research, see Ashkenazi 1997; Borneman 2009.
27 For ethnographic examples that account for the multiplicity of perspectives, see Geertz 1972; Gerholm 1988.
28 For ethnographic findings that call into question universal concepts, see Boddy 1989; Stoller 1989a.
29 For anthropological accounts of writing and note-taking during fieldwork, see Clifford 1990; Gardner and Hoffman 2006; Van Maanen 2010.
30 For theoretical reflections on the holistic perspective, see Geertz 1973; Arensberg 1981. See also Fabian 1990.
31 For a blending of perspective on culture, see Bhabha 1994.
32 For reflexive accounts, see for example Rabinow 1977; Ruby 1982. For the dialogical approach in anthropological research, see Tedlock 1987.
33 See Marcus and Cushman 1982.
34 For theoretical proposals for the role of film in ethnographic research, see Rouch 1974; Ruby 1975; Rouch and Feld 2003; El Guindi 2004.
35 For theoretical and comparative accounts of anthropological concepts, see in particular Mauss 1954; Hubert and Mauss 1964; Douglas 1966; Mauss 1972, 2003.
36 For older comparative accounts in anthropology, see Benedict 1934; Radin 1966; Douglas 1970. For a more recent discussion, see Mace and Pagel 1994.
37 For a discussion of the interconnectedness of ethnographic data and theoretical approaches, see Bateson 1941; Handelman 1990; Kreinath 2004a.
38 See Geertz 1983. For the debate on the distinction between the emic and etic perspective, see Pike 1967; Headland, Pike, and Harris 1990; McCutcheon 1999.
39 For grounded ethnographies, see Schieffelin 1976; Kapferer 1983; Daniel 1984; Bradburd 1998.
40 For anthropological approaches stressing the comparative perspective, see Douglas 1966, 1970; Dumont 1970; Bloch 1992.
41 See Driessen 1993; Strang 2006.
42 For ethnographic accounts that also represent the voices of their informants, see Fernea and Bezirgan 1977; Stoller and Olkes 1987; Abu-Lughod 1993b.
43 The diversity of local perspective is well-documented by Geertz 1957; Schieffelin 1976; Kendall 1985.
44 For the etic perspective, see Lévi-Strauss 1963; Douglas 1970.
45 For a epistemological critique of anthropological meta-representations, see Derrida 1978; Handelman 2004.
46 See Platvoet 2004; Kreinath, Snoek, and Stausberg 2006; see also Harrison 2008.
47 For comparative accounts with the attempt to combine ethnography and ethnology, see Evans-Pritchard 1963; Vogt 2002; Whitehouse 2007.
48 For a discussion of the notion of ethnocentrism, see Barth 1969; Hollis and Lukes 1982; Gellner 1985.
49 For a discussion of the notion of cultural relativism, see Herskovits 1972; Spiro 1986; Brown 2008.
50 For anthropological accounts of human rights, see Messer 1993; Goodale 2006, 2009; Donnelly 2007.
51 On the discussion of female genital mutilation, see Boddy 1989; Gordon 1991.

52 For a discussion of universal human rights and Muslim cultural rights, see Halliday 1987; Mernissi 1987; Peteet 1993; Afshari 1994; Saktanber 1997; Abu-Lughod 2002.
53 For critical accounts of the definition of ritual, see Goody 1977; Asad 1988; Gerholm 1988; Bell 1992; Snoek 2006. See also Handelman 2006.
54 For accounts of anthropological theory, see Radin 1966; Layton 1997; Barnard 2000.
55 For the contextualization of anthropological knowledge, see Fardon 1990; Strathern 1995; Faubion and Marcus 2009.
56 For a critical review of the primary focus on illiterate people in anthropology, see Wolf 1982; Fabian 1983; Goody 1986.
57 For earlier accounts of the Middle East, see Gulick 1969; Antoun 1971, 1976; Fernea and Malarkey 1975. For more recent accounts, see Eickelman 1981; Lindholm 1995; Bates and Rassam 2001.
58 See, for example, Gilsenan 1989; Lindholm 2002a. For a bibliographic survey on Muslims in the Middle East and throughout the world, see Weeks 1978; Strijp 1992; Sedgwick 2006.
59 See Huntington 1993; Lewis 1993; see also Er-Rashid 2003; Trumpbour 2003.
60 See Wallin 1854; Burton 1855; Doughty 1898. See also Cobbold 1934. For the study of the poetic representation of the Middle East in nineteenth century poetry, see Haddad 2002.
61 For early anthropological accounts, see Lane 1860; Westermarck 1899, 1914, 1926, 1933; Thomas 1932. See also Rose 1907; Scott 1913. For some later accounts, see Granqvist 1947; Von Grunebaum 1951.
62 For the most prominent critique of orientalism, see Said 1978, 1985. For a critical review, see Clifford 1980. For further discussion on orientalism, see also Turner 1984, 1994; Burke 1998; Varisco 2007.
63 For the influential distinction between the Great and Little Tradition, see Redfield 1956. For a very early adaptation of this distinction, see Geertz 1961.
64 For earlier accounts, see Geertz 1968; Gellner 1968; El-Zein 1977. For a theoretical and methodological discussion on the study of Islam in local contexts, see Eickelman 1982; Manger 1992; Bowen 1998b.
65 For an emphasis on the individual believer, see Manger 1999; Lukens-Bull 1999; Marranci 2008.
66 See, for example, Lewis 1955, 1956; Crapanzano 1973; Gilsenan 1973; El-Zein 1974; Eickelman 1976.
67 See also Birge 1937; Abun-Nasr 1965; Trimingham 1971.
68 For definitions of these and other technical terms, see the Glossary of Anthropological Terms in the appendix of this Reader.
69 For early accounts, see Evans-Pritchard 1946, 1949; Barth 1959.
70 For studies on Muslim villages, see Fuller 1961; Fernea 1965; Hansen 1967; Loeffler 1988; Delaney 1991; Friedel 1991.
71 For ethnographic studies on nomadism among Muslims, see Barth 1965; Asad 1970; Birks 1977; Tapper 1979; Abu-Lughod 1986; Bradburd 1998.
72 See Asad 1970; Bujra 1971; Tapper 1979; Ahmed 1983.
73 For the critical review of the study of Islam in Africa, see Soares 2000; Henle 2006; Launay 2006; Şaul 2006. See also McIntosh 2009.
74 For the study of syncretic forms, see Lewis 1983; Beatty 1996. For an account of hybridity, see Werbner 1996a; Werbner and Modood 1997.
75 See, for example, Gellner 1969; Rabinow 1975. For studies on Muslims in South Asia, see also Peacock 1978; Hefner 1985; Woodward 1988.
76 For the study of possession rituals in Muslim societies, see Crapanzano 1977; Boddy 1989; Kramer 1993; Lambek 1993; Matory 1994; Rasmussen 1995; Masquelier 2001.
77 For a discussion of critical anthropology, see Marcus and Fischer 1986; Marcus 1999. For a critical account of anthropological typologies, see Comaroff and Comaroff 1991; Gupta and Ferguson 1997. For an overview, see also Ortner 1984.
78 For the role of the anthropological study of symbolism, see Geertz 1973; Ortner 1973; for the anthropological accounts of individual agency, see Crapanzano 1980; Abu-Lughod 1986.
79 See Fischer 1980; Breckenridge and Van der Veer 1993.
80 See Geertz 1968; Peters 1979; Youssef 1985; Antoun 1989. For a bibliographic source on Islamic revival, see also Haddad, Voll, and Esposito 1991.
81 For anthropological accounts of the colonial encounter, see Asad 1973; Stocking 1991. See also Said 1979, 1989, 1993.

82 See Launay 1992; Soares 1996, 2005; Möller 2005; Schulz 2008. For anthropological accounts of postcolonialism, see Comaroff and Comaroff 1993; Werbner and Ranger 1996; Werbner 1998.
83 For feminist approaches of writing about women's lives, see Abu-Lughod 1993b; Behar and Gordon 1995. For ethnographic accounts of the agency of Muslim women, see Hegland 1995; Brenner 1996; Cooper 1999, Mahmood 2001a.
84 See Fernea and Fernea 1972.
85 For ethnographic studies, see Tapper 1983; Tapper and Tapper 1987; Holy 1988; Mir-Hosseini 1999; Shehabuddin 1999. For a discussion on gender and Islam, see also Mernissi 1975; Ahmed, L.1992; Marcus 1992; Haddad and Esposito 1998; Anwar 2006. See also Peteet 1994, 2005; Boellstorff 2005; Lahoucie 2006.
86 See Tapper 1983; Werbner 1988.
87 For ethnographic accounts of women's gatherings, see Weix 1998; Mahmood 2001b; Deeb 2006; Torab 2006. See also Buitelaar 1993. For the role of women in saint venerations, see Mernissi 1977; Coulon 1988; Tapper 1990; Ghadially 2005. For further accounts of saint veneration among Muslims, see also Gellner 1969; Gilsenan 1973; Reeves 1995; Schielke 2008.
88 See Ong 1990; Donnan and Selier 1997.
89 See Tapper 1985; Werbner 1986. See also Mason 1975.
90 See Abu-Lughod 1993a; Hegland 1998. See also Granqvist 1965.
91 See Donnan 1988; Aswad and Bilgé 1996.
92 For studies on the unequal access of Muslim women to the public sphere, see Hansen 1961; Antoun 1968; Abu-Zahra 1970; Wikan 1982; Combs-Schilling 1989; Bernal 1994. See also Messick 1987, 1988; Bowen 1998a; Kazemzadeh 2002. See also Ewing 1988.
93 See Poya 1999; Shehabuddin 2008; Wieringa 2009.
94 For studies on Muslim feminism, see Saktanber 1994; Abu-Lughod 1998; Fernea 1998; Göle 1998; Karam 1998; Secor 2001; White 2002b; Mahmood 2004.
95 For classical accounts on the veiling issue, see Mernissi 1987; Brenner 1996; El Guindi 1999.
96 For the discussion of the headscarf issues in light of secularism and modernity in Turkey, see Göle 1996; Navaro-Yashin 1999, 2002; Secor 2002; Silverstein 2003; O'Neil 2008. For ethnographic accounts in Europe, see Bowen 2006; Werbner 2007.
97 For Muslims in Europe, see Gerholm and Lithman 1988; Dassetto 1996; Goody 2004; Cesari and McLoughlin 2005; Norris 2006. For North America, see also Haddad and Lummis 1987; Haddad 1991, 1994; Metcalf 1996; Cesari 2004; Malik 2004; Westerlund 2004; Haddad, Smith, and Moore 2006.
98 For accounts of Muslims in multicultural societies, see Modood and Werbner 1997; Shadid and van Koningsveld 2002. For the study of transnational networks, see Werbner 2002; Allievi and Nielsen 2003; Gokariksel and Secor 2009.
99 See Cesari and McLoughlin 2005; Modood, Triandafyllidou, and Zapata-Barrero 2005.
100 See Göle 1997; Salvatore 1997; Eickelman 2000; Gilsenan 2000; Houston 2001; Asad 2003.
101 See Peletz 2002; Vahdat 2002; Thompson 2003; Çınar 2005; Houston 2006; Keyman 2007. For an earlier account, see also Von Grunebaum 1962.
102 For a discussion of the impact of globalization on Muslims, see also Kosebalaban 2005; Ahmed 2007; Mandaville 2007.
103 For anthropological accounts of Islam and postmodernity, see Fischer and Abedi 1990; Ahmed, A.S. 1991, 1992; Donnan and Ahmed 1994.
104 See El-Zein 1977. For further accounts, see Das 1984; Asad 1986; Lindholm 2002b. For an overview of the anthropology of Islam, see also Starrett 1997; Marranci 2010.
105 For a more specific emphasis on Muslims, see Lukens-Bull 2007; McLoughlin 2007; Marranci 2006, 2008.
106 In this regard, the anthropology of Islam is facing quite similar methodological questions as, for example, the emerging anthropology of Christianity (Asad 1993; Cannell 2006; Engelke and Tomlinson 2006; Keane 2007; Robbins 2007).
107 For a theoretical discussion of reflexivity in anthropology, see Babcock 1980; Ruby 1982; Bourdieu and Wacquant 1992.
108 For ethnographic accounts on the negotiation of Muslim identity, see Torab 1996; Mahmood 2001b; Horstmann 2009. For studies on Muslim discourses, see also Bowen 1993; Lambek 1993.
109 See Eickelman 1978, 1985.
110 See Messick 1986, 1988.
111 See Starrett 1995a, 1995b.

112 For a general discussion, see Schieffelin 1985; Hobart and Kapferer 2004.
113 For ethnographic accounts on the discussion of Muslim identity, see Olson 1985; Hegland 1998; Mahmood 2004; Schulz 2008.
114 See Eickelman 1982; Bowen 1998b; Lukens-Bull 2005.
115 See, for example, Eickelman 1979; Roff 1987; Starrett 1995b.
116 Ethnographic examples illustrating the position of the anthropologist are provided by Lambek 1990; Van der Veer 1992; Geros 2008; Borneman 2009.
117 For instances, see Rasmussen 2001; Saktanber 2002, Schielke 2008.
118 See Shannon 2004; Wolf 2006; Silverstein 2008.
119 For the discussion the role of the insider's perspective in the anthropology of Islam, see Geertz 1973; Das 1984; Ahmed 1986; Davies 1988; Tapper 1995; Lukens-Bull 1999; Varisco 2005.
120 For ethnographic accounts, see Horvatich 1994; Brenner 1996; Eisenlohr 2006; Werbner 2007. For a theoretical discussion, see Mandaville 2007.
121 For some classical approaches, see Cruise O'Brian 1971; Geertz 1971; Gerholm 1977; Ahmed 1980; Donnan and Werbner 1991. For a recent ethnographic account, see Rudnyckyj 2009. The introduction of market economy and the principles of capitalism in Muslim-majority countries led to different responses in the social and political transformations in their societies (McAllister 1990; Bernal 1994).
122 See Asad 1970; Tapper 1979.
123 See Eickelman 1978; Starrett 1998; Brenner 2001.
124 For the study of poetry among Muslims, see Abu-Lughod 1986; Lavie 1990; Cooper 1999.
125 See Combs-Schilling 1985; Khan 2006.
126 See, for example, Peletz 2002; White 2002a; Lukens-Bull 2005.
127 For the study of print culture on Muslim discourse and practice, see Meeker 1994; Edwards 1995; Starrett 1996; Hefner 1997.
128 For ethnographic accounts, see Eickelman and Anderson 1999; Hefner 2003; Poole and Richardson 2006; Schulz 2006.
129 For the anthropological study of television, see Öncü 1995; Abu-Lughod 2005.
130 See Schulz 2006.
131 See Hirschkind 2006.
132 For anthropological accounts of the Internet, see Stowasser 2001; Anderson 2003; Wheeler 2006. See also Bunt 2003, 2009.
133 For studies on the commercialization of Ramadān, see Armbrust 2002; Keenan and Yeni 2003; Odabasi and Argan 2009.
134 On the Islamic fashion industry in Turkey, see White 1999; Kiliçbay and Binark 2002; Akou 2007; Gokariksel and Secor 2009.
135 See also Driessen 1993.
136 For accounts by literary theorists, see Barthes 1975; Iser 1976; Eco 1979.
137 For the re-reading of ethnographic classics, see Handelman 1979; Marcus 1985.
138 For the anthropologist as author, see Geertz 1988; Fabian 1990.
139 On the discussion of writing culture, see Clifford and Marcus 1986; Abu-Lughod 1991.
140 See Yanow 2009.
141 See, for example, Habermas 1971; Said 1978.
142 For the discussion of temporalization of historical discourse, see White 1987; Koselleck 1989.
143 See El-Zein 1977; Asad 1986. See also Crapanzano 1992.
144 For the discussion of rhetoric strategies, see Crapanzano 1986; Rabinow 1986.
145 For theoretical approaches, see Foucault 1970; Bourdieu 1988.
146 For anthropological accounts, see Clifford 1983; Clifford and Marcus 1986; Strathern 1995; Turner 2002.
147 See Daniel and Peck 1996. See also Eco 1979; Fish 1980.
148 For the analysis of headscarf discourses in Turkey, see also Olson 1985; Göle 1996; Özdalga 1998; White 1999; Navaro-Yashin 2002; Çınar 2005; Kreinath 2009. See also footnote 96.
149 See also Said 1981.
150 See Bateson 1936; Geertz 1957.
151 See also Schieffelin 1996; Köpping 2004; Kreinath 2004b.
152 For studies on the ritual prayer, see also Bowen 1989; Weix 1998; Parkin and Headley 2000; Mahmood 2001b; Masquelier 2001; Henkel 2005; Soares 1996, 2005; Takim 2006; El Guindi 2008.

153 For the philosophical debate on the issue and its implications, see Ryle 1945; Wittgenstein 1953; Polanyi 1967.
154 See Said 1981; Asad 1986; Lukens-Bull 1999, 2007; Marranci 2008.
155 For the role of theory in the anthropology of Islam, see also Asad 1986; Abu-Lughod 1989, 1990a; Eickelman and Piscatori 1996; Mahmood 2001a.
156 See El-Zein 1977; Bowen 1989; Lambek 1990.
157 See Asad 1986; Abu-Lughod 1990a; Mahmood 2001b.
158 For the discussion on the unity of Islam in comparative perspective, see Von Grunebaum 1955; Gellner 1981; Roff 1999; Saeed 2007.
159 See El-Zein 1977; Lukens-Bull 2007; McLoughlin 2007.
160 See Hirschkind 2001; Mahmood 2001b.
161 See also Said 1978.
162 See Jourde 2009; Soares and Osella 2009.
163 See also Bourdieu 1977; Gell 1998; Ortner 2006.
164 See Boon 1982; Holy 1987.
165 See Handelman 1990; Hastrup 1995.
166 For research relevant to the semiotics of religion in the anthropology of Islam, see among many others Geertz 1957, 1971; El-Zein 1974, 1977; Lambek 1980, 1986, 1990; Holy 1988, 1991; Asad 1986, 1993, 2003; Werbner 1986, 1988, 1996a, 1996b, 2007; Bowen 1989, 1992, 1993, 2006; Mahmood 2001b, 2004. For reviews of anthropological literature on classical semiotic approaches to ritual, see Kreinath 2004a, 2006.
167 See Hafez 2000; Karim 2000; Poole 2002; Qureshi and Sells 2003; Poole and Richardson 2006; Ismael and Rippin 2010. See also Daniel 1960.
168 The cursory reader might overlook that these practices are not themselves the five pillars, as they do not imply one of the most important pillars—the confession of faith (*shahada*), that is, there is only one God and Muhammad is his Prophet. It is not only because this formula is rather short and spoken as a public confession in order to become a Muslim, but also that there are—for reasons that cannot be sufficiently explored here—no ethnographic studies on this topic. One reason might be that this formula is in its form too short, its content too clear, and its consequences too obvious that it did not receive the scholarly attention it would deserve.
169 See El Guindi 2008; see also Zerubavel 1981, Bloch 1987; Whitehouse 2002.
170 See also Denny 1985; Roff 1985.

References

Abu-Lughod, Lila (1986) *Veiled Sentiments: Honor and Poetry in a Bedouin Society*, Berkeley, CA: University of California Press.

—— (1989) "Zones of Theory in the Anthropology of the Arab World," *Annual Review of Anthropology*, 18: 267–306.

—— (1990a) "Anthropology's Orient: The Boundaries of Theory on the Arab World," in Hisham Sharabi (ed.) *Theory, Politics, and the Arab World: Critical Responses*, New York: Routledge.

—— (1990b) "The Romance of Resistance: Tracing Transformation of Power through Bedouin Women," *American Ethnologist*, 1/18: 41–55.

—— (1991) "Writing against Culture," in Richard G. Fox (ed.) *Recapturing Anthropology: Working in the Present*, Santa Fe, NM: School of American Research Press.

—— (1993a) "Islam and the Gendered Discourses of Death," *International Journal of Middle East Studies*, 25: 187–205.

—— (1993b) *Writing Women's Worlds: Bedouin Stories*, Berkeley, CA: University of California Press.

—— (1998) *Remaking Women: Feminism and Modernity in the Middle East*, Princeton, NJ: Princeton University Press.

—— (2002) "Do Muslim Women Really Need Saving? Anthropological Reflections on Cultural Relativism and Its Others," *American Anthropologist*, 104: 783–790.

—— (2005) *Dramas of Nationhood: The Politics of Television in Egypt*, Chicago, IL: University of Chicago Press.

Abu-Zahra, Nadia M. (1970) "On the Modesty of Women in Arab Muslim Villages: A Reply," *American Anthropologist*, 72: 1079–1088.
Abun-Nasr, Jamil M. (1965) *The Tijaniyya: A Sufi Order in the Modern World*, London: Oxford University Press.
Afshari, Reza (1994) "An Essay on Islamic Cultural Relativism in the Discourse of Human-Rights," *Human Rights Quarterly*, 16: 235–276.
Ahmed, Akbar S. (1980) *Pukhtun Economy and Society: Traditional Structure and Economic Development in a Tribal Society*, London: Routledge and Kegan Paul.
—— (1983) *Religion and Politics in Muslim Society: Order and Conflict in Pakistan*, Cambridge: Cambridge University Press.
—— (1986) *Toward Islamic Anthropology: Definition, Dogma and Directions*, Ann Arbor, MI: New Era.
—— (1991) "Postmodernist Perceptions of Islam: Observing the Observer" *Asian Survey*, 31: 213–231.
—— (ed.) (1992) *Postmodernism and Islam: Predicament and Promise*, London: Routledge.
—— (2007) *Journey into Islam: The Crisis of Globalization*, Washington, DC: Brookings Institution Press.
Ahmed, Leila (1992) *Women and Gender in Islam: Historical Roots of a Modern Debate*, Hew Haven, CT: Yale University Press.
Akou, Heather M. (2007) "Building a New 'World Fashion': Islamic Dress in the Twenty-First Century," *Fashion Theory*, 11: 403–422.
Allievi, Stefano, and Jürgen S. Nielsen (eds) (2003) *Muslim Networks and Transnational Communities in and across Europe*, Leiden: Brill.
Anderson, Jon W. (2003) "The Internet and Islam's New Interpreters," in Dale W. Eickelman and Jon W. Anderson (eds) *New Media in the Muslim World: The Emerging Public Sphere*, Bloomington, IN: Indiana University Press.
Antoun, Richard T. (1968) "On the Modesty of Women in Arab Muslim Villages: A Study in the Accommodation of Traditions," *American Anthropologist*, 70: 671–697.
—— (1971) "Three Approaches to the Cultural Anthropology of the Middle East," *Middle East Studies Association Bulletin*, 5: 24–53.
—— (1976) "Anthropology," in Leonard Binder (ed.) *The Study of the Middle East: Research and Scholarship in the Humanities and the Social Sciences*, New York: John Wiley & Sons.
—— (1989) *Muslim Preacher in the Modern World: A Jordanian Case Study in Comparative Perspective*, Princeton, NJ: Princeton University Press.
Anwar, Etin (2006) *Gender and Self in Islam*, London: Routledge.
Arensberg, Conrad (1981) "Cultural Holism through Interactional Systems," *American Anthropologist*, 83: 562–581.
Armbrust, Walter (2002) "The Riddle of Ramadan: Media, Consumer Culture, and the 'Christmasization' of a Muslim Holiday," in Donna L. Bowen and Evelyn A. Early (eds) *Everyday Life in the Middle East*, Bloomington, IN: Indiana University Press.
Asad, Talal (1970) *The Kababish Arabs: Power, Authority and Consent in a Nomadic Tribe*, London: Hurst & Co.
—— (ed.) (1973) *Anthropology and the Colonial Encounter*, London: Ithaca Press.
—— (1986) *The Idea of an Anthropology of Islam*, Washington, DC: Georgetown University, Center for Contemporary Arab Studies.
—— (1988) "Towards a Genealogy of the Concept of Ritual," in Wendy James and Douglas H. Johnson (eds) *Vernacular Christianity: Essays in the Social Anthropology of Religion. Presented to Godfrey Lienhardt*, New York: Lilian Barber.
—— (1993) *Genealogies of Religion: Discipline and Reason in Christianity and Islam*, Baltimore, MD: Johns Hopkins Press.
—— (2003) *Formations of the Secular: Christianity, Islam, Modernity*, Stanford, CA: Stanford University Press.
Ashkenazi, Michael (1997) "Informant Networks and their Anthropologists," *Human Organization*, 56: 471–478.
Aswad, Barbara C. and Barbara Bilgé (eds) (1996) *Family and Gender among American Muslims: Issues Facing Middle Eastern Immigrants and their Descendants*, Philadelphia, PA: Temple University Press.
Babcock, Barbara A. (1980) "Reflexivity: Definitions and Discriminations," *Semiotica*, 30: 1–14.

Barnard, Alan (2000) *History and Theory in Anthropology*, Cambridge and New York: Cambridge University Press.

Barth, Frederik (1959) *Political Leadership among Swat Pathans*, London: Athlone Press.

—— (1965) *Nomads of South Persia, the Baseri Tribe of the Khamseh Confederacy*, New York: Humanities Press.

—— (ed.) (1969) *Ethnic Groups and Boundaries: The Social Organization of Culture Difference*, Bergen: Universitetsforlaget.

Barthes, Roland (1975) *The Pleasure of the Text*, trans. Richard Miller, New York: Hill and Wang.

Bates, Daniel G., and Amal Rassam (2001) *Peoples and Cultures of the Middle East*, Upper Saddle River, NJ: Prentice Hall.

Bateson, Gregory (1936) *Naven: A Survey of the Problems suggested by a Composite Picture of the Culture of a New Guinea Tribe drawn from Three Points of View*, Cambridge: Cambridge University Press.

—— (1941) "Experiments in Thinking about Observed Ethnological Material," *Philosophy of Science*, 8: 53–68.

Bauman, Richard (1986) *Story, Performance, and Event: Contextual Studies of Oral Narrative*, Cambridge and New York: Cambridge University Press.

—— and Charles L. Briggs (1990) "Poetics and Performance as Critical Perspectives on Language and Social Life," *Annual Review of Anthropology*, 19: 59–88.

—— and Joel Sherzer (1974) *Explorations in the Ethnography of Speaking*, London and New York: Cambridge University Press.

Beatty, Andrew (1996) "Adam and Eve and Vishnu: Syncretism in the Javanese Slametan," *The Journal of the Royal Anthropological Institute*, 2: 271–288.

—— (2005) "Emotions in the Field: What are we Talking about?" *Journal of the Royal Anthropological Institute*, 11: 17–37.

Behar, Ruth, and Deborah A. Gordon (1995) *Women Writing Culture*, Berkeley, CA: University of California Press.

Bell, Catherine M. (1992) *Ritual Theory, Ritual Practice*, Oxford and New York: Oxford University Press.

Benedict, Ruth (1934) *Patterns of Culture*, Boston and New York: Houghton Mifflin Company.

Benthall, Jonathan (1999) "Financial Worship: The Quranic Injunction to Almsgiving," *The Journal of the Royal Anthropological Institute*, 5: 27–42.

Bernal, Victoria (1994) "Gender, Culture, and Capitalism: Women and the Remaking of Islamic 'Tradition' in a Sudanese Village," *Comparative Studies in Society and History*, 36: 36–67.

Bhabha, Homi K. (1994) *The Location of Culture*, London and New York: Routledge.

Birge, John K. (1937) *The Bektashi Order of Dervishes*, London: Luzac & Co.

Birks, J. Stace (1977) "The Mecca Pilgrimage by West African Pastoral Nomads," *The Journal of Modern African Studies*, 15: 47–58.

Bloch, Maurice (1987) "The Ritual of the Royal Bath in Madagascar: The Dissolution of Death, Birth and Fertility into Authority," in David Cannadine and Simon Price (eds) *Rituals of Royalty: Power and Ceremonial in Traditional Societies*, Cambridge: Cambridge University Press.

—— (1992) *Prey into Hunter: The Politics of Religious Experience*, Cambridge and New York: Cambridge University Press.

Boas, Franz (1925) *Contributions to the Ethnology of the Kwakiutl*, New York: Columbia University Press.

Boddy, Janice P. (1989) *Wombs and Alien Spirits: Women, Men, and the Zar Cult in Northern Sudan*, Madison, WI: University of Wisconsin Press.

Boellstorff, Tom (2005) "Between Religion and Desire: Being Muslim and Gay," *American Anthropologist*, 107: 575–585.

Bohannan, Paul, and Dirk van der Elst (1998) *Asking and Listening: Ethnography as Personal Adaptation*, Prospect Heights, IL: Waveland Press.

Boissevain, Jeremy (1974) *Friends of Friends: Networks, Manipulators and Coalitions*, New York: St. Martin's Press.

Boon, James A. (1982) *Other Tribes, Other Scribes: Symbolic Anthropology in the Comparative Study of Cultures, Histories, Religions, and Texts*, Cambridge and New York: Cambridge University Press.

Borneman, John (2009) "Fieldwork Experience, Collaboration and Interlocution: The 'Metaphysics of Presence' in Encounters with the Syrian Mukhabarat," in John Borneman and Abdellah

Hammoudi (eds) *Being There: The Fieldwork Encounter and the Making of Truth*, Berkeley, CA: University of California Press.

Borneman, John and Abdellah Hammoudi (2009) "The Fieldwork Encounter, Experience, and the Making of Truth: An Introduction," in John Borneman and Abdellah Hammoudi (eds) *Being There: The Fieldwork Encounter and the Making of Truth*, Berkeley, CA: University of California Press.

Bourdieu, Pierre (1977) *Outline of a Theory of Practice*, trans. Richard Nice, Cambridge and New York: Cambridge University Press.

—— (1988) *Homo Academicus*, trans. Peter Collier, Stanford, CA: Stanford University Press.

—— (1998) *Practical Reason: On the Theory of Action*, trans. Randall Johnson, Cambridge: Polity Press.

—— and Loïc J.D. Wacquant (1992) *An Invitation to Reflexive Sociology*, Chicago, IL: University of Chicago Press.

Bowen, John R. (1989) "Salat in Indonesia: The Social Meanings of an Islamic Ritual," *Man*, 24: 600–619.

—— (1992) "On Scriptural Essentialism and Ritual Variation: Muslim Sacrifice in Sumatra and Morocco," *American Ethnologist*, 19: 656–671.

—— (1993) *Muslims through Discourse: Religion and Ritual in Gayo Society*, Princeton, NJ: Princeton University Press.

—— (1998a) "Qur'ân, Justice, Gender: Internal Debates in Indonesian Islamic Jurisprudence," *History of Religions*, 38: 52–78.

—— (1998b) "What is 'Universal' and 'Local' in Islam?" *Ethos*, 26: 258–261.

—— (2006) *Why the French Don't Like Headscarves: Islam, the State, and Public Space*, Princeton, NJ: Princeton University Press.

Bradburd, Daniel (1998) *Being There: The Necessity of Fieldwork*, Washington, DC: Smithsonian Press.

Breckenridge, Carol A., and Peter van der Veer (1993) *Orientalism and the Postcolonial Predicament: Perspectives on South Asia*, Philadelphia, PA: University of Pennsylvania Press.

Brenner, Louis (2001) *Controlling Knowledge: Religion, Power, and Schooling in a West African Muslim Society*, Bloomington, IN: Indiana University Press.

Brenner, Suzanne A. (1996) "Reconstructing Self and Society: Javanese Muslim Women and the 'Veil'," *American Ethnologist*, 23: 673–697.

Briggs, Charles L. (1986) *Learning How to Ask: A Sociolinguistic Appraisal of the Role of the Interview in Social Science Research*, Cambridge and New York: Cambridge University Press.

Brown, Michael F. (2008) "Cultural Relativism 2.0," *Current Anthropology*, 49: 363–383.

Buckley, Peter (1994) "Observing the Other: Reflections on Anthropological Fieldwork," *Journal of the American Psychoanalytic Association*, 42: 613–634.

Buitelaar, Maria (1993) *Fasting and Feasting in Morocco: Women's Participation in Ramadan*, Oxford: Berg.

Bujra, Abdalla S. (1971) *The Politics of Stratification: A Study of Political Change in a South Arabian Town*, Oxford: Claredon Press.

Bunt, Gary R. (2003) *Islam in the Digital Age: E-Jihad, Online Fatwas, and Cyber Islamic Environments*, London and Stirling: Pluto Press.

—— (2009) *iMuslims: Rewiring the House of Islam*, Chapel Hill, NC: University of North Carolina Press.

Burke, III, Edmund (1998) "Orientalism and World History: Representing Middle Eastern Nationalism and Islamism in the Twentieth Century," *Theory and Society*, 27: 489–507.

Burton, Richard F. (1855) *Personal Narrative of a Pilgrimage to El-Medinah and Meccah*, London: Longman, Brown, Green, and Longmans.

Candea, Matei (2007) "Arbitrary Locations: In Defense of the Bounded Field-Site," *Journal of the Royal Anthropological Institute*, 13: 167–184.

Cannell, Fenella (2006) *Anthropology of Christianity*, Durham, NC: Duke University Press.

Caplan, Patricia (2003) *The Ethics of Anthropology: Debates and Dilemmas*, London and New York: Routledge.

Cesari, Jocelyne (2004) *When Islam and Democracy Meet: Muslims in Europe and in the United States*, New York: Palgrave Macmillan.

—— and Sean McLoughlin (2005) *European Muslims and the Secular State*, Aldershot: Ashgate.

Cobbold, Evelyn (1934) *Pilgrimage to Mecca*, London: J. Murray.

Çınar, Alev İ. (2005) *Modernity, Islam, and Secularism in Turkey: Bodies, Places, and Time*, Minneapolis, MN: University of Minnesota Press.
Clifford, James (1980) "Review Essay of *Orientalism* by Edward Said," *Historical Theory*, 19: 204–223.
—— (1983) "On Ethnographic Authority," *Representations*, 1: 118–146.
—— (1990) "Notes on Fieldnotes," in Roger Sanjek (ed.) *Fieldnotes: The Makings of Anthropology*, Ithaca, NY: Cornell University Press.
—— and George E. Marcus (1986) *Writing Culture: The Poetics and Politics of Ethnography*, Berkeley, CA: University of California Press.
Cohen, Abner (1972) *Arab Border-Villages in Israel: A Study of Continuity and Change in Social Organization*, Manchester: Manchester University Press.
Comaroff, Jean, and John Comaroff (1991) *Of Revelation and Revolution*, Chicago, IL: University of Chicago Press.
—— and —— (eds) (1993) *Modernity and its Malcontents: Ritual and Power in Postcolonial Africa*, Chicago, IL: University of Chicago Press.
Combs-Schilling, M. Elaine (1985) "Family and Friend in a Moroccan Boom Town: The Segmentary Debate Reconsidered," *American Ethnologist*, 12: 659–675.
—— (1989) *Sacred Performances: Islam, Sexuality and Sacrifice*, New York: Columbia University Press.
Cooper, Barbara M. (1999) "The Strength in the Song: Muslim Personhood, Audible Capital, and Hausa Women's Performance of the Hajj," *Social Text*, 17: 87–109.
Coulon, Christian (1988) "Women, Islam, and Baraka," in Donald C. O'Brian and Christian Coulon (eds) *Charisma and Brotherhood in African Islam*, Oxford: Claredon Press.
Crapanzano, Vincent (1973) *The Hamadsha: A Study of Moroccan Ethnopsychiatry*, Berkeley, CA: University of California Press.
—— (1977) "Mohammed and Dawia: Possession in Morooco," in Vincent Crapanzano and Vivian Garrison (eds) *Studies in Spirit Possession*, New York: Wiley and Sons.
—— (1980) *Tuhami: Portrait of a Moroccan*, Chicago, IL: University of Chicago Press.
—— (1986) "Hermes' Dilemma: The Masking of Subversion in Ethnographic Description," in James Clifford and George Marcus (eds) *Writing Culture: The Poetics and Politics of Ethnography*, Berkeley, CA: University of California Press.
—— (1992) *Hermes' Dilemma and Hamlet's Desire: On the Epistemology of Interpretation*, Cambridge, MA: Harvard University Press.
Crary, Jonathan (1990) *Techniques of the Observer: On Vision and Modernity in the Nineteenth Century*, Cambridge, MA: MIT Press.
Cruise O'Brian, Donald B. (1971) *The Mourides of Senegal: The Political and Economic Organization of an Islamic Brotherhood*, Oxford: The Claredon Press.
Csordas, Thomas J. (1990) "Embodiment as a Paradigm for Anthropology," *Ethnos*, 18: 5–87.
Daniel, E. Valentine (1984) *Fluid Signs: Being a Person the Tamil Way*, Berkeley, CA: University of California Press.
—— and Jeffrey M. Peck (1996) *Culture/Contexture: Explorations in Anthropology and Literary Studies*, Berkeley, CA: University of California Press.
Daniel, Norman A. (1960) *Islam and the West: The Making of an Image*, Edinburgh: Edinburgh University Press.
Das, Veena (1984) "For a Folk-Theology and Theological Anthropology of Islam," *Contributions to Indian Sociology*, 18: 239–305.
Dassetto, Felice (1996) *La construction de l'Islam européen: approche socio-anthropologique*, Paris: Harmattan.
Davies, Merryl W. (1988) *Knowing one Another: Shaping an Islamic Anthropology*, London and New York: Mansell Publishing Limited.
Davies, James, and Dimitrina Spencer (2010) *Emotions in the Field: The Psychology and Anthropology of Fieldwork Experience*, Stanford, CA: Stanford University Press.
Deeb, Lara (2006) *An Enchanted Modern: Gender and Public Piety in Shi'i Lebanon*, Princeton, NJ: Princeton University Press.
Delaney, Carol (1991) *The Seed and the Soil: Gender and Cosmology in Turkish Village Society*, Berkeley, CA: University of California Press.

Denny, Freferick M. (1985) "Islamic Ritual: Perspectives and Theories," in Richard C. Martin (ed.) *Approaches to Islam in Religious Studies*, Tucson, AZ: University of Arizona Press.

Derrida, Jacques (1978) "Structure, Sign and Game in the Discourse of Human Sciences," in Jacques Derrida (ed.) *Writing and Difference*, Chicago, IL: University of Chicago Press.

Desai, Amit, and Evan Killick (eds) (2010) *The Ways of Friendship: Anthropological Perspectives*, New York: Berghahn Books.

Donnan, Hastings (1988) *Marriage among Muslims: Preference and Choice in Northern Pakistan*, Delhi: Hindustan Publisher.

——and Akbar S. Ahmed (eds) (1994) *Islam, Globalization, and Postmodernity*, London: Routledge.

——and Frits Selier (1997) *Family and Gender in Pakistan: Domestic Organization in a Muslim Society*, New Delhi: Hindustan Publisher.

——and Pnina Werbner (eds) (1991) *Economy and Culture in Pakistan: Migrants and Cities in a Muslim Society*. London: Macmillan.

Donnelly, Jack (2007) "The Relative Universality of Human Rights," *Human Rights Quarterly*, 29: 281–306.

Doughty, Charles M. (1898) *Travels in Arabia Deserta*, Cambridge: Cambridge University Press.

Douglas, Mary (1966) *Purity and Danger: An Analysis of Concepts of Pollution and Taboo*, London: Routledge & Kegan Paul.

—— (1970) *Natural Symbols: Explorations in Cosmology*, New York: Pantheon Books.

Driessen, Henk (1993) *The Politics of Ethnographic Reading and Writing: Confrontations of Western and Indigenous Views*, Saarbrücken and Fort Lauderdale: Verlag Breitenbach.

Dumont, Louis (1970) *Homo Hierarchicus: An Essay on the Caste System*, trans. Mark Sainsbury, Chicago, IL: University of Chicago Press.

Eco, Umberto (1979) *The Role of the Reader: Explorations in the Semiotics of Texts*, Bloomington, IN: Indiana University Press.

Edwards, David B. (1995) "Print Islam: Media and Religious Revolution in Afghanistan," *Anthropological Quarterly*, 68: 171–184.

Eickelman, Dale F. (1976) *Moroccan Islam: Tradition and Society in a Pilgrimage Center*, Austin University of Texas Press.

—— (1978) "The Art of Memory: Islamic Education and its Social Reproduction," *Comparative Studies in Society and History*, 20: 485–516.

—— (1979) "The Political Economy of Meaning," *American Anthropologist*, 6: 386–393.

—— (1981) *The Middle East: An Anthropological Approach*, Englewood Cliffs, NJ: Prentice-Hall.

—— (1982) "The Study of Islam in Local Contexts," *Contributions to Asian Studies*, 17: 1–16.

—— (1985) *Knowledge and Power in Morocco: The Education of a Twentieth-Century Notable*, Princeton, NJ: Princeton University Press.

—— (2000) "Islam and the Languages of Modernity," *Daedalus*, 129: 119–135.

—— and Jon W. Anderson (eds) (1999) *New Media in the Muslim World: The Emerging Public Sphere*, Bloomington, IN: Indiana University Press.

——and James Piscatori (1996) "Social Theory in the Study of Muslim Societies," in Dale F. Eickelman and James Piscatori (eds) *Muslim Travellers: Pilgrimage, Migration, and the Religious Imagination*, London: Routledge.

Eisenlohr, Patrick (2006) "The Politics of Diaspora and the Morality of Secularism: Muslim Identities and Islamic Authority in Mauritius," *Journal of the Royal Anthropological Institute*, 12: 395–412.

El Guindi, Fadwa (1999) *Veil: Modesty, Privacy, and Resistance*, Oxford and New York: Berg.

—— (2004) *Visual Anthropology: Essential Method and Theory*, Walnut Creek: AltaMira Press.

—— (2008) *By Noon Prayer: The Rhythm of Islam*, Oxford and New York: Berg.

El-Zein, Abdul Hamid (1974) *The Sacred Meadows: A Structural Analysis of Religious Symbolism in an East African Town*, Evanston, IL: Northwestern University Press.

—— (1977) "Beyond Ideology and Theology: The Search for the Anthropology of Islam," *Annual Review of Anthropology*, 6: 227–254.

Engelke, Matthew E., and Matt Tomlinson (2006) *The Limits of Meaning: Case Studies in the Anthropology of Christianity*, New York: Berghahn books.

Er-Rashid, Haroun (2003) "Muslims and the West: A Paradigm of Polarization," in Michael J. Thompson (ed.) *Islam and the West: Critical Perspectives on Modernity*, Oxford: Rowman & Littlefield Publishers.

Evans-Pritchard, Edward E. (1937) *Witchcraft, Oracles and Magic among the Azande*, Oxford: Clarendon Press.

—— (1946) "Hereditary Succession of Shaikhs of Sanusiya Lodges in Cyrenaica," *Man*, 46: 58–62.

—— (1949) *The Sanusi of Cyrenaica*, Oxford: The Claredon Press.

—— (1963) *The Comparative Method in Social Anthropology*, London: Athlone Press.

Ewing, Katherine P. (ed.) (1988) *Shari'at and Ambiguity in South Asian Islam*, Berkeley, CA: University of California Press.

Fabian, Johannes (1983) *Time and the Other: How Anthropology Makes its Object*, New York: Columbia University Press.

—— (1990) "Presence and Representation: The Other and Anthropological Writings," *Critical Inquiry*, 16: 753–772.

Fardon, Richard (ed.) (1990) *Localizing Strategies: Regional Traditions of Ethnographic Writing*, Edinburgh: Scottish Academic Press.

Faubion, James D. (2009) "The Ethics of Fieldwork as an Ethics of Connectivity, or, The Good Anthropologist (Isn't What She Used to be)," in James D. Faubion and George E. Marcus (eds) *Fieldwork is Not What it Used to be: Learning Anthropology's Method in a Time of Transition*, Ithaca, NY: Cornell University Press.

—— and George E. Marcus (eds) (2009) *Fieldwork is Not What it Used to be: Learning Anthropology's Method in a Time of Transition*, Ithaca, NY: Cornell University Press.

Fernea, Elizabeth W. (1965) *Guests of the Sheik: An Ethnography of an Iraqi Village*, New York: Anchor Books.

—— (1998) *In Search of Islamic Feminism: One Woman's Global Journey*, New York: Doubleday.

—— and Basima Q. Bezirgan (1977) *Middle Eastern Muslim Women Speak*, Austin, TX: University of Texas Press.

Fernea, Robert A., and Elizabeth W. Fernea (1972) "Variation in Religious Observance among Islamic Women," in Nikki R. Keddie (ed.) *Scholars, Saints, and Sufis: Muslim Religious Institutions in the Middle East since 1500*, Berkeley, CA: University of California Press.

—— and James M. Malarkey (1975) "Anthropology of the Middle East and North Africa: A Critical Assessment," *Annual Review of Anthropology*, 4: 183–206.

Firth, Raymond (1936) *We, the Tikopia: A Sociological Study of Kinship in Primitive Polynesia*, London: G. Allen & Unwin.

Fischer, Michael M.J. (1980) *Iran: From Religious Dispute to Revolution*, Cambridge, MA: Harvard University Press.

—— and Mehdi Abedi (eds) (1990) *Debating Muslims: Cultural Dialogues in Postmodernity and Tradition*, Madison, WI: University of Wisconsin Press.

Fish, Stanley (1980) *Is There a Text in This Class? The Authority of Interpretative Communities*, Cambridge, MA: MIT Press.

Foucault, Michel (1970) *The Order of Things: An Archaeology of the Human Sciences*, trans. A.M. Sheridan Smith, London: Tavistock Publications.

—— (1972) *The Archaeology of Knowledge*, trans. A.M. Sheridan Smith, London: Tavistock Publications.

Frankl, P.J.L., and Y.A. Omar (1996) "The Observance of Ramadān in Swahili-Land," *Journal of Religion in Africa*, 26: 416–434.

Friedel, Erika (1991) *Women of Deh Koh: Lives in an Iranian Village*, Harmondsworth: Penguin.

Fuller, Anne H. (1961) *Buarij: Portrait of a Lebanese Muslim Village*, Cambridge, MA: Harvard University Press.

Gadamer, Hans-Georg (1975) *Truth and Method*, trans. Joel Weinsheimer and Donald G. Marshall, London: Sheed and Ward.

Gardner, Andrew, and David M. Hoffman (2006) "Fieldwork and Writing 'from' the Field," in Andrew Gardner and David M. Hoffman (eds) *Dispatches from the Field: Neophyte Ethnographers in a Changing World*, Long Grove, IL: Waveland Press.

Geertz, Clifford (1957) "Ritual and Social Change: A Javanese Example," *American Anthropologist*, 59: 32–54.

—— (1961) "Studies in Peasant Life: Community and Society," *Biennial Review of Anthropology*, 2: 1–41.
—— (1968) *Islam Observed: Religious Developments in Marocco and Indonesia*, New Haven, CT: Yale University Press.
—— (1971) "Suq: The Bazar Economy in Sefrou," in Clifford Geertz, Hildred Geertz and Lawrence Rosen (eds) *Meaning and Order in Moroccan Society*, Cambridge: Cambridge University Press.
—— (1972) "Deep Play: Notes on the Balinese Cockfight," *Daedalus*, 101: 56–86.
—— (1973) "Thick Description" in Clifford Geertz, *The Interpretation of Cultures: Selected Essays*, New York: Basic Books.
—— (1983) *Local Knowledge: Further Essays in Interpretive Anthropology*, New York: Basic Books.
—— (1988) *Works and Lives: The Anthropologist as Author*, Stanford, CA: Stanford University Press.
Gell, Alfred (1998) *Art and Agency: An Anthropological Theory*, Oxford and New York: Clarendon Press.
Gellner, Ernest (1968) "A Pendulum Swing Theory of Islam," *Archives Marocaines de Sociologie* 1: 5–14.
—— (1969) *Saints of the Atlas*, Chicago, IL: Chicago University Press.
—— (1981) *Muslim Society*, Cambridge and New York: Cambridge University Press.
—— (1985) *Relativism and the Social Sciences*, Cambridge and New York: Cambridge University Press.
Gerholm, Tomas (1977) *Market, Mosque, and Mafraj*, Stockholm: Stockholm University Press.
—— (1988) "On Ritual: A Postmodern View," *Ethos*, 3/4: 190–203.
—— and Yngve Georg Lithman (eds) (1988) *The New Islamic Presence in Western Europe*, London and New York: Mansell.
Geros, Panagiotis (2008) "Doing Fieldwork with Fear and Silences," in Heidi Armbruster and Anna Laerke (eds) *Taking Sides: Ethics, Politics, and Fieldwork in Anthropology*, New York and Oxford: Berghahn Books.
Ghadially, Rehana (2005) "Devotional Empowerment: Women Pilgrims, Saints and Shrines in a South Asian Muslim Sect," *Asian Journal of Women's Studies*, 11: 79–101.
Gilsenan, Michael (1973) *Saint and Sufi in Modern Egypt: An Essay in the Sociology of Religion*, Oxford: Clarendon Press.
—— (1982) *Recognizing Islam: An Anthropologist's Introduction*, London: Croom Helm.
—— (1989) "Very like a Camel: The Appearance of an Anthropologist's Middle East," in Richard Fardon (ed.) *Localizing Strategies: Regional Traditions of Ethnographic Writing*, Washington, DC: Smithsonian Institute Press.
—— (2000) "Signs of Truth: Enchantment, Modernity and the Dreams of Peasant Women," *The Journal of the Royal Anthropological Institute*, 6: 597–615.
Gluckman, Max (1955) *Custom and Conflict in Africa*, Oxford: Blackwell.
—— and Cyril Daryll Forde (eds) (1963) *Essays on the Ritual of Social Relations*, Manchester: Manchester University Press.
Gokariksel, Banu, and Anna J. Secor (2009) "New Transnational Geographies of Islamism, Capitalism and Subjectivity: The Veiling Fashion Industry in Turkey," *Area*, 41: 6–18.
Göle, Nilüfer (1996) *The Forbidden Modern: Civilization and Veiling*, Ann Arbor, MI: University of Michigan Press.
—— (1997) "The Quest for the Islamic Self within the Context of Modernity," in Sibel Bozdogan and Resat Kasaba (eds) *Rethinking Modernity and National Identity in Turkey*, Seattle, WA: University of Washington Press.
—— (1998) "Islamism, Feminism and Post-Modernism: Women's Movements in Islamic Countries," *New Perspectives on Turkey*, 19: 53–70.
Goodale, Mark (2006) "Toward a Critical Anthropology of Human Rights," *Current Anthropology*, 47: 485–511.
—— (2009) *Surrendering to Utopia: An Anthropology of Human Rights*, Stanford, CA: Stanford University Press.
Goody, Jack (1977) "Against 'Ritual': Loosely Structured Thoughts on a Loosely Defined Topic," in Sally F. Moore and Barbara G. Myerhoff (eds) *Secular Ritual*, Assen and Amsterdam: Van Gorcum.
—— (1986) *The Logic of Writing and the Organization of Society*, Cambridge and New York: Cambridge University Press.
—— (2004) *Islam in Europe*, Cambridge: Polity Press.

Gordon, Daniel (1991) "Female Circumcision and Genital Operations in Egypt and the Sudan: A Dilemma for Medical Anthropology," *Medical Anthropology Quarterly*, 5: 3–14.

Granqvist, Hilma (1947) *Birth and Childhood among the Arabs: Studies in a Muhammadan Village in Palestine*, Helsingfors: Söderström & Co.

—— (1965) *Muslim Death and Burial: Arab Customs and Traditions Studied in a Village in Jordan*, Helsingfors: Central Tryckeriet.

Grimshaw, Anna (2001) *The Ethnographer's Eye: Ways of Seeing in Anthropology*, Cambridge and New York: Cambridge University Press.

Gulick, John (1969) "The Anthropology of the Middle East," *Middle East Studies Association Bulletin*, 3: 1–14.

Gupta, Akhil and James Ferguson (1997) *Culture, Power, Place: Explorations in Critical Anthropology*, Durham, NC: Duke University Press.

Habermas, Jürgen (1971) *Knowledge and Human Interests*, trans. Jeremy J. Shapiro, Boston, MA: Beacon Press.

Haddad, Emily A. (2002) *Orientalist Poetics: The Islamic Middle East in Nineteenth-Century English and French Poetry*, Aldershot and Burlington: Ashgate.

Haddad, Yvonne Y. (ed.) (1991) *The Muslims of America*, New York: Oxford University Press.

—— (ed.) (1994) *Muslim Communities in North America*, Albany, NY: State University of New York.

—— and John L. Esposito (eds) (1998) *Islam, Gender, and Social Change*, New York and Oxford: Oxford University Press.

—— and A.T. Lummis (1987) *Islamic Values in the United States: A Comparative Study*, New York: Oxford University Press.

—— J.I. Smith, and K.M. Moore (2006) *Muslim Women in America: The Challenge of Islamic Identity Today*, New York: Oxford University Press.

—— John O. Voll, and John L. Esposito (1991) *The Contemporary Islamic Revival: A Critical Survey and Bibliography*, New York: Greenwood Press.

Hafez, Kai (ed.) (2000) *Islam and the West in the Mass Media: Fragmented Images in a Globalizing World*, Cresskill, NJ: Hampton Press.

Halliday, Fred (1987) "Relativism and Universalism in Human Rights: The Case of the Islamic Middle East," in David Beetham (ed.) *Politics and Human Rights*, London: Blackwell.

Handelman, Don (1979) "Is Naven Ludic? Paradox and the Communication of Identity," *Social Analysis*, 1: 177–191.

—— (1990) *Models and Mirrors: Towards an Anthropology of Public Events*, Cambridge: Cambridge University Press.

—— (2004) "Re-Framing Ritual," in Jens Kreinath, Constance Hartung and Annette Deschner (eds) *The Dynamics of Changing Rituals: The Transformation of Religious Rituals within Their Social and Cultural Context*, New York: Peter Lang.

—— (2006) "Conceptual Alternative to 'Ritual'," in Jens Kreinath, Jan Snoek and Michael Stausberg (eds) *Theorizing Rituals. Vol. I: Issues, Topics, Approaches, Concepts*, Leiden: Brill.

Hansen, Henny H. (1961) "The Pattern of Women's Seclusion and Veiling in a Shi'a Village," *Folk*, 3: 23–42.

—— (1967) *Investigations in a Shi'a Village in Bahrain*, Copenhagen: Publications of the National Museum.

Harrison, Faye V. (2008) *Outsider Within: Reworking Anthropology in the Global Age*, Urbana, IL: University of Illinois Press.

Hastrup, Kirsten (1995) *A Passage to Anthropology: Between Experience and Theory*, New York: Routledge.

Headland, Thomas, Kenneth Pike, and Marvin Harris (eds) (1990) *Emics and Etics: The Insider/Outsider Debate*, New York: Sage Publications.

Hefner, Robert W. (1985) *Hindu Javanese: Tengger Tradition and Islam*, Princeton, NJ: Princeton University Press.

—— (1997) "Print Islam: Mass Media and Ideological Rivalries among Indonesian Muslims," *Indonesia*, 64: 77–103.

—— (2003) "Civic Pluralism Denied? The New Media and *Jihadi* Violence in Indonesia," in Dale W. Eickelman and Jon W. Anderson (eds) *New Media in the Muslim World: The Emerging Public Sphere*, Bloomington, IN: Indiana University Press.

Hegland, Mary E. (1995) "Shi'a Women of Northwest Pakistan and Agency through Practice: Ritual, Resistance, Resilience," *Political and Legal Anthropology Review*, 18: 1–14.
—— (1998) "Flagellation and Fundamentalism: (Trans)forming Meaning, Identity, and Gender through Pakistani Women's Rituals of Mourning," *American Ethnologist*, 25: 240–266.
Henkel, Heiko (2005) "'Between Belief and Unbelief Lies the Performance of Salat': Meaning and Efficacy of a Muslim Ritual," *Journal of the Royal Anthropological Institute*, 11: 487–507.
Henle, Paul (2006) "Spirit Possession, Power, and the Absent Presence of Islam: Re-Viewing *Les maîtres fous*" *The Journal of the Royal Anthropological Institute*, 12, 731–761.
Herskovits, Michael J. (1972) *Cultural Relativism: Perspectives in Cultural Pluralism*, ed. by Frances Herskovits, New York: Random House.
Hirschkind, Charles (2001) "Civic Virtue and Religious Reason: An Islamic Counterpublic," *Current Anthropology*, 16: 3–34.
—— (2006) *The Ethical Soundscape: Cassette Sermons and Islamic Counterpublics*, New York: Columbia University Press.
Hobart, Angela, and Bruce Kapferer (2004) *Aesthetics in Performance: Formations of Symbolic Construction and Experience*, New York: Berghahn Books.
Hollis, Martin, and Steven Lukes (1982) *Rationality and Relativism*, Cambridge, MA: MIT Press.
Holy, Ladislav (1987) *Comparative Anthropology*, Oxford and New York: Blackwell.
—— (1988) "Gender and Ritual in an Islamic Society: The Berti of Dafur," *Man*, 23: 469–487.
—— (1991) *Religion and Custom in a Muslim Society: The Berti of Sudan*, Cambridge: Cambridge University Press.
Horstmann, Alexander (2009) "The Revitalisation and Reflexive Transformation of the Manooraa Rongkruu Performance and Ritual in Southern Thailand: Articulations with Modernity," *Asian Journal of Social Science*, 37: 918–934.
Horvatich, Patricia (1994) "Ways of Knowing Islam," *American Ethnologist*, 21: 811–826.
Houston, Christopher (2001) "The Brewing of Islamist Modernity: Tea Gardens and Public Space in Istanbul," *Theory, Culture, and Society*, 18: 77–97.
—— (2006) "The Never Ending Dance: Islamism, Kemalism and the Power of Self-Institution in Turkey," *The Australian Journal of Anthropology*, 17: 161–178.
Hubert, Henri, and Marcel Mauss (1964) *Sacrifice: Its Nature and Function*, trans. Wilfried D. Halls, London: Cohen & West.
Huntington, Samuel P. (1993) "The Clash of Civilizations?" *Foreign Affairs*, 72: 22–50.
Hymes, Dell (1962) "The Ethnography of Speaking," in Thomas Gladwin and William C. Sturtevant (eds) *Anthropology and Human Behavior*, Washington, DC: Anthropological Society Washington.
Iser, Wolfgang (1976) *Der Akt des Lesens: Theorie ästhetischer Wirkung*, Munich: Wilhelm Fink Verlag.
Ismael, Tareq Y., and Andrew Rippin (2010) *Islam in the Eyes of the West: Images and Realities in an Age of Terror*, London and New York: Routledge.
Johnson, Jeffrey C., Christine Avenarius, and Jack Weatherford (2006) "The Active Participant-Observer: Applying Social Role Analysis to Participant Observation," *Field Methods*, 18: 111–143.
Jourde, Cedric (2009) "The Ethnographic Sensibility: Overlooked Authoritarian Dynamics and Islamic Ambivalences in West Africa," in Edward Schatz (ed.) *Political Ethnography: What Immersion Contributes to the Study of Power*, Chicago, IL: University of Chicago Press.
Kapferer, Bruce (1983) *A Celebration of Demons: Exorcism and the Aesthetics of Healing in Sri Lanka*, Bloomington, IN: Indiana University Press.
Karam, Azza M . (1998) *Women, Islamisms, and the State: Contemporary Feminisms in Egypt*, London: Macmillan Press; New York: St Martin's Press.
Karim, Karim H. (2000) *Islamic Peril: Media and Global Violence*, Montreal and New York: Black Rose Books.
Kazemzadeh, Masoud (2002) *Islamic Fundamentalism, Feminism, and Gender Inequality in Iran under Khomeini*, Lanham, MD: University Press of America.
Keane, Webb (2007) *Christian Moderns: Freedom and Fetish in the Mission Encounter*, Berkeley, CA: University of California Press.
Keenan, Kevin L., and Sultana Yeni (2003) "Ramadan Advertising in Egypt: A Content Analysis with Elaboration on Selected Items," *Journal of Media and Religion*, 2: 109–117.

Kendall, Laurel (1985) *Shamans, Housewives, and Other Restless Spirits: Women in Korean Ritual Life*, Honolulu, HI: University of Hawaii Press.

Keyman, E Fuat (2007) "Modernity, Secularism and Islam: The Case of Turkey," *Theory, Culture, and Society*, 24: 215–234.

Khan, Naveeda (2006) "Of Children and Jinn: An Inquiry into an Unexpected Friendship during Uncertain Times," *Cultural Anthropology*, 21: 234–264.

Kiliçbay, Bariş, and Mutlu Binark (2002) "Consumer Culture, Islam and the Politics of Lifestyle: Fashion for Veiling in Contemporary Turkey," *European Journal of Communication*, 17: 495–511.

Köpping, Klaus-Peter (2004) "Failure of Performance or Passage to the Acting Self? Mishima's Suicide between Ritual and Theater," in Jens Kreinath, Constance Hartung and Annette Deschner (eds) *The Dynamics of Changing Rituals: The Transformation of Religious Rituals within Their Social and Cultural Context*, New York: Peter Lang.

Kosebalaban, Hasan (2005) "The Impact of Globalization on Islamic Political Identity: The Case of Turkey," *World Affairs*, 168: 27–37.

Koselleck, Reinhart (1989) *Vergangene Zukunft: Zur Semanik geschichtlicher Zeiten*, Frankfurt a.M.: Suhrkamp.

Kramer, Fritz (1993) *The Red Fez: Art and Spirit Possession in Africa*, trans. Malcolm Green, London and New York: Verso.

Kreinath, Jens (2004a) "Meta-Theoretical Parameters for the Analysis and Comparison of two Recent Approaches to the Study of the Yasna," in Michael Stausberg (ed.) *Zoroastrian Rituals in Context*, Leiden: Brill.

—— (2004b) "Theoretical Afterthoughts," in Jens Kreinath, Constance Hartung and Annette Deschner (eds) *The Dynamics of Changing Rituals: The Transformation of Religious Rituals within Their Social and Cultural Context*, New York: Peter Lang.

—— (2006) "Semiotics," in Jens Kreinath, Jan A.M. Snoek and Michael Stausberg (eds) *Theorizing Rituals. Vol. I: Issues, Topics, Approaches, Concepts*, Leiden: Brill.

—— (2009) "Headscarf Discourses and the Contestation of Secularism in Turkey," *The Council of Societies for the Study of Religion Bulletin*, 38: 77–84.

——, Jan A.M. Snoek and Michael Stausberg (2006) "Ritual Studies, Ritual Theory, Theorizing Ritual: An Introductory Essay," in Jens Kreinath, Jan A.M. Snoek and Michael Stausberg (eds) *Theorizing Rituals. Vol. I: Issues, Topics, Approaches, Concepts*, Leiden, Boston, MA: Brill.

Lahoucie, Ouzgane (2006) *Islamic Masculinities*, London: Zed Books.

Lambek, Michael (1980) "Spirits and Spouses: Possession as a System of Communication among the Malagasy Speakers of Mayotte," *American Ethnologist*, 7: 318-331.

—— (1986) "Ritual and Social Change: The Case of Funerals in Mayotte," in C. Kottak, J.-A. Rakotoarisoa, A. Southhall and P. Vérin (ed.) *Madagascar: Society and History*, Boulder: Westview Press

—— (1990) "Certain Knowledge, Contestable Authority: Power and Practice on the Islamic Periphery," *American Ethnologist*, 17: 23–40.

—— (1993) *Knowledge and Practice in Mayotte: Local Discourses of Islam, Sorcery, and Spirit Possession*, Toronto: University of Toronto Press.

Lane, Edward (1860) *An Account of the Manners and Customs of the Modern Egyptians*, London: John Murray.

Launay, Robert (1992) *Beyond the Stream: Islam and Society in a West African Town*, Berkeley, CA: University of California Press.

—— (2006) "An Invisible Religion? Anthropology's Avoidance of Islam in Africa," in David Mills, Mustafa Babiker and Mwenda Ntarangwi (eds) *African Anthropologies: History, Critique, and Practice*, London and Dakar: Zed and Codesria.

Lavie, Smadar (1990) *The Poetics of Military Occupation: Mzeina Allegories of Bedouin Identity Under Israeli and Egyptian Rule*, Berkeley, CA: University of California Press.

Layton, Robert (1997) *An Introduction to Theory in Anthropology*, Cambridge: Cambridge University Press.

Lévi-Strauss, Claude (1963) *Structural Anthropology*, trans. Claire *Jacobson* and Brooke G. *Schoepf*, New York and London: Basic Books Inc.

Lewis, Bernard (1993) *Islam and the West*, New York: Oxford University Press.

Lewis, Ioan M. (1955) "Sufism in Somaliland: A Study in Tribal Islam I," *Journal of the British School of Oriental and African Studies*, 17: 581–602.

—— (1956) "Sufism in Somaliland: A Study in Tribal Islam II," *Journal of the British School of Oriental and African Studies*, 18: 145–160.
—— (1983) "Syncretism and Survival in African Islam," in Ioan M. Lewis (ed.) *Aspetti dell'Islam 'Marginale'*, Roma: Accedemia Nazionale dei Lincei.
Lindholm, Charles (1995) "The New Middle Eastern Ethnography," *Journal of the Royal Anthropological Institute*, 1: 805–521.
—— (2002a) *The Islamic Middle East: An Historical Anthropology*, Oxford and Cambridge: Blackwell.
—— (2002b) "Kissing Cousins: Anthropologists on Islam," in Hastings Donnan (ed.) *Interpreting Islam*, London: Sage Publications Ltd.
Loeffler, Reinhald (1988) *Islam in Practice: Religions Beliefs in a Persian Village*, Albany, NY: State University of New York Press.
Lukens-Bull, Ronald A. (1999) "Between Text and Practice: Considerations in the Anthropological Study of Islam," *Marburg Journal of Religion*, 4: 1–21.
—— (2005) *A Peaceful Jihad: Negotiating Identity and Modernity in Muslim Java*, New York: Palgrave Macmillan.
—— (2007) "Lost in a Sea of Subjectivity: The Subject Position of the Researcher in the Anthropology of Islam," *Contemporary Islam*, 1: 173–192.
Lutz, Catherine, and Lila Abu-Lughod (1990) *Language and the Politics of Emotion*, Cambridge and New York: Cambridge University Press.
Mace, Ruth, and Mark Pagel (1994) "The Comparative Method in Anthropology," *Current Anthropology*, 35: 549–564.
Mahmood, Saba (2001a) "Feminist Theory, Embodiment, and the Docile Agent: Some Reflections on the Egyptian Islamic Revival," *Cultural Anthropology*, 16: 202–236.
—— (2001b) "Rehearsed Spontaneity and the Conventionality of Ritual: Disciplines of Salat," *American Ethnologist*, 28: 827–853.
—— (2004) *Politics of Piety: The Islamic Revival and the Feminist Subject*, Princeton, NJ: Princeton University Press.
Malik, Iftikhar H. (2004) *Islam and Modernity: Muslims in Europe and the United States*, London: Pluto Press.
Malinowski, Bronislaw (1922) *Argonauts of the Western Pacific: An Account of Native Enterprise and Adventure in the Archipelagoes of Melanesian New Guinea*, London: G. Routledge & Sons.
Mandaville, Peter (2007) "Globalization and the Politics of Religious Knowledge Pluralizing Authority in the Muslim World," *Theory, Culture, and Society*, 24: 101–115.
Manger, Leif (1992) "On the Study of Islam in Local Contexts," *Forum for Development Studies*, 1: 51–65.
—— (ed.) (1999) *Muslim Diversity: Local Islam in Global Contexts* Richmond, UK: Curzon Press.
Marcus, George E. (1985) "A Timely Rereading of *Naven*: Gregory Bateson as Oracular Essayist," *Representations*, 12: 66–82.
—— (1995) "Ethnography in/of the World System: The Emergence of Multi-Sited Ethnography," *Annual Review of Anthropology*, 24: 95–117.
—— (1999) *Critical Anthropology Now: Unexpected Contexts, Shifting Constituencies, Changing Agendas*, Santa Fe, NM: School of American Research Press.
—— and Dick Cushman (1982) "Ethnographies as Texts," *Annual Review of Anthropology*, 11: 25–69.
—— and Michael M.J. Fischer (1986) *Anthropology as Cultural Critique: An Experimental Moment in the Human Sciences*, Chicago, IL: University of Chicago Press.
Marcus, Julie. (1992) *A World of Difference: Islam and Gender Hierarchy in Turkey*, London: Allen & Unwin Ltd.
Marranci, Gabriele (2006) *Jihad beyond Islam*, London: Berg Publishers.
—— (2008) *The Anthropology of Islam*, London: Berg Publishers.
—— (2010) "Sociology and Anthropology of Islam: A Critical Debate," in Bryan S. Turner (ed.) *The New Blackwell Companion to the Sociology of Religion*, Chichester: Wiley-Blackwell.
Mason, John P. (1975) "Sex and Symbol in the Treatment of Women: The Wedding Rite in a Libyan Oasis Community," *American Ethnologist*, 2: 649–661.
Masquelier, Adeline M. (2001) *Prayer has Spoiled Everything: Possession, Power, and Identity in an Islamic Town of Niger*, Durham, NC: Duke University Press.

Matory, J. Lorand (1994) "Rival Empires: Islam and the Religions of Spirit Possession among the Oyo-Yoruba," *American Ethnologist*, 21: 495–515.

Mauss, Marcel (1954) *The Gift: Forms and Functions of Exchange in Archaic Societies*, trans. Ian Cunnison, Glencoe, IL: Free Press.

—— (1972) *A General Theory of Magic*, trans. Robert Brain, London: Routledge and Kegan Paul.

—— (1973) "Techniques of the Body," *Economy and Society*, 2: 77–80.

—— (2003) *On Prayer*, trans. Susan Leslie, ed. by W.S.F. Pickering, New York: Durkheim Press/ Berghahn Books.

McAllister, Carol (1990) "Women and Feasting: Ritual Exchange, Capitalism, and Islamic Revival in Negeri Sembilan, Malaysia," *Research in Economic Anthropology*, 12: 12–51.

McCutcheon, Russell T. (ed.) (1999) *The Insider/Outsider Problem in the Study of Religion: A Reader*, London and New York: Cassell.

McIntosh, Janet (2009) *The Edge of Islam: Power, Personhood and Ethno-Religious Boundaries on the Kenya Coast*, Durham, NC: Duke University Press.

McLoughlin, Seán (2007) "Islam(s) in Context: Orientalism and the Anthropology of Muslim Societies and Cultures," *Journal of Beliefs and Values*, 28: 273–296.

Mead, Margaret (1928) *Coming of Age in Samoa: A Psychological Study of Primitive Youth for Western Civilisation*, New York: W. Morrow & Company.

Meeker, Michael (1994) "Oral Culture, Media Culture, and the Islamic Resurgence in Turkey," in Eduardo P. Archetti (ed.) *Exploring the Written: Anthropology and the Multiplicity of Writing*, Oslo: Scandinavian University Press.

Mernissi, Fatima (1975) *Beyond the Veil: Male–Female Dynamics in a Modern Muslim Society*, Cambridge, MA: Schenkman.

—— (1977) "Women, Saints, and Sanctuaries," *Signs*, 3: 101–112.

—— (1987) *The Veil and the Male Elite: A Feminist Interpretation of Women's Rights in Islam*, Reading: Addison-Wesley Publishing.

Meskell, Lynn, and Peter Pels (eds) (2005) *Embedding Ethics*, Oxford and New York: Berg.

Messer, Ellen (1993) "Anthropology and Human-Rights," *Annual Review of Anthropology*, 22: 221–249.

Messick, Brinkley (1986) "The Mufti, the Text, and the World: Legal Interpretation in Yemen," *Man*, 21: 102–119.

—— (1987) "Subordinate Discourse: Women, Weaving and Gender Relations in North Africa," *American Ethnologist*, 14: 210–225.

—— (1988) 'Kissing Hands and Knees: Hegemony and Hierarchy in Shari'a Discourse,' *Law and Society Review*, 22: 637–659.

Metcalf, Barbara D. (ed.) (1996) *Making Muslim Space in North America and Europe*, Berkeley, CA: University of California Press.

Mir-Hosseini, Ziba (1999) *Islam and Gender: The Religious Debate in Contemporary Iran*, Princeton, NJ: Princeton University Press.

Modood, Tariq, and Pnina Werbner (1997) *The Politics of Multiculturalism in the New Europe: Racism, Identity, and Community*, London and New York: Zed Books.

—— Anna Triandafyllidou, and Ricard Zapata-Barrero (2005) *Multiculturalism, Muslims and Citizenship: A European Approach*, New York: Routledge.

Möller, André (2005) *Ramadan in Java: The Joy and Jihad of Ritual Fasting*, Stockholm: Almqvist & Wiksell.

Navaro-Yashin, Yael (1999) "The Historical Construction of Local Culture: Gender and Identity in the Politics of Secularism versus Islam," in Caglar Keyder (ed.) *Istanbul: Between the Global and the Local*, Oxford: Rowman & Littlefield.

—— (2002) "The Market for Identities: Secularism, Islamism, Commodities," in Deniz Kandiyoti (ed.) *Fragments of Culture: The Everyday of Modern Turkey*, London: I.B. Tauris.

Needham, Rodney (1975) "Polythetic Classification: Convergence and Consequences," *Man*, 10: 349–369.

Norris, H.T. (2006) *Popular Sufism in Eastern Europe: Sufi Brotherhoods and the Dialogue with Christianity and 'Heterodoxy'*, New York: Routledge.

O'Neil, Mary L. (2008) "Being Seen: Headscarves and the Contestation of Public Space in Turkey," *European Journal of Women's Studies*, 15: 101–115.

Odabasi, Yavuz, and Metin Argan (2009) "Aspects of Underlying Ramadan Consumption Patterns in Turkey," *Journal of International Consumer Marketing*, 21: 203–218.

Olson, Emelie A. (1985) "Muslim Identity and Secularism in Contemporary Turkey: 'The Headscarf Dispute'," *Anthropological Quarterly*, 58: 161–171.

Öncü, Ayşe (1995) "Packaging Islam: Cultural Politics on the Landscape of Turkish Commercial Television," *Public Culture*, 8: 51–71.

Ong, Aihwa (1990) "State versus Islam: Malay Families, Women's Bodies, and the Body Politic in Malaysia," *American Ethnologist*, 17: 258–276.

Ortner, Sherry B. (1973) "On Key Symbols," *American Anthropologist*, 15: 1338–1346.

—— (1984) "Theory of Anthropology Since the Sixties," *Comparative Studies in Society and History*, 126: 126–166.

—— (2006) *Anthropology and Social Theory: Culture, Power, and the Acting Subject*, Durham, NC: Duke University Press.

Otto, Ton, and Nils Bubandt (eds) (2010) *Experiments in Holism: Theory and Practice in Contemporary Anthropology*, Malden, MA: Wiley-Blackwell.

Özdalga, Elisabeth (1998) *The Veiling Issue: Official Secularism and Popular Islam in Modern Turkey*, Richmond, UK: Curzon.

Parkin, David J., and Stephen C. Headley (2000) *Islamic Prayer across the Indian Ocean: Inside and Outside the Mosque*, Richmond, UK: Curzon.

—— and Stanley J. Ulijaszek (eds) (2007) *Holistic Anthropology: Emergence and Convergence*, New York: Berghahn Books.

Peacock, James L. (1978) *Purifying the Faith: The Muhammadijah Movement in Indonesia*, Menlo Park, CA: Benjamin Cummings Pub. Co.

Peletz, Michael G. (2002) *Islamic Modern: Religious Courts and Cultural Politics in Malaysia*, Princeton, NJ: Princeton University Press.

Peteet, Julie (1993) "Arab Voices: The Human Rights Debate in the Middle East," *American Anthropologist*, 95: 236–238.

—— (1994) "Male Gender and Rituals of Resistance in the Palestinian 'Intifada': A Cultural Politics of Violence," *American Ethnologist*, 21: 31–49.

—— (2005) *Landscape of Hope and Despair: Palestinian Refugee Camps*, Philadelphia, PA: University of Pennsylvania Press.

Peters, Rudolph (1979) *Islam and Colonialism: The Doctrine of Jihad in Modern History*, The Hague: Mouton.

Pike, Kenneth L. (1967) *Language in Relation to a Unified Theory of the Structure of Human Behavior*, 2nd edn, The Hague: Mouton.

Platvoet, Jan G. (2004) "Ritual as War: On the Need to De-Westernize the Concept," in Jens Kreinath, Constance Hartung and Annette Deschner (eds) *The Dynamics of Changing Rituals: The Transformation of Religious Rituals within Their Social and Cultural Context*, New York: Peter Lang.

Polanyi, Michael (1967) *The Tacit Dimension*, Chicago, IL: University of Chicago Press.

Poole, Elizabeth (2002) *Reporting Islam*, London and New York: I.B. Tauris.

—— and John E. Richardson (2006) *Muslims and the News Media*, London and New York: I.B. Tauris.

Poya, Maryam (1999) *Women, Work and Islamism: Ideology and Resistance in Iran*, London and New York: Zed Books.

Qureshi, Emran, and Michael A. Sells (eds) (2003) *The New Crusades: Constructing the Muslim Enemy*, New York: Columbia University Press.

Rabinow, Paul (1975) *Symbolic Domination: Cultural Form and Historical Change in Morocco*, Berkeley, CA: University of California Press.

—— (1977) *Reflections on Fieldwork in Morocco*, Berkeley, CA: University of California Press.

—— (1986) "Representations are Social Facts: Modernity and Postmodernity in Anthropology," in James Clifford and George Marcus (eds) *Writing Culture: The Poetics and Politics of Ethnography*, Berkeley, CA: University of California Press.

Radcliffe-Brown, Alfred R. (1922) *The Andaman Islanders: A Study in Social Anthropology*, Cambridge: Cambridge University Press.

Radin, Paul (1966) *The Method and Theory of Ethnology: An Essay in Criticism*, New York: Basic Books.

Rasmussen, Anne K. (2001) "The Qur'an in Indonesian Daily Life: The Public Project of Musical Oratory," *Ethnomusicology*, 45: 30–57.

Rasmussen, Susan J. (1995) *Spirit Possession and Personhood among the Kel Ewey Tuareg*, Cambridge: Cambridge University Press.

Redfield, Robert (1956) *Peasant Society and Culture: An Anthropological Approach to Civilization*, Chicago, IL: University of Chicago Press.

Reeves, Edward B. (1995) "Power, Resistance, and the Cult of Muslim Saints in a Northern Egyptian Town," *American Ethnologist*, 22: 306–323.

Robbins, Joel (2007) "Continuity Thinking and the Problem of Christian Culture: Belief, Time, and the Anthropology of Christianity," *Current Anthropology*, 48: 5–38.

Roff, William R. (1985) "Pilgrimage and the History of Religions: Theoretical Approaches to the Hajj," in Richard C. Martin (ed.) *Approaches to Islam in Religious Studies*, Tucson, AZ: University of Arizona Press.

—— (ed.) (1987) *Islam and the Political Economy of Meaning: Comparative Studies on Muslim Discourse*, Berkeley, CA: University of California Press.

—— (1999) "Afterword: The Comparative Study of Muslim Societies," in Leif Manger (ed.) *Muslim Diversity: Local Islam in Global Contexts*, Richmond, UK: Curzon Press.

Rosaldo, Renato (1989) *Culture and Truth: The Remaking of Social Analysis*, Boston, MA: Beacon Press.

Rose, H.A. (1907) "Muhammadan Birth Observances in the Punjab," *The Journal of the Royal Anthropological Institute of Great Britain and Ireland*, 37: 237–260.

Rouch, Jean (1974) "The Camera and the Man," *Studies in the Anthropology of Visual Communication*, 1: 37–44.

—— and Steven Feld (2003) *Ciné-Ethnography*, Minneapolis, MN: University of Minnesota Press.

Ruby, Jay (1975) "Is an Ethnographic Film a Filmic Ethnography?" *Studies in the Anthropology of Visual Communication*, 2: 104–111.

—— (ed.) (1982) *A Crack in the Mirror: Reflexive Perspectives in Anthropology*, Philadelphia, PA: University of Pennsylvania Press.

Rudnyckyj, Daromir (2009) "Spiritual Economies: Islam and Neoliberalism in Contemporary Indonesia," *Cultural Anthropology*, 24: 104–141.

Ryle, Gilbert (1945) "Knowing How and Knowing That," *Proceedings of the Aristotelian Society*, 46: 1–16.

Rynkiewich, Michael A., and James P. Spradley (1976) *Ethics and Anthropology: Dilemmas in Fieldwork*, New York: Wiley.

Saeed, Abdullah (2007) "Trends in Contemporary Islam: A Preliminary Attempt at a Classification," *The Muslim World*, 97: 395–404.

Said, Edward W. (1978) *Orientalism*, New York: Pantheon Books.

—— (1979) *The Palestine Question and the American Context*, Beirut: Institute for Palestine Studies.

—— (1981) *Covering Islam: How the Media and the Experts Determine How We See the Rest of the World*, New York: Pantheon Books.

—— (1985) "Orientalism Reconsidered," *Cultural Critique*, 1: 89–107.

—— (1989) "Representing the Colonized: Anthropology's Interlocutors," *Cultural Critique*, 15: 205–252.

—— (1993) *Culture and Imperialism*, London: Chatto & Windus.

Saktanber, Ayşe (1994) "Becoming the 'Other' as a Muslim in Turkey: Turkish Women vs. Islamist Women," *New Perspectives on Turkey*, 11: 99–134.

—— (1997) "Between Religious Tradition and Emancipatory Politics: The Islamic Dilemma of Women's Human Rights in a Muslim-Yet-Secular Society: The Case of Turkey," *Middle East Policy*, 5: 172–190.

—— (2002) "'We Pray Like You Have Fun': New Islamic Youth between Intellectualism and Popular Culture," in Deniz Kandiyoti (ed.) *Fragments of Culture: The Everyday of Modern Turkey*, London: I.B. Tauris.

Salvatore, Armando (1997) *Islam and the Political Discourse of Modernity*, Reading, UK: Ithaca Press.

Şaul, Mahir (2006) "Islam and West African Anthropology," *Africa Today*, 53: 2–33.

Schieffelin, Edward L. (1976) *The Sorrow of the Lonely and the Burning of the Dancers*, New York: St. Martin's Press.

—— (1985) "Performance and the Cultural Construction of Reality," *American Ethnologist*, 12: 707–724.

—— (1996) "On Failure and Performance: Throwing the Medium Out of the Seance," in Carol Laderman and Marina Roseman (eds) *The Performance of Healing*, London: Routledge.

—— (2006) "Participation," in Jens Kreinath, Jan A.M. Snoek and Michael Stausberg (eds) *Theorizing Rituals. Vol. I: Issues, Topics, Approaches, Concepts*, Leiden: Brill.

Schielke, Samuli (2008) "Policing Ambiguity: Muslim Saints-Day Festivals and the Moral Geography of Public Space in Egypt," *American Ethnologist*, 35: 539–552.

—— (2009) "Being Good in Ramadan: Ambivalence, Fragmentation, and the Moral Self in the Lives of Young Egyptians," *Journal of the Royal Anthropological Institute*, 15: 24–40.

Schulz, Dorothea E. (2006) "Promises of (Im)mediate Salvation: Islam, Broadcast Media, and the Remaking of Religious Experience in Mali," *American Ethnologist*, 33: 210–229.

—— (2008) "(Re)Turning to Proper Muslim Practice: Islamic Moral Renewal and Women's Conflicting Assertions of Sunni Identity in Urban Mali," *Africa Today*, 54: 21–43.

Scott, Samuel B. (1913) "Mohammedanism in Borneo: Notes for a Study of the Local Modifications of Islam and the Extent of Its Influence on the Native Tribes," *Journal of the American Oriental Society*, 33: 313–344.

Scupin, Raymond (1982) "The Social Significance of the Hajj for Thai Muslims," *The Muslim World*, 72: 25–33.

Secor, Anna J. (2001) "Toward a Feminist Counter-Geopolitics: Gender, Space and Islamist Politics in Istanbul," *Space and Polity*, 5: 191–211.

—— (2002) "The Veil and Urban Space in Istanbul: Women's Dress, Mobility and Islamic Knowledge," *Gender, Place and Culture*, 9: 5–22.

Sedgwick, Mark J. (2006) *Islam and Muslims: A Guide to Diverse People in a Modern World*, Boston, MA: Nicholas Brealey.

Shadid, Wasif A, and P. Sjørd van Koningsveld (eds) (2002) *Intercultural Relations and Religious Authorities: Muslims in the European Union*, Leuven: Peeters.

Shannon, Johnathan H. (2004) "The Aesthetics of Spiritual Practice and the Celebration of Moral and Musical Subjectivities in Aleppo, Syria" *Ethnology*, 43: 381–391.

Shehabuddin, Elora (1999) "Contesting the Illicit: Gender and the Politics of Fatwas in Bangladesh," *Signs*, 24: 1011–1044.

—— (2008) *Reshaping the Holy: Democracy, Development, and Muslim Women in Bangladesh*, New York: Columbia University Press.

Silverstein, Brian (2003) "Islam and Modernity in Turkey: Power, Tradition and Historicity in the European Provinces of the Muslim World," *Anthropological Quarterly*, 76: 497–517.

—— (2008) "Disciplines of Presence in Modern Turkey: Discourse, Companionship, and the Mass Mediation of Islamic Practice," *Cultural Anthropology*, 23: 118–153.

Snoek, Jan (2006) "Defining Rituals," in Jens Kreinath, Jan Snoek and Michael Stausberg (eds) *Theorizing Rituals. Vol. I: Issues, Topics, Approaches, Concepts*, Leiden: Brill.

Soares, Benjamin F. (1996) "The Prayer Economy in a Malian Town," *Cahiers d'Études africaines*, 144: 739–753.

—— (2000) "Notes on the Anthropological Study of Islam and Muslim Societies in Africa," *Culture and Religion*, 1: 277–285.

—— (2005) *Islam and the Prayer Economy: History and Authority in a Malian Town*, Edinburgh: Edinburgh University Press for the International African Institute.

—— and Filippo Osella (2009) "Islam, Politics, Anthropology," *Journal of the Royal Anthropological Institute*, 15: 1–23.

Spiro, Melford E. (1986) "Cultural Relativism and the Future of Anthropology," *Cultural Anthropology*, 1: 259–286.

Spradley, James P. (1979) *The Ethnographic Interview*, New York: Harcourt Brace Jovanovich.

Starrett, Gregory (1995a) "The Hexis of Interpretation: Islam and the Body in the Egyptian Popular School," *American Ethnologist*, 22: 953–969.
—— (1995b) "The Political Economy of Religious Commodities in Cairo," *American Anthropologist*, 97: 51–68.
—— (1996) "The Margins of Print: Children's Religious Literature in Egypt," *Journal of the Royal Anthropological Institute*, 2: 117–139
—— (1997) "The Anthropology of Islam," in Stephen D. Glazier (ed.) *The Anthropology of Religion: A Handbook*, Westport, CT: Greenwood.
—— (1998) *Putting Islam to Work: Education, Politics, and Religious Transformation in Egypt*, Berkeley, CA: University of California Press.
Stocking, George W. (1983) *Observers Observed: Essays on Ethnographic Fieldwork*, Madison, WI: University of Wisconsin Press.
—— (1991) *Colonial Situations: Essays on the Contextualization of Ethnographic Knowledge*, Madison, WI: University of Wisconsin Press.
Stoller, Paul (1989a) *Fusion of the Worlds: An Ethnography of Possession among the Songhay of Niger*, Chicago, IL: University of Chicago Press.
—— (1989b) *The Taste of Ethnographic Things: The Senses in Anthropology*, Philadelphia, PA: University of Pennsylvania Press.
—— and Cheryl Olkes (1987) *In Sorcery's Shadow: A Memoir of Apprenticeship among the Songhay of Niger*, Chicago, IL: University of Chicago Press.
Stowasser, Barbara (2001) "Old Shaykhs, Young Women, and the Internet: The Rewriting of Women's Political Rights in Islam," *The Muslim World*, 91: 99–119.
Strang, Veronica (2006) "A Happy Coincidence? Symbiosis and Synthesis in Anthropological and Indigenous Knowledges," *Current Anthropology*, 47: 981–1008.
Strathern, Marilyn (1995) *Shifting Contexts: Transformations in Anthropological Knowledge*, London and New York: Routledge.
Strijp, Ruud (1992) *Cultural Anthropology of the Middle East: A Bibliography*, Leiden and New York: Brill.
Takim, Liyakat (2006) "Offering Complete or Shortened Prayers? The Traveler's Salat at the 'Holy Places'," *The Muslim World*, 96: 401–422.
Tapper, Nancy (1983) "Gender and Religion in a Turkish Town: A Comparison of two Types of Formal Women's Gathering," in Pat Holden (ed.) *Women's Religious Experience*, London: Croom Helm.
—— (1985) "Changing Wedding Rituals in a Turkish Town," *Journal of Turkish Studies*, 9: 305–313.
—— (1990) "Ziyaret: Gender, Movement, and Exchange in a Turkish Community," in Dale Eickelman and James Piscatori (eds) *Muslim Travellers: Pilgrimage, Migration, and the Religious Imagination*, London: Routledge.
—— and Richard Tapper (1987) "The Birth of the Prophet: Ritual and Gender in Turkish Islam," *Man*, 22: 69–92.
Tapper, Richard (1979) *Pasture and Politics: Economics, Conflict, and Ritual among Shahsevan Nomads of Northwestern Iran*, London: Academic Press.
—— (1995) "'Islamic Anthropology' and the 'Anthropology of Islam'," *Anthropological Quarterly*, 68: 185–193.
Tedlock, Barbara (1991) "From Participant Observation to the Observation of Participation: the Emergence of Narrative Ethnography," *Journal of Anthropological Research*, 47: 69–94.
Tedlock, Dennis (1983) *The Spoken Word and the Work of Interpretation*, Philadelphia, PA: University of Pennsylvania Press.
—— (1987) "Questions Concerning Dialogical Anthropology," *Journal of Anthropological Research*, 43: 325–244.
Thomas, Bertram (1932) "Anthropological Observations in South Arabia," *The Journal of the Royal Anthropological Institute of Great Britain and Ireland*, 62: 83–103.
Thompson, Michael J. (ed.) (2003) *Islam and the West: Critical Perspectives on Modernity*. Oxford: Rowman & Littlefield.
Torab, Azam (1996) "Piety as Gendered Agency: A Study of *Jalaseh* Ritual Discourse in an Urban Neighbourhood in Iran," *Journal of the Royal Anthropological Institute*, 2: 235–252.

—— (2006) *Performing Islam: Gender and Ritual in Iran*, Leiden: Brill.

Trimingham, J. Spencer (1971) *The Sufi Orders in Islam*, Oxford: Oxford University Press.

Trumpbour, John (2003) "The Clash of Civilizations: Samuel P. Huntington, Bernard Lewis, and the Remaking of the Post-Cold War World Order," in Emran Qureshi and Michael A. Sells (eds) *The New Crusades: Constructing the Muslim Enemy*, New York: Columbia University Press.

Turner, Bryan S. (1984) "Orientalism and the Problem of Civil Society in Islam," in Asaf Hussain, Robert Olson and Jamil Qureshi (eds) *Orientalism, Islam and Islamists*, Brattleboro, VT: Amana Books.

—— (1994) *Orientalism, Postmodernism and Globalism*, London: Routledge.

—— (2002) "Orientalism, or the Politics of the Text," in Hastings Donnan (ed.) *Interpreting Islam*, London: Sage.

Turner, Victor W. (1957) *Schism and Continuity in an African Society: A Study of Ndembu Village Life*, Manchester: Rhodes-Livingstone Institute.

Urban, Greg (1996) "Entextualization, Replication, and Power" in Michael Silverstein and Greg Urban (eds) *Natural Histories of Discourse*, Chicago, IL: University of Chicago Press.

Vahdat, Farzin (2002) *God and Juggernaut: Iran's Intellectual Encounter with Modernity*, Syracuse, NY: Syracuse University Press.

Van der Elst, Dirk, and Paul Bohannan (1999) *Culture as Given, Culture as Choice*, Prospect Heights, IL: Waveland Press.

Van der Veer, Peter (1992) "Playing or Praying: A Sufi Saint's Day in Surat," *Journal of Asian Studies*, 51: 545–564.

—— and Shoma Munshi (2004) *Media, War, and Terrorism: Responses from the Middle East and Asia*, London and New York: Routledge.

Van Maanen, John (2010) *Tales of the Field: On Writing Ethnography*, 2nd edn, Chicago. IL: University of Chicago Press.

Varisco, Daniel M. (2005) *Islam Obscured: The Rhetoric of Anthropological Representation*, New York: Palgrave.

—— (2007) *Reading Orientalism: Said and the Unsaid*, Seattle, WA: University of Washington Press.

Vogt, Franziska (2002) "No Ethnography without Comparison: The Methodological Significance of Comparison in Ethnographic Research," in Geoffrey Walford (ed.) *Debates and Developments in Ethnographic Methodology*, Amsterdam: JAI.

Von Grunebaum, Gustave E. (1951) *Mohammedan Festivals*, New York: Henry Schuman, Inc.

—— (1955) "The Problem of Unity in Diversity," in Gustave E. von Grunebaum (ed.) *Unity and Variety in Muslim Civilization*, Chicago, IL: Chicago University Press.

—— (1962) *Modern Islam: The Search for Cultural Identity*, Berkeley, CA: University of California Press.

Wallin, George Augustus (1854) "Narrative of a Journey from Cairo to Medina and Mecca," *Journal of the Royal Geographical Society of London*, 24: 115–207.

Weeks, Richard V. (1978) *Muslim Peoples: A World Ethnographic Survey*. Westport, CA: Greenwood Press.

Weiss, Holger (2002) "Reforming Social Welfare among Muslims: Islamic Voluntarism and other Forms of Communal Support in Northern Ghana," *Journal of Religion in Africa*, 32: 83–109.

Weisskoppel, Cordula (2005) "Moving Across: Looking at Multi-Sited-Ethnography in Theory and Practice," *Zeitschrift für Ethnologie*, 130: 45–68.

Weix, G.G. (1998) "Islamic Prayer Groups in Indonesia: Local Forums and Gendered Responses," *Critique of Anthropology*, 18: 405–420.

Werbner, Pnina (1986) "The Virgin and the Clown Ritual Elaboration in Pakistani Migrants' Weddings," *Man*, 21: 227–250.

—— (1988) "'Sealing' the Koran: Offering and Sacrifice among Pakistani Labour Migrants," *Cultural Dynamics*, 1: 77–97.

—— (1996a) "The Making of Muslim Dissent: Hybridized Discourses, Lay Preachers, and Radical Rhetoric among the British Pakistanis," *American Ethnologist*, 23: 102–122.

—— (1996b) "Stamping the Earth with the Name of Allah: Zikr and the Sacralizing of Space among British Muslims," *Cultural Anthropology*, 11: 309-338.

—— (2002) *Imagined Diasporas among Manchester Muslims: The Public Performance of Pakistani Transnational Identity Politics*, Oxford: James Currey.

—— (2007) "Veiled Interventions in Pure Space Honour, Shame and Embodied Struggles among Muslims in Britain and France," *Theory, Culture, and Society*, 24: 161–186.

—— and Helene Basu (eds) (1998) *Embodying Charisma: Modernity, Locality, and the Performance of Emotion in Sufi Cults*, New York: Routledge.

—— and Tariq Modood (1997) *Debating Cultural Hybridity: Multi-Cultural Identities and the Politics of Anti-Racism*, London: Zed Books.

Werbner, Richard P. (1998) *Memory and the Postcolony: African Anthropology and the Critique of Power*, London: Zed Books.

—— and Terrence O. Ranger (1996) *Postcolonial Identities in Africa*, London: Zed Books.

Westerlund, David (2004) *Sufism in Europe and North America*, London and New York: Routledge.

Westermarck, Edward (1899) "The Nature of the Arab Ginn, Illustrated by the Present Beliefs of the People of Morocco," *The Journal of the Anthropological Institute of Great Britain and Ireland*, 29: 252–269.

—— (1914) *Marriage Ceremonies in Morocco*, London: Macmillan.

—— (1926) *Ritual and Belief in Morocco*, New Hyde Park, NY: University Books.

—— (1933) *Pagan Survivals in Mohammedan Civilization*, London: Macmillan.

Wheeler, Deborah L. (2006) *The Internet in the Middle East: Global Expectations and Local Imaginations in Kuwait*, Albany, NY: State University of New York Press.

White, Hayden (1987) *The Content of the Form: Narrative Discourse and Historical Representation*, Baltimore, MD: Johns Hopkins University Press.

White, Jenny B. (1999) "Islamic Chic," in Caglar Keyder (ed.) *Istanbul: Between the Global and the Local*, Oxford: Rowman and Littlefield.

—— (2002a) *Islamist Mobilization in Turkey: A Study in Vernacular Politics*, Seattle, WA: University of Washington Press.

—— (2002b) "The Islamist Paradox," in Deniz Kandiyoti (ed.) *Fragments of Culture: The Everyday of Modern Turkey*, London: I.B. Tauris.

Whitehouse, Harvey (2002) "Religious Reflexivity and Transmissive Frequency," *Social Anthropology*, 10: 91–103.

—— (2007) "Towards and Integration of Ethnography, History, and the Cognitive Science of Religion," in Harvey Whitehouse and James Laidlaw (eds) *Religion, Anthropology, and Cognitive Science*, Durham, NC: Carolina Academic Press.

Wieringa, Saskia E. (2009) "Women Resisting Creeping Islamic Fundamentalism in Indonesia," *Asian Journal of Women Studies*, 15: 30–56.

Wikan, Unni (1982) *Behind the Veil in Arabia: Women in Oman*, Baltimore, MD: Johns Hopkins University Press.

Wittgenstein, Ludwig (1953) *Philosophical Investigations*, trans. Gertrude E. Anscombe, Oxford: Blackwell.

Wolf, Eric R. (1982) *Europe and the People without History*, Berkeley, CA: University of California Press.

Wolf, Richard K. (2006) "The Poetics of 'Sufi' Practice: Drumming, Dancing, and Complex Agency at Madho Lal Husain (And Beyond)," *American Ethnologist*, 33: 246–268.

Woodward, Mark R. (1988) "The *Slametan*: Textual Knowledge and Ritual Performance in Central Javanese Islam," *History of Religions*, 28: 54–89.

Woolard, Kathryn A., and Bambi B. Schieffelin (1994) "Language Ideology," *Annual Review of Anthropology*, 23: 55–82.

Yanow, Dvora (2009) "Dear Author, Dear Reader: The Third Hermeneutic in Writing and Reviewing Ethnography," in Edward Schatz (ed.) *Political Ethnography: What Immersion Contributes to the Study of Power*, Chicago, IL: University of Chicago Press.

Youssef, Michael (1985) *Revolt against Modernity: Muslim Zealots and the West*, Leiden: E.J. Brill.

Zerubavel, Eviatar (1981) *Hidden Rhythms: Schedules and Calendars in Social Life*, Chicago, IL: University of Chicago Press

Part I

Anthropological approaches to Islam

Jens Kreinath

In reconstructing the formation of the anthropology of Islam as a distinct subfield in the anthropology of religion, it is impossible to do justice to all facets of inquiry. This field of study emerged from anthropologists' diverse interest in the society and culture of people who explicitly identified themselves as Muslims. However, this is still too crude an approach to account fully for the historical and institutional conditions which must have existed to shape and lead to the emergence and institutionalization of this field of research. Even though the phrase 'anthropology of Islam' seemingly indicates a disciplinary approach to Islam as a specific field of research, this is too abstract and removed from the reality of social and political circumstances, as well as institutions that draw and guide the interests of anthropologists in this field of study. By the same token, the contributions of individual anthropologists who initiated or even established the anthropological discourse on Islam, while a good point of departure, fall short of comprehensive analysis. Without accounting for the institutional settings and frameworks, such as professional organizations and publications as well as research centers and funding agencies, which made such achievements in research and publication possible, the formation of an academic field and its body of knowledge might not be imaginable.

As outlined in the introduction, the subfield of the anthropology of Islam emerged within the broader context of anthropological study as well as the study of religions and cultures. Thus the anthropology of Islam, as a field of research bordering Islamic studies and the anthropology of religion, emerged as a niche for these studies. At the same time, it transgresses well-established academic disciplines, including those encompassing the study of Arabic language, philology and exegesis of Islamic textual traditions, as well as history and the social and political sciences. The anthropological study of Islamic discourse and practice therefore participates in the differentiation and expansion of academic fields of research, as well as in the historical and political processes and their outcomes that led to global transformations of power in the times of colonialism and postcolonialism.

In this respect, the formation of this field of study emerged within the context of colonial interests of political powers. However, at the same time, the work of anthropologists served as a critique and corrective for the misrepresentations generated in the political field of mainstream media and politics. Despite their work and acceptance in academic circles, the depth of understanding and correction is rarely received or understood outside these fields. Anthropologists first discovered the particular communities, customs, and traditions of Islam in times of Western hegemony. Through their professional interest in Muslims, which became an integral part of the colonial encounter, anthropologists moved from a conceptualization of Muslims in social and political terms, into a richer understanding of their cultural and artistic traditions, bound—primarily through the study of religious belief and practice—into definable groups.

Finding its academic legitimation in the complexities and dynamics in the field of study itself, namely the transformation of Muslim societies in the aftermath of the colonial encounter, the formation of the anthropology of Islam became possible, because the research methods it employed enhanced the understanding of Muslim societies. The differentiation of the anthropological approaches to Islam as a result of the differentiation in research methods allowed anthropologists to discover complexities in the experiences of Muslims in their local contexts.

The advantage of anthropology is its ability to provide a unique account of the diversity of Muslim cultural and religious practices throughout the world, from Morocco to Indonesia and South Africa to Central Asia, as well as from the Middle East to North America and Europe to Australia. Due to methods of ethnographic fieldwork and cross-cultural comparison, anthropological research can account equally well for the particularities of local traditions and the universality of global dynamics. Direct encounter with local traditions of Islam led anthropologists to conceptualize Islam from a more specified perspective, emphasizing the description or comparison of data through ethnography or ethnology. The main question in the anthropology of Islam (as in other fields of anthropological research) is what the role and relevance of description and comparison are, and whether and how they mutually enhance understanding of Muslims (as well as other cultures).

The focus on Islam as one among many religions and cultures was only possible due to the refinement of research methods, which anthropologists adjusted to the specificities and complexities of an Islam as a religion which is based on scriptural traditions and distributed within local and global contexts. In this respect, the anthropology of Islam emerged as a unique field of research insofar as it deals with the discourses and practices of textual and oral traditions with translocal dimensions and an appeal to universal claims. Since the anthropology of Islam is committed to understanding Muslims in their local communities and to employing a holistic perspective, it also has to consider the philological and historical study as well as the ritual and juridical use of scriptural traditions. This was not a major concern of early anthropologists, who focused their study almost exclusively on non-literate people in former colonies. Despite the account of literate traditions, the anthropology of Islam, more than other fields of research, has to deal with the stratification of society and the differentiation of knowledge due to the philosophical and theological implications of Islam as a monotheistic religion with universal claims.

The first sub-section, *Conceptualizing Islam*, takes up this challenge and provides important insights into the strengths and weaknesses of the descriptive and comparative accounts of Islam. Excerpts from two classic works published in the field, which emphasize either description or comparison, provide a solid starting point for studying the anthropology of Islam. In part because of the methodological differences between ethnography and ethnology and the different conceptualizations each requires, the anthropology of Islam is and continues to be a growing field of research which provides insight into an open-ended understanding of Muslims, their beliefs, and their practices.

Michael Gilsenan's work, *Recognizing Islam*, exemplifies a significant conceptualization of Islam, theorizing cultures and religion from a holistic perspective that derives its methodological potential from the description of ethnographic details. Gilsenan's personal reflections, including his own discomforts, misgivings and understandings of Muslim practices and the political implications of Islam in world politics of the time are voiced throughout his writing and are utilized as he struggles to make meaning of his findings during fieldwork.

Gilsenan's reading provides clear concepts and examples of how Islam has changed over time as he experienced it. The reading illuminates the multi-layered transformations present in Islamic societies. Gilsenan does not confine his analysis to a changing Islam, as he thoroughly describes global effects on a local context within a holistic anthropological perspective while deriving his knowledge from his encounter with the people who lived it. Moving beyond the conceptualization of Islam as a monolithic religion, Gilsenan's account offers a point of reference for reflection and self-examination.

The excerpt from Clifford Geertz's ethnological work, *Islam Observed*, poses the question of how Islam can be conceptualized in comparative terms. Starting by articulating the impact of various cultures—including regional politics as well as historical and social developments—on the practice of Islam, Geertz accounts for the changing political atmosphere and argues for a change in the study of Islam. Including the effects of both colonization and decolonization, this piece makes a case for the value of cross-cultural comparison and its difficulties. This work, a series of lectures compressed into four chapters in its entirety, was at the time an innovative and novel approach to Muslim societies and the interpretation and understanding of Islam. It remains to this day a classic text and presents an opportunity to examine the theoretical position of anthropology at that time. The noticeable shift in the framework between these two pieces is a demonstration, not only of the changing concepts of Islam by Western scholars, but also for the changing field of anthropology itself as researchers moved beyond description and interpretation to the consideration of their own production of information, its impact on knowledge, and its reception within the academic field. As we find later in this *Reader*, many of the authors rely on and criticize the works of Geertz and Gilsenan.

The theoretical framework, or approach, to any subject within anthropology thus plays an integral role in the findings and outcomes of the research project. Furthermore, theoretical changes within the discipline and its methods of analysis have an impact on anthropologists in the field as well as the communities studied. In *Approaching Islam*, we survey crossroads in the anthropology of Islam, which go along with a critical analysis of past methodological approaches and conceptions. Starting in the 1970s, scholars like Abdul Hamid el-Zein began, in his article 'Beyond Ideology and Theology', to radically question the works of well-known authors in the field of anthropology and began to outline the difficulties and problematic nature of relying on the concept of Islam as a homogenous religion for analyzing multi-faceted societies, peoples, and cultures. Drawing on the similarities between anthropological and theological notions of cosmos, god and man, el-Zein reveals the underlying theological positioning of the authors' findings in both fields of reasoning. In contrast, he presents his own arguments for new conceptions and approaches to Islam, not necessarily as a monolithic or unifying factor which binds societies and individuals over space and time, but for a more anthropological approach towards local "islams" [*sic*] incorporating anthropological precepts of economy, politics, social organization and history.

As critical scholarship about Islam grew after the Iranian Revolution in 1979, it reached new heights in the mid-1980s with Talal Asad's programmatic lecture *The Idea of an Anthropology of Islam*. Starting with a review of the most significant works of that day, Asad highlights the methodological and conceptual defects within the field of anthropology. His review and comparison of indicative works shows how easily one's own perspective and position, if not carefully considered and accounted for, can lead anthropologists away from holistic approach and analysis. Through his reflexive approach to the anthropological study of Islam, Asad extensively critiques the work of anthropologists and their lack of introspection and recognition of the impact their own traditions (both anthropological and religious), cultures, history and conceptions of Islam have on their methodological approaches, formations of and conclusions about Muslims. He highlights the subtle influences of religious and political convictions or interest in the field of anthropology of Islam and challenges scholars and students to consider their own positions when approaching this subject.

While the authors of this section take different levels of analysis in their approaches to Islam and Muslims, their works made great strides in the formation of the discipline as a whole and remain foundational works with which anthropologists of Islam are intimately familiar. However, it is important to remember that anthropological texts, methods and findings are relative to their time in history and placement within the particular school of thought or frame of reference from which they derive.

Suggested readings

Abu-Lughod, Lila (1989) "Zones of Theory in the Anthropology of the Arab World," *Annual Review of Anthropology*, 18: 267–306.

Adams, Charles J. (1976) "Islamic Religious Tradition," in Leonard Binder (ed.) *The Study of the Middle East: Research and Scholarship in the Humanities and the Social Sciences*, New York: John Wiley & Sons.

Ahmed, Akbar S. (1982) *Muslim Society: Readings in Thought and Structure*, London: Routledge & Kegan Paul.

——— (1988) *Discovering Islam: Making Sense of Muslim History and Society*, London: Routledge.

Anjum, Ovamir (2007) "Islam as a Discursive Tradition: Talal Asad and His Interlocutors," *Comparative Studies of South Asia, Africa and the Middle East*, 27: 656–672.

Antoun, Richard T. (1971) "Three Approaches to the Cultural Anthropology of the Middle East," *Middle East Studies Association Bulletin*, 5: 24–53.

——— (1976) "Anthropology," in Leonard Binder (ed.) *The Study of the Middle East: Research and Scholarship in the Humanities and the Social Sciences: A Project of the Research and Training Committee of the Middle East Studies Association*, New York: Wiley.

Asad, Talal (ed.) (1973) *Anthropology and the Colonial Encounter*, London: Ithaca Press.

——— (1993) *Genealogies of Religion: Discipline and Reason in Christianity and Islam*, Baltimore, MD: Johns Hopkins Press.

——— (2003) *Formations of the Secular: Christianity, Islam, Modernity*, Stanford, CA: Stanford University Press.

Bowen, Donna L., and Evelyn A. Early (1993) *Everyday Life in the Muslim Middle East*, Bloomington, IN: University of Indiana Press.

Bowen, John R. (1998) "What is 'Universal' and 'Local' in Islam?" *Ethos*, 26: 258–261.

Das, Veena (1984) "For a Folk-Theology and Theological Anthropology of Islam," *Contributions to Indian Sociology*, 18: 239–305.

Digard, Jean-Pierre (1978) "Perspectives anthropologiques sur l'Islam," *Revue française de sociologie*, 19: 497–523.

Eickelman, Dale F. (1981) *The Middle East: An Anthropological Approach*, Englewood Cliffs, NJ: Prentice-Hall.

——— (1981) "A Search for the Anthropology of Islam: Abdul Hamid el-Zein," *International Journal of Middle East Studies*, 13: 361–365.

——— (1982) "The Study of Islam in Local Contexts," *Contributions to Asian Studies*, 17: 1–16.

——— (1987) "Changing Interpretations of Islamic Movements," in William R. Roff (ed.) *Islam and the Political Economy of Meaning: Comparative Studies on Muslim Discourse*, Berkeley, CA: University of California Press.

Eickelman, Dale F., and James Piscatori (1996) "Social Theory in the Study of Muslim Societies," in Dale F. Eickelman and James Piscatori (eds) *Muslim Travellers: Pilgrimage, Migration, and the Religious Imagination*, London: Routledge.

Eickelman, Dale F., and Armando Salvatore (2006) "Public Islam and the Common Good," *Etnográfica: Revista do Centro de Estudos de Antropologia Social*, 10: 97–105.

El Guindi, Fadwa (2008) *By Noon Prayer: The Rhythm of Islam*, Oxford and New York: Berg.

Fernea, Elizabeth Warnock (1965) *Guests of the Sheik: An Ethnography of an Iraqi Village*, New York: Anchor Books.

Fernea, Robert A., and James M. Malarkey (1975) "Anthropology of the Middle East and North Africa: A Critical Assessment," *Annual Review of Anthropology*, 4: 183–206.
Geertz, Clifford (1975) "Mysteries of Islam," *New York Review of Books*, 22: 18–26.
Gellner, Ernest (1970–1971) "The Pendulum Swing Theory of Islam," *Philosophical Forum*, 2: 234–244.
——— (1981) *Muslim Society*, Cambridge: Cambridge University Press.
Gilsenan, Michael (1990) "Very Like a Camel: The Appearance of an Anthropologist's Middle East," in Richard Fardon (ed.) *Localizing Strategies: Regional Traditions of Ethnographic Writing*, Washington, DC: Smithsonian Institution Press.
——— (2000) "Signs of Truth: Enchantment, Modernity and the Dreams of Peasant Women," *The Journal of the Royal Anthropological Institute*, 6: 597–615.
Gulick, John (1969) "The Anthropology of the Middle East," *Middle East Studies Association Bulletin*, 3: 1–14.
——— (1976) *The Middle East: An Anthropological Perspective*, Pacific Palisades, CA: Goodyear.
Hammoudi, Abdellah (1980) "Segmentarity, Social Stratification, Political Power and Sainthood: Reflections on Gellner's Theses," *Economy and Society*, 9: 279–303.
Kessler, Clive S. (1990) "New Directions in the Study of Islam: Remarks on Some Trends and Prospects," *Jurnal Antropologi dan Sosiologi*, 18: 3–22.
Lindholm, Charles (1986) "Caste in Islam and the Problem of Deviant Systems: A Critique of Recent Theory," *Contributions to Indian Sociology*, 20: 61–73.
——— (2002a) "Kissing Cousins: Anthropologists on Islam," in Hasting Donnan (ed.) *Interpreting Islam*, London: Sage.
——— (2002b) *The Islamic Middle East: An Historical Anthropology*. 2nd edn, Oxford: Blackwell.
Lukens-Bull, Ronald A. (1999) "Between Text and Practice: Considerations in the Anthropological Study of Islam," *Marburg Journal of Religion*, 4: 1–21.
——— (2007) "Lost in a Sea of Subjectivity: The Subject Position of the Researcher in the Anthropology of Islam," *Contemporary Islam* 1: 173–192.
Mahmood, Saba (2006) "Secularism, Hermeneutics, and Empire: The Politics of Islamic Reformation," *Public Culture*, 18: 323–347.
Manger, Leif (1992) "On the Study of Islam in Local Contexts," *Forum for Development Studies*, 1: 51–65.
——— (1999) "Muslim Diversity: Local Islam in Global Contexts," in Leif Manger (ed.) *Muslim Diversity: Local Islam in Global Contexts*, Richmond, UK: Curzon Press.
Marranci, Gabriele (2008) *The Anthropology of Islam*, London: Berg Publishers.
——— (2010) "Sociology and Anthropology of Islam: A Critical Debate," in Bryan S. Turner (ed.) *The New Blackwell Companion to the Sociology of Religion*, Chichester: Wiley-Blackwell.
Mayeur-Jaouen, Catherine, and Bernard Heyberger (2006) *Le corps et le sacré en orient musulman*, Aix-en-Provence: Édisud.
McLoughlin, Seán (2007) "Islam(s) in Context: Orientalism and the Anthropology of Muslim Societies and Cultures," *Journal of Beliefs and Values* 28: 273–296.
Roff, William R. (ed.) (1987) *Islam and the Political Economy of Meaning: Comparative Studies on Muslim Discourse*, Berkeley, CA: University of California Press.
——— (1999) "Afterword: The Comparative Study of Muslim Societies," in Leif Manger (ed.) *Muslim Diversity: Local Islam in Global Contexts*, Richmond, UK: Curzon Press.
Schimmel, Annemarie (1955) "Zur Anthropologie des Islam," in Claas J. Bleeker (ed.) *Studies in the History of Religions*, Leiden: Brill.
Scott, David, and Charles Hirschkind (ed.) (2006) *Powers of the Secular Modern: Talal Asad and His Interlocutors*. Stanford, CA: Stanford University Press.
Sedgwick, Mark J. (2006) *Islam and Muslims: A Guide to Diverse People in a Modern World*, Boston, MA: Nicholas Brealey.
Starrett, Gregory (1997) "The Anthropology of Islam," in Stephen D. Glazier (ed.) *The Anthropology of Religion: A Handbook*, Westport, CT: Greenwood.
Tsugitaka, Sato (2004) *Muslim Societies: Historical and Comparative Aspects*. London: Routledge.
von Grunebaum, Gustave E. (1962) *Modern Islam: The Search for Cultural Identity*, Berkeley, CA: University of California Press.

Conceptualizing Islam

1 Recognizing Islam

Religion and society in the modern Arab world

Michael Gilsenan

Michael Gilsenan has a joint appointment at the departments of Middle Eastern and Islamic Studies and Anthropology of New York University. He held the Chair in the Study of the Contemporary Arab World at Magdalen College, Oxford from 1985 to 1995. He earned his BA in Oriental Studies in 1963 and received a D.Phil. from Oxford University in 1967. Gilsenan has conducted extended periods of research in Egypt, Lebanon, Singapore, Malaysia and Java. His fields of research include the sociology of religion, relations between violence, narrative and political power and, more recently, property, inheritance and law in the Arab diaspora in southeast Asia over the past 150 years. His most widely known publications include *Saint and Sufi in Modern Egypt: an Essay in the Sociology of Religion* (1973); *Recognizing Islam* (1983); and *Lords of the Lebanese Marches: Violence and Narrative in an Arab Society* (1996). In the following section, taken from the first and eleventh chapters of *Recognizing Islam*, including the afterword, Gilsenan writes reflexively about his first impressions and experiences with the people he encountered during his (field)work in Yemen, Lebanon and Egypt. In this article, Gilsenan uses the 'way of walking' as a metaphor for understanding the significance of cultural differences.

An anthropologist's introduction

My own experience of Islam began with a surprised and uncomfortable recognition that things are not what they seem.

As a nineteen-year-old preuniversity member of a British organization called Voluntary Service Overseas, I was doing a year of teaching in what was then (1959) the colony of Aden and the Protectorates and is now the People's Democratic Republic of Yemen. A friend and I were in Seyyun, one of the ancient towns of the great eastern wadi of the Hadhramaut, ruled by a British-appointed family of sultans and dominated by a highly influential clan of sherifs, descendants of the Prophet Muhammed.

Two young men of that family met us in the street, walking in the heat of the morning. The green band around their turbans, the flowing cream-coloured outer garments, and their trim beards all signified the holiness and precedence of their position.[1] Their wealth, from large local landholdings and overseas business in Indonesia, showed in the quality of the fine material of their clothes and in the size and equal elegance of the luxurious house to which we were being guided.

It was all an enchantment, a desert, an oasis, a holy town, an age-old tradition. The fullness of sanctity and a ritualized sense of gracious order and harmony were added to when a student of mine encountered in the street stooped respectfully to kiss the young sherifs' hands as we passed, thus marking his respect and acknowledgment of their position. The world was a perfectly formed magic garden. And I was entranced. All my images of Islam and Arab society were brought unquestioningly together.

The front door slammed behind us. The spell was broken. Our companions swiftly closed the window shutters so that no one could see us, lights were switched on, a Grundig tape recorder played Western pop music, and the strictly forbidden whiskey came out of the cupboard. Turbans were quickly doffed, and there was no talk of religion but only of stifling boredom, the ignorance of local people, the cost of alcohol, and how wonderful life had been in Indonesia.

To a naive adolescent, pious not to say sanctimonious in the face of the culture of this strange and marvelous society newly opened to him, the shock was enormous.

Was the street scene nothing but a scene? A show of holiness, a mere facade maintained by the elite, who had to hide from the very marks and duties of their authoritative position? Such signs of religion and hierarchy were used to dominate others, but, for some of the young sherifs at least, in the isolation of their houses were clearly an almost insupportable burden.

A day later I met the student, a boy in his late teens like myself. He delivered the second blow. "We kiss their hands now," he said, "but just wait till tomorrow." He was a Nasserist, a word that to the British and sherifian authorities meant subversion, communism, and an enemy to be bitterly resisted. A member of the first generation of peasants to be educated, he belonged to a cultural club in which most of the young men were sympathizers with the cause of the Egyptian president, then at the height of his power. That cause was identified as that of all Arabs against imperialism and the control of conservative and reactionary forces. He would talk to me, but I, too, was part of the apparatus of colonial administration, a fact that he realized much more clearly than I did.

The hand-kissing was a show, but a show with diametrically opposed meanings for the actors. It secreted hidden interpretations, reversals, and denials.

Both sides had strong definitions of true religion. The sherifs' whole position rested on their descent, ritual competence, and the belief in their power to bring blessing, education, and knowledge of Islamic law, all symbolized by their dress. For them the student was perilously close to unbelief and certainly tainted by socialism. The whiskey drinkers might acknowledge their own imperfect conduct but not see any link between this and a challenge to their authority. For the student, the men whose hands he kissed were not only obstacle to independence but had nothing to do with a true Islam, which had no need of sherifs, no need of reverence for wealthy merchants and landowners in green turbans or of deference to a religious hierarchy. The real Islam was free of such mediations with God and was embodied in the Qur'ān and the traditions. It was an egalitarian force for the unity of all members of the community and part of a global struggle, an Islam that went hand in hand with a fight against local sources of corruption and alien power.

That moment in south Arabia contained many of the conflicts and traces of religion that, twenty years later, I have come to write about here: class opposition, groups and individuals using the signs and codes but seeing events in quite different ways, concealed significances in social life, complex relations to wider historical changes in power relations and the economy. Finally, and not least, it draws attention to the danger of stereotypical images of another society and another religion. This is only one of the problems involved in learning about Islam in practice, where it is inextricably bound up with many dimensions of social life in ways that are frequently not at all what they initially appear to be.

These themes have run through my studies as an anthropologist, bringing new shocks and recognitions. My fieldwork has been carried out in circumstances where economic and political power, and sometimes overt violence and coercion, were crucial elements in social relations in which I myself was a participant.

In Egypt in the period 1964 to 1966 my work on the Sufi mystical brotherhoods was pursued among the urban poor, the low-paid unskilled and skilled workers, and new immigrants to the city from the countryside (Gilsenan 1973). Other members were drawn from elements of the petty bourgeoisie, who were struggling to maintain a precarious status and were living on the margins of poverty, since their small businesses, trades, clerkships, or minor civil service positions were insecure and ill rewarded. They lived in a world of major political changes as Nasserism replaced British rule and an irreversible break with the past seemed to have been made. For them Islam was all the more important as society shifted in ways difficult to grasp. Yet the sheikhs of the great Islamic University of al-Azhar in Cairo assured me that these brotherhoods had nothing to do with Islam at all and that I was not only wasting my time but giving a false impression of what the true religion is. The brotherhood members in turn regarded many of the sheikhs as quite irrelevant to an experience of the inner truths of the ways to God and to the practice of Islam in general. [...]

The perspectives on the world into which I was educated by [Lebanese] villagers with very different views and practices of their own seemed full of contradictions and unease. There appeared to be an underlying radical refusal to believe that anyone acted for anything other than personal interest, whatever the vocabulary of religion, honor, or kinship that was used, or that what was said or done was more than a cover for quite different secret intentions and purposes. Really to live in such a world involved practical mastery of both inner and outer realities as people conceived them. At the heart of reality might lie the core truth of religion, but who knew where that heart of reality lay or how to discover it? All this made for a multiplicity of interpretations, questionings, and almost theatrical social encounters. The rules and conditions of such forms might be shaped by overall social and economic conditions, but the everyday manifestations were kaleidoscopically variable. The relationship between these two dimensions is an unending problem that is present in everything that follows.

These kinds of experiences, so different and so similar, have been the main formative influences on my own construction of the meanings of Islam in society. The social classes among whom I anomalously moved are usually little considered in work on religion and belief. Historical documents give only inadequate and scattered accounts of what ordinary people are supposed to believe, and then only as seen through the eyes of literate specialists whose own position often includes the tacit or overt proposition that this cannot be true Islam. Both sheikhs and non-Muslim scholars can be found slipping into such attitudes and exclusions. That they do so is interesting and perhaps not very surprising. But such views are far too limited and partial.

The social strata of which I have spoken and among whom I have worked make up the broad mass of the population of many Islamic societies. They are usually not politically or socially dominant in a direct way, but they are of critical importance. [...]

The significance of these classes and groupings has increased enormously in the modern period. They are its creation, born out of change. Their societies have all experienced the world transformations of the past century and a half, through colonial or imperial control, the development of the world capitalist market and consequent major shifts in production, technology, land tenure, and property relations. The forms and functions of the state have expanded and altered in a whole range of forms: monarchical, military, secular socialist, attempts at realizations of different conceptions of Muslim political institutions, state socialist, state capitalist, and others. [...]

For everyone the nature and meaning of society have become a central problem. The domination exercised in the Middle East, particularly by Britain, France, and the United States, has deep repercussions. Political orders have been overturned and with them often the authority of Muslim rulers and Muslim law. The very bases of political legitimacy and claims to authority are questions of constant relevance and sharply contesting points of view. Social and cultural institutions once part of the taken-for-granted everyday world are equally open to fiercely divergent interpretation. Many of the suppositions and predispositions that make up culture have come into conscious and often very critical and self-conscious reflection. What Islam means for Muslims in the modern world is now an issue for debate and action in the context of the politics of nation states, the struggle for energy supplies, superpower rivalry, and dependency. What is the *umma*, the Islamic community, and how and where is *ijma'*, or consensus, to be formed? What is Islamic government and in what forms and institutions must it be embodied?

As the forces of nationalism and anti-imperialism have generated their own contradictions and taken sometimes acutely opposed directions that have divided, as much as unified, the idea of a pure tradition takes on a renewed vitality. Tradition: that which we have always done and believed and from which we have derived our social forms. But what is the authentic tradition with which we are to face the forces of unbelief, corruption, and oppression?

It is a confrontation. The insistence on a self-conscious examination is born out of contest. As a leading Arab intellectual has said, "Tradition is born in confrontation with military or commercial aggression. … Slavism, *brahmo saraj*, the reinterpretation of Confucius by *Kang Yu-Wei*, salafiyya—these responses are doubtless different but nonetheless display the same structure" (Laroui 1976: 87).

Tradition, therefore, is put together in all manner of different ways in contemporary conditions of crisis; it is a term that is in fact highly variable and shifting in content. It changes, though all who use it do so to mark out truths and principles they regard as essentially unchanging. In the name of tradition many traditions are born and come into opposition with others. It becomes a language, a weapon against internal and external enemies, a refuge, an evasion, or part of the entitlement to domination and authority over others. One of the single most important elements in what is often called Islamic fundamentalism is precisely this struggle over the definition of what is the tradition. This means not only a religious interpretation but a whole form of life. Such processes, as Laroui's remarks make clear, have been worldwide in the past two centuries, as capitalism has spread, and are by no means confined to Islamic communities.

The basic building blocks of these ideologies of Islamic tradition are largely shared. It is the relations between them and the stress on a particular interpretation of a given element that are significant for the distinctions between movements and groups.

The fundamentals can be set out quite simply. Islam which means submission to God, is constructed upon what Muslims believe is a direct Revelation in Arabic from God: the Qur'ān. This recitation or reading, for that is what the word *Qur'ān* means, is the miraculous source of the *umma*, the Islamic community. It is the Word. And the conception and communal experience of the Word in prayer, in study, in talismans, in chanting of the sacred verses, in *zikr* (Sufi rituals of remembrance), in the telling of beads, in curing, in social etiquette, and in a hundred other ways are at the root of being a Muslim. The directness of the relationship with Allah through the Word and its intensely abstract, intensely concrete force is extremely difficult to evoke, let alone analyze, for members of societies dominated by print and the notion of words standing for things.

It is yet more difficult when we realize that the shape and form of the letters making up the Qur'ānic verses that adorn mosques and homes, for example, are not decorative in any Western sense but are part of this essential directness of the Revelation and are felt as intrinsically full of divine energy and grace.

This recitation that gave birth to the community was given to the Prophet Muhammed, whose duty it was to transmit it to the society of early-seventh-century CE western Arabia in his role as a "warner," as the Qur'ān calls him, and as the last, or "seal," of the prophets. The Revelation had come down before, to the Jews and the Christians through their prophets, acknowledged as such in the Qur'ān, but it had been distorted by the rabbis and the priests. This is the last chance. There will be no other after it. Muhammed is not a wonder worker, the miracles are made by God, and one of the greatest miracles is the divine language of the Qur'ān itself.

Nonetheless, the figure of Muhammed obviously occupied an extraordinary position, and the family of the Prophet came to be especially revered. Often the ruler had to claim to be of that family of the Qureish, and groups of holy men, such as the sherifs I have already mentioned, based their authoritative positions on such a sacred genealogy. No other principle had been established by Muhammed before his death in CE 632, or the year 11 of the Muslim calendar, so that his succession was left problematic to his followers and to generations after.

The practice of the Prophet, the *sunna*, became a model for all Muslims, and it was recorded and elaborated in what became a large number of texts, on which, together with the Qur'ān, the Islamic law was based. The traditions of Muhammed and his Companions, known as the *hadith*, developed into a framework for defining what the community is, and this framework became the basis of education and learning as much as of practical life.

Practical is a key word in my view. For God and His *umma* are active in history. They have a covenant that is lived out not only in the five pillars—the profession of faith that "there is no God but Allah, and Muhammed is his Prophet," the observance of fasting during the daylight hours of the holy month of Ramadān, the giving of alms, the making of the five daily prayers, and going on the great pilgrimage to the holy cities of Mecca and Medina. It entails also a general sense of practical readiness for whatever the power of God disposes in small matters or in great. Believers have their guide and model in the *sunna* and the *hadith*, which deal with the most mundane aspects of everyday life and behavior as well as the general principles directing the community.

This practical readiness is far closer to a simple characterization of the Islam of my experience than is any image of either passive resignation or fanatical impulse.

The Book, the Family, the Tradition. All three are interpreted and acted on, their meanings in life fired and turned into a personal and collective enterprise. These are the fundamental elements in contemporary movements that call for a return to a true Islam. But they are by no means the only ones, and the ways in which they are understood vary widely.

Muslims have always been aware of differences and variations in the way traditions were viewed and actions demanded. In the Middle Ages local and regional pilgrimages, as well as the great pilgrimage to Mecca and Medina, were points at which people from quite separate social and economic orders gathered. The collective quest for blessing or knowledge was one that gave form and substance to the idea of the *umma*. These pilgrimages served as channels of information. Ideas and beliefs flowed through them at startling speed. Such gatherings at a shrine were frequently markets as well, centers of distribution and exchange in an economy that might have direct or indirect links over thousands of miles of caravan route. The disappearance of the caravans has not diminished the importance of modern pilgrimages. The social, political, and symbolic weight of such gatherings has, if anything, increased. The sense in which Islam forms a world ideological system has deepened and become more actual as the means of communication have developed.

Religious men in Indonesia would, by the late nineteenth century, know very well of the reformist or Sufi mystical currents in Morocco, Egypt, Syria, Iran, or India. They would know of the revolts, rebellions, constitutional movements, and peasant insurrections in the name of Islam against internal and external foes. Books were published and read by the learned men. Popular hymns, exhortations, and lives of saints could be purchased, memorized, and repeated by an ever-expanding audience. The meanings of Islam were both quickened and challenged at the same moment. The tape recordings of the Ayatollah Khomeini's speeches smuggled into Iran spread the revolutionary message in ways security apparatuses were unable to prevent. This is but the most recent example of the speed at which ideas and calls to action are diffused.

The notion and fact of diversity in the Islamic world is therefore no more a new one for Muslims than is the call for a return to the first principles, or rather, first practices, of the community. The so-called revival of Islam in the 1970s and after is not a revival at all but a continuation. Religious movements of all kinds—austere and ecstatic, legalistic and mystic, activist and quietist—have been socially and politically highly significant since the late eighteenth century, as European and capitalist influence became predominant. There have been two hundred years of what Westerners treat as a ten-year wonder. The reference is to a long history; the forms, contexts, and relations are constantly renewed.

All of this means that Islam is very much at the center of the cultural and political stage, or appears to be.

Appears to be. Memories of a hand kiss in a street in south Arabia make me hesitate. Contemporary events are dangerous guides to thought. Islam has become so much of a preoccupation of Western politics and media that we are tempted to think of it as a single, unitary, and all-determining object, a "thing" out there with a will of its own. There is a strong notion of a powerful, irrational force that, from Morocco to Indonesia, moves whole societies into cultural assertiveness, political intransigence, and economic influence.

Another version of this idea is the notion that religion is the key to the "Arab mind" or, at a wider level, that something called the "Muslim mind" or "Islamic civilization," explains a whole series of events and structures that are otherwise totally baffling and alarming. Islam is seen as the key to the secret and as part of the nature and essence of these people. The Iranian revolution is one of the most startling phenomena that have catalyzed and continue to stimulate this sense of Islam as a total and threatening mysterious presence. [...]

I want to dissolve such conceptions and give you a more cautious awareness of what the term *Islam* comes to mean in quite different economic, political, and social structures and relations.

Anthropologists see the meaning of a particular social role or myth or ritual or event as being the product of its relations and contrasts with other roles, myths, rituals, and events. The implications of this approach are that Islam will be discussed not as a single, rigidly bounded set of structures determining or interacting with other total structures but rather as a word that identifies varying relations of practice, representation, symbol, concept, and worldview within the same society and between different societies. There are patterns in these relations, and they have changed in very important ways over time. My aim is not to persuade the reader to substitute a relativized and fragmented vision for one of global unity. Rather it is to situate some of these religious, cultural, and ideological forms and practices that people regard as Islamic in the life and development of their societies.

There are […] topics and themes […] that do not appear at first glance to have much to do with Islam or religion: the furnishing of the *salon* of the Lebanese bourgeoisie; sexuality, honor, and violation linked to God's grace; the street plan of modern Cairo; tribal markets; family feuds; genealogies; and so forth. To take any element on its own or only in relation to other elements defined as "religious" would not yield its social meaning. And we have to be prepared to find that religion is often only a very minor influence.

What these topics also show is how much there is in common between the experience of the Lebanese and Egyptian working classes and petty bourgeoisie and those same classes in other societies of the Third World in which Islam does not figure at all. An Indian village is not a Lebanese village, and Rio de Janeiro is not Cairo, of course. But I think you will see that as well as the specific differences there are many things in common generated by the complex strains of a system of dependency that is worldwide. The way in which the economy, patterns in the use of public and domestic space, and conceptions of power and identity operate are at least as alike as they are distinct. Third-world societies have been exposed to the same forces in various shapes and guises, and the chapters that follow illustrate this point and show that those forces themselves may not be quite what we think:

> It has been observed that Hegel studied English political economy before thinking about Napoleonic expansionism, and it is true that it was not the Decembrists or the savants accompanying Bonaparte's expeditions who overturned societies, whether Russian or Egyptian, but English furniture.[2]
>
> (Laroui 1976: 87)

English furniture? Well, yes. Furniture, ways of sitting, modes of dress, politeness, photography, table manners, and gestures overturn societies, too. Such conventions, techniques, and ways of acting in and on the world are as important as any religion, and changes in them may be as dislocating as changes in belief. So we should be especially wary of assuming that it is Islam that is the most important area on which to focus. We do not have to accept or impose the primacy of religion over social, economic, or political factors. This […] is an attempt to demystify our standard approaches to Islam, just as my own views were so radically shaken in south Arabia.

There are many writers who, from different perspectives and disciplines, are attempting this kind of rethinking. Edward Said has launched a full-scale attack on traditional modes of Orientalist scholarship (Said 1978). Abdallah Laroui has dissected the role of Arab intellectuals from within. Groups of French and English students have subjected the texts they were brought up on to highly critical appraisal. The sense that it is time for a basic shift in the ways in which we think about Islam in society has become more and more urgent in the last two decades.

This is a reaction to previously dominant modes of thought in anthropology, political science, history, and Oriental studies. The first emphasized functional interrelations, with units usually defined as villages or tribes, and put the rest of the world "in brackets" or in a brief section on something called social change. The second, political science, stressed elites, a division between essential forms of society called traditional and modern and a view of politics very close to current Western political interests in the area. History in most cases seemed not to have caught up with the innovations in theory and method that occurred in other branches of the subject since World War II, notably in social history and the history of those classes often disregarded the narrative of events. Orientalism operated within a tradition that had become ossified, seeing texts to be commented on often with the reverence of a medieval divine, adoring Islam but suspicious of Muslims, and frequently downright hostile to and uncomprehending of political movements in the contemporary Middle East. [...]

My own basic procedure has been to use a lot of material drawn from personal experience of Islam and to try to re-create the surprise of the moment when my work really began, that moment when realization collided with illusion in south Arabia. [...]

Islamic signs and interrogations

My experience of Islam had begun with an encounter in a street in south Arabia. Green-banded turbans stood for holy sherifian descent, learning, true Islam, and membership in a religious and social elite, but their wearers, those bored young men, longed for Indonesia and felt themselves trapped in a provincial backwater, surrounded by ignorant peasants. To the boy who kissed their hands in apparent respect, those same marks of sanctity were read as signs of a control of land, alliance with the British colonial power, and a parasitical existence. Moreover, this rural worker's son had come to Nasserism through a colonial school that all unawares had served as a breeding ground for nationalist sentiment. The student who, again in apparent respect, called a young and ingenuous English teacher sir in a class devoted to subordinate clauses, saw that teacher, in his colonial uniform of white shirt, white shorts, long white socks, and heavy black walking shoes, as representing the other partner in the alliance with the green turbans.

I think that he was right on both counts. But I must qualify the term *apparent.* It is too glib to say that either the hand kiss or the address as 'sir' was mere convention and mere show. Islam needed no mediators, but the Prophet's family and the ideal of religious learning were certainly respected, whatever their local representatives happened to be. Similarly, the young English teacher was, after all, a teacher, an *ustaz,* and as such might serve as an introduction to learning for which a genuine reverence was felt. And I noticed that the boy himself was an *ustaz* and a sheikh to his laborer father by virtue of his period in school. As a learned man in his turn, he had become of a higher authority than his father in his own family, a reversal of hierarchy that in other circumstances would be unimaginable.

This anecdotal moment can be used as a lens through which to view a wider scene, or as a tangible sign that points to far greater meanings than it can itself contain. A colonial era was ending. Aden and the Protectorates, as they then were, stood as one of the last domains of the British. They lay both geographically and politically on the periphery of a shrinking empire and of the Arab world itself. Without material resources of their own, their chief importance to the imperial power was strategic, guarding the routes of the Red Sea and serving as a natural harbor and fueling station for shipping between the Indian Ocean and the Mediterranean.

Yet peripheral though Aden was in many ways, there were vaster forces to which it was intimately linked. The port was still seen as crucial to Western power in the region. The British Petroleum Company ran the gigantic refinery. There was a large Royal Air Force base and an army barracks. Within three years of my encounter there would be a full-scale urban colonial war fought in the narrow streets of Crater, the "Arab town." The sherifs would lose their position in the Hadhramaut, and the Arab world's only Marxist state would be born. No hands would be kissed.

The young descendants of the Prophet found the Hadhramaut both central and peripheral. Their families originated there. Their claims to holy lineage were rooted in a series of great holy sanctuary cities strung along the broad valley of the Hadhramaut like so many glowing pearls. There was a powerful tradition of *'ilm*, of learning, and of mediation between the Beduin tribes. City and desert interlocked in a very direct way. The sherifs dominated the local trade and the ownership of land. On the other hand, Hadhramaut had nonetheless also been a backwater for many years. Their most important economic and religious links and investments were with the east African coast, the Gulf, India, and Java. Some had made fortunes in those areas. They were part of a wide network spanning the entire Indian Ocean, a network of learning, trade, Sufism, and power.

There were other emigrants from South Arabia who did not wear the green-banded turban. People from the peasant farmer and tribal strata also went to India and the Far East, and it was in Indonesia as early as 1914 that these migrants formed the Irshadi, or Reformers Association, to combat the power of the elite in the Hadhramaut and the whole system of sanctified inequality (Bujra 1971).

One of the main signs of such opposition was to refuse all the marks of respect given to the sherifs, of which the most prominent was the hand kiss.

The signs of hierarchy were therefore already an area of struggle long before the student explained his own seeming deference as hiding opposition. But by his time it was no longer a question of confronting an inegalitarian ideology of Islam with a reformist one. It was rather a matter of attaining total independence from a local economic and political system and from a world system of domination that helped to determine it, and to give a new shape and practical form to Islam in that region.

For his generation, therefore, religion and the symbols were no longer the overall framework within which the world order could be interrogated and denied. That could only be done through a triumphing Nasserism, a form of nationalism that appeared to incarnate an irreversible move forward. The age of colonialism was passing; the age of the newly independent nations was beginning. Though the practice of Islam and what Islam really ought to be were themselves at issue locally and internationally, by the late 1950s the instruments of the struggle were seen to be anticolonial movements in which Islam was only one dimension.

Insofar as the Islam that was identified with state systems was concerned, as in South Arabia, it was viewed by the students as a reactionary force propped up by Britain and America, who had sought "Islamic pacts" as a resistance to radical nationalism. The kind of Islam represented in the conservative dynasty of Saudi Arabia, where the luxury of the few and the repressive interpretation of the Holy Law for the many seemed inextricably linked, was to be fought tooth and nail.

An armed and shining nationalism was to be at the bright center of the time. It seemed to crystallize and define the fundamental contradictions within society that the colonial system had helped to produce. What was experienced in daily life often in indirect, mediated, and blurred ways became direct and immediate in anti-imperialist ideology and politics. The student, the sherifs, and the English teacher meeting in the outpost of a declining empire at a key moment of historical transition each in his small way stood for different elements in these contradictions. [...]

Different and sometimes mutually exclusive apprehensions and practices of Islam are emerging that separate societies and classes as much as they unite them. Rhetorical unity may be easily achieved, but in the subterranean world there are social forces that push and thrust at the shell of dessicated formulas. Class divisions are becoming stronger, and this is the key process in the culture of contemporary Islam.

I may say, to take another image, that the currents below the river's surface are quicker than its seemingly lazy movement, they swirl this way and that, and run at different speeds.

But how do I come to a sense of that level of reality? These more concealed motions, marked only by tiny, almost invisible signs, are at the heart of the matter, but how to sense and show this? […]

I turn back again to my own experience. If I am asked, out of the blue, what moments crystallize my experience of Islam in its more specifically religious dimension, I know my immediate responses. They are two.

When I first went to Cairo and began, week in, week out, to go to mosques and to sit in self-conscious jacket-and-tie piety while members of the Hamidiya Shaziliya performed the *zikr*, there was one intruding element that fundamentally disturbed all my efforts at perception and a feeling for the real meaning of the event. It was not my inability to follow the hymns, or the enormous gaps in my knowledge of the language, or my incapacity to follow the chanting of the Qur'ān. It was something far more subtle and far more disorienting, yet I could not locate it.

One day I realized what the discordant phrase in the music was: neon light. All around the interior of the mosque there were verses from the Qur'ān in *neon* light. In green neon light, as it happens, but what matter the color? Neon. Advertisements, shop fronts, Piccadilly Circus, plastic, flashing, hard, cheap … A host of submerged echos flooded the mind and blocked out everything else. It drove the Qur'ān out of my ears, threw out whatever internal calm and equilibrium I had or sought, and sounded like a constantly hit flat note disrupting the whole tonal world of a symphony.

For months neon light subverted my every solemn ritual attendance. Each time I glanced up at the Qur'ānic verses, reading the Arabic, "knowing the meaning" in a dictionary sort of way, the neon would interpose itself, the medium would dominate. Then, one day, perhaps eight or nine months after my first hesitant observations of the *zikr*, I turned unthinkingly away from the swaying bodies and the rhythms of the remembrance of God and saw, not neon, but simply greenness. Greenness, and letters that did not "stand for" anything but simply were powerful icons in and of themselves. No gaps existed between color, shape, light, and form. From that unreflecting and unexpected moment I ceased to see neon at all.

This cannot be prepared for intellectually, though trained intuition plays its part. My own straining for "meaning" had done quite as much as the neon itself to ensure that I never found it. Even the word *meaning* itself is neither apt nor useful. Neither is *history.* It adds nothing much to know a history of "green" as the color of the Prophet, of the angel Khudr, of life, and to follow it through the ages. It is the direct, self-creating, and re-creating experience of greenness that "just is" for Muslims in a particularly ordinary way, both intimately the same as and distinct from our own, that is so vital.

There is nothing mystical here, nor even mysterious. There is rather the problem of finding a discursive way of expressing a timeless and endlessly repeated instant that has its own autonomy. Perhaps in phenomenology such an essence can be written out, perhaps not. No local explanation, which in any case would never be and could never be formulated, could serve to me apprehend it. And, having once passed that first of recognition of green and form, I am quite unable to what effect it had on my experience of the brotherhoods of Lebanon. It is simply there.

The other moment that has stamped my consciousness of Islam also occurred in Egypt. We were sitting in a room in a poor quarter of Alexandria, listening to a local leader of the Sufi order reading a letter from the sheikh of the order in Cairo. We had made the *zikr* in a small mosque. My attention had been mostly taken up by the attentiveness to me of a captain in the military intelligence who was far more intrigued by my presence than by any presence of the saint himself in the ritual. It was hot, and my show of pious absorption had long since become nothing more than a show.

The *khalifa*, or deputy, droned on. This and that regulation, these and those pieces of sententious advice, the interspersed laments at the corruption of cards and coffee houses. Irritation and boredom and knees that seemed locked in an unbreakable stiffness after hours of sitting cross-legged on the floor created a longing for escape.

Then, still reading the sheikh's letter aloud, the deputy said something like the following:

> I have heard that you do not use the Name of God, *Huwa* ("He," chanted as *Hū* in the *zikr*), in your ritual, and this is a great error and nullifies the whole ceremony. This is the most concentrated of all the Names used in the *zikr*. Why is that? Because if we take the Name of God, Allah and take away the first letter, we still have a divine word (that is, *Allah* becomes in Arabic *lillah* when you drop the initial alef, or *a)*, which means "for God." But this can be reduced yet further. If we take away the second letter we are left with *lahu* (which in Arabic is two letters only), "for Him." Finally we can take away the third and penultimate letter, and then we reach the ultimate, irreducible form—*Hū*, "He" (one letter in Arabic, a softly breathed *h* made by the lips forming a circle; the Arabic letter itself has a circular form, and there is a kind of homology of written and spoken, an identity of breath and sound). This is why no zikr is truly completed unless the essential *Hū* is chanted.

Breath, barely a sound, a circle, all in one word that is scarcely anymore a word.

This kind of occasion and this kind of teaching were absolutely routine and elementary and carried a long tradition behind them. Most of my friends, many of whom were semiliterate, could discourse about such guidance for hours with the appropriate quotations. Yet it indelibly marked my imagination. It imaged Islam, like a poetic image or a musical phrase that, for reasons you neither know nor need to know, will mark your barely conscious being and can never be erased, even if it may seem forgotten and is never made an object of reflection. [...]

A way of walking

This book has been a kind of excavation and a wandering. It is hard to use either of those words without seeming pretentious, but they express my experience and will have to stand for it.

The sense of moving through a city, through spaces that others define in ways the wanderer only dimly intuits and which seem sometimes frightening, sometimes empty, sometimes so full as to be overwhelming, is very strong to me. *How* should we walk, never mind where are we going? Friends in Lebanon were always amused at my striding off determinedly with long paces, eyes forward, heels clipping hard onto the path, self-conscious purpose in every move, *going somewhere* even if only—ultimate laughter—"for a walk." They knew that the appearance of purpose covered a confusion of aims, an uncertainty about what I would find or whether I would find it or whether I should even find it down that path, on that way. The only real dupe of this oh-so-determined stride was the walker himself—looking direct when he should be glancing sideways, cutting a straight line when everything—tact, manners, self-interest, knowledge—demands that he move in the slow, wide meandering stroll of his friends with frequent stops at almond trees, shoulders loose, hands arcing expansively through the air, knees almost disjointed with relaxation, having some interchange with everyone they saw, approaching on an apparently momentary wish, the house of such a one. How disoriented these drifting, stone-scuffing amblings were to me. Yet they were a central thread in the labyrinth of the village as it drew me in, though it is only now that that clearly strikes me and can emerge as words on a page, that I have the uneasy smile of one who says: "So that's how it was!"

Didn't those strolls—whose whole form denied time, effort, goal, direction, end—didn't they always follow such defined ways? They never crossed those fields, now that I come to think of it, never randomly halted at that house or in that quarter, always skirted that olive grove, never included picking grapes from that apparently wild vine or eating apricots from that tree. There were endless absences and unseens which everyone saw, just knew, except me. Innumerable possible ways we might have gone, too, though I chafed endlessly for the one I had defined as leading to that piece of information, that insight, that slice of family history, or property relationship, or death. Wasn't the way of walking my education so much more than all the moments of knowledge consciously acquired, which in any case turned out frequently to be a snare set deliberately to catch anyone whose eyes did not dart and glance as warily as a bird's? Those sentences so laboriously written down in the red-backed reporter's notebooks at one or two in the morning gave me such a sense of having achieved something concrete, having at last *found out* something. But weren't they mostly remarkable for the days it took to realize their slippery and obscure nature? They were out and out false, nuanced this way and that, incomprehensible, if seen from such an angle these were facets to what appeared plain glass: X had lied, Y was bored, Z thought he would use this curious personage with this extraordinary innocence of relations and hidden purposes to cast a misty screen across his own intentions concerning another.

It is the way of walking that now quite unexpectedly comes out to teach me about that culture and its unspoken premises, its acting on time, its assumptions about intention, and the constraints that rules, unconscious predispositions, codes, and forms place on deliberateness. To absorb that walk in one's own body was far closer to "speaking the language" than any half control over words and stumbled formulas. Behind its apparent formlessness and disinterest there was a readiness, a sense of options, even a practical and quite specific awareness of risk.

It is only now that I realize how much language I picked up in that way. Certainly only now that I understand what the German writer Walter Benjamin was doing when he spoke of "the art of wandering":

> Not to find one's way in a city may well be uninteresting and banal. It requires ignorance—nothing more. But to lose oneself in a city—as one loses oneself in a forest—that calls for quite a different schooling. Then, signboards and street names, passers-by, roofs, kiosks, or bars must speak to the wanderer like a crackling twig under his feet in the forest, like the startling call of a bittern in the distance, like the sudden stillness of a clearing with a lily standing erect at its center.
>
> (Benjamin 1978: 8–9)

All this talk of forests and bitterns filled me with the same impatience as strolling used to do in that Lebanese village. It looked a bit precious and self-conscious, or, at best, too close for my comfort to the *flâneurs*[3] of nineteenth century Paris about whom Benjamin loved to write. Anthropology ought to be straight lines to a place, like my English walk. But that isn't very practical, as my friends knew. It closes off too much, misses too much, violates too many other ways of reaching the point one hopes to reach but whose exact nature and significance one is not exactly aware. If there is a sociological imagination, it must move like Benjamin's *flâneurs*, or rather, as he himself learned to move over years and years of losing himself in order to be able to be lost, as distinct from merely confused or not knowing where he was.

Accepting that, I begin to accept his sterner and more intimidating insight with a little less fear:

> It is likely that no one ever masters anything in which he has not known impotence; and if you agree, you will also see that this impotence comes not at the beginning or before the struggle with the subject, but in the heart of it.
>
> (Benjamin 1978: 4)

I can pretend to myself this is not true, or use it as an excuse, or run away from it with a determined walk of purpose, even if my mouth is dry and I am only able to head in this direction because I am so ignorant of the fact that, to those who do know it, it is a minefield through which only ingenuousness and chance will bring me.

Better still, I can pretend to you that it is not true. That will leave both of us easier in our minds. The guide does not like to feel constantly that at the heart of the city is his powerlessness. The guided prefers the illusion of seeing and knowing. He has paid his money, spent that morning, that afternoon, and the tour was announced with all the usual signs of taking him around these and those monuments and places of interest. The faster and more directed the walk, the more he sees, the more he knows. Talk about impotence and beginnings looks suspiciously like a shuffling off of responsibility. "You propose to take me around. You set up all kinds of headings and names. You set this route, not I. You are providing the service and now you talk about impotence? A fine sort of guide that is."

Well, maybe at least if we both know that I see in that way or am coming to, that also will be more *practical*. You will less likely assume mastery in me or yourself, be less inclined to trust my apparently longest and most clearly determined strides and more inclined to look for what they rushed both of us past; be simply less uncomfortable with the profoundly discomforting and vital sense of hesitation and discontinuity and doubts, more aware that another guide would walk a different route and at a different pace, with different eyes, more acute and reflective attention, discovering whole quarters of the city of whose existence this particular guide is only in part aware. Perhaps this will bring you to disagreement and questioning, too? Why there and not here? Why not down that road, toward that crowd, those buildings? And my answer would have to be, "I'm not too sure. They are certainly, possibly, interesting. But for the moment this particular guide has traced out, no, found out as he went and even in the act of writing these few pages discovers, the only route he turns out to know."

To say that the word *conclusion* would be portentous and misleading is just to say that of course we don't conclude anything here. I hope we don't. Not because I wish to leave you with platitudes about the endless pathways of truth, the unending journey, or the tangled ways of knowledge.

Just because this sort of ending is the only practical one. For the time being.

Notes

1 No other groups could use these insignia of rank and status. That they never carried weapons was a further sign of the nature of their authority, though by this time that fact was of less practical importance than it had been.

2 Napoleon landed in Egypt in 1798 accompanied by a group of French intellectuals and scholars, as well as by an army. They were the savants referred to.

3 A master of the art of straying, a stroller, a virtuoso of wandering in the streets "botanizing the asphalt," to use Benjamin's evocative phrase.

References

Benjamin, Walter (1978) "A Berlin Chronicle," in Peter Demetz (ed.) *Reflections*, New York: Harcourt, Brace, Jovanovich.

Bujra, Abdalla S. (1971) *The Politics of Stratification: A Study of Political Change in a South Arabian Town*, Oxford: Clarendon Press.

Gilsenan, Michael (1973) *Saint and Sufi in Modern Egypt: An Essay in the Sociology of Religion*, Oxford: Clarendon Press.

Laroui, Abdallah (1976) *The Crisis of the Arab Intellectual: Traditionalism or Historicism?* trans. Diarmid Cammell, Berkeley, CA: University of California Press.

Said, Edward W. (1978) *Orientalism*, New York: Pantheon Books.

2 Islam observed

Religious development in Morocco and Indonesia

Clifford Geertz

Clifford Geertz (23 August 1926–20 October 2006) is one of the most well-known cultural anthropologists of the twentieth century. He earned his BA in Philosophy from Antioch College in 1950 after serving in the U.S. Navy during World War II. Geertz received his PhD degree from Harvard University in 1956 from the Department of Social Relations. He held several positions throughout his career. He is known for his work at the University of Chicago (1960–1970) and at the Institute for Advanced Studies at Princeton University (1970–2000) where he was also Professor Emeritus until his death in 2006. Geertz received awards with a number of honorary doctorates from various institutions, including those from Harvard University, University of Cambridge, and University of Chicago. His main ethnographic publications are: *The Religion of Java* (1960); *Peddlers and Princes: Social Change and Economic Modernization in Two Indonesian Towns* (1963); *Person, Time and Conduct in Bali: An Essay in Cultural Analysis* (1966); *Negara: The Theatre State in Nineteenth-Century Bali* (1980). He became famous with his books *The Interpretation of Cultures: Selected Essays* (1973) and *Local Knowledge: Further Essays in Interpretive Anthropology* (1983). He was awarded the National Book Critics Circle for *Works and Lives: The Anthropologist as Author* in 1988. Through his career, Geertz spent years doing fieldwork in both Indonesia and Morocco. As the founder of interpretive anthropology, Geertz was a major contributor to anthropological theory. His work has encompassed the fields of history, psychology, philosophy and literary criticism with his vigor to analyze and understand the symbols of ritual, religions and art. A key to understanding these was his method of thick description, with the goal of describing more than just the actions, but underlying motives and motivations of the people. The following extracts, which address a comparative approach to the study of Islam, are taken from the preface and from the first and third chapter of his *Islam Observed: Religious Development in Morocco and Indonesia* (1968), which resonate and are inherently related to his classic "Religion as a Cultural System" (1966).

Preface

[…] I have attempted both to lay out a general framework for the comparative analysis of religion and to apply it to a study of the development of a supposedly single creed, Islam, in two quite contrasting civilizations, the Indonesian and the Moroccan. Merely to state such a program is to demonstrate a certain lack of grasp upon reality. What results can only be too abbreviated to be balanced and too speculative to be demonstrable. Two cultures over two thousand years are hardly to be compressed into forty thousand words and to hope, besides, to interpret the course of their spiritual life in terms of some general considerations is to court superficiality and confusion at the same time.

Yet there is something to be said for sketches as for oils and at the present stage of scholarship on Indonesian and Moroccan Islam (to say nothing of comparative religion, which as a scientific discipline hardly more than merely exists), sketches may be all that can be expected. For my part, I have drawn the inspiration, if that is the word for it, for my sketch mainly out of my own fieldwork as an anthropologist in the two countries concerned. [...] Fieldwork has been, for me, intellectually (and not only intellectually) formative, the source not just of discrete hypotheses but of whole patterns of social and cultural interpretation. The bulk of what I have eventually seen (or thought I have seen) in the broad sweep of social history I have seen (or thought I have seen) first in the narrow confines of country towns and peasant villages.

[...] Anthropologists are not (or, to be more candid, not any longer) attempting to substitute parochial understandings for comprehensive ones [...]. They are attempting (or, to be more precise, I am attempting) to discover what contributions parochial understandings can make to comprehensive ones, what leads to general, broad-stroke interpretations particular, intimate findings can produce. [...]

The fact that the anthropologist's insights, such as they are, grow (in part) out of his intensive fieldwork in particular settings does not, then, in itself invalidate them. But if such insights are to apply to anything beyond those settings, if they are to transcend their parochial origins and achieve a more cosmopolitan relevance, they quite obviously cannot also be validated there. Like all scientific propositions, anthropological interpretations must be tested against the material they are designed to interpret; it is not their origins that recommend them. For someone who spends the overwhelming proportion of the research phases of his scholarly life wandering about rice terraces or blacksmith shops talking to this farmer and that artisan in what he takes to be the latter's vernacular, the realization of this fact can be a shaking experience. One can cope with it either by confining oneself to one's chosen stage and letting others make of one's descriptions what they will (in which case the generalization of them is likely to be even more uncritical and uncontrolled), or one can take up, in the absence of any particular competence to do so, the task of demonstrating that less special sorts of material and less minutely focused problems can be made to yield to the same kinds of analysis practiced on the narrowed scene. To choose the second alternative is to commit oneself to facing up to the necessity of subjecting one's theories and observations to tests quite unlike those to which anthropological arguments are normally required to submit. [...]

I have sought to see what sense I could make of the religious histories of Morocco and Indonesia in terms both of what I have concluded from my field studies and what, in more general terms, I think religion comes down to as a social, cultural, and psychological phenomenon. But the validity of both my empirical conclusions and my theoretical premises rests, in the end, on how effective they are in so making sense of data from which they were neither derived nor for which they were originally designed. [...]

Two countries, two cultures

Of all the dimensions of the uncertain revolution now underway in the new states of Asia and Africa, surely the most difficult to grasp is the religious. It is not measurable as, however, inexactly, economic change is. It is not, for the most part, illuminated by the instructive explosions that mark political development: purges, assassinations, *coups d'etat*, border wars, riots, and here and there an election. Such proven indices of mutation in the forms of social life as urbanization, the solidification of class loyalties, or the growth of a more complex occupational system are, if not wholly lacking, certainly rarer and a great deal more equivocal in the religious sphere [...]. It is not only very difficult to discover the ways in which the shapes of religious experience are changing, or if they are changing at all; it is not even clear what sorts of things one ought to look at in order to find out.

The comparative study of religion has always been plagued by this peculiar embarrassment: the elusiveness of its subject matter. The problem is not one of constructing definitions of religion. We have had quite enough of those; their very number is a symptom of our malaise. It is a matter of discovering just what sorts of beliefs and practices support what sorts of faith under what sorts of conditions. Our problem, and it grows worse by the day, is not to define religion but to find it.

[...] [T]he aim of the systematic study of religion is, or anyway ought to be, not just to describe ideas, acts, and institutions, but to determine just how and in what way particular ideas, acts, and institutions sustain, fail to sustain, or even inhibit religious faith—that is to say, steadfast attachment to some transtemporal conception of reality.

There is nothing mysterious in this, nor anything doctrinal. It merely means that we must distinguish between a religious attitude toward experience and the sorts of social apparatus which have, over time and space, customarily been associated with supporting such an attitude. When this is done, the comparative study of religion shifts from a kind of advanced curio collecting to a kind of not very advanced science; from a discipline in which one merely records, classifies, and perhaps even generalizes about data deemed, plausibly enough in most cases, to have something to do with religion to one in which one asks close questions of such data, not the least important of which is just what does it have to do with religion. We can scarcely hope to get far with the analysis of religious change—that is to say, what happens to faith when its vehicles alter—if we are unclear as to what in any particular case its vehicles are and how (or even *if*) in fact they foster it.

Whatever the ultimate sources of the faith of a man or group of men may or may not be, it is indisputable that it is sustained in this world by symbolic forms and social arrangements. What a given religion is—its specific content—is embodied in the images and metaphors its adherents use to characterize reality; it makes, as Kenneth Burke once pointed out, a great deal of difference whether you call life a dream, a pilgrimage, a labyrinth, or a carnival. But such a religion's career—its historical course—rests in turn upon the institutions which render these images and metaphors available to those who thus employ them [...]. Religion may be a stone thrown into the world; but it must be a palpable stone and someone must throw it.

If this is accepted (and if it is not accepted the result is to remove religion not merely from scholarly examination and rational discourse, but from life altogether), then even a cursory glance at the religious situation in the new states collectively or in any one of them separately will reveal the major direction of change: established connections between particular varieties of faith and the cluster of images and institutions which have classically nourished them are for certain people in certain circumstances coming unstuck. In the new states as in the old, the intriguing question for the anthropologist is, "How do men of religious sensibility react when the machinery of faith begins to wear out? What do they do when traditions falter?" [...]

In attempting to answer grand questions like this, the anthropologist is always inclined to turn toward the concrete, the particular, the microscopic. We are the miniaturists of the social sciences, painting on Lilliputian canvases with what we take to be delicate strokes. We hope to find in the little what eludes us in the large, to stumble upon general truths while sorting through special cases. At least I hope to, and in that spirit I want to discuss religious change in the two countries in which I have worked at some length, Indonesia and Morocco. They make from some points of view an odd pair: a rarefied, somewhat overcivilized tropical Asian country speckled with Dutch culture, and a taut, arid, rather puritanical Mediterranean one varnished with French. But from some other points of view—including the fact that they are both in some enlarged sense of the word Islamic—they make an instructive comparison. At once very alike and very different, they form a kind of commentary on one another's character.

Their most obvious likeness is, as I say, their religious affiliation; but it is also, culturally speaking at least, their most obvious unlikeness. They stand at the eastern and western extremities of the narrow band of classical Islamic civilization which, rising in Arabia, reached out along the midline of the Old World to connect them and, so located, they have participated in the history of that civilization in quite different ways, to quite different degrees, and quite different results. They both incline toward Mecca, but, the antipodes of the Muslim world, they bow in opposite directions. [...]

[T]o say that Morocco and Indonesia are both Islamic societies, in the sense that most everyone in them (well over nine-tenths of the population in either case) professes to be a Muslim, is as much to point up their differences as it is to locate their similarities. Religious faith, even when it is fed from a common source, is as much a particularizing force as a generalizing one, and indeed whatever universality a given religious tradition manages to attain arises from its ability to engage a widening set of individual, even idiosyncratic, conceptions of life and yet somehow sustain and elaborate them all. [...]

In both societies, despite the radical differences in the actual historical course and ultimate (that is, contemporary) outcome of their religious development, Islamization has been a two-sided process. On the one hand, it has consisted of an effort to adapt a universal, in theory standardized and essentially unchangeable, and unusually well-integrated system of ritual and belief to the realities of local, even individual, moral and metaphysical perception. On the other, it has consisted of a struggle to maintain, in the face of this adaptive flexibility, the identity of Islam not just as religion in general but as the particular directives communicated by God to mankind through the preemptory prophecies of Muhammad.

It is the tension between these two necessities, growing progressively greater as, first gradually and then explosively, the way men and groups of men saw life and assessed it became more and more various and incommensurable under the impress of dissimilar historical experiences, growing social complexity, and heightened self-awareness, that has been the dynamic behind the expansion of Islam in both countries. But it is this tension, too, that has brought Islam in both countries to what may, without any concession to the apocalyptic temper of our time, legitimately be called a crisis. In Indonesia as in Morocco, the collision between what the Koran reveals, or what Sunni (that is, orthodox) tradition has come to regard it as revealing, and what men who call themselves Muslims actually believe is becoming more and more inescapable. [...]

The overall strategies evolved in Morocco and in Indonesia during the premodern period for coping with this central dilemma—how to bring exotic minds into the Islamic community without betraying the vision that created it—were, as I have indicated, strikingly different, indeed almost diametrical opposites, with the result that the shapes of the religious crises which their populations now face are to a certain extent mirror images of one another.

In Morocco the approach developed was one of uncompromising rigorism. Aggressive fundamentalism, an active attempt to impress a seamless orthodoxy on the entire population, became, not without struggle, the central theme. This is not to say that the effort has been uniformly successful, or that the concept of orthodoxy that emerged was one that the rest of the Islamic world would necessarily recognize as such. But, distinctive and perhaps even errant as it was, Moroccan Islamism came over the centuries to embody a marked strain of religious and moral perfectionism, a persisting determination to establish a purified, canonical, and completely uniform creed in this, on the face of it, unpromising setting.

The Indonesian (and especially the Javanese) mode of attack was, as I say, quite the contrary: adaptive, absorbent, pragmatic, and gradualistic, a matter of partial compromises, half-way covenants, and outright evasions. The Islamism which resulted did not even pretend to purity, it pretended to comprehensiveness; not to an intensity but to a largeness of spirit. Here, too, one ought not to take the aim for the achievement, nor to deny the presence of unconformable cases. But that over its general course Islam in Indonesia has been as Fabian in spirit as in Moroccan it has been Utopian is beyond much doubt. It is also beyond much doubt that, whatever they may originally have had to recommend them, neither of these strategies, the prudential or the headlong, is any longer working very well, and the Islamization of both countries is consequently in some danger not only of ceasing to advance but in fact of beginning to recede. [...]

Viewed as a social, cultural, and psychological (that is to say, a human) phenomenon, religiousness is not merely knowing the truth, or what is taken to be the truth, but embodying it, living it, giving oneself unconditionally to it.

In the course of their separate social histories, the Moroccans and the Indonesians created, partly out of Islamic traditions, partly out of others, images of ultimate reality in terms of which they both saw life and sought to live it. Like all religious conceptions, these images carried within them their own justification; the symbols (rites, legends, doctrines, objects, events) through which they were expressed were, for those responsive to them, intrinsically coercive, immediately persuasive—they glowed with their own authority. It is this quality that they seem gradually to be losing, at least for a small but growing minority. What is believed to be true has not changed for these people, or not changed very much. What has changed is the way in which it is believed. Where there once was faith, there now are reasons, and not very convincing ones; what once were deliverances are now hypotheses, and rather strained ones. There is not much outright skepticism around, or even much conscious hypocrisy, but there is a good deal of solemn self-deception.

In Morocco this most frequently appears as a simple disjunction between the forms of religious life, particularly the more properly Islamic ones, and the substance of everyday life. Devoutness takes the form of an almost deliberate segregation of what one learns from experience and what one receives from tradition, so that perplexity is kept at bay and doctrine kept intact by not confronting the map with the landscape it is supposed to illuminate—Utopia is preserved by rendering it even more utopian. In Indonesia it most frequently appears as a proliferation of abstractions so generalized, symbols so allusive, and doctrines so programmatic that they can be made to fit any form of experience at all. The eloquence of felt particulars is smothered in a blanket of vacant theories which, touching everything, grasp nothing—Fabianism ends in elevated vagueness. But, formalism or intellectualism, it really comes down to about the same thing: holding religious views rather than being held by them. [...]

A few untroubled traditionalists at one pole and even fewer radical secularists at the other aside, most Moroccans and Indonesians alternate between religiousness and what we might call religious-mindedness with such a variety of speeds and in such a variety of ways that it is very difficult in any particular case to tell where the one leaves off and the other begins. In this, as in so many things, they are, like most of the peoples of the Third World, like indeed most of those of the First and Second, rather thoroughly mixed up. As time goes on, the number of people who desire to believe, or anyway feel they somehow ought to, decreases much less rapidly than the number who are, in a properly religious sense, able to. And in this rather demographic-looking fact lies the interest of religion for those of us who would like to uncover the dynamics and determine the directions of social change in the new states of Asia and Africa. [...]

The scripturalist interlude

The notion that religions change seems in itself almost a heresy. For what is faith but a clinging to the eternal, worship but celebration of the permanent? Has there ever been a religion, from the Australian to the Anglican, that took its concerns as transient, its truths as perishable, its demands as conditional? Yet of course religions do change, and anyone, religious or not, with any knowledge of history or sense for the ways of the world knows that they have and expects that they will. For the believer this paradox presents a range of problems not properly my concern as such. But for the student of religion it presents one, too: how comes it that an institution inherently dedicated to what is fixed in life has been such a splendid example of all that is changeful in it? Nothing, apparently, alters like the unalterable.

On the secular level, the resolution of this paradox lies in the fact that religion is not the divine, nor even some manifestation of it in the world, but a conception of it. Whatever the really real may be really like, men make do with images of it they take, if they are faithful, as both depictions of it and guides for relating themselves to it. [...] What happens to a people generally happens also to their faith and to the symbols that form and sustain it. [...] But of course what we are interested in is not the mere differences between the past and the present but the way in which the former grew into the latter, the social and cultural processes which connect them. [...] The problem is to understand how, given such beginnings, we have arrived, for the moment, at such endings.

For accomplishing this task, the scientific explanation of cultural change, our intellectual resources are rather meager. Systematic discussions of the transformation of societies from what we gather they used to be like to what they seem now to be like generally follow one or another of a small number of strategies, which we may call the indexical, the typological, the world-acculturative, and the evolutionary.

The simplest of these is the indexical. A number of usually rather arbitrary indices of social advance—literacy, miles of paved road, per capita income, complexity of occupational structure—are set up and the society in question measured against them. Change consists of movement from scores farther away from those characteristic of fully industrialized societies towards ones closer to them. Even when quantitative measures are not used, the style of thinking is the same: religious change consists of (say) a decline in the magical element in worship and a rise in the devotional; political in (say) greater hierarchization of authority.

The typological approach involves setting up ideal-type stages "primitive," "archaic," "medieval," "modern," or whatever—and conceiving change as a quantum-like breakthrough from one of these stages to the next. The career of a culture is portrayed in a series of snapshots taken at certain strategic points along it and arranged into a sequence at once temporal and logical.

In the world-acculturative approach, modernization is conceived in terms of borrowing from the West, and change is consequently measured by the degree to which values, ideas, and institutions which were, supposedly, perfected in the West—innerworldly asceticism, the rule of law, or the small family—have diffused to the society in question and taken root there.

And in the evolutionary approach, now coming somewhat back into favor after a long eclipse, certain world-historical trends—increasing social differentiation, increasing control over energy, increasing individualism, increasing civility—are postulated as intrinsic to human culture, and a society's movement is measured in terms of the degree to which these trends have managed, against the lethargy of history, to express themselves.

To my mind, none of these approaches seems very promising. [...]

These various strategies for studying change may, of course, be combined, and some of them, for example the evolutionary and the typological, commonly are. But taken either together or separately, they seem to me to share a common defect: they describe the results of change, not the mechanisms of it. It may well be true that, compared to the Indonesia or Morocco of 1767, the Indonesia or Morocco of 1967 is more literate, has passed from being an "archaic" society to being a "premodern" one (whatever that might mean), has been deeply influenced by Western values, techniques, and modes of thought, and displays a much greater degree of social differentiation. But to say this is to raise questions, not to answer them. What we want to know is, again, by what mechanisms and from what causes these extraordinary transformations have taken place. And for this we need to train our primary attention neither on indices, stages, traits, nor trends, but on processes, on the way in which things stop being what they are and become instead something else.

In a sense, to pose the problem as I have—how our countries got to where they are from where they were—is to do history backward. Knowing, we think, the outcome, we look for how, out of a certain sort of situation obtaining in the past, that outcome was produced. There is a degree of danger in such a procedure, for it is all too easy to reverse the reasoning and to assume that given the past situation the present was bound to arise. This is, in fact, the mistake, a kind of logical howler reinforced by scientific dreams of grandeur, that the social evolutionists, and indeed all varieties of historical determinists, make. But the reasoning does not reverse. [...] It is legitimate to look at a later state of affairs and isolate the forces that, with the finality of the already occurred, produced it out of a prior state, of affairs. But it is not legitimate to locate those forces in the prior state itself, nor indeed to locate them anywhere but in the events through which they actually operated. [...]

So far as our topic, religious change in Indonesia and Morocco, is concerned, the great difference [...] is that the classical religious styles in each case [...] are no longer more or less alone in the field but are besieged on all sides by dissenting persuasions. Attacked from the spiritual left by secularism and, much more importantly, from the spiritual right by what I am going to call, in a perhaps slightly eccentric use of the term, "scripturalism," these main-line traditions not only no longer have the hegemony they once had, they do not even have the definition. They remain, in some general, overall, vaguely pervasive way, the basic religious orientations in their respective countries, the characteristic forms of faith. Substantively, they have not changed. What has changed, if one may speak anthropomorphically for the moment, is their sense that their dominance is complete and their position is secure. This is gone and, barring extraordinary developments, gone permanently. They, or more accurately their adherents, feel themselves embattled, at once the heritors of a tested vision and embarrassingly out of date. Piety remains, but assurance does not.

To describe the religious history of, say, the last one hundred and fifty years in Indonesia and Morocco is therefore to describe a progressive increase in doubt. But doubt of a peculiar kind. With some exceptions, which may or may not represent the wave of the future (my own inclination is to think not), there has been rather little increase in skepticism in the proper sense, in atheism and agnosticism. Nearly everyone in either country still holds beliefs one can, by almost any reasonable definition, call religious, and most hold a very great many. What they doubt, unconsciously and intermittently, is their belief—its depth, its strength, its hold upon them—not its validity. I hope I am not being too subtle or paradoxical here. I do not mean to be. The point I am trying to make is an elusive one; yet in my opinion, it is also an overwhelmingly important one. On the spiritual level, the big change between the days of Mataram and Mulay Ismail and today is that the primary question has shifted from "What shall I believe?" to "How shall I believe it?" In neither country have men yet come in any vast numbers to doubt God. But they have come, if not precisely in vast numbers in quite significant ones, to doubt themselves.

I attempted to phrase this point [...] in terms of a distinction between "religiousness" and "religious-mindedness." Religious-mindedness, celebrating belief rather than what belief asserts, is actually a response, perhaps the most logical response, to the sort of doubt I am talking about. Given a dislocation between the force of classical symbols, which has lessened, and their appeal, which has not, or not as much, the indicated procedure is to base their validity on something other than their intrinsic coerciveness: namely, to be paradoxical one last time, their hallowedness—their spiritual reputation rather than their spiritual power.

The bulk of our two populations still considers either an inward search for psychic equilibrium or a moral intensification of personal presence the most natural mode of spiritual expression. The problem is that these days naturalness seems increasingly difficult actually to attain. Everything is growing terribly deliberate, willed, studied, *voulu*. [...] The transformation of religious symbols from imagistic revelations of the divine, evidences of God, to ideological assertions of the divine's importance, badges of piety, has been in each country, though in different ways, the common reaction to this disheartening discovery. And it is this process, as well as the loss of spiritual self-confidence that underlies it, that we need somehow to explain. [...]

The primary impact of colonialism was, here as elsewhere, economic. The European demand for consumption goods—coffee and sugar in Indonesia, wool and wheat in Morocco—got the period of all-out colonialism under way; the European demand for industrial raw materials—rubber in Indonesia, phosphates in Morocco—consummated it. In between, the foundations of a modern economy, an enclave economy, of course, but a modern one nonetheless, were laid down. [...]

But of course, beyond its economic impact, and largely because of it, colonialism also created a unique, not to say bizarre, political situation.[1] It was not just that the indigenous rulers were either removed or reduced to agents of foreign powers, but, more importantly, that the symbols of legitimacy, the loci of power, and the instruments of authority were rudely dissociated. [...] The main result of this odd state of affairs was twofold: a framework for national integration of a sort which had not previously existed was created; and the distinction between ruler and ruled became more than a difference in power, status, or situation, it became a difference in cultural identity. At the same time as the Protectorates and the East Indies brought Morocco and Indonesia into being as integrated states, they brought them into being as bifurcated polities.

Bifurcated societies, actually, for around the core of soldiers and colonial officials were collected the plantation managers, commercial farmers, bankers, mine operators, exporters, and merchants (plus, as envoys of conscience, a few clerics, teachers, and savants) for whom the whole enterprise was designed. Hermetic, privileged, and above all foreign, this group formed, as it wished and as it turned out, an indigestible element in each society. No colonial ideology seeking to justify imperialism by removing it to higher ground [...] could ever change this fact. [...] Beyond the economic and political, the colonial confrontation was spiritual: a clash of selves. And in this part of the struggle, the colonized, not without cost and not without exception, triumphed: they remained, somewhat made over, themselves.

In this determined maintenance of social personality religion played, as might be expected, a pivotal role. The only thing the colonial elite was not and, a few ambiguous cases aside, could not become was Muslim. The trappings of local culture could be taken on—couscous, burnouses, and moorish arches in Morocco; rijstaffel, sarongs, and wall-less drawing rooms in Indonesia. Local etiquette might be affected, local craftwork cultivated. Even the language might be learned. But it was all *Mauresque* or *Indische,* not Moroccan or Indonesian. The real line between, in the Moroccan phrasing, Nazarenes and Believers, or, in the Indonesian, Christian Men and Islamic Men, was not effaced. Indeed, it grew sharper. In a curiously ironical way, intense involvement with the West moved religious faith closer to the center of our peoples' self-definition than it had been before. Before, men had been Muslims as a matter of circumstance; now they were, increasingly, Muslims as a matter of policy. They were *oppositional* Muslims. Not only oppositional, of course; but into what had been a fine medieval contempt for infidels crept a tense modern note of anxious envy and defensive pride.

But if colonialism created the conditions in which an oppositional, identity-preserving, willed Islam could and did flourish, scripturalism—the turn toward the Koran, the *hadith,* and the Sharia, together with various standard commentaries upon them, as the only acceptable bases of religious authority—provided the content of such an Islam. Western intrusion produced a reaction not only against Christianity (that aspect of the matter can easily be overemphasized) but against the classical religious traditions of the two countries themselves. It was not European beliefs and practices, whose impingement on either Moroccan or Indonesian spiritual life was tangential and indirect, toward which the doctrinal fire of the scripturalists was mainly directed; it was maraboutism and illuminationism. Externally stimulated, the upheaval was internal.

In Indonesia, the general movement toward an Islam of the book rather than of the trance or the miracle has commonly been associated with the word *santri,* the Javanese term for a religious student. In Morocco, it has not had any single name, and indeed has been a rather less capsular development, but it has centered around the same figure, there called a *tāleb.* Neither of these movements was highly organized or integrated, indeed, until recently they were hardly organized or integrated at all. Nor was either of them new in the colonial period: there were bent scholastics disputing in the airless mosque schools of Fez and Demak almost from the time of Islam's arrival. But it was in the colonial period, the high colonial period, that they gathered strength and, culminating [...] in a kind of convulsive self-purification, threatened for awhile to drive the classical traditions not merely from the center of the stage but from the scene altogether. [...]

This tense intermixture of radical fundamentalism and determined modernism is what has made the culminating phases of the scripturalist movement[2] so puzzling to Western observers. Stepping backward in order better to leap is an established principle in cultural change; our own Reformation was made that way. But in the Islamic case the stepping backward seems often to have been taken for the leap itself, and what began as a rediscovery of the scriptures ended as a kind of deification of them. "The Declaration of the Rights of Man, the secret of atomic power, and the principles of scientific medicine," an advanced *kijaji* once informed me, "are all to be found in the Koran," and he proceeded to quote what he regarded as the relevant passages. Islam, in this way, becomes a justification for modernity, without itself actually becoming modern. It promotes what it itself, to speak metaphorically, can neither embrace nor understand. Rather than the first stages in Islam's reformation, scripturalism in this century has come, in both Indonesia and Morocco, to represent the last stages in its ideologization. [...]

Predictions in this field, however, are pointless. All a student of comparative religion can really do is to layout the general limits within which the spiritual life of a people has moved, is moving, and, the future never being wholly unlike the present, is likely to go on moving. Just how, within those general limits, it will in fact move, God, as they say, only knows.

Notes

1 The colonial period in both countries is, naturally enough, much more extensively documented than their histories generally but, also naturally enough, more subject to prejudiced and one-sided (both pro- and anti-imperialist) interpretations as well. Some of the more useful synoptic works, representing various points of view include: For Indonesia: Furnivall 1983; Burger 1939; Burger 1948-1949, 1949-1950; Wertheim 1959; Vandenbosch 1942; Kat Angelino 1931. For Morocco: Miège 1961; Berque 1962; Cerych 1964; Maurois 1931; Aubin 1906.

2 With respect to the uprisings [...], see, for West Sumatra: Radjab 1964; for central Java: Yamin 1952 and van der Kroef 1949; for Northwest Java: Kartodirdjo 1966; on North Sumatra: Snouck-Hurgronje 1906.

References

Aubin, Eugene (1906) *Morocco of Today Crowned by the French Academy*, London: J.M. Dent & Co.

Berque, Jacques (1962) *French North Africa: The Maghrib between the World Wars*, London: Faber & Faber.

Burger, Dionijs H. (1939) *De Ontsluiting van Java's Binnenland voor het Wereldverkeer*, Wageningen: H. Veenman & Zonen.

——— (1948–1949) "Structuurveranderingen in de Javaansche Samenleving," *Indonesie*, 2: 381–398, 521–537.

——— (1949–1950) "Structuurveranderingen in de Javaansche Samenleving," *Indonesie*, 3: 1–18,101–123, 225–250, 347–350, 381–389, 512–534.

Cerych, Ladislav (1964) *Européens et Marocains, 1930–1956: Sociologie d'une décolonisation*, Bruges: De Tempel.

Furnivall, John S. (1983) *Netherlands India*, New York: AMS Press.

Kartodirdjo, Sartono (1966) *The Peasants' Revolt of Banten in 1888: Its Conditions Course and Sequel*, 's-Gravenhage: Nijhoff.

Kat Angelino, Aarnold D. (1931) *Colonial Policy*, The Hague: M. Nijhoff.

Maurois, André (1931) *Lyautey*, Paris: Plon.

Miège, Jean-Louis (1961) *Le Maroc et l'Europe: 1830–1894*, Paris: Presses Universitaires de France.

Radjab, Muhamad (1964) *Perang Paderi: Di Sumatera Barat (1803–1838)*, 2nd edn, Djakarta: Balai Pustaka.

Snouck-Hurgronje, Christiaan (1906) *The Achehnese*, trans. Arthur W. O'Sullivan, 2 vols, Leiden and London: E.J. Brill, Luzac & Co.

Van der Kroef, Justus M. (1949) "Prince Diponegoro: Progenitor of Indonesian Nationalism," *The Far Eastern Quarterly*, 8: 424–450.

Vandenbosch, Amry (1942) *The Dutch East Indies: Its Government, Problems and Politics*, 3rd edn, Berkeley, CA: University of California Press.

Wertheim, Willem F. (1959) *Indonesian Society in Transition: A Study of Social Change*, 2nd rev. edn, The Hague: W. van Hoeve.

Yamin, Muhammad (1952) *Sedjarah Peperangan Dipanegara, Pahlawan Kemerdekaan Indonesia*, Djakarta: Jajasan Pembangunan.

Approaching Islam

3 Beyond ideology and theology

The search for the anthropology of Islam

Abdul Hamid el-Zein

Abdul Hamid el-Zein (1934–13 August 1979) was born to a merchant family of Alexandria, Egypt. After having earned two degrees at the University of Alexandria, in philosophy and social science, el-Zein went on to achieve two Master of Arts degrees in anthropology, one from Alexandria and the other from the American University in Cairo. As his thesis, el-Zein studied the creation of a waterwheel in a Nubian village. Submitted as his thesis to both the University of Alexandria and the American University, this work marked el-Zein as both a brilliant scholar and the beginning of his style of looking at the world in a holistic perspective able to utilize a multitude of theoretical strains. el-Zein earned his PhD at the University of Chicago in 1970. His dissertation, "The Sacred Meadows: A Structural Analysis of Religious Symbolism in an East African Town" (1974), was about the social and religious life in Lamu, Kenya. The same year, he became a member of the anthropology faculty of Temple University and within four years earned his place as associate professor. At the time of his death, el-Zein had works in progress, which included a critical survey of Orientalist and anthropological studies of Islam and a monograph on the structural linguistics of Ferdinand de Saussure and Arabian folklore, though he had published only one major work. During his short but remarkable career, he was a participant in the Comparative Study of New Nations, won numerous scholarly awards from the Woodrow Wilson and Ford Foundations, Temple University, Chicago University, the United Nations, and was a Resident Fellow at the Institute for Advanced Study in Princeton. This article below originally reviews five studies on Muslim societies and proposes for the first time an anthropology of Islam. In the three studies from his review that are presented here, he scrutinizes the theoretical foundations of their anthropological research and argues that they are bound by their own assumptions. In radically questioning the existence of universal concepts, el-Zein in the end even questions the concept of Islam.

* * *

In the course of our intellectual history, Islam came to be understood as a unified religious tradition and, in common with other institutional religions, taken as a guide to its own understanding (Levy 1957). The concept of Islam thus defined the nature of the subject matter and its appropriate modes of interpretation or explanation, but discoveries emergent within this framework have begun to contradict these premises.

In order to reveal the significance and complexity of this problem, this review first examines two apparently opposed positions on Islam: the "anthropological" and the "theological." These perspectives emerge from different assumptions concerning the nature of Man, God, and the World, use different languages of analysis, and produce different descriptions of religious life. Five anthropological studies are taken here to represent the internal variation within the anthropological perspective, while a general commentary suffices to describe the more standardized theological paradigm. Of course, the works discussed here do not exhaust the relevant studies of Islam, but they exemplify certain major approaches well enough to allow discussion of the interaction of theoretical views and ethnographic description. In all approaches, the meaning of religion as a universal form of human experience and of Islam as a particular instance is presupposed, invariable, and incontestable. Consequently, all claim to uncover a universal essence, the real Islam. Ironically, the diversity of experience and understanding revealed in these studies challenges the often subtle premise of the unity of religious meaning. It then becomes possible to ask if a single true Islam exists at all.

By virtue of its scope and sophistication, the work of Clifford Geertz offers a suitable point from which to begin the investigation. Although he proceeds by assuming a single form of religious experience and a unity of meaning within Islamic tradition, Geertz simultaneously accentuates the diversity in the actual content of religious experience as lived in the everyday world. Although they are intricately imbedded in his most recent study on Islam (Geertz 1968), the theoretical notions which permit the eventual integration of this diversity are never systematically stated or elaborated. These crucial assumptions emerge clearly only through reconstructing implicit relationships between statements presented in other works. For Geertz, human phenomena are simultaneously organic, psychological, social, and cultural. Certain universal problems and qualities of being human arise from the reality of man's biological condition and in necessary social and psychological processes. Yet when grasped by man's immediate consciousness, these existential problems and conditions appear plastic and elusive. It is through the dimension of culture, which is man's unique capacity, that these problems and processes are given meaning, organized, and controlled (Geertz 1964: 52–63; Geertz 1965: 51; Geertz 1966: 5; Geertz 1968: 16, 100; Geertz 1973: 5). These four dimensions of human reality are mutually determinative, and therefore must ultimately be integrated within a single analytic framework. But because culture particularly is the means of interpretation of all experience, it becomes the central concept in Geertz's understanding of human existence. Culture lends both order and significance to man's direct and matter-of-fact apprehension of the reality of nature and existence. In this sense, culture does not refer to a set of institutions, traditions, or customs, but involves the conceptualization of life: an intersubjective process of the interpretation of immediate experience (Geertz 1968: 93–94).

The cultural processes of giving meaning to the world are rooted in the human capacity for symbolic thought. All men impose thought or meaning upon the objects of their experience (events, images, sounds, gestures, sensations) which, when defined, become attached to symbols or the material vehicles of meaning (Geertz 1966: 5). In turn, meaning arranges these objects in intelligible forms. This expressive capacity results in the creation of cultural systems understood as patterns of symbols which must possess a certain degree of coherence in order to establish for man the structure of his own existence (Geertz 1973: 17).

For Geertz, symbols and the meanings they carry are culturally defined and socially shared. An individual is born into an already meaningful world. He inherits cultural interpretations from his predecessors, shares them with his contemporaries, and passes them on to the following generations. Therefore, symbolic thought is always social, intersubjective, and public. It cannot escape into a mysterious and inaccessible domain of private subjective meaning. So while man creates his own symbols, these symbols define for him the nature of his own reality. For Geertz, the analysis of culture consists of the study of these social, intersubjective, and culturally relative worlds. It is a positive science in the sense that it deals with symbols as empirical expressions of thought. And it is cast in phenomenological terms: his intention is to develop "a method of describing and analyzing the meaningful structure of experience ... in a word, a scientific phenomenology of culture" (Geertz 1966: 7). The emphasis of this approach is on "meaning." Because it is impossible to discover directly the ontological status of events, actions, institutions, or objects, the problem lies in grasping their meaning when brought to consciousness.

The formation of different forms of cultural systems corresponds to certain levels of the organization of thought. Geertz refers informally to the variety of possible cultural systems throughout his studies: religion, art, common sense, philosophy, history, science, aesthetics, ideology (Geertz 1964: 62; Geertz 1968: 94). In his study of Islam, common sense, religion, and science become the most essential symbolic forms in his analysis. Common sense constitutes a primary dimension through which man gives meaning to his immediate experience (Geertz 1975).

Common sense is not the mere matter-of-fact apprehension of reality but the judgments, assessments, or colloquial wisdom which structure a practical reality. This set of shared notions is not the outcome of deliberations or reflection, but emerges in the experiential engagement with reality. Common sense notions involve such basic aspects of survival that they are invariably taken for granted.

However, the relation between common sense notions, matter-of-fact reality, and human creativity is never stable. The nature of man's engagement with the world changes through time with increasing awareness and differs from place to place. Therefore, common sense notions differ and change accordingly—or when common sense simply fails to account for experience, its authority dwindles, and religion as a higher and more general interpretive order emerges (Geertz 1968: 94–95). Religion, in Geertz's view, offers a wider interpretation of the world and serves as a correction of common sense. In this sense, religion and common sense enter into a continued dialectic and must be studied as reciprocal traits of man's experiential reality.

Geertz refers to religion as the synthesis of two dimensions of human experience: "world view" and "ethos." In any culture, the collective notions, images, and concepts of the world view establish the essential reality of nature, self, and society. They define the sheer actuality of existence (Geertz 1957: 421; Geertz 1968: 97). Ethos constitutes the evaluative aspect of existence; it expresses the desired character, tone, style, and quality of social and cultural life. It concerns the way in which things are properly done (Geertz 1968: 97–98). Ethos and world view, or values and the general order of existence, continually reaffirm each other. Their interrelationship is powerfully and concretely expressed in the form of sacred symbols which not only objectify but condense multiple rays of the universe of meaning and focus them in tangible and perceptible forms. Any culture will require only a limited number of synthesizing symbols due to their immense power to enforce this integration of fact and value (Geertz 1957: 421–422).

Systems of religious symbols continually respond to the inevitable force of historical change. Geertz regards history as the continual process of formation and sedimentation of meaning. No laws or processes of history exist but the creation of meaning which, because meaning is intersubjective, constitutes a process of social transformation as well. To arrive at any general explanation, history is studied in reverse for there are no predictive and necessary sequences of meaning. Yet in spite of his rejection of grand-scale historical necessity, Geertz does impose the constraint of the concept of tradition. For most civilizations, the structure of possibilities of change is set in formative years (Geertz 1968: 11). Thus, traditions, such as Islam, emerge with the continuity of culturally shared meanings.

Yet the concept of history in Geertz's work contains an internal tension. On the one hand, historical change is the necessary field for man's continual creation of meaning through which he realizes himself as a human and cultural being. On the other hand, change is continually denied by man, whose very creation of symbols reflects the intention to fix and stabilize meanings in objectified forms. Religion reflects this struggle. In situations of extreme change such as foreign intrusion or conquest, religious symbols and beliefs may weaken in the face of upheaval and contradiction in previously coincident social conditions. Yet it is equally possible that by virtue of the commitment of faith, these symbols may persist by denying other forms of experience such as moral, aesthetic, scientific, or even practical considerations. In this sense, faith is the true counterpart of change. While belief may stabilize reality momentarily and partially, faith attempts to fix it absolutely.

It is through yet another mode of experience, science, that these other cultural systems may be understood. Because science is itself a cultural system, it too becomes a process of interpretation. Yet it constitutes a privileged mode of understanding in the sense that it grasps the reality of the entire process of human existence, unlike common sense and religion which remain limited to particular forms of experience. As a scientist, the anthropologist must not merely observe and report, he must interpret the native's interpretation of reality, or give a "thick" description (Geertz 1973). This thick description is achieved when the scientific imagination succeeds in suspending its own cultural attitudes in order to comprehend the essential nature of human experience. Scientific explanation in Geertz's view is a matter of discovering the intricacies of expression. To explain is to reorganize and clarify the complexity of meaning by revealing its order in symbolic forms (Geertz 1965: 47; Geertz 1973: 16).

The scientific understanding of religious experience is perhaps the most difficult. These moments of subjective spiritual experience demand complete involvement, and therefore are never directly communicated between subjects. Rather, the immediate religious experience usually becomes translated into common sense terms. But science, as a privileged mode of interpretation, recognizes and accounts for this process of "secondary revision" and is capable of an indirect understanding of religious symbols. Furthermore, this very rephrasing into common sense reveals to the scientific mind the relevance of religion to social action.

In *Islam Observed*, it is this scientific phenomenology of culture which Geertz applies to the analysis of the diverse cultural expressions of Islam in Morocco and Indonesia (Geertz 1968). Geertz examines the interrelationship of sacred symbols with world view, ethos, faith, common sense, and social context which constitutes the total religious experience. The precise contents of the religious system and the social order vary through time and from culture to culture. In this study, the detailed and intricate variations in the meaning of the religious experience result from both the pressure of history and the already—given distinctions in cultural or social traditions. However, the complex diversity of meaning which emerges from the comparison of Indonesian and Moroccan Islam is always intended to reveal similarities at a higher analytic level which embrace the diverse processes of formation and transformation of cultural expressions or styles of a core tradition.

The first factor of variation is simply the accidental sequence of historical events. [...] During these initial periods when Islam first put its roots into foreign lands, certain conditions in each society set the limits within which Islamic meaning might develop and change (Geertz 1968: 11). These constraints created the boundaries of possible variation which are the basis of the development of distinct "traditions" of meaning. Perhaps the most significant constraint in Geertz's analysis is the nature of the social order into which religious symbols and ideas must naturally fit in order to seem authentic (Geertz 1968: 20).

In the case of Morocco, the relevant social context consisted of an unstable pattern of settlement and continuous feuding. Religious symbols both defined and interpreted this social reality. In coincidence with a fragmented social structure, Moroccan Islam lacked a religious order or hierarchy which would determine who could and could not aspire to leadership and sainthood. Instead, personal charisma, which any man might posses regardless of social or religious status, became the sole criterion of authority and power. The symbol of authority, the saint, took on the image of the warrior zealously enforcing his own doctrine, continually striving to enhance his charisma by producing miracles, and demanding the blind obedience of as many followers as possible.

The Indonesian setting differed entirely. The population was quietly settled in towns or outlying agricultural villages, and their social relations were built upon a sense of order and cooperation. Their version of Islam involved a strict, hierarchical order of graded spirituality and corresponding rules determining who was to attain the highest stages. The saint became a symbol of self-contained order, inward reflection and self-reform. His power lay not in the brute force of his authority but in the rewards of internal insight through years of meditation.

Geertz sees these saints as metaphors or cultural constructions in which society objectifies its values, norms, ideals, and notions defining significant actions. Each embraces and condenses thousands of meanings and is able to create a symbolic unity between otherwise discordant elements (Geertz 1964: 58–59). Through the selection and comparison of these key synthesizing symbols, and through the investigation of particular historical and social dimensions of their expression, Geertz builds up the diverse patterns of existential meaning in these local *islams*. With precision, he locates the uniqueness which distinguishes one culture's experience of Islam from another's. While the saints of Morocco and the saints of Indonesia might play a similar role as condensing metaphors, their meanings will never be the same.

Despite his emphasis on the particularity and historicity of these religious experiences, Geertz continues to refer to them collectively as "Islamic" and to speak of "Islamic consciousness" and "Islamic reform." The unity which he thus imputes to the religious phenomena emerges as a consequence of his presupposed notions of human existence. For Geertz, human reality at its most fundamental level is unified. It involves the universal conditions of being. For all men, the lived-in world is an experienced world constituted through symbolically expressed meanings which are intersubjectively or socially shared. Geertz establishes not only the reality of shared experience but also the forms in which it is expressed. His work on Islam emphasizes the primacy of common sense, religion, and science. Although they vary according to the content of particular cultural expressions, the forms themselves and their interrelationships remain fixed and universal. The dynamics of these forms and the expression of their content yield the dimension of existence called history; and the continuity of meaning in time and space leads to the formation of historical traditions of meaning.

Thus all expressions of Islam find unity of meaning through two dimensions of these universal conditions: first as expressions of a particular form of experience, religion, with certain defined characteristics such as the integration of world view and ethos; and second as an historically continuous tradition of meaning in which the original expression and all those following it in time and space do not exist as complete distinct realities but as delicately related developments of an initial symbolic base linked by the social process of shared meaning. Islam is seen in terms of Wittgenstein's notion of family resemblances. Striking similarities seem to appear over many generations, yet a careful look shows that no one characteristic is held in common. Rather, features overlap and crisscross. There is less order than in a trend within a single tradition. Continuities arise in oblique connections and glancing contrasts (Geertz 1975). This unity of Islam established at the level of his philosophical premises allows Geertz to speak legitimately of an "Islamic" consciousness at the level of actual experience as well. Each individual experience contains the universal characteristics assigned to the religious form of experience and those particular shared meanings which recall an entire tradition of Islam. [...]

[Gilsenan] studies the emergence of a saint and his vision of God and human existence during a period of social upheaval in Egypt. He defines the saint as a charismatic leader, who, as Weber would have it, has a unique and personal power to shape the meaning of existence during a time of social crisis and to convince a group of people to commit themselves to his vision. Weber emphasizes, although Gilsenan does not, the revolutionary nature of the charismatic leadership and belief which "revolutionizes men 'from within' and shapes material and social conditions according to its revolutionary will" (Weber 1968: 1116). Charisma starts as a conflict with the rational-legal norms: "Hence, its attitude is revolutionary and transvalues everything: it makes a sovereign break with the traditional or rational norms: 'It has been written, but I say unto you'" (Weber 1968: 1115). The system of meaning which the charismatic leader creates must be clothed in novel, personal, and emotional insights which continuously capture the imagination of the believers and convince them to follow him without question. The essence of charisma arises in its spontaneity and dies as soon as it becomes routinized and depersonalized. Therefore, in its pure form, charisma opposes bureaucracy which represents formal, impersonal, and fixed systems of rules and meanings. [...]

In Egypt, at the time of the appearance of the Saint *Sidi Salama ar-Radi* (1867–1927), the British occupation and the influence of technological and economic success in Western societies disrupted traditional values, social structure, and religious order, particularly the significance of mystical orders shattered in the face of the rising importance of secular means of achievement. The *ulama*, the religious elite whose authority rested upon legalistic and formal theological interpretations of the *Quran*, joined with the government in an effort to revive the image of Islam by purifying its concepts and formalizing its structure. Therefore, by official decision in 1903, the mystical orders were organized as a bureaucratic system. However, in spite of this, their inherently fluid notions of affiliation allowed continuous changes in membership and segmentation of the orders themselves. The political disfavor which this incurred, combined with competition from secular education, political parties, and social clubs, brought the entire rationale of mystical orders and knowledge into question.

The Saint *Sidi Salama ar-Radi* intended to reestablish the preeminence of mysticism through the creation of a new order which would satisfy the needs of the rising middle class and offer the working class a personal expression of religion. He possessed the traditional mystic criterion of leadership: he received the teachings of an already established line of religious leaders, and claimed the gift of supernatural power of God. In this sense, the Egyptian saint strikes a compromise between the miraculous charisma which Geertz finds in Morocco and the genealogically based charisma of the *sadah*. His power is determined both by revelation and by a sacred lineage of teachers. Yet in this period of rapid modernization, the legitimization of sainthood also required formal theological knowledge. Although in the past mysticism was ambivalent concerning the worth of studying theology, it now claimed to include it. Thus, *Sidi Salama ar-Radi* incorporated miraculously the currently valued tenets of formal theology into a mystical tradition in which knowledge comes directly from God.

The order he established, the *Hamidiya Shadhiliya*, was based upon a corpus of laws which he decreed in order to define a strict hierarchy of roles and functions. Each member was responsible to the saint or to his representative. The actions of the members had to be watched carefully, and the branches of the order were to be inspected from time to time to secure their obedience of the laws. A sacred oath, the *'ahd*, that enforced an irrevocable and life-long commitment to the order was required. A structure of the saint's religious innovations then fell directly into the existing pattern of the formal bureaucratic rigidity that mysticism claimed to challenge.

Perhaps the most puzzling aspect of Gilsenan's analysis is the use of the framework of charisma to elucidate the sociological power of this saint. If the investigation is pursued, the mystic appears to lack the requirements of the concept. First, the saint was originally a member of the *Qawigjiya-Shadhiliya* order, and from that group he drew the followers who constituted the core of his new order (Mustafa 1974). Therefore, he did not found the order through the power of his personal charisma, but through systematic recruitment from members of a group already socially and politically predisposed to commitment. Secondly, the history of the *Shadhiliya* order in Egypt reveals a traditional compatibility between theological concepts and mystical knowledge (al-Din al-Shayal 1965: 162–190). *Sidi Salama*'s efforts to integrate theological formulations with mysticism were more a rephrasing of the content of an established pattern rather than a personal and revolutionary synthesis in line with Weber's definition of the charismatic leader.

And finally, the bureaucratic structure of the new order directly contradicts the nature of change which occurs through charisma. The saint, through his laws and through the sacred oath, abolished the vital process of continual reinterpretation that characterizes a charismatic message. Even Gilsenan admits that according to sociological criteria, the charisma of the saint failed to capture the nature, direction, and intensity of change in the social and political life of Egypt at that time. Instead his visions and organizations portrayed a static world which conformed to the traditional concept of formally structured religion.

Now the question of the proper role of religion in social processes arises. [...] Gilsenan explores the power of religious meaning, through charisma, to create and define the nature and historical sense of social life. In this way, he brings out the cultural significance of religion which Geertz also has emphasized. [...] In the end, the role of the charismatic saint and of religion in general was to satisfy certain social and political conditions. The degree to which these demands were met determined the success of the saint and the legitimacy of the religious system. If religious means had failed to cope with changing social relations and attitudes, other institutions would have arisen as alternative solutions. So for [...] Gilsenan the process of social change proceeds along a single path. And Islam constitutes a temporary ideological obstacle which will eventually be superseded by a more modern and rational form of society.

According to [...] Gilsenan [...], religion constrains and stabilizes its social base. Islamic societies would have remained locked into a traditional form, determined by the rigidity of their religious world view, had it not been for the external forces of change arising through contact with the West. And even at that, the expressions of Islam [...] in Egypt perpetrated their significance [...] by readjustment to new social and political conditions with the foundation of a bureaucratic mystic order. In [this] case religion did [not] itself become an innovative force.

It is Eickelman's contribution to contest this notion of religion's inherently static form (Eickelman 1976). He makes history the dominant theoretical perspective which views social reality and all cultural or symbolic systems, including religion, as in a continuous state of change. He criticizes other models of change as mere comparisons of two static states, the before and the after, without accounting for the social processes which make the transition possible. [...]

In order to reveal the complexity of these processes, Eickelman insists that social reality must be analyzed in both its synchronic and diachronic dimensions. A diachronic view of society over time preserves a sense of the uniqueness and particularity of its characteristics; a synchronic study uncovers the interrelationships among its elements that hold at one point in time but which, by virtue of a necessary incongruity between the symbolic and the social, inevitably lead to change. Thus these two points of view become complementary rather than contradictory as in many other anthropological approaches (Sahay 1972: 153–164). In this respect, Eickelman claims to follow in the footsteps of Max Weber. [...]

Eickelman's analysis of Maraboutism in Morocco reinterprets rather than re-produces these Weberian concepts. If he were to build his model on perpetual change in the strict Weberian sense, then the meanings, interests, and relevancies of the matter he studies must change. However, he states that "From an analysis of Maraboutism in its contemporary context and an attempt to comprehend the fundamental assumptions which Moroccans now make about social reality, one develops a sense of expectation of what is crucial and often absent in evidence concerning earlier periods" (Eickelman 1976: 63). This implies the use of the present to reconstruct the past, which in turn suggests a continuity of values and interests which violate Weber's notion of historical change. Eickelman further remarks that after considerable immersion in the contemporary aspects of Maraboutism, "it became clear that something was missing, that what I saw were fragments of a pattern of beliefs, once solid, that was beginning to crumble" (Eickelman 1976: 64). Again, a stable social and religious reality takes shape. Here the present is not conceived as a particular historical reality in its own right. Instead it is evaluated as incomplete against a reconstructed or presumed past totality.

Eickelman treats history as a real sequence of empirical events. He reconstructs historical facts according to documents, French travelogues, and observations of the present. These events are linked by an inherent continuum of meaning, values, and interests which reach from some point in the past into the present. This extension of historical meaning implies stability rather than change. The Moroccan cultural systems are not open to continual and unlimited variation but constrained by boundaries inherent in the notion of historical continuity.

If change takes place, it is within this bounded reality. For Eickelman the force of change in any society lies in the lack of fit between social conduct and symbolic systems which express the culturally defined universe of meaning. He feels that a tendency exists in anthropological analyses to place these two dimensions in perfect correspondence. Either the social structure is considered the essentially stable domain and the symbolic system becomes its reflection, or vice versa. In these cases, the problem of historical change is avoided. However, an interaction occurs between these two systems which indicates that they remain distinct and out of balance. This asymmetric relationship can be seen when the individual, Eickelman's basic unit of analysis, manipulates symbols in order to realize his social goals and interests, justify or acquire a social position, or accumulate power. Eickelman refers to the means of manipulation as ideologies which mediate the opposition of the symbolic and the social. Ideologies themselves must be conceived as social activities maintained through various forms of expression, including ritual action. In the process of expression and manipulation, ideologies change over time. In turn, they reshape and redefine the social order. Yet because ideology continually varies according to its historical moment of use, a social structure can never be in complete coincidence with its ideological counterpart.

All expressions of religion—in this case Islam—are dealt with in terms of the notion of "ideology" defined as an essentially instrumental and pragmatic function. Religious ideology works at two social levels: the explicit ideology articulated by intellectuals and the religious elite, and implicit ideology which consists of local and popular interpretations of religious tradition. Although they do share certain elements in common, these two dimensions continually come into conflict. With respect to a particular version of Moroccan Islam, Maraboutism, the local interpretations that Eickelman investigates are the outcome of a world view resting on five key concepts: God's will, reason, propriety, obligation, and compulsion. Although these concepts are not related to each other in any permanent pattern, they all serve to render social action both meaningful and coherent. [...]

The saint, at least for those who follow him, defines the initially unordered stream of reality by imposing meaning and coherence on the lived world. The vision of the world which he perpetuates is one of a fixed and universal reality where "everything is written from the eternity." Change becomes an illusion for the Marabout. Within this system, a player may gain or lose, reach the status of saint or be disgraced as a sinner. But in spite of these possibilities, he must remain within a total framework of the universe which he cannot change.

In order to analyze this religious ideology, Eickelman has placed it within the explanatory framework of history. However, on two accounts the very content of his study raises certain questions concerning the nature of this theoretical perspective. First, although history, and consequently all religion and Islam, are said to involve continual change, their study is based upon assumptions which claim to be universal and invariable; the fact of history itself does not change. And while the content of actual religious symbols may vary, religion is always defined as an ideology and ideology is defined as instrumental. The significance of all cultural expressions of Islam can then be interpreted in terms of these premises. It appears that in order to analyze change, the concept of change itself must be fossilized by presuppositions which define its nature and subject matter in order to make the recognition and description of any significant historical moment possible. Religion as an ideology of God's will as understood by the Moroccans dissolves history with the premise of eternity. The opposite notion, the validity of history, for Eickelman is perhaps ideology as well. A certain paradox then emerges. The study of religion as ideology must be conducted from another ideological position (Lapidus 1974: 287–299).

Not only Eickelman's work but all anthropological monographs reviewed here begin from certain fundamental, theoretical premises concerning the nature of human reality, conscious or unconscious experience, history, and religion. Each set of interdependent assumptions implies a corresponding mode of interpretation which will reveal the real meaning of the diverse cultural expressions of Islam. Yet in spite of their differences, all positions approach Islam as an isolable and bounded domain of meaningful phenomena inherently distinct both from other cultural forms such as social relations or economic systems and from other religions. Within the domain of Islam, they also construct an internal dichotomy between local or folk Islam and the Islam of the elite, or *ulama*. However, the criteria of distinction differ in order to serve each view of reality, history, and meaning.

For Geertz, different societies transform Islam to fit their own unique historical experience, and therefore at the local level there exist as many meanings and expressions of Islam as historical contexts. However, the elite, the *ulama*, separate themselves from the local interpretations or the specifications of particular historical embodiments of Islam. They reflect upon the sacred tradition with its unique experience in order to grasp the eternal essence of Islam. Yet their superior position, by definition one of separation from popular knowledge, makes it impossible for them to relate this universalism to the level of common experience. The Islam of the *ulama* is highly abstract, formal, and legalistic. Theology in this sense is more reflective than popular systems of religious meaning. At the same time it is less ritualistic and less bound to common sense experience and social action.

The mode of expression differs as well. Most folk interpretations of Islam dwell upon the meaning of natural phenomena conceived as the reflection of God and the authority of the saints. The power of these religious elements does not reside in their physical manifestation. [...] Their notion of Islam centers upon the reading of the *Quran* and the prophetic traditions which yield meanings intended to transcend any particular cultural idiom. Formal religious education becomes a process of repetition in which meanings are already defined and stabilized in the pretense of universality (Ibn Khaldun 1967). These unchanging formulations of the essence of Islam and the folk concepts which change continually according to social usage in any particular circumstance exist simultaneously in all Islamic societies.

The anthropologist taking a phenomenological approach focuses on the daily lived experience of the local Islams and leaves the study of theological interpretation to the Islamists. Therefore, he faces the problem of grasping meanings which are fluid and indeterminate. He must stabilize these meanings in order to understand them and communicate them to others. Symbols then become finite and well-bounded containers of thought, and at the moment of analysis the continuous production of meaning is stopped. Meaning becomes static through its objectification in the symbol (Waardenburg 1974: 267–285). In order to isolate these objectifications of subjective meaning, the analyst must regard the symbol itself as an objective reality which he can describe without the influence of his own symbolic patterns. Science then requires a disinterest and detachment, a certain neutrality common to the scientific community. Although the scientist's understanding is still a mode of interpretation which can only guess at the meaning of another's experience rather than enter it directly, it retains its superior validity by recognizing the process and structure of interpretation itself.

This notion of science contains certain internal contradictions. Science is considered a mode of interpretation and reflection on experience just as any other cultural form; therefore, the suspension of cultural attitudes can never be complete—the criteria of true objectivity must be a higher cultural form of experience. Furthermore, in the scientific process of reflection, not only experience but the conscious subjects as well must become objects of reflection. In this way the very creators of symbols under study become passive carriers of meaning, while the scientific and supposedly disinterested consciousness takes over the active role.

The phenomenological position implies a certain hierarchy of experience based on the degree and intensity of different forms of reflection. The greater the reflection on experience, the greater the order in the systems of meaning. And objective understanding lies in the recognition of the order of the complexity of meaning. The local *islams* involve accepted, taken-for-granted experiences, and little directed reflectivity. Theological Islam entails more reflectivity and a more ordered system of meanings. Finally, history, because it specifically requires reflection on the past, and science, in this case anthropological reflection on human experience, become the privileged mode of understanding due to their awareness of the nature of the processes of human experience. Yet within the total hierarchy, both theology and anthropology claim a higher degree of reflection than folk expressions of Islam. Therefore, they both regard these expressions as less ordered, less objective, and somehow less complete versions of the religious experience. Each, however, looks upon this diversity of experience in different ways. Theologians condemn it in order to enforce their view of the eternal meaning of Islam; anthropologists regard the various expressions as diluted forms, distorted by magic and superstition, and thus indirectly imply the existence of a pure and well-defined essence of Islam. [...]

Gilsenan, in his analysis, reveals a distinction between elite and local Islam based not on opposition and domination [...] but on complementarity. The formal and systematized laws of the *ulama* differed in both content and style from the more mystical interpretation of the people. Yet both were traditionally opposed to the overriding authority of the ruling class. While the *ulama* were considered a social minority with little claim to actual political power, the mystic orders (because they defined the popular notions and values of Islam) were capable of organizing a mass rebellion in response to any governmental threat. So in order to buttress their social power, the *ulama* allied with the mystics. Even if these two approaches to Islam did not directly support each other's system of beliefs, they at least became noncontradictory. Both forms of Islam defined for society a stable and eternal vision of the world according to the all-pervasive order and meaning of God's will. [...]

Along with the bureaucratic trend of modernization, the influence of other new systems of social relevance such as trade unions, political parties, and secular education caused the mystical orders, as well as the *ulama*, to reevaluate their own concepts of meaning and order. The saint who was the center of Gilsenan's analysis attempted to show both the *ulama* and secular forces that these rational principles could be gained only through mystical experience. Yet his own solution, to formalize and bureaucratize the mystical order, contradicted his intention to reinstate the authority of the immediate spiritual encounter. According to Gilsenan's own criteria, the saint is considered a failure. He could not adjust the preexisting structure of mysticism to the changing social order. For Gilsenan, religion is idle; it does not define true reality, but functions instead to support the pregiven reality of the social order. Both the elite and local version of Islam are ideologies, not of an ideal Islam [...], but of the rational order of secular society. Therefore, there exist two systems of meaning, the religious system and social reality. If the two systems correspond, the society remains stable; if they do not, the ideological system of religion yields to fundamental social conditions. The conflict is essential for it constitutes society's drive to modernize itself. It leads to the creation of historical consciousness, rationality, and individualism. From this perspective, the rational order of modern bureaucracy, competition, and secular life will eventually destroy and leave behind those other systems of meaning which cannot adjust to it. If in traditional society Islam defines the meaning and order of social reality, in modern society, the actual empirical conditions of social life determine the meaning of Islam.

This relation between Islam and social change forms the core of Eickelman's study of Maraboutism. He too distinguishes the elite Islam from its local expressions according to his own notion of the formation of ideological systems. In contrast to Gilsenan, Eickelman believes that any social structure, even in so-called "traditional" and conservative ones, never remains stationary but changes at each moment. This change results from the lack of fit between social conduct and symbolic systems. Their dialectical interaction produces ideological systems as a means of social manipulation manifest in actual social activities defined by specific historical contexts. In this framework, the Islam of the *ulama* is considered an "explicit" ideology transcending the influence of culturally relative values and beliefs and therefore may legitimately be referred to as "religion." Local versions of Islam, however, are understood as "implicit" ideologies as they adhere to and are intertwined with common sense notions, the untutored and accepted assumptions concerning the nature of reality specific to each social group. These interpretations then vary according to cultural background and historical moment. Systems of religious meaning thus retain their social and historical particularity. Because they never rise to a level of cross-cultural application, like the Islam of the elite which gives them the status of true ideology, local Islam is always a very culturally specific set of beliefs, rather than a fixed and wholly coherent institutionalized religion.

Both forms of Islam coexist in a state of tension. The elite continually contest the local traditions of Islam. People acknowledge the general concepts dictated by the *ulama*, but they choose to live according to more particularistic notions of Islam, which conform with the patterns of their daily experience.

This particular anthropological distinction appears to reinforce the *ulama*'s claim to a superior religious position by treating the elite version as "religion," and reducing other interpretations to implicit ideology. These distinctions between elite and popular Islam are obviously derived from the fundamental assumptions defining each anthropological paradigm. Although all positions argue the objectivity and universality of their own premises, the mere fact of a multiplicity of possible meanings at the fundamental level of the nature of Man, God, and the World challenges the notion of a single, absolute reality. Rather than being accepted as given truths, these anthropological premises might be treated as anthropologists themselves treat the tenets of Islam: as diverse, culturally relative expressions of a tradition—in this case, a "scientific" one. [...]

Recognition of the imposition of premises alien to the subject matter itself involves a reevaluation of the authority of scientific understanding. From this perspective, changes in the definition of the function or essence of Islam do not result from the accumulation of knowledge, but from the changing attitudes to religion in the West (Waardenburg 1973). The notion of the "disinterested observer" is, in fact, impregnated with the values of a scientific community. [...]

In terms of this supposedly scientific distinction between folk and elite Islam, anthropology studies the former, yet its principles of analysis resemble the latter.

Like science, theological positions which are referred to as elite Islam, regardless of how anthropologists define them in their different paradigms, assume the same detached attitude. In both science and theology, understanding the real meaning of religious phenomena comes only through a presumed separation from common subjective assumptions and from immediate involvement with the object of study. Both positions agree on the existence of a "folk" Islam as opposed to a formal Islam which, in order to be known, demands a greater degree of reflection and systematization of principles than found in popular expressions of belief. Anthropology and theology differ merely in the particular aspects of these local interpretations selected for analysis.

However, the authority claimed by theological Islam is contested by the recognition that in any given cultural system, a folk theology may be found which rivals formal theology in its degree of abstraction, systematization, and cosmological implication. It is even possible to argue that this folk Islam constitutes the real Islam and that the traditions of the *ulama* developed historically out of already established principles of the nature of spiritual reality entwined with the life of the Islamic community (el-Zein 1974). In fact, these opposing theologies are complementary. Because each form both defines and necessitates the other, the problem of determining a real as opposed to an ideological Islam becomes an illusion.

On the most general level of abstraction, folk theology involves reflection on principles of ultimate reality, nature, God, man, and history which are formally expressed in traditional literature, folk tales, heroic stories, proverbs, and poetry. For instance, in the tale of *Seif bin dhi Yazan*, the reality of the world according to Islamic principles and the existence of the Prophet was known before the actual historical birth of Mohammed and his articulation of that doctrine. Therefore, in the folk conception, counter to the view of historians and

Islamicists, direct reflection upon the order of the world, rather than the actual statements of the Prophet and *Quran*, leads the mind to the origin of that order.

[...] While in the folk tradition the order of nature and the *Quran* were regarded as metaphors, the strict and formal theological interpretation gave complete authority to the sacred book to define the order of the world (Abu-Zahra 1970: 76–105).

This total focus on the sacred text led to the development of a strong formalism and traditionalism, a common language and the construction of a bounded universe of meaning (Makdisi 1971). The *Quran* and prophetic tradition prescribed an absolute reality expressed in a privileged language in which true meaning exists. [...]

Therefore folk theology and formal theology developed from the same principle: that both nature and the *Quran* reflect the order and truth of God. Yet the two paradigms choose opposite priorities. While one locates meaning in nature and includes the *Quran* within that general order, the other finds truth first in the *Quran* and then extends that reality to the interpretation of the rest of nature. Their essential complementarity stems from a relation of mutual completion. [...] Thus both attempt to contain the flux of experience: formal theology seeks to control space by fixing time, and the other to control time by fixing space.

In the end, there are no inherent differences in the content of either folk or formal theology to suggest that one is more objective, reflective, or systematic than the other. [...]

What unifies both expressions of theology with anthropology is the structure of their means of understanding Islam. All begin from positive assumptions concerning the nature of man, God, history, consciousness, and meaning. Their interpretations of the meaning of Islam depend themselves upon already presupposed and fixed meanings which determine the universality of Islam, define and limit properly "religious" and "Islamic" phenomena, and distinguish a folk from an elite, and a real from a false Islam. [...]

Criteria of validity differ as well. The anthropological positions claim to be more objective than both the folk and the theological traditions. With respect to the folk expressions of Islam, they assume their scientific analyses to be more reflective and systematic. And although theology is recognized as highly reflective, it is not critical and therefore remains subordinate to the authority of anthropology which, being scientific, is critical as well. [...]

Both the anthropological and theological approaches outlined here assume that there is a reality of Islam which may be derived from principles of an encompassing universal reality of the nature of man or God. The importance of diversity is then overridden at the level of both the religious and the total human experience which take on absolute, fixed, and positive meanings. Because they begin from such assumptions, actual interpretations of any particular cultural situation, symbol, or passage of the *Quran* will reflect pregiven meaning in two ways. First, although particular content may vary, it must always contain the characteristic of meaning specific to a form of experience. [...] Further, even the culturally and historically relative dimensions of meaning which are said to change, change only in accordance with unchanging criteria of meaningfulness. [...] It is impossible with such a rigid framework to suggest that each expression of Islam creates its own real world of meaning.

As the previously discussed positions would all agree, man does order his world through systems of meaning. [...] One thing emerges from the diversity of interpretation: each treated the saint as a thing and artificially added to it different dimensions of meaning which varied according to the investigator's interest. Each investigator selects from the multitude of possibly identifiable features and functions of the saint one or two which are deemed distinctive and which, in the subsequent analysis, are taken as the saint. Analysis based on such highly selective reading of ethnographic data artificially collapses the complexity of the "saint" to a single dimension, leaving unexplained many possible questions about the undeniable multiplicity of the cultural construct "saint."

Much of the behavior associated with the saint and his worshippers, along with the range of meaning signifiable through the saint, may appear to be spurious, idiosyncratic, and irrelevant. At the tomb of Egypt's most important saint, for example, Gilsenan observed what appeared to be wildly inappropriate behavior amongst the worshippers. Singing, dancing, shouting, joking, even cursing, accompanied the ritual of worship on the Saint's Day—behavior unexplainable either as piety of believers or as the intelligible actions of politically and/or economically rational actors. [...] The analyst confronted with such material must either demonstrate its rational "fit" with what he has identified as the real significance of the saint, expand his definition of the "saint" to accommodate dimensions of meaning beyond simple political or economic manipulation or metaphoric condensation, or, as too often happens, he may find these data irrational and/or irrelevant accompaniments to the "essential" nature of the saint. It would seem most desirable to reexamine our original positive notion of "saint."

Elsewhere I have shown that the saint may be profitably viewed as a symbol, not in the sense of being a vehicle for meaning, but as a relational construct in which the exdimension of purity/impurity, defilement, and sacralization are articulated with a broad and variable range of content, including political, economic, and otherwise pragmatic aspects of life (el-Zein 1974). The saint thus symbolically embodies fundamental properties of a system of classification in the matrix of which all institutions (politics, economics, etc) and institutionally related behavior (manipulation of power, disposition of resources, etc) are necessarily framed. The precise opposition embodied by the saint at this level may, of course, vary from place to place, just as the content apprehended therein varies. But it is only by going beyond institutions and functions, actors, and positive meanings to the relatively simpler complexity of categorical opposition that the richness of the saint or any other "religious symbol" emerges along with its position in the logic of culture.

The positions reviewed here all accept in some way the principle of objectivity based on a separation of realities in which the subject occupies the privileged position of being able to encompass within his consciousness the reality of the object. The object in each case is a thing or set of things whose order or ultimate meaning is to be discovered through techniques which identify systematic *connections* between *things*. The things may be symbols constructed as vehicles for otherwise disembodied but contained "meanings," institutions, domains, or any other entities whose existence as entities is unquestioned. That is, we have been treating analyses of Islam which accept as fundamental the existence of "Islam," "religion," "economy," "politics," and even "saints," whose relation to each other within a given culture may vary, but whose existential "truth" is not subject to question. The goal of such analysis then becomes one of finding the "essence" of things at hand and the kind of connection which seems best to explain how these things work in a "cultural system." The exact kind of relation (conceived as a connection) which emerges as dominant varies with the nature of things studied. [...]

But what if each analysis of Islam treated here were to begin from the assumption that "Islam," "economy," "history," "religion" and so on do not exist as things or entities with meaning inherent in them, but rather as articulations of structural relations, and are the outcome of these relations and not simply a set of positive terms from which we start our studies? In this case, we have to start from the "native's" model of "Islam" and analyze the relations which produce its meaning. Beginning from this assumption, the system can be entered and explored in depth from any point, for there are no absolute discontinuities anywhere within it—there are no autonomous entities and each point within the system is ultimately accessible from every other point. In this view there can be no fixed and wholly isolable function of meaning attributed to any basic unit of analysis, be it symbol, institution, or process, which does not impose an artificial order on the system from outside. That is, the orders of the system and the nature of its entities are the same—the logic of the system is the content of the system in the sense that each term, each entity within the system, is the result of structural relations between others, and so on, neither beginning nor ending in any fixed, absolute point. The logic of such a system, the logic of culture, is immanent within the content and does not exist without it. But while the "content" might differ from one culture to another, the logic embedded in these various contents are the same. In this sense, both the anthropologist and the native share a logic which is beyond their conscious control. It is a logic which is embedded in both nature and culture, and which can be uncovered through the intricate analysis of content. Here the problem of objectivity which haunted all the studies discussed above disappears, and since it was a problem created by a notion of the transcendence of consciousness and subjectivity of the investigator, it will vanish as a phantom, leaving in its place a logic which is shared by both the subject and the object. Islam as an expression of this logic can exist only as a facet within a fluid yet coherent system; it cannot be viewed as an available entity for cultural systems to select and put to various uses. "Islam," without referring it to the facets of a system of which it is part, does not exist. Put another way, the utility of the concept "Islam" as a predefined religion with its supreme "truth" is extremely limited in anthropological analysis. Even the dichotomy of folk Islam/elite Islam is infertile and fruitless. As I have tried to show, the apparent dichotomy can be analytically reduced to the logic governing it.

The works we have discussed here seemed not to offer a means for uncovering the logic of culture or the principles which are immanent in culture and which order and articulate the thoughts and actions of culture bearers. In this sense we have not yet been led to the structure of "Islam," nor can we be, for it is a contradiction in terms to speak of the systemic "fit"—the structure—of an autonomous entity. The fact of structure can never be shown in an isolated state and is reached only by unfolding patterns of both actual and potential diversity of cultural content. In its totality, this variability reveals the absence of any positive, universal content. Working from this perspective, from which meaning is strictly relational, the analyst cannot select relevant material according to some standard of truth, but must consider systems in their entirety. In this way, the multiplicity of cultural meanings is explored and developed. There are no privileged expressions of truth. "Objectivity" must be bound to the shared structures of both the analyst and the subject regardless of the content of their respective cultural systems.

This logic of relations implies that neither Islam nor the notion of religion exists as a fixed and autonomous form referring to positive content which can be reduced to universal and unchanging characteristics. Religion becomes an arbitrary category which as a unified and bounded form has no necessary existence. "Islam" as an analytical category dissolves as well.

References

Abu-Zahra, Muhammad (1970) *Al-Quran, al-mujiza al Kubra*, Cairo: Dar al-Fikr al Arabi.

al-Din al-Shayal, Jamal (1965) *Aalam al Askandriya*, Cairo: Dar al Maarif.

Eickelman, Dale F. (1976) *Moroccan Islam: Tradition and Society in a Pilgrimage Center*, Austin, TX: University of Texas Press.

El-Zein, Abdul H. (1974) *The Sacred Meadows: A Structural Analysis of Religious Symbolism in an East African Town*, Evanston, IL: Northwestern University Press.

Geertz, Clifford (1957) "Ethos, World View and the Analysis of Sacred Symbols," *Antioch Review*, 17: 421–437.

——— (1964) "Ideology as a Cultural System," in David E. Apter (ed.) *Ideology and Discontent*, New York: Free Press.

——— (1965) "The Impact of the Concept of Culture on the Concept of Man," in John R. Platt (ed.) *New Views of the Nature of Man*, Chicago, IL: University of Chicago Press.

——— (1966) *Person, Time, and Conduct in Bali: An Essay in Cultural Analysis*, New Haven, CT: Yale University Press.

——— (1968) *Islam Observed: Religious Development in Morocco and Indonesia*, New Haven, CT: Yale University Press.

——— (1973) *The Interpretation of Cultures: Selected Essays*, New York: Basic Books.

——— (1975) "Common Sense as a Cultural System," *The Antioch Review*, 33: 5–26.

Ibn Khaldun (1967) *The Muqaddimah: An Introduction to History*, trans. Franz Rosenthal, Princeton, NJ: Princeton University Press.

Lapidus, Ira (1974) "Notes and Comments," *Humaniora Islamica*, 2: 287–299.

Levy, Reuben (1957) *The Social Structure of Islam*, 2nd edn, Cambridge: Cambridge University Press.

Makdisi, George (1971) "Law and Traditionalism in the Institutions of Learning in Medieval Islam," in Gustave E. von Grunebaum (ed.) *Theology and Law in Islam*, Wiesbaden: Harrassowitz.

Mustafa, F.A. (1974) "The Social Structure of the Shadhilya Order in Egypt," MA Thesis, University of Alexandria, Egypt.

Sahay, Arun (1972) *Sociological Analysis*, London: Routledge & Kegan Paul.

Waardenburg, Jean Jacques (1973) *L'Islam dans le miroir de l'occident*, The Hague and Paris: Mouton.

——— (1974) "Islam Studies as a Symbol and Signification System," *Humaniora Islamica*, 2: 267–285.

Weber, Max (1968) *Economy and Society: An Outline of Interpretive Sociology*, trans. Ephraim Fischoff, New York: Bedminster.

4 The idea of an anthropology of Islam

Talal Asad

Talal Asad is currently distinguished professor at the well-known City University of New York. Born in Saudi Arabia as son of Muhammad Asad, Asad was raised in Pakistan and later on went to the United Kingdom to study architecture, though finally enrolled in anthropology. After earning his Masters in anthropology at the University of Edinburgh, he attended Oxford University where he studied under the renowned anthropologist Edward E. Evans-Pritchard. Asad began his career as a lecturer at University of Hull and later joined the staff at the New School for Social Research in New York before he took up a position at the City University of New York. His ethnographic publication is *The Kababish Arabs: Power, Authority and Consent in a Nomadic Tribe* (1970). He edited *Anthropology and the Colonial Encounter* (1973) and co-edited with Roger Owen the volume *Sociology of Developing Societies: The Middle East* (1983). His more theoretical works include *Genealogies of Religion* (1993); *Formations of the Security* (2003) and *On Suicide Bombing* (2007). Beyond his articles ranging from "Notes on Body Pain and Truth in Medieval Christian Ritual," "Politics and Religion in Islamic Reform," and "Ideology, Class and the Origins of the Islamic State" to "Anthropological Conceptions of Religion: Reflections on Geertz," Asad played a major role, along with Roger Owen and Sami Zubaida, in establishing the *Review of Middle East Studies*. Throughout his work, Asad became known for his lucid critique of various modes of thinking and his bringing forward the issue of the ethnocentrism of Western classifications of other cultures, making important contributions in the areas of post-colonialism, Christianity, Islam and the study of ritual. In this programmatic lecture on the anthropology of Islam, Asad develops and refines analytical concepts for the study of Muslim traditions. Here, he argues that we should conceptualize Islam as a discursive tradition and study it by starting with its own foundation in the Qur'ān and *hadith*.

I

In recent years there has been increasing interest in something called the anthropology of Islam. Publications by Western anthropologists containing the word "Islam" or "Muslim" in the title multiply at a remarkable rate. The political reasons for this great industry are perhaps too evident to deserve much comment. However that may be, here I want to focus on the conceptual basis of this literature. Let us begin with a very general question. What, exactly, is the anthropology of Islam? What is its object of investigation? The answer may seem obvious: what the anthropology of Islam investigates is, surely, Islam. But to conceptualize Islam as the object of an *anthropological* study is not as simple a matter as some writers would have one suppose.

There appear to be at least three common answers to the question posed above: (1) that in the final analysis there is no such theoretical object as Islam; (2) that Islam is the anthropologist's label for a heterogeneous collection of items, each of which has been designated Islamic by informants; (3) that Islam is a distinctive historical totality which organizes various aspects of social life. We will look briefly at the first two answers, and then examine at length the third, which is in principle the most interesting, even though it is not acceptable.

Eight years ago, the anthropologist Abdul Hamid el-Zein struggled with this question in a survey entitled "Beyond Ideology and Theology: The Search for the Anthropology of Islam" (el-Zein 1977). This was a brave effort, but finally unhelpful. The contention that there are diverse forms of Islam, each equally real, each worth describing, was linked in a rather puzzling way to the assertion that they are all ultimately expressions of an underlying unconscious logic. This curious slippage from an anthropological contextualism into a Levi-Straussian universalism led him to the final sentence of his article: "'Islam' as an analytical category dissolves as well." In other words, if Islam is not an analytical category, there cannot, strictly speaking, be such a thing as an anthropology of Islam.

So much for an answer of the first kind. One adherent of the second point of view is Michael Gilsenan, who, like el-Zein, emphasizes in his recent book *Recognizing Islam* that no form of Islam may be excluded from the anthropologist's interest on the grounds that it is not the true Islam (Gilsenan 1982). His suggestion that the different things that Muslims themselves regard as Islamic should be situated within the life and development of their societies is indeed a sensible sociological rule, but it does not help identify Islam as an analytical object of study. The idea he adopts from other anthropologists—that Islam is simply what Muslims everywhere say it is—will not do, if only because there are everywhere Muslims who say that what other people take to be Islam is not really Islam at all. This paradox cannot be resolved simply by saying that the claim as to what is Islam will be admitted by the anthropologist only where it applies to the informant's *own* beliefs and practices, because it is generally impossible to define beliefs and practices in terms of an isolated subject. A Muslim's beliefs about the beliefs and practices of others *are* his own beliefs. And like all such beliefs, they animate and are sustained by his social relations with others.

Let us turn then to an answer of the third type. One of the most ambitious attempts to address this question is Ernest Gellner's *Muslim Society*, in which an anthropological model is presented of the characteristic ways in which social structure, religious belief, and political behavior interact with each other in an Islamic totality (Gellner 1981). In what follows, I shall deal in some detail with this text. My purpose, however, is not to assess this particular work, but to use it to extract theoretical problems that must be examined by anyone who wishes to write an anthropology of Islam. As it happens, many elements in the overall picture presented by Gellner are to be found also in other writings—by anthropologists, Orientalists, political scientists, and journalists. In looking at this text one is therefore also looking at more than a unique account. But the picture it presents is of less interest than the way it has been put together—the assumptions it draws on and the concepts it deploys.

II

There is in fact more than one attempt to conceptualize Islam in Gellner's text. The first of these involves an explicit comparison between Christianity and Islam, each broadly conceived as differing historical configurations of power and belief, one essentially located in Europe, the other in the Middle East. Such a conceptualization is central to Orientalism, but it is also to be found implicitly in the writings of many contemporary anthropologists.

One sign of this is the fact that anthropological textbooks on the Middle East—such as Gulick's or Eickelman's—devote their chapter on "Religion" entirely to Islam (Gulick 1976; Eickelman 1981). Although Christianity and Judaism are also indigenous to the region, it is only Muslim belief and practice that Western anthropologists appear to be interested in. In effect, for most Western anthropologists, Sephardic Judaism and Eastern Christianity are conceptually marginalized and represented as minor branches in the Middle East of a history that develops elsewhere—in Europe, and at the roots of Western civilization.

My disquiet about this notion of Europe as the true locus of Christianity and the Middle East as the true locus of Islam does not come primarily from the old objection to religion being represented as the essence of a history and a civilization (an objection which even some Orientalists like Becker advanced long ago) (van Ess 1980). My concern as an anthropologist is over the way this particular contrast affects the conceptualization of Islam. Consider, for instance, the opening paragraphs of Gellner's book. Here the contrast between Islam and Christianity is drawn in bold, familiar lines:

> Islam is the blueprint of a social order. It holds that a set of rules exist, eternal, divinely ordained, and independent of the will of men, which defines the proper ordering of society. ... Judaism and Christianity are also blueprints of a social order, but rather less so than Islam. Christianity, from its inception, contained an open recommendation to give unto Caesar that which is Caesar's. A faith which begins, and for some time remains, without political power, cannot but accommodate itself to a political order which is not, or is not yet, under its control. ... Christianity, which initially flourished among the politically disinherited, did not then presume to *be* Caesar. A kind of potential for political modesty has stayed with it ever since those humble beginnings. ... But the initial success of Islam was so rapid that it had no need to give anything unto Caesar.
>
> (Gellner 1981)

If one reads carefully what is being said here, one must be assailed by a variety of doubts. Consider the long history since Constantine, in which Christian emperors and kings, lay princes and ecclesiastical administrators, Church reformers and colonial missionaries, have all sought, by using power in varying ways, to create or maintain the social conditions in which men and women might live Christian lives—has this entire history nothing to do with Christianity? As a non-Christian, I would not presume to assert that neither Liberation Theology nor the Moral Majority belong to the essence of Christianity. As an anthropologist, however, I find it impossible to accept that Christian practice and discourse throughout history have been less intimately concerned with the uses of political power for religious purposes than the practice and discourse of Muslims.

I want to make it clear that I have nothing in principle against comparisons between Christian and Muslim histories. Indeed, one of the most valuable features of the recent book by Fischer on Iran is the inclusion of descriptive material from Jewish and Christian histories in his account of the *madrasa* system (Fischer 1980). This is one of the very few anthropological studies of contemporary Islam that employ implicit comparisons with European history, and consequently enrich our understanding.

But one should go beyond drawing *parallels*, as Fischer does, and attempt a systematic exploration of *differences*. For this reason, my own research over the past three years has been concerned with detailed anthropological analyses of monastic ritual, the sacrament of confession, and the medieval Inquisition in twelfth-century Western Europe, which stand in contrast to the very different connections between power and religion in the medieval Middle East (Asad 1983a; Asad 1983b; Asad 1986). Of particular note is the fact that Christians and Jews have usually formed an integral part of Middle Eastern society in a way that is not true of non-Christian populations in Europe. My claim here is not the familiar and valid one that Muslim rulers have in general been more tolerant of non-Muslim subjects than Christian rulers have of non-Christian subjects, but simply that medieval Christian and Muslim authorities ("religious" and "political") must have had to devise very different strategies for developing moral subjects and regulating subject populations. This is too large a subject to be expounded here, even in outline, but it is worth touching on by way of illustration.

Modern historians have often observed that Muslim scholars in the classical and post-classical periods displayed no curiosity about Christianity, and that in this their attitude was strikingly different from the lively interest shown by their Christian contemporaries in the beliefs and practices not only of Islam but of other cultures too (von Grunebaum 1962). What is the reason for this intellectual indifference toward Others? The explanation given by Orientalists such as Bernard Lewis is that the early military successes of Islam bred an attitude of contempt and complacency toward Christian Europe. "Masked by the imposing military might of the Ottoman Empire, the peoples of Islam continued until the dawn of the modern age to cherish—as many in East and West still do today—the conviction of the immeasurable and immutable superiority of their civilization to all others. For the medieval Muslim from Andalusia to Persia, Christian Europe was still an outer darkness of barbarism and unbelief, from which the sunlit world of Islam had little to fear and less to learn" (Lewis 1973). Perhaps that was so, but our question is best approached by turning it around and asking not why Islam was uncurious about Europe but why Roman Christians were interested in the beliefs and practices of Others. The answer has less to do with cultural motives allegedly produced by the intrinsic qualities of a worldview or by the collective experience of military encounters, and more with structures of disciplinary practices that called for different kinds of systematic knowledge. After all, Christian communities living among Muslims in the Middle East were not noted for their scholarly curiosity about Europe either, and Muslim travelers often visited and wrote about African and Asian societies. It does not make good sense to think in terms of the contrasting attitudes of Islam and Christianity, in which a disembodied "indifference" faces a disembodied "desire to learn about the Other." One ought instead to be looking for the institutional conditions for the production of various social knowledges. What was regarded as worth recording about "other" beliefs and customs? By whom was it recorded? In which social project were the records used? Thus, it is no mere coincidence that the most impressive catalogues of pagan belief and practice in early medieval Christendom are those contained in the Penitentials (handbooks for administering sacramental confession to recently-converted Christians) or that the successive manuals for inquisitors in the later European Middle Ages describe with increasing precision and comprehensiveness the doctrines and rites of heretics. There is nothing in Muslim societies to parallel these compilations of systematic knowledge about "internal" unbelievers simply because the disciplines that required and sustained such information are not to be found in Islam. In other words, forms of interest in the production of knowledge are intrinsic to various structures of power, and they differ not according to the essential character of Islam or Christianity, but according to historically changing systems of discipline.

Thus, beyond my misgivings about the plausibility of historical contrasts in terms of cultural motives—such as "potential for political modesty" on the one hand, and "theocratic potential" on the other—lies another concern, namely that there may well be important differences which the anthropologist studying other societies ought to explore, and which may too easily be obscured by the search for superficial or spurious differences. The problem with the kind of contrasts of Islam with Christianity drawn by Gellner is not that the relations between religion and political power are the same in the two. Rather, the very terms employed are misleading, and we need to find concepts that are more appropriate for describing differences.

III

So far we have looked very briefly at one aspect of the attempt to produce an anthropology of Islam: the virtual equation of Islam with the Middle East, and the definition of Muslim history as the "mirror image" of Christian history, in which the connection between religion and power is simply reversed (Gellner 1981). This view is open to criticism both because it disregards the detailed workings of disciplinary power in Christian history and because it is theoretically most inadequate. The argument here is not against the attempt to generalize about Islam, but against the manner in which that generalization is undertaken. Anyone working on the anthropology of Islam will be aware that there is considerable diversity in the beliefs and practices of Muslims. The first problem is therefore one of organizing this diversity in terms of an adequate concept. The familiar representation of essential Islam as the fusion of religion with power is not one of these. But neither is the nominalist view that different instances of what are called Islam are essentially unique and *sui generis*.

One way in which anthropologists have attempted to resolve the problem of diversity is to adapt the Orientalist distinction between orthodox and nonorthodox Islam to the categories of Great and Little Traditions, and thus to set up the seemingly more acceptable distinction between the scripturalist, puritanical faith of the towns, and the saint-worshipping, ritualistic religion of the countryside. For anthropologists, neither form of Islam has a claim to being regarded as "more real" than the other. They are what they are, formed in different ways in different conditions. In fact, the religion of the countryside is taken as a single form only in an abstract, contrastive sense. Precisely because it is by definition particularistic, rooted in variable local conditions and personalities, and authorized by the uncheckable memories of oral cultures, the Islam of the unlettered countryfolk is highly variable. "Orthodoxy" is therefore, for such anthropologists, merely one (albeit invariable) form of Islam among many, distinguished by its preoccupation with the niceties of doctrine and law, claiming its authority from sacred texts rather than sacred persons.

This dichotomy has been popularized by two well-known Western anthropologists of Moroccan Islam, Clifford Geertz and Ernest Gellner, and by some of their pupils. But what made it interesting was the further argument that there was an apparent correlation of this dual Islam with two types of distinctive social structure, something first proposed by French colonial scholarship on the Maghrib. Classical Maghribi society, it was claimed, consisted on the one hand of the centralized, hierarchical organization of the cities, and on the other of the egalitarian, segmental organization of the surrounding tribes. The cities were governed by rulers who continually attempted to subdue the dissident, self-governing tribes; the tribesmen in turn resisted with varying degrees of success, and sometimes, when united by an outstanding religious leader, even managed to supplant an incumbent ruler. The two categories of Islam fit nicely into the two kinds of social and political structure: *shari'a* law in the cities, variable custom among the tribes; *'ulama* in the former, saints among the latter. Both structures are seen as parts of a single system because they define the opponents between whom an unceasing struggle for political dominance takes place. More precisely, because both urban and tribal populations are Muslim, all owing at the very least a nominal allegiance to the sacred texts (and so perhaps also implicitly to their literate guardians), a particular style of political struggle emerges. It is possible for urban rulers to claim authority over the tribes, and for tribes to support a country-based leader who aims to supplant the ruler in the name of Islam.

To this broad schema, which was initially the product of a French "sociology of Islam," Gellner has added, in successive publications, a number of details drawn from a reading of (1) the classical sociologies of religion, (2) Ibn Khaldun's *Muqaddimah,* and (3) British anthropological writings on segmentary lineage theory. And he has extended it to cover virtually the whole of North Africa and the Middle East, and almost the entire span of Muslim history. The resulting picture has been used by him, and drawn on by others, to elaborate the old contrast between Islam and Christianity in a series of inversions—as in the following crisp account by Bryan Turner:

> There is a sense in which we can say that in religion "the southern, Muslim shore of the Mediterranean is a kind of mirror-image of the northern shore, of Europe." On the northern shore, the central religious tradition is hierarchical, ritualistic, with a strong rural appeal. One corner-stone of the official religion is saintship. The deviant reformist tradition is egalitarian, puritan, urban and excludes priestly mediation. On the southern shore, Islam reverses this pattern: it is the tribal, rural tradition which is deviant, hierarchical and ritualistic. Similarly, saint and shaikh are mirror-image roles. Whereas in Christianity the saints are orthodox, individualistic, dead, canonized by central authorities, in Islam the shaikhs are heterodox, tribal or associational, living and recognized by local consent.
>
> (Turner 1974)

Even as it applies to the Maghrib, this picture has been subjected to damaging criticism by scholars with access to indigenous historical sources in Arabic (e.g., Hammoudi 1980; Cornell 1983). This kind of criticism is important, but it will not be pursued here. While it is worth asking whether this anthropological account of Islam is valid for the entire Muslim world (or even for the Maghrib) given the historical information available, let us instead focus on a different issue: What are the discursive styles employed here to represent (a) the historical variations in Islamic political structure, and (b) the different forms of Islamic religion linked to the latter? What kinds of questions do these styles *deflect* us from considering? What concepts do we need to develop as anthropologists in order to pursue those very different kinds of questions in a viable manner?

In approaching this issue, let us consider the following interconnected points: (1) Narratives about culturally distinctive actors must try to translate and represent the historically-situated discourses of such actors as responses to the discourse of others, instead of schematizing and de-historicizing their actions. (2) Anthropological analyses of social structure should focus not on typical actors but on the changing patterns of institutional relations and conditions (especially those we call political economies). (3) The analysis of Middle Eastern political economies and the representation of Islamic "dramas" are essentially different kinds of discursive exercise which cannot be substituted for each other, although they can be significantly embedded in the same narrative, precisely because they are discourses. (4) It is wrong to represent types of Islam as being correlated with types of social structure, on the implicit analogy with (ideological) superstructure and (social) base. (5) Islam as the object of anthropological understanding should be approached as a discursive tradition that connects variously with the formation of moral selves, the manipulation of populations (or resistance to it), and the production of appropriate knowledges.

IV

If one reads an anthropological text such as Gellner's carefully, one may notice that the social and political structures of classical Muslim society are represented in a very distinctive way. What one finds in effect are protagonists engaged in a dramatic struggle. Segmentary tribes confront centralized states. Armed nomads "lust after the city," and unarmed merchants fear the nomads. Saints mediate between conflicting tribal groups, but also between the illiterate nomad and a remote, capricious God. Literate clerics serve their powerful ruler and try to maintain the sacred law. The puritanical bourgeoisie employs religion to legitimize its privileged status. The city's poor seek a religion of excitement. Religious reformers unite pastoral warriors against a declining dynasty. Demoralized rulers are destroyed by the disenchantment of their urban subjects converging with the religious and military power of their tribal enemies.

A representation of social structure that is cast entirely in terms of dramatic roles tends to exclude other conceptions, to which we shall turn in a moment. But even a narrative about typical actors requires an account of the discourses that orient their behavior and in which that behavior can be represented (or misrepresented) by actors to each other. In a dramatic play in the strict sense, these discourses are contained in the very lines the actors speak. An account of indigenous discourses is, however, totally missing in Gellner's narrative. Gellner's Islamic actors do not speak, they do not think, they *behave*. And yet without adequate evidence, motives for "normal" and "revolutionary" behavior are continually being attributed to the actions of the major protagonists in classical Muslim society. There are, to be sure, references in the text to "partners who speak the same moral language," but it is clear that such expressions are merely dead metaphors, because Gellner's conception of language here is that of an emollient that can be isolated from the power process. In the context of his description of the circulation of elites "within-an-immobile-structure," for example, he writes that "Islam provided a common language and thus a certain kind of smoothness for a process which, in a more mute and brutalistic form, had been taking place anyway." In other words, if one removes the common language of Islam, nothing of any significance changes. The language is no more than a facilitating instrument of a domination that is already in place

This purely instrumental view of language is very inadequate—inadequate precisely for the kind of narrative that tries to describe Muslim society in terms of what motivates culturally recognizable actors. It is only when the anthropologist takes historically defined discourses seriously, and especially the way they *constitute* events, that questions can be asked about the conditions in which Muslim rulers and subjects might have responded variously to authority, to physical force, to persuasion, or simply to habit.

It is interesting to reflect on the fact that Geertz, who is usually regarded as having a primary interest in cultural meanings as against Gellner's preoccupation with social causation, presents a narrative of Islam in his *Islam Observed* that is not, in this respect, very different. For Geertz's Islam is also a dramaturgical one. Indeed, being more conscious of his own highly wrought literary style, he has made explicit use of metaphors of political theater. The politics of Islam in "classical" Morocco and in "classical" Indonesia are very differently portrayed, but each, in its own way, is portrayed as essentially theatrical. Yet for Geertz, as for

Gellner, the schematization of Islam as a drama of religiosity expressing power is obtained by omitting indigenous discourses, and by turning all Islamic behavior into *readable gesture.*

V

Devising narratives about the expressions and the expressive intentions of dramatic players is not the only option available to anthropologists. Social life can also be written or talked about by using analytic concepts. Not using such concepts simply means failing to ask particular questions, and misconstruing historical structures.

As an example, consider the notion of tribe. This idea is central to the kind of anthropology of Islam of which Gellner's text is such a prominent example. It is often used by many writers on the Middle East to refer to social entities with very different structures and modes of livelihood. Ordinarily, where theoretical issues are not involved, this does not matter very much. But where one is concerned, as at present, with conceptual problems, it is important to consider the implications for analysis of an indiscriminate usage of the term "tribe."

It is the case not only that so-called "tribes" vary enormously in their formal constitution, but more particularly that pastoral nomads do not have an ideal-typical economy. Their variable socio-economic arrangements have very different implications for their possible involvement in politics, trade, and war. Several Marxists, such as Perry Anderson, have argued for the concept of a "pastoral mode of production" (Anderson 1974), and following him Bryan Turner has suggested that this concept should form part of a theoretically informed account of Muslim social structures because and to the extent that Middle Eastern countries have pastoral nomads living in them (Turner 1978).

The assumption that pastoral nomads in the Muslim Middle East have a typical political and economic structure is misleading (Asad 1970; Asad 1973; Asad 1979). The reasons for this are too involved and tangential to consider here, but a brief look at the issue will remind us of concepts of social structure different from those still being deployed by many anthropologists and historians of Islam.

Any study of the military capabilities of pastoral nomads in relation to townsmen must begin not from the simple fact that they are pastoral nomads, but from a variety of political-economic conditions, some systematic, some contingent. Types of animals reared, patterns of seasonal migration, forms of herding arrangements, rights of access to pastures and watering points, distribution of animal wealth, degree of dependence on returns through sales, on direct subsistence cultivation, on gifts and tribute from political superiors or inferiors—these and other considerations are relevant for an understanding of even the basic question of how many spare men can be mustered for war, how readily, and for how long. Among the pastoral nomadic population I studied in the deserts of northern Sudan many years ago, for example, the possibilities for mobilizing large numbers of fighting men had altered drastically from the middle of the nineteenth century to the middle of the twentieth primarily because of a large increase in small livestock, a shift to more intensive and complex herding arrangements, greater involvement in animal sales, and a different pattern of property rights. The point is not that this tribal grouping is somehow typical for the Middle East. Indeed, there are *no* typical tribes. My argument is simply that what nomads are able or inclined to do in relation to settled populations is the product of various historical conditions that define their political economy, and not the expression of some essential motive that belongs to tribal protagonists in a classic Islamic drama. In other words, "tribes" are no more to be regarded as agents than "discursive structures" or "societies" are. They are historical structures in terms of which the limits and possibilities of people's lives are realized. This does not mean that "tribes" are less real than the individuals who comprise them, but the vocabulary of motives, behavior, and utterances does not belong, strictly speaking, in analytic accounts whose principal object is "tribe," although such accounts can be embedded in narratives about agency. It is precisely because "tribes" are differently structured in time and place that the motives, the forms of behavior, and the import of utterances will differ too.

Representations of Muslim society that are constructed along the lines of an action play have, not surprisingly, no place for peasants. Peasants, like women, are not depicted as *doing* anything. In accounts like Gellner's they have no dramatic role and no distinctive religious expression—in contrast, that is, to nomadic tribes and city-dwellers. But of course as soon as one turns to the concepts of production and exchange, one can tell a rather different story. Cultivators, male and female, produce crops (just as pastoralists of both sexes raise animals) which they sell or yield up in rent and taxes. Peasants, even in the historical Middle East, *do* do something that is crucial in relation to the social formations of that region, but that *doing* has to be conceptualized in political-economic and not in dramatic terms. The medieval agricultural sector underwent important changes that had far-reaching consequences for the development of urban populations, of a money economy, of regional and transcontinental trade (Watson 1983). This is true also for the later pre-modern period, even though economic histories talk of the changes in terms of decline rather than growth. One does not have to be an economic determinist to acknowledge that such changes have profound implications for questions of domination and autonomy.

This approach to writing about Middle Eastern society, which pays special attention to the long-term working of impersonal constraints, will be sensitive to the indissoluble but varying connections between the social economy and social power. It will also continually remind us that historical Middle Eastern societies were never self-contained, never isolated from external relations, and so never entirely unchanging, even before their incorporation into the modern world system. Unlike those narrators who present us with a fixed cast of Islamic dramatis personae, enacting a predetermined story, we can look for connections, changes, and differences, beyond the fixed stage of an Islamic theater. We shall then write not about an essential Islamic social structure, but about historical formations in the Middle East whose elements are never fully integrated, *and never bounded by the geographical limits of "the Middle East"* (Lombard 1971; Dols 1977).[1] It is too often forgotten that "the world of Islam" is a concept for organizing historical narratives, not the name for a self-contained collective agent. This is not to say that historical narratives have no social effect—on the contrary. But the integrity of the world of Islam is essentially ideological, a discursive representation. Thus, Geertz has written that:

> It is perhaps as true for civilizations as it is for men that, however much they may later change, the fundamental dimensions of their character, the structure of possibilities within which they will in some sense always move, are set in the plastic period when they were first forming.
>
> (Geertz 1968: 11)

But the fatality of character that anthropologists like Geertz invoke is the object of a professional *writing*, not the unconscious of a subject that writes itself *as Islam* for the Western scholar to read.

VI

The anthropology of Islam being criticized here depicts a classic social structure consisting essentially of tribesmen and city-dwellers, the natural carriers of two major forms of religion—the normal tribal religion centered on saints and shrines, and the dominant urban religion based on the "Holy Book." My argument is that if the anthropologist seeks to understand religion by placing it conceptually in its social context, then the way in which that social context is described must affect the understanding of religion. If one rejects the schema of an unchanging dualistic structure of Islam promoted by some anthropologists, if one decides to write about the social structures of Muslim societies in terms of overlapping spaces and times, so that the Middle East becomes a focus of convergences (and therefore of many possible histories), then the dual typology of Islam will surely seem less plausible.

It is true that in addition to the two major types of religion proposed by the kind of anthropology of Islam we are talking about, minor forms are sometimes specified. This is so in Gellner's account, and in many others. Thus there is the "revolutionary" as opposed to the "normal" Islam of the tribes, which periodically merges with and revivifies the puritan ideology of the cities. And there is the ecstatic, mystical religion of the urban poor which, as "the opium of the masses," excludes them from effective political action—until, that is, the impact of modernity when it is the religion of the urban masses which becomes "revolutionary." In a curious way, these two minor forms of Islam serve, in Gellner's text, as markers, one positive, one negative, of the two great epochs of Islam—the classical rotation-within-an-immobile structure, and the turbulent developments and mass movements of the contemporary world. So this apparent concession to the idea that there may be more than two types of Islam is at the same time a literary device to define the notions of "traditional" and "modern" Muslim society.

Now, the anthropologist's presentation of Islam will depend not only on the way in which social structures are conceptualized, but on the way in which religion itself is defined. Anyone familiar with what is called the sociology of religion will know of the difficulties involved in producing a conception of religion that is adequate for cross-cultural purposes. This is an important point because one's conception of religion determines the kinds of questions one thinks are askable and worth asking. But far too few would-be anthropologists of Islam pay this matter serious attention. Instead, they often draw indiscriminately on ideas from the writings of the great sociologists (e.g., Marx, Weber, Durkheim) in order to describe forms of Islam, and the result is not always consistent.

Gellner's text is illustrative in this regard. The types of Islam that are presented as being characteristic of "traditional Muslim society" in Gellner's picture are constructed according to three very different concepts of religion. Thus, the *normal tribal religion*, "that of the dervish or marabout," is explicitly Durkheimian. "It is … concerned," we are told, "with the social punctuation of time and space, with season-making and group-boundary-marking festivals. The sacred makes these joyful, visible, conspicuous and authoritative" (Gellner 1981: 52). So the concept of religion here involves a reference to collective rituals to be read as an enactment of the sacred, which is also, for Durkheim, the symbolic representation of social and cosmological structures.[2]

The concept that is deployed in the description of the *religion of the urban poor* is quite different, and it is obviously derived from the early writings of Marx on religion as false consciousness. "The city has its poor," Gellner writes, "they are uprooted, insecure, alienated. … What they require from religion is consolation or escape; their taste is for ecstasy, excitement, an absorption in a religious condition which is also a forgetting …" (Gellner 1981: 48).[3] If one looks at this kind of construction carefully, one finds that what is called religion here is the psychological response to an emotional experience. What was indicated in the account of tribal Islam was an emotional *effect*, but here it is an emotional *cause*. In the one case the reader was told about collective rituals and their meaning, about ritual specialists and their roles; in the other attention is directed instead to private distress and unfulfilled desire.

When one turns to the *religion of the bourgeoisie*, one is confronted by yet other organizing ideas. "The well-heeled urban bourgeoisie," remarks Gellner, "far from having a taste for public festivals, prefers the sober satisfactions of learned piety, a taste more consonant with its dignity and commercial calling. Its fastidiousness underscores its standing, distinguishing it both from rustics and the urban plebs. In brief, urban life provides a sound base for scripturalist unitarian puritanism. Islam expresses such a state of mind better perhaps than other religions" (Gellner 1981: 42).[4] The echoes from Weber's *Protestant Ethic* in this passage are not accidental, for its authority is invoked more than once. In this account, the "bourgeois Muslim" is accorded a moral—or, better, an esthetic—style. His distinguishing feature is the literacy that gives him direct access to the founding scriptures and the Law. In this latter respect one is urged to see him as immersed in a moralistic, literate enterprise. Neither collective rituals nor unquenched desire, neither social solidarity nor alienation, religion is here the solemn maintenance of public authority which is rational partly because it is in writing, and partly because it is linked to socially useful activities: service to the state, and commitment to commerce.

These different ways of talking about religion—the tribal and the urban—are not merely different aspects of the same thing. They are different textual constructions which seek to represent different things, and which make different assumptions about the nature of social reality, about the origins of needs, and about the rationale of cultural meanings. For this reason, they are not merely different representations, they are incompatible constructions. In referring to them one is not comparing like with like.

But the main difficulty with such constructions is not that they are inconsistent. It is that this kind of anthropology of Islam (and I want to stress here that Gellner's eclecticism is typical of very many sociological writers on Islam) rests on false conceptual oppositions and equivalences, which often lead writers into making ill-founded assertions about motives, meanings, and effects relating to "religion." More important, it makes difficult the formulation of questions that are at once less tendentious and more interesting than those which many observers of contemporary Islam (both "conservative" and "radical" Islam) seek to answer.

An instructive example is the hoary old argument about the totalitarian character of orthodox Islam. Like Bernard Lewis and many others, Gellner proposes that scriptural Islam has an elective affinity for Marxism,[5] partly because of "the inbuilt vocation towards the implementation of a sharply defined divine order on earth" (Gellner 1981: 47), and partly because of "The totalism of both ideologies [which] precludes institutionalised politics" (Gellner 1981: 48).

Quite apart from the empirical question of how widespread Marxist movements have been among twentieth-century Muslim populations,[6] it must be said that the notion of a totalitarian Islam rests on a mistaken view of the social effectivity of ideologies. A moment's reflection will show that it is not the literal scope of the *shari'a* which matters here but the degree to which it informs and regulates social practices, and it is clear that there has never been any Muslim society in which the religious law of Islam has governed more than a fragment of social life. If one contrasts this fact with the highly regulated character of social life in modern states, one may immediately see the reason why. The administrative and legal regulations of such secular states are far more pervasive and effective in controlling the details of people's lives than anything to be found in Islamic history. The difference, of course, lies not in the textual specifications of what is vaguely called a social blueprint, but in the reach of institutional powers that constitute, divide up, and govern large stretches of social life according to systematic rules in modern industrial societies, whether capitalist or communist.[7]

In 1972, Nikki Keddie wrote: "Fortunately, Western scholarship seems to have emerged from the period when many were writing … that Islam and Marxism were so similar in many ways that one might lead to the other" (Keddie 1972). Perhaps that period of Western scholarly innocence is not entirely behind us. But the point of this example will be lost if it is seen as merely another attempt to defend Islam against the claim that it has affinities with a totalitarian system. Such a claim has been challenged in the past, and even if rational criticism cannot prevent the claim from being reproduced, the matter is in itself of little *theoretical* interest. Instead, it is important to emphasize that one must carefully examine established social practices, "religious" as well as "nonreligious," in order to understand the conditions that define "conservative" or "radical" political activity in the contemporary Islamic world. And it is to this idea that we will now turn.

VII

My general argument so far has been that no coherent anthropology of Islam can be founded on the notion of a determinate social blueprint, or on the idea of an integrated social totality in which social structure and religious ideology interact. This does not mean that no coherent object for an anthropology of Islam is possible, or that it is adequate to say that anything Muslims believe or do can be regarded by the anthropologist as part of Islam. Most anthropologies of Islam have defined their scope too widely, both those appealing to an essentialist principle and those employing a nominalist one. If one wants to write an anthropology of Islam one should begin, as Muslims do, from the concept of a discursive tradition that includes and relates itself to the founding texts of the Qur'an and the *hadith*. Islam is neither a distinctive social structure nor a heterogeneous collection of beliefs, artifacts, customs, and morals. It is a tradition.

In a useful article, "The Study of Islam in Local Contexts," Eickelman has recently suggested that there is a major theoretical need for taking up the "middle ground" between the study of village or tribal Islam and that of universal Islam (Eickelman 1982). This may well be so, but the most urgent theoretical need for an anthropology of Islam is a matter not so much of finding the right scale but of formulating the right concepts. "A discursive tradition" is just such a concept.

What is a tradition?[8] A tradition consists essentially of discourses that seek to instruct practitioners regarding the correct form and purpose of a given practice that, precisely because it is established, has a history. These discourses relate conceptually to *a past* (when the practice was instituted, and from which the knowledge of its point and proper performance has been transmitted) and *a future* (how the point of that practice can best be secured in the short or long term, or why it should be modified or abandoned), through *a present* (how it is linked to other practices, institutions, and social conditions) (MacIntyre 1981). An Islamic discursive tradition is simply a tradition of Muslim discourse that addresses itself to conceptions of the Islamic past and future, with reference to a particular Islamic practice in the present. Clearly, not everything Muslims say and do belongs to an Islamic discursive tradition. Nor is an Islamic tradition in this sense necessarily imitative of what was done in the past. For even where traditional practices appear to the anthropologist to be imitative of what has gone before, it will be the practitioners' conceptions of what is *apt performance,* and of how the past is related to present practices, that will be crucial for tradition, not the apparent repetition of an old form.

My point is not, as some Western anthropologists and Westernized Muslim intellectuals have argued, that "tradition" is today often a fiction of the present, a reaction to the forces of modernity—that in contemporary conditions of crisis, tradition in the Muslim world is a weapon, a ruse, a defense, designed to confront a threatening world (Gilsenan 1982),[9] that it is an old cloak for new aspirations and borrowed styles of behavior (Laroui 1976).[10] The claim that contemporary ideas and social arrangements are really ancient when they are not is in itself no more significant than the pretense that new ones have been introduced when actually they have not. Lying to oneself, as well as to others, about the relationship of the present to the past is as banal in modern societies as it is in societies that anthropologists typically study. The important point is simply that all instituted practices are oriented to a conception of the past.

For the anthropologist of Islam, the proper theoretical beginning is therefore an instituted practice (set in a particular context, and having a particular history) into which Muslims are inducted *as* Muslims. For analytical purposes there is no essential difference on this point between "classical" and "modern" Islam. The discourses in which the teaching is done, in which the correct performance of the practice is defined and learned, are intrinsic to all Islamic practices. It is therefore somewhat misleading to suggest, as some sociologists have done,[11] that it is *orthopraxy* and not *orthodoxy,* ritual and not doctrine, that matters in Islam. It is misleading because such a contention ignores the centrality of the notion of "the correct model" to which an instituted practice—including ritual—ought to conform, a model conveyed in authoritative formulas in Islamic traditions as in others. And I refer here primarily not to the programmatic *discourses* of "modernist" and "fundamentalist" Islamic movements, but to the established *practices* of unlettered Muslims. A practice is Islamic because it is authorized by the discursive traditions of Islam, and is so taught to Muslims[12]—whether by an *'alim,* a *khatib,* a Sufi *shaykh,* or an untutored parent. (It may be worth recalling here that etymologically "doctrine" means teaching, and that orthodox doctrine therefore denotes the correct process of teaching, as well as the correct statement of what is to be learned [Williams 1967]).

Orthodoxy is crucial to all Islamic traditions. But the sense in which I use this term must be distinguished from the sense given to it by most Orientalists and anthropologists. Anthropologists like el-Zein, who wish to deny any special significance to orthodoxy, and those like Gellner, who see it as a specific set of doctrines "at the heart of Islam," both are missing something vital: that orthodoxy is not a mere body of opinion but a distinctive relationship—a relationship of power. Wherever Muslims have the power to regulate, uphold, require, or adjust *correct* practices, and to condemn, exclude, undermine, or replace *incorrect* ones, there is the domain of orthodoxy. The way these powers are exercised, the conditions that make them possible (social, political, economic, etc.), and the resistances they encounter (from Muslims and non-Muslims) are equally the concern of an anthropology of Islam, regardless of whether its direct object of research is in the city or in the countryside, in the present or in the past. Argument and conflict over the form and significance of practices are therefore a natural part of any Islamic tradition.

In their representation of "Islamic tradition," Orientalists and anthropologists have often marginalized the place of argument and reasoning surrounding traditional practices. Argument is generally represented as a symptom of "the tradition in crisis," on the assumption that "normal" tradition (what Abdallah Laroui calls "tradition as structure" and distinguishes from "tradition as ideology") excludes reasoning just as it requires unthinking conformity

(Laroui 1976). But these contrasts and equations are themselves the work of a historical motivation, manifest in Edmund Burke's ideological opposition between "tradition" and "reason," an opposition which was elaborated by the conservative theorists who followed him, and introduced into sociology by Weber (MacIntyre 1980).

Reason and argument are necessarily involved in traditional practice whenever people have to be taught about the point and proper performance of that practice, and whenever the teaching meets with doubt, indifference, or lack of understanding. It is largely because we think of argument in terms of formal debate, confrontation, and polemic that we assume it has no place in traditional practice (Dixon and Stratta 1986). Yet the process of trying to *win someone over* for the willing performance of a traditional practice, as distinct from trying to demolish an opponent's intellectual position, is a necessary part of Islamic discursive traditions as of others. If reasons and arguments are intrinsic to traditional practice, and not merely to "a tradition in crisis," it should be the anthropologist's first task to describe and analyze the kinds of reasoning, and the reasons for arguing, that underlie Islamic traditional practices. It is here that the analyst may discover a central modality of power, and of the resistances it encounters—for the process of arguing, of using the force of reason, at once presupposes and responds to the fact of resistance. Power, and resistance, are thus intrinsic to the development and exercise of any traditional practice.

A theoretical consequence of this is that traditions should not be regarded as essentially homogeneous, that heterogeneity in traditional practices is not necessarily an indication of the absence of an Islamic tradition. The variety of traditional Islamic practices in different times, places, and populations indicates the different Islamic reasonings that different social and historical conditions can or cannot sustain. The idea that traditions are essentially homogeneous has a powerful intellectual appeal,[13] but it is mistaken. Indeed, widespread homogeneity is a function not of tradition, but of the development and control of communication techniques that are part of modern industrial societies (Williams 1974).[14]

Although Islamic traditions are not homogeneous, they aspire to coherence, in the way that all discursive traditions do. That they do not always attain it is due as much to the constraints of political and economic conditions in which the traditions are placed as to their inherent limitations. Thus, in our own time the attempt by Islamic traditions to organize memory and desire in a coherent manner is increasingly remade by the social forces of industrial capitalism, which create conditions favorable to very different patterns of desire and forgetfulness.[15] An anthropology of Islam will therefore seek to understand the historical conditions that enable the production and maintenance of specific discursive traditions, or their transformation—and the efforts of practitioners to achieve coherence.[16]

VIII

I have been arguing that anthropologists interested in Islam need to rethink their object of study, and that the concept of tradition will help in this task. I now want to conclude with a final brief point. To write about a tradition is to be in a certain narrative relation to it, a relation that will vary according to whether one supports or opposes the tradition, or regards it as morally neutral. The coherence that each party finds, or fails to find, in that tradition will depend on their particular historical position. In other words, there clearly is not, nor can there be, such a thing as a universally acceptable account of a living tradition. Any representation of tradition is contestable. What shape that contestation takes, if it occurs, will be determined not only by the powers and knowledges each side deploys, but by the collective life they aspire to—or to whose survival they are quite indifferent. Moral neutrality, here as always, is no guarantee of political innocence.

Notes

1 The changing networks of intercontinental trade which linked Dar ul-Islam to Europe, Africa, and Asia differentially affected and were affected by patterns of production and consumption within it (see Lombard 1971). Even the spread of contagious disease with its drastic social and economic consequences connected Middle Eastern political units with other parts of the world (see Dols 1977: 36–37). It would not be necessary to refer so baldly to well-known historical evidence if it were not still common for eminent scholars to write of "Islam" as a mechanically balanced social structure, reflecting its own dynamic of cause and effect, and having its own isolated destiny.

2 Gellner's resort to the Durkheimian viewpoint on religion is not quite as consistent as it ought to be. Thus, in one place we read that "the faith of the tribesman *needs* to be mediated by special and distinct holy personnel, rather than to be egalitarian; it *needs* to be joyous and festival-worthy, not puritanical and scholarly; it *requires* hierarchy and incarnation in persons, not in scripts" (Gellner 1981: 41, emphasis added). But a dozen pages later, when Gellner wants to introduce the idea of "revolutionary" tribal religion, these *needs* have to be made to disappear: "It is a curious but crucial fact about the social psychology of Muslim tribesmen," he writes, "that their normal religion is for them *at one level* a mere *pis aller*, and is tinged with irony, and with an ambivalent recognition that the *real* norms lie elsewhere" (Gellner 1981: 52, emphasis in original).

3 Such phrases might be more plausible (but not therefore entirely valid see, e.g., Abu-Lughod 1969) if applied to the condition of poor rural migrants in a modern metropolis. To describe the lower strata of medieval Muslim cities, with their organization into quarters, guilds, Sufi brotherhoods, etc., as being "uprooted, insecure, alienated" is surely a little fanciful, unless, of course, one takes the mere occurrence of bread riots in periods of economic hardship as a sign of mental disturbance among the poor. Yet, oddly enough, when Gellner does refer to the urban masses in twentieth-century cities, a totally new motivation is imputed to the uprooted migrants: "The tribal style of religion loses then much of its function, whilst the urban one gains in authority and prestige from *the eagerness of migrant-rustics to acquire respectability*" (Gellner 1981: 58, emphasis added). Now the religion of the urban poor is attributed no longer to a desire for forgetting, but to a desire for respectability.

4 Most Muslims for most of their history, as Gellner himself acknowledges, cannot be described as scripturalist puritans, yet "Islam," he claims, expresses a scripturalist state of mind better than other religions. There is surely some fuzziness here. It is clear that Gellner is identifying the *essential* tendency of Islam with what he regards as the life-style of the "well-heeled urban bourgeoisie" (Gellner 1981: 41) This equation may be appealing to some Muslims, but the attentive reader will wish to ask in what sense this social group is naturally "puritan," and indeed in what sense they are "better" puritans than, say, seventeenth-century Puritans in England and America. A natural "distaste for public festivals"? Anyone who has lived in a Muslim community, or read relevant historical accounts (e.g., Lane 1908 or Snouck-Hurgronje 1931), will know the rites of passage are more elaborate among the "well heeled urban bourgeoisie" than among the lower urban social strata. "Scripturalism" based on literacy? But the literacy of merchants is a very different thing from the literacy of professional "men of religion" (see the excellent book by Street [1984]). Besides, the traditions of Qur'anic exegesis developed by Muslim "men of religion" are far richer and more diverse than the blanket term "scripturalist" suggests.

5 In reproducing the view that there is an "elective affinity" between Islam and Marxism, Gellner appears to have missed the fact that Ibn Khaldun, the only classical Muslim theorist who deals in detail with connections between political power and the economy, warns explicitly against the government's trying to control trade or production—see Ibn Khaldun 1967: 232–234. Since the idea of government control of the economy has never been part of classical Muslim theory, but is central to classical Marxism, there is here a crucial opposition between the two.

6 Apart from the important communist parties in Iraq and Sudan (neither of which commanded a massive following), Marxism has had no real roots among contemporary Muslim populations. States like the People's Democratic Republic of Yemen are exceptions that prove the rule. (See

also Benningsen and Wimbush 1979 for an account of protracted resistances against Russian imperial power.) Marxist ideology has been associated with *some* Westernized intellectuals and *some* authoritarian states, but *never* with the *'ulama* or the well-heeled urban bourgeoisie, who are supposed by Gellner to be the historical carriers of scripturalist, unitarian, puritan Islam. It is his mistaken attempt to connect this latter kind of Islam with "Marxism," "socialism," or "social radicalism" (terms used indiscriminately) that leads him to make the implausible argument that "scripturalist rigorism or fundamentalism" is admirably suited to bringing about modernization in the Muslim world.

7 As a succinct evocation of the powers of a modern state, the following memorable passage from Robert Musil's great novel has scarcely been bettered: "The fact is, living permanently in a well-ordered State has an out-and-out spectral aspect: one cannot step into the street or drink a glass of water or get into a tram without touching the perfectly balanced levers of a gigantic apparatus of laws and relations, setting them in motion or letting them maintain one in the peace and quiet of one's existence. One hardly knows any of these levers, which extend. deep into the inner workings and on the other side are lost in a network the entire constitution of which has never been disentangled by any living being. Hence one denies their existence, just as the common man denies the existence of the air, insisting that it is mere emptiness ... " (Musil 1954: 182).

8 In outlining the concept of tradition, I am indebted to the insightful writings of Alisdair MacIntyre, in particular his brilliant book *After Virtue* (MacIntyre 1981).

9 Thus Gilsenan: "Tradition, therefore, is put together in all manner of different ways in contemporary conditions of crisis; it is a term that is in fact highly variable and shifting in content. It changes, though all who use it do so to mark out truths and principles as essentially unchanging. In the name of tradition many traditions are born and come into opposition with others. It becomes a language, a weapon against internal and external enemies, a refuge, an evasion, or part of the entitlement to domination and authority over others" (Gilsenan 1982: 15.)

10 Or as Abdallah Laroui puts it: "one might say that tradition exists only when innovation is accepted under the cloak of fidelity to the past" (Laroui 1976: 35).

11 For example, see Eickelman 1981: 201–260. In a short paper written a decade ago, I emphasized that orthodoxy is always the product of a network of power (Asad 1976).

12 Incidentally, it is time that anthropologists of Islam realized that there is more to Ibn Khaldun than his "political sociology," that his deployment of the Aristotelian concept of virtue (in the form of the Arabic *malaka)* is especially relevant to an understanding of what I have called Islamic traditions. In a recent essay, "Knowledge, Virtue, and Action: The Classical Muslim Conception of *Adab* and the Nature of Religious Fulfillment in Islam," Ira Lapidus has included a brief but useful account of Ibn Khaldun's concept of *malaka* (Lapidus 1984: 52–56).

13 Thus, in an essay entitled "Late Antiquity and Islam: Parallels and Contrasts", the eminent historian Peter Brown quotes with approval from Henri Marrou: "For in the last resort classical humanism was based on tradition, something imparted by one's teachers and handed on unquestioningly ... it meant that all the minds of one generation, and indeed of a whole historical period, had a fundamental homogeneity which made communication and genuine communion easier" (Brown 1984: 24). It is precisely this familiar concept, which Brown employs to discuss "the Islamic tradition," that anthropologists should abandon in favor of another.

14 For an introductory discussion of some problems relating to the control and effects of a typically modern form of communication, see R. Williams 1974.

15 The result among Muslim intellectuals has been described by Jacques Berque thus: "Dans Ie monde actuel et parmi trop d'intellectuels ou de militants, on se partage entre adeptes d'une authenticité sans avenir et adeptes d'une modernisme sans racines. Le francais traduit mal, en l'espéce, ce qui en arabe vient beaucoup mieux: ancâr al-macîr bilâ acîl wa ancâr al-acîl bilâ macîr" (Berque 1981: 68).

16 It should be stressed that the problem indicated here is not the same as the one treated in the many monographs that purport to describe the recent "erosion of the old unity of values based on Divine Revelation" which has accompanied the disruption of the "stable, indeed static, social world" of traditional Muslim society (see Gilsenan 1973: 196, 192). A recent example that addresses some of the questions I have in mind is Zubaida 1982, which attempts to show that Khomeini's novel doctrine of *wilayat-i-faqih,* although based on traditional *Shi'i* premises and modes of reasoning, presupposes the modern concepts of "nation" and "nation-state." Zubaida's argument does not require the assumption of traditional stability or homogeneity.

References

Abu-Lughod, Janet L. (1969) "Varieties of Urban Experience," in Ira M. Lapidus (ed.) *Middle Eastern Cities: A Symposium on Ancient, Islamic, and Contemporary Middle Eastern Urbanism*, Berkeley, CA: University of California Press.

Anderson, Perry (1974) *Passages from Antiquity to Feudalism*, London: New Left Books.

Asad, Talal (1970) *The Kababish Arabs: Power, Authority and Consent in a Nomadic Tribe*, London: C. Hurst.

——— (1973) "The Beduin as a Military Force," in Cynthia Nelson (ed.) *The Desert and the Sown*, Berkeley, CA: University of California Press.

——— (1976) "Politics and Religion in Islamic Reform," *Review of Middle East Studies*, 2: 13–22.

——— (1979) "Equality in Nomadic Systems?" in Equipe Ecologie et Anthropologie des Societes Pastorales (ed.) *Pastoral Production and Society*, Cambridge: Cambridge University Press.

——— (1983a) "Anthropological Conceptions of Religion: Reflections on Geertz," *Man*, 18: 237–259.

——— (1983b) "Notes on Body Pain and Truth in Medieval Christian Ritual," *Economy and Society*, 12: 287–327.

——— (1986) "Medieval Heresy: An Anthropological View," *Social History*, 11: 345–362.

Benningsen, Alexandre A., and S. Endres Wimbush (1979) *Muslim National Communism in the Soviet Union*, Chicago, IL: Chicago University Press.

Berque, Jacques (1981) *L'Islam: La philosophie et les sciences*, Paris: Les Presses de l'Unesco.

Brown, Peter (1984) "Late Antiquity and Islam: Parallels and Contrasts," in Barbara D. Metcalf (ed.) *Moral Conduct and Authority: The Place of Adab in South Asian Islam*, Berkeley , CA: California University Press.

Cornell, Vincent J. (1983) "The Logic of Analogy and the Role of the Sufi Shaykh in Post-Marinid Morocco," *International Journal of Middle East Studies*, 15: 67–93.

Dixon, John, and Leslie Stratta (1986) "Argument and the Teaching of English: A Critical Analysis," in Andrew M. Wilkinson (ed.) *The Writing of Writing* Milton Keynes: Open University Press.

Dols, Michael W. (1977) *The Black Death in the Middle East*, Princeton, NJ: Princeton University Press.

Eickelman, Dale F. (1981) *The Middle East: An Anthropological Approach* Englewood Cliffs, NJ: Prentice-Hall.

——— (1982) "The Study of Islam in Local Contexts," *Contributions to Asian Studies*, 17: 1–16.

El-Zein, Abdul H. (1977) "Beyond Ideology and Theology: The Search for the Anthropology of Islam," *Annual Review of Anthropology*, 6: 227–254.

Fischer, Michael M.J. (1980) *Iran: From Religious Dispute to Revolution*, Cambridge, MA: Harvard University Press.

Geertz, Clifford (1968) *Islam Observed: Religious Development in Morocco and Indonesia*, New Haven, CT: Yale University Press.

Gellner, Ernest (1981) *Muslim Society*, Cambridge and New York: Cambridge University Press.

Gilsenan, Michael (1973) *Saint and Sufi in Modern Egypt: An Essay in the Sociology of Religion*, Oxford: Clarendon Press.

——— (1982) *Recognizing Islam: An Anthropologist's Introduction*, London: Croom Helm.

Gulick, John (1976) *The Middle East: An Anthropological Perspective*, Pacific Palisades, CA: Goodyear.

Hammoudi, Abdellah (1980) "Segmentarity, Social Stratification, Political Power and Sainthood: Reflections on Gellner's Theses," *Economy and Society*, 9: 279–303.

Ibn Khaldun (1967) *The Muqaddimah: An Introduction to History*, trans. Franz Rosenthal, Princeton, NJ: Princeton University Press.

Keddie, Nikki R. (ed.) (1972) *Scholars, Saints, and Sufis: Muslim Religious Institutions in the Middle East since 1500*. Berkeley, CA: University of California Press.

Lane, Edward W. (1908) *Manners and Customs of the Modern Egyptians*, London: Dent.

Lapidus, Ira (1984) "Knowledge, Virtue, and Action: The Classical Muslim Conception of *Adab* and the Nature of Religious Fulfillment in Islam," in Barbara D. Metcalf (ed.) *Moral Conduct and Authority: The Place of Adab in South Asian Islam*, Berkeley, CA: California University Press.

Laroui, Abdallah (1976) *The Crisis of the Arab Intellectual: Traditionalism or Historicism?*, trans. Diarmid Cammell, Berkeley. CA: University of California Press.

Lewis, Bernard (1973) "The Muslim Discovery of Europe," in Bernard Lewis (ed.) *Islam in History: Ideas, Men and Events in the Middle East*, New York: Library Press.

Lombard, Maurice (1971) *L'Islam dans sa première grandeur: VIIIe–XIe siècle*, Paris: Flammarion.

MacIntyre, Alasdair C. (1980) "Epistemological Crises, Dramatic Narrative, and the Philosophy of Science," in Gary Gutting (ed.) *Paradigms and Revolutions: Appraisals and Applications of Thomas Kuhn's Philosophy of Science*, Notre Dame, IN: University of Notre Dame Press.

——— (1981) *After Virtue: A Study in Moral Theory*, London: Duckworth.

Musil, Robert (1954) *The Man Without Qualities*, trans. Eithne Wilkins and Ernst Kaiser, London: Secker & Warburg.

Snouck-Hurgronje, Christiaan (1931) *Mekka in the Latter Part of the 19th Century*, trans. James H. Monahan, Leiden: Brill.

Street, Brian V. (1984) *Literacy in Theory and Practice*, Cambridge: Cambridge University Press.

Turner, Bryan S. (1974) *Weber and Islam: A Critical Study*, London: Routledge & Kegan Paul.

——— (1978) *Marx and the End of Orientalism*, London: George Allen & Unwin.

van Ess, Josef (1980) "From Wellhausen to Becker: The Emergence of *Kulturgeschichte* in Islamic Studies," in Malcolm H. Kerr (ed.) *Islamic Studies: A Tradition and its Problems*, Malibu, CA: Undena Publications.

von Grunebaum, Gustave E. (1962) *Medieval Islam: A Study in Cultural Orientation*, 3rd edn, Chicago, IL: University of Chicago Press.

Watson, Andrew M. (1983) *Agriculture Innovation in the Early Islamic World*, Cambridge: Cambridge University Press.

Williams, Michael E. (1967) "Doctrine," *New Catholic Encyclopedia*, 4: 939–940.

Williams, Raymond (1974) *Television: Technology and Cultural Form*, London: Fontana.

Zubaida, Sami (1982) "The Ideological Conditions for Khomeini's Doctrine of Government," *Economy & Society*, 11: 138–172.

Part II

Religious practices of Islam

Jens Kreinath

Ethnographic accounts and theoretical approaches mutually complement each other as different angles of anthropological research. In the anthropology of Islam, as well as other fields of anthropology, the formation of theoretical approaches has a significant impact on the way methods of investigation are implemented, utilized, and refined for ethnographic studies. In reverse, ethnographic studies present empirical findings that allow for the criticism of theoretical frameworks and the re-evaluation of their strengths and weaknesses in light of new insights into the complexities of social life. Thus, the contributions of the former section relate to subsequent readings in a number of ways. Theoretical approaches can be used as an analytical framework to compare and contrast various ethnographic accounts of religious practices, and the relevance and shortcomings of these approaches can be debated and evaluated based on the findings presented in ethnographic case studies.

The following section on religious practices explores in considerable detail how some Muslims perform daily prayer (*salāt*), fast (*ṣawm*) during the month of Ramaḍān, take a pilgrimage (*ḥajj*) to Mecca, perform the feast of sacrifice (*ʿīd al-adḥā*), and engage in obligatory almsgiving (*zakāt*) by describing local practices and cultural contexts observed by anthropologists during fieldwork. Ethnographic accounts of these practices reflect some of the main aspects of Islam, which Muslims commonly observe and accept as foundational for their belief. The distinctness of these descriptions lies in the way they present Muslims living their religion, giving them a human face so that they become tangible and understandable in a way that would otherwise not be possible. With the exception of the pilgrimage to Mecca, the holiest city for Muslims in Saudi Arabia, to which non-Muslims usually do not have access, anthropologists are able to study the complexities of Muslim culture and witness their religious practices through their fieldwork methods. These methods require the personal and professional involvement of the anthropologist in the encounter with the people they study. Through their training in participant observation and qualitative interviewing, anthropologists approach the social and cultural life of Muslims with a focus on their subtleties and intricacies. In this regard, their findings clearly derive from the methods of investigation they employ, requiring the trust and consent of the people with whom they work.

Through participation in the daily lives and social and cultural events, which often take place on religious holidays of those whom they study, anthropologists who immerse themselves into a culture are afforded the benefits of developing personal relationships and establishing strong personal ties with the community. This implies that anthropologists, through their qualitative research methods, can only encounter a limited number of Muslims from specific segments of a society. Due to their first-hand encounter with the groups they study and the families they live with, anthropologists aim to understand daily concerns, and to describe them while empathetically trying to grasp the native's point of view in an unbiased way, abstaining from value judgments. At the same time, anthropologists focus on how people organize and interact at public events and on religious occasions, in the attempt to decipher patterns in the religious lives of Muslims. The ethnographic accounts anthropologists have produced on religious practices bear witness to the challenge of being absorbed into the religious life and, at the same time, being able to explain what insights they grasped to individuals who have not had this kind of experience. The aim of these ethnographic accounts is to give the dynamics of the social and religious life of a Muslim community a textual or visual form by connecting specific occasions and events in which religious practitioners participate with the discourses and conversations the anthropologist has with them.

These forms of religious practice are indicative of Islam having a (more or less specified) temporal order and rhythm of repetition, which follows a unique calendarical time-line to different degrees of organizational complexity and requires deliberate commitment. Practicing Muslims perform these obligations as acts of faith and, in doing so, are observant of Islam in order to index their submission to the will of God. Even though anthropologists cannot observe Islam the way Muslims do, they can observe Muslims as they practice their rituals and follow the commands of their religion. Although the anthropology of Islam cannot be reduced to questions of what Muslims do, religious practice is certainly imperative to being accepted as a Muslim and has consequences in matters of everyday social and political life. The challenge for anthropologists is that they can observe Muslims performing their religious practices only to a rather limited degree. The regulations and prescripts of Muslim practices determine the degree to which outsiders can participate and mark the distinct line between believer and non-believer. This implies that the testimonials that anthropologists give of these practices based on a direct ethnographic encounter can only be partial and are limited.

Taking into consideration that the classical ethnographic method of participant observation is lacking insofar as it can only scratch the surface of religious and cultural practices (their true meaning may only be understood by the insider), this method alone does no justice to the study of Muslim religious practices. Even though Muslim practice is visible and observable for anthropologists, its emphasis is on the faith and intention of the believer. The belief and the object of belief remain invisible to the anthropologist. Although anthropologists certainly do participate in public events related to daily prayer, fasting during the month of Ramaḍān, the pilgrimage to Mecca, the feast of sacrifice, and almsgiving, they are unable and prohibited from performing these acts as testimonials of faith under the pretense of better understanding them.

With this in mind, it is obvious that anthropological accounts of these religious practices have to rely on the information they gather through Muslim discourses and practices to which they are invited. The main insights they get come with the information and instruction they receive from their interviews with interlocutors in focus groups, who serve as brokers or agents to explain the tenets of their religion to more or less informed outsiders. This does not imply that anthropologists cannot witness or interact with Muslims performing their religious practices. For example, such interaction is possible on social occasions when praying and fasting or almsgiving and feasting enter into the public realm. However, the crucial aspect of ethnographic fieldwork on religious practices in this field of study is that anthropologists, above all, attempt to establish a personal and professional rapport with the Muslims they aim to understand, as the subsequent readings in this section show. However, anthropologists usually do not confine their interest in understanding Muslims to their interlocutors; usually, they also show interest in the social and cultural dimensions of communal religious life and the ways in which Muslim life becomes organized by patterns of temporal rhythms. Therefore, as the readings show, anthropologists spend an extended amount of time living in the respective community of their study and immerse themselves into the rhythms of everyday demands and duties, including daily jobs and chores. This allows them to see distinctive features of a community which would otherwise remain concealed. This is what anthropologists can contribute to a more refined understanding of Muslims.

For these reasons, the sequence of this section's readings follow the rhythms of the timeline according to which Muslims organize their religious lives in order to allow the reader to grasp some insights into the patterns within which Islam is practiced. As indicated in the introduction, prayer and almsgiving are, for Muslims, duties of everyday life. At time-periods specified throughout the lunar calendar, Muslims fast and sacrifice once a year, whereas they usually perform the pilgrimage to Mecca once in a lifetime. The temporal design, frequency and rhythm, as well as the public accessibility of these practices defined the parameters and determined the research the anthropologists were able to carry out. In applying different theoretical approaches and methods of inquiry suitable for analyzing ethnographic findings, the works of the anthropologists presented in this section reveal the complexity and diversity of such accounts.

As the most frequent and intimate practice Muslims perform, ritual prayers (*salāt*) occur at specified time-cycles throughout the day. Ritual prayer is the second most important pillar of Islam for Sunnī Muslims, on which the contributions to this Reader primarily focus. These prayers follow a prescribed liturgical order involving the achievement of a state of ritual purity and an orientation toward Mecca. Each of the five prayers has a specific name and follows a specific sequence. The work by Saba Mahmood, entitled "Rehearsed Spontaneity and the Conventionality of Ritual: Disciplines of Salat," engages the practice of the prayer through the conceptual framework of bodily discipline and the efficacy of ritual practice in shaping individuals' beliefs and behaviors. While Mahmood accounts for the role of women in the Islamic Revival in Cairo and their political recognition through their religious practice, Heiko Henkel explores in "Between Belief and Unbelief Lies the Performance of Salat: Meaning and Efficacy of a Muslim Ritual" the Islamic practice in the context of social dynamics in Istanbul. In giving an interpretative framework for the efficacy of this ritual, Henkel argues that religious commitment is crucial for understanding the practice of prayer within the secular nation-state of Turkey.

This first set of readings is followed by ethnographic accounts of fasting (*ṣawm*) during the month of Ramaḍān. Instituted by the Prophet, the fast is performed by Muslims as a spiritual discipline lasting throughout the month of Ramaḍān from dawn to sunset. This is the third of the five pillars or Islam. The practice of fasting is presented through two different methodological accounts from significantly different Muslim societies in East Africa. P.J.L. Frankl provides a detailed ethnographic account which explores the cultural subtleties of describing the sequences of events during the month of Ramaḍān and the fast's linguistic categories and historical documents in "The Observance of Ramadān in Swahili-Land." Samuli Schielke provides a unique look at the social dynamics in Cairo, focusing on the physical discipline the sport of football can provide male Muslims during the last hour of their daily fast during Ramaḍān. In keeping with the idea of critical scholarship, Schielke advances methodological approaches in "Being Good in Ramadān: Ambivalence, Fragmentation, and the Moral Self in the Lives of Young Egyptians" which ask about the ways in which religious practice has been presented and utilized in the identity formation of individuals, by providing venues to incorporate men into the community's traditional practices.

The subsequent depictions deal with the impact of the pilgrimage (*ḥajj*) to Mecca on different local communities. Scheduled between the eighth and twelfth day in the month of *Dhū al-Ḥijja*, the last month of the Muslim lunar calendar, the Ḥajj is a practice that Muslims should perform once during their lifetime. The pilgrimage to Mecca during the month of *Dhū al-Ḥijja* is one of the most demanding of the pillars of Islam and requires more preparation than any other. Following prescribed steps and visiting the most sacred sites of Islamic faith, including the Ka'ba, the pilgrimage to Mecca is a unifying but distinct event for all Muslims, worldwide. With about one million visitors each year, it has a significant and lasting effect on those who perform the pilgrimage as well as on their local community upon their return. In looking at the impact this yearly event has had on the local Muslim community, Raymond Scupin's "The Social Significance of the Hajj for Thai Muslims" and Barbara M. Cooper's "The Strength in Song: Muslim Personhood, Audible Capital and Hausa Women's Performance of the Hajj" address the effects of this religious obligation on the social relationships in their home countries. These two readings exemplify both the prestige system associated with performance of the Ḥajj as well as the use of media and the global social networks of Muslims that facilitate the pilgrimage to Mecca in modern times. In particular, Cooper offers insight into this practice from a complex and changing female perspective. Scupin, on the other hand, explores the social ramifications of the Ḥajj in light of the distance from Mecca for believers in southeast Asia. The Ḥajj is a globally significant form of Muslim religious practice, and its extensions into local perspectives have received considerable attention in the anthropological sphere.

The feast of sacrifice (*'īd al-aḍḥā*) is itself an integral part of the Ḥajj. Although not itself one of the pillars of Islam, the feast is a major religious event commonly accepted and practiced among Sunnī Muslims, with considerable anthropological ramifications. An integral part of the pilgrimage to Mecca, the annual feast of sacrifice begins with a ritual sacrifice on the tenth day of *Dhū al-Ḥijja* and lasts four days. This feast of sacrifice commemorates the faith of Abraham (Ibrahim) and his willingness to sacrifice his son at God's command, as it is recounted in the Qur'ān. During this feast, the meat of the sacrificial animal is distributed in equal parts to the family, neighbors and the poor. The two readings on the feast of sacrifice allow insight into the differing ways sacrifice is performed, as well as ways in which sacrifice is utilized as a means to unify communities. Dwelling on a rich body of anthropological theory, the study of the Muslim feast of sacrifice illustrates and enhances an understanding of sacrifice as a central element of religious life. "On Scriptural Essentialism and Ritual Variation: Muslim Sacrifice in Sumatra and Morocco" by John R. Bowen concerns the variations of practice at local levels, the recognition of which highlights and criticizes the works of past researchers, who reduced and reified the sacrifice to patriarchal structures and functions in Muslim societies. Pnina Werbner, in "'Sealing' the Koran: Offering and Sacrifice among Pakistani Labour Migrants," theorizes sacrifice as a ritual practice, which takes on hybrid forms in the context of labor migration. Delving into the obstacles of Pakistanis who migrated to Manchester to make a living there, Werbner conceptualizes the practice of sacrifice and hindrances to it which emerge in the Pakistani encounter with Manchester. She enquires into the identity formation of Pakistanis as an ethnic community, and asks how they have adapted to their new homeland while maintaining religious and cultural ties to Pakistan.

Although almsgiving (*zakāt*), as one of the five pillars of Islam, is a general obligation throughout the year, it becomes most significant in the distribution of sacrificed meat during the feast of sacrifice in the month of *Dhū al-Ḥijja*. As one of the major duties for Muslims, this practice entails forms of taxation on their personal property. As a charitable practice, almsgiving is a form of purifying property by giving up a portion of one's wealth. Through the giving of alms, Muslims believe they will receive blessings as a form of spiritual reward. A major religious duty often-overlooked by anthropologists of Islam, the *zakāt*, is approached from different angles in the concluding chapters of this section, by Holger Weiss's "Reforming Social Welfare among Muslims: Islamic Voluntarism and other Forms of Communal Support in Northern Ghana" and Jonathan Benthall's "Financial Worship: The Quranic Injunction to Almsgiving." Weiss discusses the practice of the *zakāt* in Ghana by recognizing the different forms of alms and the controversial aspects of institutionalizing the practice at a nation-state or global level within a local community. Benthall provides a thorough theoretical and ethnographic overview of the practice and understanding of almsgiving on both local and global levels based on his evidence from Jordan and Palestine, leading to broader questions of social justice in these regions of the Middle East.

As mentioned in the introduction, this selection of readings on religious practices among Muslims does not represent the five pillars of Islam, but is restricted to some of the most widely accepted tenets of Sunnī Islam. It is not comprehensive, and the readings are not representative of all religious practices relevant to Muslims. Not included are the pilgrimage to local shrines (*ziyāra*), the art of reciting the Qur'ān (*ʿilm al-tajwīd*), the spending time secluded in a mosque praying and reciting the Qur'ān during the month of Ramaḍān (*i'tikāf*), the celebration of Muhammad's birthday (*mawlid*), the act of the repeated invocation of the name of God as part of ritual worship (*dhikr*) common among Ṣūfī Muslims, or the passion plays (*ta'ziyyah*) during the month of Muḥarram among Shīʿa Muslims. Anthropological themes centered on Islam could further include specific studies on the body and cultural politics, food and Islamic etiquette, sexuality, gender and ritual tradition or knowledge and religious authority relevant for the selected texts. However, the selected set of readings, in one way or another, already addresses the aforementioned themes and thus there is no need to duplicate them. The selected readings, exemplary in their focus and significance, are intended to direct attention to the diversity of local forms of Islam and the ways anthropologists can approach the diversity among Muslims, even where their most fundamental ritual tenets are concerned.

Suggested readings

al Faruqi, Lois Ibsen (1987) "Qur'an Reciters in Competition in Kuala Lumpur," *Ethnomusicology*, 31: 221–228.

Al-Naqar, Umar (1972) *The Pilgrimage Tradition in West Africa: An Historical Study with Special Reference to the Nineteenth Century*, Khartoum: Khartoum University Press.

Antoun, Richard T. (1968) "The Social Significance of Ramadan in an Arab Village," *Muslim World*, 58: 36–42, 95–104.

Armbrust, Walter (2000) "The Riddle of Ramadan: Media, Consumer Culture, and the Christmasization of a Muslim Holiday," in Donna L. Bowen and Evelyn A. Early (eds) *Everyday Life in the Muslim Middle East*, revised edition, Bloomington, IN: Indiana University Press.

——— (2006) "Synchronizing Watches: The State, the Consumer, and Sacred Time in Ramadan Television," in B. Meyer and A. Moors (ed.) *Religion, Media, and the Public Sphere*, Bloomington: Indiana University Press.

Beeman, William O. (1979) "Cultural Dimensions of Performance Conventions in Iranian Ta'ziyeh," in Peter J. Chelkowski (ed.) *Ta'ziyeh: Ritual and Drama in Iran*, New York: New York University Press.

——— (2007) "Classical Persian Music, Islam and Ta'ziyeh," in Soussie Rastegar and Anna Vanzan (eds) *Muraqqa'e Sharqi: Studies in Honor of Peter Chelkowski*, San Marino: AIEP Editore.

Benthall, Jonathan (2002) "Organized Charity in the Arab-Islamic World: A View from the NGOs," in Hastings Donnan (ed.) *Interpreting Islam*, London: SAGE Publications

Bhardwaj, Surinder M. (1998) "Non-Hajj Pilgrimage in Islam: A Neglected Dimension of Religious Circulation," *Journal of Cultural Geography*, 17: 69–87.

Bianchi, Robert R. (2004) *Guests of God: Pilgrimage and Politics in the Islamic World*, Oxford: Oxford University Press.

Birks, J.Stace (1977) "The Mecca Pilgrimage by West African Pastoral Nomads," *The Journal of Modern African Studies*, 15: 47–58.

Bonte, Pierre, Anne-Marie Brisebarre, Altan Gökalp, and Sadok Abdelsalam (eds) (1999) *Sacrifices en Islam: Espaces et temps d'un rituel.* Paris: CNRS Editions.

Bowen, John R. (1989) "Salat in Indonesia: The Social Meanings of an Islamic Ritual," *Man*, 24: 600–619.

Bowen, Donna Lee, and Evelyn A. Early (eds) (2002) *Everyday Life in the Muslim Middle East.* 2nd edn, Bloomington, IN: Indiana University Press.

Brisebarre, Anne-Marie (ed.) (1998) *La fête du mouton: Un sacrifice musulman dans espace urbain.* Paris: CNRS Editions.

Burton, Richard F. (1855) *Personal Narrative of a Pilgrimage to El-Medinah and Meccah*, London: Longman, Brown, Green, and Longmans.

Campo, Juan (1987) "Shrines and Talismans: Domestic Islam in the Pilgrimage Paintings of Egypt," *Journal of the American Academy of Religion*, 55: 285–305.

Chelhod, Joseph (1955) *Le Sacrifice chez les Arabes: Recherches sur l'évolution, la nature et la fonction des rites sacrificiels en Arabie occidentale*, Paris: Presses Universitaires de France.

Combs-Schilling, M. Elaine (1989) *Sacred Performances: Islam, Sexuality and Sacrifice*, New York: Columbia University Press.

Delaney, Carol L. (1990) "The *Hajj*: Sacred and Secular," *American Ethnologist*, 17: 513–530.

Denny, Frederick M. (1985) "Islamic Ritual: Perspectives and Theories," in Richard C. Martin (ed.) *Approaches to Islam in Religious Studies*, Tucson, AZ: University of Arizona Press.

——— (1988) "Qur'an Recitation Training in Indonesia: A Survey of Contexts and Handbooks," in Andrew Rippin (ed.) *Approaches to the History of the Interpretation of the Qur'an*, Oxford: Claredon Press.

Din, Abdul K. and Abdul S. Hadi (1997) "Muslim Pilgrimage from Malaysia," in Robert H. Stoddard and E. Alan Morinis (eds) *Sacred Places, Sacred Places: The Geography of Pilgrimages*, Baton Rouge, FL: Geoscience Publications.

Donnan, Hastings (1989) "Symbol and Status: The Significance of the Hajj in Pakistan," *Muslim World*, 79: 205–216.

——— (1995) "Pilgrimage and Islam in Rural Pakistan: The Influence of the Hajj," *Etnofoor*, 8: 63–82.

Eickelman, Dale F., and James P. Piscatori (1990) *Muslim Travellers: Pilgrimage, Migration, and the Religious Imagination*, Berkeley, CA: University of California Press.

El Guindi, Fadwa (2008) *By Noon Prayer: The Rhythm of Islam*, Oxford and New York: Berg.

Fallers, L.A. (1974) "Notes on an Advent Ramadan," *Journal of the American Academy of Religion*, 42: 35–52.

Fernea, Robert A., and Elizabeth W. Fernea (1972) "Variation in Religious Observance among Islamic Women," in Nikki R. Keddie (ed.) *Scholars, Saints, and Sufis: Muslim Religious Institutions in the Middle East since 1500*, Berkeley , CA: University of California Press.

Gade, Anna M. (2002) "Taste, Talent and the Problem of Internalization: A Qur'anic Study of Religious Musicality from Southeast Asia," *History of Religions*, 41: 328–368.

Gardner, Katy (1999) "Global Migrants and Local Shrines: The Shifting Geography of Islam in Sylhet, Bangladesh," in Leif Manger (ed.) *Muslim Diversity: Local Islam in Global Contexts*, Richmond, UK: Curzon Press.

Ghadially, Rehana (2005) "Devotional Empowerment: Women Pilgrims, Saints and Shrines in a South Asian Muslim Sect," *Asian Journal of Womens Studies*, 11: 79–101.

Gordon, Joel (1998) "Becoming the Image: Words of Gold, Talk Television, and Ramadan Nights on the Little Screen," *Visual Anthropology*, 10: 247–263.

Graham, William A. (1983) "Islam in the Mirror of Ritual," in Richard G. Hovannisian and Speros Vryonis (eds) *Islam's Understanding of Itself*, Malibu, CA: Undena Publications.

Hammoudi, Abdellah (2005) *Une saison à la Mecque: récit de pèlerinage*, Paris: Seuil.

Hickey, Joseph V., Gregory R. Staats, and Douglas B. McGaw (1979) "Factors Associated with the Mecca Pilgrimage among the Bokkos Fulani," *Journal of Asian and African Studies*, 14: 217–230.

Hoffmann, Thomas J. (1999–2000) "Dis/integrating the Centre: Space, Narrative, and Cognition with Special Reference to the Hadjdj and the Ka'ba," *Temenos*, 35–36: 25–38.

Junus, U. (1966) "The Payment of Zakat al-Fitrah in a Minangkabau Community," *Bijdragen Tot de Taal-, Land-, en Volkenkunde*, 122: 447–454.

Kanafani-Zahar, Aida (1997) "Le religieux sublimé dans le sacrifice du mouton: un example de coexistence communautaire au Liban," *L'Homme: Revue française d'anthropologie*, 141: 83–100.

Katz, M. (2004) 'The Hajj and the Study of Islamic Ritual,' *Studia Islamica*, 98–99: 95–129.

Lee, Tong S. (1999) "Technology and the Production of Islamic Space: The Call to Prayer in Singapore," *Ethnomusicology*, 43: 86–100.

Long, David E. (1979) *The Hajj Today: A Survey of the Contemporary Makkah Pilgrimage*, Albany, NY: State University of New York Press.

Masquelier, Adeline M. (2001) *Prayer has Spoiled Everything: Possession, Power, and Identity in an Islamic Town of Niger*, Durham, NC: Duke University Press.

Mazumdar, Shampa, and Sanjoy Mazumdar (2002) "In Mosques and Shrines: Women's Agency in Public Sacred Space," *Journal of Ritual Studies*, 16: 165–179.

——— and ——— (2005) "The Articulation of Religion in Domestic Space: Rituals in the Immigrant Muslim Home," in Pamela J. Stewart and Andrew Strathern (eds) *Contesting Rituals: Islam and Practices of Identity-Making*, Durham, N.C.: Carolina Academic Press.

Metcalf, Barbara D. (1990) "The Pilgrimage Remembered: South Asian Accounts of the Hajj," in Dale F. Eickelman and James P. Piscatori (eds) *Muslim Travellers: Pilgrimage, Migration, and the Religious Imagination*, London: Routledge.

Möller, André (2005) *Ramadan in Java: The Joy and Jihad of Ritual Fasting*, Stockholm: Almqvist & Wiksell.

Nelson, Kristina (1982) "Reciter and Listener: Some Factors Shaping the *Mujawwad* Style of Qur'anic Reciting," *Ethnomusicology*, 26: 41–48.

——— (1985) *The Art of Reciting the Qur'an*, Austin, TX: University of Texas Press.

O'Brien, Susan (1999) "Pilgrimage, Power, and Identity: The Role of the Hajj in the Lives of Nigerian Hausa Bori Adepts," *Africa Today*, 46: 11–40.

Odabasi, Yavuz, and Metin Argan (2009) "Aspects of Underlying Ramadan Consumption Patterns in Turkey," *Journal of International Consumer Marketing*, 21: 203–218.

Østergaard Jacobsen, Kate (1996) "Ramadan in Morocco: An Analysis of the Interaction of Formal and Local Traditions," *Temenos*, 32: 113-135.

Qureshi, Regula B. (1996) "Transcending Space: Recitation and Community among South Asian Muslims in Canada," in Barbara D. Metcalf (ed.) *Making Muslim Space in North America and Europe*, Berkeley, CA: University of California Press.

Parkin, David J., and Stephen C. Headley (eds) (2000) *Islamic Prayer across the Indian Ocean: Inside and Outside the Mosque*. Richmond, UK: Curzon.

Peters, Francis E. (1994) *The Hajj: The Muslim Pilgrimage to Mecca and the Holy Places*, Princeton, NJ: Princeton University Press.

Powers, Paul R. (2004) "Interiors, Intentions, and the 'Spirituality' of Islamic Ritual Practice," *Journal of the American Academy of Religion*, 72: 425–459.

Rasmussen, Anne K. (2001) "The Qur'an in Indonesian Daily Life: The Public Project of Musical Oratory," *Ethnomusicology*, 45: 30–57.

Roff, William R. (1985) "Pilgrimage and the History of Religions: Theoretical Approaches to the Hajj," in Richard C. Martin (ed.) *Approaches to Islam in Religious Studies*, Tucson, AZ: University of Arizona Press.

Rowley, Gwyn (1997) "The Pilgrimage to Mecca and the Centrality of Islam," in Robert H. Stoddard and E. Alan Morinis (eds) *Sacred Places, Sacred Places: The Geography of Pilgrimages*, Baton Rouge, FL: Geoscience Publications.

Salamandra, Christa (1998) "Moustache Hairs Lost: Ramadan Television Serials and the Construction of Identity in Damascus, Syria," *Visual Anthropology*, 10: 227–246.

Schulz, Dorothea E. (2008) "Piety's Manifold Embodiments: Muslim Women's Quest for Moral Renewal in Urban Mali," *Journal for Islamic Studies*, 28: 66–93.

——— (2008) "(Re)Turning to Proper Muslim Practice: Islamic Moral Renewal and Women's Conflicting Assertions of Sunni Identity in Urban Mali," *Africa Today*, 54: 21–43.

Simon, Gregory M. (2009) "The Soul Freed of Cares? Islamic Prayer, Subjectivity, and the Contradictions of Moral Selfhood in Minangkabau, Indonesia," *American Ethnologist*, 36: 258–275.

Singer, Amy (2006) "Soup and Sadaqa: Charity in Islamic Societies," *Historical Research*, 79: 306–324.

——— (2008) *Charity in Islamic Societies*, Cambridge: Cambridge University Press.

Snouk Hurgronje, Christiaan (1931) *Mekka in the Latter Part of the 19th Century*, Leiden: E.J. Brill.

Soares, Benjamin F. (1996) "The Prayer Economy in a Malian Town," *Cahiers d'Études africaines*, 144: 739–753.

——— (2005) *Islam and the Prayer Economy: History and Authority in a Malian Town*, Edinburgh: Edinburgh University Press for the International African Institute.

Takim, Liyakat (2005) "Charismatic Appeal or Communitas? Visitation to The Shrines of the Imams," in Pamela J. Stewart and Andrew Strathern (eds) *Contesting Rituals: Islam and Practices of Identity-Making*, Durham, N.C.: Carolina Academic Press.

——— (2006) "Offering Complete or Shortened Prayers? The Traveler's Salat at the 'Holy Places'," *The Muslim World*, 96: 401–422.

Tangban, Ojong E. (1991) "The Hajj and the Nigerian Economy 1960–1981," *Journal of Religion in Africa*, 21: 241–255.

Tapper, Nancy (1990) "Ziyaret: Gender, Movement, and Exchange in a Turkish Community," in Dale Eickelman and James Piscatori (eds) *Muslim Travellers: Pilgrimage, Migration, and the Religious Imagination*, London: Routledge.

Thaiss, Gustav (1972) "Religious Symbolism and Social Change: The Drama of Husain," in Nikki R. Keddie (ed.) *Scholars, Saints, and Sufis: Muslim Religious Institutions in the Middle East since 1500*, Berkeley, CA: University of California Press.

Torab, Azam (1996) "Piety as Gendered Agency: A Study of *Jalaseh* Ritual Discourse in an Urban Neighbourhood in Iran," *Journal of the Royal Anthropological Institute*, 2: 235–252.

——— (2006) *Performing Islam: Gender and Ritual in Iran*, Leiden: Brill.

van de Bruinhorst, Gerard C. (2000) 'Theoretical Problems in Current Anthropological Research on Islamic Sacrifice,' *Focaal*, 36: 185-194.

Van Hoven, Ed (1996) "Local Tradition or Islamic Precept? The Notion of Zakat in Wuli (Eastern Sénégal)," *Cahiers d'études africaines*, 36: 703–722.

Yocum, Glenn (1992) "Notes on an Easter Ramadan," *Journal of the American Academy of Religion*, 60: 201–230.

Young, William C. (1993) "The Ka'ba, Gender, and the Rites of Pilgrimage," *International Journal of Middle East Studies*, 25: 285–300.

Wallin, George A. (1854) "Narrative of a Journey from Cairo to Medina and Mecca," *Journal of the Royal Geographical Society of London*, 24: 115–207.

Wegner, Ulrich (1986) "Transmitting the Divine Revelation: Some Aspects of Textualism and Textual Variability in Qur'anic Recitation," *World of Music*, 26: 57–78.

Weix, G.G. (1998) "Islamic Prayer Groups in Indonesia: Local Forums and Gendered Responses," *Critique of Anthropology*, 18: 405–420.

Werbner, Pnina (1996) "Stamping the Earth with the Name of Allah: Zikr and the Sacralizing of Space among British Muslims," *Cultural Anthropology*, 11: 309–338.

——— (2010) "Beyond Division: Women, Pilgrimage and Nation Building in South Asian Sufism," *Women's Studies International Forum*, 33: 374–382.

Daily Prayers

5 Rehearsed spontaneity and the conventionality of ritual

Disciplines of "*salāt*"

Saba Mahmood

Saba Mahmood is an associate professor of social cultural anthropology at the University of California at Berkeley. She studied under Talal Asad and was awarded her PhD in anthropology at Stanford University. After receiving a BA in architecture, Mahmood has earned four MAs, in urban planning, architecture, political science, and anthropology. She has taught at University of Chicago, Divinity School, was a visiting professor at Leiden University, International Institute for the Study of Islam, is a Harvard Academy Scholar, and earned a place on the Executive Board of the Society for Cultural Anthropology. Her areas of specialty include the anthropology of Islam, and her current research focuses on subject formation, liberalism, secularism and feminist/post-structuralist theory. She has spent a significant amount of time in Cairo, Egypt for her fieldwork, as well as Beirut, Lebanon. Her recent publications include *Pious Transgressions: Embodied Disciplines of the Islamic Revival* (2003); *Politics of Piety: The Islamic Revival and the Feminist Subject* (2005); "Secularism, Hermeneutics, Empire: The Politics of Islamic Reformation" (2004). She co-authored with Charles Hirschkind "Feminism, the Taliban and the Politics of Counter-Insurgency" (2002). In 2005, she was awarded both the Victoria Schuck Award through the American Political Science Association and received an honorable mention, Albert Hourani Book Award from the Middle East Studies Association. These join her other awards, including a Carnegie Scholars Award and the "Cultural Horizon Prize" for best-published essay in cultural anthropology by the Society for Cultural Anthropology in 2002. The article below discusses how the body is disciplined through the performance of *salāt* by questioning current theories of ritual, agency, and self. Mahmood argues for reconsideration of the Western notions of self and agency, which provides her with the key to better understand the Women's Mosque Movement in Cairo.

Introduction

One distinguishing feature of ritual action is its formal and rule-governed character, which anthropologists have often juxtaposed with informal and spontaneous activity. Even among those anthropologists who have disagreed about whether ritual action is a *type* of human behavior (e.g., Bloch 1975; Douglas 1973; Turner 1969) or an *aspect* of all kinds of human action (e.g., Leach 1964; Moore and Myerhoff 1977), there seems to be consensus that ritual activity is conventional and socially prescribed, a characteristic that sets it apart from mundane activities (Bell 1992).[1] This key opposition between formal and informal (or routine) behavior has provided the basis of other conceptual oppositions within theoretical elaborations on ritual, such as stereotypical versus spontaneous action, rehearsed versus authentic emotions, public demeanor versus private self.[2] These series of interconnected distinctions are at the center of a productive and fruitful dialogue among anthropologists concerning the variable ways in which people link conventional or ritualized behavior with informal or mundane activity in different cultural systems.

One central concern within anthropological studies of ritual has been the place of emotion in ritual performance (see Bloch 1975; Evans-Pritchard 1965; Obeyesekere 1981; Radcliffe-Brown 1964; Rosaldo 1980; Tambiah 1985; Turner 1969). Drawing on depth psychology, Victor W. Turner, for example, argues that ritual action is a means of, and space for, channeling and divesting the antisocial qualities of powerful emotions.[3] Stanley J. Tambiah, on the other hand, in breaking from such an approach, contends that ritual as conventionalized behavior is not meant to "express intentions, emotions, and states of mind of individuals in a direct, spontaneous, and 'natural way.'" Rather, according to Tambiah, ritual distances individuals from "spontaneous and intentional expressions because spontaneity and intentionality are, or can be, contingent, labile, circumstantial, even incoherent or disordered" (Tambiah 1985: 132). Following this line of thought, other anthropologists have suggested that ritual is a space of "conventional" and not "genuine" (i.e., personal or individual) emotions (Kapferer 1979). Notably, despite some obvious differences, these contrasting conceptions of the role emotions play in ritual performance share a view of ritual as socially prescribed and formal behavior and, therefore, opposed to routine and pragmatic action.[4] Ritual, in these views, is understood to be the space where individual psychic drives are either channeled into conventional patterns of expression or temporarily suspended so that a conventional social script may be enacted. Common to both these positions is the understanding that ritual activity is where emotional spontaneity comes to be controlled.

In this article, I would like to engage and extend this conversation, with special attention to how specific organizations of self and authority articulate differential relationships between informal activity and rule-prescribed social behavior (such as ritual). In drawing attention to the conceptual pairs that have informed the study of ritual, my aim is not to dismiss these oppositions, but to show the ways in which these concepts are linked in complicated and variable ways depending on the discursive and practical conditions of authority and variable conceptions of personhood. Thus, my intent here is not to propose yet another definition of ritual but to inquire into the relationships that conventional or formal acts articulate with intentions, spontaneous emotions, and bodily capacities under different contexts of power and truth.[5]

In doing so, I draw on ethnographic fieldwork I conducted among a women's piety movement based in the mosques of Cairo, Egypt. The primary focus of this movement was the teaching and studying of Islamic scriptures, social practices, and forms of bodily comportment considered germane to the cultivation of the ideal virtuous self. As I will show, for the women I worked with, the ritual act of Muslim prayer (*salāt*) did not require the suspension of spontaneous emotion and individual intention, neither was it a space for a cathartic release of unsocialized or inassimilable elements of the psyche. Rather, in interviews with me, mosque participants identified the act of prayer as a key site for purposefully molding their intentions, emotions, and desires in accord with orthodox standards of Islamic piety. As a highly structured performance—one given an extensive elaboration in Islamic doctrine—prayer (*salāt*) was understood by the women I worked with to provide an opportunity for the analysis, assessment, and refinement of the set of ethical capacities entailed in the task of realizing piety in the entirety of one's life, and was not a space conceptually detached from the daily tasks of routine living. I will argue, therefore, that the conscious process by which the mosque participants induced sentiments and desires in themselves, in accordance with a moral-ethical program, simultaneously problematizes the "naturalness" of emotions as well as the "conventionality" of ritual action, calling into question any *a priori* distinction between formal (conventional) behavior and spontaneous (intentional) conduct. [...]

Piety and conventionality

As part of the Islamic revival (*al-Sahwa al-Islamiyya*) in Egypt, the women's mosque movement emerged 20 years ago when women started to organize weekly religious lessons—first at their homes and then within mosques—to read the Quran, the *hadith* (the sayings and actions of the Prophet Muhammad), and associated exegetical literature.[6] [...]

The women's mosque movement seeks to preserve those virtues, ethical capacities, and forms of reasoning that the participants perceive to have become unavailable or inaccessible to ordinary Muslims. The practical efforts of the mosque movement are directed at instructing Muslims not only in the proper performance of religious duties and acts of worship but, more importantly, familiarizing them with the exegetical tradition of the Quran and the *hadith*. [...] Yet the women's mosque movement should not be understood as a withdrawal from sociopolitical engagement in as much as the form of piety it seeks to realize entails the transformation of many aspects of social life in Egypt.[7]

This is the first time in Egyptian history that such a large number of women, from a wide variety of socio-economic backgrounds, has played a central role in the institution of the mosque and Islamic pedagogy, both of which have been male-dominated domains. [...] Although most Egyptian women have had some measure of training in piety, the mosque movement is unique in making a religious discourse that had largely been limited to male institutions of high theology popular among women from a range of socio-economic backgrounds (Mahmood 2003).[8] It now competes with parallel secular traditions of self-cultivation available to contemporary Egyptians.[9]

[...] The conditions within which this form of piety is being realized are quite distinct from those previously encountered by women. Whether it is working in mixed-sex offices, riding public transportation, attending coeducational schools, or consuming contemporary forms of mass entertainment, women in Egypt have to deal with a variety of situations that their mothers' and grandmothers' generations did not encounter. As many of the mosque participants argued, their movement is precisely a response to the problem of living piously under conditions that have become increasingly ruled by a secular rationality. [...] My focus in this article is on the role certain forms of conventional behavior and emotional expressions play within the larger disciplinary program pursued by the mosque participants in their cultivation of piety.

Prayer and pragmatic action

The condition of piety was described by the mosque participants I knew as the quality of "being close to God": a manner of *being* and *acting* that suffused all of one's acts, both religious and worldly in character. Although the consummation of a pious deportment entailed a complex ethical disciplinary program, at a fundamental level it required that the individual perform those acts of worship made incumbent upon Muslims by God (*al-farā'id*), as well as Islamic virtues (*al-fadā'il*) and acts of beneficence that secure God's pleasure (*al-a'māl al-sāliha*).[10] Examples of the latter include practicing modesty, fulfilling social and familial obligations, and performing supererogatory prayers. The attitude with which these acts are performed is as important as their prescribed form: Sincerity (*al-ikhāls*), humility (*khushū'*), and feelings of virtuous fear and awe (*khashya* or *taqwa*), are all emotions by which excellence and virtuosity in piety are measured and marked. Many of the mosque attendees observed to me that although they had always been aware of the basic duties required of them as Muslims, it was only their attendance in the mosque groups that provided them with the necessary skills to be able to achieve excellence and higher levels of devotion in their practice.

According to the mosque participants with whom I spoke, among the minimal requirements critical to the formation of a virtuous Muslim is the act of praying five times a day. The performance of prayer (sing. *salāt*, pl. *salawāt*) is considered to be so centrally important in Islam that whether someone who does not pray regularly can qualify as a Muslim has been a subject of intense debate among theologians.[11] *Salāt* is an act of prayer the correct execution of which depends on the following elements: (1) an intention to dedicate the prayer to God, (2) a prescribed sequence of gestures and words, (3) a physical condition of purity, and (4) proper attire. While fulfilling these four conditions renders prayer acceptable (*maqbūl*), I was told it is also desirable that *salāt* be performed with all the feelings, concentration, and tenderness of the heart appropriate to when one is in the presence of God—a state called *khushū'*.

Although it is understandable that an ideal such as *khushū'* had to be learned through intense devotion and training, it was surprising to me that mosque participants considered the desire to pray five times a day (with its minimal conditions of performance) an object of pedagogy. As many of the participants reported to me, they did not pray diligently and seemed to lack the requisite will to accomplish what was required of them. Because such states of will were *not* assumed to be natural by the teachers and their followers, women took extra care to teach each other the means by which the desire to pray could be cultivated and strengthened in the course of conducting the sort of routine, mundane actions that occupied most women during the day.

The complicated relationship between the performance of *salāt* and one's daily activities was revealed to me in a conversation with three women, all of whom regularly attended lessons in different mosques of their choice in Cairo. They were part of a small number of women whom I had come to regard as experienced in the cultivation of piety. My measure for coming to such a judgment was none other than the one used by the mosque participants: They not only carried out their religious duties (*al-farā'id*) diligently, but also attested to their faith (*imān*) by continuously doing good deeds (*al-ā'māl al-sāliah*) and practicing virtues (*al-fadā'il*). As the following exchange makes clear, the women pursued the process of honing and nurturing the desire to pray through the performance of seemingly unrelated deeds during the day until that desire became a part of their conditions of being.

The setting for this conversation was a mosque in downtown Cairo. Because all three of the women work as clerks in the local state bureaucracy in the same building, it was convenient for them to meet in the neighboring mosque in the late afternoons after work on a weekly basis. Their discussions sometimes attracted other women, who had come to the mosque to pray. In this instance, a young woman in her early twenties had been sitting and listening intently, when she suddenly interrupted the discussion to ask a question about one of the five basic prayers required of Muslims, a prayer known as *al-fajr*. This prayer is performed right after dawn breaks and before sunrise. Many Muslims I know consider it the most demanding and difficult of prayers because it is hard to leave the comfort of sleep to wash and pray and also because the period within which it must be performed is very short. This young woman expressed the difficulty she encountered in performing the task of getting up for the morning prayer and asked the group what she should do about it.

Mona, a member of the group who is in her mid-thirties, turned to the young woman with a concerned expression on her face and asked, "Do you mean to say that you are unable to get up for the morning prayer *habitually and consistently*?" The girl nodded in agreement. Bearing the same concerned expression on her face, Mona said, "You mean to say that you forbid yourself the reward [*sawāb*] of the morning prayer? This *surely* is an indication of *ghafla* on your part?" The young woman looked somewhat perturbed and guilty but persisted and asked, "What does *ghafla* mean?" Mona replied that it refers to what you do in the day: If your mind is mostly occupied with things that are not related to God, then you are in a state of *ghafla* (carelessness, negligence). According to Mona, such a condition of negligence results in inability to say[12] the morning prayer.

Looking puzzled, the young woman asked, "What do you mean what I do in the day? What does my saying of the prayer [*salāt*] have to do with what I do in the day?" Mona answered:

> It means what your day-to-day deeds are. For example, what do you look at in the day? Do you look at things that are prohibited to us by God, such as immodest images of women and men? What do you say to people in the day? Do you insult people when you get angry and use abusive language? How do you feel when you see someone doing an act of disobedience [*ma'āsi*]? Do you get sad? Does it hurt you when you see someone committing a sin or does it not affect you? These are the things that have an effect on your heart [*qalbik*], and they hinder or impede [*ta'attal*] your ability to get up and say the morning prayer. [The constant] guarding against disobedience and sins wakes you up for the morning prayer. *Salāt* is not just what you say with your mouth and what you do with your limbs. It is a state of your heart. So when you do things in a day for God and avoid other things because of Him, it means you're thinking about Him, and therefore it becomes easy for you to strive for Him against yourself and your desires. If you correct these issues, you will be able to rise up for the morning prayer as well.

Perhaps responding to the young woman's look of concentration, Mona asked her, "What is it that annoys you [*bitghī zik*] the most in your life?" The young woman answered that her sister fought with her a lot, and this bothered her and made her angry most days. Mona replied:

> You, for example, can think of God when your sister fights with you and not fight back with her because He commands us to control our anger and be patient. For if you do get angry, you know that you will just gather more sins [*dhunub*], but if you are quiet then you are beginning to organize your affairs on account of God and not in accord with your temperament. And then you will realize that your sister will lose the ability to make you angry, and you will become more desirous [*rāghiba*] of God. You will begin to notice that if you say the morning prayer, it will also make your daily affairs easier, and if you don't pray it will make them hard.

Mona looked at the young woman who had been listening attentively and asked: "Do you get angry and upset [*tiz'ali*] when you don't say your morning prayer?" The young woman answered yes. Mona continued:

> But you don't get upset enough that you don't miss the next morning prayer. Performing the morning prayer should be like the things that you can't live without: for when you

> don't eat, or you don't clean your house, you get the feeling that you *must* do this. It is this feeling that I am talking about: there is something inside you that makes you want to pray and gets you up early in the morning to pray. And you're angry with yourself when you don't do this or fail to do this.

The young woman looked on and listened, not saying much. At this point, we moved back to our previous discussion, and the young woman stayed with us until the end.

The answer that Mona provided to this young woman is not a customary answer, such as invoking the fear of God's retribution for habitually failing to perform one's daily prayers. Mona's response reflects the sophistication and elaboration of someone who has spent considerable time and effort in familiarizing herself with an Islamic interpretive tradition of moral discipline. I would like to draw attention here to the economy of discipline at work in Mona's advice to the young woman, particularly the ways in which ordinary tasks in daily life are made to attach to the performance of consummate worship. Notably, when Mona links the ability to pray to the vigilance with which one conducts the practical chores of daily living, *all* mundane activities—like getting angry with one's sister, the things one hears and looks at, the way one speaks—become a place for securing and honing particular moral capacities. As is evident from the preceding discussion, the issue of punctuality clearly entails more than the simple use of an alarm clock: it encompasses an entire attitude one cultivates in order to create the desire to pray. Of significance is the fact that Mona does not assume that the desire to pray is natural, but that it *must be created* through a set of disciplinary acts. These include the effort to avoid seeing, hearing, and speaking about things that make faith (*imān*) weaker and instead engaging in those acts that strengthen the desire for, and the ability to enact, obedience to God's will. The repeated practice of orienting all acts toward securing God's pleasure is a cumulative process the net result of which, on one level, is the ability to pray regularly and, on another level, the creation of a pious self.

This understanding of ritual prayer posits an ineluctable relationship between conventional or rule-governed action and routine and practical conduct. Note that in Mona's formulation, ritual prayer is conjoined and interdependent with pragmatic and utilitarian activities of daily life, actions that must be monitored and honed as conditions for the performance of the ritual itself. Insofar as disciplining mundane conduct is integral to the consummation of ritual action, this understanding problematizes the separation that some theorists of ritual have drawn between ritual and pragmatic action (e.g., Bloch 1974; Leach 1964; Turner 1976). For women like Mona, the performance of *salāt* is one among a continuum of other practices that serve as the necessary means to the realization of a pious self and are the critical instruments in the teleological program of self-formation. This understanding was echoed in a comment I often heard among the mosque participants to the effect that the act of prayer performed for its own sake, and without adequate regard for how it contributes to the realization of piety, is "lost power" (*quwwa mafqūda*).

Mona's discussion of ritual prayer problematizes another polarity, central to a number of anthropological discussions of ritual, that between the spontaneous expression of emotion and its theatrical performance. This polarity, found in the work of Evans-Pritchard 1965 and Bloch 1975 among others, is most succinctly stated by Tambiah in the quote I cite above: "ritual as conventionalized behavior is not designed or meant to express intentions, emotions, and states of mind of individuals in a direct, spontaneous, and 'natural way'" (Tambiah 1985: 132). Demonstration of affect in ritual, according to Tambiah, should not be understood as "a 'free expression of emotions' but a disciplined rehearsal of 'right attitudes'" (Tambiah 1985: 134).[13] Tambiah's point would seem to capture well certain aspects of

Mona's understanding of ritual as a space for the enactment of socially prescribed behaviors, including those involving the expression of affect. Yet such a parceling of spontaneous emotions and disciplined gesture and attitude remains incongruous with other key aspects of the formulation of ritual prayer that Mona elaborates.

As is clear from the example above, in Mona's understanding the enactment of conventional gestures and behaviors devolves on the *spontaneous* expression of well *rehearsed* emotions and *individual* intentions, thereby directing attention to how one learns to express "spontaneously" the "right attitudes." For women like Mona, ritual (i.e., conventional, formal action) is understood as the space par excellence of making their desires act *spontaneously* in accord with pious Islamic conventions. Thus, ritual worship, for the women I worked with, was both *enacted through*, and *productive of*, intentionality, volitional behavior, and sentiments—precisely those elements that are assumed by Tambiah and others to be bracketed in the performance of ritual. Importantly, in this formulation ritual is not regarded as the theater in which a preformed self enacts a script of social action. Rather, it is one among a number of sites where the self comes to acquire and give expression to its proper form. [...]

Indeed, if, as Asad argues, the meaning of ritual cannot be fixed in terms of its formal or conventional character within European history, then the question arises: How are scholars to analyze formal and rule-governed behavior so as to understand the radically different roles it plays under different conceptions of self and authority? Thus, rather than assuming *a priori* that formal behavior necessarily stands in a particular relationship to social authority and the subject's actions, Asad's work encourages the question: What are the variable and varied relations between conventional behavior and the formation of the self under different traditions of discipline and self formation?[14] [...]

Economies of discipline

A central aspect of ritual prayer [...] is that it serves both as a *means* to pious conduct and an *end*. In this logic, ritual prayer (*salāt*) is an end in that Muslims believe God requires them to pray, and a means insofar as it is born out of, and transforms, daily action, which in turn creates or reinforces the desire for worship. Thus, the desired goal (i.e., pious worship) is also one of the means by which that desire is cultivated and gradually made realizable. In fact, in this world view, neither consummate worship nor the acquisition of piety is possible without the performance of prayer in the prescribed (i.e., codified) manner and attitude. As such, ritual worship is both part of a larger program of discipline through which piety is realized and a critical condition for the performance of piety itself.

Despite its centrality to the mosque participants, this understanding of ritual as both means and end was not one shared by all Egyptian Muslims. Consider, for example, Mona Hilmi's interpretation of *salāt*. Hilmi is a columnist who writes for *Rūz al-Yusuf*, a popular weekly magazine that represents a liberal-nationalist perspective in the Egyptian press. What prompted the appearance of her article was the arrest of several teenagers from upper-middle-class and upper-class families for allegedly participating in "devil worship" (*'abdat al-shaitān*). This incident was widely reported in the Egyptian press and, in part, prompted a discussion about the appropriate role of religion—in particular ritual worship—in Egyptian society. Hilmi writes:

> The issue is not whether people perform rituals, and acts of worship [*'ibadāt*] either to get recompense or reward [*sawāb*], or out of fear of God, or the desire to show off in front of other people. The issue instead is how rituals [*tuqūs*] and worship [*'ibadāt*] prepare

> for the creation of a type of person who thinks freely, is capable [*mauhil*] of enlightened criticism on important daily issues, of distinguishing between form and essence, between means and ends, between secondary and basic issues. The biggest challenge is how to transform love for God inside every citizen [*mawā tin wa mawa tina*] into continuous self-criticism of our daily behaviors and manners, and into an awakening of innovative/creative revolutionary thought that is against the subjugation of the human beings and the destruction of his dignity.
>
> (Hilmi 1997: 81)

Clearly Hilmi's argument engages the importance of religious practice in Egyptian society, but it is an interpretation of ritual practice that is quite distinct from the one that Mona and her friends espoused. First, Hilmi and the women with whom I worked voice clear differences about the kind of person to be created in the process of performing rituals. Hilmi imbues her view of what a human being should become with the language and goals of liberal-nationalist thought. For example, the highest goal of worship for her is to create a human being capable of "enlightened criticism on important daily issues" and "revolutionary thought that is against the subjugation of human beings" (Hilmi 1997: 81). As a result, Hilmi addresses "the citizen" (*mawā tin wa mawa tina*) in her call to duty rather than "the faithful" (*mu'min wa mu'mina*) or "slaves of God" (*'ibād Allah*), the terms more commonly used by the women with whom I worked. In contrast, for many of the mosque participants, the ultimate goal of worship was the natural and effortless performance of the virtue of submission to God. Even though women like Mona subjected their daily activities to self-criticism (as the author recommends), it was done in order to secure God's approval and pleasure rather than to hone those capacities referred to by Hilmi and central to the definition of the modern-autonomous citizen.[15] I do not mean to suggest that the discourses of nationalism have been inconsequential in the development of the mosque movement or that the modern state and its forms of power (social, political, and economic) have not shaped the lives of the women I worked with in important ways. My point is simply that the inculcation of ideals of enlightened citizenship was *not* the aim of worship for the women of the mosque movement as it seems to be for Hilmi. What these contrasting interpretations of ritual prayer reveal is not only a disagreement regarding the goals of the act, but also distinctly different presuppositions about the relationship between conventional and routine behavior in the construction of the self.

[...] For Hilmi, I would argue, it seems that the goal of creating modern autonomous citizens remains independent of the means she proposes (i.e., Islamic rituals). [...] In Hilmi's schema, I would contend, therefore, that the means (i.e., ritual *salāt*) and the end (i.e., the model liberal citizen) can be characterized without reference to each other; and a number of quite different means may be employed to achieve one and the same end. In other words, whereas rituals such as *salāt* may, in Hilmi's view, be usefully enlisted for the project of creating a self-critical citizenry, they are not necessary but *contingent* acts in the process. Hence Hilmi emphasizes the citizen's ability to distinguish between essence and form—that is, between an inner meaning conceptually independent from the outward performances that express it—and the dangers of conflating the two. In contrast, for women like Mona, ritual acts of worship, as I show above, are the *sole* and *ineluctable* means of forming pious dispositions. In other words, prescribed rituals are the means by which pious capabilities are developed and internal to their practice.

What I want to suggest is that in an imaginary like Mona's, where external behavioral forms and formal gestures are integral to the realization and expression of the self, the concept of the self and its relation to the body (its variable modes of action and expression) are quite different from the ones discussed by Hilmi. In Hilmi's view, external behavior may serve as a means of disciplining the self but, as I have shown above, remains inessential to that self.[16] Thus the conceptual articulation of formal practices in relation to oneself and others differs in these two imaginaries and, by extension, the implications for power and authority vary as well.

[...] In this article, I have tried to argue that the body's conceptual relationship with the self and others, and the ways in which it articulates with structures of authority, varies under different discursive regimes of power and truth precisely *because the body's ritual practices endow it with different kinds of capabilities.*

In order to grasp this point it is necessary, however, to understand the body and its behavioral forms not only in its capacity as a signifying medium, but also as a tool for becoming a certain kind of a person and attaining certain kinds of states (Asad 1993; Mauss 1979). Starrett is correct, of course, that the nationalist discourse treats the body as a signifying medium wherein the ordered performance of collective worship is taken to be a sign of a well-disciplined nation (as do other public events of national import) (Starrett 1995). Yet for women like Mona, as is clear from my discussion above, bodily forms are at the center of the self's potentialities, both in the subjective and social sense. What I have presented here are two distinctly different views of ritual, one in which ritual organizes practices aimed at the development and formation of an embodied self, and another in which, to borrow Asad's words, ritual "offers a reading of a social institution" (Asad 1993: 78). It is important, therefore, to recognize the disparate organizations of the body-self undergirding these different conceptions of ritual and to analyze the conditions under which parallel and overlapping traditions of reasoning and moral formation exist, not only in different historical and cultural contexts, but also within a single cultural milieu.

Habitus and (un)conscious intentions

In this article, insofar as I address the theme of bodily inculcation through ritual practice, it is worthwhile to examine briefly the utility of Bourdieu's notion of habitus for the analysis of Islamic teachings (Bourdieu 1977; Bourdieu 1980). Although Bourdieu's concept of habitus has proven to be a productive tool for discussions of embodiment, its usefulness in the analysis of the kind of disciplinary practices I have explored above, I would argue, is somewhat limited. Bourdieu proposed the notion of habitus as a means to integrate conceptually phenomenological and structuralist approaches so as to elucidate how the supraindividual structure of society comes to be lived in human experience. For Bourdieu, habitus is a "generative principle" through which "objective conditions" of a society are inscribed in the bodies and dispositions of social actors (Bourdieu 1977; Bourdieu 1980). According to Bourdieu, structured dispositions that constitute habitus correspond to an individual's class or social position and are engendered "in the last analysis, by the economic bases of the social formation in question" (Bourdieu 1977: 83). Although Bourdieu acknowledges that habitus is learned—in the sense that no one is born with it—his primary concern is with the unconscious power of habitus through which objective social conditions become naturalized and reproduced. He argues that "practical mimesis" (the process by which habitus is acquired)

> has nothing in common with an *imitation* that would presuppose a conscious effort to reproduce a gesture, an utterance or an object explicitly constituted as a model ... [instead] the process of reproduction ... tend[s] to take place below the level of

> consciousness, expression and the reflexive distance which these presuppose ... What is 'learned by the body' is not something that one has, like knowledge that can be brandished, but something that one is.
>
> (Bourdieu 1980: 73)

Apart from the socio-economic determinism that characterizes Bourdieu's discussion of bodily dispositions, what I find problematic in this approach is the lack of attention to the pedagogical process by which a habitus is learned.[17] As is clear from the ethnographic example I provide above, among the mosque participants I worked with, the body was thematized as a site of moral training and cultivation, thereby problematizing the narrow model of unconscious imbibing that Bourdieu assumes in his discussion of habitus. Yet conscious training in the habituation of virtues itself was undertaken, paradoxically, to make consciousness redundant to the practice of these virtues. This is evident in Mona's advice to the young woman when she says that one should become so accustomed to the act of praying five times a day that when one does not pray one feels just as uncomfortable as when one forgets to eat: At this stage, the act of prayer has attained the status of almost a physiological need that is fulfilled without conscious reflection. Yet it would be a mistake to say that mosque participants believe that once a virtue has taken root in one's disposition it issues forth perfunctorily and automatically. Insofar as the point is not simply *that* one acts virtuously but also *how* one enacts a virtue (with what intent, emotion, commitment, etc.), constant vigilance and monitoring of one's practices is a critical element in this model of ethical formation. This economy of self-discipline, therefore, draws attention to the role self-directed action plays in the learning of an embodied disposition and its relationship to "unconscious" ways of being.[18] Bourdieu's failure to attend to pedagogical moments and practices in the process of acquiring a habitus results in a neglect of the historically and culturally specific embodied capacities that different conceptions of the subject require. It also neglects the precise role various traditions of bodily discipline play in becoming a certain kind of a subject.[19]

In analyzing the role of conscious training in the acquisition of embodied dispositions within the practices of the mosque movement, I have found it useful to draw on an older genealogy of habitus that was first developed by Aristotle and later came to inform both the Christian and Muslim traditions.[20] Habitus in this formulation is concerned with ethical formation and presupposes a specific pedagogical process by which a moral character is acquired. In this understanding, both vices and virtues—insofar as they are considered to be products of human endeavor, rather than revelatory experience or natural temperament—are acquired through the repeated performance of actions that entail a particular virtue or vice, until all behavior comes to be regulated by the habitus. Thus habitus in this tradition of moral cultivation implies a quality that is acquired through human industry, assiduous practice, and discipline such that it becomes a permanent feature of a person's character. Premeditated learning is a teleological process aimed at making moral behavior a nondeliberative aspect of one's disposition. Bourdieu, in drawing on the Aristotelian tradition, retains the sense of habitus as durable, embodied dispositions, but he leaves aside the pedagogical aspect of the Aristotelian notion as well as the context of ethics within which the concept was developed. Thus, although Bourdieu uses habitus in a more restricted sense to focus on how ideology is inscribed on the body, the practices of the mosque participants suggest a more complicated usage in which issues of moral formation stand in a specific relationship to a particular kind of pedagogical model. [...]

Induced weeping, fear, and felicity

Let me elaborate the principle undergirding the model of ethical formation outlined above through an analysis of one of the organizing principles within the disciplinary practices of the mosque lessons: the triad of fear (*al-khauf*), hope (*al-rajā'*), love (*al-hubb*).[21] The process of cultivating and honing a pious disposition among the mosque participants centered not only around the practical tasks of daily living, but also the creation and orientation of the emotions such a disposition entailed. No other theme of the mosque lessons captured the emotive aspect of this disciplinary program better than the tripartite theme of fear-hope-love, so often evoked by the teachers and attendees. As elaborated in the mosque lessons, the principle of fear (*al-khauf*) refers to the dread one feels from the possibility of God's retribution (e.g., fires of hell), an experience that leads one to avoid indulging in those actions and thoughts that may earn His wrath and displeasure; hope (*al-rajā'*) is the anticipation of the beneficence (*hasanāt*) one accrues with God for undertaking religious duties and good deeds; and the principle of love (*al-hubb*) refers to the affection and devotion one feels for God, which in turn inspires one to pursue a life in accordance with His will and pleasure. Thus, each emotion is tied to an economy of action that follows from the experience of that particular emotion.

[...] Consider the following excerpt from a mosque lesson delivered by one of the most popular mosque teachers (*dā'iyāt*), Hajja Samia, to an audience of 500 women. Hajja Samia, a woman in her early forties, was well known for her repeated evocations of fear in her weekly lessons and was sometimes criticized by her audience for these evocations. In response, she had the following to say one morning as she wrapped up her hour-long lesson (*dars*):

> People criticize us for evoking fear in our lessons [*durus*]. But look around you: do you think ours is a society that is afraid of God? If we were afraid of Him and his fury [*qahar*], do you think we would behave in the way we do? We are all humans and commit mistakes, and we should ask for forgiveness from Him continually for these. But to commit sins intentionally, as a habit, is what is woeful! Do we feel remorse and cry at this condition of the Islamic community [*umma*]? No! We do not even know we are in this condition. The last shred of fear in our hearts has been squeezed out by the countless sins we commit, so that we do not even know the difference between what is permissible and what is not [*harām wa halāl*]. Remember that if we cannot cry out of fear of the fires of hell, then we should certainly cry at the condition of our souls!

These remarks are striking for the ineluctable relationship Hajja Samia draws between the ability to fear God and capacities of moral discernment and action. In this formulation, the emotion of fear does not serve simply as a motivation for the pursuit of virtue and avoidance of vice; it has an epistemic value-enabling one to *know and distinguish* between what is good for oneself and for one's community and what is bad (described in accordance with God's program). Notably, according to Hajja Samia, the repeated act of committing sins intentionally and habitually has the cumulative effect such that one becomes the kind of person who has lost the capacity to fear God, which, in turn, is understood as the ultimate sign of the inability to judge the status of one's moral condition.[22] For many Muslims, the ability to fear God is considered one of the critical registers by which one monitors and assesses the progress of the moral self toward virtuosity, and the absence of fear is the marker of an inadequately formed self. Hajja Samia, therefore, interprets the incapacity of Egyptian Muslims today to feel frightened of the retribution of God to be both the *cause* and the *consequence* of a life lived deliberately without virtue.

The various elements in this economy of emotion and action were clarified to me further by one of the long-time attendees of Hajja Samia's lessons. Umm Amal, a gentle woman in her late fifties, had recently retired after having worked as an administrator in the Egyptian airline for most of her life. Having raised two children single-handedly and through adversity, she had acquired a forgiving and accommodating temperament that seemed to be quite the opposite of Hajja Samia, who was often strict and unrelenting in her criticisms of the impious behavior of Egyptian women. It came as a surprise to me, therefore, when Umm Amal defended Hajja Samia's emphasis on fear in her lessons, in particular her evocations of topics such as the tortures of hell and the pain of death. I asked Umm Amal what she meant when she said that she feared God and how she thought it affected her ability to feel close to God. She responded:

> I feel fear of God not simply because of threats of hell and torments of the grave [*a'dhāb al-qabr*], though these things are also true because God mentions them in Quran. But for me the real fear of God stems from two things: from the knowledge that He is all powerful [*qudratihi*], and from the knowledge of the sins that we have committed in our lives and continue to commit without knowing. Imagine God is the Lord of all worlds. And knowing this engenders fear and awe [*khashya*] in you. This is different from fear [al-khauf] that paralyzes you, but it is fear that motivates you to seek His forgiveness and come closer to Him. Because fear that paralyzes you, or makes you feel despondent about His kindness [*rahma*] is objectionable and reprehensible [*madhmūm*]. But fear that propels you toward Him is commendable and praiseworthy [*mahmūd*]. So one who fears is not someone who cries all the time *but one who refrains from doing things that make him afraid of punishment*.... So yes, when I hear talk about fear [*kalām 'an al-khauf*] it has an effect on me because it reminds me of the acts of disobedience I have committed unknowingly, given how absorbed I have been in my life with raising my children and working, and makes me want to seek forgiveness for them. You see if I am not reminded, then I forget, and I become accustomed to making these mistakes and sins. Most of us do not sin intentionally, but we do so without knowing. Talk of fear reminds us of this and forces us to change our behaviors [*tassaruftāina*]. But the greatness of my Lord [*rabbi*] is that He continually forgives us. This causes me to love Him as much as I fear His capacity for greatness.

Umm Amal's answer is remarkable for delineating the topography of fear and love undergirding virtuous action. Notably, these emotions are not simply subjective states but linked to action. Umm Amal, therefore, draws a distinction between fear that results in inaction (considered reprehensible, *madmūm*) and fear that compels one to act virtuously (perceived as desirable or praiseworthy, *mahmūd*). Fear of God in this conception is a cardinal virtue the force of which one must feel subjectively and act on in accord with its dictates.[23] She also draws a distinction between ordinary fear (*khauf*) and fear with reverence or awe (*khashya*). *Khauf* is what you feel, as another mosque participant put it, when you walk alone into a dark unknown space, but *khashya* is what you feel when you confront something or someone whom you regard with respect and veneration, an aspect of God that Umm Amal calls "His omnipotence" (*qudratihi*).[24] Yet it is precisely the qualities that inspire *khashya* in Umm Amal that also inspire her to love God. Thus, in Umm Amal's view, love and fear of God are integrally related to her ability to recognize God's greatness both in His capacity to punish, as well as to forgive and sustain His creatures despite their tendency to err.

Umm Amal's response also speaks to the roles fear and love play in the habituation of virtues and vices. Unlike Hajja Samia, she is talking about Muslims who commit acts of disobedience (*ma'āsi*) out of negligence, rather than conscious intention. Yet even vices committed out of negligence, if done repeatedly, have the same effect as do intentionally committed vices in that once they have acquired the status of habits they can come to corrode the requisite will to obey God.[25] This logic assumes that although someone with a pious disposition can err, the repeated practice of erring from God's program results in the sedimentation of this quality in one's character. This accords with the Aristotelian understanding of habitus insomuch as the repeated performance of vices (as well as virtues) results in the formation of a virtueless (or virtuous) disposition. Fear of God is the capacity by which one becomes cognizant of this state and begins to correct it. Thus, it is repeated invocations of fear and the economy of actions following from it that train one to live piously (a spur to action), and are also a permanent condition of the pious self (*al-nafs al-muttaqi*).

Although the importance of fear to this pedagogical model of ethical formation is clear from the examples above, the question arises how this emotion is acquired and cultivated, especially because the mosque participants do not consider fear of God to be natural but something that has to be learned? According to the women I worked with, there are many avenues that provide training in fear. One is the space of the mosque lessons. I was surprised to find out that many of the attendees who came to hear Hajja Samia regularly were drawn by her ability to engender fear. When I asked one of these women why she preferred Hajja Samia's severe and strident (*mutashad-did*) style of delivery, she responded:

> We live in a society in which it is hard to remain pious and to be protective of our religion [*nihfiz' ala dīnnina*]. When we hear this kind of talk, it startles us and keeps us from getting lost in the attractions of the world. You see the path to piety [*taqwa*] is very difficult. Hajja Samia and others are afraid that unless they use [the rhetorical style of] *takhwīf* [to cause to fear], people will lose all the effort they have exerted in getting there. They want people to hold on to their efforts in the path of piety [*taqwa*] and this is why they use *takhwīf*.[26]

Hajja Samia, therefore, did not simply prescribe fear as a necessary condition for piety, but deployed a discourse and rhetorical style that elicited it as well.[27] In doing so, she punctuated her lessons with evocations of the fires of hell, trials of death, and the final encounter with God after death. This style of preaching aimed at the creation of fear in the listeners is termed *tarhīb* (and at times *takhwīf*), and its antonym *targhīb* refers to the evocation of love for God in the audience: most mosque teachers stressed the importance of maintaining a fine balance between these two rhetorical strategies. Cassette-recorded sermons that used the *takhwīf* style were also widely popular among the women I worked with because they were perceived to be particularly effective in inducing the emotion of virtuous fear (*taqwa*) in the listener.[28]

[…] The way consummate excellence was achieved in one's prayers was a topic of heated discussion among the mosque participants. One of the widely circulated booklets among the mosque groups was entitled "How to Feel Humility and Submission [*khushū'*] in Prayer?" (Maharib 1991). The booklet provided instruction to women on how to pray with *khushū'*, focusing not only on the act of *salāt* itself but also on the conditioning of one's thoughts and actions before and after its performance.[29] One of the techniques mentioned in this booklet, and extensively discussed by the mosque participants, is that of weeping during the course of prayer, especially at the time of supplications, as a means for the expression and realization of a fearful and reverential attitude (*khashya*) toward God. Weeping in this context, however, is not tantamount to crying provoked by the pain of personal sufferings. Instead, it must issue forth out of a sense of being overwhelmed by God's greatness and enacted with the intention of pleasing Him. In other words, the act of weeping in prayer is not meant to be cathartic of one's sorrow and grief, a release of stressful emotions generated by the tensions of life that Turner has described in relation to ritual practice in other contexts (Turner 1969; see also Scheff 1977). On the contrary, according to the mosque participants I know, the act of crying in prayer for the sake of venting one's feelings, rather than expressing one's awe for God, renders the ritual null and void (*bāṭil*). Similarly, Muslim theologians have long considered crying in prayer for the sake of impressing fellow Muslims to be an idolatrous act (*shirk*). Notably, the emphasis participants place on the intention with which one performs these emotions complicates those anthropological views that suggest that rituals have little to do with the practitioners' intentions or emotions (e.g., Bloch 1975; Tambiah 1985).[30] Virtuous fear and weeping are not understood by the mosque participants to be generic emotions, nor are they devoid of intentionality—rather, they are specific to the economy of motivation and action of which they are a constitutive part and, in an important sense, impart to a particular action its distinctive quality.[31]

The ability to cry effortlessly with the right intention did not come easily to most women, however, and had to be cultivated through acts of induced weeping during *salāt*. Booklets of the kind mentioned above suggest different strategies for the attainment of this state, and women are advised to try a number of visual, kinesthetic, verbal, and behavioral techniques in order to provoke the desired affect (see Maharib 1991). This entailed various exercises of imagination geared to exciting one's emotions, evoking the pious tenderness that *khushū'* entails and that leads to weeping. According to the women I know, common exercises included: envisioning that one was being physically held between the hands of God during prayer; visualizing crossing the legendary bridge (*al-sarāt*), narrow as a sharp blade, that all Muslims will be required to walk in the Hereafter but that only the pious will be able to traverse successfully; or avoiding the fires of hell that lie underneath. Other women would talk about imagining the immensity of God's power and their own insignificance. The principle underlying these exercises is that repeated invocations of weeping, with the right intention, habituate fear of God to the point that it infuses all of one's actions, in particular *salāt*. In other words, repeated bodily behavior, with the appropriate intention (however simulated in the beginning), leads to the reorientation of one's motivations, desires, and emotions until they become a part of one's "natural" disposition. Notably, in this economy of discipline, disparity between one's intention and bodily gestures is not interpreted as a disjunction between outward social performance and one's "genuine" inner feelings—rather, it is considered to be a sign of an inadequately formed self that requires further discipline and training to bring the two into harmony in accord with a teleological model of self-formation.

[...] I would argue that it would be a mistake to reduce the practice of weeping in prayer to a cross-cultural example of conventionalized behaviors that are assumed to achieve the same goal in all contexts. This is so for two reasons. First, such a view does not give adequate attention to those performances of conventional behavior that are aimed at the development and formation of the self's spontaneous and effortless expressions. As is clear from the discussion above, the pedagogical program among the mosque participants was geared precisely toward making prescribed behavior natural to one's disposition, and one's virtuosity lay in being able to spontaneously enact its most conventional aspects in a ritual context as much as in ordinary life, thereby making any *a priori* separation between individual feelings and socially prescribed behavior unfeasible. Similarly, as I have shown above, simulating "proper" intentions, did not (to use Tambiah's words) "code" real intentions but, was a disciplinary act undertaken to bridge the gap between how one "really felt" and how one was "supposed to feel"—thereby making a distinction between simulation and reality rather porous.

Second, the process of inducing fear and weeping in oneself during *salāt* complicates the separation Tambiah draws between ordinary and conventional emotions insofar as it suggests the disciplinary aspects of the most individualized and unstructured feelings and emotional expressions. As much recent anthropological literature has pointed out, given that emotions are discursively and historically constructed, it is difficult to sustain a meaningful separation between what are called "real individual" feelings and those that are a part of what Tambiah calls "institutionalized intercourse" (Lutz and Abu-Lughod 1990; Yanagisako and Delaney 1995). Thus, to understand how ritual functions in different discursive contexts of power and subject formation, it is important to interrogate the specific and differential ways in which conventional performances are linked to emotions or feelings rather than assume that they cohere in a singular and definitive manner.

Conclusion

In this exploration of the embodied practices of the mosque movement, I have analyzed the body not so much as a signifying medium to which different ideological meanings are ascribed, but more as a tool or developable means through which certain kinds of ethical and moral capacities are attained. Rather than focus on the experience of the body, I have explored the process by which an experienced body is produced and an embodied subject is formed. I use the notion of experience in this analysis to refer to the skills and aptitudes acquired through training, practice, and apprenticeship to a particular field of study.[32] Such an understanding of experience seems to capture well the principle of self-formation that informed the practices of the women I worked with, wherein through the repeated performance of certain acts they attempted to re-orient their volition, desires, emotions, and bodily gestures to accord with norms of pious conduct.

My insistence in this article on exploring differential conceptions of ritual is geared toward problematizing the attribution of essential meaning to the conventional and formal character of ritual. I direct attention to how formality is variously conceptualized in different discursive traditions and made to articulate with disparate structures of authority and models of the self. In exploring the role that the ritual act of Muslim prayer played in the formation of pious selves among the women I worked with, I have suggested that the relationship between conventional behavior and pragmatic action needs to be complicated further than anthropological theories of ritual suggest. I have proposed that the mosque participants' understanding of ritual prayer is best analyzed as a disciplinary practice that complexly combines pragmatic action (i.e., day-to-day mundane activities) with formal and highly codified behavior. Rather than assume that conventional gestures and behaviors necessarily accomplish the same goals *a priori*, I suggest the need for inquiry into the variable relationships that formal conventionalized behavior (such as ritual) articulate with different conceptions of the self under particular regimes of truth, power, and authority.

Finally, insofar as my analysis complicates the distinction between a subject's "true" desires and obligatory social conventions—a distinction critical to liberal notions of freedom—it represents a challenge to how progressive or liberal scholars think about politics. The politics that ensues from the assumption of such a disjunction necessarily aims to identify the moments and places where conventional norms impede the realization of an individual's real desires.[33] In this view, the freedom of individuals resides in their ability to act out of their "own will, reason, and interests," rather than those of convention, tradition, or direct coercion (where the latter are taken to be manifestations of the social will). Yet, as I have argued in this article, an abidance by conventional behavior cannot simply be taken as evidence of the operation of a high degree of social control and repression of the self. Rather, formal behavior, in the context of the movement I have discussed, is a condition for the emergence of the self as such and integral to its realization.

[…] My point is simply that the desire for freedom from social conventions is not an innate desire, but assumes a particular anthropology of the subject. Thus any exploration of practices of freedom must consider, not only hierarchical structures of social relations, but also the architecture of the self, the interrelationship between its constituent elements that makes a particular imaginary of freedom possible. In other words, such an analysis requires thinking through the topography of a politics of freedom adequate to variable understandings of the self and its embodied powers. It invites conceptualization of freedom as a contextual, rather than universal, practice.

Notes

1 The term *conventional* is used sometimes to refer to ordinary or standard ways of doing things, and at others to indicate behavior that is constrained by custom and social rules. In this article, I have used *conventional* in the latter sense, sometimes alternating it with phrases like "rule-governed and socially prescribed behavior."

2 Much of this debate assumes a particular model of the relation between the inner life of individuals and their outward expressions, a model predicated on a Cartesian understanding of the self as it was developed in early modern and Romantic thought in Europe. As a theatrical mode of self-presentation emerged as a legitimate and necessary form of commercial sociability in eighteenth century Europe, Romantic thinkers, for example, came to see this development in terms of the need for a necessary detachment between the inner life of individuals and their social performances. Historian Edward J. Hundert discusses this attitude in the work of Rousseau who drew a clear separation between an inner self and its social performances, inasmuch as "expressions of inner life resisted all attempts to encode it as a feature of social practices theatrically conceived, precisely because such a life was [regarded as] singular and self-defining" (Hundert 1997: 82). Hundert quotes Rousseau from *The Confessions*: "I know my own heart … I am made unlike anyone I have ever met. I will even venture to say that I am like no one in the whole world. I may be no better, but at least I am different" (Hundert 1997: 82). This view of the unique privatized subject whose essence cannot be captured in the social conventions of a given society seems to resonate with the conception of ritual action as necessarily devoid of "authentic, individualized" emotions.

3 According to Victor W. Turner, "powerful drives and emotions associated with human physiology, especially the physiology of reproduction, are divested in the ritual process of their antisocial quality and attached to components of the normative order, energizing the latter with a borrowed vitality, and thus making the Durkheimian 'obligatory' desirable" (Turner 1969).

4 Turner's statement that ritual is "prescribed formal behavior for occasions not given over to technological routine" (Turner 1976: 504) is in keeping with Tambiah's view that "if we postulate a continuum of behavior, with intentional behavior at one pole and conventional behavior at the other, we shall have to locate formalized ritual nearer the latter pole" (Tambiah 1985: 134). Malinowski acknowledged the instrumental aspects of certain rituals, but made this the basis of the distinction between magical and religious rites where the former had an instrumental and pragmatic quality (Malinowski 1922). Later, with the decline of structural functionalism, anthropologists increasingly interpreted ritual as an expressive and communicative act, the meaning of which was to be deciphered by the analyst (e.g., Clifford Geertz, Edmund Leach, Stanley J. Tambiah).

5 The conception of power I use here is indebted to Michel Foucault's later work (Foucault 1988a; Foucault 1988b; Foucault 1997). In this work, Foucault uses the term "technologies of the self" to describe a modality of power that "permits individuals to effect by their own means, or with the help of others, a certain number of operations on their own bodies and souls, thoughts, conduct, and way of being" (Foucault 1997: 224) so as to transform themselves into the willing subjects of a particular discourse. Power in this conception is understood not so much as a force that is

externally imposed on a subject, but as the capacities that the embodied self develops in accord with the authoritative standards of a particular discursive tradition. For a discussion of Foucault's later work on ethics, see Paul Rabinow's *Introduction* in Foucault (Rabinow 1997: xi–xlii).

6 By the time I conducted my fieldwork (1995–1997), the movement had become so popular that there were hardly any neighborhoods in this city of 11 million inhabitants where some form of religious lessons were not offered for women. The attendance at these gatherings varied from ten to 500 women, depending on the popularity of the woman teacher. The movement continues to be organized informally by word of mouth and has no organizational center that oversees its coordination. Indeed, even the Egyptian religious press barely mentions the increased frequency of women's activities at the mosques.

7 The Egyptian government has slowly come to recognize the crucial role such a movement is playing in institutionalizing an Islamic sociability that makes the task of securing a secular-liberal society difficult. Consequently, in the last few years, the government has begun to monitor popular mosque gatherings for views that the state considers objectionable. In addition, the Ministry of Religious Affairs now requires men and women, regardless of their prior religious training, to enroll in a two-year state-run program in order to be able to preach in mosques. For a fuller discussion of this tension between the state and the women's mosque groups, see Mahmood 2003.

8 Eickelman has also noted the increasing familiarity of the younger generation with Islamic knowledges that had up until the twentieth century been the purview of religious scholars in the Arab world. He attributes this development to the widespread consumption of mass media as well as to increased rates of literacy, both of which make access to these knowledges easier than was the case for previous generations (Eickelman 1992).

9 Despite salient differences across gender lines, I was struck by the similarity of themes emphasized in the men's and women's piety movements. Although I did not conduct fieldwork among the men's piety movement, I was exposed to many of its public forms such as the popular religious literature written by and for men, cassette-recorded sermons, and religious lessons delivered by men in mosques to male and female audience. For a comprehensive analysis of the male piety movement in contemporary Cairo, see Hirschkind 2001a; Hirschkind 2001b.

10 The acts of worship include verbal attestation to faith (*shahāda*), praying five times a day (*salāt*), fasting (*saum*), the giving of alms (*zakāt*), and pilgrimage to Mecca (*haj*).

11 See the debate between the two preeminent theologians—Imam Shafā'i and Imam Hanbal—on this issue, reported in al-Sayyid Sabiq (Sabiq 1994: 72).

12 [Editor's note: One does not only say the *salāt*, but also performs it bodily].

13 Bloch expresses a similar view when he argues, "The reason why the formalized code is unsuitable for practical day-to-day maneuvering is because formalization creates an uncharted distance between things or situations and communication" (Bloch 1974: 65).

14 For an interesting elaboration of Asad's argument about the emergence of the category of ritual as an anthropological object of study, see Scott's discussion of Sinhalese Buddhist rituals (Scott 1994: 111–136).

15 It is important to note that the mosque participants as well as Hilmi are concerned with articulating an ideal standard of moral conduct, rather than describing particular instances of individual behavior. As such, their remarks delineate a set of normative standards by which the correctness or deviancy of an act is measured or judged.

16 In a recent essay, Webb Keane addresses a parallel distinction in analyzing the different conceptions of ceremonial exchange that coexist among Protestant and non-Protestant Sumbanese (Keane 2000). For the former, ceremonial exchange is a signifying practice that has only an arbitrary relationship to the material substance exchanged in the ceremony. For the latter, the materiality of these exchanges remains embedded in, and constitutive of, social relations and personhood.

17 The correspondence Bourdieu draws between the class and social position of social actors and their bodily dispositions needs to be complicated by the fact that in any given society there are traditions of discipline and self-formation that cut across class and social positions. See Cantwell 1999 for an excellent discussion of this point. Indeed, my work with mosque groups from a wide range of socio-economic backgrounds shows that the tradition of moral formation I have described, with its corresponding pedagogical program, although inflected by relations of social hierarchy, did not in any simple way reflect the social and class position of the participants. For a discussion of this point in the context of other traditions of discipline, see Foucault 1988a and Foucault 1988b, and Rose 1997.

18 Starrett has drawn attention to the role explicit discourse plays in fixing the ideological meaning of ritual activity and to Bourdieu's neglect of this aspect. Although agreeing with Starrett's critique, my point in this article is somewhat different in that I am interested in conscious action directed at making certain kinds of behaviors unconscious or nondeliberative.

19 In discussing the utility of Bourdieu's work to medical anthropology, Arthur Kleinman has made a parallel criticism. He argues: "Indeed, as resonant and as robust as his claim for the dialectical interaction between *habitus* and social structure is ... there is still all too little theoretical work by Bourdieu on how this mediation/transformation is actualized in everyday social life. In other words, Bourdieu's accomplishment has been to evoke sociosomatics without working them out. This remains an equivalent in social theory to the 'mystical leap' between mind and body in psychosomatic medicine" (Kleinman 2004: 204). I would add that a study of the pedagogical process by which a bodily disposition is acquired is crucial to understanding how different traditions of discipline are predicated on specific kinds of relationships between various aspects of the body and the self.

20 For a discussion of the Christian adaptation and reformulation of the Aristotelian notion of habitus, see Carruthers 1990, Inglis 1999, and Nederman 1989. For a historical discussion of how Hellenic ideas came to be adopted and developed in the Islamic tradition, see Fakhry 1983 and Watt 1985.

21 For a discussion of the triad of fear-hope-love in the Sunni tradition, see McKane 1962.

22 This logic is captured well in the Quranic phrase (often repeated by the mosque participants) that describes those who commit sins habitually as doing "injustice to themselves," or *zalama nafsahu* (see Izutsu 1966: 164–172). Hence Hajja Samia's statement that the condition of habitual sinners deserves the utmost pity because their real punishment is their deficient and ill-formed characters for which they will not only pay in the Hereafter, but also in this world.

23 As Hajja Samia implies above, if Muslims possessed the virtue of fear then it would be evident in their conduct, and they would order their lives in accord with God's will.

24 This difference is also spelled out by Izutsu in his discussion of the terms *khauf* and *khashya* as they occur in the Quran (Izutsu 1966: 195–197). He shows that in most instances when *khashya* is used in the Quran, its proper object is God rather than human beings.

25 This is also the reasoning implicit in the phrase often repeated by the mosque participants: *mafish saghāra ba'd al-istimrār wa mafish kabāra ba'd al-istaghfār*, meaning "vices done repeatedly and continually acquire the status of grave sins, and a grave sin if repented properly loses its gravity (in the eyes of God)."

26 Depending on the context, I have translated the term *taqwa* as piety, virtuous fear, or fear of God. This is pursuant with the variable meanings accorded to *taqwa* in the Quran. For an analysis of the conceptual and linguistic relationship between piety and fear, see Izutsu's excellent discussion of the use of the terms *taqwa*, *khauf*, *khashya*, *rahiba* (all of which are used interchangeably) in the Quran (Izutsu 1966: 150, 195–200).

27 Rhetoric in this usage refers to the process by which the orator recruits her listeners to participate in a shared economy of action and response (Burke 1969; McKeon 1987). See Appadurai 1990 for an insightful discussion of the rhetorical practice of praise by beggars in contemporary India, based on the classical Hindu aesthetic principle of *rasa* (juice or essence), which creates a shared "community of sentiment" among enunciators of praise, those who receive it, and the audience.

28 For an extended analysis of the rhetorical practice of Islamic sermons in contemporary Egypt among male preachers and listeners, see Hirschkind 2001a.

29 For example, if one is preoccupied with issues pertaining to one's family, a common cause of distraction in *salāt*, then women are advised to undertake a number of different acts outside of *salāt*—such as repeating Quranic and supplicatory verses (*azkār*), or going out of their way to do something in the name of God, such as giving charity (*sadaqa*). Similarly, the booklet suggests a number of mental exercises to overcome laziness so as to be able to pray diligently.

30 For an analysis of ritual that departs from this point of view, especially in examining the role of intention and speech among the Sumbanese, see Keane 1997.

31 There is a large body of literature in Islamic theology that deals with the importance of intention (*al-niyya*) in the performance of religious and worldly acts. Thus the same act (such as slaughtering an animal) acquires a different status depending on the intention with which it is undertaken—from an act of worship, to an ordinary act of tending to one's hunger, to an idolatrous act (see Nawawi 1990: 23). Many of the mosque participants' discussions focused on how to render

mundane tasks of daily living virtuous by dedicating the intention accompanying those acts to God, a process that oriented one's "secular" acts to securing His pleasure. For an interesting and contrastive discussion of contemporary debates about the proper role of intention in Muslim prayer in Indonesia, see Bowen 1989; Bowen 1997.

32 The *Oxford English Dictionary* lists three different meanings of experience, one of which refers to "the state of having been occupied in any department of study or practice ...; [and] the aptitudes, skills, judgments, etc., thereby acquired." This is in contrast to experience understood as a form of consciousness or state of being. See Scott 1991 and Sharf 1998 for critiques of the use of the category of experience in a number of scholarly works to ground the analyst's epistemological authority.

33 A range of liberal thinkers, from Hobbes, to Rousseau, to Hume, to John Stuart Mill, take this disjunction to be central to their conception of individual and political freedom. In this view, the individual establishes agency and moral freedom by making contact with an inner voice, rather than responding to the will of others. For a review of classical liberal points of view on individual and political freedom, see Berlin 1969 and Christman 1991.

References

Appadurai, Arjun (1990) "Topographies of the Self: Praise and Emotion in Hindu India," in Catherine A. Lutz and Lila Abu-Lughod (eds) *Language and the Politics of Emotion*, Cambridge: Cambridge University Press.

Asad, Talal (1993) *Genealogies of Religion: Discipline and Reasons of Power in Christianity and Islam*, Baltimore, MD: Johns Hopkins Press.

Bell, Catherine M. (1992) *Ritual Theory, Ritual Practice*, New York: Oxford University Press.

Berlin, Isaiah (1969) *Four Essays on Liberty*, Oxford: Oxford University Press.

Bloch, Maurice E. (1974) "Symbols, Song, Dance and Features of Articulation: Is Religion an Extreme Form of Authority?," *Archives européennes de sociologie*, 15: 55–81.

——— (1975) *Political Language and Oratory in Traditional Society*, London and New York: Academic Press.

Bourdieu, Pierre (1977) *Outline of a Theory of Practice*, trans. Richard Nice, Cambridge: Cambridge University Press.

——— (1980) *The Logic of Practice*, trans. Richard Nice, Stanford, CA: Stanford University Press.

Bowen, John R. (1989) "*Salāt* in Indonesia: The Social Meanings of an Islamic Ritual," *Man*, 24: 600–619.

——— (1997) "Modern Intentions: Reshaping Subjectivities in an Indonesian Muslim Society," in Robert W. Hefner and Patricia Horvatich (eds) *Islam in an Era of Nation-States: Politics and Religious Renewal in Muslim Southeast Asia*, Honolulu, HI: University of Hawai'i Press.

Burke, Kenneth (1969) *A Rhetoric of Motives*, Berkeley, CA: University of California Press.

Cantwell, Robert (1999) "Habitus, Ethnomimesis: A Note on the Logic of Practice," *Journal of Folklore Research*, 36: 219–234.

Carruthers, Mary J. (1990) *The Book of Memory: A Study of Memory in Medieval Culture*, Cambridge: Cambridge University Press.

Christman, John (1991) "Liberalism and Individual Positive Freedom," *Ethics*, 101: 343–359.

Douglas, Mary (1973) *Natural Symbols: Explorations in Cosmology*, New York: Random House.

Eickelman, Dale F. (1992) "Mass Higher Education and the Religious Imagination in Contemporary Arab Societies," *American Ethnologist*, 19: 643–655.

Evans-Pritchard, Edward E. (1965) *Theories of Primitive Religion*, Oxford: Clarendon Press.

Fakhry, Majid (1983) *A History of Islamic Philosophy*, 2nd edn, New York: Columbia University Press.

Foucault, Michel (1988a) "Technologies of the Self," in Luther H. Martin, Huck Gutman and Patrick H. Hutton (eds) *Technologies of the Self: A Seminar with Michel Foucault*, Amherst, MA: University of Massachusetts Press.

——— (1988b) "The Political Technology of Individuals," in Luther H. Martin, Huck Gutman and Patrick H. Hutton (eds) *Technologies of the Self: A Seminar with Michel Foucault*, Amherst, MA: University of Massachusetts Press.

——— (1997) *Ethics: Subjectivity and Truth*, trans. Paul Rabinow, New York: The New Press.

Hilmi, Mona (1997) "Abdat al-Shaitan wa 'Abdat al-Siramik [Worship of the Devil and Worship of Ceramic]," *Ruz Al-Yusuf*, 3583: 80–81.

Hirschkind, Charles (2001a) "Civic Virtue and Religious Reason: An Islamic Counterpublic," *Cultural Anthropology*, 16: 3–34.

——— (2001b) "The Ethics of Listening: Cassette-Sermon Audition in Contemporary Egypt," *American Ethnologist*, 28: 623–649.

Hundert, Edward J. (1997) "The European Enlightenment and the History of the Self," in Roy Porter (ed.) *Rewriting the Self: Histories from the Renaissance to the Present*, New York: Routledge.

Inglis, John (1999) "Aquinas's Replication of the Acquired Moral Virtues: Rethinking the Standard Philosophical Interpretation of Moral Virtue in Aquinas," *Journal of Religious Ethics*, 27: 3–27.

Izutsu, Toshihiko (1966) *Ethico-Religious Concepts in the Quran*, rev. edn, Montreal: McGill University Press.

Kapferer, Bruce (1979) "Emotion and Feeling in Sinhalese Healing Rites," *Social Analysis*, 1: 153–176.

Keane, Webb (1997) "From Fetishism to Sincerity: On Agency, the Speaking Subject, and Their Historicity in the Context of Religious Conversion," *Comparative Studies in Society and History*, 39: 674–693.

——— (2000) "Sincerity, 'Modernity,' and the Protestants," Unpublished Manuscript, Department of Anthropology, University of Michigan.

Kleinman, Arthur (2004) "Bourdieu's Impact on the Anthropology of Suffering," *International Journal of Contemporary Sociology*, 33: 203–210.

Leach, Edmund R. (1964) *Political Systems of Highland Burma: A Study of Kachin Social Structure*, London: Athlone Press.

Lutz, Catherine, and Lila Abu-Lughod (1990) *Language and the Politics of Emotion*, Cambridge: Cambridge University Press.

Maharib, Ruqaiyya Bint Muhammad Ibn (1991) *Kayfa Taksh ana fi al-Salat [How to Feel Humility in Prayer]*, Cairo: Dar Al-'Ulum al Islamiyya.

Mahmood, Saba (2003) *Pious Transgressions: Embodied Disciplines of the Islamic Revival*, Princeton, NJ: Princeton University Press.

Malinowski, Bronislaw (1922) *Argonauts of the Western Pacific*, London: G. Routledge & Sons.

Mauss, Marcel (1979) *Sociology and Psychology: Essays*, trans. Ben Brewster, London: Routledge & Kegan Paul.

McKane, William (1962) *Al-Ghazali's Book of Fear and Hope*, Leiden: E.J. Brill.

McKeon, Richard P. (1987) *Rhetoric: Essays in Invention and Discovery*, Woodbridge: Ox Bow Press.

Moore, Sally F., and Barbara G. Myerhoff (ed.) (1977) *Secular Ritual*. Amsterdam: Van Gorcum.

Nawawi, Abu Zakarriya Yahya b. Sharaf, Muhyi al-Din (1990) *Sharh Matn al-Arba un al-Nawawiyya [Explication of the Text of Nawawai's Collection of Forty Prophetic Statements]*, Cairo: Dar al-Tauzi'a wa al-Nashr al-Islamiyya.

Nederman, Cary J. (1989) "Nature, Ethics, and the Doctrine of 'Habitus': Aristotelian Moral Psychology in the Twelfth Century," *Tradition*, 45: 87–110.

Obeyesekere, Gananath (1981) *Medusa's Hair: An Essay on Personal Symbols and Religious Experience*, Chicago, IL: University of Chicago Press.

Rabinow, Paul (1997) "Introduction," in Paul Rabinow and Robert Hurley (eds) *Michel Foucault: Ethics, Subjectivity and Truth*, New York: The New Press.

Radcliffe-Brown, Alfred R. (1964) *The Andaman Islanders*, New York: Free Press.

Rosaldo, Michelle Z. (1980) *Knowledge and Passion: Ilongot Notions of Self and Social Life*, Cambridge: Cambridge University Press.

Rose, Nikolas (1997) "Assembling the Modern Self," in Roy Porter (ed.) *Rewriting the Self: Histories from the Renaissance to the Present*, New York: Routledge.

Sabiq, Al Sayyid (1994) *Fiqh al-Sunna [The Jurisprudence of Tradition]*, Cairo: Maktabat al-Qahira.

Scheff, Thomas J. (1977) "The Distancing of Emotion in Ritual," *Current Anthropology*, 18: 483–505.

Scott, Joan W. (1991) "The Evidence of Experience," *Critical Inquiry*, 17: 773–797.

Scott, David (1994) *Formations of Ritual: Colonial and Anthropological Discourses on the Sinhala Yaktovil*, Minneapolis, MN: University of Minnesota Press.

Sharf, Robert (1998) "Experience," in Mark C. Taylor (ed.) *Critical Terms for Religious Studies*, Chicago: University of Chicago Press.

Starrett, Gregory (1995) "The Hexis of Interpretation: Islam and the Body in the Egyptian Popular School," *American Ethnologist*, 22: 953–969.

Tambiah, Stanley J. (1985) *Culture, Thought, and Social Action: An Anthropological Perspective*, Cambridge, MA: Harvard University Press.

Turner, Victor W. (1969) *The Ritual Process: Structure and Anti-Structure*, Chicago, IL: Routledge & Kegan Paul.

——— (1976) "Ritual, Tribal and Catholic," *Worship*, 50: 504–525.

Watt, W. Montgomery (1985) *Islamic Philosophy and Theology: An Extended Survey*, 2nd edn, Edinburgh: Edinburgh University Press.

Yanagisako, Sylvia J., and Carol L. Delaney (1995) *Naturalizing Power: Essays in Feminist Cultural Analysis*, New York: Routledge.

6 "Between belief and unbelief lies the performance of *salāt*"

Meaning and efficacy of a Muslim ritual

Heiko Henkel

Heiko Henkel earned his PhD in 2004 from Princeton University with his dissertation: "Pious Disciplines and Modern Lives: The Culture of Fiqh in the Turkish Islamic Tradition." He is currently associate professor of anthropology at the University of Copenhagen. Previously, Henkel taught at the University of British Columbia and Williams College. His research centers on Turkish Islamic Tradition in contemporary Germany and Turkey, Northern European social history and transformations of Western Europe and Turkey. Other topics include ritual, literacy and subject formation, security and the "good life" as well as the Western development of interventions. Henkel's current research analyzes the often acrimonious encounter of Islamic traditions with European liberal publics. His publications include "Rethinking the *Dar al-hab*: Social Change and Changing Perceptions of the Western Turkish Islam" (2004), "The Location of Islam: Inhabiting Istanbul in a Muslim Way" (2007), and "Fundamentally Danish: The Cartoon Affair as Transitional Drama" (2010). In this article below, Henkel debates on the meaning and practice of the *salāt* in Istanbul and analyzes his ethnographic account in light of contemporary theories of ritual. Based on his findings, he argues that the practice of *salāt* implies a commitment to the mainstream dogmas and interpretations of Islam.

Introduction

Among the many forms of religious practice performed by Muslims in Turkey, the *salāt*, the five-times-daily prayer (Turk. *namaz*), holds a special place. Not only is it seen by many religious Muslims as the single most important of the ritual obligations specified by the experts of Muslim *fiqh* (jurisprudence) but, together with the Muslim headscarf, it is also the most visible and perhaps most provocative aspect of everyday Muslim religious practice in Turkey. For my friend Ayşecan,[1] a middle-aged professional woman from Ankara and self-declared secularist, the prayer's dramatic gesture of submission is proof of Muslim fundamentalism, smacking of irrationality, intolerance, even violence, and the Arabic texts of the prayer and the *ezan* (call to prayer) sound to her foreign and archaic. Ayşecan's views are shared by many in Turkey and Europe, of course, who see in the insistence on the absolute truth of the Qur'ānic revelation, which is affirmed in the prayer, a commitment inherently at odds with liberal society.

To view the prayer as an archaic fixture of an outdated tradition is, however, to overlook its role in the dynamic landscape of religious commitment in contemporary Turkey. In recent decades an explicitly religious (*dindar*) middle class has increasingly been integrated into mainstream Turkish society, religious women have become active players in its institutions and public sphere, and Turkish Islam has embraced the language of human rights and liberal concepts of society. The most tangible aspect of this transformation is the triumph of the post-Islamist Justice and Development Party (AKP), which won a landslide victory in the 2002 elections with a platform combining commitment to its roots in the Islamic tradition with a program of political liberalization and the quest for EU accession.[2] These changes have occurred, this article will propose, with the aid of the *salāt*, which inserts a fixed point of reference into the diverse and changing lifeworlds of religious Muslims.

[...] In her recent study of the Islamist movement in Istanbul, for instance, Jenny White notes that

> [w]hat binds people together in the Islamist movement is neither ideology (be it political or religious) nor any particular type of organization (whether civil society or "tribe"). Rather, the movement is rooted in local culture and interpersonal relations, while also drawing on a variety of civic and political organizations and ideologies.
>
> (White 2002: 6)

White's observation is in many ways compelling and backed by her subtle and persuasive ethnographic study which shows the complex interrelatedness of a cultural heritage, the sometimes shared and sometimes distinct experiences of groups and individuals, and the particular political processes that have shaped Turkish society over the past decades. Yet it seems to me that she is missing an important aspect in her account. Much of the Turkish Muslim movement's appeal, and certainly much of its social and political relevance, stems from the fact that, by tying its diverse projects and the lives of Muslim practitioners into the wider framework of the Islamic tradition, it transcends "local culture and interpersonal relations." Through this association, it provides followers with the means of inserting their lives into meaningful narratives of a common history and cosmology and of a fate ultimately shared by a universal Muslim community. Muslim ritual, this article suggests, has been an enormously important resource for Muslim practitioners in facilitating the generation of community and continuity despite enormous social change.

In his long-neglected study *On Prayer*, Marcel Mauss observes that while the meaning of other forms of religious practice often remains opaque, "every prayer is always to some extent a *Credo* [and thus] a single prayer contains several elements of self-justification, often clearly expressed" (Mauss 2003: 22). This deliberate conjuncture of action and speech, he argues, makes prayer especially interesting as a social phenomenon as it sheds "some light on the very controversial question of the relationship between myth and ritual" (Mauss 2003: 23). [...] For the purpose of this article, Mauss' observation can thus be reformulated, admittedly with slightly different implications, as the relationship between the particular discursive tradition of Islam (Asad 1986; Asad 1993) and the highly choreographed bodily discipline of the prayer.[3]

Saba Mahmood has shown for the case of an Egyptian female piety movement that the *salāt* plays an important role in a project of "self-shaping" among Muslim practitioners (Mahmood 2001). By submitting to the discipline of *salāt*, practitioners seek to generate and maintain their capacity to submit willingly to what they see as the guidance offered by the Qur'ān. As for Mahmood's interlocutors in Egypt, for many Turkish Muslims the *salāt* is an important body technique (Mauss 1992) through which they aim to generate and maintain their commitment to the Islamic tradition. For my Turkish interlocutors, however, and I suspect for Mahmood's as indeed for Muslim practitioners elsewhere, this aspect of the *salāt* is embedded in a much wider project of generating what Turkish Muslim scholars call *İslam ahlâkı*, a term that refers both to the normative framework of proper personal conduct and to its embodiment as a stable disposition (see Karaman, Bardakoğlu, and Apaydın 2000: II, 426). Complementary to these efforts are projects of "Islamicizing" modern society (*çağı islamlaştırmak*[4]), which have taken a central part in Turkey's Muslim revival movement, and which aim at shaping ideally the entirety of the practitioner's lifeworld according to criteria derived from the Islamic tradition. [...]

Given the heterogeneity of contemporary Turkish society and the diversity of interpretative traditions within Turkish Islam, however, these projects of constructing tightly integrated lifeworlds based on particular Muslim interpretations of Islam have a paradoxical effect: as groups and individuals seek to develop the most adequate interpretations and forms of life, the ensuing diversity fractures the Islamic tradition and the Muslim community. At the same time, religious Muslims generally attribute tremendous importance to the unity of the Muslim community, corresponding to the notion of one definite path for achieving a moral life outlined in the Qur'ān. The centrifugal effects of these diverse social projects are thus seen as a major challenge. The significance of the *salāt*, I suggest, lies primarily in addressing this challenge.[5]

Taking as axiomatic that practice, especially if systematically integrated into more encompassing forms of life, shapes the practitioner over time, this article suggests that the prayer is part of a matrix of disciplines and institutions in which Muslim forms of subjectivity and social relations are forged and reproduced. [...] My point is simply that the *salāt* inserts a sequence of practice into everyday life, prompting practitioners to assert and enact belief (*imān*) as the unequivocal commitment to Islam while at the same time enabling both changing interpretations of the Islamic tradition and the affirmation of Muslim community across different interpretations of Islam. The Muslim ritual of *salāt* is thus important for the reproduction of a particular collective representation, but not necessarily in the form of a shared classificatory system, an ideology, or common projects of political and social reform. In contemporary Turkish society, and indeed at other times of great social change, the *salāt*'s most important aspect may thus be its capacity to generate and signal the commitment of practitioners to a shared framework of moral reasoning across social dividing lines. In this sense, as Michael Lambek has suggested of ritual more generally, the *salāt* "provides occasion for the unreserved assumption of responsibility and obligation in which agents, without distinction between the virtuous and the incontinent, acknowledge their agency and commit themselves to bearing responsibility for their actions" (Lambek 2000: 317).

Diversity and community

The following episode shows the pertinence of Lambek's observation for the *salāt*'s role in contemporary Turkey. In the spring of 2001, my friend Hakan invited me to spend the evening with him and a couple of friends. We met at Hakan's parents-in-law's apartment in the neighborhood of Ümraniye, where we ate dinner and watched some television with the family. At about eight o'clock, Hakan, his wife Emine, and I walked the short distance to their own apartment, leaving their small children at Emine's parents' house. When the guests, two married couples, arrived, Emine and the two women retired to one of the apartment's living rooms, where they remained for the rest of the evening. Looking at his watch, Hakan asked his guests, Hüsameddin, a lecturer in history at one of Istanbul's new private universities, and Şahin, an economist, if they had already performed the evening *salāt*. They had not, and so the three men retreated to the bathroom for the ablutions and then to one of the bedrooms of the apartment for the prayer. After a few minutes the three men joined me in the second living room. Given that Hakan had decided to retreat to another room for the prayer, I did not witness the *salāt* that evening. I saw it performed on many other occasions, however, and I will turn to the format of the prayer in a moment. Before I do that, let me return to the evening at Hakan's house.

Note the configuration in which Hakan and Emine entertained their guests that evening. Like many secular Turkish couples of their generation, they invited other couples to their apartment for an evening of informal socializing. Yet the separate socializing of women and men gave the evening a particular *dindar* (religious) Muslim character. This creation of homo-social spaces is a prominent element of urban, conservative Islam (Olson 1982). It is in an important way a form of religious practice, given that it enacts regulations of the *sharia* as interpreted by mainstream Muslim scholars in Turkey (Henkel 2007). In contrast to the performance of *salāt*, however, the enactment of *muamelat* ("social duties") and *sunna* practices (emulating the Prophet's way of life) remains mostly implicit. [...]

What [...] is the role of the *salāt*? The prayer clearly created neither instant solidarity nor a shared worldview among practitioners that evening. Furthermore my interlocutors' commitment to the Islamic tradition clearly does not explain everything about the way this evening unfolded. It is not more than one aspect of the evening, albeit an important one. What is interesting about my interlocutors' implicit and explicit references to Islam, however, is that they refer at once to diverse social projects and to a shared discursive framework, the Islamic tradition. This framework is shared not only by Turkish Muslims, of course, but by religious Muslims all over the world, and is interpreted and appropriated in different ways. The particularity of this social relation is inadequately described either as a culture or as a civilization or an ideology. It is that of a shared religious tradition, produced and reproduced by the continuing reference to the founding texts of the Qur'ān and the *hadith* (the transmitted reports of the Prophet's exemplary life, see Asad 1986: 14). As the conversation sketched above shows, the three young men clearly share neither a coherent ideology nor an organization, and their ways of life are shaped by a multitude of heterogeneous institutions, disciplines, and social networks.

Nonetheless, they are united in a shared, although normally unstated, commitment. It is here, in defining, reaffirming, and making explicit this shared commitment of Muslim practitioners to the precepts of the Islamic tradition that the *salāt* provides these practitioners with a powerful resource. In the episode sketched above, as on innumerable other occasions, it inserts this explicit and sharply defined commitment to Islam into the flow of social practice. For a variety of reasons this is no small matter. For one, it draws a clear-cut division between those who did and did not commit themselves to Islam in the prayer. Secondly, the commitment to Islam contained in the *salāt* takes place notwithstanding Şahin and Hüsameddin's differences. While it did little to ameliorate their quarrel, it inserted a shared commitment to a discursive framework, and, as Lambek notes, to a horizon of responsibility. There is yet another aspect. On another occasion Hakan had confided to me that he and a number of friends were worried because they suspected that Şahin, who had recently returned from serving his obligatory term in the Jandarma (Turkey's paramilitary police force), had become somewhat lax in his religious commitment. Hakan had added that he hoped that the influence of his friends would again strengthen this commitment. Initializing the communal *salāt* that evening, Hakan may thus also have hoped that it had a "therapeutic," indeed disciplining, effect on Şahin. Incidentally, the *salāt* may have played a somewhat similar role that evening in Hakan's relationship to Hüsameddin. Like others of my religious acquaintance outside the Islamist party, Hakan was suspicious of the real level of religious commitments among the Virtue Party's cadres. Performing the communal prayer may not altogether quell such suspicions but it introduces an objective criterion for assessing virtue (see MacIntyre 1980) as it marks the dividing line between believers (*müminin*) and others.

The choreography of prayer

The *salāt* is a highly formalized prayer, consisting of a number of clearly defined components. The four universally recognized juridical schools of *sunni* Islam (*madhabs*) differ slightly in their definition of the correct performance of the *salāt*, and within the Hanafi *madhab* (which is followed by the great majority of Turkish *sunni* Muslims) there are slight differences in the performance as it is prescribed for men and women. Strictly speaking there are, of course, also nuances in the performance that vary between one person and another and even from one performance to another. It seems to me, however, that within the Turkish context these are minor and often unintended differences. The large majority of practitioners assume that they follow universally accepted guidelines, readily available in the Turkish *ilmihal* literature, the Muslim "catechisms,"[6] as closely as possible.

The remarkable stability of the *salāt*'s format in contemporary Turkey (and to a lesser extent across Muslim communities worldwide, see Parkin and Headley 2000) can partly be explained by the historical commitment of most Turkish *sunni* Muslim communities and scholars to the Hanafi *madhab.*[7] A different, albeit related, factor is the joint endeavor of the religious establishment and the Ottoman/Turkish state since the late nineteenth century to purify and systematize the ritual practice of Turkish Muslims as part of a wider project of creating an "educated" population (Deringil 1998: 96).[8] Various motives and institutions thus converge here in their endeavor to maintain a ritual format that transcends local particularities. More pronounced are differences in the regularity of the *salāt* and the precise *modus* in which it is performed. [. . .] Given the political sensitivity of religious issues in Turkey, no statistical data are available to indicate the actual level of the *salāt*'s performance,[9] but my guess is that about one quarter of Turkish Muslims perform the ritual regularly, and a good deal more do so irregularly.

Each of the five-times-daily prayers consists of a number of prayer-cycles (*rekâts*), which in turn consist of a sequence of stations. The night *salāt*, which Hakan and his friends performed on the evening described above, has four obligatory (*farz*) and six recommended (*sünnet*) cycles. In its basic form, each prayer-session, despite its intricate format, takes just a few minutes to perform for those accustomed to its practice. However, practitioners can expand the prayer-session by additional prayer-cycles or by adding a more personalized prayer (*dua*). During one daily sequence of the five obligatory prayer-sessions, practicing Muslims like Hakan and his friends perform at least seventeen cycles and may complete the recommended thirty-eight prayer-cycles or more. The time-slot in which the night *salāt* is valid—each of the five prayers has a precisely defined window of time when it has to be performed—is defined as the time between the disappearance of the evening sky's redness and the "true dawn," which signals the onset of the morning *salāt*. Prayer times thus change with the cycle of the seasons and with geographical location. The exact beginnings and endings of the five slots in which each of the prayers has to be performed are meticulously calculated by religious scholars (although results may vary by a few minutes) and published daily in the religiously-minded newspapers and on Islamic websites. In 2001, a small, Windows-compatible computer program, not only showing the prayer times for that particular day at a particular location but also counting-down the remaining minutes for the current prayer slot, was widely distributed among those of my interlocutors who used the computer.

Table 1 Time-slots for the five obligatory salāt performances.

Morning Prayer	*Sunrise*	*Noon Prayer*	*Afternoon Prayer*	*Evening Prayer*	*Night Prayer*
from 4:23 until just before →	6:04 no prayer from sunrise until →	from 12:11 until just before →	from 16:29 until just before →	from 16:29 until just before →	from 19:44 until just before Morning Prayer

Table 1 shows the prayer times for 22 March 2001, as published by the Turkish Directorate for Religious Affairs. The time-slots begin at the times given and end just before the following time-slot begins. The communal prayer in mosques commences normally at the beginning of the prayer times; those who come late perform the prayer individually at the back.

The prayer times are distributed over the course of the day, creating a recurring, albeit gradually changing, pattern in each day. This pattern inserts the prayer's performance into the different spheres of life that the practitioner traverses during a day and in the course of his or her life (the home, the workspace, travel, or, as in my example, time spent socializing). With it comes the opportunity, in fact the obligation, to assert Muslim community in many different social settings. The steeply rising number of mosques in Istanbul (from 1984 to 2003 the number of mosques rose from 1,471 to 2,562)[10] provides a public and highly visible infrastructure for this—at least for male practitioners, given that in Turkey women generally do not use mosques to perform the *salāt.* The obligatory performance of the *salāt,* however, also poses the challenge of performing the prayer in indifferent or even hostile settings such as, for instance, many workplaces. Many of my interlocutors mentioned this as the main reason to seek employment with explicitly religious employers.

Despite the posting of prayer times in the media, the traditional call to prayer (the *ezan*) is still important in Turkey. From the mosques a *muezzin* announces the beginning of each prayer time by singing *ezan* in a stylized manner which, fortified by sound systems of varying aptitude and quality, renders it widely audible across town. With the exception of a brief period in the early Republic, the "cantillation" (Özdemir and Frank 2000: 110) of the *ezan* has always been in Arabic in Turkey. The main themes of the prayer are already introduced in the *ezan*: the affirmation of God's magnificence and singularity, and the truth of the revelation received by Muhammad. Below, the *ezan* is given in its Turkish transliteration of the Arabic original in the left column and in English translation on the right.[11]

Before being able to perform the *salāt,* the practitioner has to be in a state of ritual purity. The ritual cleaning preceding the *salāt* (the *abdest*) is in itself a painstakingly detailed procedure consisting of an elaborate but partial cleaning of the body's extremities (Headley 2000). After the ablution, the practitioner finds a ritually clean space (for instance in a mosque) or produces one with a prayer rug or simply a piece of newspaper, and turns in the direction of Mecca, the geographical centre of Islam. Women wear a headscarf, and some male practitioners wear a prayer cap, to show their particular devotion. At the outset of the *salāt,* the practitioner is required to state his or her intent (*niyet*) to perform the particular prayer: for example, the obligatory morning prayer and two additional recommended *rekâts.* As Muslim scholars point out, the formulation of the practitioner's intent links the physical act of the prayer to the conscious intent of the practitioner.

The prayer itself begins with the *tekbir*, the ubiquitous formula *allâhü ekber*—"God is magnificent"—that frames each of the subsequent stations of the prayer. In the first station,

The Muslim call to prayer

Allâhü ekber	God is magnificent
Allâhü ekber	God is magnificent
Allâhü ekber	God is magnificent
Allâhü ekber	God is magnificent
Eşhedü en lâ ilâhe illallâh *Eşhedü en lâ ilâhe illallâh*	I know and affirm without doubt: there is no god but God (twice)
Eşhedü enne Muhammeden Resûlullah *Eşhedü enne Muhammeden Resûlullah*	I know and affirm without doubt: Muhammad is God's messenger (twice)
Hayye ale's-salâh	Come, to the salāt
Hayye ale's-salâh	Come, to the salāt
Hayye ale'l-felâh	Come, to work
Hayye ale'l-felâh	Come, to work
Allâhü ekber	God is magnificent
Allâhü ekber	God is magnificent
Lâ ilâhe illallâh	There is no god but God

the *kıyam*, the practitioner recites a sequence of partly fixed, partly variable prayer formulas and verses from the Qur'ān (the *sübhâneke*, the *eûzü-besmele*, the *fatiha surah*, and then a shorter *surah* or a few verses from the Qur'ān). Like all other recitations during the prayer, these are recited silently in Qur'ānic Arabic by moving tongue and lips but without actually voicing.[12] The use of Arabic is important because it provides Muslim practitioners with a universal language, similar to the role played until recently by Latin in the Roman Catholic Church. Unlike Latin in the Christian tradition, however, Arabic is seen as the language in which God revealed the Qur'ān to Muhammad. Given the Qur'ān's status as God's unadulterated message and the fundamental significance given to the very wording of this revelation, renditions of Qur'ānic verses into other languages always remain problematic. Thus, while local translations and understandings may vary, the Arabic *Urtext* remains the principal referent.[13] The sübhâneke can be rendered into English as follows:

> My God! I declare that you are free of any shortcomings. I praise and glorify you. Your name is exalted. Your existence is above everything. Your exaltation is glorious. There is no god apart from you.

Then a verse called the *eûzü-besmele* is recited:

> I seek protection in God from the accursed Satan. In the name of God, the all-Merciful, the all-Compassionate.

This is followed by the *fatiha*, the Qur'ān's famous opening Surah:

> In the name of God, the Beneficent, the Merciful.

> Praise be to God, Master of the Day of Judgment,
> the Cherisher and Sustainer of the Worlds;
> We serve only you, and we ask only you for help
> Show us the straight path, the path of those that are blessed,
> and not that of those who accrue God's wrath and who go astray.
> Amen.

A short section from the Qur'ān is then recited, for example, Surah 112, *el-İhlâs*:

> In the name of God, the Merciful, the Benevolent!
> Say: He is God, the One.
> The everlasting God.
> He neither procreates nor is He created.
> Nothing is like Him.

This concludes the prayer's first station.

In the second station of the *salāt*, the *rükû*, the practitioner is still standing but now bows the upper body until it reaches a horizontal position. The hands are placed on the knees, and in this position, after a *tekbir*, a series of short formulas is recited.

> My God, you are almighty and perfect. (Repeated three to seven times)
> God listens to those who praise Him.
> Our Lord, praise be only to you.
> God is magnificent.

The worshipper then rises again to an upright position, and from there enters into the two prostrations (the third and fourth station of this *rekât*). In these prostrations the practitioner drops to his or her knees and bends the upper body down so that nose and forehead touch the ground. The open hands are placed on the ground right beside the head. In this position the practitioner recites further praise of God. Between the first and the second prostration the worshipper sits upright for a short while to collect his or her thoughts. With the second prostration the first *rekât* of the night prayer is concluded. It is followed by three further obligatory (*farz*) cycles, slightly different from the first. These four *rekât*s can be preceded by four recommended (*sünnet*) cycles and followed by an additional two. Like all other *salāt* performances, the night prayer ends with a greeting over the right and left shoulders. The prayer can be extended by adding a *dua* (a more individualized prayer) and/or the *tesbihat*, the meditative repetition of certain formulas in praise of God (*zikir*), in which the *tesbih* (a chain with beads, not unlike the Christian rosary) is used to keep track of the number of recitations. The prayer-session ends when the practitioner rises to his or her feet again.

The ritual process

As this sketch of the night prayer shows, its message could hardly be more explicit and straightforward: the practitioner affirms his or her commitment to the truth of the Qur'ānic revelation and submission to the command of God. This invocation is made in Arabic, in which few Turkish practitioners are fluent, but translations of the Arabic original are well known and everywhere available. The prayer, however, does more than simply affirm the practitioner's commitment to Islam; it is an invocation of central concepts of the Islamic tradition (more precisely of Islamic *akaid* or "dogma"), such as the perfection, exaltation, mercy, and all-powerfulness of God. Parts of the prayer's verses are taken directly from the Qur'ān, and the only real variant in the prayer's rigid format is the practitioner's (or prayer leader's) choice of a suitable passage of the Qur'ān after the recitation of the *fatiha*. Numerous of God's "beautiful names" are evoked (the Merciful, the Benevolent) and the practitioner pleads for God's protection against "the accursed Satan." The prayer's recitation is paralleled by the bodily movements of the practitioner; the ritual cleansing of the body, the careful preparation of the prayer space, the direction of the body toward Mecca, the solemn standing at the outset of the prayer, the bowing toward Mecca, and, most dramatically, the multiple prostrations of the *salāt* all enact and emphasize the spoken affirmation of submission and alliance.

The linguistic and non-linguistic elements of the prayer form part of the minutely choreographed ritual process that creates a ritual sphere with a clearly demarcated interior. Entry into this time-space requires from the candidate-practitioner the fulfillment of a rigid set of preconditions for which prayer manuals provide long lists. These are conditions that have to be met before the practitioner is allowed to enter the *salāt*, as well as lists with things that invalidate (*bozmak*, lit. "destroy") the *salāt*. Fulfillment of these preconditions not only prepares the practitioner for the performance of the *salāt* and orientates him or her toward the geographic center of the Muslim community within a particular temporal matrix; it also ties the practitioner into a wider regime of care for the body and the soul. The rigid boundaries of the ritual time-space of the *salāt*, however, are not only visible in the elaborate entry procedures. Once within the ritual time-space the practitioner must not abort the *salāt* prematurely or leave it by way of distraction until it is concluded. It must not be entered by anyone not properly prepared. As Humphrey and Laidlaw suggest for the Jain *puja* ritual, in the *salāt* the practitioner steps into the bodily discipline of a ritual which he or she cannot alter; components may be varied, but the whole must be performed in accordance with a minutely prescribed format (Humphrey and Laidlaw 1994: 260). Thus the *salāt* is not simply a homogenous time-space but one which obliges the practitioner to traverse it in a particular way; in this sense it is akin to a *parcours* that can only be successfully traversed in one correct mode.

The immediate effect of the ritual process of the *salāt* is that the practitioner temporarily turns any office, any living room, any street-corner, into a mosque as well as any office-clerk into a Muslim. This is not to say, however, that the *salāt* works wonders. What it seeks to ensure is that, in the clearly demarcated time-space of the prayer, a person becomes a Muslim practitioner and ceases to be an office-clerk just as the office-corner is transformed temporarily into a mosque. At least five times a day practitioners become essentially Muslims while the secular and heterogeneously constituted spaces of the lifeworld are re-defined as Muslim spaces.

Within these demarcations the *salāt* is a space of Islamic practice, clearly defined, spatially and temporally bounded, and set apart from everyday activity. This separation calls to mind the break—the establishment of a radical duality between the profanity of everyday life and the domain of the sacred (Durkheim 1995: 39)—that Durkheim saw as constitutive of ritual. In the case of the *salāt*, however, the sacred-profane dualism is somewhat misleading. Neither is the time-space of the *salāt* itself sacred (a destroyed *salāt* is not seen as a sacrilege but simply as an invalid *salāt* which thus has to be repeated) nor is the world outside of it necessarily profane. The *salāt* introduces a break between the flow of everyday life (characterized by a variety of different kinds of social disciplines, Muslim and other) and a time-space ideally characterized by pure Islamic practice. In this sense the rigidly controlled boundary surrounding the *salāt* demarcates a sphere—and thus a context—in which the practice of the *salāt* is embedded. Once there has been a transgression of this boundary that sets off this context from the world in which it is inserted, the *salāt* is by definition invalid and has to be repeated. In other words, the context established by the elaborate arrangements surrounding the prayer may not be infringed upon by the immediate social context. When the boundary is upheld, and the practitioner has fulfilled the manifold conditions thus required, the *salāt* is not simply a particular kind of practice that is inserted into the flow of everyday life but a practice that provides its own context.

It is undoubtedly the case, as John R. Bowen has noted in his discussion of the *salāt* in Indonesia, that individual performances of the *salāt* take place within different social settings and, more to the point, in the context of particular religio-political projects (Bowen 1989). These contexts shape the way the prayer is understood by practitioners as well as observers, and sometimes even change aspects of the prayer's format. However, the "social meaning" of the prayer is not, as Bowen suggests, entirely defined by this social context. Rather, by distancing the enunciation of the prayer formulas from its immediate social context and by seeking to integrate each individual performance into an elaborately evoked discursive context of Islam, the ritual of *salāt* responds to the fact that Muslim practitioners interpret the Islamic tradition within different and changing social contexts—a diversification which, of course, continuously threatens to undermine the unity of Islam as a coherent discursive framework. Bowen's argument rests on his assertion that "[t]he *salāt* is not structured around an intrinsic propositional or semantic core. It cannot be 'decoded' semantically because it is not designed according to a single symbolic or iconic code" (Bowen 1989: 615). In contrast, I find it difficult to imagine any practice more clearly structured "around an intrinsic propositional or semantic core" than the *salāt*. Nevertheless, Bowen is certainly right to point out that the meaning of utterances (even apparently straightforward ones) is not strictly speaking inherent in the text of such an utterance (inherent, in other words, in the signifier) but depends upon the way in which it is understood, both by the person making the utterance and by the listener. Again, however, what the ritual of *salāt* does is to offer a sophisticated response to precisely this predicament of human existence by providing a minutely choreographed body technique by which a particular, sharply delineated message can be inserted into the most diverse social contexts and made as unambiguous as possible.

Bowen's argument concerning the *salāt* is mirrored more broadly in the conceptualization of ritual in the anti-Durkheimian current of British anthropology, suspicious of claims that the significance of ritual lies in its reinforcement of collective representations. Caroline Humphrey and James Laidlaw's *The Archetypal Actions of Ritual*, which focuses on Jain ritual but seeks to develop a general theory of ritual practice, is an eloquent example of this current (Humphrey and Laidlaw 1994). Citing with approval Bowen's study of the *salāt*, the authors suggest that Jain ritual—and indeed ritual in general—has no underlying meaning and thus must not be seen as a social technique stabilizing a particular classificatory system (Humphrey and Laidlaw 1994: 81). It is, they suggest, only in a further act, unrelated to the ritual itself, that practitioners give meaning to the rituals they perform (Humphrey and Laidlaw 1994: 260). As a general proposition, this is not very persuasive given that a central aspect of the prayer's importance and effectiveness is its ability to address religious Muslims as it engages them in a pledge of alliance and submission. Humphrey and Laidlaw nevertheless have a point when they assert that the particular format of ritual makes it impossible for religious authorities to define any particular interpretation of the ritual; indeed, the meaning of the *salāt* cannot be defined entirely by any one of the Muslim *cemaats* with their diverse interpretation of Islam. However much the practice of *salāt* is integrated into these local

Muslim projects, the rigid and universal format of the *salāt* inevitably refers beyond any particular interpretation of Islam to a more widely shared discursive framework.

Louis Althusser pointed out that the interlocutory force of addressing individuals, or, in his terms, the power to interpellate, is the necessary condition for the transmission of ideology (Althusser 1971). Althusser rightly saw ritual (in his case the rituals of the Roman Catholic Church) as a particularly effective form of such interpellation. With regard to the transmission of "ideology" it is, however, necessary to make a crucial distinction. The *salāt*, like other forms of prayer, can become part of particular political projects and specific occasions, like political rallies. Indeed, the sermons read as part of the communal Friday prayer in Turkey are centrally composed by Turkey's Directorate of Religious Affairs (Kara 1985; Prätor 1985). The performance of the *salāt* may support these projects, mobilize their supporters, and "transmit" particular messages but, to the extent that the *salāt* maintains its rigid and virtually universal format, it transcends these specific projects by confirming the practitioners' commitment to what I called the fundamental concepts of the Islamic tradition—the existence of God and the truth of the Qur'ānic revelation. In this sense, the *salāt* "serve[s] to contain the drift of meanings," to use Douglas and Isherwood's formulation (Douglas and Isherwood 1996: 43).

[…] [T]he richness of the *salāt* does not lie in a complex symbolism; its main message, as we have seen, is unequivocal and straightforward. While the *salāt* may not, however, be particularly rich in symbolism (even its main dramatic gesture, the repeated prostration, is indexical rather than symbolical), it is ripe with references to fundamental concepts of Islam, most centrally to God's unity, magnificence, and absolute authority. The *salāt* thus affirms the absolutely fixed point of the Islamic tradition—the fundamental truth of the existence of God and his revelation. […] It is this fundamental concept at the centre of the Islamic tradition that practitioners are prompted dramatically to reaffirm in the five-times-daily practice of the *salāt*. […]

"Between belief and unbelief lies the performance of salāt"

My argument so far has been that the *salāt* provides a protected space in which practitioners first disengage with their immediate social context and then engage with and commit to the foundational concepts of the Islamic tradition. I have argued that this stylized commitment is not bound to any particular interpretation of Islam. It is now time to modify this proposition. When asked about the significance of the *salāt*, my Turkish interlocutors often told me that the *salāt* helped them to strengthen their belief (*imān*). Their explanation resonates with the often quoted saying, attributed to the Prophet, that "between belief and unbelief lies the performance of *salāt*." However, if it is the aim of the *salāt* to signal and strengthen "belief," what exactly does belief mean in this context? One important aspect of the *salāt* is surely, as Mahmood notes, its role as a Muslim discipline or self-discipline which, through continuing practice, shapes certain dispositions of religious Muslims (Mahmood 2001: 828).[14] As such, the *salāt* is part of particular social projects of Muslim communities or movements and, at the same time, constitutes a central part of a much more widely recognized matrix of instituted practices that define a transnational Muslim community. The practice of *salāt*, however, has another, more immediate effect, which is also reflected in the saying cited above. By affirming and defining the practitioner's "belief," the *salāt* establishes a web of social relations mediated by commitment to a shared discursive framework. […]

The concept of belief, as it is elaborated in the *ilmihal*, thus has two poles which are in constant dynamic relation. At one pole, belief (*imān*) pertains to the unreserved commitment to the divine rules laid out in the Qur'ān and the *sunna* of the Prophet as interpreted by Muslim scholars and ideally encompassing and shaping the entirety of the believer's existence. In practice, however, such total belief is problematic in at least two ways: firstly, as most religious Muslims are well aware, given the constraints of an imperfect world a life fully determined by Muslim piety is scarcely ever achieved; and, secondly, it is hardly possible for a large community to agree upon which shape this total commitment should take given the famously opaque aspects of the Qur'ānic revelation. The other pole of *imān* is thus much more abstract and simultaneously much more specific in its commitment to believing in God and accepting the Qur'ān as the revealed word of God. In contrast to its opposite pole, this is a limited, unambiguous, and very sharply defined commitment, and one that is easy to fulfill. Formally, a single utterance of the *şehadet kelimesi* gives access to the community of Muslims. These two poles of belief are closely related and constantly refer to each other. On the one hand, submission to God's command, even in its most abstract form, always refers beyond the act of submission in that the Qur'ān urges readers to shape their lives and society according to its precepts so as to achieve redemption and avoid God's wrath in the afterlife. This is notwithstanding the fact that these precepts can only be deduced from the Qur'ān by way of interpretation. On the other hand, the myriad ways in which Muslims interpret these precepts to shape their lives according to God's commands always refer back to the other pole, the practitioner's submission to God's authority.

[...] Apart from its role in the arduous, ill-defined, and never fully achieved projects of generating Muslim subjectivity (*İslam ahlâkı*), the *salāt* offers practitioners the opportunity to enact their membership in the Muslim community in an immediate and unambiguous way.

This Muslim concept of belief does not exist in a vacuum, of course, and its significance greatly depends upon the social context in which it is evoked. [...]

Since the 1970s, the strongly hegemonic position of the Turkish state and its Kemalist legacy has considerably weakened and, with far-reaching reforms under the stewardship of Turgut Özal, Turkish politics has taken a distinctly neo-liberal turn (Keyder 1987; Öniş 1991; Yavuz 1997). As in the earlier authoritarian era, the liberal turn is embraced by secularists and religious Muslims alike. In this new era, the classification as *mümin* is still crucial for religious Muslims like Hakan and his friends but its significance is changing. As religious Muslims have moved from the periphery into the center of Turkish society, they increasingly share economic interests and consumer patterns, workplaces and neighborhoods, middle-class life-styles and sensibilities with their secularist peers. In this context, the *salāt* gains particular significance as it offers a highly mobile body technique with which the particular social relationship between practitioners can be affirmed and the individual's disposition as believer can be shaped within the heterogeneous lifeworlds of contemporary Turkey.

Conclusion

Although I disagree with my friend Ayşecan in her assessment of the *salāt* as irrational and archaic, I can hardly quarrel with her over the fact that she feels provoked by it. It is, after all, a practice that marks commitment not only to the central dogmas of mainstream interpretations of Islam in Turkey and to the revealed nature of the Qur'ān but also to social projects to which she feels strongly opposed. Moreover, the *salāt* generates forms of solidarity from which she is explicitly excluded. As a secularist Muslim, she feels, not altogether unreasonably, that her way of being a Muslim is challenged by the performance of *salāt*. But what the *salāt* does not do, and this is what I hope to convince my friend of, is to commit practitioners to any particular political project or interpretation, say, of the place of women in society. On the contrary, the enacted commitment to a sharply defined consensus offered by the performance of *salāt* enables religious Muslims to experiment with new interpretations of Islam and new ways of life without abandoning the shared discursive framework of a community of believers. At the same time that the *salāt* provides a powerful resource, however, it also poses a considerable challenge to religious Muslims in calling upon them to organize their lives in such a way that the propositions of the *salāt* remain meaningful. The *salāt* itself is not enough to maintain these conditions. The context in which the revealedness and absolute truth of the Qur'ān remain a convincing proposition is created by a much more encompassing project of inserting Muslim institutions and practices into modern lives. So far, Turkish religious Muslims seem to be very successful in this project.

Notes

1 I have used pseudonyms for all my Turkish interlocutors.

2 The Justice and Development Party (AKP), which emerged in 2001 from the reformist wing of Turkey's banned Islamist Virtue Party (FP), won 34.1 per cent of the vote. The 10 per cent threshold for entering parliament meant that the party gained a dominating majority of seats, eclipsing the presence of Turkey's entire political establishment in parliament. Ironically, another regenerated classic of Turkish politics, the post-Kemalist People's Republican Party (CHP), re-entered parliament as the sole opposition party.

3 One of the limitations of Mauss's brilliant exposé is that, like many subsequent anthropologists, he saw prayer, like ritual in general, as "above all a means of acting upon sacred beings" (Mauss 2003: 56). The realm of efficacy is thus very limited. If we couple Mauss's insights on the important role of prayer with another of his brilliant insights, the importance of "body techniques" (Mauss 1992) in shaping and socializing individual bodies, the realm of efficacy is considerably expanded.

4 The phrase is taken from an editorial of the journal *İslam* by Seyfi Say 1997. It is a pun on the secularist use of the term *çağdaş* (contemporary), implying a presence that has overcome its outdated and unenlightened religious past. *Çağı islamlaştırmak* is thus a contradiction in terms within this view, although not for the editors of *İslam*.

5 David Parkin and Stephen Headley's edited volume *Islamic prayer across the Indian Ocean: inside and outside the mosque* addresses some of the issues addressed in this article (Parkin and Headley 2000). Headley's afterword especially provides a stimulating and rich comment on the significance of the *salāt* (Headley 2000) The main conceptual axis around which the volume is organized, the dualism of "inside and outside the mosque," is much less prominent in Turkey than "across the Indian Ocean."

6 The Muslim *ilmihals* are somewhat similar to Christian catechisms in that they compile what are seen as the most central tenets of Islam and of proper Muslim conduct. These descriptions of correct Muslim practice are today available from a variety of sources (written by Turkish scholars or translated from the Arabic). In the Ottoman/Turkish context, *ilmihals* became widely distributed in the later nineteenth century as part of an attempt to regulate popular Muslim practices (Kelpetin 2000).

7 The Qur'ān already mentions *salāt* (a term used for prayer in Arabic even before the ascent of Islam) but does not offer a systematic description. The two major Bukhari and Muslim *hadith* collections, compiled in the ninth century CE, transmit a great number of comments attributed to the Prophet concerning the importance and the right performance of *salāt*. It was during this period that the standardized format of the prayer took shape (Monnot 1995: 927). Monnot's entry on the *salāt* in the *Encyclopaedia of Islam* contains considerable useful detail, most of which is pertinent for the *salāt* as it is performed in Turkey.

8 Such standardization is by no means characteristic of all Turkish Muslim rituals. Sufi rituals, for instance, take different forms in different circles, although here a certain standardization seems to have taken place as well. As Nancy and Richard Tapper note, the celebration of the Prophet's birthday, which is very popular in Turkey, has a very fluid format (Tapper and Tapper 1987: 77–82). Not surprisingly, perhaps, the quasi-official *İlmihal* published by the Turkish Diyanet Vakfi mentions the *mevlud* not under "ritual" (*ibadet*) but under the theologically insignificant category of "ceremonies" (Karaman, Bardakoğlu, and Apaydın 2000).

9 For instance, David Shankland's informative study *Islam and Society in Turkey* (Shankland 1999) and Özdemir and Frank's *Visible Islam in Modern Turkey* (Özdemir and Frank 2000) give no estimate of religious adherence.
10 Numbers for the 1980s and 1990s are given in İstanbul Büyükşehir Belediye [n.d.]: 60. The number for 2002 is given on a webpage called Camiler Kenti Istanbul on the site www.Istanbul.com.
11 The Arabic transliteration is taken from Karaman, Bardakoğlu, and Apaydın 2000: I, 267, who also provide a Turkish translation. For a useful account of the *ezan* and other central aspects of Islamic worship in Turkey, see Özdemir and Frank 2000.
12 This silent performance seems to be specific to the Turkish case (see Monnot 1995: 928).
13 The English rendering of the prayer formulas poses the dilemma of whether a translation directly from the Arabic should be used or a translation of one of the commonly used Turkish translations. I have opted here for the latter, but I have found that the differences are not very significant. I am here relying mostly on the Turkish renditions of the prayer formulas as they appear in Tavaslı (n.d).
14 Asad 1993 suggests that this is paralleled in the case of medieval Christian practices.

References

Althusser, Louis (1971) "Ideology and Ideological State Apparatuses," in Louis Althusser (ed.) *Lenin and Philosophy, and Other Essays*, New York: Monthly Review Press.

Asad, Talal (1986) *The Idea of an Anthropology of Islam*, Washington, D.C.: Georgetown University, Center for Contemporary Arab Studies.

——— (1993) *Genealogies of Religion: Discipline and Reasons of Power in Christianity and Islam*, Baltimore: Johns Hopkins Press.

Bowen, John R. (1989) "*Salāt* in Indonesia: The Social Meanings of an Islamic Ritual," *Man*, 24: 600–619.

Deringil, Selim (1998) *The Well-Protected Domains: Ideology and the Legitimation of Power in the Ottoman Empire, 1876–1909*, London: I.B. Tauris.

Douglas, Mary, and Baron Isherwood (1996) *The World of Goods: Towards an Anthropology of Consumption*, London: Routledge.

Durkheim, Émile (1995) *The Elementary Forms of the Religious Life*, trans. Karen E. Fields, New York: The Free Press.

Headley, Stephen C. (2000) "Afterword," in David J. Parkin and Stephen C. Headley (ed.) *Islamic Prayer across the Indian Ocean: Inside and Outside the Mosque*, Richmond, Surrey: Curzon.

Henkel, Heiko (2007) "The Location of Islam: Inhabiting Istanbul in a Muslim Way," *American Ethnologist*, 34: 57–70.

Humphrey, Caroline, and James Laidlaw (1994) *The Archetypal Actions of Ritual: A Theory of Ritual Illustrated by Jain Rite of Worship*, Oxford: Clarendon Press.

İstanbul Büyükşehir Belediye (n.d.) *Grafiklerle 1990'larda İstanbul*, İstanbul: İstanbul Büyükşehir Belediyesi Kültür İşleri Daire Başkanlığı Yayınları.

Kara, Ismail (1985) "Tanzimat'tan Cumhuriyet'e Islamcılık Tartışmaları," *Tanzimat'tan Cumhuriyet'e Türkiye Ansiklopedisi*, 5: 1405–1420.

Karaman, H., A. Bardakoğlu, and Y. Apaydın (ed.) (2000) *İlmihal.* 2 vols. İstanbul: İslam Araştımaları Merkezi.

Kelpetin, H. (2000) "İlmihal," *İslam Ansiklopedisi*, 22: 121–125.

Keyder, Çağlar (1987) *State and Class in Turkey: A Study in Capitalist Development*, London: Verso.

Lambek, Michael (2000) "The Anthropology of Religion and the Quarrel between Poetry and Philosophy," *Current Anthropology*, 41: 309–320.

MacIntyre, Alasdair C. (1980) *After Virtue: A Study in Moral Theory*, Notre Dame: University of Notre Dame Press.

Mahmood, Saba (2001) "Rehearsed Spontaneity and the Conventionality of Ritual: Disciplines of Salāt," *American Ethnologist*, 28: 827–853.

Mauss, Marcel (1992) "Techniques of the Body," in Jonathan Crary and Sanford Kwinter (ed.) *Incorporations*, New York: Zone.

——— (2003) *On Prayer*, trans. Susan Leslie, Oxford: Berghahn Books.

Monnot, Guy (1995) "Salāt," *Encyclopedia of Islam*, 8: 925–934.

Olson, Emelie A. (1982) "Duofocal Family Structure and an Alternative Model of Husband-Wife Relationship," in Çigdem Kağıtçıbaşı and Diane Sunar (ed.) *Sex Roles, Family and Community in Turkey*, Bloomington: Indiana University Turkish Studies.

Öniş, Ziya (1991) "Political Economy of Turkey in the 1980s: Anatomy of Unorthodox Liberalism," in Metin Heper (ed.) *Strong State and Economic Interest Groups: The Post-1980 Turkish Experience*, Berlin: Walter de Gruyter.

Özdemir, Adil, and Kenneth Frank (2000) *Visible Islam in Modern Turkey*, New York: St. Martin's Press.

Parkin, David J., and Stephen C. Headley (ed.) (2000) *Islamic Prayer across the Indian Ocean: Inside and Outside the Mosque*. Richmond: Curzon.

Prätor, Sabine (1985) *Türkische Freitagspredigten: Studien zum Islam in der heutigen Türkei*, Berlin: Klaus Schwarz.

Say, S. (1997) "Asil İrtica ..." *İslam*, 164: 10.

Shankland, David (1999) *Islam and Society in Turkey*, Huntingdon: Eothen Press.

Tapper, Nancy, and Richard Tapper (1987) "The Birth of the Prophet: Ritual and Gender in Turkish Islam," *Man*, 22: 69–92.

Tavaslı, Yayınları (n.d.) *Duâlı Namaz Hocası*, İstanbul: Tavaslı Yayınları.

White, Jenny B. (2002) *Islamist Mobilization in Turkey: A Study in Vernacular Politics*, Seattle: University of Washington Press.

Yavuz, M. Hakan (1997) "Political Islam and the Welfare (Refah) Party in Turkey," *Comparative Politics*, 30: 63–82.

Fasting during the month of Ramadān

7 The observance of Ramadān in Swahili-Land[1]

P. J. L. Frankl[2]

P.J.L. Frankl was a scholar of Swahili who was affiliated to the African Studies Centre in Leiden. His main fields of research are the historical and ethnographic study of language, culture and religion in Swahili-Land with a particular emphasis on the colonial period and literary forms of Swahili culture. He published the majority of his works together with his life-long colleague and friend Yahya Ali Omar. Their articles cover a wide range of topics: "Mombasa under the BuSa'idi: A Leaf from the Taylor Papers" (1991); "*Shairi La Washona-Nguo was Mambasa* 'The Tailors of Mombasa': A Nineteenth Century Satire from Central Swahili Land" (1994); "The Word for 'God' in Swahili: Further Considerations" (1995); "An Historical Review of the Arabic Rendering of Swahili Together with Proposals for the Development of a Swahili Writing System in Arabic Script (Based on the Swahili of Mombasa)" (1997); "*Kashu Langu* 'My Strongbox': A Popular Song from Swahili Mombasa" (1998); "The Idea of 'The Holy' in Swahili" (1999); "Siku ya Mwaka: The Swahili New Year (with special reference to Mombasa)" (2000). They also published *Three Prose Texts in the Swahili of Mombasa* (1998). The following text provides lucid ethnographic details and explains how Muslims practice Ramadān in Swahili-Land by using various historical and linguistic sources.

Introduction

In the Islamic calendar Ramadān is the month of the year during which Muslims throughout the world observe strict fasting between dawn and sunset; this is the fourth of the five pillars of Islam. "The fast of the month of Ramadān is obligatory [Arab. *fard* or *wājib*] for every believer provided he [or she] be of sound mind, an adult, and able to support it" (al-Nawawi 1914: 99). With regard to Ramadān the entire Islamic world follows the same religious practices in all essentials; where non-essentials are concerned there is variety in local usage. The account which follows is mainly concerned with the observance of Ramadān in Swahili-Land, with special reference to Mombasa.[3]

At the end of the nineteenth century the population of Mombasa was small and almost entirely Muslim;[4] today, towards the end of the twentieth century, the population and size of the town have increased enormously, largely because, since the 1960s especially, many inhabitants from the interior have settled and been settled in central Swahili-Land with varying degrees of permanence. As a consequence about half of the population resident within the boundaries of Mombasa Municipality is now, perhaps, Muslim, although the proportion is approximately ninety-five per cent in Mombasa's Old Town. The autocthonous Swahili are the largest single group of Muslims in Mombasa, but there are other African Muslims too, as well as Omanis, Ḥaḍramis, Comorians, Baluchis and Indians; during Ramadān all are especially conscious of Islamic bonding.

The year: solar and lunar

In the past the Swahili people of the East African coast observed both their own solar year and an Islamic lunar year. The Swahili solar year was agricultural and nautical, but during the second half of this century it has fallen into desuetude, having been more or less replaced by the Gregorian year (Frankl and Omar 1993).

The Islamic year "consists of twelve lunar months or 354 days, leaving a discrepancy of eleven days between it and the solar year. As this is never rectified by the introduction of intercalary months, there is no correspondence between the Islamic calendar and the seasons, and we find the fast of Ramadān, for instance, occurring at all times of the year, as it works its way round" (Burt 1910: 147). Consequently over a period of thirty years a Muslim will experience the full range of weather conditions during Ramadān.

The Swahili people have divided the Islamic lunar year into two unequal parts:

1 *mala-mtana*, the eleven months during which it is lawful for Muslims to eat during the day (although, for example, many pious Muslims fast on Mondays and Thursdays throughout *mala-mtana*), and
2 Ramadān.

Ramadān is the ninth month of the Islamic year, but for the Swahili it is, in practice, the last (see Appendix). "Most [African Muslims] have adopted the Arabic names for months; however when a month has a special significance it invariably acquires a local descriptive name which is the one commonly used. Thus in Swahili Shawwal, which follows Ramadān and opens with the breakfast festival (*'īd al-fiṭr*), is called *mfungo mosi*, 'the first releasing,'[5] the next month 'the second releasing,' and so on up to the ninth" (Trimingham 1980: 65).

Fasting

An outline of the legal regulations which apply to fasting in general and Ramadān in particular as applicable to Muslims of the Shāf'ī school, the legal school to which the Swahili people belong, may be found elsewhere (Juynboll 1914: 113 sqq; al-Nawawi 1914: 95–103). The other three Sunni law schools differ only in detail from the Shāf'ī.

kula mfungo:[6] activities before the fast

The phrase *kula mfungo* has been defined as "the feasting and amusement which is kept up for three days before the commencement of Ramadān" (Krapf 1882: 223). Another Swahili phrase with a similar meaning is *kuvunda jungu* "to receive food from a relative or friend to mark the end of the eleven non-fasting months"—literally "to break the large earthenware cooking pot" (Sacleux 1939: 195). During these last days of Sha'bān a typical Swahili family, or a group of friends, would have gone on an outing to their *shamba* "orchard" on the mainland, for example north to Kisauni (nowadays a densely populated suburb), west to Changamwe (much of which has since become industrialised) or, perhaps, south to Mtongwe (most of which now comprises the Kenya Navy Base) in order to *kula mfungo*, i.e. to picnic, to enjoy one another's conversation, and generally to relax in a congenial atmosphere before the commencement of the fast.

Returning from the *shamba*, *vyama* "associations of like-minded people" might vie with one another in *ngoma* "drumming accompanied by singing and dancing." The membership of many of these *vyama* consisted of Swahili women.[7]

As the twentieth century draws to a close few such rural estates remain in the possession of the Swahili people, but it has become accepted for Muslim groups to picnic on public beaches, or in the Shimba Hills. Nowadays the last three days before Ramadān have generally been replaced by the last weekend (i.e. Saturday and Sunday) before Ramadān.

'Abd al-Ḥamīd el-Zein (1935-1979) had, for a student of Swahili, the potential advantage of being both a Muslim and an Arabic speaker. He carried out research in Lamu,[8] northern Swahili-Land, in the late 1960s, laying much emphasis on the influence exerted there by the Ḥaḍramī sharifs (who claim to be descended from the Prophet Muhammad). He gives a vivid description of the annual picnic which takes place in Lamu on the last day of Sha'bān. The *madrasa* has already closed, and early in the morning, before breakfast, the male children of the town gather in front of the Riyāḍah mosque dressed in *k'anzu* (an ankle-length garment, usually white) and *kofia* (a skull cap). They wait there until the youngest sharif of the Riyāḍah emerges from the mosque carrying a red flag with white borders and inscribed in Arabic *Yā Ḥabīb 'Alī al-Ḥabashī!* (O Ḥabīb 'Alī al-Ḥabashī!).[9] As soon as the flag comes out the children form up and walk off hand in hand to their picnic site near the beach, singing a hymn in praise of the Prophet Muḥammad. This is a day for all the male children of Lamu who eat with the sharifs, while non-sharif adults eat by themselves. After a day of feasting, swimming and playing the procession of singing children and sharifs returns to the Riyāḍah mosque in time for the sunset prayers, after which people wish one another well for the month of Ramadān (el-Zein 1974: Chap. 6, 224-227).

On the eve of Ramadān small groups of Muslims throughout the world of Islam assemble at mosques, or on roof-tops or at road-sides to search the night sky.[10] In Mombasa parties returning from their *shambas* would dance their way back to the town, singing: *kongo, kongo, mgeni wetu*! "Our guest, [you are] very welcome!"—the "guest" being the month of Ramadān.[11] This practice was known as *kwenda kutwaa mwezi* "going to fetch the new moon."

In this connection, Shaykh Abd Allah Saleh al-Farsi, a much loved *qāḍī* wrote:

> *kwa kuimbia mwisho wa Shaaban vyuoni na misikitini 'Marahaban ya shahra Ramadhan,' au 'Karibu mgeni...,' na nyinginezo—upumbavu huo na kichekesho; bali kilizo kwa wanaojua. Uzushi tu huu. Huo mwezi wa Ramadhan unawasikia wanavyoukaribisha hivyo?*
>
> To sing at the end of Sha'bān 'welcome, O month of Ramaḍān,' or 'be welcome, guest... ,' and so forth in [our Swahili] schools and mosques is foolishness and is something to make one laugh; on the contrary for those who know something about the matter it is something to make one weep. This is merely an invention, for can the month of Ramaḍān hear [the greeting] when it is thus welcomed?
>
> (al-Farsey 1397/1977: 30).

Islamic schools

On the 24th and 25th of Sha'bān each pupil used to bring three *pesa* to the teacher (who earned no salary as such).[12] This levy was called *mfungo*. From the 27th of Sha'bān every *chuo* "school" was on holiday until the 1st of Ramaḍān (Hinawy 1964: 34). A further levy was imposed during the last ten days of Ramaḍān (see below, *laylat al-qadr*). Nowadays most teachers at Islamic schools receive reasonable salaries, and so the payments mentioned by Shaykh Mbarak Hinawy are no longer made.

The month of Ramadān

In Mombasa the beginning of every Ramadān is marked by the firing of two cannon shots from Ngomeni (the Portuguese-built fort) by the Kenya Navy (formerly the Royal East African Navy).[13] However this is to simplify the matter for it has been recorded that the beginning and end of Ramadān in East Africa are matters "over which there has been controversy" (Trimingham 1964: 92); over thirty years later this continues to be the case. Discussing the commencement of Ramadān Shaykh al-Amin bin Ali al-Mazru'i, the eminent *qāḍī* of Mombasa, wrote that the month begins either if the new moon has been sighted by all the people, or if the *qāḍī* accepts the testimony of reliable witnesses, or if the month of Sha'bān has attained thirty days; if the new moon is sighted in only one place the people of that town and all within a radius of 560 miles must begin the fast (al-Mazru'i 1353/1934: 52).[14]

Some Swahili divide the month into three periods of ten days each. In Mombasa the first period may be referred to as *fungu la waArabu* "the decade of the Arabs" (who are considered wealthy), followed by *fungu la waSwahili* "the decade of the Swahili" (folk of moderate means), and finally *fungu la waGunya* "the decade of the Bajuni" (who live in the extreme north of Swahili-Land). Some Ḥaḍramīs say that, devotionally, one should try to focus on *toba* (repentance) during the first decade, on *imani* (belief) during the second, while the final ten days should emphasise *ibada* (worship).

For all Muslims Ramadān is the most important month of the year. Many a Swahili male marks it sartorially by wearing a clean white *k'anzu* and a *kofiya*.[15] Ramadān was, and to some extent still is, a holiday month—employees entitled to annual leave endeavoured to take that leave during Ramadān, while Swahili travellers in the interior of Africa would make sure that they returned to the coast before the end of Sha'bān.[16] A number of Swahili poets derive inspiration from the Ramaḍān theme (e.g. Sengo and Sengo 1979).Some self-employed Swahilis prefer not to ply their trade during Ramadān.[17] In other parts of the Islamic world where the population is wholly or almost wholly Muslim, e.g. in Najd, central Arabia, "trade and industry are largely at a stand-still during Ramadān" (Plessner 1955: 417); however Mombasa is now in many respects a westernised town, and most Muslims in paid employment have to take that fact into account when fulfilling their religious obligations.

Many Ḥaḍramī restaurant-owners shut their establishments for the entire month, some considering the closure to be an opportunity for redecoration.[18] Restaurants owned by Indian Muslims remain open for business during the hours of fasting but, formerly, would have draped a red curtain as a warning across the entrance; whether this is, or is not, a custom found in Muslim establishments in the Indian sub-continent I cannot say. What is certain is that during my visit to Mombasa in Ramadān 1415/1995 no such red curtains could be seen. There is an allusion to this practice in a stanza composed in 1368 AH/AD 1948 by Shaykh Abdallah al-Husni:

> 8. *Imekuwa Ramadhani * ukenda migahawani*
> *ni paziya milangoni * ndani wat'u wajiliya.*
>
> When Ramadhan comes
> you will see if you go to the restaurants
> curtains draped across the doorway
> inside folk are eating brazenly.

(Frankl and Omar 1995: 140)

For several months before the onset of the fast housewives buy in commodities such as rice and sugar for, however difficult the eleven non-fasting months, there are always more than enough supplies of food during Ramadān—oxymoron though that statement may be. The truth of this observation is embodied in the old Swahili saw: *Ramadhani ni shekhe * huja na karama zake* "the month of Ramadān is like a shaykh that comes accompanied by miracles."

Ramadān was a unique month not only because of the abundance of food. Muslim landlords would waive the rent due for this month, since it was deemed that one who rented accommodation would almost certainly be poor. Furthermore the *zaka* (Arab. *zakāt*, the annual alms-tax for Muslims) is often paid during this month.[19]

If a young person is caught breaking the fast without a valid reason children will gather round that person singing:

> *kobe! kobe! la mtana!*
> *na kiteweo ni p'anya wa jana!*
>
> A tortoise! the tortoise is eating [during] the day-time! [Its] relish is a rat [killed] yesterday!' (One who breaks the fast is called 'tortoise' because the tortoise munches constantly throughout the day).

In practice, almost all Muslims will fast,[20] although some will fast but neglect the prayers. Such backsliders are confronted with the old Swahili aphorism: *afungaye aseswali * saumu yake batali* "the one who fasts but does not pray, his fasting is invalid." Again there are those who do not pray during the eleven non-fasting months, but who go to the mosque during Ramadān—of such it is said: *alikuwa akiswaliya uji* "he only prayed because of the food" (for an observation on *uji* as a synonym for break-fast see Note 23 below).

All day and every day in Ramadān men and women will go about their tasks saying or chanting a kind of *du'a'* (a prayer or litany) heard chiefly during this month, beseeching God for remission of one's sins in this world and for salvation in the world to come. This *du'a'* is also heard in the mosques after prayers.

During the mornings of Ramadān towns and cities with populations which are predominantly Muslim are quiet until about nine or ten o'clock. In the afternoons housewives venture out to buy fresh food for the approaching break-fast at sunset. Swahili ladies were never seen in Mombasa's central municipal market, for they went to their own local markets such as the *soko ya waungwana* near the Anisa Mosque; men and women now go to temporary street markets known as Arsani (probably from the Arabic *'arsa* "a vacant lot") where dates, fresh vegetables and an astonishing range of freshly baked Swahili bread and other food may be purchased for break-fast at sun-set.

During the afternoons housewives would be busy cooking. Many Swahili dishes are prepared during Ramadān which are rarely tasted during the eleven months of *mala-mtana*, for example *tambi za mapapayu* "slices of unripe pawpaw cut into long slender threads (like vermicelli) and then cooked in *tui la nazi* 'coconut milk' with sugar added." Readers familiar with other Islamic societies can doubtless make similar observations—in Ethiopia "each region or group has its Ramaḍān speciality" (Trimingham 1952: 228).

Also, early in the afternoons, fresh *tembo la tamu* "sweet unfermented wine made from the sap of coconut palms" is collected. Later that same afternoon vendors would go through the lanes of Mombasa's various *mitaa* "neighbourhoods" crying *tembo! tembo!* The liquid, stored in a *kitoma* "pumpkin," would be ladled out to customers, taken home and used in the baking of such delicacies as *mahamri* and *vitambua*-which are kinds of Swahili bread.

kufungua[21] muadhini

At sunset, just as the *muadhini* (Arab. *mu'adhdhin, muezzin*) proclaims the call to evening prayer the first food is tasted; this is known as *kufungua muadhini.* In the crowded mosques the sunset prayers, which in the other eleven months begin almost immediately after the call to prayer, are delayed for some ten or fifteen minutes to enable food (dates[22] and some cooked delicacies) to be eaten, together with something to drink such as fruit juice or coffee. This is a time for fellowship and good-natured banter.

futari[23] and daku[24]

The main meal is *futari* "break-fast," eaten at home after the evening prayers have been said. Travellers and others who are alone at this time are not forgotten, the landlord or a neighbour inviting them to break-fast for the duration—a custom known as—*futurisha wat'u* "inviting people to break-fast." When I stayed in Mombasa during Ramadān 1415/1994 I had the pleasure and the privilege of being invited to break-fast by a Swahili family whom I have known for some thirty years. I would leave my rooms at the sunset call to prayer and walk through virtually deserted streets and lanes to my host's residence where the *salāt al-maghrib* "evening prayers" had already been said. I was welcomed in the sitting room with a glass of fresh, chilled fruit juice and some dates. After a chat of some fifteen minutes or so a member of the household, usually one of the children, would greet us and say that the meal was ready. The food was always varied and plentiful, but without extravagance. One writer observed that in Ethiopia as elsewhere in Africa "overeating is the rule in Ramaḍān" (Trimingham 1952: 228). It is only proper to add that my own experiences have been an exception to the rule—if rule it be. After eating, hands were washed and we returned to the sitting room where we chatted until the call to *salāt al-'isha'*, "the night prayers," when my host and his grandson went to the local mosque.

A further meal known as *daku* (Arab. *saḥūr*) may be eaten before dawn.[25] It is of interest that while some other Islamic societies who do not speak Arabic use the Arabic word *saḥūr* to refer to this meal, the Swahili language has its own name. The owner of the house whose hospitality and friendship I enjoyed while staying in Mombasa visited me faithfully night after night at about ten o'clock with my *daku*, in this instance a tray of delicacies prepared by his wife, and he would usually remain for half an hour or so to chat. In the past, before the hour of *daku*, drummers used to go from house to house beating their *vigoma* "small drums" so that people wishing to eat might not miss the meal (Johnson 1939: 69). There might also be a song.[26] On the first day after Ramadān, i.e. on the first of *mfungo mosi* (the first of *shawwāl*), those who had beaten the *vigoma* would go round the houses of the *mtaa* for the last time carrying a *k'apu* "a large basket" into which housewives would place *mtele* "husked rice," or money, as a kind of *zakāt 'l-fiṭr* "alms on the feast day which ends the fast." The practice remains, though in an attenuated form.

bembe[27]

Between *futari* and *daku* there may be *bembe*, tasty snacks brought before sunset and served about ten or eleven o'clock at night and shared with one's friends—*bembe* being supplied by or brought to one's friends as tokens of esteem and affection. The concept of *bembe* appears to be peculiarly Swahili and is not, it seems, found in other African-Islamic societies. In Mombasa it seems that the word *bembe* is not confined to Ramaḍān. For example if a relative or close friend arrives from abroad with the intention of staying in the town for a few days only, he or she may be sent *bembe* if time is short and an opportunity of offering hospitality does not present itself; or again, *bembe* may be sent to a couple moving into a new house.

A second meaning of the word *bembe* has been defined, somewhat misleadingly it has to be said, as "food and confectionery cooked by a woman for her lover, and sent to him during Ramaḍān" (Krapf 1882: 24; also Sacleux 1939: 103). In this sense *bembe* is actually a large meal sent by a fiancée's family to the fiancé's home on one evening only during the final ten days of the fast. Once intelligence of the fiancée's intention has been received, the fiancé's family will not prepare *futari* on that day, for they know that they will be the recipients of a gargantuan meal, a meal so enormous that it is possible to invite many relatives and friends.[28]

kilalo

During Ramadān there is, or was, a mutually beneficial arrangement between the Swahili of Mombasa and the neighbouring people of the Nyika.[29] Nyika men would travel to Mombasa in order to walk through the lanes of the town in the early morning crying *kilalo*! *kilalo*! The purpose of their cry was to offer their services as dishwashers in those households without *maboi* "house-servants." The Swahili housewife temporarily in need of domestic help would engage a Nyika man who, in exchange for washing the dishes, would be given *kilalo*, that is to say *chakula kilicholala* "left-overs" (or *mwiku* during the eleven non-fasting months)—for quite often during Ramadān quantities of food are left over, even though most Muslim families do try to avoid *isrāf* "extravagance."

Shaykh al-Amin's fulminations

So much stress on cooking and eating during the month of fasting caused Shaykh al-Amin bin Ali, soon to be appointed *qāḍī* of Mombasa, to fulminate against what he considered to be overemphasis. His chosen medium was the short-lived Mombasa newspaper *Sahifa* which he edited. In Ramaḍān 1349 (1931) he wrote:

> *Ama sisi, mt'u ambaye katika mala-mtana alikuwa akifunguwa kanwa kwa kipande cha mkate na kikombe cha chai, huwa katika Ramadhani hatosheki illa kwa uji wa maziwa na nyama ya kuchoma na mikate mizuri kwa mituzi ya k'uku, khalafu aje ale daku kwa viteweo yot'e; mbali bembe atakalokula baina ya futari na daku, farne, faluda, maji mazuri ya sharbati au ya zabibu.*
>
> As for us [the Swahili of Mombasa], somebody who, in the other eleven months, breakfasted on a slice of bread and a cup of tea will only be satisfied during Ramaḍān with wheatmeal porridge boiled in milk, and shish kebab, and many varieties of fine bread dipped in chicken broth; and again, when it is time for *daku* that same person will eat [cooked rice] with many kinds of side dishes; there is also *bembe*, which that person eats between *futari* and *daku*, with *farne*,[30] *faluda*,[31] sherbet and raisin syrup.
>
> (al-Mazru'i 1955: 12)

Night-time entertainments

Muslims are "inclined to make up during the night for the deprivations of the day" (Gibb and Kramers 1961: 469). In Mombasa, after the *salāt al-'ishā'* "night prayers," teams of youths would compete in a tug-of-war (*-vuta bugu*),[32] young men would box (*-pigana ndondi*) egged on by chanting supporters, while adult males would play cards (*-teza karata*), the card games being played either privately between friends or as a fierce competition between representatives of the various *mitaa* "neighbourhoods"—the final rounds of the competition taking place during the last two nights of Ramadān. Nowadays during the evenings of the fasting month young boys race around Mombasa's by-ways on rented bicycles.

During the 1990s these night-time entertainments have become less frequent in Mombasa, partly because of an increasing crime rate in the town, partly because lack of sleep impairs efficiency in a competitive, Western-dominated society, and partly because of the influence of television and videos.

In northern Swahili-Land, according to Charles Sacleux—greatest of all the Swahili lexicographers, students gave their teacher a *tumba*, a kind of small bag made of plaited coconut fronds in which they would carry *maandazi* (a Swahili specialty) to their teacher in the evenings at the time of leaving the mosque, thus ensuring that he had something with which to break the fast (Sacleux 1939: 910).

Religious activities

During Ramadān, much time is spent on religious study. For this is the month during which the Holy Qur'ān was revealed to the Prophet Muhammad: *Ni mwezi wa Ramadhan ulioteremshiwa Qur'āni* (al-Mazru'i 1353/1934: 64) "the month of Ramadān, wherein the Koran was sent down" (Arberry 1955: I, 52). In the *darasa*, "religious classes," Muslims study *tafsīri* (Arab. *tafsīr*) "interpretation and commentary on Qur'ānic texts."[33] The *tafsīri* in Mombasa's Mbaruku mosque, after the afternoon prayers, was especially popular, but other mosques had their *tafsīri* classes too. Immediately after the night prayers many will stay on in the mosque to pray the supererogatory *tarawehe* prayers (Arab. *salāt al-tarāwīḥ*).

After the *tarawehe* prayers some of the congregation in some of the mosques will remain to attend a *darasa* "a religious class" which, in this context, takes the form of a recitation of one *juzuu* (Arab. *juz'*) "a thirtieth part of the Holy Qur'ān," and thus all thirty parts may be conveniently read within the space of one month (the Swahili alone will go to a particular house for this purpose). Night after night every person present will recite, when it is their turn to do so, one *kara* (from the Arabic consonantal root *qr'* "read")[34]—"a sub-division of a *juzuu*." The person who is most knowledgeable in *'ilm al-tajwīd* "the art of reading the Holy Qur'ān in accordance with established rules of pronunciation and intonation" will stop the recitation every time an error occurs, and the reader who has erred must then re-read that portion correctly. When the last verse of the *kara* is reached, all will recite it in unison. The next *kara* then begins, and so on, until the whole *juzuu* has been correctly recited. The following night the next *juzuu* is read in the same manner. The origin of this practice is the belief that the Prophet Muhammad read back to the angel Jibrīl (Gabriel) the verses which the angel had imparted to him; indeed, the Swahili refer to Jibrīl as *Mu'allim Jibrīl* "Teacher Jibrīl." On the last night of Ramadān, after the reading of the final *juzuu*, the host will lay on a feast for all who have shared in the readings throughout the holy month. Details of the *darasa* in Lamu during the 1960s are available elsewhere (el-Zein 1974: 227–235).

Laylat al-qadr: "The Night of Power"

Muslims believe that some time during the last ten nights of Ramadān the Holy Qur'ān was first revealed to the Prophet Muḥammad.

> *Hakika Sisi Tumeteremsha [Qur'ān] katika Lailat il-Kadr;*
> *Ni lipi la kukujaza ni ipi hiyo Lailat ul-Kadr?*

Lailat ul-Kadr ni bora kuliko mezi elfu.

(al-Mazru'i n.d.: 61)

Behold, we sent it down on the Night of Power;
And what shall teach thee what is the Night of Power?
The Night of Power is better than a thousand months …

(Arberry 1955: II, 346)

The precise night is now unknown, but the received wisdom is that it was probably one of the odd (i.e. not even) dates during the last ten days of the month—especially the 23rd, 25th, 27th and 29th. During these times especially, pious Muslims endeavour to perform good deeds, many spending all their time secluded within a mosque-a practice known in Arabic as *i'tikāf* "applying oneself zealously to the service of God."

In addition to the levy paid by pupils at the end of Sha'ban (see above, Islamic schools), a further levy, this time of eight *pesa* (twelve cents), was paid to the *chuo* teacher on the 24th and 25th of Ramadān—the payment being known as *muharama* (Hinawy 1964: 34).

zakat 'l-fiṭr

During the days before the end of Ramadān the head of each household donates *zakāt 'l-fiṭr*, an obligatory gift based on the number of Muslims in one's household. The gift consists of two and a half *p'ishi* of "food commonly consumed in the place" (al-Nawawi 1914: 90)—which, in Swahili-Land, is rice—or the equivalent in cash, and is donated to poor and needy people. The purpose of *zakāt 'l-fiṭr* is to ensure that no Muslim goes without food on the feast day.

'īd: "The Feast-Day"

One of the three festivals which provide a framework for the Swahili year is *'īd al-fiṭr* "the feast of the breaking of the fast," and this is celebrated throughout the Muslim world. Once the new moon has been sighted in Lamu the people there hold a service in the Riyāḍah mosque known as *iḥyā'* ("revival," "a return to life"). This has been detailed elsewhere (el-Zein 1974: Chap. 6, 235–239). In Mombasa the end of the fast, and thus the commencement of the feast, is marked by the firing of two cannon shots from Ngomeni[35]—heard clearly in the Old Town during the final break-fast. As has been mentioned above, there is not always unanimity in East Africa as to when the fast has ended. In the morning after sunrise, the first day of *mfungo mosi* (Arab. *shawwāl*), special *'īd* prayers (Arab. *salāt al-'īd*) are said in all the mosques.[36]

In 1321/1903

> the *Baraza* at the Jubilee Hall.[37] [Mombasa] took place as usual on Monday, the day of Id-el-Fitr. The Hall had been prettily decorated with flags and palms, and punctually at half past nine Sir Charles Eliot and the officers of the [British East Africa] Protectorate ["in full uniform with medals and decorations"] arrived [having met at the adjacent Mombasa Club at 9.15 a.m.], were saluted by a guard of honour ... the Swahili band meanwhile playing the British national anthem. The Wali [Sālim bin Khalfān Āl-BūSa'īdī] and the Assistant Wali ['Alī bin Sālim Āl-BūSa'īdī] received his guests at the entrance.[38] After the customary hand-shaking, speeches, syrup, coffee and rose water, the pleasant gathering dispersed.
>
> (African Standard, Mombasa Times, 23, xii: 1903, 4)

Similarly, in Zanzibar town

> the fast of Ramadān was brought to a close on Sunday evening when just before sunset keen and interested eyes spied the new moon. Immediately salvoes of artillery and a *feu de joie* were fired from the Palace square where H.H. the Sultan's troops were massed, and the big flags flew out from different flag staffs on shore and from every craft in harbour. The firing was repeated at seven o'clock the next morning and at noon. H.H. the Sultan held a *baraza* for the Arabs in the morning, followed by the feasting of many thousands, and the troops were paraded in the Palace square in the afternoon. On Tuesday morning His Highness held a *baraza* for Europeans, followed by a reception of the British Indian and Parsee communities. Each afternoon the customary great crowds have gathered in the *Nazi-Moja* [i.e. *mNazi mMoja*], bent on the amusements common to every fair all the world over, the most popular being the many native dances showing the wide range of origin of many of the natives living in the island.... The illuminations in the Palace square and the display of fireworks have attracted large crowds each evening.
>
> (Gazette for Zanzibar, 23:xii: 1903, 1)

Shortly after *'īd 'l-fiṭr* 1415/1995 a revived *Baraza ya waMiji* ("The twelve Swahili tribes of Mombasa in Council") held a festive meal in Mombasa's Old Town to celebrate the end of the fast.

In Lamu (northern Swahili-Land) the end of Ramadān is also celebrated. After *salāt 'l-'asr* "the afternoon prayers" the sharifs of the Riyāḍah mosque hold a service in the adjacent *ribāṭ* ("hospice") during which traditional religious songs are sung to the accompaniment of flutes and drums (el-Zein 1974: 239–244).

Meanwhile, as an entertainment for lesser mortals, *gwaride* "military-style bands" would parade in the town, stopping outside certain houses in order to solicit money from the occupants.

> 7. *na swala tumeziwata * misikiti twaipita*
> *kwa ngoma na tarumbeta * wala hatuoni haya.*
>
> We have abandoned the prescribed prayers
> We pass by the mosques
> With drums and trumpets and we feel no shame.
>
> (Frankl and Omar 1995: 140)

On the occasion of *'īd* Muslims wear their best clothes. In Swahili-Land men of standing would sport an embroidered *k'anzu*, over which might be worn a *joho* or a *bushti* "types of cloak" or, if a *qāḍī*, a *juba*; women and children would wear new dresses.[39] In Mombasa the *uwanda wa Makadara*, "the open space in Makadara between the Mbaruku mosque and the Baluchi mosque" becomes a fair-ground for the three days of the *'īd*, and is known as *bembeyani* "the place of swings [and roundabouts]." Children are given coins (or low-value currency notes) by relatives and friends, when the age-old greeting *'īd mubārak* "a blessed *'īd*" is exchanged, with *mkono wa idi* "the *'īd* handshake."

Muslim women observe a supererogatory fast for six consecutive days immediately following *'īd al-fiṭr* (and a good many men too, but on a voluntary basis). Thus during the first week of *mfungo mosi* (Arab. *shawwāl*) one person might enquire of another: *je, sita unayo?* "Are you observing the six-day fast?"

After the end of Ramadān the spectre of Hunger returns to haunt the poor. This is embodied in the somewhat complicated two lines of a verse sung during the *vigoma* "drumming" towards the end of the last night of the fast, just before *daku* (i.e. just before the very last meal of the month):

> *fungate*[40] *imekwisha*
> *Dari Suudi*[41] *sokota mt'u wako.*[42]
>
> Ramadān has finished now. O Hunger, [you can begin again] to make your victim suffer your pangs.

Despite cataclysmic changes during the past century and a half, Ramadān continues to be the most important month in the Islamic year, and its observance remains an integral part of the Swahili way of life.

Appendix: the Islamic calendar

TAKWIMU (Swahili)		*TAQWIM (Arabic)*	
1	*mfungo mosi*	10	*shawwāl*
2	*mfungo pili*	11	*dhū 'l-qa'dah*
3	*mfungo tatu*	12	*dhū l'-hijjah*
4	*mfungo nne*	1	*muharram*
5	*mfungo tano*	2	*safar*
6	*mfungo sita mala-mtana*	3	*rabī' 'l-awwal*
7	*mfungo sabaa*	4	*rabī' 'l-thāni*
8	*mfungo nane*	5	*jumāda 'l-ūlā*
9	*mfungo tisiya*	6	*jumādā 'l-ākhira*
10	*rajabu*	7	*rajab*
11	*shaabani*	8	*sha'bān*
12	*ramadhani*	9	*Ramadān*

Notes

1 With special reference to Mombasa. Unless otherwise stated the Swahili of this article is in *kiMvita*, the Swahili of Mombasa.
2 In consultation with Yahya Ali Omar.
3 Probably the earliest written reference emanating from Mombasa to the observance of Ramadān (or, more precisely, to the end of the fast) is dated 1240/1825. In 'A Journal of the British Establishment of Mombasa' Acting Lieutenant James Emery R.N. wrote on 21st May 1825: "Yesterday [i.e., 1st Shawwāl 1240] I went to the fort and found the Arab flag flying which I hauled down immediately and hoisted the English. I sent to the Sultan [Sulaymān bin 'Alī al-Mazrū'ī] to know who hoisted it. He said he gave orders to hoist it not knowing it was wrong, it being Ramathan. ... He then asked me to allow him to hoist the Arab flag for three days during the feasts" (Emery 1825 [Emery disallowed the request]).
4 *Parliamentary Papers* LX (1898): "Report by Sir A. Hardinge on the condition and progress of the East Africa Protectorate from its establishment to 1897" (C. 8683), 8.

5 *Mfungo mosi*: Some intellectuals have argued that, logically, the spelling should be *mfungu mosi*, and no doubt they are correct; however the common people say *mfungo*.

6 *Mfungo*, apparantly, is also the name of a dance, being one of the dances named in the Schedule to the Mombasa Municipality (Native Dances, Processions and Strolling Musicians) By-laws, 1934 (Kenya Proclamations, Rules and Regulations 1934, General Notice No. 1304).

7 *Vyama*: some of the *vyama vya wanawake* "women's association," such as *Banu Saada* (properly *banāt Sa'adah*) and *Ibinaa* (properly *banāt 'l-waṭan*) became well known in Mombasa (Strobel 1975: 227 sqq); others, such as *Dari Suudi*, were less well known.

8 Lamu: this is the spelling employed by Arabs and Europeans; the Swahili have Amu.

9 Ḥabīb 'Alī al-Ḥabashī, a Ḥaḍramī sharīf, was a scholar who died in Lamu in 1333 AH/AD 1915; he was the uncle of the founder of the Riyāḍah mosque (Lienhardt 1959: 231).

10 "The yearly fast [in Zanzibar] begins with the new moon of Ramazan; crowds assemble in the open places and upon the terrace roofs till the popping of pistols and matchlocks and salvos from the squadron warn the faithful that the crescent has appeared" (Burton 1872: I, 390).

11 *Kongo* is a word of welcome extended to a guest who has come from a distance (Sacleux 1939: 436); *kongo mwezi*: "the first quarter of the moon" (Krapf 1882: 170).

12 *Pesa*: 'the pesa was a small copper coin of India, since 1845 introduced to the Suahili coast' (Krapf 1882: 302). Swahili-Land had its own copper currency during the reign of Sayyid Barghash bin Sa'īd, with a 1-pesa coin issued in 1299/1882, and a second issued in 1304/1887. The Barghash pesa circulated in Mombasa until well into the twentieth century.

13 A similar custom prevails in Riyāḍ, or did when I was teaching there in the 1970s.

14 "... A sight of the moon in any place renders obligatory the commencement of the fast in that neighbourhood, but not in places situated at a great distance" (al-Nawawi 1914: 95).

15 Variants of the *k'anzu* and the *kofia* are worn by men in many Islamic societies

16 A recent novel by a Zanzibari writer refers to Ramadān thus: "Uncle Aziz did not stay long [in the East African interior]. It was his intention to return to the coast before the start of Ramadhan, to fast and rest in his own home. The disposal of the goods before the end of the month [of *Shabani*] would allow him to pay his porters off, in time for the new year [i.e. *mfungo mosi*] and all the expenses of Idd [*al-fiṭr*]" (Gurnah 1994: 92).

17 For example, the elderly shoemaker from Siyu who has made and repaired my sandals for over thirty years closes his "shop" during the fasting month.

18 During Ramadān all eating establishments in the Kingdom of Saudi Arabia are shut during the hours of daylight.

19 *Zakāt* is a fixed portion on certain kinds of one's wealth which Muslims must give away annually for the benefit of the poor—it is obligatory charity, and is not to be confused with *sadaka* (Arab. *sadaqāt*) voluntary charity.

20 In West Africa "the fast is observed fairly strictly, for African life is so open that it is difficult to conceal the fact that one is not fasting [!]" (Trimingham 1959: 78).

21 *-Fungua*: cease fasting—the antonym being *-funga* used intransitively.

22 Dates: "During the month of Ramadān the Sunna recommends breaking the fast as soon as possible, by eating some dates, if one has any, or, if not, by drinking a little water" (al-Nawawi 1914: 99). The Deeds Register of the Waqf Commissioners in Mombasa (folio 249) records that part of the proceeds of a *waqfed* property in Mombasa are to be spent on the Salim bin Khalfan [al-BūSa'īdī] mosque in Malindi "for the defraying of Ramadān expenses for opening of the fast." To this end the Imām of the mosque receives an annual cheque before the onset of the fast to be used for the purchase of dates.

23 *Futari*: break-fast; at the turn of the century the Swahili ate twice a day during the eleven months of *mala-mtana*—at about ten in the morning (*kunwa uji* "drinking gruel") and again at about four in the afternoon (*kula wali* "eating boiled rice"). It is of considerable interest that the two meals eaten during Ramadān—*futari* (including *uji* "gruel") and *daku* (including *wali* "boiled rice")—are a survival of the earlier practice during *mala-mtana*. Today European conventions have influenced Swahili eating habits in that break-fast during the eleven non-fasting months is now taken early in the morning and consists of a cup of tea with a slice of bread or toast (*kunwa chai* "drinking tea"); however, even today, many Africans have porridge for their breakfast. A mid-day meal, also in imitation of the European practice, is now the norm in Swahili-Land.

24 *Daku*: the etymology of this word is uncertain. Krapf hazards *ndaa k'uu* "great hunger" (Krapf 1882: 44); this is also the suggestion of no less an authority than Sacleux "grand faim" (Sacleux

1939: 44)—but that etymology must be considered as speculative. The Arabic-derived suggestion in Johnson is, in our opinion, improbable (Johnson 1939: 69).

25 A record of what was eaten by the Swahili people of the Mrima (southern Swahili) coast reads: *vyakula vyao uji na maandazi na tambi, ao hupika muhogo na ndizi na nyama, ao samaki wa kupaka, na usiku katika sa'a ya tatu wanakula daku—wali na nyama mpaka sa'a nne, na desturi hiyo mpaka mwezi wa ramaḍani ishe* (Velten 1903: 287). "Their food is gruel and buns and rice flour or cooked cassava, bananas, and meat, or fish roasted with coconut. From the third hour to the fourth they eat the *daku* meal of rice and meat; and this is their custom until the end of Ramadhan" (Mtoro bin Mwinyi Bakari 1981: 192).

26 Examples of *daku* songs, the words but not the music, have appeared [sic!] in print; they were collected in Kilwa Kivinje, on the Mrima coast (Hasani bin Ismail 1968: 41–43). Imprisoned in Beirut during the late 1980s, Terry Waite wrote: "The holy month of Ramadān has begun ... Outside in the street someone is beating a drum while a male voice chants a haunting melody ... It is an hour or so before daybreak, so the chanting must be designed to wake those who wish to eat" (Waite 1994: 262).

27 *Bembe*: (see also Velten 1903: 287; Sacleux 1939: 103). The word remains current throughout Swahili-Land although, of course, it is unfamiliar to second-language speakers who do not have this custom in their culture. A line from a nineteenth century song runs:

*moyo watamani bembe * kwa mwezi wa Ramathani*
my heart longs for *bembe* during the month of Ramadān.

(Taylor Papers: XI, 24)

A word which may, perhaps, carry a similar meaning to the first of the two given meanings of *bembe* is *mfungo* "fasting-gift; a present sent to a friend in the middle of Ramadān" (Taylor 1891: 114; also Sacleux 1939: 547).

28 It is not the custom for Muslims to marry during Ramaḍān.

29 Nyika: the people of the *nyika*—the "desolate wilderness" some twenty kilometers inland from Mombasa. Since the second World War the Nyika people [not all of whom live on the *Nyika*] have preferred the name Mijikenda (Sperling 1988: 12, fn. 3). The waNyika/Mijikenda are nine closely related but distinct peoples who share a common linguistic and cultural heritage.

30 *Farne*: Sacleux 1939: 216.

31 *Faluda*: Sacleux 1939: 214.

32 *-Vuta bugu*: this form of tug-of-war is now virtually unknown, and in the Mombasa of the 1930s it seems to have been confined to Mjuakale (the old, northern, part of the Old Town). On Wasini Island the term was *-vuta jugwe* (we are obliged to Sayyid Abd al-Rahman bin Mwinyi Alawi [Mu'allim Sagaff] for this regional variant).

33 *Darasa*: "religious classes"; the subjects taught in the *darasa* during the eleven non-fasting months consist of such demanding topics as *fiqh* "jurisprudence," *nahw* "syntax," *sarf* "morphology"; but during *mfungo sita* (Arab. *rabī' 'l-awwal*), the month in which some Muslims celebrate the Prophet Muḥammad's birth, the *maShekhe* teach *sīra* "the life of the Prophet."

34 *Kara*: the definition in the *Standard Swahili-English Dictionary* is incomplete, and thus misleading (Johnson 1939: 174). Shaykh al-Amin's publications employ the romanised variant *maqra* (e.g. al-Mazru'i 1980).

35 Ludwig Krapf wrote in 1844: "Sobald der Neumond sichtbar ist, so hat das Fasten der Muhamedaner ein Ende, auf der Festung in Mombas werden Kanonen abgefeuert, und wer eine Flinte hat, nimmt Theil an dem Gewehrfeuer." [As soon as the new moon is visible the fast of the Muslims comes to an end; cannon are fired from the fort in Mombasa, and whoever has a musket fires that] (Krapf 1858: 218).

36 On 9th May 1826 (corresponding to 1st Shawwāl 1241) James Emery, Commandant of the British Establishment in Mombasa, wrote in his journal: "This morning being a day of praying and feasting with the Mohammedans" (Emery 1825 [see Note 3 above]).

37 Jubilee Hall, Mombasa: so named to commemorate the diamond jubilee of Queen Victoria in 1897.

38 In the 1820s the 'Sheik [Liwali] of Mombas' paid the expenses of the feast on 'īd 'l-fiṭr (Owen 1833: ii, 154).

39 Dresses: during the two great festivals it is commendable "to use scent, and dress in one's best clothes as on Friday" (al-Nawawi 1914: 65).

40 *Fungate*: the Swahili honeymoon, lasting seven days as the word indicates, but here used to denote the month of Ramadān.
41 Dari Suudi: here used to denote Hunger—but see also Note 7 above.
42 A literal translation of these two lines is not meaningful.

References

al-Farsey, Abdallah Saleh (1397/1977) *Bid-a [Innovation]*, Mambasa: Adam Traders.

al-Mazru'i, al-Amin bin Ali (1353/1934) *Hidayat al-atfal [Guidance for Children]*, Cairo.

——— (1955) "Mazungumzo ya Saumu [A Chat about Fasting]," in al-Amin bin Ali al-Mazru'i (ed.) *Uwongozi [Guidance]*, Mambasa: East African Muslim Welfare Society.

——— (1980) *Tafsiri ya Qur'ani Tukufu [Commentary on the Holy Qur'an]: al-Faatihah/al-Baqarah*, Nairobi: Shungwaya Publishers.

——— (n.d.) *Juzuu ya Amma*, Mambasa: Haji Mohamed & Sons.

al-Nawawi, Muhyi al-din Abu Zakariya Yahya (1914) *Minhaj et-talibin: A Manual of Muhammadan Law According to the School of Shafii*, trans. Lodewijk W. van den Berg and E.C. Howard, London: W. Thacker.

Arberry, Arthur J. (1955) *The Koran Interpreted*, London: George Allen & Unwin.

Burt, M.F. (1910) *Swahili Grammar and Vocabulary*, London: Society for Promoting Christian Knowledge.

Burton, Richard F. (1872) *Zanzibar: City, Island, and Coast*, 2 vols, London: Tinsley Brothers.

el-Zein, Abdul H. (1974) *The Sacred Meadows: A Structural Analysis of Religious Symbolism in an East African Town*, Evanston, IL: Northwestern University Press.

Emery, James B. (1825) "A Journal of the British Establishment of Mambasa 1824–1826," *PRO/ADM*, 52: 3940.

Frankl, P.J.L., and Yahya Ali Omar (1993) "Siku ya Mwaka: New Year's Day in Swahili-Land (With Special Reference to Mombasa)," *Journal of Religion in Africa*, 23: 125–135.

——— (1995) "Mashairi ya Waadhi [Verses of Admonishment]: The People of Mombasa Rebuked," *Afrikanistische Arbeitspapiere: Swahili Forum*, 42: 138–157.

Gibb, Hamilton A.R., and Johannes H. Kramers (1961) *Shorter Encyclopaedia of Islam*, 2nd edn, Leiden and London: E.J. Brill & Luzac.

Gurnah, Abdulrazak (1994) *Paradise*, London: The New Press.

Hasani bin Ismail (1968) *The Medicine Man: Swifa ya Ngwumali* trans. Peter Lienhardt, Oxford: Clarendon Press.

Hinawy, Mbarak Ali (1964) "Notes on Customs in Mombasa," *Swahili*, 34: 17–38.

Johnson, Frederick (1939) *A Standard Swahili-English Dictionary (Founded on Madan's Swahili-English Dictionary)*, Oxford: Oxford University Press.

Juynboll, Th. (1914) *Handbuch des islamischen Gesetzes: Nach der Lehre der Shafi'itische Schule*, Leiden and Leipzig: Brill & Harrassowitz.

Krapf, Johan L. (1858) *Reisen in Ostafrika [Travels in East Africa]*, Korntal and Stuttgart: F.A. Brockhaus.

Krapf, J. Ludwig (1882) *A Dictionary of the Swahili Language*, London: Trübner & Co.

Lienhardt, Peter (1959) "The Mosque College of Lamu and its Social Background," *Tanganyika Notes & Records*, 53: 228–242.

Mtoro bin Mwinyi Bakari (1981) *The Customs of the Swahili People*, trans. J.W.T. Allen, Berkeley, CA: University of California Press.

Owen, W.F.W. (1833) *Narrative of Voyages to Explore the Shores of Africa*, 2 vols, London: Richard Bentley.

Plessner, M. (1955) "Ramadan," *Encyclopaedia of Islam*, 2: 417–418.

Sacleux, Charles (1939) *Dictionnaire Swahili-Français*, Paris: Institut d'Ethnologie.

Sengo, Tigita Sh.Y., and F.T. Sengo (1979) *Mashairi ya mfungo wa Ramadhani [Poems about the Fast of Ramadan]*, Arusha & Dar es-Salaam: Eastern Africa Publications.

Sperling, David C. (1988) "The Growth of Islam among the Mijikenda, 1826–1933," PhD Thesis, SOAS, University of London, London.

Strobel, Margaret A. (1975) "Muslim Women in Mombasa: 1890–1973," PhD Thesis, University of California, Los Angeles.

Taylor, William E. (1891) *African Aphorisms or Saws from Swahili-Land*, London: Society for the Promotion of Christian Knowledge.
Trimingham, John S. (1952) *Islam in Ethiopia*, London: Oxford University Press.
——— (1959) *Islam in West Africa*, Oxford: Clarendon Press.
——— (1964) *Islam in East Africa*, London: Oxford University Press.
——— (1980) *The Influence of Islam upon Africa*, London and New York: Longman.
Velten, Carl (1903) *Desturi za Wasuaheli [The Customs of the Swahili People]*, Göttingen: Vandenhoeck & Ruprecht.
Waite, Terry (1994) *Taken on Trust*, London: Hodder & Stoughton.

8 Being good in Ramadān

Ambivalence, fragmentation, and the moral self in the lives of young Egyptians

Samuli Schielke

Samuli Schielke is currently a research fellow and head of the research group "In Search of Europe: Considering the Possible in Africa and the Middle East" at Zentrum Moderner Orient (ZMO) in Berlin, and an external lecturer in the Master Visual and Media Anthropology program at the Free University of Berlin. He received his PhD in social sciences from the University of Amsterdam in 2006 and from 2006–2007 did postdoctoral work with the Department of Anthropology and African Studies. Egypt has been his primary area of research, focusing on the contradictions and margins of the Islamic revival as well as cosmopolitan imaginations in Egypt. He has authored and edited a number of publications on festive culture and Sufism in Egypt: "Policing Ambiguity: Muslim Saints-Day Festivals and the Moral Geography of Public Space in Egypt" (2008), "Dimensions of Locality: Muslim Saints and Their Places" (with Georg Stauth, 2008) and "Mystic States, Motherly Virtues, Female Participation and Leadership in an Egyptian Sufi Milieu" (2008). His most recent publications "Boredom and Despair in Rural Egypt" (2008) and "Ambivalent Commitments: Troubles of Morality, Religiosity and Aspiration among Young Egyptians" (2009) address religiosity and everyday life of the younger generation in Egypt. Together with Daniela Swarowsky, he produced a documentary, "Messages from Paradise #1: Egypt–Austria: About the Permanent Longing for Elsewhere" and has shown a number of ethnographic photography exhibits. The article below shows how the fasting during the month of Ramadān is shaped by different personal trajectories and cultural ideals. He argues that an anthropological study of subjectivity and morality of Muslims should not only search for the notion of perfection, but also for the ambivalences and ambiguities of their ethical standards.

Introduction

For young men in the northern Egyptian village of Nazlat al-Rayyis,[1] the holy month of Ramadān is a privileged time for football. Every afternoon before fast-breaking time, youths gather to play at schoolyards or other open spaces. At the secondary school, a Ramadān tournament of local amateur clubs attracts up to a hundred spectators, who sit from early afternoon until shortly before sunset in the shade, watching the usually two or three consecutive matches that take place in an afternoon. I was amazed at first by this display of what seemed to me an extreme exercise of physical endurance in face of a fasting that involves complete abstinence from food, drink, smoking, and sex from dawn to sunset. But when I discussed the subject with the young men, they said that playing football during the hours before fast-breaking is not very arduous at all. On the contrary, concentrating on the game makes one forget the feelings of hunger and thirst.[2] The hours before the fast-breaking can be long, and male students and civil servants especially often have a lot of free time in Ramadān.

Football is not only about killing time, however. It is also seen as a form of the sociality (*lamma*) and amusement (*taslîya*) that characterize Ramadān in Egypt as much as fasting and praying do. Despite the ascetic character of fasting, Ramadān in Egypt is surrounded by a festive atmosphere. Streets are decorated with flags, colourful strips of paper, lights, and lanterns. In the evenings—especially towards the end of Ramadān—people invite friends and relatives, the cafés are full, and in the cities a veritable season of cultural events characterizes the second half of the month. But festive as they may be, Ramadān gatherings nevertheless express a spirit of religious and moral discipline. Forms of entertainment deemed immoral or un-Islamic—flirting and making out, consumption of alcohol and cannabis, pornography—largely stop during the holy month. In the cities, bars are closed. In the villages, internet cafés are empty. The trade in cannabis that otherwise flourishes in cities and villages alike reaches a seasonal low. Other forms of entertainment that are not seen as immoral as such are suspended in Ramadān because they have no place in the rigid schedule of fasting. Popular celebrations such as saints-day festivals (*mûlids*) and weddings are not celebrated at this time.[3] These forms of entertainment, temporarily unavailable during the holy month, are partly replaced by football. "The football matches," a friend of mine argued, "are for the youths a way to compensate for not being able to go after girls, smoke marijuana and drink beer. It's a way to fill the emptiness that they otherwise fill with immoral entertainment."

Ramadān football is an ambivalent exercise. It is one of the gatherings so characteristic of the sense of community that prevails in the month of fasting, and a way to kill time that is not deemed immoral or un-Islamic. But at the same time it shows a very complex understanding of religion and morality. Not only does it mix ascetic discipline with fun and entertainment, it is also part of a time of exceptional morality that, by its nature, will only last as long as Ramadān lasts, and that by virtue of its temporally limited nature indirectly legitimizes less consistent approaches to religion and morality for the rest of the year.

Since the Islamic revival of the 1970s, rigid religious moralism has become a leading tone of the debates in Egypt on norms and values. Daily life, however, continues to be characterized by the ambiguity between and an uneasy co-existence of religious morality and discipline, communal respect and reputation, the expectations and promises of consumerism and romantic love, and the limitations of practical circumstances. This tension is most strongly present among the youth, whose life experience has become (or perhaps has always been) highly fragmented, characterized by contradictory values and expectations, and often by strong crises and shifts in lifestyle and attitudes.

While subjectivity, religiosity, and morality have become a central topic of the anthropology of Muslim societies, the issues of ambivalence and fragmentation have so far been given relatively little attention. Notably Talal Asad, Michael Lambek, Charles Hirschkind and Saba Mahmood have—with somewhat different emphases—argued for an anthropology of morality that, rather than focusing on codes, commands, and prohibitions, should have as its focus the ways in which moral personhood and responsibility are created and practiced (Asad 1993; Lambek 2000; Hirschkind 2001; Hirschkind 2006a; Hirschkind 2006b; Mahmood 2005). Morality, in this sense, is about the conscious cultivation of virtues with the aim of developing a virtuous self. The problem of these approaches is that although they give considerable attention to practical judgment in the face of conflict, debate, and contestation, they look at the practice of morality and religion primarily from the perspective of coherence. [...] Yet if we are to understand the ambiguity of Ramadān football, we must find a way to account for views that are neither clearly nor consistently in line with any grand ideology, and lives that are full of ambivalence—not only between moral and amoral aims, but also between different, at times mutually hostile, moral aims. [...]

My own research on Muslim saints-day festivals (Schielke 2006) indicates that while in earlier, more mystical traditions of Islam ambivalence was accommodated as part of a normative order that did not require a comprehensive and universalizing discipline, modernist and reformist approaches that emphasize rationality and purity often take the abolition of ambivalence as a key task. Their attempt to do so, however, actually leads not to more clarity but to more fragmentation.

In this paper, I argue that moral subjectivity is a very important issue indeed, but there is a risk—especially when morality and piety come together—of favouring the complete, the consistent, and the perfect in a way that does not do justice to the complex and often contradictory nature of everyday experience. To develop this theoretical critique, I shall depart somewhat from the conventions of academic writing: I will present my empirical case first and only afterwards conclude with a detailed critical discussion, informed by my empirical argument, of current research in the field. For the sake of clarity, I single out one particularly influential and good example of the study of piety and subjectivity—Saba Mahmood's *Politics of Piety* (Mahmood 2005)—which, I believe, offers inspiring directions for the anthropological study of religion, but falls into the trap of what Katherine Ewing has called "the illusion of wholeness" (Ewing 1990).

Ramadān morality

Ramadān, in Muslim belief, is a blessed, holy month which constitutes a special period of piety that involves much more than just fasting. There is a general sense of increased social, moral, and pious commitment during Ramadān. In the evenings, the mosques are often packed with believers participating in the voluntarily *tarâwîh* prayers, in addition to canonical ritual daily prayers that can extend over more than an hour after the evening (*'ishâ*) prayer. In the streets of the cities, wealthy citizens offer large-scale services of free food at fast-breaking time, known as "tables of the Merciful" (*mawâ'id ar-Rahmân*).

Arduous to maintain especially in summer heat, fasting is seen by many as a spiritual exercise in disciplining carnal desires. Furthermore, many people ascribe to the feeling of hunger, a strong power in facilitating social responsibility towards the poor. The central and most important motivation for fasting, however, is the prospect of Paradise. Ramadān is a time when God rewards believers most generously and forgives their sins. For the duration of Ramadān, "the gates of Paradise are open and the gates of Hell are closed."[4] According to a *hadith* (authoritative tradition) of the Prophet Muhammad, distributed as a poster by the local Branch of the Muslim Brotherhood,

> Whoever fasts and stands for prayer in the month of Ramadān with faith and entrusting God with counting the reward, the sins he has previously committed are forgiven. And whoever stands for prayer in the Night of Destiny (*Laylat al-Qadr*)[5] with faith and entrusting God with counting the reward, the sins he has previously committed are forgiven.[6]

Other traditions state that the obligatory prayer counts seventy times its value during Ramadān, that voluntary prayer gains the same reward as an obligatory one, and that a prayer in *Laylat al-Qadr* is better than that of a thousand months. On the other hand, the consequences of not observing Ramadān are severe. Intentionally breaking the fast without a legitimate reason cannot be recalled or equaled out by anything, and both good and bad deeds count their double in reward and punishment during Ramadān.[7]

Not surprisingly, then, Ramadān is "the season of worship" (*mûsim al-'îbâda*), a time when people try to be good—that is, observe religious commandments and moral virtues more rigorously than they usually do. People who otherwise rarely pray try to fulfill this obligation during the holy month, especially in the beginning and around *Laylat al-Qadr*. Since it is believed that anger, curses, and insults break the fast, people attempt to avoid them during Ramadān, and in arguments and fights (which are numerous in Ramadān as people often have short tempers due to fasting), people often use the phrase "Oh God, I'm fasting!" (*Allâhumma ana sâyim*)[8] to avoid using foul language but also to call oneself and others to calm down.

During the holy month, one must abstain from all the other minor and major misdeeds that may be forgivable at other times. If God's reward and blessings are very close during Ramadān, so are His wrath and punishment. This belief involves not only practices deemed as immoral and sinful, such as drinking, flirting, adultery, watching pornography, lying, stealing, and violence. It also implies restrictions upon practices with more ambiguous status, notably cinema, music, and dress. Many women opt for a more conservative dress during Ramadān (by not using make-up, for example), and some people abstain from listening to pop music and watching movies, arguing that "they are *harâm* (forbidden) during Ramadān."

This focus on reward and piety is framed, however, by the general sense of gathering, joy, and entertainment of which the afternoon football matches are only one example. A month of fasting, Ramadān is also a privileged time of eating as people compensate for the fasting in daytime with special delicacies in the evening. The consumption of meat and sugar skyrockets. Special television programs and, in the cities, cultural events in theatres and tents offer a wide range of Ramadān entertainment. At night, cafés, promenades, and parks are packed with people, including many more women and families than usually. People generally spend more money in Ramadān, and towards the end of the month, with *'îd al-fitr* (the feast of breaking the fast) approaching, consumption reaches an intensity similar to that of Christmas in the West.

This "Christmasization of Ramadān," as it has been called by Walter Armbrust (Armbrust 2000), and the character of Ramadān as a time of exceptional morality have been regularly subjected to criticism both from religious authorities and from ordinary citizens who feel that the "true" spirit of Ramadān is lost in the midst of all this. They argue that Ramadān should be a time of spirituality and discipline that helps to create a "committed" (*multazim*) Muslim character and society free of vices and unnecessary spending, orientated to the purpose of individual and collective self-improvement (Abû l-Ma'âtî 2006: 7; al-Khashshâb 2006: 7; Matar 2006: 23–24; Sha'bân 2006: 4; al-Shurbâsî 2006: 1428–1431).

The popular practice of Ramadān, both in its ascetic and festive variations, does not focus on progressive improvement of society and self. Firmly based on the authoritative sources of Islam but with a different emphasis than offered by established religious discourse, its focus is explicitly on reward (*thawâb*), the forgiving of sins, and the ultimate aim of entering Paradise in the afterlife. During Ramadān, people frequently discuss in detail the correct form of voluntary prayers and the exact details of fasting in order to maximize the reward of praying and fasting. This is a highly utilitarian understanding of religion that implicitly allows Ramadān to be established as a moral and pious exception from not so perfect everyday life. If Ramadān is a time of exceptional reward when God forgives one's previous sins, one may commit some sins and slip a little from one's obligations during the rest of the year—in a year's time, after all, it is Ramadān again.

The ways in which most people practise Ramadān do not require an ethical subjectivity that aims at the perfection of a purified, God-fearing self capable of keeping right and wrong clearly apart in one's judgment of one's own and others' conduct. This is, however, the ideal promoted by the Salafi reformist movement and, to a less radical extent, established public-sector religious functionaries. It is, more importantly, closely connected with the (for the time being) hegemonic ideology of developmentalist nationalism, which, despite some severe compromises it has undergone in the process of economic liberalization, continues to posit the ideal of a rational, committed, and disciplined citizen who, much like the ideal Salafi believer, has "awareness" (*wa'y*), that is, clear and authoritative knowledge and a correspondingly sound ethical disposition. This is a notion of society, religion, and the subject which, in its secular and Islamist varieties alike, centres on discipline, clarity, and consistence in service of a grand purpose (Schielke 2006; Schielke 2007). [...] The moral subject in this practice of and vernacular discourse on morality is one who acts appropriately according to the time and the occasion in order to find a more or less acceptable temporary balance between God's commands, social customs and values, personal desires, and economic pressures, a balance in which the weight of different constituents can change depending on the social context of a practice, the time of the year, and one's personal biography. [...] [I]n the end it is precisely the temporary rigour of the holy month that establishes and legitimizes the flexible nature of norms and ethics for the rest of the year.

This can be best seen in the time of *'îd al-fitr*, the feast of breaking the fast that marks the end of Ramadān. In line with the established traditions of ritual Law, Muslims take the Feast as an occasion to reward themselves for withstanding the trial of fasting. But the extent and ways in which they do so can significantly depart from individual and collective self-improvement and reform. The Feast marks not only a reward for fasting, but also the return to a normal order of affairs. On the first Friday after Ramadān, at the congregational Friday noon (*gum'a*) prayer, the sermons invariably circle around one issue: reminding the believers that they must follow the commandments of their creed not only during Ramadān, but for all of the year, that the Feast does not mean that one is allowed to revert to one's bad habits. And yet every year when Ramadān football gives way to other forms of entertainment, the same young men who pray and fast during Ramadān now celebrate in ways that would have been out of the question a few days earlier. The sales of hashish skyrocket, cafés with satellite dishes start showing porn again, and, most visibly and dramatically, youths gather in parks, promenades, and public places to celebrate in an excited and tense atmosphere that often leads to outbreaks of sexual harassment with young men aggressively touching and grabbing women passing by (Malek 2006).

But the power of the moral shift of the Feast lies not simply in the reversion to bad habits. More importantly, it marks the shift from a period of observance during which the sins of the previous year are erased, to a more complex order of morality. Sexuality is a strong case in point. While, according to Islamic rituals, sexual intercourse is allowed in the night during Ramadān, the rigorous and often tiring schedule imposed by fasting leaves little time and energy for sex. On the first evening of the Feast in 2004, I met with young men from the village in a café. They were sitting outside in the alley, while inside, behind mostly closed doors, middle-aged family fathers were watching porn on a French satellite channel.[9] The youths explained that the married men were "warming up" to go home and have sex with their wives after a month's abstinence. Since the young unmarried men did not have wives waiting for them at home, they were doing their best to annoy and make fun of the older men, who were slightly but not very uncomfortable with the situation, exposed, on the one hand, confirmed in their striving for potency, a very important male virtue, on the other. But also for the young men the Feast meant a return to male virtues based on virility and sexuality after temporarily devoting themselves to the more ascetic virtues of piety and sportsmanship during Ramadān. Many of them had girlfriends and prospective brides whom they were courting, and those who did not were nevertheless busy with romantic and erotic fantasies, as well as attempts to make contacts with girls, with strategies ranging from flirting to aggressive harassment. The end of Ramadān meant that they were free to resume "going after girls" (*yimshi wara l-banât*), a practice deemed morally questionable but all the same essential for their male self-esteem and their expectations of romantic love.

Moral registers

The moral universe in which Ramadān morality is embedded is characterized by a profound ambivalence that is not only a coincidental result of circumstances but actually provides the foundation of situational moral action and an ethical subjectivity that is based on a coexistence of various motivations, aims, and identities that can and often do conflict but do not constitute exclusive opposites.

Young people in the village, often strongly influenced by Salafis and Muslim Brothers in their religious beliefs, generally share a literalist understanding of religion as a clear, exact set of commandments and prohibitions that leave little or no space for different interpretations or negotiation. In their everyday practice, however, they also express other ideals that may more or less clearly contradict their religious discourse.

The life experiences and expectations of the young men of Nazlat al-Rayyis are characterized by several moments of ambivalence that consider not only others' expectations of them but also, as far as I can tell on the basis of their accounts, their own expectations of themselves. Ideals of rigid sexual morality coexist and compete with the imaginaries and experiments of romance and sex, wishes of self-realization with the aspirations for social status, ideals of moral integrity with the drive for material well-being. In fact, people often speak in very different tone and with very different arguments and style about different topics. While young men often ridicule Salafi activists with their long beards, short-hemmed *gallâbiyas* (long loose gowns worn by men), and painstakingly precise ritualism, at the same time their idea of a profoundly religious person is usually identical with the image of the Salafi. A talk, very critical and satirical, about social values can turn suddenly very serious and dogmatic when the subject of religion crops up. On the other hand, people can argue for very conservative and strict standards of gender relations at one time, but express rather liberal ideals of romantic love at other times. In short, morality is not a coherent system, but an incoherent and unsystematic conglomerate of different moral registers that exist in parallel and often contradict each other. There are several key moral registers, each with values, terminologies, discourses, and fields of their own, that play a role in the lives and discourses of the young men with whom I did fieldwork. The most important among them are as follows:

1 Religion, understood as a set of clear norms, often referred to as "Qur'ān and the Sunna," that is, the two central sources of Islam. Religion, in this understanding, is essentially a normative system that defines all acts as either permitted (*halâl*) or prohibited (*harâm*) on the base of evidence from the Scripture.
2 Social justice, generally with a clear socialist overtone problematizing issues such as corruption, privatization of public-sector enterprises and public services, nepotism, authoritarian rule, economic exploitation, the lack of opportunities of people with state education, and the ridiculously low salaries of civil servants.

3 Community and family obligations, usually referred to with "respect" (*ihtirâm*), including one's social standing in the community, good behaviour, responsibility for one's family, recognition of authorities and hierarchies, and wealth.
4 Good character (*tîba, gada'âna*), based on the readiness to help friends, avoidance of conflicts, and a general sense of joviality and sympathy. Good character is often seen by young men as a more "true" virtue than respect, which, in their view, often is based purely on money and can conceal an essentially vicious character.
5 Romance and love, celebrating passion and emotional commitment and describing "pure love" as an all-sacrificing obsession that disregards both self-interest and other moral ideals.
6 Self-realization, expressed in the aim of finding a well-paid job and a place in life and, to a lesser degree, of widening one's horizon of experience.

Morality in this sense is not only unsystematic and ambiguous, it is also accompanied by declaredly amoral aims and strategies that people deem necessary to fill the "emptiness" of the everyday and to reach material well-being. Some of the most important amoral registers are money and the necessity of earning an income (which, for example, force a respectable and God-fearing civil servant to live on bribes), sex and desire, and fun and excitement, including the consumption of alcohol and drugs. On the other side, there are also recurring topoi which in a moralizing tone at once establish a moral register and offer an excuse—most notably so a critique of materialism which consists of claiming that "in this village" or "in our society" all that really counts is money and that true moral values have no importance anymore. By insinuating that if it were not for all this money and materialism, people really would be able to live happy, spiritual lives in justice and harmony, the critique of materialism at once establishes the registers of religion and social justice and explains why it is not possible to live according to them.

Romantic love and sexuality, to stay with an example that is deemed crucially important by the young men I have followed in my fieldwork, form an ethical discourse with specific virtues and teleologies of the subject, that is, ways to become and be a good human being (see Foucault 1990: 25–32). Romance is strongly present not only in everyday experience, but also in the public media in the form of love songs, films, soap operas, and so on. While the plots and the kinds of problems that the heroes of love songs and stories face certainly move within a moral universe that makes them meaningful and understandable to their audiences, they definitely cannot be reduced to the religious discourse of legitimate and illegitimate relationships, the vernacular ethics of patriarchal family, or the forms of double morality that measure different actions on different scales depending on gender, social status, and the context of the action. Love represents an ethics of desire and commitment (which can reach the degree of obsession) that stands in stark contrast to the religious discourse on chastity and the social practice of parental control over marriages.[10] But committed to the ideals of romance as the young men are, they can simultaneously be very convinced about the necessity of gender segregation and the absolute prohibition of adultery (*zinâ*) in Islam. The interesting point here is not just the fact that despite the religious discourse on chastity premarital sex does take place quite often, but the ambivalent coexistence of partly opposing teleologies of the subject, on one level striving for a sinless and pure disposition that excludes erotic relationships before marriage, on another level aiming for a romantic and erotic relationship that in the end (not at the beginning) may lead to marriage, while on a further level committed to ideals of family hierarchies and respect that exclude girlfriends from the role of potential wives exactly because their participation in romantic affairs makes them "bad" (*wihsha*) and unrespectable.[11]

The practice of all these contradictory and conflicting expectations and ideals is necessarily situational and inconsequent. Love stands in a continuous tension to the register of gender segregation and sexual morality and the register of family responsibilities. The communal quality of respect is often seen as a mere mask based on material values and detached from the virtue of good character. The ideal of social justice stands in a striking juxtaposition to a reality where nepotism, bribes, and illegal trade are often the only and usually the most lucrative way to make a living. The over-arching normativity of religion, finally, is continuously relativized by references to other registers that, rather than questioning or subverting religious norms, circumvent them.

Ramadān, in this mosaic of a moral universe, is a site of higher order, a moral exception which through the exercise of fasting establishes a clear hierarchy and a clear teleology: the commands of God and the prospect of Paradise. By the logic of its exceptional nature, it cannot and need not be a permanent state of affairs. My point here is that this is not merely a compromise that allows for amoral practices for the sake of material necessity. Romantic love, social respect, good character, and self-realization constitute moral registers and ethical teleologies of the subject that are by no means amoral; on the contrary, they imply normative expectations in their own right. While during Ramadān they can be temporarily subordinated to the superior normativity of religion, in the everyday their relationship is one of competitive coexistence.

Living according to the Book

This coexistence is increasingly troubled—but not replaced—by the current turn of many young people towards a Salafi revivalist understanding of religion as an all-encompassing ritual and moral discipline that has as its declared aim the abolition of ambivalence and the imposition of clarity (see also Lincoln 2006: 56–60). Good life, in this understanding, must and can only be based on full and comprehensive application of *al-kitâb wa-s-sunna*, that is, the Qur'ān and the Prophet's tradition *qua* definitive manuals of moral action. This, however, does not mean that people would actually live in this way, and therein lies both the power and the fundamental trouble of the Salafi ideal of religiosity. On the one hand, people can hold to it without actually having fully to realize it, and its being unrealized allows it to remain pure and simple while life is messy and complex. On the other hand, however, it can become a serious obstacle in people's lives, a debate-killing argument that can lead people into serious crises and dead ends. [...]

With its emphasis on direct knowledge and application of religious "facts," Islamic reformism opens up powerful possibilities of critique while excluding or marginalizing others by positing them beyond discussion. Other styles of being religious exist, but they are increasingly stigmatized as incomplete or erroneous. Spaces of ambiguity are increasingly dependent on silence, double standards, and cognitive dissonance. While values can be debated, declaring them religious often ends the debate. All other moral registers have either to accept or ignore the supremacy of religion, but they cannot openly contest it.

What makes this troubling for young men is the way the current wave of religiosity often leaves people hanging in a situation where they accept the promise of religion for a better life both in this world and the Hereafter, but cannot measure the promise in any legitimate way, or search for alternative solutions should the reality fall short of the promise. The problems this causes are best seen in the fragmentation of people's biographies. Young age is often characterized by strong changes in beliefs and attitudes, and it is usually at young age that people choose to become "committed" (*multazim*) Salafis who not only meticulously fulfill religious obligations such as praying and fasting, but also apply a wider pious discipline to all aspects of their lives, changing their style of dress, giving up smoking,[12] starting to socialize primarily with other Salafis, and adapting a distinctive jargon. Becoming an active Salafi with the corresponding comprehensive discipline is usually marked by a strong break between a "sinful" (*'âsî*) past and a "committed" present—therefore disqualifying the more ambivalent forms of morality. But we must be careful not to take the way from ambivalence and imperfection to clarity and commitment as the regular and typical one. The perfectionist nature of the piety movement produces much starker contrasts between commitment and deviance than the temporal relativism of Ramadān morality. The result is not necessarily a general shift from Ramadān piety to comprehensive piety, but rather the increasing intensity of the juxtapositions and shifts. People always live complex lives; a person's identity is in practice dialogical, made up of different voices and experiences (Gregg 2007; van Meijl 2006). In consequence, people commonly shift between different roles and identities. This can become a problematic and troublesome experience, however, when one or some of the ideologies of the self a person holds to are based on a demand for strict and exclusive perfection—as the Salafi revivalist notion of subjectivity based on "commitment" (*iltizâm*) is.

Salafis, just like everybody else, live everyday lives loaded with ambiguities and contradictions. To a certain degree Salafi discourse allows for pragmatic solutions legitimized by the Islamic legal category of necessity (*darûra*). Shaving one's beard for conscription is a common case of such compromises for the sake of necessity that young Salafi men face. The problem, however, is that this by no means lessens the pressure on pious self-perfection. On the level of emotional and spiritual commitment, there is little space for negotiation. The rigour of Salafi piety that makes it so attractive in the mess of the everyday also makes it difficult to maintain in the face of ambivalent feelings. Take, for example, the story of Mustafa (a pseudonym), a man in his early twenties who after a period of excessive consumption of hashish and a lifestyle deemed irresponsible and unrespectable by his friends and family turned to Salafi religiosity in order to find a clear distinction between right and wrong.

I first met Mustafa some time before his military service and shortly after he had given up his practice of Salafi piety. While he continues to hold to Salafi ideas on religion when asked, he now regularly shaves, has returned to smoking, prays irregularly, and maintains contact with female friends in a way which Salafis would consider unacceptable (but which is considered well within the limits of respectable behaviour by his friends). It has not been an easy shift for him: he frequently reports intense feelings of guilt and failure because of the temporary suspension of his commitment (he does indicate that he hopes to return to a more pious lifestyle after the end of his military service). Neither his move from deviation to commitment, nor his slip (as he describes it) from commitment to ambivalence are in any way unusual. I know people who have gone through periods as a Muslim Brotherhood activist at school, a left-wing atheist as a university student, and a liberal believer attached to ideas of Nasr Abû Zayd[13] as a family father. There are some women whom I came to know as veiled and conservative young students but who have since given up veiling and have grown increasingly critical of what they see as misguided religious moralism, without, however, turning against religion as such. Others again have begun to wear a more covering dress and adopted a more "committed" (*multazima*) lifestyle after completing their studies, seeing this not as a break, however, but rather as a ripening process. Some men I know have become radical and strictly committed Salafis who make a clear break with their past, grow their beards, and (try to) stop smoking after spending wild student years with girlfriends, alcohol, and drugs. Some among them remain Salafis, while others later shave their beards again and return to an ambiguous, "ordinary" lifestyle.

It is for the people for whom pious commitment is only a period in their life that the Salafi aim of comprehensive purity is most troubling. They often tell of having experienced a period of intense happiness and satisfaction as active Salafis but then losing the drive, facing everyday problems at work or with state authorities (who view Salafis with great suspicion), and reverting to their old habits. In the following period, they often report a feeling of failure and guilt. With their earlier standards and norms no longer sufficient or legitimate in their eyes, they are nevertheless not able to hold the drive for purity so central for Salafi piety. Troubled by the loss of his earlier almost euphoric sense of piety and commitment, Mustafa says:

> Yesterday I heard a sermon on the computer that made me think about my priorities. You have to be self-vigilant and repent every day to our sublime and exalted Lord, and renew your promises to our Lord. I felt a state of lethargy. When I heard the same tape earlier I cried. So why didn't I cry yesterday? Because my heart is black. Why am I like this? I remember an example Shaykh Salâh told me: Let's assume that next to the chimney of an oven there is a freshly painted wall. What will happen to that wall? On the first day it blackens a little. On the next day it blackens more. On the third day it blackens more, and so on. The same thing in the heart, which stays polished and clean with the obedience to sublime and exalted God. When you give up worship (*'ibâdât*) the heart keeps being blackened by dirt.

For one thing, this account describes pious commitment as a fragile form of continuous self-suggestion rather than as cumulative self-perfection. Furthermore, it pinpoints how the Salafi discourse of piety with its tremendous emphasis on purity makes it very difficult to find a balance with different desires if the drive of self-suggestion recedes—as it often does. There is neither return to the relative comfort of the negotiated ambiguity of living for God in Ramadān and for oneself for the rest of the year, nor comfort in the rigid understanding of religion. Since religion stands totally beyond critique, people can only search for faults in themselves. And since the Salafi interpretation of religion insists that there are no interpretations of religion, only plain objective Religion on the one side and erroneous deviations on the other, rural young people rarely have access to other interpretations of religion that would allow them to reconcile their ambivalent experiences with their religious faith.

As a consequence, the wave of Salafi religiosity with its insistence on purity and perfection actually intensifies the fragmentation and contradictions in young people's lives. While wishing to be good Muslims living by the Qur'ān and the Sunna and going to Paradise in the Hereafter, the young men in the village still also wish to fall in love, to be excited, to get high, to be wealthy, to get abroad, to have sex, and many other things. Some of these aims do not contradict the young men's religious convictions. But those that do are becoming more and more difficult to include as legitimate elements of a necessarily ambiguous and complex life. Instead, they become increasingly separate and mutually antagonistic.

Flaws of perfection

With football as a paradigmatic case of Ramadān piety and morality, we reach rather different conclusions than we would have with, say, the practice of prayer (see, e.g., Henkel 2005; Möller 2005: 380). Of course, Ramadān is about prayer as much as it is about football, and, if given the choice, most Muslims would certainly name prayer as the more important part (although the most important, undoubtedly, would be fasting, which gives both prayer and football their special "taste" during Ramadān). But my point is that in looking at what may seem a marginal practice and a way to kill time instead of focusing on a core ritual, we may actually learn more about the moral and religious world to which both belong. A focus on key religious practices and the attempt to fulfill them is likely to produce analyses that highlight the moment of perfection. A focus on the margins of these practices, on the contrary, is likely to shed more light on the much less perfect social experiences and personal trajectories that all too easily remain obscured by the strong tendency of religious discourse—both in first and third person—to describe the normative as the normal. [...]

Much of the recent research on morality, piety, and subjectivity is characterized by what I see as a problematic tendency to privilege the aim of ethical perfection. Here I single out the currently perhaps most prominent example of such a tendency: Saba Mahmood's (Mahmood 2003; Mahmood 2005) work on the piety movement in Egypt, which, closely aligned with the work of Talal Asad (Asad 1986; Asad 1993; Asad 2003) and Charles Hirschkind (Hirschkind 2001; Hirschkind 2006a; Hirschkind 2006b), has gained great (and for a large part deserved) acclaim within the anthropology of Islam (see, e.g., Bautista 2008).

Mahmood argues that rather than positing a liberal autonomous subject as a natural starting-point of the study of religious and moral subjects, we need to look at the creation of an ethical self through embodied religious practices and accept that there are religiously and culturally preconditioned moral subjectivities that differ from those prescribed by liberal and feminist theory. [...]

Critical of both the denunciatory tone of many studies on Islamist piety movements, on the one hand, and of the search for moments of resistance and subversion, on the other, Mahmood refers to Aristotle to call for a focus upon the way people attempt to learn and live moral dispositions. Acting within a moral universe that provides certain kinds of legitimate arguments and forms of action, the women active in the piety movement consciously attempt to develop a docile and pious character. In doing so, Mahmood argues, they are neither making free choices of the autonomous, liberal kind, nor are they passive objects of manipulation. To avoid such simple oppositions and the ideological weight they carry, we should look at the kind of actions and arguments that are available to people and the ways they relate individual dispositions to ethical practice.

A key category in Mahmood's study of the piety movement is habitus; however, in a very different sense from that popularized by Pierre Bourdieu (Bourdieu 1984: 168–177). Mahmood criticizes Bourdieu for missing the Aristotelian point of *habituation*, the active acquiring of an ethical disposition by the means of bodily habit. Habitus, according to Mahmood, involves the active capacity of forming and transforming the self through bodily practice [...]

Mahmood's analysis, as important as it is in many ways, is flawed in three respects: firstly, in its taking committed religious activists as paradigmatic representatives of religiosity; secondly, in its focus on the *attempt* to realize a docile, God-fearing ideal which leaves out the actual consequences of that attempt; and, thirdly, in its hermetic approach to "culture" and "tradition." The first is a limitation which *Politics of Piety* (Mahmood 2005) shares with many other studies on religious practice, especially in the context of Islam, where perhaps too many works have been devoted to religious activists, on the one hand, and intellectuals who attempt to revise the very basics of religious morality, on the other. The problem of such studies is that by limiting the scope of religious expression either to a strive towards perfection or a fundamental critique of religious norms, they unintentionally reproduce the bias of the committed groups they study. If we are to understand the ambiguous logic of

Ramadān morality and the fragmentary outcome of the Salafi project of perfection, we will have to look at that majority of people who are not actively committed to religious or political activism, who do share a recognition of the supreme authority of religion but do not practise it as an over-arching teleological project of ethical self-improvement (see Marsden 2005: 251–261; Masquelier 2007; Otayek and Soares 2007: 17–19).

More importantly, we will have to avoid Mahmood's second and perhaps more profound flaw of looking at the declared attempt, but overlooking its outcome. In a way, Mahmood offers us an analysis that takes practice as a central category but does not tell us much about actual practice itself. "Practice" in Mahmood's usage is primarily a conceptual category describing "the relationships [people] establish between the various constituent elements of the self (body, reason, volition, and so on) and a particular moral code or norm" (Mahmood 2003: 846). As a result, she can tell us much about the intended outcomes of the project of piety, but only little about its actual consequences. As Gary Gregg points out, the fact that a person has fashioned a perfect pious identity "does not predict how consistently his or her experience will conform to its contours" (Gregg 2007: 297–298). What happens when claims and ideals such as those formulated by the women of the piety movement come to be practised as guidelines in a life that has other, competing orientations and is characterized not by the primary purpose of perfection but rather by a struggle to find one's place in life?

Piety does not proceed along a unilinear path. It is an ambivalent practice that is often related to specific periods in life, especially those marked by crises. While it does not leave one unchanged, the endeavour of pious self-suggestion does not seem to build such strong dispositions that they would simply override other parts of an individual's personality. This is, of course, common knowledge in Egypt, as it is probably everywhere. But when we try to conceptualize the constitution of moral selves, we are easily tempted to take the more perfect and consistent life-stories as the more paradigmatic ones. I posit that it is precisely the fragmented nature of people's biographies which, together with the ambivalent nature of most moral subjectivities, should be taken as the starting-point when setting out to study moral discourse and ethical practice.

A third flaw in Mahmood's argumentation is that she too easily identifies the moral universe of the pious women with that of an Islamic discursive tradition that offers a set of references to the Scripture and ways of argumentation and reasoning (see Asad 1986). While there is no doubt that a such discursive tradition exists—or, more accurately, is produced and imagined by the people who as Muslims talk about Islam (Schielke 2007)—the problem is that a focus on "discursive tradition" makes it very easy to view religion as if it were a coherent entity, dynamic within but clearly demarcated to the outside. The focus on the inner dynamics and traditions of Islam easily insinuates a determining force of "culture" that is contradicted by those often highly idiosyncratic ways of positing oneself in the world that I have encountered among the young men of Nazlat al-Rayyis. To state that people are primarily acting within their discursive traditions understates the complexity, reflectivity, and openness of their worldviews and life experiences, especially so in a globalizing world characterized by the registers of consumerism, nationalism, human rights, and romance just as much as it is articulated by the striving for pious discipline and communal respect (Gregg 2007; Marsden 2005).

Developing her concept of ethics and self-formation, Mahmood notes in brackets that as far as specific conceptions of the self are concerned, "there may be different kinds that inhabit the space of a single culture" (Mahmood 2005: 139). The short exploration of moral subjectivities among the young men of Nazlat al-Rayyis that I have undertaken in this paper suggests that while this statement clearly is true (although it is very unlikely that such a clearly demarcated thing as "a single culture" exists), it does not go far enough. Not only do different conceptions of the self inhabit the space of a single culture, they are also present in the life experience of a single individual, to some extent simultaneously, to some extent periodically. An anthropological study of morality and ethical subjectivity has to take this inherent ambivalence as a starting-point. Rather than searching for moments of perfection, we have to look at the conflicts, ambiguities, double standards, fractures, and shifts as the constitutive moments of the practice of norms.

Notes

1 Nazlat al-Rayyis, where I have conducted a large part of my fieldwork for this article, is a large village between the Rosetta branch of the Nile and Lake Burullus, some 30 kilometres from the Mediterranean coast. A centre of schools and services for surrounding hamlets, it is nevertheless clearly rural in character, unlike many other villages of similar size. The population is entirely Muslim and divided into two economic groups of approximately equal size: farmers and fishermen who earn their living on Lake Burullus. This economic distinction is also an important base for identity, especially for the fisher families, who identify themselves as such even when they earn their living as workers, civil servants, and so on. By rural standards, Nazlat al-Rayyis appears to have relatively high levels of literacy and education. The village also has a long history of political activism. In the colonial period, it was a Wafdist stronghold, and in the republican period it has had a high level of leftist and communist activism. Today it has a strong and active branch of the Muslim Brotherhood. The people with whom I conducted the fieldwork for this paper mostly come from fishermen families but aim for careers in trade or the public sector. They have middle or high education, but their actual work and careers often fall short of their qualifications and expectations.

2 Trying it out myself, I found out that fasting and football indeed do go well together, to the degree that I once almost missed fast-breaking because of a match. The bigger problem for me was the absolutely superior level of the youths compared to my very modest skills and condition.

3 While there is no provision in Islamic rites against celebrating weddings in Ramadān, it is unusual to do so. This, like so many religious sensibilities, derives less from any specific textual traditions than a common sense that designates practices and times with specific qualities which, while not mutually exclusive, don't harmonize well.

4 *Al-Bukhârî: Sahîh*, book of fasting (*as-sawm*), chapter 5; *at-Tirmidhi: al-Jamiʿ as-sahîh*, book of fasting (*as-sawm*), chapter 1, *hadith* 682. (Because of the great variety of different printed and electronic editions of the Sunnite *hadith* collections, I refer to the *hadiths* by chapters rather than page numbers. References to canonical *hadith* collections are by editor, short title, and chapter.)

5 One of the last ten nights of Ramadān, when according to Islamic belief the revelation of the Qur'ān to Muhammad began. The exact date of *Laylat al-Qadr* is not known, but it is commonly celebrated on the night before the 27th of Ramadān.

6 Reported in slightly different versions by *ad-Dârimî: Sunan*, book of fasting (*as-sawm*), chapter 54 (*Fadl qiyâm shahr Ramadân*); *at-Tirmidhî: al-Jamiʿ as-sahîh*, book of fasting (*as-sawm*), chapter 1, *hadith* 683; *al-Bukhârî: Sahîh*, book of fasting (*as-sawm*), chapter 6.

7 For *Laylat al-Qadr*, see *Mâlik ibn Anâs*: *al-Muwatta'*, book of retreat in the mosque (*al-iʿtikâf*), chapter 6 (*mâ jâ' fî laylat al-qadr*), *hadith* 15; for intentionally breaking the fast, *Bukhârî: Sahîh*, book of fasting (*as-sawm*), chapter 29; for double reward, Muslim: *Sahîh*, book of fasting (*as-siyâm*): chapter of the merit of fasting (*fadl as-siyâm*), *hadith* 164.

8 Similarly, bystanders can also appeal to people involved in an argument with the phrase "Because you're fasting" (*ʿashân inta sâyim*).

9 Owing to the exposed character of cafés and the recent spread of internet in the countryside, pornography has largely disappeared from regular cafés and moved to internet cafés and private homes.

10 It is often difficult to draw a clear line between arranged and love marriages because a degree of negotiation is at play in most cases (see Hart 2007).

11 While men can more easily employ common standards of double morality to manoeuvre between different ethical ideals, women experience much more pressure to fulfil conflicting ideals of chastity and attractiveness.

12 While smoking cigarettes is not seen as a vice in Egyptian society, the Salafi movement makes a strong point about smoking being *harâm*.

13 The hermeneutic approach to the study of the Qur'ān employed by the Egyptian academic Nasr Abû Zayd, which caused a scandal that forced him to emigrate to Europe, has significant popularity among people searching for alternatives to what they deem a narrow-minded, fundamentalist interpretation of their religion.

References

Abû l-Ma'âtî, 'Â. (2006) "Min khawâtir ash-Sha'râwî ar-ramadanîya: hikmat as-siyâm fî ramadan [Al-Sha'râwî on Ramadan: The Wisdom of Fasting in Ramadan]," *al-Akhbâr*, 28 September: 7.

Al-Khashshâb, U. (2006) "Fî multaqâ l-fikr al-islâmî: al-intisâr 'alâ shahawât an-nafs tadrîb lil-intisâr fî ma'ârik al-hayât [At the Podium of Islamic Thought: The Victory over Desires of the Lower Soul is a Training for Victory in the Battles of Life]," *al-Akhbâr*, 28 September: 7.

Al-Shurbâsî, A. (2006) "as-Sawm madrasat tahdhîb [Fasting is the School of Cultivation]," *al-Azhar* 79: 1428–1431.

Armbrust, Walter (2000) "The Riddle of Ramadan: Media, Consumer Culture, and the Christmasization of a Muslim Holiday," in Donna L. Bowen and Evelyn A. Early (eds) *Everyday Life in the Muslim Middle East*, rev. edn, Bloomington, IN: Indiana University Press.

Asad, Talal (1986) *The Idea of an Anthropology of Islam*, Washington, DC: Georgetown University, Center for Contemporary Arab Studies.

——— (1993) *Genealogies of Religion: Discipline and Reasons of Power in Christianity and Islam*, Baltimore, MD: Johns Hopkins Press.

——— (2003) *Formations of the Secular: Christianity, Islam, Modernity*, Stanford, CA: Stanford University Press.

Bautista, Julius (2008) "The Meta-Theory of Piety: Reflections on the Work of Saba Mahmood," *Contemporary Islam*, 2: 75–83.

Bourdieu, Pierre (1984) *Distinction: A Social Critique of the Judgement of Taste*, trans. Richard Nice, London: Routledge & Kegan Paul.

Ewing, Katherine P. (1990) "The Illusion of Wholeness: Culture, Self, and the Experience of Inconsistency," *Ethos*, 18: 251–278.

Foucault, Michel (1990) *The History of Sexuality. Vol. 2: The Use of Pleasure*, trans. Robert Hurley, New York: Vintage Books.

Gregg, Gary S. (2007) *Culture and Identity in a Muslim Society*, Oxford and New York: Oxford University Press.

Hart, Kimberly (2007) "Love by Arrangement: The Ambiguity of 'Spousal Choice' in a Turkish Village," *Journal of the Royal Anthropological Institute*, 13: 345–362.

Henkel, Heiko (2005) "'Between Belief and Unbelief Lies the Performance of Salat': Meaning and Efficacy of a Muslim Ritual," *Journal of the Royal Anthropological Institute*, 11: 487–507.

Hirschkind, Charles (2001) "The Ethics of Listening: Cassette-Sermon Audition in Contemporary Egypt," *American Ethnologist*, 28: 623–649.

——— (2006a) "Cassette Ethics: Public Piety and Popular Media in Egypt," in Birgit Meyer and Annelies Moors (eds) *Religion, Media, and the Public Sphere*, Bloomington, IN: Indiana University Press.

——— (2006b) *The Ethical Soundscape: Cassette Sermons and Islamic Counterpublics*, New York: Columbia University Press.

Lambek, Michael (2000) "The Anthropology of Religion and the Quarrel between Poetry and Philosophy," *Current Anthropology*, 41: 309–320.

Lincoln, Bruce (2006) *Holy Terrors: Thinking about Religion after September 11*, Chicago, IL: University of Chicago Press.

Mahmood, Saba (2003) "Ethical Formation and Politics of Individual Autonomy in Contemporary Egypt," *Social Research*, 70: 837–866.

——— (2005) *Politics of Piety: The Islamic Revival and the Feminist Subject*, Princeton, NJ: Princeton University Press.

Malek (2006) *Su'âr Wasat al-Madîna al-jinsî [Downtown Sexual Harassment]*, [Accessed 25 June 2007]. Available online http://malek-x.net/node/268.

Marsden, Magnus (2005) *Living Islam: Muslim Religious Experience in Pakistan's North-West Frontier*, Cambridge: Cambridge University Press.

Masquelier, Adeline (2007) "Negotiating Futures: Islam, Youth, and the State in Niger," in Benjamin F. Soares and René Otayek (ed.) *Islam and Muslim Politics in Africa*, New York: Palgrave Macmillan.

Matar, I. (2006) "Okaziyôn al-maghfara [Discount Redemption]," *Rúz al-Yúsuf*, 29 September: 23–24.

Möller, André (2005) *Ramadan in Java: The Joy and Jihad of Ritual Fasting*, Stockholm: Almqvist & Wiksell.

Otayek, René, and Benjamin F. Soares (2007) "Introduction: Islam and Muslim Politics in Africa," in Benjamin F. Soares and René Otayek (eds) *Islam and Muslim Politics in Africa*, New York: Palgrave Macmillan.

Schielke, Samuli (2006) "Snacks and Saints: Mawlid Festivals and the Politics of Festivity, Piety and Modernity in Contemporary Egypt," PhD Thesis, University of Amsterdam.

——— (2007) "Hegemonic Encounters: Criticism of Saints-Day Festivals and the Formation of Modern Islam in Late 19th and Early 20th Century Egypt," *Die Welt des Islams*, 47: 319–355.

Sha'bân, K. (2006) "as-Siyâm wa-sh-shabâb [Fasting and the Youth]," *al-Akhbâr* 9 October: 4.

Van Meijl, Toon (2006) "Multiple Identifications and the Dialogical Self: Urban Maori Youngsters and the Cultural Renaissance," *Journal of the Royal Anthropological Institute*, 12: 917–933.

Pilgrimage to Mecca

9 The social significance of the *hajj* for Thai Muslims

Raymond Scupin

Raymond Scupin is the Chair of the Anthropology and Sociology Department at Lindenwood University. Additionally, he serves as the director of the Center for International and Global Studies. He received his BA in history, Asian studies and anthropology from University of California, Los Angeles, in 1972 and continued his education at University of California, Santa Barbara receiving both his MA and PhD from that institution. He is a member of the Human Rights Council of the American Anthropological Association (AAA) and the Society for the Anthropology of Religion (SAR). He received an award as a Fulbright Fellow in addition to receiving a grant from the National Endowment of the Humanities (NEH) for the Philosophy of Social Sciences. Scupin has lectured at the University of California, Santa Barbara, as well as being a visiting lecturer at the Ramkhamhaeng University in Bangkok, Thailand, and Northern Kentucky University. His areas of research include Islam, ethnicity, religion and globalization, publishing essays in these fields along with writings in Asian Studies. He is most well known as author of several textbooks in anthropology, *Cultural Anthropology: A Global Perspective* 8th edition (2012); and *Anthropology: A Global Perspective* 7th edition (2012) with Christopher DeCorse. Scupin has also edited a number of volumes, including *Religion and Culture: An Anthropological Focus* 2nd edition (2008) *Peoples and Cultures of Asia* (2006) as well as *Race, Ethnicity: An Anthropological Focus on the United States and the World* (2012). Dr. Scupin was honored with the Missouri Governor's award for excellence in teaching in 1999 and in 2007, he received the President's Scholar Award. The article below is one of the first and few articles that address the impact of the *hajj* on the Muslim community and their social stratification in Thailand. It also provides some important statistical information about the participation of Thai Muslims in the *hajj*. Scupin argues that the participation in the *hajj* clearly led to a system of prestige, in which the *hajjī* came to be recognized by the members of their local Muslim community.

Introduction

The significance of the impact that Southeast Asian Muslims returning from the *hajj* have had on their own societies has long been recognized, and the increase in numbers of pilgrims has greatly widened their circles of influence. While in the mid-nineteenth century approximately 2,000 pilgrims were counted annually departing from Indonesia for Mecca (Roff 1970: 155–181), by the early twentieth century the opportunities for making the *hajj* increased dramatically, with tens of thousands of Indonesians and

Malaysians becoming pilgrims. Some of these pilgrims remained in Mecca for some time to study and were exposed to Middle Eastern Islamic fundamentalism. On their return they became the dynamic leaders of Islamic reformist or fundamentalist movements in Southeast Asia. This essay, based upon fifteen months of ethnographic research on the Muslim population in Bangkok, assesses the social and cultural significance of the *hajj* for the Muslim population in Thailand in the recent past. First the Thai Muslim population will be identified, followed by a brief discussion of the variant forms of Islamic ideology in those communities. Finally this assessment will attempt to delineate future trends in Thai Muslim participation in the *hajj*.

The Muslim population in Thailand

Thai scholars and government officials tend to classify the Muslim population of Thailand into two categories: Malays and non-Malays (Haemindra 1976). This classification is a consequence of the unique cultural and historical situation of the Muslims of Thailand. The gradual Islamization of Indonesia and Malaysia, that occurred over several centuries, was simultaneous to the southward expansion of the Thai kingdom. Historically tributary Malay states, such as Patani were progressively transformed into provinces dependent upon and incorporated into the Thai Buddhist Kingdom. The Muslim majority of these provinces has retained the Malay cultural heritage and Malay is the dominant language in these southern provinces where very few individuals speak, much less read, Thai. Although Thai authorities have continually attempted to assimilate this indigenous minority, their efforts have had a very limited effect as indicated by the ongoing irrendentist and separatist political activities. These "incorporated" Muslims, usually referred to as "Malay" Thai Muslims, make up approximately 85 percent of the population in the four southern provinces of Thailand.

The "non-Malay" Thai Muslims are those of Indian, Pakistani, Iranian, Cham (from Cambodia), Indonesian, Chinese, and Malay descent living in areas where Thai Buddhists are the majority. For all practical purposes, most of these Muslims have been assimilated into the mainstream of Thai culture. Their native language is Thai, and in general, the economic, educational, social, political, and cultural conditions appear to have been conducive to the Thaiification. Uniform institutionalized socialization processes and intermarriage have had a leveling effect on most vestiges of traditional ethnicity. Consequently, outside of religion, the general social structural and cultural features exhibited by these Muslims are essentially the same as those of the dominant Thai Buddhist group.

Islam and reform in Thailand

In the twentieth century an Islamic reform movement arose, centered in Bangkok, the capital of Thailand, but with its origin in the Middle East and the ideological developments in that part of the Muslim world. A few Thai Muslims had gone to study at al-Azhar and, while in Egypt, were exposed to the reformist thought of Muhammad ʿAbduh and Rashid Ridā. But it was mainly through the mediation of Muslim intellectuals in Malaysia and Indonesia that this reformist ideology reached Thailand. In Malaysia the Kaum Muda movement was beginning to instill Islamic reformist ideals in certain segments of the Muslim population (Roff 1961). Simultaneously, the Muhammadijah movement led by Ahmad Dachlan et al. was having a dramatic influence on the form of the Islamic tradition in Indonesia (Peacock 1978; Noer 1973).

Initially, reformist ideas came to Thailand as an indirect result of Dutch colonial policy in Indonesia. An Indonesian refugee named Ahmad Wahab, who had been exiled by the Dutch authorities in the early part of the twentieth century, immigrated to Bangkok. Prior to his immigration, Wahab had spent a considerable amount of time in the Middle East as a student, familiarizing himself with the then current religious thought and practices (including the postulates of ʿAbduh and Ridā). Upon returning to Indonesia, he became active in the Muhammadijah movement. Involved in anti-colonial political activities against the Dutch, he was subsequently exiled and settled in Bangkok in 1926.

After Wahab had mastered the Thai language, he began teaching reformist thought in his new environment. Successful in attracting many followers and students, he set up informal study groups and, though there was no fixed fee for the teaching, the interest was so great that he and his family were supported by his students. From his base he eventually established the first Islamic reform association in Thailand, *Ansorisunna.* This association issued a monthly periodical, edited by Wahab, that had an impact on the literate sector of the Muslim population in Bangkok. Through it he directed an active reformist campaign, presenting the ideals of the *Al-Manār* reformists to the Thai Muslims.

It was through Wahab's students and followers that Islamic reformist ideas were galvanized and translated into a religious movement. One of the individuals affected by Wahab's teaching was Direk Kulsiriswasd (Ibrāhīm Qureyshī), a central figure in contemporary Muslim theology in Thailand. Direk became involved in the Islamic reformist movement in the 1950s, and throughout his career as a businessman he produced influential tracts on Islamic religious and cultural affairs. In addition to several academic articles on different aspects of Islamic history and culture in Thailand, he completed a massive four volume Thai translation of the Qur'ān and finished a translation of al-Bukhāri. Direk became the foremost intellectual leader of the reformist movement from the 1950s into the 1980s.

This reform movement, that attracted primarily an urban-based following rather than a rural constituency, especially among the newly educated groups, created internal cleavages in the Thai Muslim communities, resulting in two broadly-based ideological factions known as *khana mai* (new, reformist group) and *khana kau* (old traditionalist group). Reformist Muslims emphasized *ijtihād* and *ʿaql*—the rational interpretation of the Qur'ān and *hadīth* by the individual Muslim. The *khana mai* Muslim reformist opposed the procedure of *taqlīd*—or adherence to the norms of traditional authority. These reformist ideals ran counter to the ideology espoused by the conservative *ʿulamā'* and the *khana kau* Muslims. The religious conflict between the reformists and traditionalists resulted in both direct and indirect transformations in the form and content of Islam in Thailand.

The *khana mai* reformists were attempting to purify the Islamic traditions and purge popular religious concepts and rituals which had become amalgamated with Muslim theology. Reformists view "folk Islam" as it exists in Southeast Asian Muslim communities as the most visible symbol of *jumūd* or decadence within the Islamic tradition. The *khana mai* hold that this state of affairs was due to a lack of comprehension of the genuine tenets of Islam. "Folk Islam" was a dramatic concern to Southeast Asian Muslim reformers because of the intermingling of elements from rural indigenous spiritualism, and also because of the influence from the other great religious traditions such as Hinduism and Buddhism which preceded the Islamic tradition. For Islam, in its initial penetration of the area, was acceptable to many Southeast Asians only in so far as it would assimilate the Hindu, Buddhist, and other indigenous spiritualistic beliefs. Yet as more Muslims in Thailand were exposed to reformist literature the tolerance for "folk Islam" diminished greatly. This reformist movement, then, also had an immediate effect on the participation of Thai Muslims in the *hajj.*

Disputes about the *hajj* and related practices

Until recently, very few Thai Muslims were able to make the *hajj* compared proportionately with the number of pilgrims from Malaysia and Indonesia. Historically, the chief means of transportation to Saudi Arabia for Thai Muslims was by ship—the pilgrims travelled to Penang in Malaysia to board British vessels. This trip was an extremely inconvenient and expensive venture, especially for those who did not live near Malaysia. Following World War II, the economic conditions improved, precipitating an increase in the number of Thai Muslims observing the *hajj*. Responding to this increase, the Thai government licensed a private shipping company to provide the transport to Saudi Arabia. Later, several other shipping companies—all of them non-Muslim enterprises—began to compete, offering "package deals," whereby an individual paid a lump sum for everything, including ship passage and accommodations upon arrival in Saudi Arabia. Some of them launched vigorous advertising campaigns and even went so far as to pay commissions to returned *hajjīs* if they sold the "package" to other Muslims. This fierce competition and related business practices led to widespread abuse, corruption, and confusion. The complaints of Muslims reaching Saudi Arabia ranged from finding that there were no accommodations to not being able to obtain return passage despite pre-payment and all kinds of guarantees.

The *khana mai* Muslims took up this issue in their ideological campaign in the 1960s.[1] They criticized the Thai government and the *khana kau* Muslim representatives within it for allowing these businesses to exploit the pilgrims. Some of the younger reformists alleged that the *khana kau* leadership colluded with the shipping companies out of pure unadulterated self-interest, charging that many *khana kau hajjīs* would lose their commissions and their vested economic interest if these companies were restrained by the government. The reformists also rallied against the advertising blitzes that resulted in economic disaster for many Thai Muslims. Many of them were encouraged to mortgage their lands or homes and, when they returned from Mecca without any funds, this created additional burdens for the communities at large and presented obstacles for further economic development.

Although some of the reformists' allegations were not based on substantiated evidence, the overall effects of these charges stimulated the *khana kau* Muslim leaders in the Islamic affairs segment of the Thai bureaucracy to press the government on this matter. As a result, the government assumed closer supervision of the pilgrimage process and began to take measures to prevent such problems. It established the Thai Maritime Navigation Company Ltd , as a state enterprise, charging it with the responsibility of safe and efficient transport of Thai Muslims to Mecca. The government also set up a committee, under the chairmanship of the Under-Secretary of State of the Ministry of Communications—with members drawn from other government ministries—to supervise the transport of pilgrims and to find measures to assist and protect them (Ministry of Foreign Affairs Thailand 1976). The problem with these resolutions is that, like much governmental legislation, they came too late, since in the meantime air transportation had replaced transport by sea.[2]

Another more general concern expressed by the *khana mai* reformists regarding the *hajj* was the socio-economic status of the returned pilgrim. Traditionally, in both the rural and urban Muslim communities of Thailand, *hajjīs* held a position of great respect. They performed almost no physical labor and devoted most of their time to religious affairs. Fraser notes that in Rusembilan, a village in Patani, there was a prohibition on physical labor for the *hajjīs*. Since many of them owned rice paddies and coconut plantations, other people would work on their fields and divide the harvest equally with them (Fraser 1960: 163–165). In the urban areas the status of the *hajjīs* was also one of great respect and eminence. Many of them were trained in the traditional *fiqh* and ritual obligations. At the conclusion of their studies, they were expected to make the *hajj* as an integral part of their formal education. On all appropriate occasions these *hajjīs* were invited to religious ceremonies to lead the prayers. They wore the traditional sarong and turban indicating their status, and were not expected to contribute any food or other items for the ceremonies, often being reimbursed by the host even for their moderate taxi expenses.

Hajjīs were often invited to lead Muslim communal feasts, in both rural and urban areas, and to preside over life-cycle events and other rituals considered to be non-Islamic by the reformist *khana mai*. These communal feasts are prevalent throughout Southeast Asia and have been described in depth and detail by anthropologists (Geertz 1960; Burr 1972). In Thailand, these celebrations are referred to as *thambun* feasts and, to some extent, parallel Buddhist practices. During the period we are describing, these festivities were an integral feature of Muslim practices throughout Thailand, and the *hajjīs*' participation in these rituals greatly enhanced their status in the eyes of the participants.

The reformists were opposed to the privileged status traditionally claimed by the *hajjīs*. Many of the *khana mai* Muslims performed the pilgrimage themselves but most of them declined to use the *hajjī* title. In Bangkok, almost none of the *khana mai* wore the traditional sarong or white turban which made the *khana kau hajjī* the most conspicuous Muslims in the city. The reformists maintained that neither the Qur'ān nor the *hadīth* support the notion of a priestly class in Islam and insisted emphatically that according to fundamental Islamic doctrine all persons are equal in the eyes of God. According to them, this basic egalitarianism provides no room for the use of pretentious titles which distinguish the privileged from the underprivileged, and they, therefore, objected strongly to using the *hajj* as a device to increase the discrepancy in social status among the believers.

According to the reformers, this group of *hajjīs* attempted to emulate the Buddhist monks. Separated from the economic burdens of other Muslims, their status paralleled to some extent the position of Buddhist monks who collect food in their begging bowls or obtain it at various religious ceremonies. These *hajjī* practices were, in the eyes of the reformists, an unnecessary drain on the resources of the Muslim community and a waste of valuable manpower. The criticism that this now unproductive manpower could contribute towards the economic development of the Muslim communities, is similar to the critique leveled at the Thai Buddhist *sangha* or monkhood by some economic theorists of the more industrialized nations.

As part of this critique of the *hajjī* prestige system the reformists also attacked the educational system. The *khana mai* viewed the learning of elaborate ritual techniques and advanced chanting methods, of memorizing Arabic verses and studying *fiqh* as an education largely irrelevant in the modern Thai environment. They sought a transformation of these Muslim schools into innovative learning environments with a sound scientific basis.

The present situation

The reformists' criticism of the *hajjī* system has had an effect, albeit a limited one, on the Muslim tolerance for this system. The pilgrimage seems to have become less effective as a means of gaining status. Aside from the reformist critique, other factors contributed to this phenomenon. First, because of the relative ease of journeying to Mecca in the past few years, many Muslims, both *khana mai* and *khana kau*, have been able to perform the pilgrimage, and the larger number of *hajjīs* has made the *hajjī*-status somewhat less special and less prestigious than it was in the past. Moreover, even the traditional leaders came to realize that the pilgrimage caused serious economic hardship for some people and began to raise questions about it. A case in point was what happened to many of the Muslims owning rice paddies in the now suburbanized area of South and Southeast Bangkok, who suddenly gained what appeared to be vast amounts of capital from the sale of their land to large real estate brokers for the development of middle class housing. One of the first reactions of several of these *nouveau riche* Muslims was to fulfill a lifetime dream of going to Mecca, often expending large amounts of money to highlight their newly acquired prestige, and then ending up within a number of years without any capital resources and nothing more to show for their short-lived wealth than the white turban of the *hajjī*. Although the recent events were, in a sense, more dramatic because of the sudden gain of wealth, the basic problem was not so different from that which arose when in prior years some Muslims sold their rubber plantations in order to make the *hajj*, and ended up in a rather destitute situation.

The conservative *'ulamā'* or *khana kau* leadership's attitude toward making the *hajj* seems to have changed to some extent in so far as they have become more circumspect in bestowing prestige on any person simply because he has made the *hajj*. They now rather seek to insure that status and prestige is reserved for those *hajjīs* who strictly demonstrate competence in traditional Islamic thought and who are strictly upholding Islamic practices, the latter including, according to the *'ulamā'* giving support to these leaders' religious judgments and opinions.

Whatever the changes, the *hajjī* prestige system is still very much alive in Thai Muslim communities, and in many circles no life-cycle event or religious ceremony is performed without the *hajjīs*' presence in leading roles. Furthermore, the imam and other religious officials of the mosque and the Islamic bureaucracy are recruited and elected from the *hajjī* class.

Statistics for the last decade or so for Thai Muslim participation in the *hajj* are shown in Table 1.

Obviously there was a precipitous decline in *hajj* participation from Thailand during the period 1975–1978. During that period airfares from Thailand to Saudi Arabia increased dramatically. Following that period airfares have declined and Thai Muslim *hajj* participation

Table 1 Thai Muslim participation in the *hajj*[3]

Year	*Number of Thai pilgrims*
1969	2,399
1970	4,263
1971	4,981
1972	2,448
1973	2,057
1974	3,456
1975	654
1976	192
1977	233
1978	421
1979	1,906
1980	2,978
1981	2,753

has grown. Other economic factors are extremely important when attempting to explain the increase and decrease in numbers of Thai Muslims fulfilling their religious obligation—making the *hajj*.[4]

Because of increasing energy costs and declining agricultural productivity in Thailand the rate of inflation has spiraled since 1979 (U.S. Department of State 1980). The Thai government has been seeking ways to mitigate the effects of this cost-of-living spiral by controlling utility and transportation prices. The long term consequences of this policy on international travel is indeterminate at this juncture. And yet if past indicators are anything like the future, and if the cost of air travel to Saudi Arabia increases along with other consumptive goods there will be a commensurate decline in Thai Muslim *hajj* participation. Thai Muslims do not look forward to that prospect.

Notes

1 This section describes the situation they faced at that time and the changes they sought to bring about. The last section of the article will deal with the present conditions and a few very tentative suggestions as to likely developments in the future.

2 Only those Muslims who hold round trip tickets of Saudi Arabian airlines or Thai International airways are granted visas in order to make the *hajj*. Some Thai Muslims have complained that this monopoly restricts competition and tends to keep airfare prices artificially high.

3 The statistics for the years 1969–1972 were drawn from David E. Long 1979: 134. The statistics for the years 1973–1981 were obtained through the Hajj Research Center of King Abdulaziz University in Jeddah. I would like to thank Dr. Syed Abedin of the Institute of Muslim Minority Affairs for his assistance in gathering these data.

4 Dr. Ladd Thomas a political scientist who has been doing research on Muslims in South Thailand has indicated that the participation of the Muslims in South Thailand in the hajj corresponds to economic cycles related to the rubber industry. Whenever the economic climate is on an upswing more Muslims participate in the *hajj*.

References

Burr, Angela (1972) "Religious Institutional Diversity, Social Structure and Conceptual Unity: Islam and Buddhism in a Southern Thai Coastal Fishing Village," *Journal of the Siam Society*, 60: 183–215.

Fraser, Thomas M. (1960) *Rusembilan: A Malay Fishing Village in Southern Thailand*, Ithaca, NY: Cornell University Press.

Geertz, Clifford (1960) *The Religion of Java*, Glencoe, IL: Free Press.

Haemindra, Nantawan (1976) "The Problem of the Thai-Muslims in the Four Southern Provinces of Thailand (Part 1)," *Journal of Southeast Asian Studies*, 7/8: 197–225.

Long, David E. (1979) *The Hajj Today: A Survey of the Contemporary Makkah Pilgrimage*, Albany, NY: State University of New York Press.

Ministry of Foreign Affairs Thailand (1976) *Islam in Thailand*, Bangkok: Ministry of Foreign Affairs.

Noer, Deliar (1973) *The Modernist Muslim Movement in Indonesia: 1900–1942*, Singapore: Oxford University Press.

Peacock, James L. (1978) *Purifying the Faith: The Muhammadijah Movement in Indonesian Islam*, Menlo Park, CA: Benjamin Cummings.

Roff, William R. (1961) "Kaum Muda—Kaum Tua: Innovations and Reaction Among the Malays, 1900–1941," in Kennedy G. Tregonning (ed.) *Papers on Malayan History*, Singapore: University of Malaya in Singapore.

——— (1970) "Southeast Asian Islam in the Nineteenth Century," in Peter M. Holt, Ann K. Lambton and Bernard Lewis (eds) *The Cambridge History of Islam*, Cambridge: Cambridge University Press.

U.S. Department of State (1980) *Foreign Economic Trends and Their Implications for the United States: Thailand*, Washington, D.C.: U.S. Department of State.

10 The strength in the song

Muslim personhood, audible capital, and Hausa women's performance of the *Hajj*

Barbara M. Cooper

Barbara M. Cooper currently is a professor with the Department of History, Rutgers University. She earned her BA at St. John's College and attended Boston University for her PhD in history. Cooper conducted most of her field research on the continent of Africa in the Hausa-speaking region of Niger. Her work has explored the history of gender, religion and family life among the Hausa during the twentieth century. She is currently working on a history of discourses of motherhood and debates about fertility in the francophone Sahel. She has multiple publications including "Chronic Nutritional Crisis and the Trope of the Bad Mother" in *A Not-So Natural Disaster: Niger 2005* (2009); *Evangelical Christians in the Muslim Sahel* (2006) and *Marriage in Maradi: Gender and Culture in a Hausa Society in Niger 1900–1989* (1997). In 2007, she received the Herskovits Award for *Evangelical Christians in the Muslim Sahel*, an award she was also nominated for in 1998 for her *Marriage in Maradi*. The article below, originally published in 1999, employs the oral and musical traditions of Niger to decipher the changing role of the *hajj* for Hausa women. By considering economic and infrastructural changes, Cooper shows how Hausa women can enhance their social status because they are able to perform the *hajj* on their own.

Introduction

> Narrators are, in more than one sense, formed by their own narrations.
>
> (Tonkin 1992)

Two hackneyed phrases in English capture a certain impatient and impersonal sensibility regarding capital in the West: time is money, and talk is cheap. These phrases make little or no sense in Hausa-speaking Niger, so far as I can tell, where the classic adage regarding capital is *magana jari ce* (speech is wealth). While this expression is commonly invoked in celebration of Hausa literary arts (indeed, a well-known publication promoting literacy is so named), in this essay I would like to take seriously for a moment the understanding that oral performance can be a form of capital. The Hausa language has many words for wealth, but the word generally used to mean investment capital is used in this proverb. What would it mean to say that the act of speech is a kind of investment, or that oral performance can be thought of as a transaction involving wealth? The finest gift I ever received in Maradi was a song. Of course, one receives many gifts as a researcher: eggs, soap, chickens, taxi fare, cloth. One struggles mightily to ascertain what sorts of gifts might be appropriate to give in return. In this essay I would like, after a fashion, to make a return gift commensurate with the kind of wealth that was given to me—a celebration of a life through the power of song, an evocation of the potency of what can be heard but not seen.

Hajjiya Malaya sang this song for me one pleasant September morning in 1989 as we sat in the cool dark of her modest *banco* (mud) home in the compound of numerous female kin of the Sarki, the traditional ruler of the department of Maradi (a territory that had been an autonomous and bellicose kingdom prior to colonial rule). She broke into song in the midst of an otherwise unremarkable conversation about her life in which I asked her about the pilgrimage to Mecca indicated by her title. At the time I was astounded at this "breakthrough into performance" (Hymes 1981). Although my surprised expression made her laugh, it did not keep her from continuing her song cheerfully and at a breathtaking clip. The melody soared from a high lilting tone praising Allah and her kinsman the Sarki and then swooped down into a much lower range and a more somber mode in her punctuated refrain praying for her adoptive son Mahaman Lawali. Her voice was surprisingly clear and strong for a woman in her nineties. Here, then, is the wealth she shared with me:

A Song to My Son, Mahaman Lawali
Bismillahi arahamani
I begin with the name of Allah
because of God's work
blessings on Lawali.

Let me keep Mahaman, Allah,
Let me keep Mahaman, Allah,
I bring prayers to the King, Allah,
I carry them to the place of Allah's prophet,
For me, leave me Mahaman Lawali.

Let me keep Mahaman
So that if he should grow up he can make me a place to sleep,
If he makes porridge, he will give me some,
If he makes gruel,
He will give me some in the morning.

I say to Mahaman,
Your mother has no money,
But Allah made a way for her,
I say, Allah made a way for me,
The Sarki [the traditional ruler of Maradi, her kin] sent me to
God's house, Lawali.

Allah gave me the will, I threw [stones at Satan],
I passed the day in the fields of Adam, Mahaman,
I saw the rocks of Mount Arafat,
I slept at Muzdalifa, Mahaman.
In the morning I went to throw stones at Satan,
We went to throw stones at Satan, and then there I was at God's
house, Lawali.

Allah gave me the will to make the circuit of the Kaba,
I did the Tawaf, I did Safa and Marwa [Sa'y], Mahaman,
I went to visit the tombs at Medina, Lawali,
I say I went to Medina and made a visit.

You know, your mother has no anger, Lawali,
Truly, threshing makes the grain ready,
We took nothing but the purest, Lawali.
I tell you, my mother's kin,
I have no evil feelings,
For I am still praying to God
To give each one their share of strength.

(Malaya 1989)

I have provided here the central core of Hajjiya Malaya's song, which she repeated with minor variations many times. The song was recursive, with her social, emotional, and spiritual reflections strung creatively and spontaneously upon the more linear strand of her movement through the rituals of the *hajj*.[1] Rather than simply narrating the trip in song, Hajjiya improvises on the dual themes of the pilgrimage proper and the social relations in which its successful completion is embedded. The song is therefore multilayered: it is an invocation to God, echoing no doubt the prayers she offered up in Mecca for the as-yet-unborn child; it is a gift to her new son, with whom she shares her experience upon her return; and it serves both to entertain and to edify her female friends and kin at the celebration of his birth and naming (*bikin suna*) and at other such family gatherings. The moral message it conveys can therefore be understood, as Beverly Mack (1997) has recently argued concerning the poetic works of female Sufi scholars of Nigeria, as a kind of *zakat* (alms) offered for the instruction and moral uplift of the community at large.

Like other, more narrative accounts of women's pilgrimage experiences that I collected, this song opens with an expression of gratitude for the sponsorship enabling her to make the trip; it traces the geography of the *hajj* ritual in speech; it locates the experience of the *hajj* in local social tensions and relations; and its primary emphasis is on the spiritual experience of God's special protection in Mecca. It is also a prayer, an aspect of the song/poem that gives it particular poignancy and a sense of the speaker's direct and personal relationship to Allah. Many members of Malaya's kinship and friendship networks were familiar with this song, which she had performed for them on numerous occasions. Hajjiya Malaya's poetic rendition of her *hajj* brings into focus many of the issues surrounding both the pilgrimage proper and women's oral reenactments of their pilgrimage experience on returning home. I will use her song to explore the cultural forms Maradi women seem to borrow from more broadly in making public their pilgrimage experiences, the social context of such performances, and the sociopolitical implications of women's growing access to the moral and cultural capital signaled in the title *hajjiya*.

Hausa women's performance of the *hajj* is historically quite new.[2] While individuals of all social backgrounds have, particularly recently, managed to perform the pilgrimage, it remains closely identified with material success through trade and with access to capital on a scale out of most women's reach. Indeed, today the term used to describe a successful male merchant in Niger is *Al Hajj*, regardless of whether he has performed the pilgrimage or not. The literature on the Hausa diaspora emerging from the *hajj* assumes, by and large, that the pilgrim is male, and where women appear at all they enter as the "wives of pilgrims," not as pilgrims in their own right. It's clear that until this century most pilgrims from West Africa were indeed male, and this has left an interesting imprint on Hausa pilgrim communities, since male pilgrims have married local Arabic-speaking women; the women and children may speak Arabic, while young men only learn Hausa as they move into adulthood for trade (Works 1976: 61).

Prior to independence, women's limited access to substantial trade capital along with their obligation to care for young children and elderly kin made pilgrimage particularly difficult for them.[3] Women have been able to make the trip more recently because of state subsidies for religious travel and because air travel has reduced the time they must be absent to perform the rites at Mecca.[4] Subsidizing the *hajj* is one way a single-party state in an overwhelmingly Muslim region (Niger is 90 percent Muslim) can gain some legitimacy. As will become clear in a moment, sponsorship of the *hajj* is an important form of symbolic capital in this region, something lost neither on politicians in postcolonial capitals nor on traditional rulers in more provincial locales such as Maradi.

I came to this consideration of Hausa women's pilgrimage accounts in the course of collecting detailed life histories of women in the Maradi region for a historical study exploring the articulation of material struggles with cultural contests. I discovered that many of the women I worked with did not seem to have a sense of their life experience as containing a story worth telling, or at any rate a story amenable to a public recounting in the context of an interview. [...]

Much of my work up to this point has focused on a particularly rich vein around the question of shifting marriage obligations in the region (Cooper 1997). [...]

However, there was another, seemingly unrelated, lode in my interviews, presenting women with an occasion to talk strikingly openly about themselves and their own lives. This emerged when I asked women with the title *hajjiya* to tell me about their pilgrimage. This question elicited lengthy responses that might continue uninterrupted for several minutes, responses that I came to discover had their own characteristic shape. In other words, it seemed to me that I had stumbled on an indigenous Hausa oral form—the pilgrimage account—and because the women I spoke with knew how to tell such a tale they delivered their accounts comfortably and probably in something close to the form they had delivered them on other occasions. I do not claim that these oral performances were not tailored in many ways for me as an audience, for clearly they were. I do suggest, however, that as a younger woman curious about Mecca I made a reasonably familiar audience, and that the ease with which Maradi women responded to this question probably reflected their sense that this was a question they had answered safely and engagingly in the past.

What we have in Hajjiya Malaya's song is an engagement with modernity and the articulation of an individuated form of identity in the absence of the literacy and print media so often taken for granted as inevitable elements in the rise of modernity and the elaboration of the supra-local forms of communal identity implicated in it.[5] Theorists of literacy and globalization have assumed to a remarkable extent that transformations in societies are driven in predictable ways by technology, in particular the technologies of writing, print, and other media such as television. The novel uses to which the *hajj* phenomenon puts transport, communication, and finance technology should already give us pause here. The *hajj* today rests on an almost unimaginable technological and administrative infrastructure involving transport, communication, Islamic banks, medical practitioners, massive slaughterhouses, and sanitation crews—none of which could have been predicted in a narrow understanding of the expansion of technology under capitalism.[6] The technologist reading of social transformation also contains other unwarranted assumptions. First, all spaces are assumed to be uniformly susceptible to distanciation or "space-time compression"—the collapse of space into a shared, homogeneous experience through technologies allowing simultaneity (Giddens 1990; Harvey 1989). However, Mecca will never be homologous with, say, Los Angeles or Frankfurt—indeed it presents an alternative, recentered modernity in which the collapse of time becomes, in a sense, the triumph over all time and space through ritual.

Second, such work implicitly sees the postmodern subject emerging from the encounter with global modernity as formed by the media understood largely as emanating from a Euro-American center. [...] Yet it is not altogether clear that the particular transformation in thought evidenced in Hajjiya Malaya's song could be understood to derive from predictable properties of an expansive and dispassionate technology or even from the needs of industrial society. The newly public persona in Hajjiya Malaya's song derives from the unpredictable and opportunistic adaptations of an extraordinarily resilient Hausa cultural economy articulated orally through a passionately expressed Islamic idiom in the context of women's new access to the *hajj*. If there are technologies at play here, they are the airplane and the boom box.

From the poetics of hegemonic culture to the medium of colonial resistance

The pleasure of song, combined with the mnemonic qualities of verse, has made songs an important part of how Islam has been promoted in the Hausa-speaking region. [...] [Women's] pilgrimages to local shrines and tombs clearly resonate with Hajjiya Malaya's *hajj* to Mecca, and the poetic form she employs possibly draws on the kinds of oral poems and songs women learned in the wake of the jihad of Usman 'dan Fodio.

In other ways this oral song resonates with the more masculine genre of the written poem expressing a longing to perform the *hajj*. West African rulers from Mansa Musa to Askia Muhammad have long drawn on the *baraka* (spiritual force) that performance of the *hajj* invests in them to shore up their power and prestige (Lewis 1980: 135–136). By the same token the criticisms of many Islamic reformists gained force through their performance of the *hajj*, making it possible to topple nominally Muslim rulers. Performance of the *hajj* could serve both to reinforce the claims of standing rulers (see Barkindo 1992 on the state-sponsored *hajj* tradition of Kanem/Bornu) and to justify the attacks of reformists (see Hiskett 1984: 168, 170, 227, 235, 237). Thus the performance of the *hajj* has long played a role in political legitimation—whether to protect existing rulers or to justify revolt in West Africa. The emphasis of the nineteenth-century jihadists in Hausaland on Islamic orthodoxy enhanced the appeal and salience of the *hajj*. Ironically, the tremendous political and military demands of the era also made it impossible for the leaders of the jihad to absent themselves long enough to perform the *hajj*.[7] A poetic tradition emerged in Hausaland wherein the expression of longing to go to Mecca also served to evoke a nostalgia for a more perfect Islamic community.[8] [...]

The *hajj*, then, is not simply a form of spiritual capital for those who succeed in performing it. It serves also as a powerful and broadly held metaphor for both the individual spiritual quest and the collective emulation of an ideal Islamic community. These themes obviously have particular salience in the context of colonial domination under a non-Muslim power. Like the rituals themselves, the *hajj* as poetic trope serves to evoke the past through an alternative political and spiritual geography in order to recuperate a reformed and renewed future. The familiar litany of the ritual performances of the *hajj* then becomes a way of evoking a utopian Islamic community, particularly with the onset of colonial intrusion.[9]

When Hajjiya Malaya evokes the landscape of the *hajj* in poetic form she conjures this utopian vision as well, a vision in which the duties of one generation to the other are upheld, in which each one has "their share of strength," and in which jealousy and competition are neutralized by prayer. The poem, more effectively than straight narrative, permits her to evoke an ideal space, one that imaginatively maps the spiritual topography of Mecca onto her social relations in Maradi. The tremendous yearning in her song—for the health of Lawali, for the proper outcome of their relationship, and for the eventual happiness of her jealous kin—draws force from the poetic traditions she, an illiterate woman, unconsciously imbibes in this predominantly oral rather than literate environment. If the poems of longing for Mecca seem to have a more obvious political referent than Hajjiya Malaya's poem, that is because the political sphere in which her poem has most salience—the interior court of the Sarki's palace—is largely invisible to the outsider.

The counterhegemonic poetics of popular performance

The consideration of these alternately didactic and ecstatic literate genres does little to help us understand the more performative qualities of Hajjiya Malaya's song. Hajjiya Malaya [...] was not herself literate. If these poetic traditions, once translated into vernacular songs, made their way into the broader understanding of Islam in the region and contributed to shaping local oral forms, they nevertheless cannot fully explain the shape and power of Malaya's oral performance. I shall turn, then, to consider some of the oral forms, all of which antedate Islam in this region, that also inform her composition.

I suspect that I was given this song because I had asked Hajjiya on another occasion whether she knew any women who were professional praise-singers. She was much amused, and pointed out that she herself was well known for her songs (*wa'ko'ki*). She was not a *zabaya* (a woman, often of a relatively low-status background, who earns her living from singing at the ceremonies marking major life events). On the contrary, Hajjiya Malaya was an aristocrat maintained modestly at the expense of the traditional ruler of Maradi, the Sarki. However, she clearly saw her work as related to that of a praise-singer, a sense reinforced by the song's careful enunciation of the Sarki's sponsorship as well as her public performance of the song before audiences similar in composition to those at a family celebration. One way of making sense of this performative kinship would be to note that Malaya repays the Sarki's patronage by making public his generosity. In the case of this song about going to Mecca his generosity has pious overtones, since sending clients and kin to Mecca is one way a devout Muslim can gain merit.

Praise-singers occupy an ambivalent place in Hausa culture. As generally lower-status individuals engaged in something akin to a craft for pecuniary reward, they are sometimes looked down on by others. On the other hand, their proximity to the wealthy and powerful lends them a certain allure of power. Furthermore, their ability to subtly (or not so subtly) sabotage the reputations of their patrons and sponsors in song gives praise-singers very real influence over the wealthy. In a sense, the song of the praise-singer is the most public statement possible of the actions, standing, and moral fiber of her patrons; it serves, in effect, as an audible statement of account of local symbolic capital.

It was in reflecting on the nature of the power of professional praise-singers that I began to fully appreciate the force of Hajjiya Malaya's song and the importance of audible capital. I became acutely aware of the public quality of such songs one afternoon when I was recording what I thought was a private performance of praise songs by a well-known singer, Hajjiya Zabaya. The sound of her songs carrying over the walls of the compound prompted numerous neighbors to respond by sending her an endless stream of gifts of grain, food, cash, and cola. Sounds, messages, loyalties, and favors—all carried beyond the compound walls into the surrounding neighborhood to create an audible public performance. Evidently simply to hear the praise-singer's song was to be drawn into social exchange.

Hajjiya Malaya's song in praise of the Sarki, then, has an importance that might easily escape the eye. Once I had recorded it many of her friends and relatives asked me if they could have a copy of the tape, alerting me to the circulation of ideas, commentary, and critique in audible forms. In Maradi, cassette tapes are an important way in which the internal spaces of homes are breached, making it possible for seemingly private arenas to overlap and intersect with, even to compete with, the more apparently public spaces of the mosque, the market, and the political meeting. Alternative interpretations of Islam are debated through such recordings, Christian proselytizing is advanced through "cassette ministries," and popular culture makes its irreverent commentary on contemporary politics through the circulation of cassettes. If spectacle remains important to the negotiation and performance of culture and politics, one neglects the audible at one's peril in a region in which *daraja* (respectability) is associated with a certain distancing from vulgar (or rather visible) public display.

If in her song Hajjiya Malaya praises the Sarki, she simultaneously makes public her own standing and moral fiber. When such qualities are made known broadly they give rise to obligations and expectations. The Sarki is expected to continue to perform as a beneficent and pious ruler. Hajjiya makes herself known as a successful pilgrim, a client, and a devout woman who deserves continued support. Most importantly, she establishes in a very public fashion her relationship to her adoptive son. While the adoption of the children of close kin is not unusual in this region, sustaining moral claims on those children can be difficult. By making public through song her adopted son's debts to her and responsibility for her in her old age, Malaya in effect weakens the potential claims of others on him. Particularly relevant here are her own close kin, whose jealousies are forestalled through her prayer that "each one" will receive "their share of strength." They also, then, become publicly indebted to her for her prayers. [...]

The song, then, is far from being a simple record of a trip to Mecca. The dynamics generated by this public song of praise and prayer make the song and the singer important agents within the local political field.

Hajjiya's particular casting of the oral *wa'ka* is unusual, however. Hausa language does not distinguish between song and written poetry, employing the same term, *wa'ka*, for both, suggesting that any oral/literate typology will elide some important historical commonalities between written poetry and songs. Nevertheless, some attention to the differences between the contemporary conventions and expectations of the *wa'ka* as oral song (*wa'kar baka*) as opposed to the *wa'ka* as written poem (*rubatucciyar wa'ka*) is called for in order to appreciate the novelty of this song. In a comparative study of oral songs (composed largely by women) and published *wa'ka* poems (written largely by men), Beverly Mack notes that in general low-status Hausa women singers use songs to "say and do what other women cannot, criticizing the status quo, and encouraging behavior that is not normally condoned" (Mack 1986: 185). The oral *wa'ka*, she points out,

> is appropriate to the praise song for prestigious individuals, naming and wedding celebrations, spirit-possession cult ritual, pacing domestic tasks, etc. It is suited to the non-religious—the ritual, entertainment, and quotidian situation. These extemporaneously delivered *wakoki* are basic to Hausa entertainment in both private and in public settings. (Mack 1986:182)

The written poems, on the other hand, are often didactic and conservative even when written by literate women. […]

By composing a clearly religious song, Hajjiya Malaya has violated the expectations of the oral *wa'ka*. She has taken a genre largely devoted to entertainment and transgression (or "idle chatter") and used it in ways that bridge (or perhaps heal) the postjihad rupture between the feminine oral *wa'ka* and the more masculine written poem. Her song takes on some of the didactic and spiritual qualities of the written form, teaching her audience about the rites of the *hajj*, for example, while upholding the conservative values of respect for elders. In other words, she has co-opted into the oral form some of the qualities of the more prestigious masculine written form. She has, in effect, adopted something of a masculine persona, despite the clearly feminine and maternal concerns of the poem. Indeed, it is precisely the moral force of the maternal combined with the religious sanctity of the *hajj* itself that make it possible in this instance for a woman who has little or no formal schooling in Islamic scholarship to presume to compose such a deeply spiritual song on such a personal theme. […]

Both storytelling and the singing of *wa'ka* songs can potentially bring opprobrium or disapproval upon the women who perform them. Both are performed at night, when women traditionally visit one another. However, women's evening movements are also carefully scrutinized for fear of affairs. Common elements of Hausa stories trouble some Muslims, who find the spirits who populate the stories as well as the characters' often wild and improper antics inappropriate. Similarly, some singers' performances bear a kinship to *bori* spirit possession activities if they are accompanied by drumming on calabashes and vivid body movements (Mack 1983: 223). Both the oral *wa'ka* and the *tatsuniya* tradition are potentially at odds with conservative readings of proper Islamic practice. This explains somewhat why women's songs and poems are often didactic in nature, for their educative function vitiates any criticism they might bring on their authors. Conversely, if a woman hopes to teach others appropriate behavior, poetry rather than songs or tales will generally serve her well by lending cultural legitimacy to her didacticism (Furniss 1996: 16).

Hajjiya Malaya's song, then, stands in interesting tension with the song and folktale traditions. In seizing on the performative resource of storytelling while recasting the tale as one more clearly in line with the kinds of genres generally seen as appropriate by Muslim men, she is carrying forward a tradition in which women are creative, active agents while reworking it to conform to more masculine notions of piety and propriety. No one could mistake her song for a *tatsuniya*, of course, for it is not set out, as folktales are, with the formulaic verbal markers of an invented fantasy ("*Ga tan ga tanku; Ta zo ta wuce*"). Indeed, the force of her song requires that it have reference to a real event prescribed by Islam whose incredible dimensions are miraculous rather than fantastic. The performance of the *hajj* account, then, draws on the tradition of storytelling by firelight, but it goes further by turning the tale into an account of a real event. It is significant that women whose life stories are not authorized by existing genres find a rare justification for seizing the stage to recount a part of their lives publicly when the account centers on the performance of the *hajj*.[10] This observation calls for a consideration of Muslim Hausa women's religious practice and the extraordinary role of the pilgrimage in their lives.

Islamic practice: feminine variants and the universal hajj

West African Islam, and indeed African Islam in general, has historically tolerated a strong strand of saint veneration. Islamic practice in many regions of Africa may entail pilgrimage to tombs of local saints (Lewis 1980: 74). Such local pilgrimage cults are often very important to women, perhaps because the pilgrimage to Mecca has been, by and large, impossible for them until quite recently. Certainly among the Hausa it is clear that women's experience of Islam has been shaped by *ziyara*, or visiting saints' tombs.[11] Such local pilgrimages are often multivocal and have been powerful to women precisely because they draw on familiar ritual practices even as they contribute to women's greater integration into Islam. Indeed the *hajj* rites in Mecca themselves draw on and recast pre-Islamic pilgrimage traditions (Peters 1994: 3–59). The highly textured quality of the rituals in and near Mecca explains, perhaps, how this preeminently Muslim practice can simultaneously resonate with pre-Islamic rites elsewhere.

The importance of women's local rituals to their understanding and practice of Islam has contributed to the readiness with which both Muslims themselves and scholars of Islam have presumed that the tremendous variations in how women practice Islam mean that Muslim women are less pious and, in a sense, less Muslim than their male counterparts. Women stand in, then, for locality, particularity, national authenticity, and diversity in Islam. These qualities, however rationalized and valorized, tend to undermine women's standing in a religion stressing unity and universality. This reality no doubt prompted Robert and Elizabeth Fernea's revisionist article, "Variation in Religious Observance among Islamic Women," in which they enumerate the diverse forms of female worship, including the *zar*, *qraya*, *maulid*, and *azza*, seeing these as peculiarly feminine contributions to shared local conceptions of Islam (Fernea and Fernea 1972: 391–401). They propose that these need not be seen as failed or deviant forms of Islam, but should be understood as localized expressions of common core beliefs.

Women's Islamic practice, then, exhibits tremendous variation. The preceding consideration of popular or counterhegemonic Hausa performance practice suggests that, indeed, many Muslim Hausa women engage in practices from *bori* cult activities to storytelling and singing that some Muslim Hausa men might regard as unorthodox. Such variation, in turn, is precisely what politicians and scholars, often male, tend to attack. For this reason, the uniformity of the performance of the *hajj* has the effect, for women, of providing one place where their practice of Islam is unassailable.[12] This means that, whether women use their newfound *baraka* to gain sanction for their own practices or to attack the prevailing practices of others, they have increasingly at their disposal an extremely potent form of religious capital, one based on performance rather than on scholarly training.

Globalization, multiple modernities, and Muslim personhood

Numerous scholars who work in Muslim regions have insisted recently that modernity be understood as multiple, complex, and frequently engaging what one might call a dialectical ambivalence toward the West (Watts 1996; Lazreg 1994; Metcalf 1990). Göle rightly warns that to read such alternate modernities through the lens of resistance is to miss the creative reappropriations and new subjectivities they entail (Göle 1997). It seems inadequate to see Muslim subjectivities of the contemporary moment as being primarily or initially emanations of or reactions to the Western secular subject—we must break free of the solipsism that reduces all discourses to responses to the West (for a particularly suggestive treatment of this issue see Larkin 1997). We must ask ourselves whether there are modernities outside the reflexive/reactive "alternatives" to the West, modernities that emerge out of global phenomena and postcolonial histories but which engage different kinds of understandings of wealth, personhood, and the public sphere than are commonly taken for granted in much work on modernity and globalization.

Like Barbara Metcalf (1990), I see the *hajj* as inviting an intriguing autobiographical impulse, but in the case of the oral performances of the *hajj* I collected I do not think a credible case can be made for their origins in Western media or modernist literary forms, if only because the paucity of print matter and the low incidence of literacy in the Maradi region (in striking contrast with northern Nigeria and South Asia) render any such linkage implausible. More importantly, however, the imprint of preexisting Hausa cultural forms is so clearly evident here that any potentially novel influence of print culture on subject formation appears insignificant by comparison. My purpose in this essay in dwelling on one song in particular is to drive this point home as forcefully as possible. Globalization is deeply imbricated in local social concerns and is articulated within and through local cultural forms in unpredictable ways. My work with women around their experiences of the *hajj* has taught me that globalization is not readily or productively collapsed into subsumption under Western or even Northern capital. The expansion of Islam has long been an extraordinarily powerful globalizing force (see, e.g., Abu-Lughod 1989), one that cannot be reduced to resistance to the West or more loosely to the "relativization" imperative, to use Robertson's ungainly formulation.[13] Furthermore, globalization does not annihilate locality: cultural forms at more proximate scales are given heightened, not reduced, salience with globalization. Rather than producing deterritorialization, the modern *hajj*, I would argue, produces a resacralization of familiar terrain and a powerful recentering around Mecca. Finally, within this complex nexus linking the individual with scales from the household and neighborhood to the global community of Islam, the renegotiation of gender can be performed without any reference to or articulation of a feminist stance in dialogue with the West. Women's growing access to the performance of the *hajj* as a form of moral capital has figured in subdued local struggles to recalibrate women's social position, influencing local understandings of women's position within Islam.

Women's increasing ability to fulfill their obligation to perform the *hajj* has tremendous political-economic implications, raising the important question of which women are best positioned to take advantage of the shifting and shrinking spiritual geography of the late twentieth century. In Hajjiya Malaya's case her links to the fading but still relevant aristocracy of the Maradi region provided her with indirect access to the wealth of the Nigerois state. Elderly women in general have a stronger moral claim to those periodic pockets of accumulated capital that make pilgrimage possible, reinforcing the strong gerontocratic element in Hausa social life. But not all of the women I encountered who had gained the title *hajjiya* were elderly or aristocratic. All Muslim women in Maradi who have any success in trade make saving money for their pilgrimage a very high priority, so that for women as well as for men successful completion of the pilgrimage is a mark of commercial success. A new class of prominent female merchants, the *hajjiyoyi* (the plural form for *hajjiya*), has emerged in Maradi; their pious title shields them somewhat from criticism for their visibility in the commercial realm. Furthermore, the association of pilgrimage with age enhances their occasionally dubious claims that they are postmenopausal and therefore no longer subject to the constraints on movement and visibility taken for granted as appropriate for younger women. Among the educated elite of the civil-servant class the title *Madame* competes with the title *hajjiya* as a mark of social distinction—once again access to the resources of the state creates differential access to moral capital. Finally, and intriguingly, several young women who earn their keep through sexual services have managed to dignify their lifestyles through the acquisition of the title *hajjiya*. Women gain access to the capital necessary to perform the pilgrimage through a variety of means, from clientage to wage labor to successful trade. They then translate that experience into forms of capital that are recognized in Maradi proper and thereby convert themselves, in a sense, into recognizably Muslim persons. Attention to just such locally specific cultural transactions, through which real individuals interact with global processes, are critical to sustaining a rich sense of human agency, personhood, and individual worth.[14]

Obviously in a region as poor as Niger these multiple transactions (cash into pilgrimage, experience into song, unseen woman into visible Muslim person) generate tremendous competition for scarce capital. Not everyone succeeds in going to Mecca: of my 110 female informants only 17 had performed the *hajj* in a sample deliberately skewed toward elderly women and urban women who were active in trade. While this is a startling increase over the number of women who performed the pilgrimage in past centuries, it continues to be the case that only a small percentage of the population succeeds in fulfilling this religious obligation. Women in urban centers with access to the resources of the state clearly have an advantage over women who are locked in marginal farming enterprises in rural areas. We need to begin to gain a clearer picture of how global phenomena such as the *hajj* influence the generation and circulation of wealth and status, amplifying existing social differentiation while simultaneously altering the terms on which distinctions (such as gender, age, and sexuality) are marked and understood.

Given the importance of the *hajj* to the circulation of symbolic and moral capital, I suggest that to make sense of this particular globalizing process we must let go of traditional understandings of profit maximization and qualify the assumption that globalization is driven by the predictable march of technology in the service of capital conventionally understood. Transport, communications, medical and food processing technologies are, in the *hajj*, put to uses that fall well outside the purview of conventional corporate expansion or even of the more labile impulses of post-Fordist flexible accumulation. As any world traveler will note in perusing flight magazines, commercial airlines have little interest in expansion into the African market beyond South Africa and a few select eco-tourist havens. The significant but seasonal linkage between Saudi Arabia and a host of sites throughout the Islamic world, then, remains utterly invisible by such a reckoning. If governments throughout the wider Muslim world invest heavily in *hajj* infrastructure, so also do individual Muslims. Indeed, the topic of the *hajj* reliably produces heated debates among Maradi's Muslims about economic rationality.[15] For pilgrims from one of the most impoverished countries on the globe, the *hajj* often represents their most vivid encounter with technology, wealth, and cosmopolitan culture. Women and men who perform the *hajj* not only may return with a new sense of themselves as Muslims, but also will be burdened with numerous expensive gifts, from VCRs to videocameras to brocaded wall hangings of the Great Mosque. As Mariane Ferme observes of "Alhaji Airplane" upon his return to Sierra Leone from Mecca, his

> dream of modernization going hand in hand with religious piety was shaped by his own spiritual and physical pilgrimage, but was also consistent with the rest of the community's perception that material wealth and "advancement" were aspects of the integration in a more cosmopolitan Muslim community.
>
> (Ferme 1994: 28)

Technology and commodities in themselves, then, tell us little about the uses to which they will be put, the kinds of modernity that will emerge, or the forms of subjectivity that will accompany those modernities. To borrow Appadurai's useful vocabulary, if the *hajj* presents an immensely complex "ethnoscape" of human movement of tremendous historical depth (Appadurai 1990), it also presents us with a contemporary "finanscape" whose contours are largely invisible to the West and whose logic is poorly captured in traditional models of profit maximization. The contemporary pilgrimage is made possible through a landscape of technology put to unpredictable uses, and it is justified at the national scale through "ideoscapes" that assert the primacy of the national even as the traveler's supra-local Muslim identity is reinforced. What does the individual pilgrim make of this complex experience? And what is the relationship between the individual subjectivity that crystallizes out of the experience and the "mediascapes" in which it is embedded? That is, what are the "proto-narratives of possible lives" (Appadurai 1990: 9) that emerge, and how are they generated?

I suggest that the verbal reenactment of the *hajj* provides Maradi's women-largely illiterate, for the most part poorly schooled in Islam, and often marginalized by local understandings of the role of women in Islam—with an alternative means of access to the cultural and spiritual capital of Islam. The performance of the *hajj* provides such women with a moral endowment. The Hajjiya can successively and repeatedly draw from this endowment to produce the oral *zakat*, a kind of audible capital that authorizes both her autobiographical impulse and her affiliated social claims. To argue that the *hajj* presents women with such a moral endowment is not, of course, to suggest that everyone will be willing to accept this currency—the piety in which women's social claims are thus modestly veiled is amenable to the satirical and subversive critique that is so familiar a mark of Hausa popular oral arts. Nevertheless, Hausa men may have done some Islamic schooling at local *makaranta* (Koranic schools), and therefore have access to the foundational textual basis of Islam. Those few with higher learning can themselves in their person embody Islam and Islamic practice as *mallamai*, professional Muslim scholars. Women in Maradi, on the other hand, often see themselves and are often seen by men locally as inferior Muslims, first because of their limited access to the most important loci of Islamic capital and second because of the association of feminine practices with innovation and particularity rather than Islamic universality. But for women, particularly older women who came of age before schooling for girls became more common after 1970, access to a pure form of Islam comes through performance, what Shii scholar Ali Shari'ati refers to as *harakat*: "As the Qur'an is Islam in words, and the Imam is Islam embodied in a human figure, so the *hajj* is Islam in *harakat* (setting out, movement)" (quoted in Fischer and Abedi 1990: 159). This essay has illustrated how one woman translated that movement into a replicable and memorable performance, a text that made it possible for her to become audible within a milieu where her commitment to Islam might otherwise remain unseen or be undervalued. In doing so, as Elizabeth Tonkin rightly points out, she struggles to become both the author and the product of her own narration (Tonkin 1992).

Notes

1 The performance of the *hajj* (pilgrimage to Mecca) is known as the fifth pillar of Islam, along with the declaration of faith, the five daily prayers, the tithe, and the fast of Ramadān. The ritual requirements of the *hajj* are easy enough in principle to summarize, as the European traveler Burkhardt did in 1829 for the benefit of his European readers:

> The principal duties incumbent upon the Hajji are: 1. that he should take the Ihram [state of ritual purity made visible through special white pilgrim dress]. 2. be present, on the 9th of Dhu al-Hajj [the twelfth month of the Muslim calendar], from afternoon till sunset at the sermon preached at Arafat [the wuquf standing ceremony]; 3. attend a similar sermon at Muzdalifa, at sunrise on the 10th of Dhu al-Hajj; 4. on the 10th, 11th and 12th of Dhu al-Hajj throw on each day twenty-one stones against the devil's pillars at Mina; 5. perform the sacrifice at Mina; or, if he is too poor, substitute for it a fast at some future time; and 6. upon his return to Mecca visit the Ka'ba and [if he is combining the Hajj and the Umra] visit the Umra [which entails

circumambulating the "House" for the final four of seven times (*tawaf*) and running between the hills of Safa and Marwa seven times (Sa'y)].

(quoted in Peters 1994: 257)

Most pilgrims also visit the prophet's tomb at Medina at the same time.

2 Trade in West Africa has long been linked to the performance of the *hajj* via the Sahara desert; Muslim identity, occasionally enhanced through performance of the *hajj*, facilitated the activities of trans-Saharan traders from the fourteenth to the nineteenth centuries. A land route skirting the southern edge of the Sahara opened up with the expanded security of the Sokoto Caliphate in the mid-nineteenth century. Such pilgrims were less likely to be aristocrats or merchants and might simply be pious farmers. In the early decades of this century the *hajj* was intimately linked to popular resistance to colonial rule. Large populations of Hausa have ended up in Chad, Sudan, and ultimately Mecca as a result of the strong West African reading of the obligation to perform the *hajj*. For the West African *hajj* see al-Naqar 1972; Barkindo 1992; Works 1976; and Yamba 1995. For more general treatments of Islam in Africa see Hiskett 1984 and Lewis 1980. For comparative anthropological and historical studies of pilgrimage see Eickelman and Piscatori 1996 and Morinis 1992. Peters 1994 offers a study of the *hajj* as seen from Mecca.

3 For an exception that proves the rule see Mack 1988.

4 Pilgrimage by Hausa speakers rose spectacularly after independence. In 1928 and 1933 Nigerian Muslims were so few that they did not make their way into official records in Saudi Arabia; by 1966 Nigeria clearly ranked among the top twenty nations sending pilgrims, and by 1972 it was second only to Yemen in the number of its pilgrims (Long 1979: 130–131). Most of those pilgrims would have been Hausa speakers, including many Nigerois from across the border in Niger.

5 See, e.g., Havelock 1980; Goody 1986; McLuhan 1964; Anderson 1991; and Gellner 1983.

6 A recent *hajj* guidebook is revealing about the quality of modernity to be encountered on the *hajj* today: advertisements for modern architectural firms and cutting-edge fertility clinics jostle with Saudi government announcements regarding the Hajj Research Centre at King Abdul Aziz University, the Mina Development Project, and completed and projected construction projects. The maps are a bewildering tangle of pedestrian tunnels, freeways, and parking complexes (Farsi 1988). Fischer and Abedi offer a Rabelaisian depiction of the intricacies of this modern bureaucratic machinery interspersed with contrasting glimpses of a more rustic *hajj* circa 1964 (Fischer and Abedi 1990: 168–170).

7 Theological works by the jihadists revived the long-simmering question of whether jihad was equally, if not more, meritorious than the performance of the *hajj* (al-Naqar 1972: 46–47, 56–61). In combination with popular belief in the mystical powers of the leaders to "fly" to Mecca miraculously (al-Naqar 1972: 63 n. 8), these essentially apologetic works exonerated the leaders of the jihad from the obligation to perform the *hajj* under the particular circumstances obtaining at that time. Such theological argumentation did little, one supposes, to relieve the genuine longing of such committed believers to perform the *hajj*.

8 Shehu Usman 'dan Fodio's beautiful poem "Ma'ama'are" is paradigmatic. For its historical context see Hiskett 1984: 160; for a lovely translation see Furniss 1996: 195–196.

9 Caliph Attahiru composed a famous poem enjoining his people to retreat before the advancing "Christian" forces of the British into the safe territory of the holy land, in effect inverting the original spatial referents of Muhammad's *hijra* (Hiskett 1984: 269–270). Later scholars and ordinary Muslims drew on the poetic tradition to express discontent under British colonial rule; for an evocative poem by a commoner see Works 1976: 12.

10 Of course, women undoubtedly share aspects of their own lives with one another and with trusted men in intimate settings. My point is rather that any more open and public account must be safe and that the performance of a *hajj* account provides a measure of sanctity affording a sense of security. The interview situation in which I, as a researcher, work is by definition public, regardless of how confidential the conversations I elicit may seem.

11 For a description of such practices in relation to the *'yan taru* movement see Boyd 1989: 77.

12 Delaney argues that the visual marginalization of female pilgrims in Mecca through their retention of local dress serves to reinforce Turkish women's marginalization at home (Delaney 1990: 521). Hausa female pilgrims, like Hausa men, did mark their ritual status with special pilgrim clothing they referred to as ihram; neither they nor Hausa men seemed to regard their performance of the *hajj* as in any way inferior. None of them remarked on other women's clothing one way or the other, which is striking given the importance of dress in the normal course of events in Maradi.

Care is taken during the rituals to protect women and the elderly, particularly during the stoning ceremonies; however, there seems to me to be no sense among Hausa pilgrims that women's performance is any less meritorious than men's.

13 Robertson's theories are summarized in Waters 1995, a useful overview of current globalization theory.

14 I suspect that Appadurai's preference in his recent reflections on the intimate violence of ethnic conflict for the term "person" over the Foucauldian term "subject" bears on this issue, for the question of how dehumanization occurs is in many ways related to the question of how personhood is constructed or ruptured (Appadurai 1998: 241 n. 13). While I have used both personhood and subjectivity here, I have, like Appadurai, a preference for the former in this context because of its resonance within the anthropology of performance and ritual.

15 Does it make sense for an individual to perform the hajj repeatedly in such an impoverished region? Hausa asked themselves. Would it make more sense to invest in schools, in mosques, or in an income-generating activity? Where does a successful individual draw the line in sponsoring the trips of others? And who should have priority? See Tangban 1991 on what he sees as the dubious rationality of Nigeria's investment in the *hajj*.

References

Abu-Lughod, Janet L. (1989) *Before European Hegemony: The World System A.D. 1250–1350*, New York: Oxford University Press.

Al-Naqar, Umar Abd al-Razzaq (1972) *The Pilgrimage Tradition in West Africa: An Historical Study with Special Reference to the Nineteenth Century*, Khartoum: Khartoum University Press.

Anderson, Benedict R. (1991) *Imagined Communities: Reflections on the Origin and Spread of Nationalism*, rev. and extend. edn, London and New York: Verso.

Appadurai, Arjun (1990) "Disjuncture and Difference in the Global Cultural Economy," *Public Culture*, 2: 1–24.

—— (1998) "Dead Certainty: Ethnic Violence in the Era of Globalization," *Public Culture*, 10: 225–247.

Barkindo, Bawuro (1992) "The Royal Pilgrimage Tradition of the Salifawa of Kanem and Borno," in Jacob F. Ade Ajayi and John E.Y. Peel (eds) *People and Empires in African History: Essays in Memory of Michael Crowder*, London: Longman Academic.

Boyd, Jean (1989) *The Caliph's Sister: Nana Asma'u, 1793–1865, Teacher, Poet, and Islamic Leader*, London: Frank Cass.

Cooper, Barbara M. (1997) *Marriage in Maradi: Gender and Culture in a Hausa Society in Niger, 1900–1989*, Portsmouth, NH: Heinemann

Delaney, Carol L. (1990) "The *hajj*: Sacred and Secular," *American Ethnologist*, 17: 513–530.

Eickelman, Dale F., and James Piscatori (eds) (1996) *Muslim Travellers: Pilgrimage, Migration, and the Religious Imagination*. London: Routledge.

Farsi, Zaki M.A. (1988) *Makkah al Mukarramah: City and Hajj Guide*, Jeddah: Zaki M.A. Farsi.

Ferme, Mariane (1994) "What 'Alhaji Airplane' Saw in Mecca, and What Happened When he Came Home: Ritual Transformation in a Mende Community (Sierra Leone)," in Charles Stewart and Rosalind Shaw (eds) *Syncretism/Anti-Syncretism: The Politics of Religious Changes*, London and New York: Routledge.

Fernea, Robert A., and Elizabeth W. Fernea (1972) "Variation in Religious Observance among Islamic Women," in Nikki R. Keddie (ed.) *Scholars, Saints, and Sufis: Muslim Religious Institutions in the Middle East since 1500*, Berkeley, CA: University of California Press.

Fischer, Michael M.J., and Mehdi Abedi (eds) (1990) *Debating Muslims: Cultural Dialogues in Postmodernity and Tradition*. Madison, WI: University of Wisconsin Press.

Furniss, Graham (1996) *Poetry, Prose, and Popular Culture in Hausa*, Washington, DC: Smithsonian Institution Press.

Gellner, Ernest (1983) *Nations and Nationalism*, Ithaca, NY: Cornell University Press.

Giddens, Anthony (1990) *The Consequences of Modernity*, Cambridge: Polity Press.

Göle, Nilüfer (1997) "The Gendered Nature of the Public Sphere," *Public Culture*, 10: 61–81.

Goody, Jack (1986) *The Logic of Writing and the Organization of Society*, Cambridge: Cambridge University Press.

Harvey, David (1989) *The Condition of Postmodernity: An Enquiry into the Origins of Cultural Change*, Oxford: Blackwell.

Havelock, Eric A (1980) "The Coming of Literate Communication to Western Culture," *Journal of Communication*, 30: 90–98.

Hiskett, Mervyn (1984) *The Development of Islam in West Africa*, London and New York: Longman.

Hymes, Dell H. (1981) *"In Vain I Tried to Tell you": Essays in Native American Ethnopoetics*, Philadelphia, PA: University of Pennsylvania Press.

Larkin, Brian (1997) "Indian Films and Nigerian Lovers: Media and the Creation of Parallel Modernities," *Africa: Journal of the International African Institute*, 67: 406–440.

Lazreg, Marnia (1994) *The Eloquence of Silence: Algerian Women in Question*, New York: Routledge.

Lewis, Ioan M. (1980) "Introduction," in Ioan M. Lewis (ed.) *Islam in Tropical Africa*, 2nd edn, Bloomington, IN: Indiana University Press.

Long, David E. (1979) *The Hajj Today: A Survey of the Contemporary Makkah Pilgrimage*, Albany, NY: State University of New York Press.

Mack, Beverly B. (1983) "'Waka Daya Ba Ta Kare Nika' [One Song Will not Finish the Grinding]': Hausa Women's Oral Literature," in Hal Wylie, Eileen Julien and Russell J. Linnemann (eds) *Contemporary African Literature*, Washington, DC: Three Continents Press.

——— (1986) "Songs from Silence: Hausa Women's Poetry," in Carol Boyce Davies and Anne Adams Graves (eds) *Ngambika: Studies of Women in African Literature*, Trenton, NJ: Africa World Press.

——— (1988) "Hajiya ma'daki: A Royal Hausa Woman," in Patricia W. Romero (ed.) *Life Histories of African Women*, London: Ashfield.

——— (1997) "Muslim Women's Education as Zakat in Northern Nigeria." Paper presented at the Fortieth Annual Meeting of the African Studies Association (ASA), November 13–16, 1997, Columbus, Ohio. New Brunswick, NJ: Rutgers University, ASA.

Malaya, Hajjiya (1989) *A Song to my Son, Mahaman Lawali*, recorded by Barbara M. Cooper in Maradi, Niger.

McLuhan, Marshall (1964) *Understanding Media: The Extensions of Man*, Cambridge, MA: MIT Press.

Metcalf, Barbara D. (1990) "The Pilgrimage Remembered: South Asian Accounts of the Hajj," in Dale F. Eickelman and James Piscatori (eds) *Muslim Travellers: Pilgrimage, Migration, and the Religious Imagination*, London: Routledge.

Morinis, E. Alan (1992) *Sacred Journeys: The Anthropology of Pilgrimage*, Westport, CT: Greenwood Press.

Peters, Francis E. (1994) *The Hajj: The Muslim Pilgrimage to Mecca and the Holy Places*, Princeton, NJ: Princeton University Press.

Tangban, Ojong E. (1991) "The Hajj and the Nigerian Economy 1960–1981," *Journal of Religion in Africa*, 21: 241–255.

Tonkin, Elizabeth (1992) *Narrating our Pasts: The Social Construction of Oral History*, Cambridge: Cambridge University Press.

Waters, Malcolm (1995) *Globalization*, London and New York: Routledge.

Watts, Michael J. (1996) "Islamic Modernities? Citizenship, Civil Society and Islamism in a Nigerian City," *Public Culture*, 8: 251–290.

Works, John A. (1976) *Pilgrims in a Strange Land: Hausa Communities in Chad*, New York: Columbia University Press.

Yamba, C. Bawa (1995) *Permanent Pilgrims: The Role of Pilgrimage in the Lives of West African Muslims in Sudan*, Edinburgh: Edinburgh University Press.

Feast of sacrifice

11 On scriptural essentialism and ritual variation

Muslim sacrifice in Sumatra and Morocco

John R. Bowen

John R. Bowen received his PhD from the University of Chicago in 1984. He is currently Dunbar-Van Cleve Professor in Arts and Science at Washington University in St. Louis, Missouri, and teaches anthropology and religious studies. His research interests are the comparative social studies of Islam across the world, including how Muslims work across plural sources of norms and values. The geographical foci of his research are the Gayo Highlands of Aceh, Indonesia, France, and Britain. His most recent publications include *Islam, Law and Equality in Indonesia: An Anthropology of Public Reasoning* (2003); *Can Islam be French?* (2008); and *Why the French Don't Like Headscarves* (2007). In 2005, Bowen was Carnegie Scholar for his research project titled "Shaping French Islam." He also serves on a number of committees, including as chair of the Council of European Studies and the Evaluation Committee of the Social Science Research Council, New York, and is President of the Scientific Council, French Network of Institutes for Advanced Studies. In addition, Bowen was member of a number of editorial boards for a diverse selection of journals, from the *Critique International* and *Journal des Anthropologues* in Paris, *Studia Islamika of Jakarta, Annual Review of Anthropology* and *American Anthropologist.* The article below employs a comparative approach to study the Muslim feast of sacrifice. Using Morocco and Indonesia as his points of reference, Bowen alludes to the heritage of Clifford Geertz in the anthropological study of Islam, by combining ethnography and ethnology. With an attempt to account for historical dimensions, he argues that Muslims shape their ritual duties differently in different cultural settings, because their obligations do not necessarily derive from Islamic scriptures, rather from local processes of adapting and transforming scriptural elements to local circumstances.

Introduction

The ritual forms practiced by Muslims have long raised thorny interpretive problems for anthropologists and Islamicists. Muslims shape their religious rituals to local cultural concerns and to universalistic scriptural imperatives. Islamic rituals thus fit comfortably neither in an ethnographic discourse of bounded cultural wholes nor in an Islamicist discourse of a scripture-based normative Islam.[1]

To the anthropologist looking for distinctively local forms of knowledge and practice, Muslim rituals of prayer, sacrifice, and pilgrimage may appear to be of little cultural interest. Anthropologists often ignore such events in favor of more explicitly localized rituals, thereby skewing the ethnographic record away from Muslim religious life. In Indonesia, for example, there is a rich tradition of studying mortuary ritual among non-Muslim peoples, reaching at least from Hertz's seminal essay (Hertz 1960) to recent studies by Metcalf 1982 and Volkman 1985. Yet when it is Muslims who die, interest seems to fade, despite the vigor and salience of Indonesian Muslims' debates about ritual in this century.[2] Much the same could be said for the study of Muslim prayer, worship, sacrifice, and alms in southeast Asia or, for that matter, in the Middle East.[3] Anthropologists have preferred distinctively local elements—marabouts, mullahs, or meditation—to those ritual and scriptural forms that most explicitly link Muslims across societal boundaries.

Although the field of Islamic studies does focus on shared Muslim traditions, it does so in such a way as to render it weakest precisely where anthropology is strongest: in the study of how rituals take on locally specified social and cultural meaning. Islamicists (see, e.g., Denny 1985; Graham 1983; Lewis 1988 are, of course, well aware of the diversity of Muslim religious and cultural lives. But the discourse of Islamic studies—which itself is, explicitly or otherwise, embedded in a framework of comparative religious studies—assumes generalized or essentialized images of Islam that may be set alongside other, similarly essentialized, religious traditions (see Smith 1963). Islamicists base their general accounts of Islam largely on scripture and on a relatively narrow range of Middle Eastern social forms. These forms are assumed to play out, more or less accurately, a single, scripturally embodied Islamic culture.[4] [...]

Moroccan sacrifice and patriarchy

Given the difficulty of encompassing Muslim ritual within the boundaries of the classical ethnographic account, it may be tempting for the anthropologist who takes the local force of Muslim ritual seriously to adopt a version of the Islamicist position. Such is the case in M.E. Combs-Schilling's book *Sacred Performances*, in which the author brilliantly relates how the 'Alawi kings of Morocco made the annual Muslim feast of sacrifice into a sanctifying ritual of state (Combs-Schilling 1989).

The annual feast of sacrifice (Arab. *'īd al-adhā*) commemorates the willingness of Abraham (Ibrāhīm) to sacrifice his son at God's command. God's command to sacrifice to him and to him alone is issued in the Qur'ān (Surah 22:34–38; 108). The collection of reports of the prophet Muhammad's deeds and statements (the *hadīth*) specifies how Muhammad carried out this command during the month of pilgrimage. These reports are important sources for Muslims' ideas and practices regarding, inter alia, which animal is the best victim, what to say when killing the victim, and who benefits from the sacrifice.[5] [...]

Combs-Schilling's noteworthy achievement is to link the public form of the sacrifice both to the persistent prestige of the monarchy and to the pervasive patriarchy of Moroccan society. She does so by weaving back and forth between political history and public ritual, and the result is convincing and elegant (though more celebratory of royal legitimacy than it is discerning of royal repression). Moroccan sacrificial ritual does appear to powerfully concentrate the force of scripture, political history, and gender oppositions on the family, the community, and the royal house.

But the author's argument does not stop at the boundaries of Moroccan political culture. She claims that the feast of sacrifice is inherently patriarchal, not only in its Moroccan practice but in its essential form and interpretation, and that it is indicative of the inherent patriarchy of Islam. Because of its patriarchal quality, the story of Ibrāhīm's encounter with God is the paradigmatic myth of Islam. Ibrāhīm meets his God on the mountaintop, away from women, and there "constructs a sacrificial intercourse and birth" between a human male and a Father God, mediated by a son and a highly phallicized ram (Combs-Schilling

1989: 239). Islam sanctified patriarchy and patrilineality, argues Combs-Schilling, by way of what she calls "Islam's central orienting myth (Ibrāhīm's sacrifice) and central orienting practice (the yearly performance of Muhammad's rite of sacrifice)" (Combs-Schilling 1989: 58). Moroccan Islam is "the most coherent" (Combs-Schilling 1989: 270) of all Islams (and, indeed, of all monotheisms [Combs-Schilling 1989: 255–271]) because, by making sacrifice socially and politically as well as religiously central, Moroccan Islam became the most publicly and thoroughly patriarchal of all Islams.

By viewing the public form of the Moroccan feast of sacrifice as a synecdoche for all of Islam, Combs-Schilling has eliminated the possibility of alternative, culturally specific elaborations of Muslim tradition. Moroccan ritual, itself presumed to have a single, univocal meaning, is viewed not as a particular North African (or Middle Eastern) elaboration of religious ideas, but as the direct embodiment of Islam's essence. The ritual's patriarchal message is taken to govern Muslim lives everywhere with a universal inevitability. [...]

Ritual variation

We could enrich the Moroccan case and at the same time recognize its cultural specificity by adopting a different analytical perspective. I would suggest that such a perspective differentiate among three levels of analysis: the public forms of ritual, ritual's overall social meaning, and the comparison of ritual form in two or more societies.

The public voice of ritual is precisely the focus of Combs-Schilling's study of Morocco, where the public use of scripture does indeed reinforce a political and domestic patriarchy. But in North African and Middle Eastern societies these public, usually male voices are often accompanied, or countered, by the voices of women, whether in the poetic articulation of plaints and desires (Abu-Lughod 1986) or in the practical construction of marriage unions (Bourdieu 1977). Both sets of meanings and forms contribute to the overall sense that any ritual makes.

Gender revisited

Evidence from other Moroccan studies suggests that the total social meaning of the feast of sacrifice in Morocco may be more complex and multivocal than Sacred Performances would indicate. Abdellah Hammoudi's account of Moroccan sacrifice is based on fieldwork in a village near Marrakesh (Hammoudi 1988). Focusing on local social actions and meanings, it provides an alternative perspective to that of Combs-Schilling's macrohistorical study, particularly with respect to the ritual representation of gender in the feast of sacrifice. While Combs-Schilling presents women only as passive observers of the sacrifice, at most dabbing some of the blood on their faces (Combs-Schilling 1989: 231), Hammoudi reveals the important role women play in sanctifying the sacrificial victim, at least in some Moroccan communities. In Hammoudi's account, the public role of the married men is complemented by the ritually crucial activities of women in preparing the victim for slaughter. Women purify the victim with henna, thereby transforming it from ordinary animal to sacrificially appropriate victim (Hammoudi 1988: 175–188). After the victim has been killed, the women gather its blood not just to share in its power but because they use it, over a long period of time, to guard the home and to combat illnesses (Hammoudi 1988: 91–92, 197). The sacrifice is thus linked to domestic affairs through the mediation of women in at least these two important ways, despite the public domination of the ritual by men (and here Hammoudi's account reinforces that given by Combs-Schilling).

Women's actions during the sacrifice thus imply a more complex set of gender ideas than are revealed in the public events. But the ritual of sacrifice is only one moment in a complex ritual cycle found in parts of Morocco, Algeria, and Tunisia. The cycle stretches from the feast of sacrifice to the celebration of Ashūrā on the tenth day of the following month, Muharram. Between the two feast days comes a series of carnivalesque processions and masquerades in which characters representing women, Jews, workers, and other figures flaunt sexuality and, in classic ritual-of-reversal fashion, violate the sanctity of the sacrifice by wearing the skin of the sacrificial victim (Hammoudi 1988: 16). The masquerade highlights the social contradictions between classes as well as those between male and female. These representations of otherness and of social contradiction "give the lie to that rigor of purity that the sacrifice tries to impose (despite the feminine ritual that accompanies it and timidly contests it) and unveils the rigor of the real" (Hammoudi 1988: 248). Stressing the resemblance to European forms of carnival, Hammoudi argues that these rites are part of the overall process by which Moroccans have made Muslim sacrifice their own (Hammoudi 1988: 16).

The publicly patriarchal character of sacrifice and the explicit links to the Ibrāhīm myth, emphasized by Combs-Schilling, are also documented by Hammoudi. But these public forms now appear as pronouncements that disguise the activities and counter representations made by women and in this respect resemble men's pronouncements on the social links established through marriage as studied by Pierre Bourdieu (Bourdieu 1977: 30–71). To put it in terms suggested by James Scott, the all-male character of ritual and speeches is the "public transcript," but not the only transcript, of the events at hand (Scott 1990). Moroccan ritual activity, at least in some places, is not the unambiguous proclamation of patriarchy but a structured combination of official patriarchy and other forms, either domestic (such as the henna preparations for the victim) or interstitial (such as the masquerades).

Combs-Schilling's argument for the inherent patriarchy of the ritual derives much of its force from the sexual symbolism of the victim and its killer. Nearly every married male Moroccan slays a ram, she reports (1989: 223), and she makes much of the ram's symbolic hypermaleness (phallus and horns). Yet here, too, other Moroccan data suggest a good deal of internal variation, the significance of which would require further exploration. Hammoudi reports that the cases he observed involved the sacrifice of a sheep (Hammoudi 1988: 91) and that, although a ram is the first choice in principle, a lamb is the second choice, and in some places a castrated goat is frequently used, without the castration appearing to damage the cultural effectiveness of the event (Hammoudi 1988: 168–170). Brown, describing the sacrifice at Salé as it was in the 1930s, mentions only the use of sheep for the sacrifice (Brown 1976: 93). He also observes that the killing of sheep was often done by butchers when not done by "someone in the household" (Brown 1976: 93), suggesting that Salé Moroccans, at least in the 1930s, attached less direct importance to the act of killing than Combs-Schilling suggests.

Variation across cultures

The array of Moroccan ritual forms that surround sacrifice thus appears as an adaptation and elaboration of ritual in keeping with a local sense of social reality, not as the univocal embodiment of an Islamic essence. One would expect other peoples as well to have adapted, elaborated, and transformed elements of the broader Islamic tradition. Comparisons between distinct Muslim peoples should allow us to discern the range and limits of variation in ritual form within and across Muslim societies. We would then be able to distinguish, at least provisionally, a general model of the ritual, realized in many locales, from forms and emphases that are characteristic of one particular culture. Combs-Schilling's argument could be recast within a multilevel comparative framework so as to retain her insightful Moroccan analysis without either essentializing Islam or overprivileging local knowledge.

Ideally, one would undertake a series of comparative studies of the feast of sacrifice in several societies. I make only one such comparison here, that between the public forms and interpretations found in Morocco by Combs-Schilling and the corresponding forms I have studied among the Gayo of highland Sumatra, Indonesia, at the other end of the Muslim world. I begin by testing Combs-Schilling's assertions about the feast of sacrifice (and Islam) by asking two questions. First, is the act of killing inevitably the most salient event of the ritual (or can other elements of the ritual be highlighted)? Second, is the cultural focus of the ritual inevitably patriarchy (or can its message be quite different)?

This comparison resembles that undertaken by Clifford Geertz in *Islam Observed* (Geertz 1968)—there, as here, comparing Indonesia and Morocco—but it differs in its point of departure. Geertz began with contrasts between Javanese and Moroccan cultures, especially with regard to mysticism and authority. I begin here with a religious obligation that Muslims recognize and seek to fulfill in Morocco, Indonesia, and elsewhere. My emphasis is less on global cultural typifications (Moroccan or Indonesian styles) than on the diversity of ideas and forms within as well as among Muslim peoples. I will therefore emphasize not only the contrast between Gayo and Moroccans but also the process of differentiation among Gayo forms.

Feasts and family in Isak Gayo sacrifice

[…] Beginning in the 1930s, reform-minded Gayo religious scholars who adhered to the Indonesia-wide modernist or "young group" (Indonesian [Ind.] *kaum muda*) position challenged the way that Gayo performed religious duties. A vigorous debate continues between modernist and traditionalist (Ind. *kaum tua*, "old group") scholars over these issues. In their public behavior, residents of the main highlands town of Takèngën tend to follow modernist prescriptions, while in many, perhaps most, Gayo villages, men and women carry out ritual practices of long standing and often identify themselves as of the "old group."

Gayo refer to the feast of sacrifice in diverse ways. It is the "holiday of sacrifice" (Gayo *reraya qurbën*) or the "great holiday" (Gayo *reraya kul*) in explicit contrast to the holiday celebrating the end of the fasting month of Ramadān, which is called simply "holiday" (Gayo *reraya*) or, in Indonesianized Arabic, *idul fitri* (Arab. *'īd al-fitr*). Upward of 100 Gayo undertake the pilgrimage each year, and in the highlands, during the holiday period, Gayo often talk about the sacrifices the pilgrims are carrying out in the city of Mina simultaneously with their own. In these contexts Gayo also may refer even to the local event as the "pilgrimage holiday" (Gayo *reraya haji*). Some Gayo, usually of modernist leanings, seek to emphasize the scriptural commandments regarding the sacrifice and to downplay local traditions, and these men and women might use the Arabic designation *'īd al-adhā*. These differing labels suggest contrasting conceptions of the event itself.

In the largely traditionalist village community of Isak, where I have done most of my work, households sacrifice various kinds of animals: chickens, ducks, sheep, goats, water buffalo.[6] Nearly all Isak households perform a sacrifice. At the very least, a household will kill one of its chickens or ducks, or buy a chicken or duck from another household. If times are very bad, two households may jointly hold a feast and share a duck. As long as the throat can be cut and the meat eaten, I was told, the sacrifice meets the demands of God. (In principle, said some half-jokingly, even a grasshopper would do as a sacrifice.)

Just prior to cutting the victim's throat, the sacrificer dedicates the animal to one or more relatives. In 1978 my neighbor Abang Das sacrificed a buffalo for the benefit of his parents and grandparents. Just before cutting the animal's throat he pronounced the Basmala ("In the name of God, the Merciful, the Compassionate") and the confession of faith ("I attest that there is no deity but God and that Muhammad is his Messenger") and then dedicated the buffalo as follows: "This is the sacrifice for my father [name], for my mother [name], and for their families." He then said his own name followed by "In the name of God; God is Great" ("*Bismillah Allah Akbar*") three times. At the completion of the dedication he slit the buffalo's throat.

In contrast to those in Morocco, most of these sacrificial events receive little notice and are hardly public. The sheep, chicken, or duck is killed in back of the house, with no more ceremony than the quiet utterance of a dedication and the Basmala. A buffalo will often be killed in a public place with many men helping tie the animal down. Who actually cuts the throat is not of great importance; a man may delegate the job to someone else. In their social practice, Gayo thus distinguish between the knife wielder (Hubert and Mauss's "sacrificer") and the person in whose name the sacrifice is performed (the "sacrifier") (Hubert and Mauss 1964: 9–28).[7]

Nor is the event interpreted in patriarchal terms. The sacrifice is carried out for the household as a unit: women as well as men speak of "their" sacrifice, and couples decide jointly on a list of people who will receive its spiritual benefit. In the case of a buffalo, the beneficiaries usually include the parents on both sides and daughters as well as sons. Widows also carry out sacrifice (without being socially redefined as men), and when a wealthy female trader sacrificed a buffalo everyone spoke of it as her sacrifice, not her husband's (he was also part of the household). This set of features alone makes the Gayo case markedly different from the Moroccan, where the physical act of throat cutting iconically signifies the virility, power, and self-sufficiency of the male as opposed to the female.

The throat cutting is not the most publicly salient moment of the ritual, then, nor are the Moroccan patriarchal messages communicated here. The focus of social attention is instead on transmitting benefit (Gayo and Ind. *pahla*) to oneself or to one's deceased relatives by means of the sacrifice and, especially, at the ritual meals (Gayo and Ind. [singular] *kenduri*) held afterward.

The Kenduri

The *kenduris* held on the feast of sacrifice vary considerably in their size. A household in which only a chicken or duck has been killed consumes the cooked animal with a minimum of ritual: at most, the household head or a learned relative recites a short prayer. A household that has sacrificed a sheep invites guests from among neighbors and relatives. If a buffalo has been killed, the entire village is automatically invited. In the last case, guest house-holds bring raw foods (milled rice, coconuts, and sugar), which the hosting household and its close relatives prepare for eating. Contributing guests also receive a bit of the raw meat from the sacrificed animal.

At feasts where a buffalo or sheep is eaten, a religiously learned man leads a group recitation of short Qur'ānic verses, recites a long petitionary prayer (punctuated by choruses of "*Amīn*"), and, for good measure, repeats, for God's hearing, the names of the beneficiaries of the just-completed sacrifice. These recitations play an instrumental role in securing the benefit of the sacrifice; they also reaffirm relations of sociability among the participants (see Robertson Smith 1972: 265).

Some ritual meals are attended by upward of 100 people. These large meals feature night-long recitation sessions called *samadiyah* (Arab. *shamad*, "eternal, everlasting").[8] The men and women who attend the sessions chant several of the shorter Qur'ānic verses as well as statements in praise of God. These recitations please God, who then relieves the torment of the deceased. (The number of guests times the number of repetitions yields the overall benefit.) The learned man who leads the guests in chanting will have been given a list of the people to whom the merit should be transmitted; he then embeds these names in a long prayer (sometimes saying the names very softly), thereby directing the evening's merit to the intended beneficiaries. These sessions are held on several nights after the death of any adult in the community as well as on the feast of sacrifice.

In Isak in each of the four years when I was present for the *'īd al-adhā*, three or four households each sacrificed a buffalo, sponsored a village-wide feast, and held an all-night recitation session. They held the feasts at different times so that men or women with ties to more than one village would be able to satisfy their multiple obligations. These major feasts were occasions for relatives who had moved away from Isak to return and join in transmitting merit to those who had died before them. The sponsors whom I knew well spoke to me about the dead who were to benefit from the night's sessions; these were times for reflection and remembrance as well as for contributing to the welfare of relatives and neighbors.

These events of transmission (at the moment of killing, the afternoon *kenduri*, and the night-time *samadiyah*) are what sacrifice is most importantly about to most Isak Gayo. Indeed, they generally reserve the phrase "to sacrifice" (Gayo *gelé qurbën*; literally, "to cut the throat of a sacrificial animal") for occasions when a goat or buffalo is killed and served at a *kenduri*. *Kenduris* are a general framework for ritual in Gayo society (and elsewhere in the archipelago).[9] Most *kenduris* combine the recitation of prayers with the burning of incense and the offering of special foods; both incense and foodstuffs help to transmit the message of the meal to the intended spiritual recipient. *Kenduris* are held on Muslim calendrical holidays (the Prophet's birthday and *'īd al-fitr*) and for a wide variety of practical purposes: to fulfill a vow, to request help from ancestors in healing a sick person, or to call on God to ensure the safe passage of a deceased person's spirit into the next world. By making the feast of sacrifice into a kind of *kenduri*, Isak Gayo have configured it as an event of transaction and communication.

This configuring is of relatively recent date, however. Around 1900, Gayo sacrifice had an entirely different relation to the broader Muslim tradition than it does today. The feast of sacrifice was not celebrated (Snouck-Hurgronje 1903: 327).[10] One sent benefit to the dead by means of the *kikah* sacrifice (Arab. *caqiqa*). Although in Isak today, as in most other Indonesian Muslim communities, the *kikah* is carried out as part of a child's initiation into the world seven days after birth, in 1900 it was performed after an individual's death (Snouck-Hurgronje 1903: 314).

Only in the 1930s, and at the insistence of modernist teachers, did Isak people begin to offer the *kikah* sacrifice as part of the child's initiation ritual. At about the same time they began to observe the feast of sacrifice, which they interpreted in the transactional terms with which they were familiar. Even in the 1980s, some Isak people would omit the *kikah* from the child's seven-day ritual, reasoning that they could always make a sacrifice at the feast of sacrifice in its place.[11]

Families and judgment day

Not only do the words sent to God generate spiritual benefit for deceased relatives, but the sheep or buffalo that has been sacrificed also provides a future material benefit. On judgment day (Gayo *kiamat*, Arab. *al-kiyāma*) the persons named as sacrificial beneficiaries will be able to ride on the animal to the place of judgment, the Meraksa field (Arab. *al-mahshar*). Only one person can ride a goat or sheep to the Meraksa field, but seven can ride on a buffalo.

A buffalo sacrifice thus provides the opportunity to bring together parents, children, and grandchildren on the back of the afterlife vehicle, and if they had the resources, most Isak would stage a buffalo feast sometime during their lives.

Isak couples shape their sacrificial strategies with afterlife sociability in mind, trying to provide a vehicle for themselves, their children, and, if possible, their parents and grandparents. Parents feel a particularly strong obligation to provide a vehicle for a child who died young, as do children for those parents and grandparents who did not have the resources to make sacrifices in their own names. I heard stories about children who would not acknowledge their parents on the day of judgment because the parents had not bothered to sacrifice for them. "Without a sacrifice there is no tie between parents and children," said one woman. The prospect of future abandonment by one's children horrifies most people and provides further encouragement to perform the sacrifice. It also leads people to include in their dedications even those parents or children who already have a vehicle provided for them, in order to ensure that family ties will be preserved during the harsh times of judgment. In the past, I was told, just before a sheep was sacrificed all the close relatives of the beneficiary would grasp its tether rope, thereby strengthening their ties in the afterlife.

In Isak, as in Morocco, the sacrificial victim is something more than the sign of the household's obedience to God. In Isak the ritual is framed as a *kenduri*, at which spiritual and future material benefits are produced by sacrifices in the name of God and by the chanting of his words. The ritual also connects the men and women of one generation with those of another through the shared sacrificial animal. The ritual projects this cross-generational, bilateral continuity onto the eschatological plane by generating images of families riding together toward the place of judgment.

Isak transactions and images contrast sharply with the centralized dynastic meanings and father-son pairs of Morocco. Gayo and Moroccans conceive of the events in Islamic terms. Both views are articulated through the performance of the feast of sacrifice and through the rich imagery of the past (Ibrāhīm's sacrifice) and the future (the Day of Judgment). Isak Gayo project that imagery out from the ritual event to the family's fate in the afterlife; Moroccans concentrate that imagery on the immediate structure of domination in the kingdom, the community, and the family.

Modernism and public discourse

One could argue that Moroccans might know scripture better than Isak Gayo, hence their greater patriarchy. Such an assertion would not prove the case for an inevitably patriarchal and killing-focused ritual. But even if one accepts its premise, Gayo internal contrasts do not support it. Gayo modernist scholars are no closer to the Moroccans than are Isak residents. Modernists in the main town of Takèngën do emphasize the commemorative meaning of the event, but the message they derive from the event is one of obedience and devotion, not patriarchy and killing. [...]

The modernists' emphasis on hewing close to scripture does not mean that their ways of understanding and observing the feast of sacrifice were formulated outside local social and cultural debates. To the contrary, Takèngën modernists developed their religious practices in a dialogue with existing ritual observances. Precisely because most Gayo historically came to understand the feast of sacrifice in terms of feasting and transaction, modernists have worked to rid the feast day of those elements. They do not hold *kenduris* on the feast of sacrifice (although they do on other occasions), and they emphasize the sharp distinction between the living and the dead.

In 1989 I observed the celebration of the feast of sacrifice in the Baléatu neighborhood of Takèngën. Baléatu residents are strongly associated with the modernist Muslim organization Muhammadiyah, whose school is located next to the neighborhood prayer-house. When asked about the purpose of the ritual, Baléatu residents invariably referred to God's command in the Qur'ān to follow the example of Ibrahīm. (Isak residents, by contrast, usually mentioned the importance of providing a vehicle for the afterlife.)

For these modernists, to follow the example of Ibrāhīm means to adopt his attitude of selfless and sincere devotion, *ikhlas* (Arab. *ikhlās*). One scholar explained that one receives merit from the sacrifice only if it is done with the proper intent, "for the sake of God and not for a worldly reason." He called the notion that the sacrifice becomes a vehicle for the afterlife "amusing."

In recounting the story of Ibrāhīm, Balbatu narrators emphasized his prior decision to give something away in devotion to God, not the moment of sacrifice (the Moroccan narrative emphasis). "Prophets had always sacrificed," explained one scholar, by which he meant they had always been willing to surrender something, "but the prophet Ibrāhīm said that he would sacrifice his child if one were born to him; the idea came to him in a dream."[12] The subtle difference between offering to give up a child if he receives one, on the one hand, and being commanded to slay his already-possessed child, on the other, is indicative of a difference in cultural emphasis, between the proper attitude of abnegation in Indonesia and the act of killing in Morocco.

The general town sequence of the feast of sacrifice resembles that followed in Isak: public worship, followed by the killing of the sacrificial animal, followed by meals. But the form and meanings of each stage are quite different. In Isak each household approaches the event as an opportunity to transmit spiritual and material benefits to its relatives and members. The key events are the act of dedicating the victim and the several *kenduris* which one might attend, both in the day and at night. For Baléatu residents the congregational worship is the most important element in the ritual, the killing of the victim is strongly played down, and the meals consist of casual home repasts and communal enjoyment of food in a nonritualized setting.

This shift in emphasis is social and political as well as religious. In Isak the events considered to be of the greatest ritual importance take place in homes (feasting and reciting); in Baléatu greater religious importance is paid to events taking place in the streets, at the open-air site for congregational worship, and in the neighborhood prayer-house. The spatial contrast indicates a shift in the social focus of the key ritual event, from the private, if shared, interests of the household to the general interests of the community as a whole. This shift in turn makes it possible for the Takèngën ritual to be more closely integrated into the ideology and control apparatus of the Indonesian state.

Public worship

The congregational worship service on the morning of the feast day, relatively unimportant in Isak, is the culmination of several days of activity in Baléatu. Although in 1989 many Baléatu people did take time to obtain a goat for sacrifice, they were more concerned with their preparations for the morning worship service (for which some purchased new clothes) and the visiting of neighbors and graveyards afterward. The feast day was preceded by a night of *takbīr*, of proclaiming God's greatness. A convoy of cars drove around and around the town, led by a loudspeaker car from which the *takbīr* was called out over and over again. The evening's amplified proclamations, following a day of recommended fasting, built up a sense of expectancy for the next morning's worship. By about six o'clock on the following morning several of the best Qur'ān reciters had arrived at the site for the congregational worship, a broad field, next to the Takèngën town mosque, with a stage at one end. The reciters began to chant the *takbīr* over loudspeakers and continued to do so for over an hour, while men, women, and children gradually filled up the worship space in front of the stage. The district finals of the national Qur'ān recitation contest had just ended and had created a particularly receptive atmosphere for this part of the service. The reciters on the stage were all winners of past years' contests, and the crowd of worshipers clearly enjoyed their skills. Men and boys filled the space closest to the stage; women and girls, an area behind them. Men, women, and children were dressed in their finest: men in fine sarongs, often of silk, and some wearing sport coats; women in brightly colored blouses and sarongs. On two worship occasions, *'īd al-adhā* and *'īd al-fitr*, women in the town dress in their most splendid clothes (following a command of the prophet Muhammad, they say); for other worship services they wear white garments that leave only their faces visible. The worship service was preceded by a welcoming address from the district military commander, setting the event in its governmental frame. The sermon, which follows worship, generally takes as its topic the willingness of the prophet Ibrāhīm to sacrifice his son to God. On this particular occasion the sermon giver talked about the importance of sacrifice in all areas of life and specifically for the success of the country's development. He stressed the value of *ikhlas*, sincere devotion, in such sacrifices, likening efforts at infrastructural development to the obedience displayed by the prophet Ibrāhīm. [...]

To take its public character first: Takèngën modernists have sought to change people's ideas in a variety of public arenas. In the 1930s modernist teachers challenged traditionalists to public debates (a new form). Sermons and afternoon Qur'ān lessons became the occasions for open criticism of existing ritual practice. Modernist leaders urged that people practice public, congregational worship instead of older transactional forms—after someone's death, for example, or at the feast of sacrifice.

These modernist-led public forms were rather easily put to the service of particular political agents and parties. In the late 1930s the newly powerful Gayo ruler of the Bukit domain in Takèngën, the largest political domain in the town area, ordered that the worship at the feast of sacrifice take place in front of his residence, with the worshipers prostrating themselves in its direction (Bowen 1991: 87). Other, anticolonial leaders could also avail themselves of modernist-led events to advance the cause of nationalism. Public gatherings to plan the celebrations of *'īd al-adhā* and *'īd al-fitr* were transformed into celebrations of a new nationalist spirit; religion in its new public form provided the perfect forum and cover for anticolonial politics (Bowen 1991: 100).[13]

The second quality of Indonesian modernism that renders it particularly open to political exploitation is what one might call the intransitive quality of its discourse. Modernist speeches and sermons emphasize proper piety: one should sacrifice, be devoted, offer praise—to God, of course, but more importantly because such actions are intrinsically valuable (value-rational rather than ends-rational, in Weber's terms). This form of discourse is easily claimed by the state as its own, when a request for everyone to sacrifice (meaning give something up) can sound vaguely religious even when the goals are clearly secular. In Indonesia proper attitudes have been particularly important to state ideology.[14]

Eating together

Isak and Baléatu celebrants also differ in how they kill the victim and consume its meat. Residents of Baléatu wish to clearly distinguish their practices from the Isak-type forms that they find un-Islamic. For this reason they have played down the instrumental religious significance of the killing and the meals, emphasizing instead the general values of family and community.

Whereas in Isak the morning worship is followed by sacrifice and ritual meals, Baléatu residents return home to express the depth of family ties. In Abang Evi's household (my own when I live in Baléatu) the parents seated themselves on a couch in the living room. In descending order of seniority, each family member and each of several close family friends kneeled in front of the parents, burying his or her head in their hands and receiving their blessings, wishes, and outpourings of emotion. The mother in particular found herself moved to tears and to long plaints over the bowed heads of her grandchildren: "you have to learn to behave better"; "you are the youngest and so you always catch it—do not take it to heart, little one." Each member of the family kneeled in the same fashion before all those senior to him or her, sometimes just for a moment and sometimes for longer exchanges of caresses and tears.[15]

On this day and the next, men and women in the neighborhood celebrated the holiday in the Baléatu prayer-house and the adjacent Muhammadiyah school. Cassette recordings of the *takbir* were played over the prayer-house loudspeaker, and children lined up at the school to take their turns at an amplified *takbir*. Town scholars spoke to the schoolchildren about Ibrāhīm's sacrifice. At the prayer-house, several men gathered to slaughter a cow and several goats that had been donated for the occasion. Neighborhood women prepared two large meals: one for the neighborhood children and all the children living in the Takèngën town orphanage, and a second for the neighborhood adults. Both meals were held in the prayer-house. Most residents of the neighborhood had contributed money and a portion of their own sacrificial meat toward the meals. A few better-off residents had given goats. About 60 men and 30 women attended the second neighborhood meal. After everyone had eaten they began to chant the *takbīr*. Women began to pound out a slow rhythm on gongs. Two men rose and danced the Gayo *tari guël* dance once performed by new bridegrooms. No prayers or dedications were uttered; the mood of the occasion was one of social celebration rather than ritual action. [...]

The ethic of avoiding self-interest also shaped the way that individuals carried out their obligation to sacrifice. Abang Evi's brother, Abang Gemboyah, who had returned from Jakarta for the holiday, had enjoyed spending much of the day before the sacrifice buying two goats, one for his own household's sacrifice and one for the meal at the prayer-house. Once he had purchased the goats he turned them over to a family friend. The next day the friend killed them at his own house, without Abang Gemboyah being present, and cooked one of the goats for the family's evening meal. The meal, eaten outdoors at their patchouli-oil plant just out of town, included no prayers, merely enjoyment of the meat that, by virtue of its purchase, had already been consecrated to God.

Both brothers downplayed the roles of sacrifier and sacrificer. They were not present for the killing and made no specific dedication (although, of course, the sacrificer uttered the obligatory Basmala when cutting the throat). For Abang Gemboyah the important religious moment came when he purchased the goats, a purchase that was of additional religious value because of the gift of the second goat. He explained that the sacrifices had to be done without any self-interest (*pamrih*), precisely the opposite of the predominant view in Isak.

Baléatu religious modernists see sacrifice as proof of one's sincere and selfless willingness to obey God. The prominence of the *takbīrs*, the morning worship, and the historical sacrifice by Ibrāhīm all support this central theme. But town modernists also characterize what they do in explicit contrast to village ways of celebrating. Baléatu people emphasize the sharp divide between the world of the living and the world of the dead, recognizing only a thin strand of communication across it, mainly through prayer to God. Practices that, in Isak, involve transactions with spiritual agents are, in Baléatu, located firmly among the living only. (Isak-born town modernists often remember such spirit transactions with a shudder, pretending that they belong to the pre-Islamic past of the highlands.) Celebrating the relations among family members is done in the home through cathartic obeisances and not by way of the sacrificial victim. Eating together (lexically distinguished from holding a ritual meal) is purely and simply that, with no suggestion that the meal or accompanying prayers are directed toward a spirit. Food is given away to orphans as a social demonstration of the sincere devotion to God that should be the sole animating force of religious actions taken during the holiday.

Underlying the contrasts between the village model of transaction and the modernist model of selfless sacrifice are some common Gayo social ideas. In both village and town the sacrifice highlights bilateral ties that link generations: in Isak these ties are represented primarily through afterlife imagery; in Baléatu, through family confessions. These social images of bilaterality contrast sharply with the Moroccan messages of patriarchal power and exclusive male access to divine sources of fertility and creativity.[16]

Indonesian resonances

The value of *ikhlas* and the relatively low emphasis placed on gender distinctions also characterize other Indonesian societies and are celebrated in Indonesian works of scriptural commentary. The emphasis on *ikhlas*, on the correct attitude of selfless devotion, is found in influential Javanese commentaries on the feast of sacrifice (Woodward 1989: 84–87). Nakamura paraphrases a sermon given on Java in 1965 by a modernist preacher, who stressed that sacrifice was worthy because of the ikhlas with which it was made, again on the model of Ibrāhīm (Nakamura 1983: 173–174).

The possibility for women to carry out a sacrifice on *'īd al-adhā* is explicitly defended in Indonesian religious scholarship. The influential modernist scholar Hasbi ash-Shiddieqy, in a work on the *feast of sacrifice*, underscores the legitimacy and indeed the importance of allowing women to carry out a sacrifice (Ash-Shiddieqy 1950). The author interprets the words of earlier Muslim scholars as indicating that a woman who owns an animal to be sacrificed ought to kill it herself or at least act as formal witness to the killing (Ash-Shiddieqy 1950: 26). Ash-Shiddieqy also makes the case that sacrifice generates merit for the sacrifiers. He argues that, because the prophet Muhammad stated that the sacrifice on *'īd al-adhā* was from him, his relatives, and his followers, we receive benefit (Ind. *pahla*) from the sacrifice (Ash-Shiddieqy 1950: 24).[17] Although this interpretation, by a modernist scholar, does not sanction the idea of transmitting benefit to specified others, it does introduce into respectable religious discourse the notion that the sacrifice confers a spiritual benefit.[18] The general emphasis in the two Gayo cases thus points toward a more general, regional religious culture that transforms the shape and understanding of its Muslim rituals.

Conclusions

In carrying out sacrifice, worship, or other religious rituals, Muslims engage in a dialogue between potentially conflicting cultural orders: the universalistic imperatives of Islam (as locally understood), and the values embedded in a particular society. The case at hand illustrates some of the difficulties of and methods for understanding that dialogue. [...]

Together, the Moroccan and Gayo cases show how Muslims have shaped a particular set of ritual duties in sharply contrasting ways, with cultural foci that do not derive in any direct way from Islamic scripture, but rather are the products of adapting, elaborating, and transforming scriptural and other elements in directions that make sense locally. This tacking back and forth between conflicting visions is, if anything is, the historical essence of Muslim ritual life. [...]

Notes

1 Similar problems are posed in the study of other scripture-based religions as well. For anthropologists these problems emerge most clearly in discussions of the Great and Little Tradition paradigm and its vicissitudes. For a Europeanist perspective see Brandes 1990.

2 See Bowen 1984, for example, on the debates over the talqin, a catechism read to the deceased after burial. Geertz 1957 justly famous article on Javanese funerals did not directly consider the form of the Islamic ritual.

3 On anthropology's tendency to ignore Islamic ritual in the Middle East see Eickelman 1989: 258 and Tapper and Tapper 1987. Among several recent works attempting to fill this gap are Tapper and Tapper's study of Prophet's birthday celebrations in Turkey (Tapper and Tapper 1987) and Antoun 1989 and Gaffney's sermon analyses (Gaffney 1987). Combs-Schilling 1989 is examined below.

4 One can see this approach embodied most vividly, and effectively, in the *Shorter Encyclopedia of Islam* (Gibb and Kramers 1953), whose entries are mainly terms from scripture or from classical Middle Eastern writers. The conflation of Islam and classical Middle Eastern culture is further exemplified by the Islamicist Bernard Lewis' recent book *The Political Language of Islam* (Lewis 1988). The book is not an investigation of how Muslims in different places and times construct political languages but an essay on the language, which turns out to be the lexicons of some Arabian Muslim scholarly texts.

5 An alternative Islamicist approach is illustrated by Smith and Haddad's survey of Islamic writings about death, with, again, no mention made of regional variation or the practices surrounding death (Smith and Haddad 1981).

6 Isak residents strongly prefer sheep to goats (although the latter are somewhat more plentiful) on the grounds that goats scavenge and dislike water and thus are relatively unclean. One man said that if you penned a goat for 44 days its "stolen food" would pass through its system, leaving the animal clean and good to sacrifice. Takengen Gayo often choose goats, perhaps in deliberate rejection of village preferences or perhaps with the horns of the ram sacrificed by Muhammad in mind.

7 The distinction was also salient in late nineteenth century coastal Aceh, where the sacrifier often handed the victim over to a man of religious learning (an *ulama*) and asked that he carry out the sacrifice (Snouck-Hurgronje 1906: I, 243).

8 The word comes from the second line of Surah al-lkhlas (Surah 112), the section of the Qur'ān that is most frequently chanted in the *samadiyah* session.

9 See McAllister 1987 on Malaysia, as well as Geertz 1960 and Woodward 1989 on the Javanese *slametan*, which for these purposes is similar to the *kenduri*.

10 In lowland Aceh, however, the feast of sacrifice was observed (Snouck-Hurgronje 1906: I, 243).

11 On the historical connections in the Arab world among the feast of sacrifice, the '*aqiqa*, and other sacrificial events, see Chelhod 1955; on these links among Pakistanis, see Werbner 1988.

12 For the Moroccan emphasis I rely on Combs-Schilling's treatment—which one presumes was obtained from Moroccan narrators, though the sources for her myth interpretation are unspecified (Combs-Schilling 1989: 233–244)—and the version of the dream cited by Hammoudi, in which Ibrāhīm is ordered to slay the child he already has (Hammoudi 1988: 193).

13 The political importance of public worship has been still more explicit in Aceh, where congregational worship has served as the icon of the perfect society (Siegel 1969).

14 Such is the case, for example, with the concept of "mutual assistance" (*gotong-royong*), a pseudotraditional term that has been hitched to many wagons, from Sukarno's authoritarian regimes to Suharto's development programs (Bowen 1986).

15 Although this family ceremony is not held in Isak, a similar ceremony held on '*īd al-fitr*, in which individuals ask forgiveness from their elders (and, as equals, from other people), is observed by all Gayo and by most Muslims in Indonesia.

16 On Java the *'īd al-adhā* does form part of a royal cult, but one quite different from the Moroccan. The holiday is one of three occasions for royal processions, during which the sacrificial element is left in the background and the dominant theme is the path to mystical knowledge and union (Woodward 1989: 205–214).

17 The *hadīth* is number 4845 in the collection by Muslim 1971: III, 1087–1088.

18 Sacrifice has not been a topic of scholarly dispute in the Gayo highlands, although many other religious topics have been debated at length (Bowen 1993). One reason may be that the Qur'ān does not explicitly condemn the idea that a sacrifier benefits from the sacrifice (and, as I have just shown, the *hadīth* literature could be used to support this idea). Rather, the Qur'ān (Surah 22:34–38) is critical of two practices, neither of which is characteristic of Isak observations of *'īd al-adhā*: sacrificing to a being other than God and claiming that the flesh and blood of the victim reach God.

References

Abu-Lughod, Lila (1986) *Veiled Sentiments: Honor and Poetry in a Bedouin Society*, Berkeley, CA: University of California Press.

Antoun, Richard T. (1989) *Muslim Preacher in the Modern World: A Jordanian Case Study in Comparative Perspective*, Princeton, NJ: Princeton University Press.

Ash-Shiddieqy, M. Hasbi (1950) *Tuntutan Qurban*, 3rd edn, Jakarta: Bulan Bintang.

Bourdieu, Pierre (1977) *Outline of a Theory of Practice*, trans. Richard Nice, Cambridge: Cambridge University Press.

Bowen, John R. (1984) "Death and the History of Islam in Highland Aceh," *Indonesia*, 38: 21–38.

——— (1986) "On the Political Construction of Tradition: Gotong Royong in Indonesia," *Journal of Asian Studies*, 45: 545–561.

——— (1991) *Sumatran Politics and Poetics: Gayo History, 1900–1989*, New Haven, CT: Yale University Press.

——— (1993) *Muslims through Discourse: Religion and Ritual in Gayo Society*, Princeton, NJ: Princeton University Press.

Brandes, Stanley (1990) "Conclusion: Reflections on the Study of Religious Orthodoxy and Popular Faith in Europe," in Ellen Badone (ed.) *Religious Orthodoxy and Popular Faith in European Society*, Princeton, NJ: Princeton University Press.

Brown, Kenneth L. (1976) *People of Salé: Tradition and Change in a Moroccan City, 1830–1930*, Cambridge, MA: Harvard University Press.

Chelhod, Joseph (1955) *Le Sacrifice chez les arabes: Recherches sur l'évolution, la nature et la fonction des rites sacrificiels en Arabie occidentale, etc*, Paris: Presses Universitaires de France.

Combs-Schilling, M. Elaine (1989) *Sacred Performances: Islam, Sexuality and Sacrifice*, New York: Columbia University Press.

Denny, Frederick M. (1985) *An Introduction to Islam*, New York: Macmillan.

Eickelman, Dale F. (1989) *The Middle East: An Anthropological Approach*, 2nd edn, Englewood Cliffs, NJ: Prentice Hall.

Gaffney, Patrick (1987) "Authority and the Mosque in Upper Egypt: The Islamic Preacher as Image and Actor," in William R. Roff (ed.) *Islam and the Political Economy of Meaning: Comparative Studies on Muslim Discourse*, Berkeley, CA: University of California Press.

Geertz, Clifford (1957) "Ritual and Social Change: A Javanese Example," *American Anthropologist*, 59: 32–54.

——— (1960) *The Religion of Java*, Glencoe, IL: Free Press.

——— (1968) *Islam Observed: Religious Development in Morocco and Indonesia*, New Haven, CT: Yale University Press.

Gibb, Hamilton A.R., and Johannes H. Kramers (1953) *Shorter Encyclopedia of Islam*, Ithaca, NY: Cornell University Press.

Graham, William A. (1983) "Islam in the Mirror of Ritual," in Richard G. Hovannisian and Speros Vryonis (eds) *Islam's Understanding of Itself*, Malibu, CA: Undena Publications.

Hammoudi, Abdellah (1988) *La victime et ses masques: essai sur le sacrifice et la mascarade au Maghreb*, Paris: Éditions du Seuil.

Hertz, Robert (1960) *Death and the Right Hand*, trans. Rodney Needham, New York: Free Press.

Hubert, Henri, and Marcel Mauss (1964) *Sacrifice: Its Nature and Function*, trans. Wilfried D. Halls, London: Cohen & West.

Lewis, Bernard (1988) *The Political Language of Islam*, Chicago, IL: University of Chicago Press.

McAllister, Carol (1987) "Matriliny, Islam, and Capitalism: Combined and Uneven Development in the Lives of Negeri Sembilan Women," PhD Thesis, Anthropology Department, University of Pittsburgh.

Metcalf, Peter (1982) *A Borneo Journey into Death: Berawan Eschatology from its Rituals*, Philadelphia, PA: University of Pennsylvania Press.

Muslim, Imam (1971) *Sahih Muslim: Being Traditions of the Sayings and Doings of the Prophet Muhammad as Narrated by his Companions and Compiled under the Title al-Jami-us-sahih*, trans. Abdul H. Siddiqui, 4 vols, Beirut: Dar al-Arabia.

Nakamura, Mitsuo (1983) *The Crescent Arises over the Banyan Tree: A Study of the Muhammadiyah Movement in a Central Javanese Town*, Jogyakarta: Gadjah Mada University Press.

Robertson Smith, William (1972) *The Religion of the Semites: The Fundamental Institutions*, New York: Schocken Books.

Scott, James C. (1990) *Domination and the Arts of Resistance: Hidden Transcripts*, New Haven, CT: Yale University Press.

Siegel, James T. (1969) *The Rope of God*, Berkeley, CA: University of California Press.

Smith, Jane I., and Yvonne Y. Haddad (1981) *The Islamic Understanding of Death and Resurrection*, Albany, NY: State University of New York Press.

Smith, Wilfred Cantwell (1963) *The Meaning and End of Religion: A New Approach to the Religious Traditions of Mankind*, New York: Macmillan.

Snouck-Hurgronje, Christiaan (1903) *Het Gayoland en zijne bewoners [Gayoland and Its Inhabitants]*, Jakarta: Landsdrukkerij.

——— (1906) *The Achehnese*, trans. Arthur W. O'Sullivan, 2 vols, Leiden and London: E.J. Brill, Luzac & Co.

Tapper, Nancy, and Richard Tapper (1987) "The Birth of the Prophet: Ritual and Gender in Turkish Islam," *Man*, 22: 69–92.

Volkman, Toby A. (1985) *Feasts of Honor: Ritual and Change in the Toraja Highlands*, Urbana, IL: University of Illinois Press.

Werbner, Pnina (1988) "'Sealing' the Koran: Offering and Sacrifice among Pakistani Labour Migrants," *Cultural Dynamics*, 1: 77–97.

Woodward, Mark R. (1989) *Islam in Java: Normative Piety and Mysticism in the Sultanate of Yogyakarta*, Tucson, AZ: University of Arizona Press.

12 "Sealing" the Koran

Offering and sacrifice among Pakistani labour migrants

Pnina Werbner

Pnina Werbner is Professor Emerita of social anthropology at Keele. Werbner received her degrees of MA Econ in anthropology and PhD in anthropology from University of Manchester. Her fieldwork spans Britain, Pakistan and Botswana, with a key focus being on urban anthropology. Her research interests are in the anthropology of Muslim ritual and religion, culture and economy, migration and diaspora, cosmopolitanism and citizenship. Throughout her career, she has published and edited numerous volumes on theoretical interest among others: *Debating Cultural Hybridity and The Politics of Multiculturalism in the New Europe* (1997), *Embodying Charisma: Modernity, Locality and the Performance of Emotion in Sufi Cults* (1998), *Women, Citizenship and Difference* (with Nira Yuval-Davis, 1999) and *Anthropology and the New Cosmopolitanism* (2008). Her research is documented in her three monographs: *The Migration Process: Capital, Gifts and Offerings among British Pakistanis* (1990, 2002); *Imagined Diasporas among Manchester Muslims* (2002) and *Pilgrims of Love: the Anthropology of a Global Sufi Cult* (2003). She has advised various research and editorial boards and presented keynote addresses throughout Europe, Australia, Pakistan and the USA. In the excerpts below, Werbner critically reviews anthropological theories of sacrifice and takes them as frameworks for analyzing her ethnographic findings among Pakistani Muslims in Manchester. She argues that one can conceptualize the ritual transformation in this community as a "naturalization" of ritual and a ritualization of social relations.

Offering, sacrifice and ritual mediation

Sacrifice, wrote Robertson Smith is "a banquet in which gods and men share together" (Robertson Smith 1886: 134). Whether a group of commensals creates its gods in its image or merely renews them in renewing itself (Durkheim 1915: 375), acts of sacrifice or offering have always been regarded as taking place in the context of "natural" groups of kindreds or locally based communities. For labour migrants this "natural" community cannot simply be "renewed"; it must be reconstructed. Moreover, its very reconstruction is problematic, for it implies a shift in commitments: from migrants' natal home to their new place of domicile.

The performance of sacrifices or ritual offerings away from home effects for Pakistani labour migrants a crucial transition. The very structure of the ritual dictates that its efficacious performance is contingent on the mediated ritual support of significant others; kin, friends, neighbours and the poor. The holding of sacrifices and offerings, hitherto unambiguously associated with "home" in its broadest affective and moral sense, is predicated, in other words, on the reconstruction of a moral universe, and in order to achieve this reconstruction, migrants must reconstitute crucial moral categories of the person. Once reconstructed, rituals of offering and sacrifice come to be powerful focuses for sociability. A family's current intimate circle, as well as its widest network of acquaintances, is gathered in order to seek blessing, redemption or atonement.

In substituting a "sacrificial schema" for a prior evolutionary model of sacrifice, Hubert and Mauss recognised the highly complex but nevertheless ordered variation in sacrificial procedures, even within a single society. Crucial to this schema was a distinction between sacrifices of sacralization and desacralization, and although de Heusch has recently criticised this contrast (de Heusch 1985: 213), it remains—perhaps in modified form—fundamental for an analysis of the transformation through sacrifice of relations between the gods, the sacrificer and the congregation participating in the ritual.

The distinction emerges quite clearly in an analysis of the ritual offerings and sacrifices performed by Punjabi Muslim labour migrants. Only offerings and sacrifices of "sacralization" are conceived to be possible, even desirable, in Britain. Sacrifices in which the primary intent is of "desacralization" continue to be held exclusively at home, in Pakistan. This reluctance to perform "desacralizing" sacrifices locally is important, for it reveals the autonomous force of a ritual, once its symbolic structure and meaning have become embedded in a local social context. The "naturalization" of ritual, its incorporation into novel social contexts, is thus not automatic; ritual cannot be said to simply sanction or buttress current social relations. [...]

When Pakistani labour migrants in Manchester hold rituals locally they are, in effect, expressing the nature of their relationships with other Pakistanis living locally. They are also staking a symbolic claim in their Manchester home and its permanency. These congregational or indexical aspects of the ritual are extremely significant, for certain rituals cannot be held, as mentioned, without the ritual services of a broader congregation. I am thus concerned here with the role of fellow migrants as *ritual mediators*, effecting a desired transformation in the condition of individuals and their families.

Pakistan and Britain

Pakistanis in Britain invest a good deal in their homes in Pakistan. Many migrants send home regular cash remittances, build "*pakka*" brick and cement houses in their natal villages or nearby towns, and continue to arrange marriages between their children and the children of siblings still resident at home, in accord with the Islamic preference for parallel and cross cousin marriage. They also continue to foster ceremonial exchange relations with friends and relatives at home, returning to Pakistan periodically on prolonged visits, laden with British gifts for a vast number of kinsmen and friends. They invest, in addition, in land, tractors, cars, tube wells and other agricultural or commercial enterprises. It is therefore, perhaps, not surprising to find that the same labour migrants continue to make ritual offerings and sacrifices at home, and to bury their dead at home, transporting corpses at some cost from Britain to Pakistan, and forming regional burial societies for this purpose.

It may be possible to argue, in light of this, that ritual behaviour simply reinforces sanctions and more pragmatic links. These in turn stem, perhaps, from migrants' sense of alienation from the receiving society. Yet, although it is undoubtedly the case that ritual "investments" in Pakistan parallel other forms of investment, it cannot be claimed that pragmatic or economic calculations are prior to the ritual accompanying them, for both stem from an integral set of experiences and moral ideas regarding where the most highly valued social relations are. This fundamental perception of the locus of valued relations dictates both ritual *and* economic behaviour.

This perception is subject to change. Although many Pakistanis continue to hope that they will ultimately return home, to Pakistan, most of them are in Britain for good. They have brought their families over, they own property in Britain, and many have invested in businesses locally. While they may have arrived as short-term "target" migrants, their stay in Britain has been prolonged indefinitely. Time and circumstances are, from this perspective, crucial determinants of transition. Under some circumstances the locus of valued relations shifts towards Britain, and migrants tend to invest *both* in Britain *and* in Pakistan. Once the transition has occurred, the holding of offerings and sacrifices in Britain becomes commonplace and is taken for granted, while many migrants also bury their dead locally. Although the ultimate symbolic priority of the country of origin remains axiomatic and is rarely questioned, individual "practical" and symbolic investments thus become more evenly distributed between Pakistan and Britain.

My paper concerns the moral transition to being doubly rooted, in Pakistan and in Britain, and its implications for locally based relations between Pakistani labour migrants resident in a single British city. It is worth noting here that while the rituals discussed are symbolically predicated on the amity of the attendant congregation, the congregation itself is a temporary one, a network focused on a household or family. The congregants are selected from a family's current friendship circle, and even close kinsmen may be excluded if they are involved in a quarrel or dispute. Clearly, the congregational aspects of such rituals vary a great deal from performance to performance, depending on personal circumstances, class background and a host of other factors. My concern here, however, is not with this congregational *variation,* which I discuss elsewhere, but with the ontological basis of the ritual—what are the preconditions for holding it, and what effects it is perceived to achieve.

[I focus on] two related processes: the "naturalization" of rituals transferred to a new context, and the "ritualization" of social relationships among labour migrants in town (Gluckman 1962: 24–25). This ritualization takes on a special significance in the urban industrial context. If in rural societies ritual arguably serves to highlight specific roles where multiplex relations prevail, among urban labour migrants such ritualization transforms the segmental relationships between neighbours, workmates or business acquaintances into morally diffuse relationships. Urban ritual overcomes, in other words, the spatial dispersion and segmentation of social relationships by gathering together a varied congregation which is, nevertheless, united in moral support for an individual or family.

From a religious perspective, it is possible for Muslims to perform acts of personal sacrifice or offering anywhere. There is no ancestral shrine, as for many African labour migrants, no central consecrated altar, as for some Semitic people.[1] These rituals are, nevertheless, contingent on a moral spatial order. Performed in order to seek blessing or a release from affliction, they require the support of a circle of significant others. They cannot be performed in an alien land, in the midst of strangers. Similarly, a man is not buried in the wild, but amidst those with whom he belongs.

The countering of affliction and the seeking of divine blessing are, moreover, crucially mediated for Pakistanis through socially significant categories *beyond* a migrant's immediate set of kinsmen. As Muslims, Pakistani migrants believe that the gaining of atonement, expiation or divine blessing requires an act of giving away, of selfless generosity. The act of communication in sacrifice or offering is only fully possible through the mediation of the poor. Without them a sacrifice or offering is incomplete.

There is more to home therefore than just a sentimental attachment. Fundamental acts of Islamic piety are perceived to be possible only in a society where certain social categories exist, and are explicitly recognised. Yet the "poor" are said to be absent in places such as

Manchester. For labour migrants the performance of sacrifices and offerings away from their natal home sometimes represents, then, a compromise, a distortion of the meaning of these acts. They cast doubt on the validity and efficaciousness of the rites outside their "natural" setting.

More generally, the transfer of rituals away from their "natural" context is associated for labour migrants with a heightened consciousness of the cultural presuppositions underlying the rituals. The taken for granted features of rites become an object of conscious reflection, as migrants grapple to resolve emergent dilemmas around hitherto normal, expected or "natural" aspects of the rituals they perform. Migration, like homecoming or strangerhood, brings into focus the implicit rules and norms hitherto left unquestioned and unexamined (Schütz 1944; Schütz 1945). Not just the meaning, but also the countering of misfortune is thus problematic for labour migrants (see Mitchell 1975).[2] The effective means of redress have to be extended and reinterpreted for, in an urban industrial environment, many of migrants' social relations are segmental or recent.

As a big city, Manchester has a heterogeneous Pakistani migrant population. Many of migrants' friendships have been forged locally, in the context of work or neighbourly interaction. Few migrants have remained encapsulated in networks of home boys or fellow villagers (*grain*). There are, nevertheless, crucial variations in migrants' perceptions of the long-term significance of their residence in the city. These perceptions are expressed ritually in differing symbolic orientations. Migrants who make sacrifices locally or bury their dead in Britain tend to sustain much broader networks of friends and acquaintances locally. Like the "Red" and "School" described by Philip Mayer, migrants vary in their "rootedness," in their very perception of where home is, and in the experience of the surrounding social environment in which they live.

Despite these differences, however, certain ritual acts continue to be performed only in Pakistan by all migrants. These acts, "for the life," like the act of sending a dead man's body home, give ideological priority to the home country, its people, its very soil, over the alienness of the diaspora. [...]

It is difficult to specify all the circumstances in which such a shift in the perception of valued relations may occur. Pakistani migrants of city origin appear to hold rituals of offering, though not necessarily of sacrifice, wherever they live, as long as they have built up a network of local friends. Among villagers, however, the transition is probably related to the maturation of families and the re-emergence of the three-generational household in Britain. Where migrants have large numbers of relatives living nearby this contributes to their sense of being settled but it is the location of very close family members—parents, siblings or children—which seems most crucial. Clearly then, there is no single isolated social characteristic which determines the transition but, as I argue below, over time migrants are drawn into the performance of rituals locally, often almost despite themselves.

Core rituals

The ritual I focus on here is known as *khatam quran*, the sealing of the Koran, or the communal Koran reading. It is held primarily by women in the domestic domain and is an important locus of interhousehold women-centred sociability (see Werbner 1988, Werbner 2002). It is thus a feature of migrant life mostly absent during the all-male, initial phase of migration, and only introduced into Britain with the arrival of wives and families. [...]

The *khatam quran*, although perhaps the most central domestic ritual performed by Pakistanis in Manchester, is a relatively simple, unelaborate ritual. In times of danger, thanksgiving or transition Pakistanis convene their fellow migrants for a ritual of formal prayer and commensality. [...] It is performed by a congregation composed mostly of women who are gathered in the house of the ritual convener. Between them the assembled guests read the entire Koran in one sitting. Each of the participants reads one or more chapters (*spara*) out of the thirty in the Koran. The reading is dedicated to the person convening the event, and is regarded as a service performed by the readers for the convener and his or her family. After the reading of the Koran has been completed at least once, an offering of food is made which is distributed to the guests. In Pakistan a share of the food is set aside for the poor as charity (*sadqa*), but this is not done in Manchester as "there are no poor people here." By custom, the Koran should be read with absolute accuracy, so as not to confuse Arabic words which vary only slightly in their spelling. A high degree of ritualism thus characterises one part of the proceedings. Otherwise, the structure of the ritual is very simple, and it contains little figurative elaboration.

Despite this apparent simplicity, however, the ritual embraces central religious and moral ideas and forms the basic model for a series of other rituals, all concerned with the two themes of sacrifice and prayer. The analysis of labour migrants' perceptions of the ritual, and of related rituals, brings into sharp focus what they consider are the fundamental features of the rites. It thus highlights the crucial elements of sacrifice and offering from a novel angle, lending some credence to certain approaches in the general debate about sacrifice and offering.

Symbolically, the moral attachment of a family to its current home and surroundings is tangibly expressed during *khatme quran* through a transformation of secular into sacred space. One room in the convener's house—and, by extension, the whole house—assumes, temporarily, certain features of a mosque. Shoes are taken off at the threshold to the room and people read the Koran seated on the ground. Along with the burning of incense, these observances serve to define the space as holy or sacred. The following description sets out the basic features of the ritual.

> When I arrived at S.'s home the ritual had already begun. Downstairs, a few men were occupied in last minute preparations for the meal, assisted by one of the women. Upstairs, eight women were reading the Koran in one of the bedrooms. Mattresses had been laid on the floor and a white cloth spread over them. The women were seated on this sheet, their heads completely covered by chiffon scarves (*dupatta*). Their shoes had been left on the threshold of the room, where they lay in a large heap. The room was filled with the aroma of burning incense. A pile of books on a raised surface in the midst of the seated women represented the chapters of the Koran still to be read. Each woman sat with a book containing one chapter in her hand, reading the Koran in a soft murmur. The little talking there was took place in hushed voices, but mostly the women concentrated on getting the reading over with.
>
> When they had completed reading the whole Koran, the women came downstairs to join their husbands, who had arrived as the reading was nearing completion. All the guests gathered together for a joint meal. Before the meal was brought to the table, a prayer was said in private over a portion of the food, asking God for forgiveness in case any mistake had been made in the proceedings.
>
> Since this was a *khatam* held by middle-class migrants, mainly urban in origin, men shared in the meal. There was some joking, as when the convener left the room to bring some more food; "she is going to pray" the men joked, amidst much laughter.

> The reason for the *khatam* was never openly stated during the proceedings. It was, apparently, held because the couple convening the event were recently married (although the husband had been living in Britain for many years); they had recently arrived from Pakistan, had been unemployed but had both found jobs and were able to repay their debts.
>
> It was, in other words, a *khatam* held as thanksgiving after a period of hardship and change, and it marked the couple's residence together in a new home. The congregation attending were all friends, with the exception of the convener's brother.

The food prayed over at the completion of a Koran reading consists, usually, of water, milk, a sweet dish, rice and fruit. The fruit is distributed first, immediately after the reading is completed, while the readers are still reclined on the floor. The selection blessed is representative of abundance, purity and the essential ingredients of a meal. The portion of the food prayed over is distributed first in order to ensure that it is entirely consumed, and none thrown away.

The countering of misfortune

Khatam quran rituals are held in order to ask for forgiveness (*bakhsh*), thanksgiving (*shukriya*), and divine blessing (*barkat*, or Arab. *baraka*). Although the three notions appear at first glance to be different, the ideas surrounding them are closely linked (see also Hubert and Mauss 1964: 14). The emphasis depends on the occasion. If the *khatam quran* is held to celebrate recovery from an illness, it is held for *shukriya*, thanksgiving. Since, however, there has been, it is believed, an unwanted intervention by God or spirits, a sin possibly committed either knowingly or unknowingly, an act of expiation is also involved. The convener is thus seeking to rid himself of the condition which caused the misfortune or affliction (*bala*, *musibat*) while at the same time seeking *barkat*. Hence, *khatam quran* rituals are intended to transform the state of the convener from that induced by negative intervention or lack of divine protection into one of *barkat*—endowed through positive divine intervention.[3] *Barkat* is thus the obverse of affliction. This opposition is expressed in the formal structure and permutations of different offerings or sacrifices Pakistanis make.

The *khatam quran* ritual is divided into two key phases: in the first phase the Koran is read. This is the phase of consecration. In the second phase, food, which constitutes, in part at least, an offering, is presented to the assembled congregation. The two phases, although closely linked, represent two separate religious acts, each surrounded by a set of theological and cosmological beliefs.

The central feature of the first ritual phase is the recitation of the Koran. This recitation is considered to have immense power. The divine force invoked in the recitation has the power to expel evil spirits and to protect against them. The reading of the Koran also evokes *barkat*, which is then imparted to the food served. *Barkat* (or *baraka* in Arabic) is a "beneficent force, of divine origin, which causes superabundance in the physical sphere and prosperity and happiness in the psychic order" (Colin 1960: 1032). The text of the Koran is charged with *barkat*.[4] A *khatam quran* is intended to transform the state of the convener into one of *barkat*, which is also shared by those reading the Koran in his or her name. The complete recitation of the Koran, especially if done in a short time, is considered a meritorious achievement. Pakistanis say they read the whole Koran because they "cannot be quite sure what particular passage suits the occasion," and this is particularly so where danger is present. The Koran, they say, includes a saying for every type of occasion, but the location and meaning of these passages is known only to God. By reading the Koran in its entirety they ensure that they have read the appropriate passage. In this way they hope to influence God, which is the intention of the *khatam*.

This type of explanation clearly stresses the magical power of the Koran in influencing God and the spirits. This magical aspect is indicated by the great emphasis placed on accurate reading. There must be no change of *zabar* or *pech* (minor vowel marks in Arabic), for this might change the meaning of the word. Indeed, the Koran is read in Arabic, which few Pakistanis understand (although most migrants have, of course, read the Urdu translation of the Koran).

In an alternative explanation, the morality of the Koran is emphasised. The Koran contains "all the laws and sayings needed to live a good life." When moving to a new house, I was told, it is right that the whole Koran be read. Where the Koran has been read, one is reluctant to sin or, if one does sin, one feels guilty about it.

Sacrifice and the mediation of the poor

Going against the magical aspect of the Koran as a book containing *barkat* is the notion of intention or *niyat* (Arab. *niya*) central to Islamic religious observance. While much emphasis is placed on the accurate reading of the Koran, the reading is followed by a prayer over the food asking God for forgiveness for any errors made in the proceedings. My informants were clear that the intention supersedes the ritualistic aspects of the event. Perhaps the most important difference between the two phases of the ritual—the Koran reading and the offering made—relates to this distinction. Paradoxically, perhaps, the reading of the Koran represents the more ritualistic phase, while the commensal meal and the associated offering given away to the poor is closely tied to the intention of the convener. And, moreover, the difference between the way in which offerings are made is linked to subtle differences in intention rather than in the form of food or money given away. Was the *khatam* held for *shukriya* (thanksgiving), for *barkat,* during illness, to consecrate a new house? The intention is all important.

The problem of how to manage misfortune or deal with affliction is at the heart of all these observances. Pakistanis believe that nothing happens without the will (*raza*) and knowledge of God. Hence their view of affliction and misfortune is closely related to their view of the moral order, of good and evil in the eyes of God. A serious illness or misfortune is believed to be caused by the intervention of evil spirits and these can only be exorcised through God's help. Indeed, they should not have afflicted a person in the first place unless he or she lacked divine protection. In cases where *khatme quran* or sacrifices are performed for a person who is seriously ill or has a chronic illness or an unnatural condition (such as barrenness in women), or in times of misfortune or trouble, the ritual is held for the explicit purpose of expelling evil spirits through the recitation of the Koran and through almsgiving. Some migrants, who deny the presence of evil spirits even in the case of serious illness, talk instead of the presence of misfortune or danger caused in their view by sin. It is the misfortune, *musibat* (or *bala*), which a person rids him- or herself of through almsgiving and prayer. Reading the Koran is seen both as a protection against such misfortune and as a means of exorcising evil spirits.

Not all *khatme quran* are associated, however, with exorcism, or even primarily with expiation since, as we have seen, many are intended to seek divine blessing or as thanksgiving, after the danger has departed. As will be seen, the ritual stress dictates the ritual form. In de Heusch's terms, is the intended effect "conjunction" or "disjunction" (de Heusch 1985: 213)?

A crucial, feature of sacrifice in this regard has to do with what parts of a sacrificial victim or offering are consumed and what parts are given away or destroyed.[5] From this perspective, the significance of the commensal meal following the Koran reading cannot be understood apart from other practices of Pakistani sacrifice. Hence, true sacrifice, i.e. the ritual slaughtering of an animal, may take a number of different forms. In Manchester, many Pakistani migrants perform animal sacrifices locally on two main occasions: at the annual *Eid Zoha* festival and after the birth of a child, particularly a son. The first sacrifice is known as *qurbani*, the second as *haqiqa*. The structure of the *qurbani* sacrifice represents an explicit model for the proper division of an animal in personal sacrifice, where the ritual act is intended to be both piacular and for the sake of divine blessing.

Qurbani sacrifices are performed to commemorate the binding of Ismail by his father Ibrahim (the Islamic version of the binding of Isaac by Abraham in the Old Testament). This myth, whether in its biblical or koranic form, exemplifies the principle of substitution of a life for a life in sacrifice. According to Islamic tradition the *bakra* (sacrificial victim) is supposed to be divided into three equal parts, with a third shared by the family of the sacrificer, a third by kinsmen and friends, and a third given away to "the poor." In Manchester, since "there are no poor" two-thirds are given away to kinsmen and friends.

As performed locally, the victim is slaughtered in the very early hours of the morning of the festival, either by the local Muslim butcher or by the sacrificer himself, who accompanies the butcher to the local abattoir. Often several families join in making a single sacrifice, usually a lamb. The victim is then cut up by the butcher and divided into portions. After the morning prayers members of a family gather for a mid-day meal, and in this a third of the victim is shared. The sacrificer allocates the rest of the meat, usually divided into two pound portions, among his neighbours and friends living in Manchester. Usually, he knocks on the door of each house he visits and hands the meat over to the person on the threshold, telling him or her that it is *qurbani*. If the people are close friends he enters the house, but if they are mere acquaintances he will usually hand over the meat on the threshold to whoever opens the door. In some cases I found that people were not quite sure of all the families who had presented them with *qurbani* that year. It may happen that the meat is handed over on the doorstep to one of the children who does not remember the name of the donor. Knowing who brought *qurbani* is not very important, for no expectation of reciprocity is implied, and no debt has been incurred. The sacrifice is made in the name of God (*khuda da nam*) by the sacrificer and his family, in order to gain merit, or to expiate sin.[6]

The *qurbani* sacrifice contrasts significantly with another form of personal sacrifice known as *sadqa* (Arab. *sadaqa*, a term also used for almsgiving in general). *Sadqa* sacrifices are always performed in Pakistan. They are preceeded by a *khatam quran* and are held, I am told, "for the life": if someone is mortally ill, or has escaped a very bad accident, a *sadqa* sacrifice is made. The idea appears to be one of substitution, and the unusual aspect of this type of sacrifice for Pakistanis is that the animal is given away to the poor *in its entirety*. Neither the sacrificer nor any of his kinsmen are supposed to partake of the sacrificial victim. To do so would be to detract from the efficacy of the ritual act. In cases of abnormal illness, I was told, the meat is not even given to the poor but is thrown away.

Two beliefs are implicit in *sadqa* sacrifice among Pakistanis. On the one hand, as the name of the sacrifice—*sadqa*—indicates, the sacrifice is an extreme act of almsgiving. On the other hand, it is also an act of expulsion of evil spirits or misfortune. For Pakistanis there is no belief that a sacrifice should be burnt or destroyed, nor is there a view that the "life of the flesh is in the blood" (Leviticus 17:11). There is, moreover, no sacred altar or shrine. The idea that God is partaking directly of any tangible substance, such as the blood of the animal, is abhorrent (see Weir 1908). The blood of a sacrificial victim is for Muslims *haram*, i.e. prohibited and sacred. Their view appears to be that blood removes all the impurities from the animal before it is shared and consumed. In other words, the flow of the blood is a purificatory element of the sacrifice. […]

The gift to the poor completes and seals the act of offering a sacrifice (for a structural analysis of the processual form of a sacrifice see Werbner 1989). Communication in sacrifice is therefore achieved for Pakistanis indirectly, via the poor, and through an act of giving. Thus, one informant told me:

> Many people (i.e. the poor) only see meat when it is given to them. That is a benefit to God in an indirect way. One feeds somebody poor and God likes it. No, the blood has no meaning. Giving blood in sacrifice is a thing among Hindus, they give blood to *Kali*, these are pagan customs. But not in Islam.

The central mediatory role played by "the poor" in atonement and expiation presents labour migrants with an intractable dilemma in their desire to perform certain ritual acts outside their "natural" setting; for their perception of the poor reflects, profoundly, the way in which labour migrants reconstitute their moral universe.

Who are "the poor" (*lokan gharib*)? For Muslims the poor may include any person, even members of one's own kin group or village, such as widows or orphans. They do not form a clear category of outsiders, and this is made quite explicit in the Koran. The notion of the poor cuts across the categories of family, friends and fellow villagers, such as low caste or landless labourers, to embrace the widest humanity Pakistanis recognise: the beggars around Saints' tombs, or the residents of orphanages, leper homes, etc. I was frequently told that I could not imagine real poverty, living in Britain. There are, moreover, no persons in Britain willing to define themselves as poor and take the remains of a commensal meal or sacrifice. It is worth noting here that although the part of the meal given away to the poor is the equivalent of the *juta*, or leftovers, given among Hindus to lower castes, the Islamic idea of giving to the poor is not as clearly predicated on a notion of immutable hierarchy. It does, however, imply real inequality in wealth and property, and it is significant that in Britain, where few people are entirely destitute, there are no Muslims willing to define themselves as belonging to this category.[7]

Pakistani labour migrants universally direct their almsgiving towards Pakistan. If they hold *khatam quran, qurbani* or *haqiqa* rituals in Manchester, it is because they feel that the further crucial social category of friends is present here. Without sharing among friends, there is no commensal meal, no *barkat*, no communication with the divine. It is possible to hold all these rituals by proxy, through kinsmen at home, in Pakistan. The sacrificer sends the money for a meal to be prepared or a beast slaughtered in his name. Many migrants, especially more recent arrivals of village origin, virtually always perform these rituals at home. Perhaps for them, more than for middle-class, urban migrants, the poor are a known and personalised group. The village or home neighbourhood remains the focus of their significant relations; they remain rooted back home symbolically, emotionally, experientially. Yet over time, they too come under increasing communal and social pressure to reconstitute a moral universe in Britain. Before going on to discuss this process, let me return briefly to the meal which follows the communal reading of the Koran and its ritual significance.

The rootedness of labour migrants

In Manchester, the meal following the Koran reading is shared in its entirety among the assembled guests. For some migrants this makes the significance of the meal problematic and even negates its role as an offering. They regard the meal primarily as an act of hospitality. Other migrants claim, however, that the food is an offering (*niyaz*) given in the name of God, and usually following a vow (*mannat*) made in times of affliction or personal crisis. Certain universal features surrounding the meal confirm its continuing ritual significance: the "sealing" of the Koran is invariably followed by a distribution of food; the food is prayed over, usually consists of primary elements, and must not be thrown away. In addition a portion of food—usually fruit—is often sent home with guests and this food is known as *tobarak* or *bakshish* (from the Arabic roots for blessing or request). The intention of the offerer appears to be the chief determinant of the designation of the offering.

Clearly, however, the ambivalence apparent in migrants' exegesis regarding the *khatam* meal reflects the fact that in Britain the meal is not appropriately apportioned. We have seen that the nature of divine intervention is related to the form of sacrificial distribution, that a structured relation exists between the consumption of the offering and the contrast between good and evil intervention. This may be represented in Figure 1.

Whereas the commensal meal following the Koran reading imparts *barkat*, the full ritual efficacy of the meal as a piacular offering (*niaz*) can only be achieved through a sharing of a portion of the food with the poor. In other words, it can only be achieved in Pakistan, at home. [...]

Hence, as migrants' stay in Britain is prolonged and extended, misfortune, affliction and particularly death draw them into the local community. A death is followed by three funerary *khatme quran* at prescribed intervals and they are intended to seek forgiveness and merit (*sawab*) for the deceased, and thus to facilitate his or her entry into heaven. During the funerary

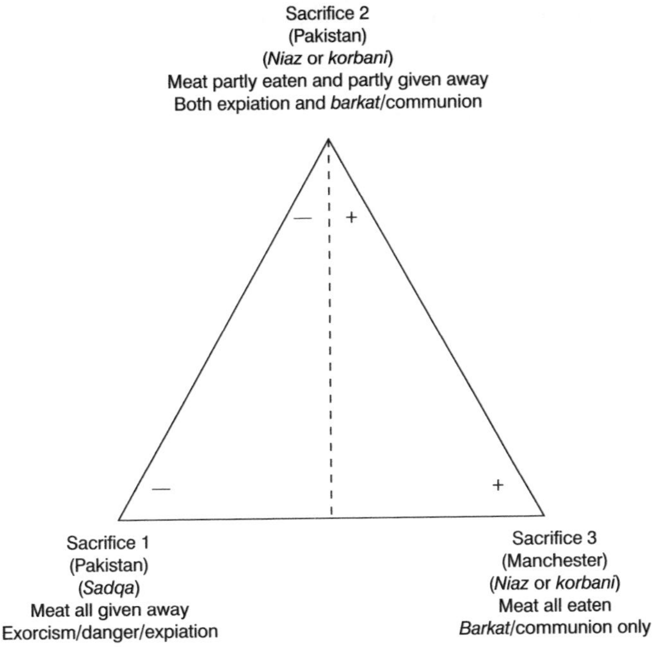

Figure 1

khatam the congregants repeat a certain Islamic prayer 125,000 times (Urdu *savalak*) over the chickpeas or date stones which, according to one version, represent the sins of the deceased. Symbolically, then, funerary *khatam* rituals, which are held with increasing frequency as the local community ages, are more elaborate than personal *khatam* rituals.

A further, and major, difference between a death *khatam* and one convened for personal offering is indexical: whereas personal offerings are exclusive affairs, drawing together an intimate circle of friends, funerary *khatme* are large, open and inclusive. While certain people are invited, anyone is welcome to attend them (on the significance of indexicality and inclusiveness in ritual see Turner 1974: 185; Werbner 1977: XXX-XXXI).

Death is also the occasion for the collection of *chanda,* contributions, made in order to send the corpse to Pakistan, accompanied by a close relative. In recent years migrants from certain parts of Pakistan have founded formal death associations (see Werbner 1985, Chapter 10). Thus, paradoxically perhaps, the ritual acts surrounding death both draw migrants into a locally constituted moral community while at the same time institutionalising the link back home. The independent force of ritual belief is most evident here, for ritual precipitates the formation of enduring organizational structures, whose significance may come to extend well beyond the reason for their formation. As migrants' sojourn is extended indefinitely, the ad hoc collections which took place previously in factories or neighbourhoods are being replaced by formal arrangements. For many migrants, therefore, the myth of return is no myth: in death migrants return home on their final journey.

Conclusions

This paper has been about the extension of moral space, and the transformation of newly formed relations into moral relations. The two processes implied in this transformation were, I argued, the "naturalization" of ritual in a novel setting, and the "ritualization" of labour migrants' local relations. I focused in the paper on one particular widely practiced ritual and spelt out its symbolic significance in some detail. One outcome of analysing the ritual in the context of labour migration, i.e. outside its "natural" context, is its elucidation of the underlying symbolic logic of Islamic sacrifice.

The Pakistani case is not unique. Short term labour migrants, it seems, rarely perform certain ritual acts away from home. Almost everywhere, they make personal offerings and sacrifices at home, and almost everywhere they prefer, if possible, to bury their dead at home. Not surprisingly, therefore, burial societies are a very widespread form of migrant association. Less recognised, perhaps, has been the common tendency to make personal sacrifices at home. Once again, this tendency is not unique to Muslims. [...]

Nevertheless, as the migrants' stay is prolonged and extended, there is a shift in their symbolic orientation. Compelling reasons grounded in migrants' beliefs and current circumstances create a need to make offerings and sacrifices away from home. In this paper I have shown that although Pakistani migrants may hold certain rituals by proxy in Pakistan, this denies critical beneficial features of the rites involved. Only relative newcomers, who believe their stay in Britain is truly temporary, prefer this option.

The cultural dynamics implicit here have comparative implications: short-term labour migrants depend upon others still resident at home to sustain their cultural heritage and perform for them a whole complex of ritual acts. They may stress diacritical emblems such as dress or language, and may seek the company of fellow migrants, but they do not attempt to replicate the religio-cultural environment they abandoned. Long-term sojourners, by contrast, recreate and revitalize—within the constraints of their new environment—the richness and complexity of their original culture. This is particularly so when the culture of origin is urban and universalistic, as it is for Pakistanis. Hence, the prevalence and focal role of domestic rituals amongst long-term migrants. Hence also the re-introduction of religio-ideological debates and conflicts in the public sphere, and the increasing popularity of literary cultural events. The sinking of local roots leads not, in other words, to the denial of the migrants' cultural heritage, but to its renewed celebration.

Notes

1 Hence the destruction of the temple and the dispersion of the Jews in 70 A.D. brought Jewish sacrifice to an abrupt end.
2 I discuss further dimensions of this problem in Werbner 1986; Werbner 1988. Clearly, relationships between kinsmen in town may undergo a critical change. Thus Mitchell points out that in town rivalry within the kin group is replaced by support and cooperation in the face of wider oppositions (Mitchell 1975: 379). Richard Werbner, in a critical reappraisal of Mitchell's view, argues that rather than reaching the "rawest grievances," the "ministering of relatives at expiatory feasts in a town is an aspect of the bid for mutual support in the midst of potentially hostile strangers" (Werbner 1972: 229–231). Conflicts between Pakistani kinsmen in town do seem often to persist, hence the continuous stress on friendship.
3 In this Islamic sacrifice and offering may differ from that of some African societies (for a comparative overview see de Heusch 1985). Evans-Pritchard's denial of the ritual significance of the commensal meal following a sacrifice is well-known, but the significant variations in the distribution and disposal of the victim on different occasions by the Nuer would seem to imply that its consumption by a congregation does have a ritual import. Nuer sacrifice, in other words, does not end with the immolation of the victim (Evans-Pritchard 1956).
4 Discussions of the Muslim notion of "*baraka*," are too manifold to be listed here. The most extensive anthropological discussion is still probably that of Westermarck for Morocco, who also discusses at length the "*baraka*" present in the Koran 1: 139 and in sacred passages (Westermarck 1968 [1926]: 205–219).
5 The full elaboration and complexity of the procedures regarding the distribution of a victim is discussed by Luc de Heusch 1985 and Richard Werbner 1989. Werbner argues that this distribution mediates the movement, not only of gods *vis-à-vis* people, but of different categories of people *vis-à-vis* each other.
6 The gaining of merit in Islam should not be confused with the gaining of merit amongst Hindus and Buddhists. The Islamic belief is in an active a watchful God, meting out punishment and reward at will. In conjunction with this is the notion of expiation and forgiveness, or purification from sin, the annulment of previous sins. The notion of merit in Islam is associated with eschatological beliefs regarding divine punishment after death, for it is then that the good and evil deeds a person has committed during his lifetime are weighed, and his destination to hell or heaven decided. Reward and punishment after death are at the centre of Islamic faith, but even after death forgiveness may be sought from God for the dead man. Hence, redemption remains a possibility to the very end, as it does not in Hinduism or Buddhism.
7 I am grateful to Tom Selwyn and Roger Ballard for drawing my attention to parallels in Hindu and Sikh practice.

References

Colin, George S. (1960) "Baraka," *Encyclopedia of Islam*, 1: 1032, Leiden: E.J. Brill.
de Heusch, Luc (1985) *Sacrifice in Africa: A Structuralist Approach*, trans. Linda O'Brien, Bloomington, IN: Indiana University Press.
Durkheim, Émile (1915) *The Elementary Forms of the Religious Life*, trans. Joseph W. Swain, London: George Allen & Unwin.
Evans-Pritchard, Edward E. (1956) *Nuer Religion*, Oxford: Clarendon Press.
Gluckman, Max (1962) "Les rites de passage," in Max Gluckman (ed.) *Essays on the Ritual of Social Relations*, Manchester: Manchester University Press.

Hubert, Henri, and Marcel Mauss (1964) *Sacrifice: Its Nature and Function*, trans. Wilfried D. Halls, London: Cohen & West.

Mitchell, J. Clyde (1975) "The Meaning in Misfortune for Urban Africans," in John Friedl and Noel J. Chrisman (eds) *City Ways: A Selective Reader in Urban Anthropology*, New York: Harper & Row.

Robertson Smith, William (1886) "Sacrifice," *The Encyclopedia Britannica* 9th edn, 21: 131–138.

Schütz, Alfred (1944) "The Stranger: An Essay in Social Psychology," *The American Journal of Sociology*, 49: 499–507.

——— (1945) "The Homecomer," *The American Journal of Sociology*, 50: 369–376.

Turner, Victor W. (1974) *Dramas, Fields, and Metaphors: Symbolic Action in Human Society*, Ithaca, NY: Cornell University Press.

Weir, T.H. (1908) "Sacrifice (Islamic)," *Encyclopedia of Religion and Ethics*, 11, New York: C. Scribner's Sons.

Werbner, Pnina (1985) "The Organisation of Giving and Ethnic Elites: Voluntary Associations amongst Manchester Pakistanis," *Ethnic and Racial Studies*, 8: 368–388.

—— (1986) "The Virgin and the Clown Ritual Elaboration in Pakistani Migrants' Weddings," *Man*, 21: 227–250.

—— (1988) "Taking and Giving: Female Bonds and Conjugal Roles in a Pakistani Immigrant Neighbourhood," in Sallie Westwood and Bhachu Parminder (eds) *Enterprising Women: Ethnicity, Economy, and Gender Relations*, London: Tavistock.

—— (2002) *The Migration Process: Capital, Gifts and Offerings among Manchester Pakistanis*, 2nd edn, Oxford: Berg Publishers.

Werbner, Richard P. (1972) "Sin, Blame and Ritual Mediation," in Max Gluckman (ed.) *The Allocation of Responsibility*, Manchester: Manchester University Press.

—— (1977) "Introduction," in Richard P. Werbner (ed.) *Regional Cults*, London and New York: Academic Press.

—— (1989) *Ritual Passage, Sacred Journey: The Process and Organization of Religious Movement*, Washington, DC: Smithsonian Institution Press.

Westermarck, Edward (1968 [1926]) *Ritual and Belief in Morocco*, New York: University Books.

Almsgiving

13 Reorganizing social welfare among Muslims

Islamic voluntarism and other forms of communal support in Northern Ghana

Holger Weiss

Holger Weiss is presently professor of general history with Åbo Akademi University, Finland. Additionally, he is a docent in global history at Åbo University, Helsinki. His specialties of research include Muslims and the secular state in Ghana, African nationalists, the Comintern (1921–1935) and consumption, identity and networks during the era of the Atlantic slave trade. He has published widely on the social welfare systems among Muslims including "*Zakat* in Northern Ghana: Not an Institution but a Goal to be Achieved" (2000), "Social Welfare in Muslim Societies in Africa" (2002), "Begging and Almsgiving in Ghana" (2007) and "Between Accommodation and Revivalism: Muslims, the State and Society in Ghana (2008). He is editor of *Social Welfare in Muslim Societies in Ghana* (2001). The following article explores the current practice of welfare in Northern Ghana in light of Muslim pre-colonial support systems. Based on his interviews, he inquires how Ghanaians assist the poor and are hospitable towards strangers. Focusing on the local settings in Ghana, he indicates which factors lead to the Islamization of the economy and political arena. He also ponders upon the impact the creation of an Islamic social welfare system has on the Muslim world.

Introduction

Islam and the Muslim community had a rather restricted social impact in Northern Ghana until the twentieth century. Some Muslim scholars were engaged in teaching children and had opened Qur'anic schools, but nothing more. During the latter half of the twentieth century, however, the contribution of the Muslim communities, and especially Muslim NGOs, in providing basic social welfare became more important. As elsewhere in Muslim Africa, the rise of Muslim (or Islamic) NGOs in Ghana has been to a large extent a reaction to Christian missionary activities and their capacity to combine religious, educational, health and social activities. Of equal importance has been the need for the Muslim community to establish organizations and associations in order to be taken into account by the colonial and postcolonial independent governments in their dealings with the various religious communities. However, as the Muslim community was not a unified group—either in Ghana or elsewhere in Muslim Africa—the outcome has been an upsurge of a great variety of associations and organizations.[1] The common factor of these Muslim NGOs has been their commitment to Islam. Some, in particular those organizations that have a direct link to the various forms of Islamism, would call for a "revitalization" of "true" Islam, i.e., reject all forms of innovation (*bida*). For such organizations, any pre-Islamic ways of communal support, for example, would be viewed with suspicion, if not rejected. However, there exists another opinion among Muslim scholars concerning how to come to terms with pre-Islamic ways of communal support, namely that of accommodation. Thus, as [...] some Muslim scholars do see a possible link between pre-Islamic forms of communal support and the provision of social welfare through Muslim NGOs and especially *zakāt* in today's Northern Ghana.

The background for the debate among Muslim scholars in Ghana about the need for a Muslim agenda in providing social welfare stems from the poor performance of the post-colonial state in Ghana. Ghana, like many other developing countries in Africa and Asia, has been hit by economic turmoil and stagnation during the last twenty to thirty years. At the same time, there has been an increased effort by politicians and economists to provide a variety of solutions to the economic, political and societal crisis in the non-western world, ranging from the neo-liberal Structural Adjustment Programmes of the World Bank and IMF to socialist concepts of state planning during the Cold War period. In between these two positions, Islamic economists have tried to explain and address economic problems as well as provide an "Islamic" solution to poverty in predominantly Muslim countries. The general line of argument among the various Islamic economists has been to provide scope for individual economic initiatives and markets, just as proponents of liberalization do, but without losing sight of the responsibilities of the state and the public sector (Pfeifer 1997: 155). There is, however, no uniform concept of what constitutes an Islamic economy.[2] Whereas most of the writings of the early Islamic economists rejected Western economic models and tried to establish an Islamic version based on a return to Islamic values and ethics,[3] modern Islamic economists have rejected in turn the "revivalist" model and attempted to come to terms with Western economic theory without losing their genuine Islamic concepts of faith.[4]

Social justice forms the cornerstone of the Islamic economic system and an elaborate social security system is perceived as an integral part of an Islamic economy. Islamic economists have argued that an Islamic social security system can, and should, be financed only through legal methods of taxation, in particular through *zakāt*.[5] [...]

Basing an Islamic social welfare system upon *zakāt* is even more complicated—if not impossible—in states such as Ghana, where Muslims are a minority. In non-Islamic or non-Muslim countries, the duty to collect *zakāt* is transferred to other public institutions, such as the mosque, and today also to non-governmental societies or NGOs. Such a situation is a rather new one. Muslim NGOs engaged in collecting *zakāt* have only existed since the 1980s.[6] [...] Of equal importance, although most often forgotten in modern discourse, has been the traditional way of providing organized social welfare through *awqaf* establishments and through the *sūfī* orders (See Kogelmann 1999).

Especially in non-Muslim countries, the local mosque has been and continues to be the foremost institution to collect and distribute *zakāt*. Other avenues have been and are the Islamic schools, and a third way has been for people to send *zakāt* back to their families and communities in their home countries. [...]

There exists a clear link between the proliferation of Islamic or Muslim NGOs in Africa and the search for alternative development approaches embedded in Islamic economics and the negotiation of Westernization. [...]

The most popular modern manual on Islamic economics is perhaps Yusuf al-Qardawi's *Fiqh az Zakat* (al-Qardawi 1999). Thus Islamic economics has been presented as an Islamic welfare state policy and has also been discussed among African Muslim scholars. Not surprisingly, the upsurge of Islamic economics in Africa has been closely linked, on the one hand, with the politicization of Islam and, on the other hand, with the Islamization of society. The outcome of the rise of various Islamist movements in Africa has been the demand for the implementation of Islamic law and economics.[7]

As in other parts of Sub-Saharan Africa, there has been an increasing amount of activity among Muslim NGOs in Ghana during the last thirty years. Here, as elsewhere, Islamic economics and a "revitalization" of an "Islamic way of life" or even "Islamic order" has been put on the agenda by some of these organizations and activists. Among others, there has been an increased emphasis on the question of poverty within the Muslim community and the possibilities of change to a better way of life—if only proper "Islamic" organizations and instructions would be outlined. Thus, [...] [o]ne problem, it seems, has been the lack of an institutionalization of the collection and distribution of *zakāt*: there are no *zakāt* committees and *zakāt* funds to educate people about *zakāt* and enforce its collection in Ghana (see further Weiss 2000). On the other hand, voluntary almsgiving or *sadaqa* is well established among the Muslim community in Ghana; in fact, some scholars even argue that the open-handedness of the Muslims after Friday prayers has created an image among non-Muslims that Islam "encourages the institution of begging" (Dretke 1968: 76; Mumuni 1994: 19).

One reason for the non-existence of an institutionalization of the collection and distribution of *zakāt* has been the lack of consensus among Muslim scholars; another common argument is that people are too poor to pay *zakāt*. However, it will be argued [...] that one reason for the non-institutionalization of *zakāt* is that there never existed any Islamic order in pre-colonial Ghana on which the collection and distribution of *zakāt*, and by extension a kind of public social welfare, could be built. What existed was based on non-Islamic models and perceptions. Yet, though there were no Islamic institutions, this did not mean that there existed no traditional support system. Interestingly, all my Muslim informants in Dagomba underlined the fact that there is, after all, not much difference between the moral obligation of Islam to give support to the poor and needy and the traditional, pre-Islamic ways of support. In fact, what can be identified is a fusion rather than a clash of these two moral orders. The latter part of this article will, therefore, discuss the impact and outlines of pre-Islamic or "traditional" ways of giving and sharing and their possible connections to an Islamic moral order. In the end, the question is about how to alleviate poverty and the potential of Muslim NGOs and local Muslim communities to accomplish this task. [...]

Muslim social welfare

[...] [T]he situation in Ghana makes a good case study on the impact of contesting trends within a Muslim community on how to provide social welfare. A common notion among social scientists in Ghana—but also the general public—has been that the Muslim population in Ghana is worse off than the rest of the population. [...]

In view of this notion about the state of Islam in Ghana, the rise of Muslim consciousness that has occurred there during the last decades is not surprising. Many of the Muslim scholars I have interviewed would still refer to the "little knowledge in Islam" of the population, i.e., the fact that most people who would claim to be Muslims would do so "by mouth but not by heart," although one can note a change in the mentality of many Muslims.[8] Before the advent of Islamist and Wabhabi-inspired Muslim organizations during the 1960s, Sufism—especially the Tijanīya order—had spread among the Muslims in Ghana. The first doctrinal rift among the Muslim community occurred when the Ahmadiyya mission started its operations on the Gold Coast during the 1920s, but their impact has mainly been felt in some localities along the coast.[9]

A much more sincere doctrinal rift within the Sunni Muslim community was caused by the dissemination of Islamist and Wahhabi ideas. The influence of Islamism and Wahhabism in Ghana goes back to the late 1950s and early 1960s, namely when Egypt and Saudi Arabia opened their diplomatic missions in Ghana. Several organizations were established during the 1970s and 1980s to champion the cause of Wahhabiyya, such as the Islamic Research and Reformation Centre, the Supreme Council for Islamic Affairs, the Islamic Charity Centre for Women Orientation.[10] In 1997, the Ahlus-Sunnah wal-Jama'ah was established as an umbrella organization for all Wahhabi organizations in Ghana.[11]

The coming of Wahhabi scholars accentuated the question, among others, of *zakāt* and institutionalized almsgiving. Already during the late 1960s Muslim scholars in Tamale debated about the establishment of a *zakāt* fund in Tamale, but, due to the lack of consensus among the *ulamā'*, the attempt was aborted—and so far no such fund exists on a local, regional or national level in Ghana (Weiss 2000). [...] In 1999 there were at least two calls for the establishment of such a fund—one by the National Chief Imam of the Ahlus-sunnah and another by the chargé d'affaires of the Royal Kingdom of Saudi Arabia,[12] but still there is no consensus about the subject and thus no central *zakāt* fund, no central collection and no central distribution of *zakāt*.

However, one might ask why there is such an overwhelming emphasis on and debate about *zakāt*. The simple reason for this is that a common factor of all the Muslim NGOs in Ghana has been their lack of generating internal financing of their projects. Thus, most of the Muslim NGOs receive substantial, if not total, financial assistance from external (foreign) sources, among others from various Zakah Funds from the Gulf states as well as Libya and Iran (See further Abu 2000). Thus, there exists the danger of becoming dependent on outside money—a problem not too unfamiliar to many African NGOs. What is even more problematic is that much of the funding channelled to Muslim NGOs in Ghana is to some extend earmarked. Thus, whereas the local community would like to improve their livelihood or establish a school or hospital, foreign Muslim donors are much more likely to finance the building of a mosque or the establishment of an Islamic call (*dawa*) centre. [...]

The failure of Ghanaian Muslim NGOs to generate internal sources for their projects raises the question why the Muslim community in Ghana is not able to provide funds through the collection of *zakāt* or the obligatory alms. According to my informants, the dissent among the Muslim community as well as its members marginal financial resources are the main reason for the non-existence of an institutionalization of the collection and distribution of *zakāt* (Weiss 2000: 146). However, it could also be argued that one reason is the lack of an Islamic order that would have existed in pre-colonial Ghana, especially in the two nominally "Muslim" states of Gonja and Dagomba, where the collection and distribution of *zakāt* would have been supervised by state officials. Although the rulers in these two states converted to Islam, the political, social and administrative structures of the kingdoms were not changed or reformed to become "Islamic states." Thus, Islamic law, Islamic taxation or Islamic institutions, like the *Bayt al-Māl,* were never established.[13] What did exist was based on non-Islamic models and perceptions. Yet, though there were no Islamic institutions, this did not mean that a traditional support system was absent.

Outlines of a pre-colonial, "traditional" support system

Zakāt has never been collected as a religious tax in Northern Ghana or in the pre-colonial kingdoms of Gonja and Dagomba. To be precise: none of the pre-colonial states in the North ever established any form of taxation but the incomes of the ruling class were extracted through various forms of tribute and *corvée* labour. Both states were based upon what might be termed war economies and both states were "predatory" ones in the sense that the economic basis of the ruling class did not rest upon production—farming, livestock or trade—but extortion (Wilks 1985). The Muslim community, which contained both Gonja and Dagomba scholars and traders, had close links to the ruling class, some of the scholars having close ties to the court, others receiving gifts from the rulers on a more or less regular basis. These gifts were usually called *sadaqa,* as Wilks was told by his informants in Yendi (see further Wilks 1968) Therefore, if *zakāt* was collected and distributed it was a private matter that was handled within the Muslim community, not a public affair where the state would have been engaged in its supervision.

However, there existed in pre-Islamic Northern Ghanaian societies other ways of distributing the fruits of the harvest through the *tindanas* (earth priests) and the rulers/chiefs. Such a local tradition is similar, but not identical, with the *ushr,* which is applied when *zakāt* is calculated and collected after the harvest.[14] Both archival sources and interviews suggest that something like a pre-colonial, non-Muslim or traditional way of support could be identified. Whether one would define it as a moral economy is another question. There clearly exists among the local people the notion of a "traditional support system" based both on local concepts of hospitality towards any stranger and on mutual assistance in times of need and want. As one of my informants, Haji Ali Hussein Zakariya, declared, "we do not have an organized system of support. Our support system is mainly based on our traditional public support systems" (Interview 16). [...]

In most cases, the argument was that the *tindana* either "owned" the land or had a central position concerning the use of land, whereas the rulers in most cases had to consult the *tindana* in cases of land and religious matters. The *tindana,* whose office in most cases was hereditary, performs the sacrifices to the gods. According to Cardinall, each year there was a general sacrifice, which varied in size. Cows and sheep were slain which were the proceeds of the sale of the baskets and calabashes of grain paid by the people to the *tindana* as rent for their farms (Cardinall 1921: 25).

However, the question of payments of rent or tribute to the *tindana* or the ruler seems to have been a more complicated one. I am able to present only some general observations. [...]

The tentative outline of a pre-colonial and non-Muslim support and tribute system might give some answers concerning the non-establishment of an Islamic order in pre-colonial states, [...] where the rulers were, at least nominally, Muslims. First, the division between a non-Muslim political public order and a rather private Muslim one is apparent. None of the systems of tribute was based on Islam. Second, there seems to have been no need to establish an Islamic order. The non-establishment, for example of a *bait almāl,* was due to the fact that the state itself was not a Muslim one but also due to the Suwarian tradition upheld by the Muslim community in the Volta region. However, the existence of some kind of organized support and tribute system, although not an Islamic one, might on the other hand make an institutionalization of *zakāt* possible. Yet, is it possible to build an Islamic institution on a non-Muslim tradition?

Assistance to the poor and hospitality towards strangers

Whereas it could seem that there is a long way to go before *zakāt* will be collected in Ghana, almsgiving as such, or what could be termed "alms of everyday life," namely *sadaqa,* has a solid position among the Muslims in Ghana. One could argue that *sadaqa* does not differ so much from the pre-Islamic ways of assisting the needy and the poor of the community. According to one of my informants, there were many commendable practices among the Dagomba before the advent of Islam, among others the giving of gifts. Gifts were seen as symbols of love and concern for others in the society and this practice was compared with pounding yam:

> If you pound yam and you do not add water, the yam does not come together. But when you add water then all particles stick together. Hence to concretise love, gifts were physical symbols to express real friendship and togetherness in the society. Whether you want to enter into friendship, [...] a woman into marriage or seek for chieftaincy—gifts were signs of intent and action.[15]
>
> (Interview 9)

My informants underlined that the giving of gifts in pre-Islamic society was as important as it is in Muslim societies and they seem to see no difference in the pre-Islamic and the Islamic practice.

Even more important, almost all of my informants held the position that pre-Islamic or traditional ways of giving support did and do not conflict with Islam (Interview 3), although some claimed that with the imposition of Islamic law the traditional support system had been given "divine" sanction (Interview 9). According to the informants, the traditional system of support in Dagomba consisted of six components: to be open-handed to visitors, to give offerings to passers-by, to assist poor households, to share the fruits of the harvest, to give assistance to women and to give assistance during the farming season.

Almost all highlighted in one or another way the cardinal duty to assist visitors, as it has been and still is practised in Dagomba. Such a custom, it is declared, is in tune with a tradition in Islam that states that a Muslim should honour his guest for three days. In most homes a room was designated for visitors. Thus any time a visitor arrived, the room was opened for any visitor without discrimination. Whether known or unknown, the visitor was first served water by the host. Then, if it appeared that the visitor was from a far distance, he was served with a meal before he was asked "Where are you coming from? What is your mission?" Then the visitor was asked whether he had especially come to visit the host or if he was in search of another person or if he had a specific socio-economic problem. If the visitor had any problems, it was the host's responsibility to assist the visitor to the best of his abilities. The host would first give the visitor a place to stay, he would give him water to wash himself with and would feed him until the visitor's mission was accomplished, regardless of the time it might take. The Dagomba were said to have honoured their guests for more than three days on occasion, even before the advent of Islam in Dagomba. However, as some informants claim, all members of the community ensured that all the needs of the visitor were taken care of as long as he stayed with them. Whenever somebody had a visitor, he would inform all his relatives and friends, who would take up the responsibility of care, which was seen as a collective responsibility (Interviews 3, 5, 6, and 17). Instead, as one of my informants claims:

> Our forefathers loved strangers more than anyone else. The rationale behind the love for visitors was that after he had departed he would give good compliments about their hospitality to other people and to his own family
>
> (Interview 6)

Second, according to some of my informants, it was the practice in Dagomba that, when a farmer saw someone passing by his farms, he would offer him roasted yam or corn to eat before the person continued his journey. The reason for such a custom, it is said, was that the farmer did not know if the traveller would meet any other person in course of his journey who would have food to share with him. In those days food was easily prepared and sold to travellers (Interviews 3, 10 and 17). A similar custom was the cooking of the eleventh meal:

if there were ten people in a family, they would make provision for eleven, so that any visitor who might appear after the meal would be fed (Interview 2).

Third, there was the custom in Dagomba that when no fire was observed in the evening at a nearby house, cereals such as com, millet and guinea-corn would be sent to that household without enquiring whether it had food or not. In some cases bowls of food would also be sent. In other cases, the neighbours would send some people to investigate the situation, and if the household was in difficulties, would send assistance. As my informants explained to me, in Dagomba dinner is highly respected and the lack of it is seen as disheartening. One of them pointed to the fact that "Islam, too, talks of the rights of the neighbour. This, I believe, was an enforced tradition among the Dagomba before the encounter with Islam" (Interview 3, see also Interviews 6, 7 and 11).

Further "traditional" ways of support occurred after harvest when farmers used to assist particularly those who did not have good yields. For instance, I was told, those with a good harvest will assist those with poor yields, in particular elderly people and poor relatives, with a bag or a basket of maize, guinea-corn, cassava or a bag of these items. In some cases it turned out that those without a yield would have received more assistance than those who had a good harvest (Interviews 2, 6, 7, 10 and 17). Some of my informants identify as a particular target women, who, once they joined a household through marriage, would be taken care of as long as they belonged to the household (Interview 5). In addition to sharing the fruits of the harvest, people were said to have given assistance to one another whenever one of them was "overwhelmed" with his farm, i.e., unable to control his farm and to start the weeding. In such a case, the head of the household would call upon his neighbours and they would come to his aid. This mutual assistance was called "*da-kpariba.*" In similar ways one could count on the help of the neighbours in other cases, like digging wells or building houses (Interviews 7, 10, 11, 12 and 17).

Last, but not least, perhaps one of the most important reasons why even Muslims in the North are not too eager to insist on an institutionalization of the collection and distribution of *zakāt* might be that the prevailing system of voluntary, private almsgiving is perceived as being quite sufficient. One day during my last stay in Tamale my friend revealed that each year he gives quite a substantial amount of money as alms to an old lady. In this way he fulfils his obligation to pay *zakāt* and at the same time—as he underlined to me—he is able to provide for the livelihood of one person who otherwise would have to beg. It is most likely that he is not the only rich farmer who in such a way supports needy persons. For both the giver and the recipient, such an informal way of handling alms seems to be preferred—as it is an act "for the sake of Allah" it is for the benefit of both the giver (as he or she will receive the blessing of Allah) and the recipient. Even more important: both the giver and, to a lesser extent the recipient, is able to control the transaction—a situation which might not be the case when *zakāt* is institutionalized.

Conclusion

The provision of social welfare has increasingly come under pressure in many African countries. Numerous African governments find it difficult even to support a basic health and education system. This crisis of the African welfare state—although one might question the term "welfare"—started during the 1970s. Since then, most of the African states have been forced to cut state provision to an absolute minimum, which usually does not include any aid for the poor. In such a situation it became the task of NGOs to take over the role of the state as providers of social welfare. However, this development is not particular to Africa and the situation in the continent resembles much of the discussion in the West about whether the state should play an active role in the provision of social welfare.

The Ghanaian case fits perfectly into the wider story of financial constraints of the state and of rising activities of NGOs. Ghana was more or less bankrupt in the 1970s, witnessed a spectacular economic revival during the late 1980s and early 1990s, but has been hard hit since the late 1990s because of a slump in gold and cocoa prices on the world market. At independence, Kwame Nkrumah and the other founding fathers had huge expectations for state provision of social welfare, yet with the economic collapse during the 1960s and 1970s the possibilities that the state could play an active role became increasingly limited.

The role of NGOs in Ghana has developed into one where local, national and trans-national NGOs all have their stake in providing social welfare. Whereas no one would question these organizations in their provision of health and educational services, there is a problem with regard to these organizations being non-governmental, i.e., both in theory and in practice outside the ultimate control of the state and governmental planning. Although the upsurge of NGOs in Africa may be viewed as a welcome development of a vital civil society, there are some problems connected with the activities of Muslim NGOs. In Nigeria and Mali, there has been an upsurge of Muslim NGOs during the last two decades, closely linked to the politicization of Islam. Such a development has so far been absent in Ghana.

The case point of this study is that Muslim NGOs in Ghana can be viewed from two sides: one where the focus is on the local and national impact of these organizations, another where the focus is on their international contacts and networks. As with Christian or secular NGOs, Muslim NGOs have to an increasing extent taken over the role of the state in providing basic social welfare in slums and rural settlements. As with Christian NGOs, the most visible sign of the Muslim NGOs is their building of mosques and prayer grounds. It is not unusual, when travelling through the country, to see newly built and painted mosques in the middle of a village or neighbourhood where no other house has ever seen any paint.

Some of the activities of Muslim NGOs in Ghana are problematic, especially when analysed from the point of the provision of social welfare. The hands of many national Muslim NGOs are tied by their donors, and social welfare projects have to be "sold" to the donors in a package that also includes the building of a mosque and educational centres. Usually then the mosque is built quite quickly, whereas the establishment of a clinic, health centre or school is much more problematic as these institutions have to be maintained and the salaries of the staff to be paid. However, none of the Muslim NGOs in Ghana are able to gather enough local resources to sustain the already existing activities and finance new projects.

Many Muslim scholars in Ghana, especially those who are affiliated to one or more Muslim NGOs, have thus started to argue that the obligatory or mandatory alms, *zakāt*, should be channelled through the Muslim NGOs. This debate has an international dimension. Islamic economics and the Islamization of the economy has been a key argument of some Muslim scholars in Pakistan and the Middle East since the colonial period, but this discussion has spread beyond these regions since the late 1970s.

The call for an Islamization of the economy and the political arena as well as the creation of an Islamic social welfare system has echoed throughout the Muslim world, backed by some Middle Eastern countries, such as Libya, Saudi Arabia, Kuwait and Iran. In African countries, such as Nigeria and Mali, the rise of Islamism was one outcome of this call. In Ghana, Muslim NGOs and Muslim scholars would not call for an Islamization of the political sphere. However, what is argued is the need for a change among the Muslims: to observe the rules and the spirit of the Law. Such a call marks a definite break with earlier forms of Islam in Ghana, namely that of accommodating to the existing political, social and economic structures. [...]

The hesitation of some Muslim scholars to call for an immediate institutionalization of *zakāt* might also be because the "traditional" system of providing social welfare—namely by giving alms in private—has been efficient to some extent. Clearly, there were two groups who benefited through private spending: the *imams* and *mallams* themselves, who traditionally would be the recipients of *zakāt*, and the "visible" beggars, who occasionally—but seemingly regularly enough—would receive *sadaqa* or voluntary alms. An institutionalization of *zakāt* would not necessarily be backed by these groups, especially not if the *zakāt* collected is spent on the upkeep of hospitals, kindergartens, orphanages and schools.

The strength of the so-called traditional way of providing social welfare has been its local background and roots. A Muslim Dagomba is able to fulfil his obligations as a Muslim—by giving alms, calling them *zakāt* or *sadaqa*—without having to break with local customs and traditions. Even more important, by spending alms a person is able to strengthen his or her social position in the community—a rich person is able to give and share, a poor person not. Alms are given "for the sake of Allah" if the giver is a Muslim, but as important is often the rather worldly intention of the giver: alms are given so that Allah might hear the prayer to achieve a certain goal or to accomplish a certain task. Why, therefore, establish an institution to take over the relationship between the giver and the recipient, as the existing forms of communal provision of social welfare have more or less been able to accomplish their task?

Interviews (as referred to in the text)

Interview 2 (10. January 2000): Group interview with scholars of the Ambariyya Islamic School: Shaikh Abubakr Tanko Ishaak, assistant director of the Amariyya Institute and director of the Supreme Council of Islamic Research, Northern Regional Branch; Shaikh Iddrisu Abdul-Hamid, chief examiner, Ambariyya Institute and member of the Supplement Committee of the Supreme Council of Islamic Research, Northern Regional Branch; Shaikh Mukhtar Ahmad Muhammad, Chairman of the *Dawa*-Committee, Supreme Council of Islamic Research, Northern Regional Branch; Shaikh Yussif Idriss Adam, secretary-general of the Ambariyya Institute and member of the board of the Islamic Supreme Council, Northern Regional Branch; Shaikh Abubakar Idriss Abdallah, supervisor of the Ambariyya Institute and member of the board of the Islamic Supreme Council, Northern Regional Branch.

Interview 3 (30. January 2000): Haji Tamin Ibrahim, Teacher at Madrasat Arabiyya Islamiyya (Tamale); Chairman of the Islamic Educational Unit, Northern Region; secretary of the Regional Chief Imam Abdulai Adam; member of the Central mosque in Tamale.

Interview 5 (31. January 2000): Haji Dawda Mustapha, Mudir (director) of Madrasatu Arabiyya Islamiyya.

Interview 6 (1. February 2000): Group interview with Shaikh Abdul-Rahim Abu Bakar, Chief Imam of Zogbele, member of the *dawa* of the Central Mosque, Alhaji Abdulaj One Oner, Special Advisor to Islamic schools in the Northern Region, chairman of the Muslim Youth, Tamale, and Shaikh Jabir Abdallah, second imam of Zogbele, member of the *dawa* of the Central Mosque, director of Markaziyya Islamic school.

Interview 8 (2. February 2000): Abdul Hamid Tahir, Regional Missionary, Ahmadiyya Muslim Jama'at, Tamale.

Interview 9 (2. February 2000): Shaikh Baba Abdallah Duah, district chairman of the Islamic council, educational unit; operator of anwar Duah Islamic school; member of the *dawa* of the Central Mosque.

Interview 10 (2. February 2000): Interview with scholars of the Nuriyyah Islamic Institute: Mahamah Alhassan, teacher, assistant Headmaster; Salihu Aswad Bawah, teacher, representative of the Islamic Council for Development and Humanitarian Services, treasurer of the Supreme Council for Islamic Research, Northern Regional Branch; Sa'ad Abdul-Rahman, secretary of the Supreme

Council for Islamic Research, Northern Regional Branch; Muhammad Jalal ad-Din Ahmad, teacher, member of the Supreme Council for Islamic Research, Northern Regional Branch.

Interview 11 (5. February 2000): Ali Umar, Chief Imam of Salaga.

Interview 12 (6. February 2000) Haji Isa (Issah) Usman, head of the *dawa* (Ahl al-sunna) in Yendi, Chief Imam of the Old Imam's mosque in Yendi.

Interview 15 (6. February 2000): Haji Asimana Kassim, Chief and Imam of Kushegu, sheikh of the dawa and Tijani community in Yendi.

Interview 16 (7. February 2000): Haji Ali Hussein Zakkariyya, Executive Director, Community Development and Youth Center; Assistant Development Manager, Islamic Education Unit, National Headquarters, Tamale.

Interview 17: Afa Razaq Taufeeq Abdallah (letter dated June 2000).

Notes

1 For an outline of Islamic NGOs in Africa, see Salih 2001.

2 For an overview of Islamic economics, see Kuran 1986 and Pfeifer 1997.

3 For example Siddiqi 1948; Qutb 1953 and Mannan 1970.

4 See further Naqvi 1981; al-Buraey 1985; Ahmad 1991; Chapra 1992; Naqvi 1994; al-Qardawi 1999.

5 *Zakāt* or obligatory almsgiving is one of the five pillars of Islam, together with the declaration of faith, the five daily prayers, fasting and the pilgrimage to Mecca and Medina. In an ideal setting, every Muslim should set apart a certain portion of his or her annual income and savings above a fixed amount of minimal wealth, called *nisab*, and spend it upon religious duties and on needy members of the community. The collection, control and distribution of *zakāt* should be handled by the *imām*, the head of the Muslim community, and those whom he appoints to collect it.

6 Islamic or Muslim NGOs have, on the other hand, existed in Africa since the late 1970s. However, none of these organizations were engaged in the collection of *zakāt* at this point (Salih 2001: 8).

7 See further Westerlund 1982; Hunwick 1997; Westerlund 1997. According to Elizabeth Hodgkin, one must, however, distinguish between two different kinds of movement, one that she defines as Islamic resurgence and one called "Islamism" (Hodgkin 1998: 198–199). Whereas the former movement strives for an increase in religious observance and fervour but recognizes different Islamic identities, the goal of the latter is to bring Islam into every aspect of human life, political, social, economic and cultural. "Islamism" is rather similar to earlier reform or revivalist movements in Islamic history in its demand for the purification of Islam and rejection of non-Islamic innovations. The key demand of today's "Islamists" is, however, the perception of Islam as a total religion. As a total religion, which does not accept any division between religious and secular life, such a condition can only be achieved by a purification of the state, namely by creating an Islamic order through the institution of Islamic Law as State Law and in the end by creating an Islamic state. However, as Hodgkin emphasizes, the latter demand, namely that of the establishment of an Islamic state, does not have to be a uniform demand, as many Islamic movements do not see the seizure of state power as among their aims.

8 I started my fieldwork and research in Northern Ghana in May 1999. So far, I have been able to interview 33 imams and Muslim scholars in Tamale, Salaga and Yendi during my three visits in May 1999, January–February 2000 and November 2001. During my second visit to Ghana, I also started to do research in the Ghana National Archives in Accra and the Regional Archives in Tamale as well as the Institute of African Studies, University of Ghana, Legon. The research has been conducted with the assistance of two colleagues, Haji Mumuni Sulemana at the University of Ghana, Legon and Afa Razaq Taufeeq Abdallah in Tamale. The 2001 notes have been transcribed, translated into English and published as *Zakāt in Northern Ghana. Field Notes 1* (Weiss, Sulemana, and Abdalla 2001). The original tapes are deposited in the library of the Department for the Study of Religions, University of Ghana.

9 On the Ahmadiyya in Ghana, see Fisher 1963, on their activities in Wa, see Wilks 1989.

10 Mumuni 1994: 51–53; personal communication November 2001.

11 Mumuni, personal communication November 2001.

12 "Speech of the National Imam," *The Muslim Searchlight* 1,3 (24. September–7. October 1999): 6; "Muslim Central Fund Proposed," *The Fountain*, November–December 1999.

13 See further Goody 1953; Goody 1967; Levtzion 1968; Ferguson 1972; Wilks 1965; Staniland 1975; Wilks 1985; Wilks 2000.

14 The *ushr* is one-tenth of the total amount of grain harvested and is given in kind as *zakāt*. However, if the fields are watered through irrigation, then the one-half of the *ushr* is given as *zakāt*. Some researchers, like Michael Watts, consider the collection of *zakāt*-grain as the backbone of a state controlled famine-reserve system that existed in pre-colonial African Muslim States (Watts 1983).

15 Similarly views are expressed in interview 15.

References

Abu, Muhammd A. (2000) "Ghana Untilizes Zakat Money for Community Projects," Available online http//www.Islamiq.com:/news/features/print.php4?news=1_11102000.

Ahmad, Ziauddin (1991) *Islam, Poverty and Income Distribution: A Discussion of the Distinctive Islamic Approach to Eradication of Poverty and Achievement of an Equitable Distribution of Income and Wealth*, Leicester: Islamic Foundation.

Al-Buraey, Muhammad (1985) *Administrative Development: An Islamic Perspective*, London: Routledge & Kegan Paul.

Al-Qardawi, Yusuf (1999) *Fiqh az-Zakat: A Comparative Study*, London: Dar Al Taqwa.

Cardinall, Allan W. (1921) *The Natives of the Northern Territories of the Gold Coast: Their Customs, Religion and Folklore*, London: G. Routledge & Sons.

Chapra, M. Umer (1992) *Islam and the Economic Challenge*, Leicester: Islamic Foundation.

Dretke, James P. (1968) "The Muslim Community in Accra: An Historical Survey," MA thesis, University of Rhana, Legon.

Ferguson, Phyllis (1972) "Islamization in Dagbon: A Study of the Alfanema of Yendi," PhD thesis, University of Cambridge, Cambridge.

Fisher, Humphrey J. (1963) *Ahmadiyyah: A Study in Contemporary Islam on the West African Coast*, London: Oxford University Press.

Goody, Jack (1953) "A Note on the Penetration of Islam into the West of the Northern Territories of the Gold Coast," *Transactions of the Gold Coast and Togoland Historial Society*, 1: 45–46.

——— (1967) "The Over-Kingdom of Gonja," in Cyril D. Forde and Phyllis M. Kaberry (eds) *West African Kingdoms in the Nineteenth Century*, London: Oxford University Press.

Hodgkin, Elizabeth (1998) "Islamism and Islamic Research in Africa," in Ousmane Kane and Jean-Louis Triaud (eds) *Islam et islamismes au sud du Sahara*, Paris: Karthala.

Hunwick, John (1997) "Sub-Saharan Africa and the Wider World of Islam: Historical and Contemporary Perspectives," in David Westerlund and Eva E. Rosander (eds) *African Islam and Islam in Africa: Encounters between Sufis and Islamists*, London: Hurst.

Kogelmann, Franz (1999) *Islamische fromme Stiftungen und Staat: Der Wandel in den Beziehunen zwischen einer religiösen Institution und dem marokkanischen Staat seit dem 19. Jahrhundert bis 1937*, Würzburg: Ergon.

Kuran, Timur (1986) "The Economic System in Contemporary Islamic Thought: Interpretation and Assessment," *International Journal of Middle East Studies*, 18: 135–164.

Levtzion, Nehemia (1968) *Muslims and Chiefs in West Africa: A Study of Islam in the Middle Volta Basin in the Pre-Colonial Period*, Oxford: Clarendon Press.

Mannan, Muhammad Abdul (1970) *Islamic Economics Theory and Practice*, Lahore: Muhammad Ashraf.

Mumuni, Sulemana (1994) "Islamic Organizations in Accra: Their Structure, Role and Impact in the Proselytization of Islam," M.Phil. thesis, University of Ghana, Legon.

Naqvi, Syed N.H. (1981) *Ethics and Economics: An Islamic Synthesis*, Leicester: Islamic Foundation.

——— (1994) *Islam, Economics, and Society*, London and New York: Kegan Paul International.

Pfeifer, Karen (1997) "Is There an Islamic Economics?," in Joel Beinin and Joe Stork (eds) *Political Islam: Essays from Middle East Report*, Berkeley, CA: University of California press.

Qutb, Sayyid (1953) *Social Justice in Islam*, trans. John B. Hardie, Washington, DC: American Council of Learned Societies.

Salih, M.A. Mohamed (2001) *Islamic NGOs in Africa: The Promise and Peril of Islamic Voluntarism*, Occasional Paper, Centre of African Studies, University of Copenhagen.

Siddiqi, Selim A. (1948) *Public Finance in Islam*, Lahore: Muhammad Ashraf.

Staniland, Martin (1975) *The Lions of Dagbon: Political Change in Northern Ghana*, Cambridge: Cambridge University Press.

Watts, Michael J. (1983) *Silent Violence: Food, Famine and Peasantry in Northern Nigeria*, Berkeley, CA: University of California Press.

Weiss, Holger (2000) "Zakat in Northern Ghana: Not an Institution but a Goal to be Achieved," *Hemispheres*, 15: 141–157.

Weiss, Holger, Hajj Mumuni Sulemana, and Afa Razaq Taufeeq Abdalla (eds) (2001) *Zakat in Northern Ghana: Field Notes 1. Interviews conducted during January and February 2000*, Helsinki: Department for African Studies, Institute for Asian and African Studies, University of Helsinki.

Westerlund, David (1982) "From Socialism to Islam? Notes on Islam as a Political Factor in Contemporary Africa," in *Research Report of the Nordiska Afrikainstitutet*, Uppsala: The Scandinavian Institute of African Studies.

——— (1997) "Reaction and Action: Accounting for the Rise of Islamism," in David Westerlund and E.E. Rosander (eds) *African Islam and Islam in Africa: Encounters between Sufis and Islamists*, London: Hurst.

Wilks, Ivor (1965) "A Note on the Early Spread of Islam in Dagomba," *Transactions of the Historical Society of Ghana*, 8: 87–98.

——— (1968) "Muslim Office in Dagomba, Field Notes: Yendi Project, No. 11," Legon: Institute of African Studies, University of Ghana and Program of African Studies, Northwestern University.

——— (1985) "The Mossi and the Akan States, 1500 to 1800," in Jacob F. Ade Ajayi and Michael Crowder (eds) *History of West Africa*, 3rd edn, Basingstoke: Longman.

——— (1989) *Wa and the Wala: Islam and Polity in Northwestern Ghana*, Cambridge: Cambridge University Press.

——— (2000) "The Juula and the Expansion of Islam into the Forest," in Nehemia Levtzion and Randall L. Pouwels (eds) *The History of Islam in Africa*, Athens, OH: Ohio University Press.

14 Financial worship

The Qur'ānic injunction to almsgiving

Jonathan Benthall

Jonathan Benthall is an honorary research fellow with the Department of Anthropology, University College London. In 1968, he earned his MA in English language and literature from the University of Cambridge and was the director of the Royal Anthropological Institute (RAI) from 1974 to 2000. From 1985 through 2000, he served as the founding editor with *Anthropology Today*. Benthall remains a member of the publications committee with the RAI and is an Associate Fellow with the Humanitarian and Conflict Response Institute, University of Manchester. His areas of research include contemporary Islam and humanitarian aid, international aid systems and the growth of new quasi-religious movements and interactions with traditional religions. Presently his emphasis is on faith-based organizations, specifically Islamic charities. Recently he has published *Disasters, Relief and the Media* (1993, new edition 2010) and *Returning to Religion: Why a Secular Age is Haunted by Faith* (2008). He is editor of *The Best of Anthropology Today* (2002) and published together with Jérôme Bellion-Jourdan *The Charitable Crescent: Politics of Aid in the Muslim World* (2003, new paperback edition 2009). He received the Anthropology in Media Award of the American Anthropological Association (AAA) in 1993 as well as the 2001 Patron's Medal from the Royal Anthropological Institute (RAI). The article below provides a theoretical and scriptural contextualization of the Qur'ānic injunction for the tradition of the *zakāt*. By scrutinizing different Islamic traditions of almsgiving in Palestine and Jordan, Benthall argues that Muslim welfare organizations provide alternative and powerful channels of social and religious solidarity.

* * *

"Those who interpret the Qur'ān without knowledge will have their place prepared for them in the fire of hell"; so runs a statement attributed to the Prophet Muhammad.[1] My excuse for taking the risk is that little has been published in Western scholarship on Islamic traditions of almsgiving (*zakāt*) and philanthropy[2] and virtually nothing by cultural anthropologists. They have indeed neglected the wider issue of philanthropy in general, though one bygone anthropologist shrewdly observed: "Real progress is progress in charity, all other advance being secondary thereto" (Marett 1935: 40). It seems that for a comparative study of charity we have to go back to as early an anthropologist as Westermarck (Westermarck 1908).[3] Some cultural anthropologists with close links to the world of non-governmental organizations—most trenchantly, de Waal—have subjected contemporary Western organized charity to an "immanent critique" (de Waal 1997), but much remains to be done to establish a fully comparative perspective. Within economic anthropology, a significant literature inspired by Marshall Sahlins sought to identify redistribution as an essential function of chiefdoms (Sahlins 1958). It was this style of insight which may have inhibited anthropologists from following up Westermarck's interest in comparing different traditions of charity as ethical systems. However, a long-standing theoretical anthropological interest in voluntary associations, dating back to Robert Lowie and W. Lloyd Warner (Caulkins 1996), has recently been rekindled, with the growing salience of the voluntary sector and a new, currently influential political attachment to "civil society" as a counter-balance to nation-states.

A more specific reason for studying Islamic organized charity is that, as is well known, the Islamist movements of the Middle East and North Africa have achieved their salience and popular support through blends of religious, political and welfarist activism. Studies of the voluntary sector in Egypt (ben Néfissa 1995; Ibrahim 1988; Rugh 1994; Sullivan 1992) and Arab Israeli villages (Israeli 1993a) testify that, relatively speaking, Islamist voluntary associations are capable of delivering effective welfare and relief services in certain contexts where the state has been unable or unwilling to provide them. To take but one example, when Egypt was hit by serious floods in November 1994, the government's response was slow and ineffective and it was the Muslim Brothers and similar organizations which gave refuge in the mosques to families who had lost their roofs.[4] This is not to deny that in some Muslim states such as Iran there is almost certainly massive corruption in the philanthropic sector owing to accumulations of capital in its hands (Waldman 1992); but at the Islamic grass-roots in a number of countries an analogy may be drawn with the South American Christian "base communities," that is to say, groups of marginalized people who start by coping with small local issues and seek to work their way slowly up to larger ones (Sullivan 1992: 8, 157–158).

There seems to be quite a widespread view that, to quote a French sociologist, the founding Muslim Brothers were "more inspired by the methods of Leninism than by Muslim tradition" (Badie 1992: 171), and I have heard this said of present-day Islamists by U.S. State Department spokesmen.[5] A historical analogy with Methodism in England or the Democratic Party in the United States would be nearer the mark. Granted, Islamist organizations are sometimes taken over by demagogues and men of violence, but so are popular movements of all descriptions. Should the ethical injunction to give aid to others be regarded as an independent determinant of Islamist movements?

Supporting evidence might be adduced from the strength of the *waqfs* or religious foundations in Islamic history, or from the early history of the Muslim Brothers (Mitchell 1969). However, the Qur'ān itself and its interpretations also provide important evidence for that contention.

Little in the Sunna—the sum of the actions and judgments (*hadiths*) of the Prophet, from which precedents and guides for later Muslim practice were derived—would contradict what is to be found in the Qur'ān on these matters. But I have several reasons for concentrating on the Qur'ān itself in this article. First, studying the Sunna is a branch of knowledge where distinguishing the more from the less authentic requires almost a lifetime's devotion (Burton 1994), whereas the Qur'ān is a universally standard text with only minuscule variant readings. Second, the mainstream of Muslim scholars contend that, though the Sunna illuminates the Qur'ān, the Qur'ān has ultimate precedence. It is, after all, considered to be the eternal and immutable speech of God, primary revelation as opposed to the secondary revelation that Christian doctrine holds most of the New Testament to be. And third, there seems today to be a renewed emphasis on the Qur'ān. Sayyid Qutb, the influential Egyptian ideologue, persuaded many that the Qur'ān contained all the necessary answers to the world's problems

(Carré 1984), a position not unfairly characterized by its detractors as fundamentalist. But I shall not forget a discussion with a devout Berber schoolteacher in a village in Morocco in the spring of 1997. In a context of economic crisis and widespread disillusion with the government's claims to be moving towards more democracy and freedom of expression, he claimed with confidence that all over the Muslim world ordinary people are now reading their Qur'āns and discovering that its teaching is at variance with the reality of regimes that claim to be Islamic. [...]

In this article I shall first outline the Qur'ānic injunction to almsgiving and some variations in interpretation, and then consider how it is attended to today in a number of Islamic states.

All Qur'ānic studies have to be carried on in a setting where even the most abstruse details can acquire heated political overtones, a kind of Jerusalem of the intellect where scholars behave like guests at a diplomatic reception, some of them quietly ignoring the existence of others (see Berg 1997). Whereas a number of anthropologists have analysed the use of Qur'ānic verses and *hadiths* in ethnographic context (e.g. Antoun 1989; Bowen 1993; Fischer and Abedi 1990), there is no reason why textual analysis of the Qur'ān itself should not also be attempted, in emulation of the long-established contribution of anthropology to studies of the Bible. It is not necessary to accept the authority of the Qur'ān oneself, to try to understand the meanings and importance which it has for many Muslims.

In contemporary Muslim societies we see a spectrum between complete incorporation of *zakāt* by the state, as in Pakistan or Sudan, and its marginalization to the individual's private conscience, as in Morocco or Oman—with a number of intermediary solutions; as in Jordan, which has established a directorate of *zakāt* under the Ministry of Religious Affairs but where local *zakāt* committees are also allowed to raise and distribute charitable funds. But *zakāt* is the third of the Five Pillars of the Religion (*arkān ad-dīn*) which are recognized by all branches of Sunni Islam, and it means the religious duty to give up a fixed proportion of one's wealth for specified good causes.[6]

Zakāt derives from the verb *zakā*, which means to purify (also with the connotation of growth or increase).[7] The meaning is usually taken to be that, by giving up a portion of one's wealth, one purifies that portion which remains, and also oneself, through a restraint on one's greed and imperviousness to others' sufferings. The recipient, likewise, is purified from jealousy and hatred of the well-off. Thus the action of giving alms has this moral function as well as fulfilling needs. The traditional proportion required is one-fortieth of one's assets per year, but a large scholarly literature sets out different proportions for different kinds of wealth. Muslims with wealth below a certain fixed threshold (*nisāb*) do not have to pay *zakāt*. In addition, there is an annual requirement on everyone to pay a small *zakāt al-fitr* (*fitr* = breaking of the fast) or *fitrah* to the needy at the end of Ramadān. This is supposed to correspond to one bushel, or about 2.2 kilos, of the local staple food, or the equivalent in cash. There is wide agreement about the general principles of *zakāt*. It is a kind of "financial worship," and without its observance the efficacy of prayer is negated. It is closely associated with prayer in many verses of the Qur'ān.[8] During Ramadān, the exercise of fasting is supposed to remind believers of what it would be like to be poor and hungry, and they are called on to be more than usually generous. Alms given during Ramadān are said to be seventy times more meritorious than at other times of the year. We are merely vice-regents or trustees over the resources available to us. A *hadith* warns that he who sleeps with a full stomach while his neighbour goes hungry will be deprived of God's mercy; and there are numerous stories of good rulers such as the second Caliph, Omar, who used to go round Mecca at night with a sack of flour making sure that everyone had enough to eat. *Zakāt* as a religious duty is to be distinguished from *Sadaqa*, which is the giving of alms more voluntarily.

The two terms are, however, closely associated throughout the Qur'ān, so closely that in the key Surah 9:60 which specifies the permitted beneficiaries of *zakāt*, the word *Sadaqa* is actually used in the text but it is generally interpreted as referring to *zakāt*.

Who should benefit from *zakāt*? The distribution of *zakāt* funds is a matter for choice only within specified limits. There are eight permitted classes of beneficiaries of alms, listed as follows (Surah 9:60):

1. The poor (*al-fuqarā'*).
2. *Al-masākīn*—usually interpreted as the needy or very poor, a word paraphrased in Surah 90:16 as "those down in the dust" (*dhā matrabatin*).
3. "The officials appointed over them," usually interpreted as the people appointed to administer the *zakāt* and negotiate with outlying groups.
4. "Those whose hearts are made to incline [to truth]" (*al-mu'allafati qulūbuhum*), interpreted as helping those recently or about to be converted, and mollifying powerful non-Muslims whom the state fears, as an act of prudent politics.[9]
5. Most Islamic commentators seem to have thought that "captives" means Muslims captured by enemies who needed to be ransomed, but Christian Décobert argues that it means men from other tribes enslaved by the Meccans and Medinans (Décobert 1991: 226).
6. Debtors—particularly, argues Décobert, because those who cannot repay their debts lose rank and become clients of their creditors.
7. Those in the way of God, that is to say in *jihād*, teaching or fighting or in other duties assigned to them in God's cause.
8. "Sons of the road" (*ibn as-sabīl*), travellers.

As with the other world religions, Islam encompasses a great deal of disagreement between authorities about matters of interpretation, and this verse of the Qur'ān provides a good example of the different readings that have arisen. I shall give some instances of these, as well as of consensus where it can be found, without attempting to cover the whole topic thoroughly.[10]

It is often stated that the recipients of *zakāt* must be Muslims (e.g. by the Egyptian scholar 'Uthman Hussayn Abd-Allah, quoted by Abu-Sahlieh 1994: 261), but this proposition is frequently rebutted today. Abdul-Aziz Al-Khayyat, a leading Jordanian Islamic scholar, told me that it is clear that the phrase *al-fuqarā'* must mean in Arabic "all the [category of the] poor," and therefore it must include the non-Muslim poor. The difference of view is reflected in the respective policies of two major British Muslim relief agencies: Islamic Relief extends *zakāt* funds to non-Muslims in Africa, while Muslim Aid restricts its aid to Muslim beneficiaries only.[11]

Abd-Allah proposes the following sub-groups of poor: orphans and foundlings, widows and divorcees, prisoners and their families, unemployed and homeless people, students, those who cannot afford to marry, disaster victims, and those in need of free medicines or dignified funerals. Al-Khayyat stresses a distinction between the poor (category 1) and the very poor (category 2). The very poor are people deprived of any kind of ownership who are not even able to evaluate their own needs. The merely poor may just not be able to meet their expenditure out of their income, and account must be taken, in assessing their need, of their obligations to their families and of their social status (al-Khayyat 1993: 184).

Category 3, the *zakāt* administrators, now allows charitable institutions to receive *zakāt* provided they are set up to help one of the permitted classes of beneficiary. This provision has sometimes given rise to a large proportion of *zakāt* being applied for state purposes by certain rulers, in a way which would now be considered abusive; but that was generally in states where no other taxes were levied by governments.[12] The practice may still be flourishing today in a country like Pakistan, where *zakāt* has been absorbed into the state taxation system and a measure of official corruption has been diagnosed (Novossyolov 1993; Roy 1992: 179 sqq.).[13]

Category 4 is interpreted by al-Khayyat as applying to anyone sympathetic to Islam (al-Khayyat 1993: 185). Abd-Allah, however, contends that this category applies to missionary education, propaganda to combat secularism or communism or Zionism or Christian missions, assisting new converts to Islam, and assuring the support or neutrality of people in power. Some interpretations allow the building of mosques as an object for disbursal of *zakāt* funds.

Abd-Allah adopts a sharply political interpretation of category 5, the captives, claiming that this function of *zakāt* includes helping Muslims in their struggle against colonialism and supporting Muslim minorities living in non-Muslim tyrannies—a point of view I have not come across elsewhere, and which would squarely place such donations outside the category of "non-political charity" in a country such as Jordan where this distinction is insisted on by the state. Similar interpretations have been offered for category 7, "those in the way of God."

"Debtors" (category 6) has been restrictively interpreted by some as meaning only those debtors "who by financing good works have become impoverished" (Schimmel 1992: 35). "Travellers" (category 8) seem to Abd-Allah to include the sub-category of refugees; al-Khayyat includes youth hostels, and also says that even if a traveller is rich in his own country, as long as there is a need he is eligible for a share of *zakāt* (al-Khayyat 1993: 186, 181).

Opinion seems to be moving in the Islamic world towards what might be called a liberalization of the definition of eligible beneficiaries. Traditionally, it seems that *zakāt* donors have expected to try to meet local needs before looking further afield, and this practice is still the norm in many Muslim communities. However, with the growth of the mass media and organized relief agencies, some Islamic scholars have ruled that it is permissible and indeed desirable to spend *zakāt* funds wherever the need is greatest. This is the principle which results in large Saudi *zakāt* funds being disbursed overseas by the International Islamic Relief Organization (IIRO).[14] [...] The consensus seems to be that Islam calls on all people to work and the characters and reputations of poor people may be taken into account in deciding whether or not they deserve help. Schemes for relieving unemployment are eligible for *zakāt* subsidy (al-Khayyat 1993: 181). People who are unable to work deserve to be helped (see e.g. Surah 51:16–19; 70:24–25).

How should *zakāt* be collected? The categories of beneficiary are mentioned in the Qur'ān, but the way it is to be collected only in the Sunna. Al-Khayyat says that this was because God foresaw that there would be new forms of money and wanted to ensure that there was flexibility (al-Khayyat 1993: 180 sq.). "If the Qur'ān had specified the sources of income, a lot of awkwardness would have arisen." In his book, he devotes many pages to a review of the different rates that should be levied on livestock, trees and crops, minerals, factories, dwelling houses, stocks and bonds, and even silk-worms and bee-hives. There is general agreement that possessions required for the owner's basic needs—including a house, clothing, tools and perishable goods—are not *zakāt*-able. Also, *zakāt* is not payable until an asset has been held for one year.

The argument for flexibility in calculating *zakāt* percentages rests on the principle that the less the amount of labour exerted and capital invested, the greater should be the levy. For instance, a *hadith* states that when a piece of land is watered by rain or springs or other naturally occurring water, the rate of *zakāt* on the product will be one tenth, whereas when the land is watered by wells the rate should be one twentieth (Mannan 1986: 255). The *zakāt* on treasure trove should be as much as one fifth because it has incurred no labour (Mannan 1986: 257).

These niceties are perhaps of somewhat theoretical interest in that, with very few exceptions (such as Saudi Arabia and Pakistan), *zakāt* in modern Muslim countries amounts to a voluntary or optional payment. The British-based organization Islamic Relief has published a simplified "Everything you need to know about Zakah" in its newsletter (*Partnership*, Winter 1996: 3). Modern necessities such as a family car and business furniture are not *zakāt*-able. Investment property is.

The original threshold for *zakāt* (*nisāb*) set by the Prophet was 88 grams of gold. Islamic Relief calculates this as the equivalent of £740. According to the British advice, this obligation is over and above any liability to state taxes. This view is supported by Al-Khayyat but disputed by other experts.[15]

Zakāt is often described in devout literature as mandatory, but there are no penalties set out in the Qur'ān or the Sunna to enforce payment or impose penalties on defaulters. Gradually, reliance came to be placed on the believer's sense of responsibility and fear of God (*taqwā*), a process accompanied by the secularization of the state as Muslim countries came under Western influence and control.[16] In those Muslim countries where *zakāt* has become an entirely private matter, stress is laid on those verses in the Qur'ān which set store on the disbursal of alms in secret (e.g. Surah 2:271).[17]

Almsgiving seems to be emphasized by preachers throughout the Muslim world. For instance, Richard Antoun, who did ethnographic fieldwork in a village in northern Jordan during a number of stays between 1959 and 1962, analysed the themes addressed by the local preacher in his Friday *khutbas* or congregational sermons. This young sheykh, who was independent-minded but on the whole non-political, did not ignore questions of ritual and theology, but gave the strongest emphasis to questions of local-level ethics. Of the sample of twenty-six sermons analysed by Antoun, over half had an ethical orientation of some kind, and of these, three were concerned specifically with alms and charity. Sermons on *zakāt* were given annually before harvest time and at the end of Ramadān, but the same topic might be addressed at any time of year in response to a day-to-day event, for instance the miserliness of a particular local individual (Antoun 1989: 90–94). What Antoun calls "normative Islam … the message of Islam as it is rendered every Friday in mosques throughout the Muslim world" needs to be understood if we are to interpret adequately the late twentieth-century Islamic revival.[18]

My own research in Jordan and the West Bank in early 1996 gives evidence of some Jordanian and Palestinian *zakāt* committees working with some effectiveness in the context of an active and varied voluntary sector. Jordan's middle path (see above) gives state recognition to *zakāt* but does not enforce it. In 1944, a law was passed making it obligatory, but this was repealed in 1953 (al-Khayyat 1993: 91 sqq.) Payments are now voluntary; tax relief is obtainable for this and indeed for all donations to recognized charities.

The *nisāb* (threshold) is set at 500 Jordanian dinars (1 JD = about £1) per year, which effectively removes the obligation from about half the adult population. In 1994, JD 1 million was apparently collected by the central *zakāt* fund and JD 2 million by 150 local committees (*Jordan Times*, 11 February 1995). The central fund supports educational and income-generating projects, old people's homes, rehabilitation projects for handicapped people, soup-kitchens and the like.

The most impressive *zakāt*-funded programme which I visited was in Nablus, the historic town in the West Bank which has suffered particularly from the Arab-Israeli conflict over many years. This has been run since 1982 by a committee which has drawn support from

Jordan and other Arab countries. Large sums, up to £10 million, have been raised. The committee has bought buildings—a cow farm, a sheep farm, a dairy for pasteurization—and also invests in land and real estate to bring in income. It has founded one of the best equipped clinics in the West Bank. According to my informants, about 3,500 income payments, at a minimum of US $50 per month, are paid out and grants made to 750 students at secondary and university level. '*Id* (festival) gifts are presented to 7,500 families. They added that the Nablus committee makes a point of being non-political and not giving any preference to devout Muslims. [...]

Spending the month of Ramadān in Jordan, I discussed the question of *zakāt* with a wide variety of Jordanians ranging from the pious to "nominal Muslims," and from rich to poor. It became clear that a large proportion of them, when they hear the word, assume it to refer to the *zakāt al-fitr* (see above), a practice which is widely observed among believers and only a trivial financial commitment for well-to-do families, though not trivial for a poor man with many children. Many people will make gifts during Ramadān to poor people in their immediate neighbourhood or social circle, ignoring the *zakāt* committees. Others hold that in a modern state such as Jordan with a tax system, the *zakāt* obligation is obsolete. One of the prominent royal charities, the Queen Alia Fund, has instituted a kind of secular *zakāt* system during Ramadān.[19]

I also visited members of a *zakāt* committee in the south of Jordan (the town of Wadi Musa) where most of the population of settled Bedouin are not affluent and the question of paying on assessment of wealth does not arise. Money is, however, collected from shopkeepers and owners of sheep and goats, and distributed locally. Ethnographic study of the actual collection and distribution of *zakāt* in a Muslim community would be a worthwhile project, but its difficulty and sensitivity should not be underestimated. One aspect is that beneficiaries are often unwilling to disclose that they have been helped, for fear of compromising their eligibility for public welfare benefits. Another is that special religious merit is gained by giving alms in secret.[20] The economic importance of religious alms in Jordan should not be exaggerated, for significant funds are also raised for charitable purposes by means of a national lottery, despite the Islamic prohibition of gambling. [...]

Zakāt is a major support in the standard Islamic case against the evils of both capitalism and communism. It "draws the sting of Marxism," Kenneth Cragg writes, depriving it of a legitimate argument against private property and property of any scandalous features; it turns the main contradiction in capitalism into a happy spiral of redistribution, and it answers with clarity the communist denial of the right to possess. It solves the problem of poverty by leave of the rich, and punishes those who hoard and monopolize and try to corner markets (Cragg 1956: 153). Under the ideal scheme which wide observance of *zakāt* would make possible, the rich do not become poor, but the poor cease to be poor.

Zakāt is a reminder that all wealth belongs to God, but there are several verses in the Qur'ān which tolerate economic inequalities even though the dignity and fundamental equality of all human beings as children of Adam is also recognized. Wealth, so the argument goes, is to be cherished in moderation, but not to be (as we might say today) fetishized. The Qur'ān condemns the emulous multiplication of wealth (Surah 102:1–2; see also Surah 104) and ostentation (according to ancient tradition, Muslims should have no table utensils of gold or silver, and neither gold nor silver should be worn by males). Provided that believers obey the rules enjoined, there is no need for them to feel guilty about their inability to measure up to an ideal morality: there is no need for the well-to-do either to give away all their wealth or to feel guilty about not being poor. Nor would Islamic teaching commend, as does the Christian Gospel, the widow who gives away her last farthings.

This point of view is put in a somewhat parodic form by a contemporary Pakistani Islamic economist who writes that a Muslim's "capacity for contribution to social welfare … is to be measured by the amount one is able to spare after enjoying the standard of living which is commonly enjoyed by men of one's rank and station in life" (quoted by Kuran 1989: 173; Kuran 1990). Put like this, the precept is at least an accurate sociological observation of how members of the upper and middle classes in all stratified societies do in fact engage in almsgiving, with rare exceptions.

The Qur'ān does not downgrade money in the style of many passages in the New Testament. It is crammed with injunctions about the right spending of money. Over one hundred verses of the Qur'ān deal with these matters (e.g. Surah 2:195; 70:23–25). Islam is the only one of the three Abrahamic religions that explicitly urges the believer not only to be generous in almsgiving but also to persuade others to be charitable (Surah 107).

Some of the literature on *zakāt* (e.g. al-Khayyat 1993) presents it as almost a panacea for the world's ills, allied with Islamic economics and the prohibition of bank interest or *riba* as the opposite of *zakāt* (Carré 1984: 155). *Zakāt's* importance seems to be one principle on which almost all devout Muslims are united.[21]

The striking claim was made by Sayyid Qutb that *zakāt* was a superior concept to the Western concept of charitable alms.[22] Qutb maintained that *zakāt* had nothing to do with charity, which was a non-Islamic concept (Carré 1984: 151; Mitchell 1969: 253). Though repudiating socialism as also non-Islamic, Qutb held that Islam disapproved both of people being in need and of class distinctions. *Zakāt* was "the outstanding social pillar of Islam," enabling individuals' efforts to be steered towards a common goal. By contrast, a gift provokes the hatred of the recipient towards the donor.

A similar idea, but completely outside the Islamic social context, was articulated earlier in the century by Mauss in *The Gift*: the unreciprocated gift, while bringing moral credit to the donor, actually wounds the recipient (Mauss 1990 [1925]). Islamic apologists argue that the poor can accept their due with no loss of dignity.

It is certainly fair to claim that the doctrine of *zakāt*, in so far as it was ever realized, introduced the first system of social security. […]

It is difficult to see how in any modern society the one-sidedness of alms, the absence of Maussian reciprocity, can be avoided. But in some ways the Arab world is still relatively "face-to-face" in character, so that the needy beneficiary of largesse can reciprocate by means of services and homage to patrons. For pious Muslims, their good acts are preparing a place in Paradise. […] The poor are always praying that they will get help; and if you are the person who gives help, then the benefit of the prayer will go to you and your family and even to your wealth itself (al-Khayyat 1993: 13–14). […]

As a matter of degree and emphasis it is a fair claim that "Among sacred books, the Qur'ān seems to be the only one in the world which sets out precisely [in Surah 9:60] the basic principles of the budget and expenses of the state" (Hamidullah 1959: II, 617). It is doubtful too whether any other world religion has an equivalent to the Islamic principle that a hungry person has the right to share in the meal of one who is well fed. If one is refused, one has the right to use force and, should one happen to kill one's adversary, one is considered innocent as one was struggling for a legitimate right (Boisard 1985: 101). Similarly, thieves may plead in defence that they have been forced to steal out of necessity, and the penalty should then fall on whoever has allowed them to fall into such dire need (Carré 1984: 149).[23]

In practice, *zakāt* has been marginalized. There is not a single Islamic state which exhibits it functioning in practice as it should, as a system of automatic redistribution. Crown Prince Hassan of Jordan's proposal for an international *zakāt* system, whereby the richer Muslim states would help poor Muslims, remains on the table and has not been taken up with any alacrity by Jordan's richer neighbours. There are great inequalities, and a serious measure of chronic poverty, in Jordan itself; and even greater inequalities in the Islamic world in general. The *per capita* income of the two wealthiest members of the Arab League, Kuwait and Qatar, is nearly 75 times that of the two poorest members, Sudan and Somalia (*Jordan Times*, 11 February 1996), though of course these disparities are by no means confined to the Islamic world. Many reformers in Jordan and other Islamic countries are impatient with religious rhetoric and see the only solution in secularization and the adoption of Western values.

Hitherto I have discussed the Qur'ānic texts on *zakāt* largely as a didactic source. An anthropologist or historian may alternatively opt to interpret them as a deep structure encapsulating the representations and practices or *idéologique* (Terray 1994) of early Islam. Décobert takes as his starting point the *hadith* according to which when the Prophet died he left no worldly estate except a mule for travelling, his weapons for fighting and a small plot of land to be held in charitable trust. Devout Muslims are fighters who have given up their goods and travelled from their kin and land in the "way of God," so that they have come to depend on the work of others, whether as booty or alms. Every Muslim thereby recapitulates the flight of the Prophet and his Companions from Mecca to Medina, and those who give generously on leaving the mosque are participating in this ideal circle (Décobert 1991: 370). Alms are a "loan to God" (Surah 2:245). "The share given to others permits their enrichment so that they can proceed to reimpoverish themselves" (Décobert 1991: 241). [...]

As noted at the beginning of this article, it is possible to look for an *idéologique* as underlying every discourse on almsgiving. However, since almsgiving is also underpinned by fundamental imperatives of compassion and sharing, it tends to slip away from such dissection, and I shall conclude by briefly examining the ambiguities which result in the Islamic context. [...]

In Jordan, as in Britain, some of the country's most prestigious public figures vie for prominence in philanthropy (see for instance page 3 of the *Jordan Times* almost every day). On one possible reading, all these efforts are economically marginal, since the whole nation is dependent on Euro-American aid and on its delicate political position as a buffer state.

However, these patrons also use their positions to introduce innovations and help raise professional standards. For instance, the Young Women's Muslim Association is in effect a vehicle for Crown Princess Sarvath's charitable projects in Jordan. One of these is a day-care centre near Amman for mentally handicapped children, which has done much to stimulate reform of the treatment of such children in Jordan: conventionally, they were regarded by families as a source of stigma and often hidden. The children in this centre, often with multiple handicaps, are enabled to acquire skills and confidence and many of them progress to a sheltered factory where they are trained to make furniture and even to compete in the normal job market. The charismatic director, Ghusoon Diab El-Kareh, brings to the work her up-to-date professional training in the USA, but also her religious conviction that handicapped people are specially blessed.

The style of the Jordanian Islamists is very different. One of the established principles of the Muslim Brothers, founded in Egypt in 1928, was "avoidance of the domination of notables and important men; since rising movements attract them and mean riches and benefits for them" (Husaini 1956: 43). One should not be naive about the political advantages of humility in times of adversity, but it would seem that moderate Islamist organizations in the Middle East have impressed many recent researchers, including some ideological enemies (Israeli 1993b: 32, 35), with their personal modesty, dedication and accessibility. Here again we can refer back to the Qur'ān, with its stress on *niyyah* or intention,[24] and its theological insistence on human dignity. In keeping with the Islamists' more general critique of what they see as objectionable features of Western domination and Arab governments, the Jordanian and Palestinian *zakāt* committees that I have mentioned seek to build up communal trust (a word I heard repeated many times when I met them) through door-to-door welfarism.[25]

Again, these organizations can be construed as self-interested—for instance, in providing alternative channels of solidarity for rising professionals excluded from the influence of dominant families, or in legitimizing new versions of Arab-Islamic patriarchy. However, there is no system of ethical teaching about civic duties which cannot be analysed in similar fashion, even that of secularized elites to whom the religious origins of their presuppositions about duties and rights may seem no more than a remote historical memory.

Notes

1 ibn Abbess (quoted in Speight 1988: 66).

2 An exception is Stillman 1975. Ziba Mir-Husseini (pers. comm. 1997) points out that *zakāt* was also a neglected topic in classical *fiqh* (Islamic jurisprudence) sources, where it was generally discussed under the category of *'ibadah* (worship) rather than *mu'āmalāt* (contracts), i.e. defined as a religious duty, like fasting or prayer, left to the individual without the state's involvement. This could have been partly because *fiqh* was developed by private scholars who did their best to keep their distance from the state apparatus. Early twentieth-century states tended to be inspired by Western rather than by Islamic traditions. The stress on *zakāt* in late twentieth-century Islamic discourses is relatively new.

3 But see also Mauss 1990 [1925], Parry 1986. Historians of Europe have been rather more attentive, e.g. Geremek and Kolakowska 1994.

4 Egyptian press reports extracted in Ayeb 1995.

5 Historically it must be untrue, for the Bolsheviks had no interest in private philanthropy, and the network of Russian charitable organizations was totally abolished by the Soviets as inimical to the principles governing human relationships in a socialist state (Madison 1960: 536).

6 The other four pillars are, in order: the *shahāda*, or "there is no god but God, and Muhammad is his prophet"; *salāt*, observance of the five daily ritual prayers; *sawm*, fasting in the month of Ramadān; and *hajj*, performance of the pilgrimage to Mecca once in a lifetime by those able to do so.

7 This summary of mainstream Sunni teaching on *zakāt* is distilled from a number of published sources cited here and interviews with experts in Jordan, Palestine and London.

8 According to Al-Khayyat there are eighty-two references in the Qur'ān to more general issues of almsgiving and spending, and thirty-two references specifically to *zakāt* (al-Khayyat 1993: 8).

9 For comment on this category, see Décobert 1991: 222–225.

10 For an example of this discussion, see Hamidullah 1959: II, 617–628.

11 Jérôme Bellion-Jourdan, personal communication. [Note: Since this article was first published in 1999, Muslim Aid decided to follow the lead of Islamic Relief.]

12 As in the Ibadate imamate of Oman in the late nineteenth century, where *zakāt* became more like a type of Danegeld than a form of religious alms (Wilkinson 1987: 180).

13 Abd-Allah suggests that the administrators of *zakāt* have a right to a maximum of one-eighth per year (they being merely one of the eight categories of beneficiary).

14 I understand that in Saudi Arabia, as a substitute for tax, individuals, and in particular businesses, are officially invited, but in effect required, to contribute to *zakāt* funds around the time of Ramadān.

15 The issue is complicated by the provision in Islamic law for a special tax to be levied on non-Muslims in return for their protection by the state: the head-tax (*jizyah*). Islamic law also provides for a land tax (*kharāj*) and for customs duty levied on traders (Mannan 1986: 246–252).

16 This article focuses on Sunni Islam. Shi'as have another religious tax known as *khoms* (one-fifth), which is levied annually on net income and wealth and paid to Shi'a *'ulamā* (scholars), allowing them, unlike their Sunni counterparts, to remain independent of the state. In theory, half of it should go to the *sayyids* (direct descendants of the Prophet) and the needy, and the other half to the leading Shi'a clergy. In practice, Shi'as often send the entire *khoms* to a chosen, trusted cleric for the funding of seminaries, mosques, hospitals, teachers' and students' salaries, poverty relief, etc. The

Islamic Republic of Iran has tried to claim the right to both *khoms* and *zakāt*, so far without success (Ziba Mir-Husseini, pers. comm. 1997, and see Naqvi 1991: 241–252).

17 Indeed, the words of Christ's Sermon on the Mount—"When you do some act of charity, do not let your left hand know what your right hand is doing" (Matthew 6:3) has become one of a number of Christian adages which are well known to many Muslims within the corpus of prophetic *hadiths*.

18 In Morocco, I am told by friends (though I have not witnessed its practice) that an agricultural equivalent of *zakāt* called '*ushr*—that is, "tenth", the same as the Jewish and Christian "tithe"—is still quite widely observed as a proportion of the harvest which is given locally to religious causes, village schools and the poor.

19 The institution to which I gave most attention during my research, the Jordanian Red Crescent, is outside the *zakāt* system and in its constitution entirely non-confessional; but, as argued elsewhere, it is deeply affected by tensions between its Arab/Islamic cultural roots and the non-confessional International Red Cross and Red Crescent Movement (Benthall 1997). Further consideration of the intricate relations between charity and politics in Jordan is outside the scope of this article.

20 There are no doubt, as in the West, also practical advantages to the donor in anonymous giving, such as not wanting to appear to be wealthy and not wanting to attract requests for gifts (Schervish 1994).

21 Even Qaddafi, the Libyan leader, among many other more mainstream political figures, defined *zakāt* as the core of the supposed Islamic alternative to capitalism and communism (Esposito 1992: 82).

22 Qutb was a brilliant Egyptian literary critic who visited the United States to study its educational system and came back an implacable critic of what he saw as Western racism, consumerism, secularism and abuse of women's dignity. He wrote a number of polemical tracts advocating a return to the literal text of the Qur'ān and excoriating all actual Muslim states as no better than non-Muslim ones, plunged in ignorance. He was imprisoned for conspiracy in 1954 and later hanged. His books, especially Qutb 1964 are widely read among Sunni radicals today.

23 This principle is adduced by moderate Islamists, such as the Muslim Brothers in Jordan, as an argument against introducing the rigours of Islamic criminal law, which predicates a more equitable society.

24 "What matters is the intention of your hearts" (Surah 33:5). A famous *hadith*, "Actions are according to their intentions," is inscribed over a gate at Al-Azhar University in Cairo. A statement of personal intention is a formally necessary step in the performance of all rituals and prayers.

25 It seems likely that in some other Arab communities where militant Islamism is strong, certain Islamic charitable associations are occasionally used as fronts for organizing violence.

References

Abu-Sahlieh, Sami A. Aldeeb (1994) *Les musulmans face aux droits de l'homme*, Bochum: Dr. Dieter Winkler.

Al-Khayyat, A.-A. (1993) *Az-Zakāt w-ataTbīqāt-hā w-istishmārāt-hā [Zakat and its Applications and Profitable Uses]*, Amman: Ministry of Awqaf and Islamic Affairs.

Antoun, Richard T. (1989) *Muslim Preacher in the Modern World: A Jordanian Case Study in Comparative Perspective*, Princeton, NJ: Princeton University Press.

Ayeb, Habib (1995) "Les inondations de novembre 1994 en Égypte," *CEDEJ Égypt MondeArabe*, 22: 159–178.

Badie, Bertrand (1992) *L'état importé: l'occidentalisation de l'ordre politique*, Paris: Fayard.

ben Néfissa, Sarah (1995) "Associations égyptiennes: un libéralisation sous contrôle," *Monde Arab*, 150: 40–47.

Benthall, Jonathan (1997) "The Red Cross and Red Crescent Movement and Islamic Societies, with Special Reference to Jordan," *British Journal of Middle Eastern Studies*, 24: 157–177.

Berg, Herbert (1997) "The Implications of, and Opposition to, the Methods and Theories of John Wansbrough," *Method and Theory in the Study of Religion*, 9: 153–173.

Boisard, Marcel A. (1985) *L'humanisme de l'islam*, 3rd edn, Paris: A. Michel.

Bowen, John R. (1993) *Muslims through Discourse: Religion and Ritual in Gayo Society*, Princeton, NJ: Princeton University Press.

Burton, John (1994) *An Introduction to the Hadiths*, Edinburgh: Edinburgh University Press.

Carré, Olivier (1984) *Mystique et politique: lecture révolutionnaire du Coran par Sayyid Qutb, frère musulman radical*, Paris: Editions du Cerf.

Caulkins, D. Douglas (1996) "Voluntary Associations," in David Levinson and Melvin Ember (eds) *Encyclopedia of Cultural Anthropology*, New York: H. Holt.

Cragg, Kenneth (1956) *The Call of the Minaret*, New York: Oxford University Press.

de Waal, Alexander (1997) *Famine Crimes: Politics and the Disaster Relief Industry in Africa*, London: James Currey.

Décobert, Christian (1991) *Le mendiant et le combattant: l'institution de l'islam*, Paris: Éditions du Seuil.

Esposito, John L. (1992) *The Islamic Threat: Myth or Reality?*, New York: Oxford University Press.

Fischer, Michael M.J., and Mehdi Abedi (ed.) (1990) *Debating Muslims: Cultural Dialogues in Postmodernity and Tradition*, Madison WI: University of Wisconsin Press.

Geremek, Bronislaw, and Agnieszka Kolakowska (1994) *Poverty: A History*, Oxford: Blackwell.

Hamidullah, Muhammad (1959) *Le prophète de l'islam*, Paris: J. Vrin.

Husaini, Ishaq M. (1956) *The Moslem Brethren*, Beirut: Khayyat.

Ibrahim, Saad E. (1988) "Egypt's Islamic Activism in the 1980s," *Third World Quarterly*, 10: 632–657.

Israeli, Raphael (1993a) *Muslim Fundamentalism in Israel*, London: Brassey's.

——— (1993b) *Fundamentalist Islam and Israel*, Lanham, MD: University Press of America.

Kuran, Timur (1989) "Economic Justice in Contemporary Islamic Thought (Part 1)," *International Journal of Middle East Studies*, 21: 171–191.

——— (1990) "Economic Justice in Contemporary Islamic Thought (Part 2)," *International Journal of Middle East Studies*, 22: 376–377.

Madison, Bernice (1960) "The Organization of Welfare Services," in Cyril E. Black (ed.) *The Transformation of Russian Society: Aspects of Social Change since 1861*, Cambridge, MA: Harvard University Press.

Mannan, Muhammad A. (1986) *Islamic Economics Theory and Practice*, London: Hodder & Stoughton.

Marett, Ralf R. (1935) *Head, Heart and Hands in Human Evolution*, London: Hutchinson.

Mauss, Marcel (1990 [1925]) *The Gift: The Form and Reason for Exchange in Archaic Societies*, trans. Wilfred D. Halls, London: Routledge.

Mitchell, Richard P. (1969) *The Society of the Muslim Brothers*, London: Oxford University Press.

Naqvi, Ali M. (1991) *Manual of Islamic Beliefs and Practice*, Qom: Ansiriyan Publications.

Novossyolov, Dimitri (1993) "The Islamization of Welfare in Pakistan," in Dale F. Eickelman (ed.) *Russia's Muslim Frontier*, Bloomington, IN: Indiana University Press.

Parry, Jonathan (1986) "*The Gift*, the Indian Gift and the 'Indian Gift'," *Man*, 21: 453–473.

Qutb, Sayyid (1964) *Ma`ālim fi al-Tarīq [Signposts along the Road]*, Cairo: Kazi Publications.

Roy, Olivier (1992) *L'échec de l'islam politique*, Paris: Éditions du Seuil.

Rugh, Andrea B. (1994) "Reshaping Personal Relations in Egypt," in Martin E. Marty and R. Scott Appleby (eds) *Fundamentalism and Society: Reclaiming the Sciences, the Family, and Education*, Chicago, IL: University of Chicago Press.

Sahlins, Marshall D. (1958) *Social Stratification in Polynesia*, Seattle, WA: University of Washington Press.

Schervish, Paul G. (1994) "The Sound of one Hand Clapping: The Case For and Against Anonymous Giving," *Voluntas*, 5: 1–26.

Schimmel, Annemarie (1992) *Islam: An Introduction*, Albany, NY: State University of New York Press.

Speight, R. Marston (1988) "The Function of Hadith," in Andrew Rippin (ed.) *Approaches to the History of the Interpretation of the Qur'an*, Oxford: Clarendon Press.

Stillman, Norman A. (1975) "Charity and Social Service in Medieval Islam," *Societas*, 5: 105–115.

Sullivan, Denis J. (1992) *Private Voluntary Organizations in Egypt: Islamic Development, Private Initiative, and State Control*, Gainesville, FL: University Press of Florida.

Terray, Emmanuel (1994) "Review of C. Décobert: *Le mendiant et le combattant: l'institution de l'islam*, Paris: Éditions du Seuil, 1991," *Annales. Histoire, Sciences Sociales*, 49: 977–980.

Waldman, Peter (1992) "Clergy Capitalism: Mullahs Keep Control of Iranian Economy with an Iron Hand," *Wall Street Journal*: May 5.

Westermarck, Edward (1908) *The Origin and Development of the Moral Ideas*, London: Macmillan.

Wilkinson, John C. (1987) *The Imamate Tradition of Oman*, Cambridge: Cambridge University Press.

Part III

Methodological reflections on the anthropology of Islam

Jens Kreinath

After considering accounts on the diversity of Muslim religious practices, it is vital to reflect upon how anthropologists represent and conceptualize their material. Although the readings illustrated how anthropologists immersed themselves into a community they worked with and how they established a rapport with the people they studied, the query continues to exist: under what conditions do anthropologists conceptualize and represent the insights they generate during fieldwork, and how do they present their findings to broader academic and non-academic audiences? As indicated before, the recognition of religious and cultural differences between insider and outsider, believer and non-believer, is important in considering the anthropology of Islam. This recognition enhances the understanding and appreciation of social and cultural diversity as a major objective of anthropology in general and the anthropology of Islam in particular.

The ethnographic accounts of religious practices presented in the Part II of this volume showed that there are significant differences in the performance and understanding of religious practices among Muslims. The way these differences came to the fore was not simply through the different geographic and cultural areas these anthropologists studied. These peculiarities also exist because the anthropologists who carried out their research did so at different times and within unique social and political contexts, utilizing different methods of inquiry and employing distinct styles of writing. The competence anthropologists can bring to the field, and the breadth of understanding in their use of participant observation, allows them to sense formerly unseen subtleties and grasp hidden rhythms and structures that organize everyday Muslim life. Research and writing techniques employed by anthropologists are critical; they must do justice to the epistemological issues at stake in grasping these rhythms and structures.

In whatever way this question is addressed, the stance anthropologists take regarding the field of study and the object of research impacts how anthropologists carry out research and present it to more or less academically informed audiences. A critical methodological question for anthropologists working on Islam is how they come to terms with and account for their own positionality toward Muslims and Islam. More than in any other discipline of the social sciences, anthropologists may, intentionally or not, impede or interfere with the field of study due to the assumptions they make or the convictions they hold. Regardless of whether this position remains implicit, the methodological questions remain: how does an anthropologist relate to their field of study, and how do they represent the insights that they gain through their research? Answers to these questions are the means by which they gather and analyze ethnographic data, allowing others to see how the people studied perceive themselves.

Because anthropology aims to take different angles of interpretation into consideration and to integrate a multiplicity of perspectives, there is perhaps no other way to study human subjects in a holistic manner. At the same time, it seems impossible for anthropologists to fully distance themselves from the social and political conditions in which they work. Even if they aim to reach detached objectivity on neutral grounds, this approach would impact how they interact with people in the field. As the former readings indicated, it is probably the other way around; anthropologists must identify themselves with the people they study if they wish to gain refined insights and enhanced understandings. Furthermore, by placing themselves and their research within the social and political surroundings in which they live, and the hierarchies and networks of the academic fields and institutions with which they more permanently work, anthropologists walk a fine line on the border between the insider and the outsider.

It would be easy to discard these problems if they were perceived as posing an unjustified epistemological critique, or holding a bias which would obscure scientific objectivity and reduce it to notions of power and knowledge. However, the question of how anthropologists find access to their resources of knowledge and how they are empowered to use methods of inquiry remains. Anthropology therefore works to provide answers to this question by examining who is controlling the academic field of study and to what degree an anthropologist can control the accuracy and relevance of the representations they produce. Such considerations on methodology are crucial to the anthropology of Islam, since it has necessarily questioned how anthropologists contribute to the body of knowledge written on Muslims, and how their knowledge and insights derive from the web of social relationships and sources of knowledge to which they have access. Methodology is concerned with reflections on the way anthropologists collect, organize and analyze their ethnographic data and apply, contest and refine the theoretical frameworks of their research questions. It deals with the kinds of questions anthropologists ask, the sorts of observations they make, and the types of interests they articulate.

It is therefore about the process by which anthropologists come to their results and draw their conclusions. In light of the fact that methodology is concerned with foundational questions regarding the methods of research and styles of representation, methodological reflections lead to practices and discourses involving anthropologists within an academic field. The position and interest of anthropologists in relation to both their field and their object of study is critical to methodological reflection, as are concerns about these exact issues and, by extension, the ways anthropologists disseminate their results through written publications and filmed documentations, and other media or means of communication. Both directions are crucial insofar as they reveal and determine the relationship between how anthropologists collect and present ethnographic data to the broader academic field and to the public. The readings presented in this section are concerned with the roles that religious practice and commitment play in ethnographic research and anthropological discourse in ethnological analysis.

The following writings allow for reflection on the relation between ethnographic accounts of religious practice and the ethnological implications for anthropological discourse in the formation of theoretical approaches. As demonstrated in the previous sections, the paths by which anthropologists approach Islam and Muslims alike have a considerable impact on the way in which they perform their fieldwork, formulate their questions, test their hypotheses, and analyze their data, and present their results. This means, in methodological terms, that anthropology as a social-scientific discipline differs from other more text-oriented disciplines in the study of Islam through its method of ethnographic fieldwork. Anthropological research relies on methods of discovery and inquiry, such as participant observation and qualitative interviews with focus groups. The outcome and results of the kind of research anthropologists perform are not predictable from the outset; their aim is to find out how the people they study see themselves.

In focusing on specific themes, issues and concerns of a local Islamic community through a holistic and inclusive perspective, anthropologists attempt to avoid unfounded comparisons, generalizations, and conclusions. They aim to provide empirical accounts that strive to give a broader picture. Further, ethnographic and ethnological works contain descriptions and conceptualizations, which may or may not be relevant to Muslims themselves, even though anthropologists emphasize and focus on the peculiarities and complexities of everyday life. Yet, it is important to consider the questions Muslims ask about themselves and their practices, as well as the role of anthropology as a discipline, with its own methods of inquiry originating in the Western hemisphere. It is imperative to consider how these two—in part conflicting conceptualizations—matter for modes of reasoning, methods, and discourses in the anthropology of Islam.

As outlined throughout the book, the anthropology of Islam incorporates questions not only about what Islam is, but also furthers the understanding of Muslims by observing and participating in their religious practices and openly interviewing informants. The overall aim, therefore, is to discover the local practices and discourses of Islam unique to the understandings and interpretations of their respective contexts. Equipped with the methods of participant observation and qualitative interview with focus groups, the anthropologist's perspective has considerable impact on this endeavor. Anthropological methods and theories—ethnographies and ethnologies alike—inform and guide researchers and fieldworkers as they formulate findings and approach answers to questions and hypotheses. It is thus central to reflect upon the placement of the anthropologist within the field of research and the theoretical framework of anthropology in Western academia and the social sciences.

The first two readings in the subsection *Situating Anthropology* are about the peculiar stance anthropologists take in relation to the object of study. This concerns whether religious commitment matters, and what its importance is for the possible outcome of ethnographic research. Starting with a critique of the Orientalism of Western and non-Muslim anthropologists, Akbar S. Ahmed proposes a new approach to Islam from an Islamic perspective. In the selected excerpts from his booklet *Toward Islamic Anthropology: Definition, Dogma and Directions*, he argues in favor of an approach based on Islamic principles while questioning the ideological implications and cultural hegemonies of a predominantly Western anthropology. Incorporating and uniting Muslim practitioners' beliefs with scholars' worldviews into an anthropological theoretical position, Akbar favors a reflexive method and proposes new guidelines and directions of study for an Islamic anthropology. This reading not only offers an opportunity to explore and reflect upon the theoretical design of the presented ethnographies, but also allows for an examination of the role of worldviews and the incorporation of such into scholarly research and findings. In contrast, Richard Tapper, in his review article 'Islamic Anthropology' and the 'Anthropology of Islam,' counters this approach and criticizes the theoretical positioning and methodology of Ahmed and anthropologists with a similar ideological agenda. Considering the works of anthropologists who incorporate Islamic principles into an anthropological approach and distinguishing the anthropological methods and theories from these proposals, Tapper outlines the fundamental differences found in the methodological parameters employed in the divide between Islamic anthropology and the anthropology of Islam. His work considers the development of Islamic anthropology and conceptual differences of a social scientific approach, which includes long-term participant observation and can ask complex questions about Islamic practices, perspectives and understandings of Islam when evaluating people, traditions, and societies.

In the final section, *Representing Islam*, reflections on the epistemology and rhetoric of anthropological research are encountered. In the concluding chapters of his classical account of U.S. reports on the Islamic Revolution of Iran, *Covering Islam*, Edward Said revisits his notion of Orientalism and reviews its theoretical insights in the wake of the politically charged events of 1979 Iran. He considers the development of an intensified Western interest in Islam and Muslim societies, as well as historical and political environments in which the first accounts of the anthropology of Islam emerged. Critically assessing financial interests, media representations, and political economy and their impact on the academic study of Islam, Said problematizes the relationship between power and the production of knowledge by Western media outlets and past scholarship. Furthermore, he scrutinizes the establishment and political construction of Islam and the Middle East within and beyond academic fields of study, and how these developments are reflected in news coverage in the West, through which politicians in the Western hemisphere acquired many erroneous, stereotypical and general preconceptions. This type of critical survey may serve to strengthen serious scholarship in the anthropology of Islam, drawing attention to inconsistencies and providing valuable insights for a reflexive awareness of the venues and positions influencing anthropologists and the people with whom they work.

In the excerpts taken from the introduction and conclusion of *Islam Obscured: The Rhetoric of Anthropological Representation*, Daniel Varisco employs a perspective which is both literary and anthropological to present a thorough survey of the development of Islamic and Middle Eastern studies, outlining the distinctive differences between schools of thought so easily confused in anthropological studies of Islam. Reviewing prior expressions of Islam through anthropological perspectives, Varisco revisits the critiques of anthropology and the "writing about culture" debate. Providing a critical and comprehensive overview of anthropological works in the field, his reading serves as a valuable tool to explore a variety of perspectives, positions and theories over time and across various regions of the world. Varisco finally affords a tempered voice and normalizing perspective for the concerns and quandaries of anthropologists working within, writing about, and representing the field, explicitly supporting the anthropological study of religion and calling for the uncomfortable and difficult questions the anthropology of Islam must ask and address.

Conceptual differences in the ways anthropologists present their data have a considerable impact on the types of questions they subsequently ask, and lead them to refine and redefine the objectives, designs, and therefore the outcomes of future research projects. These readings, which demonstrate the conceptual differences in their style of writing and representation, should provide further insights into understanding basic critiques of anthropology as a field of study and enhance the ways in which anthropology criticizes its own presumptions and representations in the attempt to overcome set boundaries and rigid paradigms of Western ideologies, colonial encounters and forms of cultural hegemony. Through these types of debates about methodology, theoretical positioning, and rhetorical analysis, the anthropology of Islam seeks to improve its techniques and refine its understandings of Muslims, focusing on the ways in which they live, perceive and organize their social lives and religious practices.

Suggested readings

Abaza, Mona, and Georg Stauth (1988) "Occidental Reason, Orientalism, Islamic Fundamentalism," *International Sociology*, 3: 343–364.

Abu-Lughod, Lila (1990) "Anthropology's Orient: The Boundaries of Theory on the Arab World," in Hisham Sharabi (ed.) *Theory, Politics, and the Arab World: Critical Responses*, New York: Routledge.

Afary, Janet, and Kevin B. Anderson (2005) *Foucault and the Iranian Revolution Gender and the Seductions of Islamism*, Chicago, IL: University of Chicago Press.

Ahmed, Akbar S. (1984) "Defining Islamic Anthropology," *RAIN*, 65: 1–4.

——— (1986) "Toward Islamic Anthropology," *American Journal of Islamic Social Sciences*, 3: 181–230.

——— (1991) "Postmodernist Perceptions of Islam: Observing the Observer" *Asian Survey*, 31: 213–231.

——— (ed.) (1992) *Postmodernism and Islam: Predicament and Promise*, London: Routledge.

Anderson, Jon W. (2003) "The Internet and Islam's New Interpreters," in Dale W. Eickelman and Jon W. Anderson (eds) *New Media in the Muslim World: The Emerging Public Sphere*, Bloomington, IN: Indiana University Press.

Asad, Talal (ed.) (1973) *Anthropology and the Colonial Encounter*, London: Ithaca Press.

——— (2003) *Formations of the Secular: Christianity, Islam, Modernity*, Stanford, CA: Stanford University Press.

Beeman, William O. (2005) *The "Great Satan" vs. the "Mad Mullahs": How the United States and Iran Demonize each other*, Westport, CT.: Praeger Publishers.

Bourdieu, Pierre (1988) *Homo Academicus*, Stanford, CA: Stanford University Press.

Bräunlein, Peter J. (2006) "'Islam Observed' – 'Islam Obscured': Lokale Religionsforschung aus translokaler Perspektive," *Zeitschrift für Religion- und Geistesgeschichte*, 58: 132–154.

Burke, III, Edmund (1998) "Orientalism and World History: Representing Middle Eastern Nationalism and Islamism in the Twentieth Century," *Theory and Society*, 27: 489–507.

Clifford, James (1980) "Review Essay of *Orientalism* by Edward Said," *Historical Theory*, 19: 204–223.

—— and George E. Marcus (1986) *Writing Culture: The Poetics and Politics of Ethnography*, Berkeley, CA: University of California Press.

Çınar, Alev (2005) *Modernity, Islam, and Secularism in Turkey: Bodies, Places, and Time*, Minneapolis, MN: University of Minnesota Press.

Davies, Merryl Wyn (1985) "Towards an Islamic Alternative to Western Anthropology," *Inquiry*, June: 45–51.

——— (1988) *Knowing one Another: Shaping an Islamic Anthropology*, London and New York: Mansell.

Djait, Hichem (1985) *Europe and Islam: Cultures and Modernity*, Berkeley, CA: University of California Press.

Donnan, Hastings, and Akbar S. Ahmed (eds) (1994) *Islam, Globalization, and Postmodernity*, London: Routledge.

Eickelman, Dale F. (2000) "Islam and the Languages of Modernity," *Daedalus*, 129: 119–135.

——— and Jon W. Anderson (1997) "Print, Islam, and the Prospects of Civic Pluralism: New Religious Writings and their Audiences," *Journal of Islamic Studies*, 8: 43–62.

Er-Rashid, Haroun (2003) "Muslims and the West: A Paradigm of Polarization," in Michael J. Thompson (ed.) *Islam and the West: Critical Perspectives on Modernity*, Oxford: Rowman & Littlefield Publishers.

Euben, Roxanne L. (1997) "Premodern, Antimodern or Postmodern? Islamic and Western Critiques of Modernity," *Review of Politics*, 59: 429–459.

Fischer, Michael M.J., and Mehdi Abedi (eds) (1990) *Debating Muslims: Cultural Dialogues in Postmodernity and Tradition*, Madison, WI: University of Wisconsin Press.

Göle, Nilüfer (2003) "Contemporary Islamist Movements and New Sources for Religious Tolerance," *Journal of Human Rights*, 2: 17–30.

Hafez, Kai (2000) "Islam and the West: The Clash of Politicised Perceptions," in Kai Hafez (ed.) *The Islamic World and the West: An Introduction to Political Cultures and International Relations*, Leiden and Boston: Brill.

——— (2000) "The Middle East and Islam in Western Media: Towards a Comprehensive Theory of Foreign Reporting," in Kai Hafez (ed.) *Islam and the West in the Mass Media: Fragmented Images in a Globalizing World*, Cresskill, NJ: Hampton Press.

Halliday, Fred (1993) "'Orientalism' and Its Critics," *British Journal of Middle Eastern Studies*, 20: 145–163.
Houston, Christopher (1998) "Alternative Modernities: Islamism and Secularism on Charles Taylor," *Critique of Anthropology*, 18: 234–240.
Hughes, Aaron W. (2007) *Situating Islam: The Past and Future of an Academic Discipline*, London: Equinox.
Hussain, Alaf (1984) "The Ideology of Orientalism," in Asaf Hussain, Robert Olson and Jamil Qureshi (eds) *Orientalism, Islam and Islamists*, Brattleboro, VT: Amana Books.
Ismael, Tareq Y., and Andrew Rippin (2010) *Islam in the Eyes of the West: Images and Realities in an Age of Terror*, London and New York: Routledge.
Kessler, Clive S. (1990) "New Directions in the Study of Islam: Remarks on Some Trends and Prospects," *Jurnal Antropologi dan Sosiologi*, 18: 3–22.
Keyman, E Fuat (2007) "Modernity, Secularism and Islam: The Case of Turkey," *Theory, Culture & Society*, 24: 215–234.
Lewis, Bernard (1972) "The Study of Islam," *Encounter*, 38: 31–41.
——— (1988) *The Political Language of Islam*, Chicago, IL: University of Chicago Press.
——— (1993) *Islam and the West*, New York: Oxford University Press.
Malik, Iftikhar H. (2004) *Islam and Modernity: Muslims in Europe and the United States*, London: Pluto Press.
Mani, Lata, and Ruth Frankenberg (1985) "The Challenge of Orientalism," *Economy and Society*, 14: 174–192.
Mauroof, S. Muhammad (1981) "Elements for an Islamic Anthropology," in Ismail R. Al-Faruqi and Abdullah O. Naseef (eds) *Social and Natural Sciences: The Islamic Perspective*, Sevenoaks: Hodder & Stoughton.
McLoughlin, Seán (2007) "Islam(s) in Context: Orientalism and the Anthropology of Muslim Societies and Cultures," *Journal of Beliefs and Values* 28: 273–296.
Momin, Abdur-Rahman (1989) "Islamization of Anthropological Knowledge," *American Journal of Islamic Social Sciences*, 6: 143–153.
Mutman, Mahmut (1992) "Under the Sign of Orientalism: The West vs. Islam," *Cultural Critique*, 23: 165–197.
Osella, Filippo, and Benjamin F. Soares (2010) *Islam, Politics, Anthropology*, Chichester: Wiley-Blackwell.
Soares, Benjamin F., and Filippo Osella (2009) "Islam, Politics, Anthropology," *Journal of the Royal Anthropological Institute*, 15: 1–23.
Poole, Elizabeth, and John E. Richardson (2006) *Muslims and the News Media*, London and New York: I.B. Tauris.
Pruett, Gordon E. (1984) "'Islam' and Orientalism," in Asaf Hussain, Robert Olson and Jamil Qureshi (eds) *Orientalism, Islam and Islamists*, Brattleboro, VT: Amana Books.
Rahman, Fazlur (1982) "The Academic Study of Islam: A Muslim Islamicist's Point of View," in Richard C. Martin (ed.) *Islam and the History of Religions*, Berkeley, CA: University of California Press.
——— (1982) *Islam and Modernity: The Transformation of an Intellectual Tradition*, Chicago, IL: University of Chicago Press.
Sadowski, Yahya (1997) "The New Orientalism and the Democracy Debate," in Joel Beinin and Joe Stork (eds) *Political Islam: Essays from Middle East Report*, London: I.B. Tauris.
Said, Edward (1978) *Orientalism*, New York: Vintage.
——— (1985) "Orientalism Reconsidered," *Cultural Critique*, 1: 89–107.
——— (2003) "The Clash of Definitions," in Emran Qureshi and Michael A. Sells (eds) *The New Crusades: Constructing the Muslim Enemy*, New York: Columbia University Press.
Salvatore, Armando (1997) *Islam and the Political Discourse of Modernity*, Reading: Ithaca Press.
——— (1998) "Discoursive Contentions in Islamic Terms: Fundamentalism vs. Liberalism?" in Ahmed Moussalli (ed.) *Islamic Fundamentalism: Myths and Realities*, Reading: Ithaca Press.
Schulze, Reinhard (2000) "Is there an Islamic Modernity?," in Kai Hafez (ed.) *The Islamic World and the West: An Introduction to Political Cultures and International Relations*, Leiden and Boston: Brill.
Scullion, Rosemarie (1995) "Michel Foucault the Orientalist: On Revolutionary Iran and the 'Spirit of Islam'," *South Central Review*, 12: 16–40.
Smith, William C. (1957) "Islam in the Modern World," *Current History*, 32: 321–325.

Spickard, James V. (2001) "Tribes and Cities: Towards an Islamic Sociology of Religion," *Social Compass*, 48: 103–116.

Turner, Brian S. (1978) *Marx and the End of Orientalism*, London: Allen and Unwin.

——— (1984) "Orientalism and the Problem of Civil Society in Islam," in Asaf Hussain, Robert Olson and Jamil Qureshi (eds) *Orientalism, Islam and Islamists*, Brattleboro, VT: Amana Books.

——— (1994) *Orientalism, Postmodernism and Globalism*, London: Routledge.

——— (2002) "Orientalism, or the Politics of the Text," in Hastings Donnan (ed.) *Interpreting Islam*, London: Sage.

Vahdat, Farzin (2003) "Critical Theory and the Islamic Encounter with Modernity," in Michael J. Thompson (ed.) *Islam and the West: Critical Perspectives on Modernity*, Oxford: Rowman & Littlefield Publishers.

Varisco, Daniel M. (2007) *Reading Orientalism: Said and the Unsaid*, Seattle, WA: University of Washington Press.

Waardenburg, Jacques (1965) "Some Institutional Aspects of Muslim Higher Education and Their Relation to Islam," *Numen*, 12: 96–138.

——— (1973) *L'Islam dans le miroir de l'occident*, The Hague and Paris: Mouton.

——— (1979) "Official and Popular Religion as a Problem in Islamic Studies," in Pieter H. Vrijhof and Jacques Waardenburg (ed.) *Official and Polular as a Theme in the Study of Religion*, The Hague: Mouton.

——— (1998) "Observations on the Scholarly Study of Religions as Pursued in Some Muslim Countries," *Numen*, 45: 235–257.

Waldman, Marilyn R. (1985) "Primitive Mind/Modern Mind: New Approaches to an Old Problem Applied to Islam," in Richard C. Martin (ed.) *Approaches to Islam in Religious Studies*, Tucson, AZ: University of Arizona Press.

Wiegand, Krista (2000) "Islam as Ethnicity? The Media's Impact on Misconceptions in the West," in Kai Hafez (ed.) *Islam and the West in the Mass Media: Fragmented Images in a Globalizing World*, Cresskill, NJ: Hampton Press.

Yegenoglu, Meyda (2006) "The Return of the Religious: Revisiting Europe and its Islamic Others," *Culture and Religion*, 7: 245–261.

Situating anthropology

15 Toward Islamic anthropology

Definition, dogma and directions[1]

Akbar S. Ahmed

Akbar S. Ahmed is currently the Ibn Khaldun Chair of Islamic Studies at the American University in Washington, DC. He earned his PhD at the School of Oriental and African Studies, University of London. He is a leading expert and spokesman on contemporary Islam and has regular appearances in the news throughout the United States and Europe. He was appointed the first Chair of Islamic Studies at the U.S. Naval Academy at Annapolis. His recent research focuses on Muslims in America. His fieldwork among Muslims includes Pakistan and Bangladesh leading to his publications on *Pukhtun Economy and Society: Traditional Structure and Economic Development in a Tribal Society* (1980) and *Religion and Politics in Muslim Society: Order and Conflict in Pakistan* (1983). His more general works include *Toward Islamic Anthropology: Definition, Dogma and Directions* (1987); *Discovering Islam: Making Sense of Muslim History and Society* (1988), the basis of the BBC series, "Living Islam"; *Postmodernism and Islam: Predicament and Promise* (1993); *The Future of Anthropology: Its Relevance to the Contemporary World* (1999); *Islam Under Siege: Living Dangerously in a Post-Honor World* (2003); *After Terror: Promoting Dialogue Among Civilizations* (2005) and *Journey into Islam: The Crisis of Globalization* (2007). His most recent work, *Journey into America: The Challenge of Islam* was published by Brookings Press in 2010. The excerpts taken from *Toward Islamic Anthropology* articulate a critique of Western biases in the anthropological study of Islam by stressing its colonial heritage. Based on the attempt to locate anthropology within the framework of Islamic history and theology, Ahmed outlines the proposal for an Islamic Anthropology after commenting on Western anthropology.

The science of anthropology

This study is speculatory and concerns a difficult and complex subject. Its task is made more difficult as it defends a metaphysical position, advances an ideological argument and serves a moral cause. It will, therefore, remain an incomplete part of an on-going process in the debate on key issues in contemporary Muslim society.

The major task of anthropology[2]—the study of man—is to enable us to understand ourselves through understanding other cultures. Anthropology makes us aware of the essential oneness of man and therefore allows us to appreciate each other. It is only quite recently in history that it has come to be widely accepted that human beings are fundamentally alike; that they share basic interests, and so have certain common obligations to one another. This belief is either explicit or implicit in most of the great world religions, but it is by no means acceptable today to many people even in "advanced" societies, and it would make no sense at all in many of the less-developed cultures. Among some of the indigenous tribes of Australia, a stranger who cannot prove that he is a kinsman, far from being welcomed hospitably, is regarded as a dangerous outsider and may be speared without compunction. [...] Many citizens of modern states today think of people of other races, nations or cultures in ways which are not very different from these, especially if their skin is differently colored or if they hold other religious or political beliefs (Ahmed 2010). [...]

I do not here discuss in detail the historical development of social anthropology; full accounts are available elsewhere (see for example Beattie 1977). But it will be easier to see why contemporary social anthropology is the kind of subject it is if we have some idea of what has led up to it. As a branch of empirical, observational science, it grew up in the context of the world-wide interaction which has vastly increased in the past century. What is most familiar is often taken for granted, and the idea that the study of living human communities was of legitimate scientific interest in its own right became evident when detailed information began to be available about hitherto remote and unfamiliar human societies. These societies had been speculated about since time immemorial, but they could not be scientifically investigated until new, easier and quicker ways of getting about the world made it possible for scholars to visit and observe them.

Initially, the reports of eighteenth- and nineteenth-century missionaries and travelers in Africa, North America, the Pacific and elsewhere provided the raw material upon which the first western anthropological works, written in the second half of the nineteenth century, were based. Before then there had been plenty of conjecturing about human institutions and their origins to say nothing of earlier times in the eighteenth century. Hume, Adam Smith and Ferguson in Britain, and Montesquieu, Condorcet and others on the Continent, had written about primitive institutions. Although their speculations were often brilliant, these thinkers were no empirical scientists; their conclusions were not based on evidence which could be tested. On the contrary, their speculations were deductively argued from principles which were for the most part implicit in their own cultures. They were really philosophers and historians of Europe, not anthropologists as we would now understand the term.

The common view was that civilized men could have nothing profitable to learn from studying the way of life of a lot of "savages." It is reported that even at the end of the nineteenth century the famous Sir James G. Frazer, when asked if he had ever seen one of the primitive people about whose customs he had written so many volumes responded with "God Forbid!" In an important sense these writers were the forerunners of modern social anthropologists—although attitudes today are dramatically different.

Modern social anthropology owes much to these nineteenth-century scholars, in spite of their misconceptions. Although they were mainly preoccupied with the reconstruction of a past which was lost forever, they were like their successors, interested in social institutions and the interrelations between the cultural and social institutions of different societies [...]

As the quantity of ethnographic information increased, and its quality gradually improved, it began to dawn on some scholars that this material was too important to be used merely to illustrate preconceived ideas about primitive peoples or about presumed earlier stages of human society. More and more this extensive ethnography was seen to demand some sort of comparative analysis in its own right. Practical concerns stimulated this interest. Colonial administrators and missionaries began increasingly to see that their work would benefit by an understanding of the social and cultural institutions of the populations they dealt with. Some of the best of the earlier monographs on the simpler societies were written by serving missionaries and administrative officers (Ahmed 1980b; Ahmed 1983; Ahmed and Hart 1983). [...]

It was with the change of interest from the reconstruction of past societies to the investigation of contemporary societies that modern social anthropology began. From this time forward social anthropologists were no longer satisfied with the collection of isolated pieces of information about particular customs or institutions, however skillfully these might be woven into theoretical schemes, or however wide-ranging the comparisons based on them. [...] So, for the first time, the question arose: how are these unfamiliar social and cultural systems to be understood?

The answer was attempted by French sociologists with their analytical and intellectual traditions. Eighteenth- and nineteenth-century French writers about human society were much concerned with the "nature" of society and of human social institutions. Their interest lay rather in what human society essentially is than in the history of its development, either generally or in particular cases. [...] What makes these entities something more than merely the totality of the component parts is the fact that these parts are related to one another in certain specific and recognizable ways. In the case of human communities, the more or less enduring relationships between different peoples are what we refer to when we speak of societies.

The French thinkers argued that if societies were systems, they must be made up of interrelated parts. They also thought that these parts must be related to one another and to the whole society of which they were parts, in accordance with laws analogous to the laws of nature, which in principle at least, it should be possible to discover. So the understanding, of societies, and of Society with a capital "S," like the understanding of the physical organisms with which they were either explicitly or implicitly being compared, was to be achieved by discovering the laws of social organization that operated to maintain the whole structure. This "organismic" approach to the study of human societies has some grave limitations and can be misleading. But it did point to the important truth that the customs and social institutions of human communities are somehow interconnected, and that changes in one part of the system may lead to changes in other parts. When this was understood it became possible to ask, and sometimes even to answer, questions about real human societies—questions which arose less readily so long as the "piecemeal" view of human cultures, which had hitherto been dominant, prevailed. Thus an anthropologist faced with a custom such as mother-in-law avoidance, which is found in many societies far remote from one another, was no longer content merely to record it for purposes of comparison with other apparently similar customs elsewhere. He now asked about the implications of the institution for husband-wife relations, or for the pattern of residence. This "organismic" approach reached its most sophisticated expression in the writings of the French sociologist, Émile Durkheim, who is still one of the most important influences in social anthropology (Durkheim 1923).

Our concern here is to stress that the two most important strains from which the fabric of modern social anthropology is woven are the fact-finding, empirical, graphic tradition represented by British and by much German and American anthropology and the "holistic," analytical intellectualism of French social philosophy.

Can we then, at this point, give a preliminary statement of what modern social anthropology is about? Anthropology is by definition the study of man. But no one discipline can possibly study man in all his aspects, though some anthropologists have written as though it could. On the whole, social anthropologists have concentrated on the study of man in his social aspect, that is in his relationships with other people in living communities. The multifarious dimensions of the social and cultural life of more complex, literate societies have for the most part been left to historians, economists, political scientists, sociologists, and a host of other specialist scholars.

Of course, the anthropologist is interested in people; they are the raw material he works with. As a social anthropologist however, his main concern is with what these people share with other people, the institutionalized aspects of their culture. For this reason social anthropologists are not interested in every social relationship in the societies they study; they concentrate mainly on those which are habitual, relatively enduring features of the societies in which they occur.

The emphasis today is essentially empirical and functional. Contemporary social anthropology is centrally a study of relationships between different kinds of people, and at a higher level of abstraction, of relationships between relationships. [...]

We shall find that in modern social anthropology the emphasis is contextual and relational. Recent social anthropology may claim to have contributed most significantly to this kind of contextual understanding in the Western social sciences. But anthropologists are today being increasingly associated with practical problems outside the classroom and their solutions.

The United Nations Organization (UNO) and the governments in the British Commonwealth, the United States, and elsewhere have made much use of trained social anthropologists. They have done this in various ways. First, they have added trained sociologists or social anthropologists to their permanent staffs. Thus the anthropologist becomes a civil servant. As such, his primary business is with practical problems upon which he brings to bear the techniques and special knowledge with which his professional training has equipped him. Government anthropologists have been asked to advise on such matters as labor migration, succession to political authority in particular tribes, and the likely social consequences of proposed land reforms. An anthropologist who takes such a post becomes a sort of anthropological general practitioner. [...]

A second way in which a government can make practical use of social anthropology is to employ a professional, on contract for a period of a year or two, to carry out a specific piece of research. This method can work well when a particular problem is considered sufficiently important to justify the expense of full-scale, professional study. An anthropologist, who has made a special study of religious institutions, might be hired to investigate the emergence in a particular area of a separatist movement; or an expert on political organization might be engaged to make a study in a community for which major administrative changes were proposed. [...]

A third method by which governments have availed themselves of information provided by anthropological investigations is by supporting, encouraging, or merely tolerating research by workers academically attached to universities or other research-sponsoring bodies. [...]

Anthropology and the colonial encounter

Modern Anthropology is seen by its Marxist and Third World critics as a product of colonialism which is true to the extent that anthropology and anthropologists have sometimes aided the colonial enterprise overtly or indirectly.

Ethnographic investigation and colonial enterprise have gone hand in hand from the beginning. In Bonaparte's expedition to Egypt were 150 scientists including ethnographers with pen and notebook in hand. This first contact between colonizing Europe and colonized Asia or Africa laid the foundation of ethnographic methodology for these continents. The ethnographic interest in colonized people was to culminate in the exhaustive studies of African, Asian and Oceanian society.

The Orientalist (the Western scholar of peoples and customs of the Orient) contributed to the image of the Oriental. During the colonial decades a cumulative picture of the Orient formed in Western minds. Let me cite the author of *Orientalism* for a description of the Oriental, "The Oriental is irrational, depraved (fallen), childlike, 'different.'" In contrast, "the European is rational, virtuous, mature, 'normal'" (Said 1978: 40). [...]

Not all colonial ethnography is defective, although its political assumptions are compromised. Sometimes political officers administering tribal groups were more sympathetic to their charges than some of the postcolonial native officials who succeeded them. Perhaps some of these colonial officers were themselves men of sensitivity and perception. These qualities, together with assignments to peripheral provinces of the colonial administrations, made them marginal to the great metropolitan empires. They posed questions difficult to answer in the context of colonialism.[3] Morocco for the French and India for the British were the "jewels" in the colonial crown. It is no coincidence that the best officers were assigned there. Some of them proved to be excellent ethnographers.

A study of their relationship with the cultural system that produced them, and the more traditional one that attracted the colonial officers who administered tribal groups, would be rewarding. It would tell much about the colonial power and also a great deal about the virtues and vices of tribal groups.

In an important sense anthropological writing is auto-biographical. Studies today have illustrated the psychological reasons why "Arabists"—the European traveler-scholars to Arab lands—reacted to the Arabs as they did. Their lineage, schooling, and childhood helped form their reaction. It would be instructive to be aware of the relevant biographical aspects of the anthropologist's life. We might have a more comprehensive picture of the group if we knew the relationship between the author and his subject.

Deeper studies of the famous "Arab" scholar-travelers are now being written.[4] Their relationship to Islam, for instance, obviously determined their attitudes to its adherents. We know that Doughty hated Islam, which to him symbolized everything decadent and corrupt. In contrast, Blunt almost became a Muslim, such was his fascination with Islam. Some officer-scholars were motivated by forces that lay deep in family psychology and childhood memory. For instance, it is widely recognized that T.E. Lawrence, the illegitimate son of a nobleman, attempted to live out his fantasies through his Arabian adventures. He was "getting even" with the world through the Arab legend in a distant land where he had princes and chiefs at his beck and call. The Lawrence saga is poor historiography but excellent press.

The scholar-travelers wore native clothes and spoke the native language. In their flamboyant behavior and eccentric appearance, they imagined they found acceptance far from home (Burton's moustache which had provoked adverse comment at Oxford was appreciated by tribal chiefs). Rejected in some childhood memory, they would indulge every fantasy in the East. They were not adult men playing at boys, but boys playing at men. Kings and chiefs were made and unmade by them (from Edwardes to Lawrence they prided themselves on this power) and they created grand sounding titles from exotic places for their heroes: Edwardes of Bannu, Gordon of Khartoum, Roberts of Kandahar and Lawrence of Arabia. They were not just Orientalist villains destroying native custom and trampling on native culture. The picture is more complex.

Orientalists were only partly racist; a number of them sought identity among and with tribal groups, and sometimes the former was subordinated to the latter. However, the romance was one-way only. European colonial scholarship was not politically innocent. Its aim was to understand the colonials better in order to dominate them more efficiently. [...]

Anthropological fieldwork

The work of the traditional anthropologist is to study other cultures. Through them he learns to understand his own culture, and equally important, himself. He remains essentially a seeker. In the distant village and among strange people he comes face to face with himself—a chilling prospect. In that encounter is reflected his true self. His writing too reflects the encounter. The Pukhtuns say, "What we see in ourselves, we see in the world." Perhaps anthropologists would do well to keep the Pukhto proverb in mind.

Progress in the natural sciences often involves setting up experimental situations in the laboratory, and then seeing whether what happens confirms or disproves hypotheses previously formulated. Social scientists cannot usually test their hypotheses about human institutions in quite this way. Their laboratory is society itself, and where a researcher is dealing with human beings, other considerations besides the desire for knowledge, such as the subject's general well-being, legal and moral standards, and the national interest must have primacy. For this reason it is rarely feasible in social science to set up experimental situations on the natural science model. It is even less feasible to arrange that such situations are repeated under conditions which are for all practical purposes identical, as natural scientists do. The human experience is unique and not transferable to the chemist's experimental laboratory.

Social anthropologists must test their hypotheses about social and cultural institutions and their interconnections in the course of fieldwork in societies and situations which they have no power to control. Their tools are observation, interpretation, and comparison rather than experiment. This does not mean that anthropologists can do without theory. It is as essential to anthropology as it is to other scientific disciplines.

Whether we like it or not, social anthropology has become a specialist subject. It has its own theoretical equipment, some account of which has been given in preceding sections, and it has by now a considerable body of comparative material to draw upon. No one who writes about the social institutions of a small-scale community without knowledge of contemporary theory in social anthropology and without some knowledge of the social and cultural institutions of comparable societies elsewhere, can hope to produce a scientifically adequate account. Without specialist training he cannot know the most important things to look for, the most useful questions to ask, or the best techniques for obtaining answers. [...]

Living in a hut or tent within the village, the anthropologist gradually begins to understand what is happening around him. As his knowledge of the language and his acquaintance with the community advance, things begin to make sense. An overheard conversation is understood; a pattern of behavior is fitted to a learned social relationship. With luck he now has a few friends in the community, people who are willing to take time and trouble to explain things to him, to take him around the neighborhood and to introduce him to others. From this point onward, the pace accelerates. The anthropologist gets to know most of the members of the community as separate individuals, differing in temperament and in social status (and in their degree of interest in his work). He learns their often intricate ties of kinship and marriage; he comes to understand what they think about one another, about the world they live in, and about him. He learns not only what are the appropriate questions to ask, but of whom to ask them. He begins to feel "at home" in the community. He now knows it in some respect more thoroughly than he has ever known any community, even the one he grew up in. He has made the breakthrough into another culture: as a field anthropologist, he has arrived. He has accomplished the major characteristic of anthropological "participant observation." [...]

It is easy for anthropologists who have worked among such peoples to romanticize their experience and many do. The experience is an unforgettable one. The ideal social anthropological fieldworker is adaptable, tactful, good humored, and possessed of a sense of perspective. Above all, he is patient and considerate. He is, after all, a guest (though usually an uninvited one) in the community he is studying, and he must show the same respect and courtesy to his hosts as he expects to receive from them. [...]

The intensiveness of modern fieldwork, and the social anthropologist's increasing specialization, imply that he must become more and more dependent on other workers. In the communities which he studies, there are nearly always a few people who can read and write, and most fieldworkers engage one or two assistants, sometimes more, and pay them salaries. These assistants may not only serve as permanent informants and advisers; often they can make useful local contacts as well as collecting information and carrying out surveys under the anthropologist's supervision. The social anthropologist must participate as fully as he can in the everyday life of the community he is studying; he must live in it and get to know its members as people, as nearly as possible on equal terms. [...]

No foreign anthropologist can ever be wholly assimilated to another culture; he can never quite become one with and indistinguishable from the people he is studying. Nor is it desirable that he should. "Stranger value" is an important asset. People often talk more freely to an outsider, so long as he is not too much of an outsider. Also, in a society where there are distinct social groups or classes, and especially when these are hierarchically arranged in terms of power and prestige, too close identification with one group or class may make easy contact with others difficult or impossible. [...]

Theoretical frames in Western anthropology

[...] It may be said that the anthropologist's first task is descriptive. In any empirical inquiry, we must know what the facts are before we can analyze them. Although the distinction between description and analysis is indispensable, it can be misleading, especially in the social sciences. The difference is not simply between studies which imply abstraction and those which do not. Even the most minimal descriptions include abstractions, generally unanalyzed and implicit. This is because descriptions tend to be in general terms, and general terms are the names of classes, that is, of abstractions, and not the names of things. Description does more than describe, it also explains. Theories are involved in even the simplest descriptions. Not only do they determine the kinds of facts which are selected for attention, but also they dictate the ways in which these facts shall be ordered and put together. The important question is not whether an account of a social institution (or of anything else) implies generalization and abstraction, for this it does. The critical questions are: What is the level of abstraction, and what are the kinds of theories involved? It is especially necessary to be explicit in social anthropology, for the social situations it deals with are often unfamiliar ones. Anthropologists have thus devised different models to explain society which combine theory and empirical inquiry.

Thus the American anthropologist, Robert Redfield, developed the idea of the "folk" culture, and the French social anthropologist, Claude Lévi-Strauss, has distinguished the "statistical mode" (the analyst's representation of the system being described) from the "mechanical model," the same system as its participant members regard it.

Lévi-Strauss's use of the term "statistical" is significant. "What actually happens" is susceptible to quantitative treatment in a way in which data of other kinds, such as beliefs and values, are not. Modern social anthropologists are required to do more than merely describe people's behavior qualitatively; they are also expected to support their assertions about what people do (or say they do) with some quantitative evidence. [...]

Islamic anthropology

It would appear from the above arguments that anthropology is, if not the child, a creation of the West and more specifically Western imperialism. This is not so. The work of Ibn Khaldun is reflected—with theoretical frame and supporting data—in that of some of the most influential contemporary Western theorists including Karl Marx, Max Weber, Vilfredo Pareto and Ernest Gellner. Weber's typology of leadership, Pareto's circulation of elites, and Gellner's pendulum swing theory of Muslim society betray the influence of Ibn Khaldun. It is indeed a tragedy that the science of sociology or anthropology did not develop after Ibn Khaldun. And Ibn Khaldun was not alone. There were al Biruni, Ibn Battuta and al Mas'udi, to name a few.

Of these perhaps al Biruni (973–1048) deserves the title of father of anthropology (I have explored this in "Al Beruni: The First Anthropologist" [Ahmed 1984]). If anthropology is a science based on extended participant observation of (other) cultures using the data collected—for value-neutral—dispassionate analysis employing the comparative method, then al Biruni is indeed an anthropologist of the highest contemporary standards (Ahmed 1984); Said 1979; Said and Zahid 1979). His work on (Hindu) India—*Kitab al Hind*—remains one of the most important source books for South Asia. The most perceptive of contemporary Hindu scholars, including mavericks like Nirad Chaudhri, quote him approvingly (Chaudhri 1965). So, almost a thousand years before Malinowski and Geertz, al Biruni was establishing the science of anthropology. Therefore, the study of society by Muslims, Islamic sociology or anthropology, is not a new or Western science.

We may define Islamic anthropology loosely as the study of Muslim groups by scholars drawing on the ideal universalistic principles of Islam—humanity, knowledge, tolerance—relating micro village tribal studies in particular to the larger historical and ideological frames of Islam. Islam is here understood not as theology but sociology. The definition thus does not preclude non-Muslims.

Certain conceptual points must first be clarified. What is the world view of the Muslim anthropologist? In the ideal the Muslim orders his life according to the will of God. In actuality this may not be so. Does he see society as motivated by the desire to perform the will of God or not? If so, the Muslim must strive to bring the actual into accord with the ideal.

Let us pose these questions in the context of the two major—sometimes overlapping—theoretical positions in the Western social sciences. These divisions are between the "methodological individualists" and the "methodological holists." Briefly, the individualists examine man in society as an actor maximizing and optimizing. Social interaction is seen as series of transactions in which "value gained and lost" is recorded in individual "ledgers" (Barth 1966: 4).

The "holists," on the other hand, view man as motivated by configurations of economy and society which transcend the individual. These divisions are not rigid and are made more complex by the different schools of anthropology.

Such debates must be directed to scientific inquiry in order to discover the dynamics of society. For society is dynamic and studies of social phenomena which are not directed towards clarifying it are reduced to academic exercises.

Which framework is applicable when analyzing a Muslim social actor? Does he behave as an individualist recording units of value gained and lost in a personal ledger? Or does he respond to social configurations of which he is part? With Muslims we may suggest the latter in most cases, all things being equal.

Islam teaches us to deal with the major concern of human beings which is to relate to our environment. And our relationships with people—individuals and groups—are the main features of our environment. Islam, then is a social religion. The implications for the Muslim are clear. He—or she—is part of the *ummah,* the community, to which he gives loyalty and which provides him with social identity. In the ideal, he belongs in part to his immediate group, in part to the larger *ummah.*

For the Muslim, rules of marriage, inheritance and an entire code—covering the most intimate details of human behavior—are laid down explicitly. The organization of society and the behavior of its members are predetermined. For Muslims, therefore, the dilemmas of this world are reduced. Man's mission is to reconcile society with the instructions of God. Debates between one or another school of thought thus become merely academic exercises.

Life, God has repeated, has not been created in jest. It is a struggle to better humanity, to improve the moral quality of our brief span on earth. The struggle to do so is called *jihad.*

The Muslim remains part of the *ummah,* the community. A too blatant expression of individual ambitious desire will provoke disapproval from the community. Which is not to say individuals do not break rules or behave in an entirely non-Muslim manner. But we are concerned with Muslim groups and not individuals. This social ethos is in contrast to the West where man is an individual first and last. Politics, business and even private life in the West are an expression of this individuality. It is this contrast which sometimes makes it difficult for the two civilizations to see eye to eye on certain key issues.

How do Muslims tackle the subject of the anthropology of Islam as Muslims—as believers. Ali Shariati has attempted an answer:

> Religion is, therefore, a road or a path, leading from clay to God and conveying man from vileness, stagnation and ignorance, from the lowly life of clay and satanic character, towards exaltation, motion, vision, the life of the spirit and divine character. If it succeeds in doing so, then it is religion in truth. But if it does not, then either you have chosen the wrong path, or you are making wrong use of the right path.
>
> (Shariati 1979: 94)

Anthropology, I am arguing, can assist in illuminating "the right path." But the primary problem before us is not the balancing of options but finding out what they are.

The two myths pertaining to the Muslim social world which continue to provide material to attack Muslims are the status of women (their lack of rights, their suppression and, connected to this, polygamy in the society) and the continuing tyranny, anarchy, and despotism of Muslim politics (the paperback version of Wittfogel's *Oriental Despotism* [1957] displays a picture of a mosque on its cover, Wittfogel 1981). We have seen how anthropologists often reflect the second in their depiction of Muslim political life. The first point is less well advertised, as the literature has been largely by male anthropologists who have had little access to Muslim women.

Minor religious injunctions or customs are exaggerated and ridicule Islam. For instance, Muslims are prohibited from eating pork as it is not considered *halal* or pure. Many other animals are also considered impure or *haram.* This is one of the features best known about Muslim, by non-Muslims. Yet these minor social injunctions can become major theological issues when discussing Islam. The prohibition is typically used as the subject of caricature and satire. It has become one of the symbols dividing the Western (pork eating) and Muslim (non pork-eating) world.

What methodological position would Islamic anthropology adopt to tackle these issues? One answer—and perhaps the easiest way out—is to be eclectic. But eclecticism is self-defeating, not because there is only one direction in which it is heuristically useful to move, but so many. We must choose—what Shariati calls—"the right path" (Shariati 1979).

There has been a suggestion by Muslim anthropologists that there is not one Islam but many Islams (el-Zein 1974; el-Zein 1977), a suggestion taken up by Western anthropologists (Eickelman 1981). I disagree with this position. There is only one Islam, and there can be only one Islam, but there are many Muslim societies. We must then not look for numerous "Islams" but we must attempt to place the multitude of Muslim societies within the framework of one universal Islam (Ahmed 1988). [...]

In a recent study I have suggested we examine not the macro level of society—powerful dynasties, large armies, high finances—nor the typical anthropological village but an intermediate level—the district (Ahmed 1982; Ahmed 1983). On this level three key and distinct categories of society interact: the representatives of the central government (whether army or civil), traditional leaders (based on land or genealogy) and religious leaders (usually the *mullahs*). For this purpose we may construct the Islamic district paradigm (Islam here is understood in a sociological not theological sense). In particular, roles such as that of the *mullah*, one of the least understood and least studied must be carefully researched. We have two distinct images of the *mullah*. One derives from the Western prototype, the "Mad Mullah," from Swat to Sudan. The image of a fanatic was fostered by the British as the *mullahs* stood against them when other groups in society had quietly acquiesced. The other image is that of saintly figures incapable of wrong, as suggested by Muslim writers. The truth is somewhere in between.[5] It is at this distinct level of society where we may predict and foretell the shape of things to come in Muslim society. The Islamic district paradigm will help us do so.

A perception such as that of the Orientalist anthropologist re-opens a fundamental question regarding anthropology. Is one function of anthropology to serve as a bridge between different cultural systems helping us to understand others and thereby ourselves? If so, such perceptions as that of Barth, may not be the best material for the bridge. Some third-world anthropologists would argue that it is already too late for any bridge-building exercises (see Asad 1973). However scientific the analysis, human beings are sensitive to cultural arrogance disguised as scientific jargon.

The anthropologist in some ways is an ambassador of his world to the village he is visiting. He not only interprets the native group to his world but his own world to them. If he is not conscious of his relationship he may create problems for future social scientists in that area or working with his group.

The question raises a related issue. Is good anthropology—from the point of view of the native, at least—sympathetic anthropology? Not necessarily. Anthropologists must record society as it *is* not as it *should be*. But I think it is imperative that anthropology be fair. Not only the warts on the face of society need to be emphasized. It is for this reason we may today read *The Sanusi of Cyrenaica* and find it a fair account although it was written by a colonial officer a generation ago (Evans-Pritchard 1973). Some understanding of the virtues of a people especially as anthropologists see them, along with a scientific analysis, are important to the discipline.[6]

It is worth noting that anthropology as a discipline is yet to grow in the Muslim world. Muslim anthropologists of stature are few and far between. Notable examples are Nur

Yalman of Turkey and Imtiaz Ahmed of India. Nur is almost unique in that his topic of study was a Buddhist village in Sri Lanka. He is unique in that for once in the contemporary world Islam is observing and not being observed. Imtiaz Ahmed, an Indian Muslim examines his own people. He reflects the major sociological problems confronting Indian Muslims, in particular the continuing interaction with the larger Hindu cultural system. His work discusses the growth of caste-like structures among Muslims.[7] The aim of anthropology remains to move from the specific to the general, to draw universal conclusions from specific situations.

The Muslim intellectual confronting the world today is sometimes moved to despair. He is ill-equipped to face it. His vulnerability diminishes him in his own eyes. He wanders between two worlds, one dead, the other powerless to be born. His wounds are largely self-inflicted. At the root of his intellectual malaise lies his incapacity to come to terms with Islam in the present age. [...]

Recommendations

Muslims cannot dismiss Western—or more correctly non-Muslim—scholarship out of hand. They must come to terms with it. [...] If Muslims are to object to such scholarship, they can only do so by creating their own alternative body of knowledge rather than by verbally berating Western scholarship.

Anthropology is important to the study of Muslim society. It has much to offer in helping to understand and solve contemporary social problems. For instance, I have argued that the distribution of aid to the Afghan refugees in Pakistan would benefit if anthropological expertise were available (Ahmed 1981). Sometimes the lacuna between the "actual" and the "ideal" in Muslim society is wide. A good example is the actual status of Muslim women among certain groups, which contrasts with the ideal (Ahmed and Ahmed 1981). Anthropological studies can help to compare the two positions in the hope of attempting a bridge. Take another example, ethnic tensions which are often read as expressions of political challenge to most nation states, may be minimized by a national understanding of different local cultures and their social characteristics.

Muslims are not living in a social vacuum. They are living in a world sometimes operating on different levels within their own society, and outside their society, on levels that, are sometimes hostile, sometimes neutral. They have to meet the challenge on every one of these levels. For better or for worse, Muslims are being "observed."[8] And the observations often indicate lack of understanding and are sometimes hostile (Said 1981). A generation after Said however there is good news in the emergence of Muslim anthropologists coming of age and into their own (see for example Amineh Hoti 2006).

Keeping the above in mind, it is therefore recommended that:

1 Simple, lucid sociological accounts of the life of the Prophet and early Muslim societies be prepared by Muslims. The books should address a wide audience—both Muslim and non-Muslim—and neither be too academic nor too abstruse (see above discussion).[9]
2 One major standard anthropological text book of high standard should be produced and then translated into the major languages of the Muslim world. It should be used at the BA level and include sections on each major cultural zone.
3 Anthropological monographs on each major Muslim region are produced for distribution in the Muslim world.[10] Initially, Morocco for the Maghrib, Pakistan for South Asia, and Indonesia for Southeast Asia as distinct cultural-geographical types may be selected.

These monographs should be simple, lucid, with attractive photographs and used in colleges and universities.

4 Visits of Muslim anthropologists within Muslim countries should be arranged and encouraged and joint projects initiated. For instance, the study of the Berbers and the Pukhtuns is a logical and exciting study.

5 Long-term studies should be conducted comparing the major social categories which would help us better understand and reach conclusions regarding Muslim society and its immediate contemporary problems.

6 The social categories to be examined could be peasants, tribes and cities. For the first, I recommend a village in Pakistan (preferably the most populous Province, Punjab) and an Egyptian village typically dependent on irrigated networks. For the tribes, the Berbers and the Pukhtuns would be a natural study, and for the cities, Cairo, Madinah and Lahore.

7 Practical and development-orientated social studies should be framed in order to enable us to better plan for Muslim society in the current age.

8 I recommend that the ethnographic and anthropological content from the writings of the great Muslim writers is extracted and compiled in a discrete set of volumes. In this exercise classic Islamic scholars will have to assist the anthropologist.

A great store of anthropology exists in the writing of the classic Muslim scholars. It is disguised as history in one text, as memoirs in another, and straightforward ethnography in the third. It needs to be mined.

Such academic endeavor will assist us in creating a core of Islamic anthropological literature for the future. I agree with Arab intellectuals that we must possess major journals and create "educational institutions capable of challenging places like Oxford, Harvard or UCLA" (Said 1978: 323). Otherwise Muslims will continue to be subordinated to the intellectual trends of the West.

Conclusion

By failing to predict the contemporary Islamic re-emergence or assess its importance, Western scholars of Islam and its peoples were encouraged to make one of their most spectacular mistakes in recent times. They assumed secular trends in Muslim society as a logical development after the Second World War. Such was the direction pointed out by the Orientalists a generation ago (Gibb 1980). However, the scholars of modern times seem to follow blindly in the footpaths of their predecessors and fall into the same errors. A Western scholar of Iran, for example, wrote recently that

> Although it is difficult to be certain, the trend seems to be away from physical resistance movements such as those during Muharram of 1963, and more towards ideological resistance through involvement and participation in the decision-making apparatus of the government.
>
> (Thaiss 1972: 366)

The paper concluded that:

> Religiously oriented individuals, who may oppose the government nevertheless, join its ranks in the hope that they will have the opportunity to implement policies that will be more in accord with their view that Islam is an all-encompassing system of beliefs"
>
> (Ibid).

And this from an Iran expert on the eve of the Islamic revolution that brought down the Shah and in an explicit way rejected his secular policies.

Muslim scholars trained in the West commit the same mistake. Aziz Ahmad concluded a paper on Islam in Pakistan thus: "The *ulema* having suffered a setback in 1970, Islamic Socialism, in which Islam is largely decorative and diplomatic, has for the time being at least gained a complete victory over the religious parties" (Ahmad 1972: 272). The vigor of the Islamic revival has repudiated the predictions of, and surprised, Islamic scholars. To his credit Clifford Geertz was one of the few Western writers who saw differently.[11]

Having conceded the vigor of the Islamic revival, Muslims must now plan directions for it in order to best utilize its finer and dynamic impulses related to knowledge. They must, as Shariati suggests, prepare to discover what "the right path" means today and should mean in the future.

However, the right path needs to be, by definition, broad and inclusive. Therefore, we need to be cautious in how we apply the term Islamic Anthropology. Attaching a label on something does not guarantee quality. There can no more be an Islamic Anthropology, as there can a Jewish or Hindu Anthropology. There is only good or bad anthropology—which ultimately must depend on the solidity of the fieldwork and the standard of analysis. Some of the best work on Muslim society has come from non-Muslim anthropologists.

The Islamic anthropologist would do well to remember Socrates' statement, "I am not an Athenian or a Greek, but a citizen of the World." In the end the anthropologist must transcend himself, his culture, his universe, to a position where he is able to speak to and understand those around him in terms of his special humanity and knowledge irrespective of color, caste or creed.

This sentiment is reflected in the last great address of the Holy Prophet of Islam at Arafat: "Allah has made you brethren one to another, so be not divided... An Arab has no preference over a non-Arab, nor a non-Arab over an Arab; nor is a white one to be preferred to a dark one, nor a dark one to a white one, except in righteousness."

Notes

1 Author's Note: These are excerpts from "an exploratory exercise" specifically written for Muslim scholars as part of the Islamization of Knowledge project launched three decades ago as a first step to encourage them to engage with ideas in the discipline of anthropology (Ahmed 1987). In order to proceed, I believed it was important to lay out the outline of western anthropology as accurately and correctly as possible. I therefore borrowed extensively from the introduction to the subject by John Beattie, a leading Western anthropologist (Beattie 1977); a fact I gratefully acknowledged. As a reciprocal gesture, I happily contributed the Foreword to the excellent study on Waziristan by John Beattie's son, Hugh Beattie 2001. Much here is dated, but much remains relevant to issues in Muslim scholarship.

2 From *anthropos*, Greek for man.

3 An example of a political officer who sympathized with his tribes and compared their code of behavior favorably to Western civilization was Sir Evelyn Howell (see Ahmed 1980a).

4 For an interesting psychological insight into the famous Arabist Western scholar-travelers see Tidrick 1981; for the impressions of Arab women of these "Arabists" see Pastner 1978.

5 For a political study of a *mullah* operating within traditional tribal networks in Waziristan, see Ahmed 1983.

6 Not only are some members of the First World—anthropologists and others—guilty of lack of sympathy for the Third World. The colonial mentality was never a monopoly of the West. The *kala sahib*—black sahib, one feature of Empire in South Asia—still lives. A good example of a Third World writer living in and writing for the First World is V.S. Naipaul. His characteristic features—sharp powers of observation and brilliant skill at description combined with cynicism and contempt for his subject—are displayed to the full in his book on Muslim society (Naipaul

1981). His method is what I call "First World contemporary colonial," that is, fly into the local Intercontinental hotel, pick up a taxi and drive around for a few hours or days picking up trivia before moving to the next place. In the course of his interviews, he uses the most objectionable methods such as lying—as to the Ayatullah Shirazi in Iran (Naipaul 1981: 49–53)—and repeating private conversations confided by his hosts whether Indian housewives or petty officials in Pakistan. To him these people, whose lives are sunk in personal and public chaos and irreversible poverty, appear to do little more than, hawk, fart, nose-pick, deceive (themselves), and despair. Despair—the word sounds like a death-knell—is repeated again and again in his world. His people are caricatures of a caricature. This is Naipaul's world view of the Third World. Muslims are no exception. Yet nowhere have I read an expression of personal gratitude for people who are with such limited resources so generously hospitable to him; no word of sympathy for their aspirations and struggle; no suggestion of hope for their goals. The "First World contemporary colonial" visits these people with a set objective in mind: he is extracting a new book from their lives. He cannot be distracted by humanity and its suffering (For a rebuttal of Naipaul by a Muslim scholar see Khurshid Ahmad 1982).

7 The name of Muhammad Mauroof (Professor and Chairman, Department of Anthropology, Cheyney State University, Cheyney) author of "Elements For an Islamic Anthropology" should also be mentioned (Mauroof 1981).

8 Clifford Geertz, one of the more sympathetic observers, titled his book, *Islam Observed* (Geertz 1968). The interest in Islam has affected publishing. Studies of Muslim society are now big publishing business. Publishers assess that to add "Islam" to a title is to guarantee sales. Hence titles like *Islam and Development* (Esposito 1980) have appeared recently in the market. But not only the West is guilty of commercializing Islam: Pakistan filmmakers recently produced a film with the unlikely title of "*Khuda aur Mahabbat*"—God and love—starring Pakistan's most popular actor, Muhammad Ali, and actress Babra Sharif.

9 For example, as a model, see Professor Ismail R. al Faruqi's translation of Haykal's *The Life of Muhammad* (Haykal 1976). For interesting work along these lines, see some of the recent publications of the newly formed Islamic associations like The Islamic Foundation, Leicester; the Institute of Policy Studies, Islamabad and the International Institute of Islamic Thought, Washington, D.C.

10 For an attempt at bringing together the Islamic tribes under one cover in anthropology, see Ahmed and Hart 1983.

11 Clifford Geertz writes for the benefit of his overhasty Western colleagues: "We have a while to wait yet, I think, even in Tunisia or Egypt, before we see an explicit movement for a 'religionless Islam' advancing under the banner, 'Allah is dead'" (Geertz 1968: 115).

References

Ahmad, Aziz (1972) "Activism of the Ulema in Pakistan," in Nikki R. Keddie (ed.) *Scholars, Saints, and Sufis: Muslim Religious Institutions in the Middle East since 1500*, Berkeley, CA: University of California Press.

Ahmad, Khurshid (1982) "What an Islamic Journey: Review of V.S. Naipaul: *Among the Believers: An Islamic Journey*, New York: Alfred A. Knopf, 1981," *The Muslim World Book Review*, 2: 13–22.

Ahmed, Akbar S. (1980a) "Introduction," in Evelyn Howell (ed.) *Mizh: A Monograph on Government's Relations with the Mahsud Tribe*, Karachi: Oxford University Press.

——— (1980b) *Pukhtun Economy and Society: Traditional Structure and Economic Development in a Tribal Society*, London and Boston: Routledge & Kegan Paul.

——— (1981) "Afghan Refugees, Aid and Anthropologists," *International Asian Forum: International Quarterly for Asian Studies*, 12: 77–92.

——— (1982) "Order and Conflict in Muslim Society: A Case Study from Pakistan," *Middle East Journal*, 36: 184–204.

——— (1983) *Religion and Politics in Muslim Society: Order and Conflict in Pakistan*, Cambridge: Cambridge University Press. Re-printed as *Resistance and Control in Pakistan*, London: Routledge, 2004.

——— (1984) "Al-Beruni: The First Anthropologist," *Royal Anthropological Institute Newsletter*, 60: 9–10.

——— (1987) *Toward Islamic Anthropology: Definition, Dogma and Directions*, Lahore: Vanguard Books. (Originally published 1986).

——— (1988) *Discovering Islam: Making Sense of Muslim History and Society*, London: Routledge.

——— (2010) *Journey into America: The Challenge of Islam*, Washington, DC: Brookings Press.

——— and Zeenat Ahmed (1981) "*Tor* and *Mor*: Binary and Opposing Models of Pukhtun Femalehood," in T. Scarlett Epstein (ed.) *Rural Women: Asian Case Studies*, Oxford: Pergamon.

——— and David M. Hart (ed.) (1983) *Islam in Tribal Societies: From the Atlas to the Indus*, London: Routledge and Kegan Paul.

Asad, Talal (ed.) (1973) *Anthropology and the Colonial Encounter*, London: Ithaca Press.

Barth, Frederik (1966) *Models of Social Organization*, Royal Anthropological Institute Occasional Paper 23, London: Royal Anthropological Institute.

Beattie, John (1977) *Other Cultures: Aims, Methods and Achievements in Social Anthropology*, London: Routledge and Kegan Paul.

Beattie, Hugh (2001) *Imperial Frontier: Tribe and State in Waziristan*, Abingdon: Routledge.

Chaudhri, Nirad C. (1965) *The Continent of Circe*, London: Chatto & Windus.

Durkheim, Émile (1923) *The Division of Labor in Society*, trans. George Simpson, London: G. Allen & Unwin, Ltd.

Eickelman, Dale F. (1981) *The Middle East: An Anthropological Approach* Englewood Cliffs, CT: Prentice-Hall.

El-Zein, Abdul Hamid (1974) *The Sacred Meadows: A Structural Analysis of Religious Symbolism in an East African Town*, Evanston, IL: Northwestern University Press.

——— (1977) "Beyond Ideology and Theology: The Search for the Anthropology of Islam," *Annual Review of Anthropology*, 6: 227–254.

Esposito, John L. (ed.) (1980) *Islam and Development: Religion and Sociopolitical Change*, New York: Syracuse University Press.

Evans-Pritchard, Edward E. (1973) *The Sanusi of Cyrenaica*, Oxford: Clarendon Press.

Geertz, Clifford (1968) *Islam Observed: Religious Development in Morocco and Indonesia*, New Haven, CT: Yale University Press.

Gibb, Hamilton A.R. (1980) *Muhammedanism*, 2nd edn, Oxford: Oxford University Press.

Haykal, Muhammad H. (1976) *The Life of Muhammad*, trans. Ismail R. Al-Faruqi, Indianapolis, IN: North American Islamic Trust Publications.

Hoti, Amineh (2006) *Sorrow and Joy among Muslim Women: The Pukhtuns of Northern Pakistan*, Cambridge: Cambridge University Press.

Mauroof, S. Muhammad (1981) "Elements for an Islamic Anthropology," in Ismail R. Al-Faruqi and Abdullah O. Naseef (ed.) *Social and Natural Sciences: The Islamic Perspective*, Sevenoaks: Hodder & Stoughton.

Naipaul, Vidiadhar S. (1981) *Among the Believers: An Islamic Journey*, New York: Alfred A. Knopf.

Pastner, Caroll M. (1978) "Englishmen in Arabia: Encounters with Middle Eastern Women," *Sign*, 4: 309–323.

Said, Edward W. (1978) *Orientalism*, New York: Pantheon Books.

—— (1981) *Covering Islam: How the Media and the Experts Determine how we see the Rest of the World*, New York: Pantheon Books.

Said, Hakim M. (ed.) (1979) *Al-Beruni: Commemorative Volume*, Karachi: Hamdard Academy.

—— and Ansar Zahid (1979) *Al-Beruni: His Times, Life and Works*, Karachi: Hamdard Academy.

Shariati, Ali A. (1979) *On the Sociology of Islam: Lectures*, trans. Hamid Algar, Berkeley, CA: Mizan Press.

Thaiss, Gustav (1972) "Religious Symbolism and Social Change: The Drama of Husain," in Nikki R. Keddie (ed.) *Scholars, Saints, and Sufis: Muslim Religious Institutions in the Middle East since 1500*, Berkeley, CA: University of California Press.

Tidrick, Kathryn (1981) *Heart-Beguiling Araby*, Cambridge: Cambridge University Press.

Wittfogel, Karl A. (1981) *Oriental Despotism: A Comparative Study of Total Power*, New York: Vintage Books.

16 "Islamic anthropology" and "anthropology of Islam"

Richard Tapper

Richard Tapper is Emeritus Professor of Anthropology in the University of London, where he taught at the School of Oriental and African Studies from 1967 to 2004. He conducted extended field research in Iran, Afghanistan and Turkey, with special interests in pastoral nomadism, ethnicity, tribe/state relations, the anthropology of Islam, documentary film and Iranian cinema. His recent books include: *Frontier Nomads of Iran: A Political and Social History of the Shahsevan* (1997) and *Islam and Democracy in Iran: Eshkevari and the Quest for Reform* (co-authored with Ziba Mir-Hosseini 2006). He has edited eight volumes, including *Islam in Modern Turkey: Religion, Politics, and Literature in a Secular State* (1991) and *Ayatollah Khomeini and the Modernization of Islamic Thought* (2000). Significant articles include "The Birth of the Prophet: Ritual and Gender in Turkish Islam" (co-authored with Nancy Tapper 1987). This review article questions various proposals for an Islamic anthropology as being ideological and biased. In taking a reflexive perspective, Tapper however takes up the challenge posed by these proposals and argues that the aim of an anthropology of Islam is to study how Muslims construct and present themselves as Muslims in their discourses and practices.

Anthropology and the Islamic Middle East

The anthropology of Islam, as a sub-field of the anthropology of religion, is some decades old. I understand it to be the application of the methods of cultural/social anthropology to the study of Islam as a world religion and associated sets of social institutions. There has been a variety of approaches and a number of reviews of them (notably Asad 1986; Eickelman 1981, Eickelman 1989; el-Zein 1977), and I do not intend to add another review here. I shall concentrate rather on one particular kind of approach that has recently come into prominence: so-called Islamic anthropology.

There are several contending varieties of Islamic anthropology, set out in at least four books and numerous articles published during the 1980s.[1] I shall concentrate on four works: the book by Ilyas Ba-Yunus and Farid Ahmad, which, despite its title *Islamic sociology*, is in essence a proposal for Islamic anthropology; the two main publications on the theme by Akbar Ahmed (*Toward Islamic Anthropology* and *Discovering Islam*); and the book by Merryl Wyn Davies (*Knowing one another*). Proponents differ as to whether Islamic anthropology should confine its attention to Muslim societies or should have a universal(-ist) scope; in other words, Islamic anthropology is not necessarily intended as the anthropological study of Islam, analogous to economic or political anthropology, any more than marxist or feminist anthropology means the anthropology of Marxism or feminism (Ardener 1985).[2] Rather it means, broadly, doing anthropology inspired by methods drawn in some way from Islam. What the competing versions of Islamic anthropology share is a basis in Islamic texts—they are, in other words, Islamic approaches to the study of anthropological texts, rather than anthropological approaches to the study of Islamic texts.[3]

Previous writings on Islamic anthropology have been proposals and mutual criticism by Muslims; there has been little critical comment from non-Muslim anthropologists, who have mostly either chosen to ignore Islamic anthropology or welcomed it rather patronizingly, without serious discussion, as a promising new development.[4] It should be said that most of the proposals have not apparently been addressed to anthropologists or other academics in the first place, but rather to a wider, non-academic, and primarily Muslim audience. Nonetheless, I would argue that it is important for Islamic anthropology to be seriously discussed by anthropologists and that something can be learned from such discussion whether or not it is found to be of positive value to the development of anthropological ideas generally.

The problem

It is easy to sympathize with Akbar Ahmed's *cri de coeur:*

> The Muslim intellectual confronting the world today is sometimes moved to despair. He is ill-equipped to face it, his vulnerability diminishes him in his own eyes. He wanders between two worlds, one dead, the other powerless to be born. His wounds are largely self-inflicted. At the root of his intellectual malaise lies his incapacity to come to terms with Islam in the twentieth century.
>
> (Ahmed 1986: 61)

These sentiments are (pre-)echoed in numerous Muslim publications—and indeed are common place in Third World intellectual writings. The sub-text is articulated thoughtfully and at some length by Wyn Davies and others. Given the relation between knowledge and power (knowledge brings power, and power defines knowledge), dominated groups come to resent being studied and "known" by others. Third World intellectuals, emerging from a history of Western economic, political, cultural, and academic dominance, have come to reject these dominations and the way they are linked in "Orientalist" discourses and definitions of knowledge. For Muslims, Islam and Muslim identity, long damaged or threatened by Western and materialist values, must be reasserted at all levels, including that of knowledge. The issue raised by Islamic anthropology (as by other critical anthropologies) is the relation between anthropology and its subjects (traditionally, the West studying the rest; the orientalist gaze): objectification and explanation (science) or empathy and understanding (humanity). More precisely, Islamic anthropology poses the question: can Islam (and the culture and society of Muslims) be studied and understood by non-Muslims? In other words, what is the nature and possibility of an anthropology of Islam?

A critique of Western knowledge, social science, anthropology

The proponents of Islamic anthropology offer a critique of Western (social) theory, to accompany their Islamist critique of Western society, culture, and values. Western social theory, anthropology included, is ethnocentric and tainted by its imperial history and connections. Anthropology is the child of Western colonialism; its subject-matter, assumptions, questions, and methods are dictated by imperial interests; and its practitioners come from imperial backgrounds and biases (through structures of funding, jobs, publication, readership) or Third World (Western-oriented/supported) elites. The traditional subjects of Western anthropology are the primitives. In the post-colonial era, as the number of unstudied primitives has diminished, anthropology has entered crisis and terminal decline. Since Third World countries gained independence, the peoples studied have insisted on doing their own anthropology, defining their own approaches, and studying and criticizing the cultures and theories of the West.

In his booklet for the International Institute of Islamic Thought, Ahmed's critique is confined largely to unsupported statements about "the notorious ethnocentricity of Western anthropology" (Ahmed 1986) and to the invidious polemical trick of comparing the ideals of one society (the Muslim world) with the evils of another (AIDS, drugs, and crime in the West). His prescription seems to be: if only they would become Muslim, all these problems would go away. But are there no social problems in Islamic societies?[5]

Ba-Yunus and Ahmad, writing for the Cambridge (UK)-based Islamic Academy, offer a more sustained criticism of what they see as the three major approaches in Western social theory, finding them divergent and in need of reconciliation, and all flawed by their commitment to positivism, objectivity, and scientific detachment. Structural functionalism ignores conflict and produces ethnocentric modernization-Westernization theory. Marxian and conflict-based approaches overstress economic processes and larger structures. Symbolic interactionism and "self-theory" focus vainly on the unpredictable individual. Sociology is supposedly universal, but the sociology of the Third World does not take account of Third World perceptions and social realities, for example, those of Muslims; its ethnocentrism typically underrates the role of religious experience. Further, sociology is commonly too theoretical and pretends to be value-free; rather, it should be practical and applied and acknowledge the necessity of values (Ba-Yunus and Ahmad 1985).

Wyn Davies conducts a rather broader review of Western scientific thought in general and anthropology in particular, emphasizing how anthropology lacks unity (except as regards its basis in Western civilization) and rigor. She invokes Thomas Kuhn's and Michel Foucault's contributions to the understanding of how knowledge is produced. Western paradigms of knowledge have shifted, but on a background of continuity—Fernand Braudel's *longue dureé*. The non-Europeans studied by anthropologists have had no say in how anthropological discourse has developed and how it has constructed reality. Western discourse is secular and sees religion as a human creation; this Western view, and the original Christian view of Islam, means the West cannot understand Muslim civilization. Typical reactions by Muslim apologists, she says, divert energies from the creation of a proper Muslim agenda. The central tradition of anthropology is fieldwork: participant-observation of the primitive (a fundamental concept). The point of the conventional criticism of the link with colonialism was anthropology's failure to observe and criticize the colonial center; and despite its new awareness of all these epistemological problems, modern anthropology still fails to comment effectively on Western society and international relations.

The major elements in this critique of Western theory are entirely conventional.[6] A response must begin by admitting that there is, or was, some truth in every point; but they are failings that characterize few anthropological studies of Islam and Muslim societies over the last couple of decades or so. The critics (as with other critical anthropologies) too often resort to misrepresentation and selectivity, the depiction of outdated stereotypes, and the erection of straw men. This is not the place for a point by point rebuttal, but it is worth marking some central issues, particularly those which affect the plausibility of the proposals for an Islamic anthropology to be discussed below.

Thus, Ahmed uses Beattie's 1964 *Other Cultures* as a source book for current Western anthropology (Beattie 1964),[7] while Wyn Davies, even if her version is more considered and up-to-date, can still refer to Raymond Firth's 1951 *Elements of Social Organization* as a standard text (Firth 1951). Small wonder then that they present such caricatures of a discipline "in crisis and decline," in which the only anthropologists are Westerners; in which anthropologists study only non-Western societies or only primitive societies; in which anthropology is necessarily ethnocentric, using Western categories and assumptions to study cultures to which they do not apply; in which anthropology is functionalist, arid scientism, concerned only with objective analysis and explanation, and opposed to both subjectivism and application; and in which this atheist functionalism puts religion on the same level of analysis as economics, politics, and kinship. In fact, in the last two decades anthropology has thankfully moved beyond reacting to such tired criticisms and has established new conventions of ethnographic reflexivity and theoretical self-awareness. This is not so say such conventions are unassailable in their turn, but there is no apparent awareness of them among the proponents of Islamic anthropology.

Nor are they free from the contradictions of those who both berate Orientalists for homogenizing "the Orient" (as against "the West") without recognizing cultural and other differences, and then accuse those such as anthropologists, who do recognize and study differences, of dividing in order to rule. Such native critics, moreover, usually come from an educated elite, whose authority to speak for or about all their co-nationals or co-religionists is as debatable as that of any outsider. Some Orientalists are justifiably accused of "exoticizing" their subjects, over-emphasizing the cultural distance between a Christian West and a Muslim East; yet modern Muslim radicals such as Wyn Davies appear to be doing just the same in their desire to claim the study of the Muslim world for Muslims alone.[8]

As many have pointed out, European and Middle Eastern cultures have common roots and orientations and have developed in dialogue with each other. Even if modern Western world views were molded by renaissance/enlightenment/colonial heritages, they are still very firmly grounded in the traditions of Greco-Roman philosophy and Semitic-monotheistic religions that they share with the Islamic Middle East. Differences are variations on a theme. More liberal Muslim apologists point to the role of medieval Islam in preserving and developing this heritage during the European Dark Ages, and to the important contributions of earlier Muslim scientists, ethnographers, and social theorists. Mutual misunderstandings between the Muslim world and the West through the centuries have arisen in contexts of political competition, from the Crusades to the spread of European commercial and political dominance in the nineteenth century. Despite diverging paradigm shifts in European and Muslim thought, there are still basic continuities and possibilities of dialogue and mutual understanding. Indeed, I would venture to suggest that the Muslim world as such, which inevitably shares many of its traditions with the West, cannot produce a truly radical critique of it. This would appear to be evident if we contrast both traditions with more distant Indian, Chinese, or Japanese, or radically different Native American, Australian, or African traditions, where any elements of common heritage with the West are comparatively recent and shallow-rooted.

Defining Islamic anthropology

Even if a distinctive radical critique of Western society and social science is not to be expected—and certainly has not yet appeared—from Islamic quarters, Muslims from Middle Eastern countries are among the non-Westerners best able to respond with alternatives to Western representations of their cultures. Their economic and political power is now often such that they can at least set the terms of what is to be studied and by whom. Their dilemma is: whose terms, with what questions? If anthropology, then should it be through categories derived from Western training and literature, or from Muslim or other indigenous sources? Or should anthropology be rejected altogether as a Western product?

One important Muslim response since the 1960s has been the attempt to *Islamize* the social sciences, including anthropology, that is, to appropriate them for Islam, by insisting that Muslim societies can only be studied by Islamic anthropology or by those conversant with Islamic textual sources.

There are common themes to the several different versions of Islamic anthropology: for example, the proposal to construct the ideal society, and social theory, from a particular reading of Koran/sunna values and principles; the affirmation of the eternal validity of this Islam; and the presentation of Islam as the middle way between Western extremes. But there are radically different and conflicting assumptions among the versions.

Ba-Yunus and Ahmad propose Islamic sociology as an activist Islamic program for sociologists:

> seeking the principles of human nature, human behaviour and human organization [it] must not be allowed to become an end in itself. It has to be applied for the sake of the promotion of Islam within individuals, around them in their societies, and between and among societies.
>
> (Ba-Yunus and Ahmad 1985: 35–36)

The approach must be based on Koranic assumptions: that God created nature; that Man is made of opposites, with free-will, the ability to learn, and superiority to the rest of nature; that society is based on the family, divine laws, an instituted authority, and economic activity; and that history is a dialectical process of conflict and consensus resulting in the Prophet. It also should be a comprehensive sociological approach which will encompass and reconcile the extremes of other contemporary approaches. Further,

> Islamic sociology would be comparative and critical, i.e., it must accept, as a preoccupation, the task of comparing human societies—Muslim as well as non-Muslim—with [the ideal] and discovering the degrees of departure of these societies from this model.
>
> (Ba-Yunus and Ahmad 1985: xiii)

The ideal picture of Islamic social structure must be constructed, with Islam as ideology, culture, or way of life, a process of deliberate obedience to God's laws, the only alternative to capitalist democracy and socialism, one that is midway between, but not a mixture. Islamic ethnography then examines actual variations; the reference point is the ideal Islamic middle path of customs relating to family and marriage (contract, choice, sex, polygyny, gender, tribes), economy (property, wealth, market, inheritance, gambling, interest, poor tax, nationalization), and polity (state, authority, justice, consultation). Capitalism, democracy, and socialism as social systems and associated social theories failed because they had no mechanism of commitment; commitment in Islam is ensured by prayer and fasting rituals. The overall picture is of an openly ideological Islamic sociology; theory and comparison (of present Muslim societies, and also of/with present Western societies, ideologies, and sociologies) refer to an ideal Islamic society, and practice concerns how to achieve it.

For Akbar Ahmed, Islamic anthropology is

> the study of Muslim groups by scholars committed to the universalistic principles of Islam—humanity, knowledge, tolerance—relating micro village tribal studies in particular to the larger historical and ideological frames of Islam. Islam is here understood not as theology but sociology. The definition thus does not preclude non-Muslims.
>
> (Ahmed 1986: 56)

Wyn Davies' proposals are, to me, the most articulate, sustained and radical. For her, Islamic anthropology is

> the study of mankind in society from the premises and according to the conceptual orientations of Islam. ... [It is] a social science, concerned with studying mankind in its social communal relations in the diversity of social and cultural settings that exist around the world today and have existed in the past. The focus of its attention is human action, its diversity of form and institutionalization; it seeks to understand the principles that order, organize and give it meaning.
>
> (Wyn Davies 1988: 82, 113)

The Western anthropology of Islam is ahistorical: it sees Islam as an abstracted ideal and ignores literary traditions and spiritual hierarchy; but one object of Islamic anthropology is to produce alternative categories and concepts and then enter a dialogue with Western anthropology. What are the relevant Islamic concepts, their history, and their context? *Tawhid* (unity) is central, and dichotomy alien. Drawing from the Sunna (*hadith*, *fiqh*, *shariah*), Wyn Davies proposes *ulema* (the learned) and *ummah* (community, society) as central elements. Man is *nafs* (living entity), with *fitrah* (natural, God-given disposition), *khilafah* (status of vice-regentship), and *din* (religion as way of life). God created human diversity, with two referents: *shariah* (laws) and *minhaj* (way of life). The *shariah* defines parameters within which many ways of life are possible. The Islamic frame is universal; European ethnography failed to come to terms with diversity from the start, and created the notion of "primitive" (Wyn Davies 1988). The Islamic perspective cannot start with despising other ways. There is no room for "otherness," nor for either relativist or rationalist extremes, but it calls for a distinctive synthesis between them. Concepts and values to form the basis of Islamic anthropology must be worked out carefully in order to avoid submission to the intellectual premises of Western scholarship:

> Unless we are clear about the context in which the categories of Islamic anthropology and social analysis are to be operated and investigated, a discussion of the categories themselves will have little significance and there will be plenty of space for mental inertia and force of habit to regard what is offered as merely a gloss upon conventional Western anthropology. It is not just the categories but the entire way of thinking about them and manipulating them that must be Islamic.
>
> (Wyn Davies 1988: 128)

The first concept is *ummah*: communities at all levels. Every *ummah* has a *din* (religion as way of life). The purpose of investigation is to ascertain the function of community:

> as a system that facilitates the harmonious embodiment of moral values as a constructive environment for right action, or hinders or deforms the purposive intent of moral values within a way of life and therefore impairs the ability or opportunity for right action.
>
> (Wyn Davies 1988:129)

Next come *shariah*, *minhaj*, and institutionalization—all these are the foundation of ethnography in Islamic anthropology. Wyn Davies outlines the practice of an Islamic ethnographer in the field: to seek to identify the *shariah* and *minhaj*, and then a variety of values; then to ask practical questions relating to development and response to crisis. Participant observation and other methods will be used, along with dialogue with the subjects, study of their history, and classification and comparison. Islamic anthropology's concepts of man and of community with their entailments make it "a distinct and different discourse of knowledge from western anthropology" (Wyn Davies 1988: 142). Distinct also are its boundaries with other disciplines; unlike Western anthropology, Islamic anthropology is basic social science.

Wyn Davies comments on earlier proponents of Islamic anthropology. Nadia Abu-Zahra is commended for bringing the interpretation of the Koran to the interpretation of Muslims' actual behavior. Akbar Ahmed is castigated for including Nur Yalman's study of Sri Lanka under the rubric of Islamic anthropology. Talal Asad is praised for criticizing the conceptual premises of Western anthropology and their application to Islam, and for noting the different focuses of knowledge: Islam on the moral person, the West on the nature of society. Others merely provide an addendum to Western anthropology, as a response to colonialism, but accept the basic Western approach as universal; or promote the indigenous social scientist with his/her special access and insights (Soraya Altorki, Akbar Ahmed). Even the more radical have only partial approaches; Ali Shariati, for example, uses familiar terminology in a new way. Wyn Davies herself starts with a new set of terms, to avoid confusion, and to deny the presumed universality of dominant Western terms and their usage. But the new terms should not be geared only to Muslims and Muslim society, like those of Ba-Yunus and Ahmad. For Islamic anthropology, she proposes borrowing Ibn Khaldun's term *'ilm al-'umran*, with complex historical and geographical resonances which she examines in detail.

Problems with Islamic anthropology

In my view, there is little to object to in the methods of research proposed for Islamic anthropology; they replicate traditional anthropological practice. The main difficulties for an anthropological reading of the Islamic anthropology program have to do with its acknowledged ideological commitment, and, in the case of Wyn Davies, her proposed terminology; and the question why, if the program has in fact nothing substantively new to offer, the proponents feel it necessary to indulge in this particular exercise of appropriation and relabeling.

Thus Ba-Yunus and Ahmad's program for ethnographic research is an entirely conventional—indeed outdated—investigation of the topics of kinship and family, economics, and politics. It seems, however, that religion and ritual, the fourth topic of the old structural-functionalist quartet, are not to receive the same attention: religion (Islam or other) is equated with the system as a whole, or at least the rules and ideals that define it (Ba-Yunus and Ahmad 1985). One has to add that the Koranic assumptions on which their Islamic sociology is to be based, parallel closely those of Christian creationism.

As for Ahmed's Islamic anthropology, while the teachings and ideals he outlines as relevant to the study of society are admirable, though highly generalized, when he comes to specific prescriptions for a new view of Muslim societies, he offers a taxonomy whose debt to Islamic ideals is far from clear, plus a set of "models" whose inadequacies I have demonstrated elsewhere.[9] In his objections to Western writings on Islam he lays himself open to criticism in his own terms. In effect, the Islamic anthropology he proposes constitutes another "Orientalism"; the only difference from the original is that his ideological commitment is made explicit. It is significant that in his view some of the best Islamic anthropology is produced by Western non-Muslims (Gellner, Geertz, Gaborieau) and one Japanese (Nakamura); those Muslims he praises for their Islamic anthropology include the modern Yalman as well as the medieval al-Biruni and Ibn Khaldun,[10] but as Wyn Davies points out, the former's Islamic background (if any) is not evident in his work, while the latter two hardly constitute anthropologists in the conventional sense accepted by Ahmed.

Wyn Davies herself is to be congratulated for recognizing the epistemological problems with anthropology and its heritage, and for attempting to make her own assumptions explicit. Her own proposals are disappointing, however, consisting largely of a new terminology of Koranic/Islamic Arabic terms which simply translate standard English social science analytical categories. The guiding concepts and assumptions listed, for example, *tawhid*, the unity of God extended to the unity of mankind (surely a basic assumption of all anthropology), are ideals and eternal values. The central analytical concepts *ummah*, *din*, *shariah*, *minhaj* translate directly into community, culture, norms, customs; the new concept of "consonance" is hardly clarified or elaborated. The concepts of "society" or "relationship," for which there are plentiful Arabic (Koranic?) translations, are oddly omitted. Following her own logic, in fact, Islamic anthropology should be conducted only in Arabic, and avoid not only all Western terms but all ways of relating them in syntax and semantics (Wyn Davies 1988).

Despite claims for the distinctiveness of an Islamic anthropology, the methods Wyn Davies proposes, though more contemporary than those of Ba-Yunus and Ahmad, are strictly conventional to modern anthropology: use of participant observation, dialogue, text, statistics, indigenous language, etc. Islamic anthropology is a holistic (that is, functionalist) study of all levels, including international relations and boundaries (that is, ethnicity). Disciplinary boundaries with sociology and history are to be torn down, but significantly there is no mention of anthropology's relations with psychology and philosophy. The reader is subjected to long passages of preaching on the superiority of the Islamic approach, which to a non-Muslim anthropologist appears as a closed and circular system; and there is no mention of problematic areas such as gender or Koranic punishments. The concept of ideal type is acknowledged as a basic principle, with the problem that comparison of empirical cases with the ideal is to be based in ideology. Islamic anthropology slips from a concern with variation within the *shariah*, to allowance and tolerance for all ways, but in effect we are offered Islamic ethnocentrism disguised as universalist relativism. The empirical study of values is even vitiated by predetermining the categories of analysis to be used, rather than attempting to understand subjects in their own terms. In her book Wyn Davies adduces no cases where these approaches and methods have been tested in practice.

Thus there seem to be three broad approaches, though proponents do not necessarily stick to one of them. In the first, Western anthropology is to be adopted, but under the guidance of Muslim ideals; who, though, is to decide what those ideals are? The second is associated with Muslim apologists who point out that Islam too has produced anthropologists and that the roots of the best Western concepts and ideals are to be found in the Koran and the Sunna. The third approach is radical: Islamic anthropology should reject Western anthropology and start afresh with a distinctive Islamic approach; the Sunna is the basis for a distinct set of (purified) values, ideals, and analytical concepts.

In all versions Islamic anthropology sets up an ideal and compares societies with it. But there is disagreement on whether Islamic anthropology can be the study of Islamic societies only or of all societies. For some, Islamic anthropology is explicitly a way of analyzing permissible Islamic forms of society and culture, and of comparing non-Islamic forms with them.

A prime argument of Islamic anthropology is that, because of its basis in Islam, it is logically, theoretically, and morally superior to other approaches. Sometimes it seems to be no more than a slogan; or at best a *vade mecum* for anthropologists who happen to be Muslim, to guide their values and choices in practical and ethical decisions, for example, in the issues such as ethnocentrism versus cultural relativism, the application of anthropology in practice and development, and the various dilemmas to be faced during field research. Being addressed to Muslims, can Islamic anthropology be seriously discussed by those not committed to it? It would be too easy to dismiss Islamic anthropology as incapable of a serious contribution to the field of anthropology and not worth study except as a distinct indigenous perception.[11] However, it is difficult for non-Muslims to comment except to point to flaws and similarities with what it is supposed to replace.

Any ideological version of anthropology clearly plays on the ambiguity between the notions of anthropology as a view, whether personal or ideological, of human nature, society, and values, and as a comparative and theoretical academic discipline whose practitioners attempt to detach themselves from or reflect upon personal or ideological biases. In many ways Islam (as religion, theology, sociology, theodicy, philosophy) is an anthropology; it can appeal only to those who accept its basic tenets. Is the notion of Islamic anthropology thus a tautology or a contradiction in terms?

The proposals for an Islamic anthropology which we have outlined have the virtue of being explicit in their values and ideological commitments. Anthropologies which claim to be non-ideological are constantly subject, internally and externally—at least in the current postmodernist atmosphere—to debate over basic assumptions. Any ideological anthropology, by contrast, tends to be dogmatic and allows little debate, except internally; it can neither ask the most interesting questions asked by other anthropologies, nor can it itself ask any interesting new questions—it can only provide answers. At present these answers fall short of a thorough, unequivocally Islamic anthropological study of either Muslim or non-Muslim society which can be demonstrated as a significant advance on non-Muslim anthropological studies of Islamic societies.

Islamic anthropology is no more easily dismissed than any other "-ism"; it should be taken seriously because it addresses a wide audience, avows its ideological base, and invites critical discussion. At the same time the motivations of its proponents should be questioned. As noted above, the authors are primarily addressing a Muslim non-academic audience, presumably even less familiar with recent developments in anthropology than they seem to be themselves. They would appear to be mainly interested in furthering their own positions, as anthropologists, within the world of Islamic intellectuals, and not in promoting their appropriation of the discipline for Islam within the world of anthropologists. It has to be said that, if they did attempt the latter, their arguments would carry no weight. They can no more claim universality for a non-believer than can any other explicitly ideological anthropology or "-ism."

Islamic intellectuals with different origins and backgrounds (Pakistani, Turkish, Iranian, Arab, British) have produced different anthropologies and emphasized different Islamic concepts. What of non-intellectual Muslims—is their Islam and their approach to the analysis of society less valid as an anthropology? Wyn Davies' Koranic prescription for Islamic anthropology—"know one another" (Wyn Davies 1988), seeing fieldwork as a dialogue and exchange of understandings—is to be preferred to other approaches in which the tyranny of a Great Tradition approach predominates.

The challenge of Islamic anthropology to non-Muslim anthropologists is essentially a continuing warning to keep under review basic concepts and assumptions and any tendencies to "-ism" or ideology; but it does also raise the perennial question of whether a critical anthropology, that can stand outside all these "-isms," is possible.

The anthropology of Islam: a personal view

Some of the most incisive critiques of Western anthropological writings on Islam, the best and most persuasive reflections and suggestions, have come from scholars originating in the Muslim world but trained in the West, such as Abdul Hamid el-Zein 1977 and Talal Asad 1986. Whether or not they are Muslim, they have not intruded their beliefs into their anthropology, any more than did Evans-Pritchard or the other "Oxford Catholics." The anthropological study of religion is not theology. It is not necessarily against either theology or religion. But good anthropology does have subversive potential; it asks awkward questions about the political and economic interests and the personal connections of powerful ideologues at all levels of society; it also asks how ideologies are constructed and how language and other systems of symbols are manipulated. The best anthropological studies of Islam, by Muslims as well as non-Muslims, have resisted the tyranny of those (whether Orientalist outsiders, or center-based *ulama*) who propose a scripturalist (Great Tradition) approach to the culture and religion of the periphery; they aim to understand how life (Islam) is lived and perceived by ordinary Muslims, and to appreciate local customs and cultures (systems of symbols and their meanings) as worthy of study and recognition in their social contexts, rather than as "pre-Islamic survivals" or as error and deviation from a scriptural (Great Tradition) norm.

The anthropology of Islam involves translating and humanizing ordinary believers' cultures, as well as analyzing the production and use of Islamic "texts." The elements of the Great Tradition (formal duties and beliefs, texts, and the officials and others who produce them) have also been subject to study in their social and cultural contexts, allowing the relevance of political manipulations, economic constraints, and tribal/kinship/ethnic allegiances and rivalries. All these matters can be investigated only by extended and intensive participant observation; and it is debatable whether they are best studied by an *insider* (one who is from the community studied, who shares its culture and religion, but may not have the skills or indeed the inclination to bring to the surface what is taken for granted); by a *compatriot* (one who may be separated from the subjects by language, culture, class, and associations, but who may be reluctant to acknowledge this distance); or by a complete *outsider* (one who may have to start from scratch in language and the rest, and take much longer, but who at least brings a fresh eye and "stranger value" to the field).

The anthropology of Islam studies how Muslims (individuals, groups, societies, nations) present/construct themselves as Muslims (as a major constituent of their identity), for example, through markers of various kinds: diet (proscription of pork and alcohol), myth and genealogy (holy descent), reverence for the prophet *(mevluds* in Turkey), conflict (Shi'a/Sunni), and discursive traditions.[12] Some of these markers are clearly textual, though all of them could be seen as texts in a broad sense, and hence matter for discussion within the context of anthropological approaches to the study of Islamic texts. This observation clearly also re-introduces the problem of what is the "Islam" that anthropologists study, on which there has been a continuing debate. Is it a unity or a diversity? Is it what professing Muslims say and do? Is it a Koran-based set of ideals, identified by theologians or by sociologists—that is, a Great Tradition? Is the anthropology of Islam the study of Muslim societies; or of Islam as a religion (texts, practice, beliefs, history)? These may be hackneyed problems, but they certainly have not yet been resolved, and I would maintain that consideration of the recent writings on Islamic anthropology throws some fresh light on them.[13]

Acknowledgments

This is a revised version of a paper delivered at the Middle East Studies Association Annual Meetings in Washington, November 1991, and at a public lecture for the Centre of Near and Middle Eastern Studies, School of Oriental and African Studies, London in December 1991; a later version was presented to a panel at the American Anthropological Association meetings in Washington in November 1993. It has benefited from comments received on those and other occasions, especially from Dale Eickelman, the panel discussant at MESA, from readings by Ziba Mir-Hosseini and Ali Tayfun Atay, and from two anonymous readers for *Anthropological Quarterly*. Faults and misconceptions remain mine. I am grateful to Daniel Martin Varisco and Greg Starrett for inviting me to participate in the MESA and AAA panels respectively, and to SOAS for giving me time and financial support for my visits to Washington.

Notes

1 The books are Ba-Yunus and Ahmad 1985; Ahmed 1986; Ahmed 1988a; Wyn Davies 1988. Articles include Mauroof 1981; Elkholy 1984; Ahmed 1984; Wyn Davies 1985; Ma'ruf 1986; Ma'ruf 1987; Momin 1989; see also some chapters in Shariati 1979.

2 See Shirley Ardener's distinction between "feminist anthropology" and the "anthropology of women" (Ardener 1985).

3 To avoid confusion, Islamic anthropology should perhaps be called "Islam*ist*" anthropology, by analogy with, for instance, Marxist anthropology, and with the contemporary usage of "Islamist" for political and intellectual movements inspired by Islam. A related issue, which will not be dealt with here, is whether anthropologists studying Muslim societies must be capable of reading and understanding the Arabic texts on which Islam is based. Those who insist on this necessity are sometimes guilty of a common Arab and Arabist presumption that Islam(ic) = Arab(ic). Its opponents also point to the irrelevance of studying Arabic texts for the study of that still large majority of Muslims who cannot read or understand those texts themselves.

4 See for example Hart 1988; Young 1988; and favourable reviews cited by Ahmed 1988b. Exceptions include Ma'ruf 1987; Sulani 1988; Eickelman 1990.

5 See Tapper 1988; and the exchange of letters with Ahmed in Ahmed and Tapper 1989. In his foreword to the booklet the late President of the Institute, Ismail al-Faruqi, outdoes Ahmed in his misrepresentation of "Western anthropology." In his later book (Ahmed 1988a) Ahmed does recognize that all is not well with Islamdom either.

6 See Hymes 1972; Asad 1973; Diamond 1974; Said 1978.

7 Otherwise, his representation of Western anthropology consists of dropping some arbitrarily chosen names in a manner which indicates he has either not read their works or not understood them; see reviews by Ma'ruf 1987; Tapper 1988; Momin 1989.

8 For comments on the critique of Orientalism, see, for example, Eickelman 1989: 22–44; 153, 374, 392–395.

9 Reviews in Tapper 1981 and Tapper 1985. For comments on these reviews, see Street 1990.

10 See also Mauroof 1981.

11 As Ahmed observed of Crone and Cook 1977. "For Muslims it is easy to dismiss the book as nonsense. I disagree. With its academic pretension (written by Professors of London University and

published by Cambridge University Press) Islamic scholars would do well to prepare a reply. If not, their silence will be taken as an incapacity to prepare a suitable answer" (Ahmed 1986: 51).

12 See Asad 1986. One virtue of Ahmed's "theory of history" is his suggestion always to look at the "other" which each leader/group/movement faces (and in terms of which it defines and redefines itself): the Ottomans and Christian Europe, Shi'i Safavids and their Sunni rivals, Pakistan and India, though he refrains from proceeding with Islam and Christianity; Judaism and the others; modern Islamic fundamentalists and the West, nineteenth-century nationalists versus the imperialists (Ahmed 1986). See also Tapper 1984 and Tapper and Tapper 1987.

13 I wrote this article with the hope of engaging proponents of Islamic anthropology in the debate which they professed to desire. Some of the responses I have had to an earlier version of the article have unfortunately confirmed my fears that it would be both misread and misrepresented, and that serious academic debate might not be possible.

References

Ahmed, Akbar S. (1984) "Al-Beruni: The First Anthropologist," *Royal Anthropological Institute Newsletter*, 60: 9–10.

——— (1986) *Toward Islamic Anthropology: Definition, Dogma and Directions*, Ann Arbor, MI: New Era Publications.

——— (1988a) *Discovering Islam: Making Sense of Muslim History and Society*, London: Routledge.

——— (1988b) "Response to Sulani (1988) with Reply by Sulani," *Muslim World Book Review* 9: 64–66.

Ahmed, Akbar S., and Richard Tapper (1989) "Islamic Anthropology," *Man*, 24: 682–684.

Ardener, Shirley (1985) "The Social Anthropology of Women and Feminist Anthropology," *Anthropology Today*, 1: 24–26.

Asad, Talal (1986) *The Idea of an Anthropology of Islam*, Washington, DC: Georgetown University, Center for Contemporary Arab Studies.

——— (ed.) (1973) *Anthropology and the Colonial Encounter*, London: Ithaca Press.

Ba-Yunus, Ilyas, and Farid Ahmad (1985) *Islamic Sociology: An Introduction*, London: Hodder & Stoughton.

Beattie, John (1964) *Other Cultures: Aims, Methods and Achievements in Social Anthropology*, London: Cohen & West.

Crone, Patricia, and Michael A. Cook (1977) *Hagarism : The Making of the Islamic World*, New York: Cambridge University Press.

Diamond, Stanley (1974) *In Search of the Primitive: A Critique of Civilization*, New Brunswick, NJ: Transaction Books.

Eickelman, Dale F. (1981) *The Middle East: An Anthropological Approach*, Englewood Cliffs, NJ: Prentice-Hall.

——— (1989) *The Middle East: An Anthropological Approach*, 2nd edn, Englewood Cliffs, NJ: Prentice Hall.

——— (1990), "Review of Merryl Wyn Davies: *Knowing One Another: Shaping an Islamic Anthropology*, London: Mansell, 1988.," *American Anthropologist*, 92: 240–241.

El-Zein, Abdul Hamid (1977) "Beyond Ideology and Theology: The Search for the Anthropology of Islam," *Annual Review of Anthropology*, 6: 227–254.

Elkholy, Abdo A. (1984) "Towards an Islamic Anthropology," *Muslim Education Quarterly*, 1: 78–94.

Firth, Raymond (1951) *Elements of Social Organization*, London: Watts.

Hart, David M. (1988) "Review of Akbar S. Ahmed: *Toward Islamic Anthropology: Definition, Dogma and Directions*, Herndon: International Institute of Islāmic Thought, 1986," *Bulletin of Middle East Studies Association*, 15: 1–2.

Hymes, Dell H. (1972) *Reinventing Anthropology*, New York: Vintage Books.

Ma'ruf, A. Mohammad (1986) "Towards an Islamic Critique of Anthropological Evolutionism," *American Journal of Islamic Social Sciences*, 3: 89–107.

——— (1987) "The Rescuing of Muslim Anthropological Thought," *American Journal of Islamic Social Sciences*, 4: 305–320.

Mauroof, S. Muhammad (1981) "Elements for an Islamic Anthropology," in Ismail R. Al-Faruqi and Abdullah O. Naseef (eds) *Social and Natural Sciences: The Islamic Perspective*, Sevenoaks: Hodder & Stoughton.

Momin, Abdur-Rahman (1989) "Islamization of Anthropological Knowledge," *American Journal of Islamic Social Sciences*, 6: 143–153.

Said, Edward W. (1978) *Orientalism*, New York: Pantheon Books.

Shariati, Ali A. (1979) *On the Sociology of Islam: Lectures*, trans. Hamid Algar, Berkeley,CA: Mizan Press.

Street, Brian V. (1990) "Orientalist Discourses in the Anthropology of Iran, Afghanistan and Pakistan," in Richard Fardon (ed.) *Localizing Strategies: Regional Traditions in Ethnographic Writing*, Edinburgh: Scottish Academic Press.

Sulani, Abu Lilia (1988) "Review of Akbar S. Ahmed: *Discovering Islam: Making Sense of Muslim History and Society*, London: Routledge & Kegan Paul Ltd., 1988," *Muslim World Book Review*, 8: 12–15.

Tapper, Richard (1981) "Review of Akbar S. Ahmed: *Pukhtun Economy and Society: Traditional Structure and Economic Development in a Tribal Society*, London and Boston: Routledge & Kegan Paul, 1980," *Asian Affairs*, 12: 328–330.

——— (1984) "Holier than Thou: Islam in Three Tribal Societies," in Akbar S. Ahmed and David M. Hart (eds) *Islam in Tribal Societies: From the Atlas to the Indus*, London: Routledge & Kegan Paul.

——— (1985) "Review of Akbar S. Ahmed: *Religion and Politics in Muslim Society: Order and Conflict in Pakistan*, Cambridge: Cambridge University Press, 1983," *Man*, 20: 562–563.

——— (1988) "Review of Akbar S. Ahmed: *Toward Islamic Anthropology: Definition, Dogma and Directions*, Ann Arbor: New Era Publications, 1986," *Man*, 23: 567–568.

Tapper, Nancy, and Richard Tapper (1987) "The Birth of the Prophet: Ritual and Gender in Turkish Islam," *Man*, 22: 69–92.

Wyn Davies, Merryl (1985) "Towards an Islamic Alternative to Western Anthropology," *Inquiry*, June: 45–51.

——— (1988) *Knowing one Another: Shaping an Islamic Anthropology*, London and New York: Mansell.

Young, William C. (1988) "Review of Akbar S. Ahmed: *Toward Islamic Anthropology: Definition, Dogma and Directions*, Ann Arbor: New Era Publications, 1986," *American Journal of Islamic Social Sciences*, 5: 289–291.

Representing Islam

17 Covering Islam

How the media and the experts determine how we see the rest of the world

Edward Said

Edward Said (1 November 1935–25 September 2003) received his PhD degree in English Literature from Harvard University in 1964. He was a distinguished professor with Columbia University. His was most well-known for his work *Orientalism* (1978), his activism surrounding the Palestinian cause and support for a State of Palestine and being one of the founding members of postcolonial criticism which still influences Middle Eastern studies. His publications include *Orientalism* (1978); *The Question of Palestine* (1979); *Nationalism, Colonialism and Literature* (1990); *From Oslo to Iraq and the Road Map* (2004) as well as the film *In Search of Palestine* for the BBC. He received multiple honorary degrees and awards for his work in literature including the Lannan Literary Award for Lifetime Achievement as well as Harvard's Bowdoin Prize. He was the first American to be awarded the Sultan Owais Distinguished Culture Prize.The excerpts taken from the third and concluding chapter *Covering Islam* (1981) dwell on the insights from his work on *Orientalism* and question the reliability of and political agenda of media coverages of the 1979 Islamic Revolution in Iran. He scrutinizes the epistemological assumptions implied in various academic attempts to interpret Islam. Said also inquires the political implications of anthropological and other scholarly approaches to the study of contemporary Islam. By employing a critical epistemology, he argues that everyone working on the interpretation of cultures in general and Islam in particular will face the choice whether to commit oneself to the service of power and ideology or to critical scrutiny and moral sense.

The politics of interpreting Islam: orthodox and antithetical knowledge

Given the present circumstances, with neither "Islam" nor "the West" at peace with each other or with themselves, it may seem exceptionally futile to ask whether, for members of one culture, knowledge of other cultures is really possible. Seek knowledge even as far as China, runs a well-known Islamic precept, and at least since the Greeks it has been a common practice in the West to assert that so long as knowledge pertains to what is human and natural, knowledge must be sought. But the actual result of this search, so far as thinkers in the West are concerned, has usually been believed to be flawed. Even Bacon, whose *Advancement of Learning* is considered to have inaugurated modern Western thought in its most enthusiastic, self-encouraging modes, in effect expresses all sorts of doubts that the various impediments to knowledge (the Idols) can ever really be removed (Bacon 1915). Bacon's respectful disciple Vico says explicitly that human knowledge is only what human beings have made; external reality, then, is no more than the "modifications of the human mind" (Vico 1968: 96). The prospects for objective knowledge of what is distant and alien diminish still further after Nietzsche.

As against this skeptical and pessimistic current, students of Islam in the West (and, though I shall not discuss them, students of the West within the Islamic world) have generally tended to be disquietingly optimistic and confident. Early modern Orientalists in Europe seemed to have had little doubt that the study of the Orient, of which the Islamic world was a part, was the royal road to universal knowledge. [...]

Ernest Renan prefaced his discussion of "Mahomet et les origines de l'islamisme" with remarks on the possibilities opening up before what he called "la science critique." Geologists, historians, and linguists, Renan said, can get at "primitive"—that is, basic and original—natural objects by examining their traces delicately and patiently: Islam is a particularly valuable phenomenon because its birth was comparatively recent and unoriginal. Therefore, he concluded, to study Islam is to study something about which one can acquire both a certain and a scientific knowledge (Renan 1851).

Perhaps because of this happy attitude, the history of Islamic Orientalism is relatively free from skeptical currents and until quite recently has been almost entirely free from methodological self-questioning. Most students of Islam in the West have not doubted that despite the limitations of their time and place, a genuinely objective knowledge of Islam, or of some aspect of Islamic life, is achievable. On the other hand, few modern scholars would be as explicitly arrogant as Renan in their views of what Islam is: no professional scholar, for instance, would candidly say like Renan that Islam is knowable because it represents a fundamental case of arrested human development. Yet I have not been able to find any contemporary example of the Islamic scholar for whom the enterprise itself was a source of doubt. In part, I think, the guild tradition of Islamic studies, which has been handed down genealogically for about two centuries, has both protected and confirmed individual scholars in what they did, regardless of the methodological perils and innovations challenging scholars in most other humanistic fields.

A representative instance of what I mean is a recent essay, "The State of Middle Eastern Studies," published in the summer 1979 issue of the *American Scholar* by a well-known British scholar of Islam, now resident and working in the United States. Taken as a whole the essay is the product of a mind going over routine things in a lazy, not particularly interesting way (Lewis 1979). What still strikes the non-specialist, however, aside from the surprising indifference of this writer to intellectual issues, is the account of Orientalism's supposed cultural pedigree. [...]

Employing little more than unsupported assertion this writing directly contravenes everything that has ever been written either by a fair number of Orientalists themselves, or by historians of Europe from the Renaissance to the present, or by students of the history of interpretation, from Augustine onwards. Even if we leave aside "the new and totally different" and therefore (by assumption) pure intellectual curiosity—which no one else who has tried to read and interpret a text has ever been fortunate to possess—there is much too much to be accepted on faith here. From reading such cultural and colonial historians as Donald Lach or J.H. Parry, one would conclude that European interest in alien cultures was based on actual encounters with those cultures usually as a result of trade, conquest, or accident (Lach and Flaumenhaft 1965; Lach 1965; Parry 1949; Parry 1963; Panikkar 1959; Abu-Lughod 1963; Miyoshi 1979). "Interest" derives from need, and need rests on empirically stimulated things working and existing together—appetite, fear, curiosity, and so on—which have always been in play wherever and whenever human beings have lived.

Besides, how does one interpret another culture unless prior circumstances have made that culture available for interpretation in the first place? And these circumstances, so far as the European interest in alien cultures is concerned, have always been commercial, colonial, or military expansion, conquest, empire. Even when Orientalist scholars in nineteenth-century German universities studied Sanskrit, codified the *hadith,* or explained the caliphate, they relied less on the fiction of pure curiosity than on the universities themselves, the libraries, other scholars, the social rewards that made their careers possible. Only Dr. Pangloss or a member of Swift's Academy of Projectors at Lagado in *Gulliver's Travels* would locate the drive for acquiring enormous European empires and the knowledge that went with them, principally in "the gratification of new intellectual curiosity." Small wonder, then, that benighted non-European natives have viewed the scholars' "intellectual curiosity" (Lewis 1979) with such suspicion, for when was a Western scholar ever in a non-Western country except by dint, however symbolic and indirect, of Western power over that country?[1] It is an indication of *this* Orientalist's peculiar ignorance and conceit that he seems unaware of the debate raging within the field of anthropology over the complicity between imperialism and ethnology; even so mandarin a figure as Lévi-Strauss has expressed misgivings, if not regrets, about imperialism being a constitutive aspect of ethnological field work.

If we dismiss out of hand the protestations about pure curiosity, we will still conclude, I believe, that the whole argument being advanced about Middle East studies is actually a defense of their essentially unflawed capacity—historically and culturally—for telling the truth about distant and alien societies. Later in the same essay this point is further elaborated with reference to the dangers of "politicizing" the field, which, it is alleged, only some scholars and some departments have managed to avoid. Politics here seems associated with narrow partisanship, as if the real scholar is above petty squabbles, being preoccupied only with ideas, eternal values, and high principles; significantly, no examples are given. The interesting point about this entire essay, nevertheless, is how it calls for science and scientific procedures in name only. When it comes to *what* the truth of nonpolitical Middle East studies is, or could be, the author simply says nothing. In other words, the attitudes, the postures, the rhetoric—in fine, the ideology—of scholarship is what counts. Its content is simply not spelled out, and what is worse, there is a deliberate attempt to conceal the connections between scholarship and what we might call worldliness, for the sake of maintaining the fiction of nonpartisan and unpolitical scholarly truth.

This tells us more about the author than it does about the field he purportedly is writing about, an irony that has dogged all modern European or Western attempts to write about non-Western societies. Not that all other scholars have been aware of the difficulty. In 1973 the Middle East Studies Association (MESA), in collaboration with the Ford Foundation, commissioned a team of experts to survey the entire field in order to assess its current state, its needs, its prospects, and its problems (Paul 1978).[2] The result was a large, densely written volume called *The Study* of *the Middle East: Research and Scholarship in the Humanities and the Social Sciences,* edited by Leonard Binder and published in 1976. Since the book is a collective work it is inevitably uneven in quality, but one is struck throughout by the general air of crisis and urgency, something totally missing from the essay in the *American Scholar.* For this group of scholars, no less distinguished than their British colleague, Middle East studies is an embattled field: there is not enough attention devoted to it, not enough money, not enough scholars. (Ironically, one member of MESA's Research and Training Committee, which first conceived the study, had written a study of the Middle East studies field a mere handful of years earlier for the United States government, in which he had derogated the need for specialized studies on Islam or the Arabs: this was a field, he said, that was culturally and politically of only secondary importance to the United States (Said 1978: 288–290). But underlying all the problems they mention is one which Leonard Binder treats candidly in his introduction. [...]

He grants at once that every scholar has "value orientations" that come into play when scholarship is produced. But then, he says, "the normative orientations of the disciplines" reduce the distracting effect of personal "ad hoc judgments" (Binder 1976: 21). Binder neither explains how "the disciplines" do things, nor does he specify what it is about "the disciplines" that so easily transforms human judgments into Olympian analyses. As if somehow to deal with these questions, he tacks on a statement at the end of his argument that is unnecessarily opaque and totally discontinuous with what has come before it: The disciplines, he says, "also present us with methods for exploring those moral issues which arise in the context of the area." Which moral issues? What methods? What context of which area? No explanation is given. His conclusion instead is of such utterly bewildering seriousness that one is left with a reassuring sense of confidence in "the disciplines"—and no sense at all of what "the disciplines" are really about.

Even when the coarse political pressures impinging upon Middle East studies are acknowledged, there is a disquieting tendency to spirit those pressures away and reestablish the canonical authority of Orientalist discourse. It bears repeating that that authority comes directly from a power within Western culture allowing students of the Orient or Islam to make statements about Islam and the Orient that, for a great many years, have been virtually unchallengeable. For who except the Orientalists spoke and continue to speak for the Orient? Neither the nineteenth-century Orientalist nor, in the twentieth century, a scholar like Leonard Binder has doubted that "the field"—and not, it must be noted, the Orient itself or its people (except as objects or informants)—has always supplied Western culture with all that it needed to know about the Orient; consequently anyone who spoke the discipline's language, deployed its concepts, managed its techniques, and acquired its credentials would be able to get beyond prejudice and immediate circumstances in order to make scientific statements. And that sense of self-sufficient, self-correcting, self-endorsing power gave and still gives Orientalism its remarkably unself-conscious rhetoric. According to Binder, the disciplines, not the people of the Orient, state the normative issues in general terms; the disciplines, not the desires of the people of that area nor the morality of everyday life, "present us with methods for exploring those moral issues which arise in the context of the area" (Binder 1976: 21).

On the one hand, therefore, "the disciplines" are institutions more than they are activities; on the other hand, they regulate and normalize what they study (which in a sense they have also created) far more readily than they analyze themselves or reflect on what they do. The net result, I think, could only by a kind of tautological indulgence be described as full knowledge of another culture. True, there have been important achievements in the study of Islam: texts have been established and positivistic descriptions of classical Islam have been made very precise. But so far as the *human* dimension of contemporary Islam or the predicament of any interpretative activity is concerned, neither has been greatly illuminated or helped by "the disciplines" of contemporary Middle East studies.

Virtually nothing about the study of Islam today is "free" and undetermined by urgent contemporary pressures. This is very far from the unpolitical objectivity alleged by many Orientalist scholars about their work; and it is almost as far both from the mechanical determinism of vulgar materialists, who see all intellectual and cultural activity as determined in advance by economic forces, and from the happy confidence of specialists who put all their faith in the technical efficiency of "disciplines." Somewhere between those extremes the interpreter's "interests" work themselves out and are reflected out into the culture at large.

But here, too, there is less diversity and freedom than we would like to believe. For what is it that makes a topic of interest out of what might otherwise be an academic or antiquarian concern if not power and will, both of which in Western society (as in all others in differing degrees) tend to be organized, to be capable of certain kinds of implementation, to exercise a redoubtable institutional authority of their own over and above narrow and pragmatic immediacy? A simple instance will make the point quickly [...].

For the general public in America and Europe today, Islam is "news" of a particularly unpleasant sort. The media, the government, the geopolitical strategists, and—although they are marginal to the culture at large—the academic experts on Islam are all in concert: Islam is a threat to Western civilization. Now this is by no means the same as saying that only derogatory or racist caricatures of Islam are to be found in the West. I do not say that, nor would I agree with anyone who did. What I am saying is that negative images of Islam continue to be very much more prevalent than any others, and that such images correspond not to what Islam "is" (given that "Islam" is not a natural fact but a composite structure created to a certain extent by Muslims and the West in the ways I have tried to describe), but to what prominent sectors of a particular society take it to be. Those sectors have the power and the will to propagate *that* particular image of Islam, and this image therefore becomes more prevalent, more present, than all others. [...]

The difference is that Islamic programs have yet to be "revised": they are still dominated by outmoded, impossibly vague concepts (like "Islam" itself) and an intellectual idiom that are out of touch with what has gone on generally in the human sciences and in the society as a whole. It is still possible to say things about Islam that are simply unacceptable for Judaism, for other Asians, or for blacks, and it is still possible to write studies of Islamic history and society that blithely ignore every major advance in interpretative theory since Nietzsche, Marx, and Freud.

The result is that very little of what goes on in the study of Islam has much to say to scholars interested in the methodological problems of general historiography, say, or in textual analysis. [...] Precisely this marginality, this willed irrelevance for the general culture, of Islamic studies makes it possible for scholars to go on doing what they have been doing, and for the media to take over the dissemination of racist caricatures of the Islamic peoples. Since the middle 1980s, however, studies of political Islam—most of them aggressive studies of fundamentalism, terrorism, and antimodernism as principal aspects of Islam—have flooded the market. Most of them draw on a handful of scholars (like Bernard Lewis) to mobilize popular opinion against the "threat" of Islam. In this way the scholarly constituency perpetuates itself, while the clientele for Islam as news continues to get the massive doses of Islamic punishment, gratuitous violence, terrorism, and harem capers it has been fed for decades.

When the experts venture into the public eye it is as experts, brought in because an emergency has caught "the West" unprepared. Their pronouncements are neither cushioned nor refined by any residual cultural feeling for Islam, as in Britain or France. They are viewed as technicians with "a solid set of 'how-tos'" (the phrase is Dwight MacDonald's) (MacDonald 1962: 360–392) to present to the anxious public. [...]

The market for expertise is so attractive and lucrative that work done on the Middle East is directed almost exclusively at it. This is one reason that in none of the established journals (nor for that matter in recent books by established scholars) is there any attention paid to the basic questions *Why* Middle East and Islamic studies? and *For whom* are they being transacted? The obliteration of the methodological consciousness is absolutely coterminous with the presence of the market, for news as well as whole clienteles of security-conscious consumers (governments, corporations, foundations): one simply does not ask why one does what one does if there is an appreciative, or at least a potentially receptive, clientele. Worse yet, the scholar stops thinking in terms of the region and the people about whom studies are being conducted. Islam, if it is "Islam" that is being studied, is not an interlocutor but in a sense a commodity. The overall result is a kind of institutional bad faith. The scholarly honor and integrity of the field are upheld against critical outsiders, scholarly rhetoric is willfully arrogant about denying political partisanship, and scholarly self-congratulation fortifies present practices (principally in popular journalism) indefinitely.

What I have been describing is an essentially lonely enterprise, which means in this case that the scholar works reactively in answer to what various interests seem to require of him or her; he or she is guided more by a guild orthodoxy than by the exigencies of genuine interpretation, and, above all, the general culture ghettoizes his or her work, rendering it marginal except during times of crisis. Neither of the two necessary conditions for knowing another culture—uncoercive contact with an alien culture through real exchange, and self-consciousness about the interpretative project itself—is present, and this absence enforces the solitude, the provinciality, and the circularity of covering Islam. Significantly, these things also make it evident that covering Islam from the United States, the last superpower, is not interpretation in the genuine sense but an assertion of power. The media say what they wish about Islam because they can, with the result that Islamic fundamentalism and terrorism and "good" Muslims (in Bosnia, for instance) dominate the scene indiscriminately; little else is covered because anything falling outside the consensus definition of what is important is considered irrelevant to United States interests and to the media's definition of a good story. The academic community, on the other hand, responds to what it construes as national and corporate needs, with the result that suitable Islamic topics are hewn out of an enormous mass of Islamic details, and these topics (extremism, violence, and so forth) define both Islam and the proper study of Islam so as to exclude everything not fitting neatly between them. Even when on occasion the government or one of the university Middle East departments or one of the foundations organizes a conference to deal with the future of Middle East studies (which is usually a euphemism for "What are we going to do about the Islamic world?"), the same battery of concepts and goals keeps turning up. Little is changed.

A great deal is staked on this repetition, not least a fairly well run system of patronage. The senior experts in the field, whether from the government, the corporation world, or the university, tend to have connections with one another and with compliant donors. A young scholar depends on this network for his or her subventions, to say nothing of employment and the possibility of publication in the established journals. To venture unfriendly critiques of the recognized scholars or of their work, in this field more than in the fields of general history or literature, is to risk too much. Book reviews as a result are insipid and mainly complimentary; criticism is uniformly couched in the most pedantic language possible, and nothing is ever said about methodology or assumptions. The most curious omission—and the most routine—is the analysis of the connection between scholarship and the various forms of power in the society for which this scholarship is produced. And the moment a voice is heard that challenges the conspiracy of silence, ideology and ethnic origins become the main topic: He(or she) is a Marxist; or, he (or she) is a Palestinian (or an Iranian, or a Muslim, or a Syrian)—and we know what *they're* like.[3] As for the sources themselves, they are always treated as if they were inert; thus in discussing a contemporary Islamic society or a movement or a figure, the scholar refers to what is being discussed mainly as *evidence*, rarely as something entitled to its own integrity or to its right, in a sense, to reply. Interestingly, there has never been any systematic attempt by Western experts on Islam to deal methodologically with Islamic writing on Islam: Is it scholarship? Is it evidence? Is it neither?

Yet despite this rather arid state of affairs, or perhaps even because of it, some knowledge of value about Islam is produced, and some independent minds manage to get through the desert. In the main, however, the over-all marginality, the overall *intellectual* incoherence (as opposed to guild consensus), the overall interpretative bankruptcy of most—though by no means all—writing on Islam can be traced to the old-boy corporation-government-university network dominating the whole enterprise. [...] For why else could so peculiar a structure of knowledge about Islam develop and thrive, so intertwined, well established, untroubled by one failure after another?

The most effective way of understanding the precise quality of this vision, which has the force of unquestioned faith, is to compare it once again with the situation obtaining in Britain and France, those two predecessors of the United States in the Islamic world. In both countries there has always been a cadre of Islamic experts, of course, with a longstanding advisory role in formulating—and even executing—government as well as commercial policy. But in both instances there was an immediate task at hand: the administering of rule in colonies. This was the case until the end of World War II. The Islamic world was viewed as a discrete series of problems, and knowledge about those problems was on the whole positivistic as well as directly engaged. Theories and abstractions about the Islamic mind, in France about the *mission civilisatrice,* in Britain about self-rule for subject peoples, intervened here and there in the conduct of policy, but always after the policy was in place and on the ground, so to speak. Discourse about Islam played the role essentially of justifying the national (or even a private economic) interest in the Islamic world. This is why today in France and Britain great scholars of Islam are public figures whose *raison d'etre,* even now that the colonial empires have been dissolved, is to maintain a French or a British interest in the Islamic world. For a number of other reasons such scholars on the whole tend to be humanists, not social scientists, and their support in the general culture comes less from the postindustrial cult of expertise (which exists in both countries) than from broad intellectual and moral currents in the society. Rodinson in France is a great philologist who is also a well-known Marxist; the late Hourani in England was a famous historian and a man whose work represents an evident liberalism (Said 1980: 386–393). Such persons are now disappearing, however, and in both France and England, American-style social scientists or specialized antiquarians are likely to replace them in the future.

Similar scholars in the United States are known only as Middle East or Islamic experts; they belong to the class of experts, and their domain, insofar as they are concerned with modern societies in the Islamic world, can be regarded as the intellectual equivalent of crisis management. Much of their status derives from the notion that for the United States the Islamic world is a strategic area, with all sorts of *possible* (if not always actual) problems. During their many decades of administering Islamic colonies, both Britain and France naturally produced a class of colonial experts, but this class did not in turn produce an adjunct to it equivalent to the network of the Middle East studies-government-corporate alliance that exists in the United States. Professors of Arabic or Persian or Islamic institutions did their work in British and French universities; they were called on for advice and even participation by the colonial departments and by private business enterprises; they occasionally held congresses; but they do not seem to have created an independent structure of their own, sustained and even maintained by the private business sector or directly by foundations and the government.

Knowledge and coverage of the Islamic world, therefore, are defined in the United States by geopolitics and economic interests on—for the individual—an impossibly massive scale, aided and abetted by a structure of knowledge production that is almost as vast and unmanageable. What is the student of Arabian or Trucial States tribes to do about the interposition between him or her and those tribes of the oil company's presence, about the active talk and promotion of rapid-deployment forces (see the *Newsweek* cover story "Defending the Oilfields: The U.S. Military Buildup," on 14 July 1980) for the Gulf area, about the whole apparatus of Middle East "hands" at the State Department, the corporations and foundations, the array of senior Orientalists professors? Of what sort can knowledge of another culture actually be when it is so hemmed in by the hypothetical urgencies of "the crescent of crisis" on the one hand and by the thriving institutional affiliations between scholarship, business, and the government on the other? [...]

All of these things—politics, pressures, markets—make themselves felt in various ways. The need for expertise about the contemporary Middle East produces many courses, many students, and a marked emphasis upon accepting and maintaining the instrumental perspectives of knowledge that are both lucrative and immediately applicable. Another result is that methodological investigations simply do not occur: a student wishing to make a career in Middle East studies will first of all dread the long and arid years necessary for obtaining a PhD (with no certainty that he or she will get a teaching job as a result); then he or she will acquire an MA or an international-studies diploma in a subject attractive to the biggest employers (the government, the oil companies, the international investment houses, contracting firms); finally, the work will tend to be done as quickly as possible in the form of a case study. All this isolates study of Islam or the Middle East from other intellectual and moral currents in the scholarly community. The media will seem like a more promising stage upon which to display expertise than, for instance, a general intellectual journal, and in the media, as habitués know, you are either a partisan (an extremely limiting thing) or you are an expert, called on to make judgments about Shi'ism and anti-Americanism. The role of expert furthers one's career obviously enough, unless one has already done well in business or in the government.

This may seem like a parody of how knowledge gets produced, but it fairly describes the extreme narrowing of focus and the disastrous thinning of substance in knowledge of Islam. Above all, it explains why it is that far from challenging the vulgar stereotypes circulated in the media. The academic experts on Islam are as a body neutralized in their isolated, immediately functional role as status symbols of relevant authority on Islam, and also dependent on the whole system constituting and legitimating their function within it; and it is this system which the media, in their reliance upon stereotypes based on fear and ignorance, reflect.

If what I have been describing seems intellectually restrictive—as indeed it is—it does not prevent the production of a huge amount of material on the Middle East, on Islam, and indeed on other parts of the Third World. In other words, we have to do with what Foucault, in another connection, has called "an incitement to discourse" (Foucault 1978: 34). Very different from a simple interventionary censorship, the intellectual regulation of discourse about distant and alien cultures positively and affirmatively encourages more of itself. This is why it has persisted despite changes taking place in the world, and this is why it has continued to draw recruits to its service.

All in all, present coverage of Islam and of non-Western societies in effect canonizes certain notions, texts, and authorities. The idea that Islam is medieval and dangerous, as well as hostile and threatening to "us," for example, has acquired a place both in the culture, and in the polity that is very well defined: Authorities can be cited for it readily, references can be made to it, arguments about particular instances of Islam can be adduced from it—by anyone, not just by experts or by journalists. And in turn such an idea furnishes a kind of *a priori* touchstone to be taken account of by anyone wishing to discuss or say something about Islam. From being something out there, Islam—or rather, the material invariably associated with it—is turned into an orthodoxy of *this* society. It enters the cultural canon, and this makes the task of changing it very difficult indeed.

So much for the orthodox coverage of Islam, coverage whose affiliations with power give it strength, durability, and above all, *presence.* Yet there is another view of Islam circulating which belongs to the category of what might be called *antithetical knowledge* (Bloom 1973).[4]

By antithetical knowledge I mean the kind of knowledge produced by people who quite consciously consider themselves to be writing in opposition to the prevailing orthodoxy. As we shall see, they do so for varying reasons and in different situations, but all of these people have a pronounced sense that how and for what reason they study Islam are questions that require deliberation and explicitness. In these antithetical interpreters, the methodological silence of Orientalism, which has usually been overlaid by layers of optimistic confidence in value-free objectivity, is replaced by urgent discussion of the political meanings of scholarship. [...]

What is most important, in my opinion, [...] is that [...] knowledge is essentially an actively sought out and contested thing, not merely a passive recitation of facts and "accepted" views. The struggle between this view, as it bears upon other cultures and beyond that into wide political questions, and the specialized institutional knowledge fostered by the dominant powers of advanced Western society is an epochal matter. It far transcends the question whether a view is pro- or anti-Islamic, or whether one is a patriot or a traitor. As our world grows more tightly knit together, the control of scarce resources, strategic areas, and large populations will seem more desirable and more necessary. Carefully fostered fears of anarchy and disorder will very likely produce conformity of views and, with reference to the "outside" world, greater distrust: this is as true of the Islamic world as it is of the West. At such a time—which has already begun—the production and diffusion of knowledge will play an absolutely crucial role. Yet until knowledge is understood in human and political terms as something to be won to the service of coexistence and community, not of particular races, nations, classes, or religions, the future augurs badly.

Knowledge and interpretation

All knowledge that is about human society, and not about the natural world, is historical knowledge, and therefore rests upon judgment and interpretation. This is not to say that facts or data are nonexistent, but that facts get their importance from what is made of them in interpretation. [...] For interpretations depend very much on who the interpreter is, who he or she is addressing, what his or her purpose is in interpreting, at what historical moment the interpretation takes place. In this sense, all interpretations are what might be called *situational:* they always occur in a situation whose bearing on the interpretation is *affiliative.*[5] It is related to what other interpreters have said, either by confirming them, or by disputing them, or by continuing them. No interpretation is without precedents or without some connection to other interpretations. [...]

Knowledge of other cultures, then, is especially subject to "unscientific" imprecision and to the circumstances of interpretation. Nevertheless, we can say tentatively that knowledge of another culture is possible, and it is important to add, desirable, if two conditions are fulfilled—which, incidentally, are precisely the two conditions that today's Middle East or Islamic studies by and large do not fulfill. One, the student must feel that he or she is answerable to and in uncoercive contact with the culture and the people being studied. As I said earlier, most of what the West knew about the non-Western world it knew in the framework of colonialism; the European scholar therefore approached his subject from a general position of dominance, and what he said *about* this subject was said with little reference to what anyone but other European scholars had said. For the many reasons I have enumerated earlier in this book and in *Orientalism,* knowledge of Islam and of Islamic peoples has generally proceeded not only from dominance and confrontation but also from cultural antipathy (Said 1978). Today Islam is defined negatively as that with which the West is radically at odds, and this tension establishes a framework radically limiting knowledge of Islam. So long as this framework stands, Islam, as a vitally lived experience for Muslims, cannot be known. This, unfortunately, is particularly true in the United States, and only slightly less true in Europe.

The second condition complements and fulfills the first. Knowledge of the social world, as opposed to knowledge of nature, is at bottom what I have been calling interpretation: it acquires the status of knowledge by various means, some of them intellectual, many of them social and even political. Interpretation is first of all a form of making: that is, it depends on the willed intentional activity of the human mind, molding and forming the objects of its attention with care and study. Such an activity takes place perforce in a specific time and place and is engaged in by a specifically located individual, with a specific background, in a specific situation, for a particular series of ends. Therefore the interpretation of texts, which is what the knowledge of other cultures is principally based on, neither takes place in a clinically secure laboratory nor pretends to objective results. It is a social activity and inextricably tied to the situation out of which it arose in the first place, which then either gives it the status of knowledge or rejects it as unsuitable for that status. No interpretation can neglect this situation, and no interpretation is complete without an interpretation of the situation. […]

A great effort has to be made to pierce the barriers that exist between one situation, the situation of the interpreter, and another, the situation that existed when and where the text was produced. It is precisely this conscious willed effort of overcoming distances and cultural barriers that makes knowledge of other societies and cultures possible—and at the same time limits that knowledge. At that moment, the interpreter understands himself or herself in his or her human situation and the text in relation to *its* situation, the human situation out of which it came. This can occur only as the result of self-awareness animating an awareness of what is distant and alien but human nonetheless. It scarcely needs to be said that this whole process has very little to do either with "the new and totally different knowledge" (Lewis 1979: 366) alluded to by the conventional Orientalist, or with Professor Binder's self-correcting "disciplines" (Binder 1976).

One thing more needs to be said in this rather abstract description of the interpretative process at the end of which knowledge—by no means a stable thing—is arrived at. There is never interpretation, understanding, and then knowledge where there is no *interest.* This may seem like the most pedestrian truism, but it is exactly this fairly obvious truth that is usually ignored or denied. […]

Therefore, the first thing to be aware of in reading a text produced in an alien culture is its distance, the main condition of its distance (in both time and space) being quite literally, although not exclusively, the presence of the interpreter in his or her time and place. As we saw, the orthodox Orientalist or "area studies" approach is to equate distance with authority, to incorporate the foreignness of a distant culture into the authoritative rhetoric of a scholarly discourse, which has the social status of knowledge, with no acknowledgment of what that foreignness exacted from the interpreter and no acknowledgment of what structure of power made the interpreter's job possible. I mean quite simply that, almost without exception, no writer on Islam in the West today reckons explicitly with the fact that "Islam" is considered a hostile culture, or that anything said about Islam by a professional scholar is within the sphere of influence of corporations, the media, and the government, all of which in turn play a very large role in making interpretations and, subsequently, knowledge of Islam desirable and "in the national interest." [...]

As an aspect of interpretation, "interest" can be glossed a good deal further and much more concretely. No one simply happens upon Islam, Islamic culture, or Islamic society. For the citizen of a Western industrial state today, Islam is encountered by virtue either of the political oil crisis, or of fundamentalism and terrorism, or of intense media attention, or of the longstanding tradition of expert—that is, Orientalist—commentary on Islam in the West. Take the case of a young historian who wishes to specialize in modern Middle Eastern history. He or she comes to study that subject with all three factors in play, all of them molding and shaping the situation in which "the facts"—the supposedly raw data—are apprehended. In addition, there are the individual's own history, sensibility, and intellectual gifts to be figured in. Taken together these constitute a significant measure of his or her interest in the subject: sheer curiosity is tempered by such things as the promise of consulting work for the State Department, the military, or oil companies, a wish to appear at conferences, on television, on lecture platforms, and to become a famous scholar, a desire to "prove" that Islam is a wonderful (or for that matter, a terrible) cultural system, an ambition to serve as a bridge of understanding between this culture and that, a desire to know. The texts, the professors, the scholarly tradition, the specific moment, add their imprint to what this young historian is going to study. In the end there are other things to be considered too. If one has studied the history of nineteenth-century Syrian land tenure, for instance, it is extremely likely that even the driest and most "objective" treatment of the subject will have some contemporary policy relevance, particularly for a government official who is anxious to understand the dynamics of traditional authority (which is connected to land ownership) as a counterweight to Baath party power in contemporary Syria.

But if, in the first place, some effort is made to have uncoercive contact with a distant culture, and secondly, if the interpreter is consciously aware of the interpretative situation in which he or she is to be found (that is, if the interpreter understands that knowledge of another culture is not absolute but is relative to the interpretative situation in which that knowledge gets produced), then it is more than likely that the interpreter will feel the orthodox view of Islam and of other "alien" cultures to be an acutely limited one. By comparison, antithetical knowledge of Islam seems to go a reasonable distance toward overcoming the limitations of orthodox views. Precisely because the antithetical scholars reject the notion that knowledge of Islam ought to be subservient to the government's immediate policy interests, or that it should simply feed into the media's image of Islam as supplying the world with terrifying militancy and violence, they highlight the complicity between knowledge and power. And in doing so they seek to establish other relationships with Islam than those ordained by the imperatives of power. Looking for alternative relationships means looking for other interpretative situations; hence, a far more scrupulous methodological sense is developed.

In the end, though, there is never any simple escape from what some critics have called the interpretative circle. Knowledge of the social world, in short, is *always* no better than the interpretations on which it is based. All our knowledge of so complex and elusive a phenomenon as Islam comes about through texts, images, experiences that are not direct embodiments of Islam (which is after all apprehended only through instances of it) but representations or interpretations of it. In other words, all knowledge of other cultures, societies, or religions comes about through an admixture of indirect evidence with the individual scholar's personal situation, which includes time, place, personal gifts, historical situation, as well as the overall political circumstances. What makes such knowledge accurate or inaccurate, bad, better, or worse, has to do mainly with the needs of the society in which that knowledge is produced. There is, of course, a level of simple factuality without which no knowledge can occur: after all, how can one "know" Islam in Morocco without knowing Arabic, Berber, and something about the country and its society? But beyond that, knowledge of Moroccan Islam is not a mere matter of correspondence between there and here, an inert object and its beholder, but an interaction of the two (usually) for a purpose *here:* for example, a learned article, a lecture, an appearance on television, advice to the policymaker. Insofar as the purpose is fulfilled, knowledge is considered to have been produced. There are other uses for knowledge (including even the use of uselessness), but the main ones tend to be very functional or instrumental.

My thesis […] has been that the canonical, orthodox coverage of Islam that we find in the academy, in the government, and in the media is all interrelated and has been *more* diffused, has seemed *more* persuasive and influential, in the West than any other "coverage" or interpretation. The success of this coverage can be attributed to the political influence of those people and institutions producing it rather than necessarily to truth or accuracy. I have also argued that this coverage has served purposes only tangentially related to actual knowledge of Islam itself. The result has been the triumph not just of a particular *knowledge* of Islam but rather of a particular *interpretation* which, however, has neither been unchallenged nor impervious to the kinds of questions asked by unorthodox, inquiring minds. […]

Except for the purposes of conquest, "Islam" is not what it is generally said to be in the West today. Immediately, then, we must provide an alternative: if "Islam" tells us far less than it ought to, if it covers up more than it covers, where—or rather, how—are we to look for information that encourages neither new dreams of power nor old fears and prejudices? […] [U]nderlying every interpretation of other cultures—especially of Islam—is the choice facing the individual scholar or intellectual: whether to put intellect at the service of power or at the service of criticism, community, dialogue, and moral sense. This choice must be the first act of interpretation today, and it must result in a decision, not simply a postponement. If the history of knowledge about Islam in the West has been too closely tied to conquest and domination, the time has come for these ties to be severed completely. About this one cannot be too emphatic. For otherwise we will not only face protracted tension and perhaps even war, but we will offer the Muslim world, its various societies and states, the prospect of many wars, unimaginable suffering, and disastrous upheavals, not the least of which would be the victory of an "Islam" fully ready to play the role prepared for it by reaction, orthodoxy, and desperation. By even the most sanguine of standards, this is not a pleasant possibility.

Notes

1 There are numerous examples of this, from the career of William Jones, to the Napoleonic expedition to Egypt, to a whole series of nineteenth-century scholar-traveler-agent types: See Said 1978: *passim*. See also the revelations about Snouck-Hurgronje in note 6, Introduction.

2 See the penetrating review of the work by Turner 1978: 20–22. Following Turner's review, in the same issue of *MERIP Reports*, James Paul estimates the cost of the MESA volume at $85.50 per page (Paul 1978: 22).

3 For an instance of how ethnic origins are cited as "credentials" by a typical Middle East studies expert, see Hurewitz 1980.

4 The phrase is partly Harold Bloom's, although of course he uses it in a very different context and calls it "antithetical criticism": see his book Bloom 1973: 93–96.
5 I have discussed the notion of *affiliation* in Said 1979.

References

Abu-Lughod, Ibrahim A. (1963) *Arab Rediscovery of Europe*, Princeton, NJ: Princeton University Press.
Bacon, Francis (1915) *Of the Advancement of Learning*, trans. George W. Kitchin, London: J.M. Dent & Sons.
Binder, Leonard (1976) "Area Studies: A Critical Assessment," in Leonard Binder (ed.) *The Study of the Middle East: Research and Scholarship in the Humanities and the Social Sciences: A Project of the Research and Training Committee of the Middle East Studies Association*, New York: Wiley.
Bloom, Harold (1973) *The Anxiety of Influence: A Theory of Poetry*, New York: Oxford University Press.
Foucault, Michel (1978) *The History of Sexuality*, trans. Robert Hurley, New York: Pantheon Books.
Hurewitz, Jacob C. (1980) "Another View on Iran and the Press," *Columbia Journalism Review*, 19: 19–21.
Lach, Donald F. (1965) *Asia in the Making of Europe*, Chicago, IL: University of Chicago Press.
——— and Carol Flaumenhaft (1965) *Asia on the Eve of Europe's Expansion*, Englewood Cliffs NJ: Prentice-Hall.
Lewis, Bernard (1979) "The State of Middle East Studies," *American Scholar*, 48: 366–367.
MacDonald, Dwight (1962) "Howtoism," in Dwight MacDonald (ed.) *Against the American Grain*, New York: Random House.
Miyoshi, Masao (1979) *As We Saw Them: The First Japanese Embassy to the United States (1860)*, Berkeley, CT: University of California Press.
Panikkar, Kavalam M. (1959) *Asia and Western Dominance*, London: Allen & Unwin.
Parry, John H. (1949) *Europe and a Wider World, 1415–1715*, London and New York: Hutchinson's University Library.
——— (1963) *The Age of Reconnaissance*, Cleveland, OH: World Pub. Co.
Paul, James (1978) "Editor's Note," *MERIP Reports*, 68: 22.
Renan, Ernest (1851) "Mahomet et les origines de l'islamisme," *Revue des deux mondes*, 12: 1063–1101.
Said, Edward W. (1978) *Orientalism*, New York: Pantheon Books.
——— (1979) "Reflections of Recent American 'Left' Literary Criticism," *Boundary*, 28: 26–29.
——— (1980) "Reply," *Columbia Journalism Review*, 19: 68–69.
Turner, Bryan S. (1978) "Review of Leonard Binder (ed.): *The Study of the Middle East: Research and Scholarship in the Humanities and the Social Sciences*, New York: Wiley, 1976," *MERIP Reports*, 68: 20–22.
Vico, Giambattista (1968) *The New Science*, trans. Thomas G. Bergin and Max H. Fisch, Ithaca, NY: Cornell University Press.

18 Islam obscured

The rhetoric of anthropological representation

Daniel Varisco

Daniel Varisco is professor of anthropology at Hofstra University. He earned both his MA and PhD degrees in anthropology from the University of Pennsylvania, in 1975 and 1982 respectively. His geographical areas of research include Yemen, Egypt, and Qatar. His areas of study include representations of Islam, fundamentalism and "Islamism," as well as the history of agriculture, irrigation, astronomy and time-keeping in the Middle East, the impact of the internet and cyberspace, and the debate over "Orientalism". He has conducted significant work in the country of Yemen on water resource use, the history of coffee and qat as well as work as a development consultant. His recently published books include *Reading Orientalism: Said and the Unsaid* (2007); *Islam Obscured: The Rhetoric of Anthropological Representation* (2005) and *Medieval Folk Astronomy and Agriculture in Arabia and Yemen* (1997) as well as co-editing with G. Rex Smith *The Manuscript of al-Malik al-Afdal: al-'Abbas b. 'Ali Dawud b. Yusuf b. 'Umar b. 'Ali Ibn Rasul* (d. 778/1377): *A Medieval Arabic Anthology from the Yemen.* In 2009 he published "Inventing Islamism: The Violence of Rhetoric" in *Islamism: Contested Perspectives on Political Islam* and in 2010 his article "Muslims and the Media in the Blogosphere" was published in *Contemporary Islam.* The excerpts discuss various attempts to represent Islam in an anthropological key. By outlining various issues and themes of an anthropology of Islam, he shows what the anthropological approach can offer to the study of Islam. He concludes with a pointed critique of Clifford Geertz arguing that anthropologists cannot observe Islam, but only Muslims as they articulate and express themselves in their practices and discourses.

Anthropology and Islam

> But to conceptualize Islam as an object of *anthropological* study is not as simple as some writers would have one suppose.
>
> (Asad 1986: 1)

[...]

I have no interest in telling you what Islam *is*, what it really *must be*, or even what it *should be*. In what follows I am more attuned to what Islam hopefully is not, at least not for someone who approaches it seriously as an anthropologist and historian. I bear no obvious axe to grind as either a determined detractor against the religion or an overanxious advocate for it. Personally, as well as academically, I consider Islam a fascinatingly diverse faith, a force in history that must be reckoned with in the present. The offensive tool I do choose to wield, if my figurative pen can stand a militant symbol, is that of a critical hammer, an iconoclastic smashing of the rhetoric that represents, overrepresents, and misrepresents Islam from all sides. By avoiding judgment on the sacred truth of this vibrant faith, I shift intention toward an I-view that takes no summary representation *of* Islam as sacred.

Like any revelation that expects to be taken seriously, Islam is about truth in all its various forms. It has become fashionable in the postexistential, poststructural, post-colonial, and temporarily postmodern climate of much intellectual criticism to ignore truth claims, reducing them to mere representation or simply by sinking into the quagmired once-metaphysical debate over what truth could possibly mean. Nietzsche is not my theoretical niche; nor do I wish to follow Foucault into self-contained deciphering of discourse or Derrida down the deconstructive path of linguistic relativism. Although I have no meta-truth to reveal, neither do I smugly assume that Islam is not or could not be true in the experiential sense knowable only to a believer. For Muslims the truth is best seen, as Fazlur Rahman wisely suggests, from the inside (Rahman 1968: xx).[1] As an anthropologist, I am prepared to follow Abdul Hamid el-Zein and leave such verification of truth to the theologians (el-Zein 1977: 242).[2] My concern at the offset is with the outside, the rhetoric of representing Islam as a religion through the lens of anthropological or sociological narratives. Much of what has been written and is still sadly said, with academic air as well as media flair, is so overflowing with half truths and untruths wrapped around grains of truths that the dynamics of one of the world's largest and fastest growing religions are obscured. [...]

Although certainly not the dominant voices representing Islam, anthropologists and sociologists today figure in the process because of what they are able to learn by observing the behavior and rhetoric of Muslims in social contexts, usually in non-Western societies. Yet few scholars outside anthropology, as well as many within the general ranks, are aware of the ways in which the rhetoric in this corpus has changed against the backdrop of postmodern critique of ethnography as a genre and the shifting paradigms within the field. Contemporary anthropology is not the exotica and erotica trope that so many people assume it always used to be.

So why not write an intellectual history of the anthropological study of Islam in order to say who did what, when, where, and how (I prefer to leave the why to the psychoanalysts)? This was my initial impulse: compile a comprehensive bibliography, plot the trajectory through specific ethnographic texts and theoretical discussions, end up with a 700-page tome that only a few well-endowed libraries would buy. Such a project, were I ever to return to it, could easily become one of those always-looking-for-something-I-missed stories that never ends. Instead I decided to return to a few overarching anthropological treatments of Islam. This led me to choose these four authors and their seminal texts. Rather than survey what anthropologists of varying persuasions have said about Islam or summarize the gists for student consumption, I decided to contextualize these texts based not only on reading of relevant ethnographies but also from my own ethnographic experience and historical research on various aspects of Islamic traditions in the Middle East.

Several post-participation observers have returned from the field to offer suggestions on how anthropology could or should treat Islam, but these must be fleshed out of ethnographic monographs, journal articles, and extended book reviews. Surprisingly, only a few anthropologists have been tempted to propose a way of looking at Islam in the cultural aggregate. The seminal text—widely recognized both within and without the discipline of American anthropology—that stands for an "anthropology" of Islam remains Clifford Geertz's far too-well-traveled *Islam Observed* (Geertz 1968). Across the Atlantic the main anthropological/sociological theorist of Islam has been Ernest Gellner, who in *Muslim Society* weaves his model of representation out of a many-colored philosophical cloak with strands from David Hume, Max Weber, Ibn Khaldun, and a host of Enlightenment mentors (Gellner 1981). The perspective of a Muslim feminist was provided to Western readers by Moroccan sociologist Fatima Mernissi, whose *Beyond the Veil* is one of the first "sociological" analyses of Muslim gender roles (Mernissi 1987). Another Muslim scholar, the British/Pakistani anthropologist Akbar Ahmed, looks at his own religion inside out in *Discovering Islam*, building in principle on an avowedly "Islamic" mode of anthropology (Ahmed 1988). These are not the only English language studies presentable under the rubric of an "anthropology of Islam," but I believe that they have been the most widely read and consulted in the latter part of the twentieth century.[3] Regardless of their age, all remain in active print and prominent library use in the early measure of the twenty-first century. As an anthropologist reading and rereading other anthropologists, I offer here a critique of the rhetoric of representing Islam in the texts of Geertz, Gellner, Mernissi, and Ahmed.

[...]

Another compelling motivation for a book in the format of textual critique is the need to speak out to colleagues and the general public about the continuing reprehensible representations of Islam and Middle Eastern people in Western society at large and in the news media. Deeply rooted ethnocentric prejudice and an unwillingness to see beyond political expedience have contributed to a demonization of Islam as a religion of violent terror alongside the older Judaeo-Christian charge of heretical error. Several prominent media icons of the Christian right have gone so far as to label the prophet Muhammad a "terrorist" and the Quran as the "enemy's book."[4] Recent collective cultural memories, whether premeditated or self-mediated, comprise an inescapably politicized litany: oil embargo, hostage crisis, mad mullahs, shoe-string budgeted airplane hijackings, skyscraper terrorism, Hamas suicide bombers, and the uncivilized clash with a post-red, green menace of fundamentalist militants. The cycle of blaming victims and victimizers, from CNN crossfiring to talk-radio jockeying and Internet chat rooms, ensures that "Islam" will be viewed suspiciously as a "problem" by Americans and Europeans for the foreseeably intolerant future.

What went wrong? How did the ideologically driven politics of nationalism and neocolonial birth pangs lose out in causal terms to the rantings of religious extremists and the martyrdom of children? The pundits have mostly played a blaming game. Echoing the patriotic rhetoric of President George W. Bush after 9/11, historian Bernard Lewis traces the troubles of the Islamic world to a "lack of freedom," seemingly the failure of predominantly Muslim countries to have the same governmental ancestry as France or the United States (Lewis 2002: 159). Were Muslims secular in a Western mode, the argument implies, they too could become enlightened enough to reform their religion into irrelevance. For a political scientist like Martin Kramer, the sandtrap lies with the entire Middle East Studies establishment reinvented in the wake of Edward Said's critique of media-friendly establishment scholars like Bernard Lewis. Middle East specialists who recognized and lamented the ethnocentrism and racism of an imperially aligned "Orientalism" are faulted for a "failure to anticipate Islamism" (Kramer 2001: 47). Being a blindsided expert on Islam in this scenario becomes tantamount to being a geologist who fails to predict the timing of an earthquake or a stockbroker who does not foresee a recession. Op-ed speak aside, there was hardly a need for academic scholars studying Islam—certainly not those who have no expertise as "political" scientists—to predict the swell of political unrest couched in religious rhetoric throughout the Muslim world. No one, not even the most sophisticated intelligence operatives in the world, was able to predict the attack on the Twin Towers. Were American security advisors waiting for an Ivory Tower directive to tell them the obvious: American policy toward the Middle East has continually generated violent reactions? Asking what went wrong in order to trounce one's opponents is disingenuous; the real question should be why ongoing global power plays resulting in political instability, economic disparity, cultural defamation, and misplaced self-interest should be labeled failures of religion. What went wrong is what usually goes wrong: someone else gets the blame for not being on the right side of God.

Frustration over political and economic events has mired much representation of Islam, the religion, into a referendum on cultural difference. Uncovering the inescapable truths about what—as Edward Said some time ago most forcefully brought to the public's attention—happens in "covering" Islam is not yet a done deed. There is, fortunately, fair and objective commentary on various aspects of Islam, even if one must first sort through the blatantly biased accounts and recycled rubbish of commercially littered books on "Islam" and "Arab" in the post-9/11 publishing world. Most of this coverage, especially the newsstand variety, has been little influenced by what anthropologists have observed in the behavior and speech of ordinary Muslims. Nor has the rhetoric of readily available anthropological texts, when consulted, been subjected to sustained critique from within the ranks of anthropologists with field experience. This makes it all the more important to know both how anthropologists have represented Islam and what more could be said based on the potential of ethnographic research and comparative cultural analysis. [...]

Introductory books about Islam often begin with a ritualized list of the "five pillars," providing an easy fill-in question for standard tests given students in Islam 101 classes. These five pillars, a useful bundling that postdates the time of Muhammad, say little about the message of Islam, apart from the *shahada,* the witness to there being only one God and one final prophet. Prayer *(salat),* alms *(zakat),* fasting *(sawm),* and pilgrimage *(hajj)* are duties, highly symbolic religious acts necessary for Muslim observance. Missing from this picture, however, is an expanded creed, a statement of faith that would flesh out this ritual count. Certainly the *shahada* is the central message of Islam, but only in the boiled-down sense of John 3:16 for born-again Christians. Islam is a monotheism and Muhammad is its definitive prophet: this should be a starting point, not a conclusion. A peculiarly "Western" way of viewing Islam has been to reduce it, following the path of Wilfred Cantwell Smith, to an orthopraxy, a religion united by practice rather than shared belief (Smith 1957: 28).[5] Given the extraordinary depth of Islamic thought, is the idea of an Islamic orthodoxy really so toxic to non-Muslims? Muslim theologians formed a complex set of beliefs from the message revealed in the Quran and statements *(hadith* literature) attributed to Muhammad. The Quran speaks of morality, the cosmic battle between good and evil, the wiles of the Devil, the resurrection of the dead, judgment day, the relationship between men and women, and many practical aspects of daily life. To assume that the adumbrated five pillars is analogous to the Ten Commandments or the Nicene Creed is thus to shortchange knowledge of the very beliefs that make the ritual duties significant. What Muslims have done with their *sunna* is certainly as doctrinally relevant as what scholastic icon Saint Thomas Aquinas did with his *Summa.*

If the reader wants to know what Muslims believe, the best way is to ask Muslims themselves.[6] With estimates now rising well over a billion, minus the obvious high percentage of those still being taught how to be Muslim, this is not hard to do. After over fourteen centuries of existence and global expansion there is a diverse and widely variant range of views that have been in one way or another defined as Islamic. Islam has long been an active missionary religion, so there are books and tracts with particular doctrinal and political spins in all the major languages. Some of these have been translated into English and other European languages; several of the basic theological texts are now available on the Internet. It is easy to find information about Islam; the trick is sifting through the rhetoric that represents the religion. Inevitably, pragmatic visions of tolerance aside, the nature of Islam as a revelation claiming to provide ultimate truth for all humanity results in a competition with other universalistic religions, such as Christianity, as well as those particular religious groups who desire only to be left alone and unconverted. My concern, as an anthropologist, is not with entering into this subjective and emotionally charged fray, but simply assessing how those of us who study Muslims in ethnographic context represent "Islam" as such. [...]

A central concern [...] is to explain a certain area of anthropological representation to non-anthropologists and anthropological colleagues who are interested in the subject of Islam. It is important to remember that interest in the "ethnology" or customs of contemporary Oriental peoples, especially Muslims, has a long pre-anthropological history. Medieval travelers, including pious pilgrims, crusading knights, and merchants, sometimes left accounts of the Muslims they passed by. Ironically, the most well-traveled medieval representation of Muslims was *The Travels of Sir John Mandeville*, a fictitious autobiographical account attributed to a fourteenth-century English knight. The irony is not that an errant knight would describe Islam, but that he would do so in a rather favorable light, remarking that Muslims were more devout and honest to their religion than Christians of his day had become to their faith (Mosley 1983: 104–110). By the nineteenth century Christian missionaries had settled into the Holy Land and produced hundreds of books with titles like William Thomson's (1858) *The Land and the Book or, Biblical Illustrations Drawn from the Manners and Customs, the Scenes and Scenery of the Holy Land*. The thrust of most this literature was unabashedly apologetic. "The remarkable reproduction of Biblical life in the East of our day is an unanswerable argument for the authority of the sacred writings" avers Rev. Henry J. Van-Lennep; "they could not have been written in any other country, not by any other people than Orientals" (van Lennep 1875: 5). The Bedouin sheikh, feared as a thief while actually traveling in Palestine and Syria, still served as a potent reminder of how the biblical patriarchs must have lived. Nomads, camels, tents, veiled wives: the stereotyping of Muslims proceeded textually by imagining an idyll of those who were probably least devout in the region. There are also the custom-packed accounts of swashbuckling adventurers, most notably Richard Burton's description of a surreptitious trip to Mecca in 1853, replete with maps and illustrations exposing the most sacred site of Muslims (Burton 1855-1856). So extensive was this corpus of traveling texts that the bibliography of a major anthology on *Peoples and Cultures of the Middle East: An Anthropological Reader*, published more than a century after Burton's text, contains more references to travel accounts than to ethnographies (Sweet 1970).

Until the 1970s there was little anthropological discussion of "Islam" as a religion in Middle East ethnography. The Dutch scholar Christian Snouck-Hurgronje and the Finnish sociologist Edward Westermarck were among several individuals who wrote about Islam from firsthand experience, but not in the modern sense of participant observation for an extended period of time *in situ* (Ellen 1983: 54).[7] The first modern ethnographic account of an Islamic context may be Evans-Pritchard's *The Sanusi of Cyrenaica*, based on field research in Cyrenaica during World War II (Evans-Pritchard 1949).[8] Eric Wolf, a cultural anthropologist, published his "functional" argument in 1951 about the origins of Islam in Mecca, but he had never conducted research in an Islamic context, nor did he know the plentiful Arabic sources firsthand (Wolf 1951).[9] This thesis was followed up by Barbara Aswad, who cited Orientalist sources rather than drawing on her fieldwork in a Syrian village (Aswad 1970).[10] The respective authors of a 1955 article entitled "Zur Anthropologie des Islam" (Schimmel 1955) and a 1961 article labeled "An Analysis of Islamic Civilization and Cultural Anthropology" (von Grunebaum 1961) turn out to be two Arabist historians, Annemarie Schimmel and Gustave von Grunebaum. The French scholar Joseph Chelhod carried out limited ethnographic research in the 1960s, but he was primarily an Arabist teasing anthropological insights out of Arabic texts.[11]

Why was there so little anthropological interest in Islam? Michael Gilsenan, reflecting on his anthropological education at Oxford in the 1960s, asks "Where was the Middle East?" (Gilsenan 1990); his blunt but astute answer is "nowhere" (Gilsenan 1990: 225).[12] At the time academic rendering of Islam was still in the hands of Orientalists, scholars who could read the literature in Arabic or the relevant language, historians, and the evolving field of religious studies. Up to that point, probably the most widely distributed anthropological book on the Middle East as a whole had been Carlton Coon's *Caravan* (Coon 1951); Coon was in fact a physical anthropologist who visited Yemen briefly but never conducted ethnographic fieldwork (Coon 1951).[13] The start of the 1960s witnessed the first installment of the revised *Encyclopaedia of Islam,* the most authoritative—in the strict sense—representation of Islam in a Western language. Yet virtually none of the articles in the first new volume were written by ethnographers.[14] Richard Antoun, in a mid-1970s survey of prior anthropological research, explained the reluctance of anthropologists to deal with Islam as a result of disciplinal tunnel vision— leaving Islam to the Orientalists—and the poor Arabic language skills of fieldworkers (Antoun 1976: 159–166).[15] At the same time, Muslim anthropologist Abdul Hamid el-Zein provided a critique of previous anthropological discussion of Islam, making a provocative case for a refined study of the various "islams" actually observable (el-Zein 1977). [...]

If there is one dominant theme connecting ethnography with Islam, primarily in the North African context, this would be Islamic mystics, Sufis, and marabouts, starting with Evans-Pritchard's pioneering study of the Sanusiyya order in Libya (Evans-Pritchard 1949). Another British anthropologist, Ernest Gellner, wrote a major study of the political role of marabouts, playing off the more orthodox "doctor" of great-tradition Islamic law against the little-tradition rural "saint" (Gellner 1972). Clifford Geertz looked at sufism as a symbolic dimension of Islam in Morocco and Indonesia in his seminal *Islam Observed* (Geertz 1968). One of his students, Vincent Crapanzano, condensed the discussion of a mystic named Tuhami to a psychoanalytic portrait (Crapanzano 1973), while another student, Dale Eickelman, detailed life in a Moroccan pilgrimage center (Eickelman 1976). On the other English-speaking side of the Atlantic, Ioan M. Lewis surveyed sufism in Somalia (Lewis 1984) and Michael Gilsenan analysed an Egyptian sufi order in Egypt (Gilsenan 1973). Once again, it seems as though anthropology came to Islam via the exotic, as though the mundane was too obvious, perhaps too boring, to require explanation.

Without question, the most comprehensive study of Islam in a local community from this period is Egyptian anthropologist el-Zein's ethnography on the religious aristocracy of Lamu, an island off Kenya (el-Zein 1974). The value of el-Zein's analysis is that the religious symbols and retold myths he encountered are contextualized within the definable social structure and observable behavior of real Muslims. Moving beyond the Durkheimian ritual of searching for the social function in local religion, el-Zein probes the pragmatic hermeneutics of masters and slaves in ritualizing Islamic stories of creation and the prophet Muhammad (el-Zein 1974). The ethnographer provides a painstakingly detailed account of how Islam is practiced. An entire chapter is devoted to his observation and participation in Ramadān mosque readings of the Swahili creation myth (el-Zein 1974: 221–280). We learn not only what various local groups say the myth means to them, but the seating arrangements of those who attend, their greeting behavior on the way to and from the mosque, even the role of children. Text is wedded to context in a manner no study of Islam had previously achieved.

The last three decades of twentieth-century ethnographic studies reveal a major shift in approaching Islamic cultures. Paralleling a trend in the discipline at large, female ethnographers began publishing on issues of gender and sexuality. These included anthropologists with their own genealogical roots to Muslim societies, such as Lila Abu-Lughod, Soraya Altorki, Fadwa El Guindi, Shahla Haeri, Ziba Mir-Hosseini, and Fatima Mernissi, to name but a few. Impressive contextualization of Islamic ritual in African societies can be found in the work of Ladislav Holy, Michael Lambek, and Robert Launay, as well as in Indonesia, exemplified in the studies John R. Bowen, Robert Hefner, and Mark Woodward. There are now specific studies of the major rituals, such as pilgrimage, fasting, prayer, *mawlid* (celebration of the Prophet's birthday) and sacrifice.[16] Egyptian anthropologist el-Sayyed el-Aswad offers, a detailed ethnographic portrait of folk cosmology in an Egyptian village (el-Aswad 2002). Some anthropologists have also linked their fieldwork to the literate tradition, such as Brinkley Messick's study of legal texts and decision making in the Yemeni town of Ibb or my own work on Islamic folk astronomy and agriculture (Messick 1993; Varisco 1993; Varisco 1997). In more recent years, anthropological studies have appeared on the resurgence of a politicized Islam, starting with the aftermath of the Iranian revolution and expanding to the global phenomenon of "Islamism" now dominating the news.[17] Even Salman Rushdie's *The Satanic Verses* gets anthropological coverage (Ahmed 1992: 169–177; Rosen 2002: 158–173; Werbner 1996).

Contemporary ethnographers are attuned to the global dimensions of popular culture in Islamic societies. In a volume on *New Media in the Muslim World: the Emerging Public Sphere,* Dale Eickelman and Jon Anderson suggest that

> by looking at the intricate multiplicity of horizontal relationships, especially among the rapidly increasing numbers of beneficiaries of mass education, new messages, and new communication media, one discovers alternative ways of thinking about Islam, acting on Islamic principles, and creating sense of community and public space.
>
> (Eickelman and Anderson 1999: 16)

John R. Bowen examines contemporary religious poetry in Sumatra (Bowen 1997). Presentation of Islamic issues in the print media has been one of the major concerns in the work of David Edwards in Afghanistan (Edwards 1995) and Gregory Starrett in Egypt (Starrett 1995; Starrett 1998).[18] Anthropologists are also participants observing the same television programs, films, and videos as their informants.[19] Jon Anderson, whose original fieldwork was in Afghanistan, has traced the trajectory of Islamic websites on the Internet from creolized pioneers, especially Muslim graduate students, to more officializing discourses of formal institutions (Anderson 1999).[20] Ethnography has come a long way from its kinship tunnel vision with Bedouins on camelback. [...]

With all due respect to Geertz and Gellner, I encountered Islam long before I met Muslims. At first, it was the childhood attraction to the Islam of the Arabian Nights, Sir Richard Burton's Meccan escapades, and my grandmother's attic full of *National Geographic.* Then it was the Islam of Orientalist scholars, as I applied myself to learning classical Arabic as a graduate student. Marrying the granddaughter of a Syrian qadi made more real the Islam I had been absorbing piecemeal. Yet, when I arrived in Yemen in 1978 to begin eighteen months of ethnographic fieldwork on traditional irrigation and water rights, my understanding of Islam was still obscured by biased misrepresentations, well meaning but partial representations and a simple lack of exposure. In the field I learned quite quickly that what Muslims do is not reducible to what books, even their own, say they should do.[21] But I also developed a passion for knowing what the texts were saying. As a personal confession, I have at times felt more at home in manuscript libraries poring over esoteric Arabic texts than playing the obvious outsider talking with villagers. Working with texts, I have developed a healthy—at least in my mind—skepticism about the "truth" of anything written. Working with people who think they have the truth only makes it more evident that texts and words should be approached as means and not ends.

The Islam I observed in a highland Yemeni village was not just the routinized five-pillar variety. All of the major rituals involved were obviously part of the context, but the value of living there was that I could observe the day-by-day behavior of real people rather than just read about the ideals. As an outsider, an American at that, I did not feel out of place or on display. Perhaps I was fortunate to live in an isolated village before the political madness of suicide bombings. The fact that my wife, also an anthropologist, is a native Arab speaker and Muslim certainly helped smooth our joint acceptance as resident outsiders. Maybe it was also the mundane focus of my research on agriculture and irrigation, readily understandable on a pragmatic level by these expert farmers. I had not come to Yemen to study "Islam," but neither had I decided ahead of time to ignore anything that came along in the process of being there. The men I spent the bulk of my time with were rarely involved in theological disputation, certainly not with me. What they did or chose not to do was their Islam and that, at least at the time, seemed the most natural thing in the world. [...]

Thus, to be a Muslim is to be so in a specific time and place, to live like anyone else through the cycle from birth to death. In this sense the notion of "observing" Islam is a telling oxymoron, especially from the angle of an anthropologist who has been to the field. Muslims can be observed; their material culture can be documented; their words read and lexicated; their behavior witnessed. "Islam" in the abstract sense of a religion or civilization can only be represented. The temptation to converge thought and sight is so engrained in our linguistic usage that representation easily gets reified as what must really be there. "Being there," for me, broke the spell of this epistemological chimera. There are good Muslims and bad Muslims, devout Muslims and indifferent Muslims. These do not get properly represented under the umbrella of an essentialized and homogenized "Islam." If the only Islam wanted is the ideal, then read a book or listen to a sermon. For the common humanity shared by us all, regardless of religion, culture, or ethnicity, it is necessary to observe others as they live their lives or read the arguments of those who have done exactly this. [...]

Muslims observed: the lessons from anthropology

There was a time, now almost a generation ago, when there were relatively few ethnographic data collected by trained anthropologists working in Islamic societies, when anthropological approaches to religion focused on "primitive" non-worldwide religious systems, and when those who did devote their scholarship to Islam did so almost exclusively as exegetes of texts. This was the academic setting that *Islam Observed* addressed, Ernest Gellner embellished, Fatima Mernissi skirted, and Akbar Ahmed derided. Edward Said, I should add, covered it and condemned it. Fortunately, there is now a sizeable presence of ethnographic analysis of Muslim societies; unfortunately, it is rarely known or cited outside of the narrow confines of specialized subfields in anthropology. Islam, mainly one geographical zone of it, appears in several summations of Middle East anthropology, but no one has yet charted the intellectual trajectory of an anthropology of Islam as such.

Perhaps there is no need. Imagine the absurdity of writing an anthropology of Christianity by tracing all the ethnography conducted in "Christian" contexts. What would such a far-fetched and novel text be called? *Christianity Observed, Christian Society, Beyond the Bread and Wine, Discovering Christianity?*[22] What precisely would an anthropologist contribute to a topic that has several fields devoted exclusively to it? That Christianity in Spain is carnivalesque and its variants in Lebanon are confessionally mired? That flux and reflux made medieval serfs into Victorian Sunday school teachers? That *the* Christian view of woman is *vagina dentata,* not the Holy Virgin Mother? That a Christian could write about his own dogmas with an empirically intact conscience? I suggest that simple essentializing of the long history of the faith into ideal types, beyond repeating the obvious sectarian splits, offers nothing new. It is easy to create unity out of diversity but seldom does it serve an analytical purpose.

It is my main contention that the selected examples of now "classic" anthropological approaches to Islam obscure the effective understanding of Islam as a cross-cultural faith embedded, quite deeply at times, in numerous cultural traditions. My emphasis throughout has been on the negative, highlighting what has gone wrong textually. To carry the metaphor further afield, we have just walked through—far too briskly, at times—a minefield of interpretive problematics and flawed rhetoric. My ultimate aim is not to die a martyr's death on an academically inclined and intellectually predefined battlefield, but to properly detonate the unexploded myths and seductive biases. Iconoclastic deconstruction will never get an author to the right side just because it avoids the wrong side. Now comes the really difficult part: charting a course of safe passage that will stay clear of the same, and perhaps irritatingly resistant, fallacies so prevalent in the texts of Geertz, Gellner, Mernissi, and Ahmed. Having objected to the obscuring of Islam, what is it that anthropologists have, can, and should do to improve their perspectives and methods for a more enlightened but less enrooted understanding of the religion of Muslims? [...]

The questions I frame here address the anthropology of Islam; they are intended for anyone interested in what anthropologists can do, as well as a call to action for colleagues in my discipline. It is, after all, an informed interdisciplinary appraisal, more than any single academic field of view, that holds the most promise. [...]

Whether or not an approach to religion is anthropological or sociological is a bit of a red herring. To a certain extent the answer is as trite as the discipline in which a researcher has been trained. But the interchange of labels is too rampant to be dismissed as simple cross-border interchange. Consider that French scholar Jean-Pierre Digard provides "perspectives anthropologiques" in a French journal of "sociologie," while calling what he does "ethnologie" (Digard 1978: 497). In France Jacques Berque and Pierre Bourdieu teach "sociologie." In Britain a number of social anthropologists regard what they do as a type of sociology, a notable example being Ernest Gellner.[23] Since Gellner was trained as a philosopher and harbored lifelong suspicions of any notion that could be called Wittgensteinian, I suppose one category is as good for him as another. American academics are generally more disciplined. Clifford Geertz is an unabashed anthropologist, although he relies to a great extent on sociologists like Weber and Parsons (Geertz 1968). Even in formal ethnographies, the bread and butter of anthropological communication, the distinction can be fuzzy. Dale Eickelman, who conducted an ethnographic study of a pilgrimage center in Boujad, Morocco, identified his primary goal as making "sociological sense" (Eickelman 1976: 4).[24] Given that most readers have a relatively clear idea of what sociology is about but little knowledge of what anthropologists do, the word choice may in fact be pragmatic rather than programmatic. [...]

The terminological confusion is compounded by that fact that a nontheological, or at least nonexegetical, study of religion is commonly labeled "sociology," even by anthropologists. I suspect this is due in large part to the sociological credentials of scholars like Durkheim and Weber, who are as likely to be read by anthropologists as by someone trained specifically in the modern discipline of sociology. Marx himself should be included in this intellectual trajectory, although reducing his meager contributions to the study of religion as "sociological" seems as uneconomical as it does Whiggishly self-serving. As Talal Asad has warned, there is a danger in applying indiscriminately to Islam such widely distributed concepts as Durkheim's sacred and profane or Weber's ideal types (Asad 1986: 12). The issue is not how useful such concepts could be, but the need to recognize the cultural specificity of the contexts in which they are commonly made. There is so much debate about the methodological problems in past sociological models of religion that borrowing contested terms may simply beg the theoretical questions. Arguing about religion, it might be said, readily becomes the opiate of social scientists, whatever their formal training. [...]

The primary source material for an ethnographer is what people do and say in the ethnographer's presence. One need not be trained as an anthropologist to observe Muslims or describe their behavior. There is a large and potentially useful corpus of description left in print and archives by travelers. Victorian Edward Lane, for example, spent considerable time in Egypt during the first half of the nineteenth century and eventually wrote *An Account of the Manners and Customs of the Modern Egyptians,* a descriptive account of just about everything a curious English gentleman abroad might find interesting (Lane 1973). Much of this is valuable documentation, but it is no more "ethnography" in the modern sense than Darwin's *On the Origin of Species* substitutes for modern genetics. If the primary field method of anthropology is reducible to mere observation, it is open to anyone willing to travel and reflect. Clearly, there should be more at stake. Just as critical historiography involves more than merely reading a historical text, so ethnography goes beyond writing down observations of curious customs. [...]

Being an ethnographer does not make a scholar objective, nor erase cultural presuppositions, but it is certainly a leg up over being a blatant religious partisan or armchair theorist.

A proper case in point is Daniel Bradburd's *Being There: The Necessity of Fieldwork,* an autobiographical account of living with the Komachi nomads of southeastern Iran in 1974 and 1975. Like many anthropologists who have done research in the Middle East, Bradburd did not set out to study Islam. His academic focus was set on household economy among pastoralists, but the Komachi happened to be Muslims as well as nomads. The older travel literature describing the Komachi spoke of them as fanatical Persians who hated Christians, while an earlier ethnographic study of nomads in the general area made it seem as though they would be irreligious (Bradburd 1998). Yet Dan Bradburd and his wife, Ann Sheedy, found that the Komachi "truly lived in a Shi'ite world," not only in the outmoded "little tradition" sense, but with direct ties to formal religious practice (Bradburd 1998: 57). Bradburd's account, readably anecdotal, is a passionate defense of participant observation as the anthropological method *par excellence.* Being there was not an end in itself, not an act of domination—certainly not from the standpoint of the Komachi—but an opportunity to build a "meaningful model" of what they saw from within a give-and-take situation where that model could be mulled over and corrected. Imagine a historian who could go back in time and interview an author, even witness the events being described in a text: that is the potential of ethnographic fieldwork for understanding how Islam is lived in a specific social setting.

Perhaps the most original contribution an ethnographic approach can offer is charting how beliefs and ideas are put into practice: not how they are supposed to be or should be, but how they unfold in an observable manner in one small place at one particular time. Ladislav Holy, for example, studied the Berti of Northern Darfur in western Sudan for a little over three years between 1961 and 1986. As an African society far off from the metropolitan centers associated with "great tradition" or normative Islam, the Berti could all too easily be dismissed as idiosyncratic syncretists, mixing Islam with earlier indigenous religious beliefs. Holy found that even the most pious members of the group were tolerant of actions that Islamic precepts would appear to prohibit. As an example, most Berti did not think the Quranic prohibition of wine applied to the local millet beer. While local religious scholars abstained from drinking beer themselves, they never preached against it and would even offer a bowl to guests. "The tolerant attitude to the sinful ways of others derives from the fact that the pious do not feel themselves in any way implicated by the acts of others," explains Holy (Holy 1991: 219). Yet, other local customs would be railed against by the pious, especially when these hindered their ability to perform religious duties. Only by being there, observing behavior and its consequences, could the anthropologist begin to unravel the local meaning of behavior responsible to textual precedent.

Holy, like many recent ethnographers, follows the Malinowskian dictum to map out what is happening from the native point of view. Rather than dismiss Berti practice as "little" in contrast to a "great" tradition that hardly exists in the local context, his focus is on the various ways in which Islam is lived in concrete, pragmatic terms. This requires building up from observation of specific behavior and following existing debates rather than measuring local practice according to a textualized ideal of what should be the case. "For the student of religion who does not want to change, condemn or justify existing beliefs and practices but to understand what they mean to those to whom they belong," argues Holy, "there is little point in classifying them according to how closely or remotely they approximate the ideal" (Holy 1991: 6). Muslims, like everyone else with human credentials, disagree in practice. The point is not whether they should, but how the artificial category of "religion"—certainly a foreign notion to the Berti themselves—masks the complex negotiation of individual and communal concerns on a day by day basis.

A major objection raised about analyses of local versions of Islam is that there appears to be an endless number of versions. Scholars who want to see the broad picture complain that ethnographic snapshots often confuse the issue. Certainly it is problematic to use the study of a single community as panoptic for a region, ethnic grouping, or even Islam as such. This is a major criticism of the essentializing of Geertz, Gellner, Mernissi, and Ahmed. But, sampling problems and overstretched interpretations aside, anthropological studies are capable of bringing new and original information to the ongoing debates. As John Bowen cogently argues, "local studies give us a window onto the rhetorics and forms that mediate between 'local' and 'translocal' phenomena."[25] I do not think there is a danger of knowing too much about variations in Islamic practice. The critical issue is balance, using observable social contexts to rein in the tendency to substitute the ideal for the real.

Ethnography is not a panacea for essentializing, but it does offer an important corrective at times. It is both process, an interactive method of getting information, and a product that literally re-presents that information in a frame not of the native's choosing. In the process the modern ethnographer is a cross between photographer and artist. A photographer usually attempts to capture a scene as it exists at a given moment, to freeze reality in a frame for remembrance. But the artist reinterprets the observable reality in order to highlight some aspects and ignore others, to imagine rather than duplicate an existing image. Photographing social behavior may be objective in intent, but the interpretive lens of the ethnographer always filters what seems so natural at a given moment. In a sense, participant observation tends to be objective only as the observer becomes consciously aware of the cultural and discipline-training biases in his field of vision. Lived experience cannot be simply observed, since only certain events will be recorded and judged to be relevant. There is no one program for deciding which observations to draw on, certainly not What Always Works 101 in graduate training.

Consider one specific and mundane event from my own fieldwork experience in rural Yemen. One local man did not know, let alone comprehend, the exact words in the prayer ritual, despite the fact he was a native speaker and had been brought up as a Muslim. When he prayed, it was obvious to the people around and to the ethnographer that he would mumble over passages that were easy to memorize. How then, should I as an outside observer of behavior represent this? From what I could see and learn through conversation, and that was hardly an omniscient perch, his fellows were tolerant of this behavior, did not attribute it to unbelief and accepted the fact that he was sincere even if not very bright. [...] For a Muslim not from the area the man's ignorance might even be taken as a sign of heresy to be corrected.

How should this discrete event involving a particular individual be represented? Unlike my sociological colleagues, I have no access to statistical data on how many men in the local sampling area were ignorant of the words as they prayed. Not being a psychologist, I cannot say what traumatic childhood event might have been blocking his memory or informing his attitude? Since I am not an *imam,* it does not offend me morally that a man could sincerely follow the ritual and do so improperly. I could, as a good historian, examine the available *fatwa* collections and see if such a case has a precedent in Islamic legal tradition; this would at least make an impressive footnote. As an ethnographic observation it may in fact be so irrelevant as not to warrant inclusion in a discussion of local ritual behavior or it may be a major bit of evidence in arguing for how individual variation plays out in ritual behavior. Whether to represent this event and how to do it are clearly subjective choices. The datum does not speak for itself, even if I allow it to become a published datum for others to interpret for themselves.[26] Once presented in print, even as I do so here, I can hardly anticipate all the possible ways in which my representation will itself be represented. Old stories about parrots, as the infamous Bororo case well illustrates, fly even in the face of reason. [...]

Anthropologists observe Muslims. Ethnographic fieldwork is done at tree level, no matter the view of the forest an individual researcher brings with him or her. This requires the ethnographer to know how to distinguish one tree from another. Essential to this process is the ability to communicate with people in their own language. Working through an interpreter can yield bits of information, but the extra layer of filtering removes the creative dynamics of communication. Most anthropologists enter the field with a minimum of language training; nor are all ethnographers competent linguists. The four books examined in this study show the range of possibilities. Geertz learned enough Indonesian to function in Java and Bali, but there is no indication he developed more than a smattering of colloquial Arabic; none of his sources in *Islam Observed* are direct Arabic or Berber sources (Geertz 1968). In *Saints of the Atlas,* Gellner makes no mention of how be obtained his information from Berber informants, apart from the admission that he possesses "a bad ear and no linguistic training" (Gellner 1969: 305).[27] His bibliography suggests that the majority of sources consulted were in French. Fatima Mernissi, a Moroccan Arabic speaker, and Akbar Ahmed, a native of Pakistan, clearly had an advantage in their fieldwork by collecting information in their respective native languages (Mernissi 1987; Ahmed 1980). [...]

Because fieldwork is a highly personal experience, there is no magical formula for success. It helps if the local people are willing to put up with a stranger in their midst. It does not help to walk into a village and assume that everyone is a potential informant with nothing better to do than sit and answer questions, speaking very slowly in the most basic elementary Arabic. Living in a remote village can be lonely; being the constant center of attention for inquisitive onlookers and myriad curious children can wear down even the most resilient demeanor. [...]

Adjusting to intrusions of cultural space is often not half the problem of dealing with the emotional consequences of joining a community where death and illness take a prominent role. One of the most painful memories of my own experience in Yemen was returning one day about two years after my fieldwork and spotting a good friend. On a previous visit I had taken a photograph of him with his young daughter. It was such a striking picture that I had it enlarged while back in the states. Normally, I followed the routine of inquiring about family and friends, but this time in my own excitement I rushed to my friend and handed him the picture. As he glanced at the image, I knew immediately from the pain in his eyes that something was wrong. I later learned that his daughter had died, run over in a tragic car accident in the village, only a few weeks before. Najwa and I often gave photographs we took of village people back to them as gifts, which we would sometimes see on a wall as we visited homes. We eventually noticed that when a person died the photograph was almost always taken down or turned to face the wall. It was only after this experience with my friend that I understood the reason. In a society where the dead are not embalmed and displayed for mourners, pictures of the recently deceased invoke emotional pain. The quotidian world bedevils the best of intentions. [...]

The essential problem in the study of Islam is precisely that: essentialist reduction of a diverse religious tradition across cultures into an ideal essence. To clarify my iconoclastic leanings, let me endorse the caveat given by Talal Asad: "The argument here is not against the attempt to generalize about Islam, but against the manner in which that generalization is undertaken" (Asad 1986: 5). I do not wish to be dismissed, even nominally, as a nominalist. My problem is with "Islam" with a capital "I." Geertz thinks he has observed it, Gellner has theorized it into a philosophical whole, Mernissi attacks what it does to the Muslim female, and Ahmed discovers it all over again for his English readers. In a provocative article published a quarter of a century ago, Muslim anthropologist Abdul Hamid el-Zein wondered in print "if a single true Islam exists at all" (el-Zein 1977). Unlike Akbar Ahmed, this was not an attempt to Islamicize anthropology or probe the theological ground foretold by Evans-Pritchard, but a challenge to scholars who blithely assume the existential "truth" of concepts. "But what if ..." asked el-Zein, analysis of Islam "were to begin from the assumption that 'Islam,' 'economy,' 'history,' 'religion,' and so on do not exist as things or entities with meaning inherent in them, but rather as articulations of structural relations, and are the outcome of these relations and not simply a set of positive terms from which we start our studies?" (el-Zein 1977: 251) If so, he reasoned, it would do no good to start with a textbook version of the five pillars, Ibn Khaldun, David Hume or Max Weber, because all this is what Islam is supposed to be. For el-Zein, true to his anthropological roots, it was important to start with the "native's model of Islam" as it is articulated in a given social context. This is not because the native is "right," a nonsensical term for non-theologian el-Zein, but in order to see how Muslims adapt what analysts call "religion" to everyday life.

It is worth revisiting el-Zein's argument, not only because it tends to be ignored or misunderstood, but as an important reminder of what it means to study Islam ethnographically.[28] Among those who miss the point and stumble on this easily decontextualized phrasing is Talal

Asad, who begins his brief lecture on "The Idea of an Anthropology of Islam" by dismissing el-Zein's "brave effort" as "unhelpful" (Asad 1986: 2).[29] Asad asserts that el-Zein is the victim of a logical paradox: claiming that diverse islams are equally real and at the same time that they "are all ultimately expressions of an underlying unconscious logic" (Asad 1986: 2). Sensing the taint of "Lévi-Straussian universalism," Asad faults el-Zein for dissolving the very analytical category, Islam, that he is searching for (Asad 1986: 2). I think there is less disagreement between the basic arguments of el-Zein and Asad than this entails. El-Zein would have agreed heartily with Asad's bottom line: "It is too often forgotten that 'the world of Islam' is a concept for organizing historical narratives, not the name for a self-contained collective agent" (Asad 1986: 11). The real problem, unstated by Asad, is a disagreement over the nature of "culture," arguably the most debated and fought over concept in the history of anthropological theory. [...]

Advocating a "phenomenological" approach at the time, el-Zein believed that underlying the diverse "contents" of cultures was an embedded "logic" in the very nature of culture. Thus, there is a sense in which both the anthropologist and the native, although from different cultures content-wise, share "a logic which is beyond their conscious control" (el-Zein 1977: 252).[30] Unfortunately, el-Zein did not elaborate in this brief review of several texts about Islam what this logic entails; he passed away soon after the article was published. The critics, however, ignore el-Zein's practical application of this theoretical frame in his excellent ethnography on Lamu. The logic he was talking about refers to the structured relation of symbols in the narratives and speech of Muslims he observed and queried. Religious symbols, like Muhammad, Adam and Eve, or the Quran, are not approached as "entities nor fixed essences" but rather serve as "vehicles for the expression and articulation of changing values in varying contexts" (el-Zein 1974: xx). In the context of Lamu, for example, he analyzes the ways in which masters and slaves, decidedly different social categories, appropriate the symbol of the Prophet Muhammad as light (*nur*) to articulate opposing worldviews. Influenced, but not blindly so, by the structuralism of Claude Lévi-Strauss and interpretive anthropology of Clifford Geertz, el-Zein was seeking a way to go beyond the surface functions to a deep structure of the religious ideology. [...]

When Abdul Hamid el-Zein conducted his search for the anthropology of Islam, he wanted to do it "beyond ideology and theology" (el-Zein 1977). For el-Zein, but definitely not for Akbar Ahmed, the anthropological approach to Islam was diametrically opposed to the theological. This was far from a confession of disbelief, but a recognition that theologians—whether Muslim or not—have "different assumptions concerning the nature of Man, God, and the World, use different languages of analysis, and produce different descriptions of religious life" (el-Zein 1977: 449). Ironically, as el-Zein noted, both theologians and anthropologists often end up by validating boxed versions of an essentialized Islam: theologians condemn local variants from the orthodox norm they validate, while anthropologists tend to reduce local practice to superstition and syncretism that distort the assumed pure essence of the religion. The anthropologist is not likely to study Islamic theology in order to determine its spiritual truth, but it is almost nonsensical that an ethnographer would attempt to study Muslims without knowing seminal texts like the Quran, *hadith* collections and relevant legal texts.[31] [...]

Western analysis of Islam has been plagued from the start by a competitive religious ideology, political and economic rivalry and the fact that by the nineteenth century European imperialism had come to dominate much of the Islamic world, especially the Middle East. In his influential *Orientalism* and later in *Covering Islam,* Edward Said argued that a hegemonic discourse of Orientalism pervaded academic and popular discourse to such an extent that Muslims and other Orientals were not allowed permission to narrate their own stories or determine their own destinies (Said 1979; Said 1981). In the following decades the loosely defined fields of postcolonial and subaltern studies elaborated on the implications of European colonial power and its neocolonial rebirth. Whether or not it was discourse, economic power, or political ideology that should be blamed for victimizing Muslim societies, it is seldom doubted today that the study of Islam still suffers from ethnocentric and racial stereotypes that infiltrate even the most avowedly objective of published studies.

For some cultural critics, there is a lingering postmodern suspicion that scholars cannot overcome the embedded ethnocentrism and racism brought to Islam as outsiders.[32] If objectivity is to be defined only as virginity, then the possibility of a neutral, nonprejudiced interpretation of Islam from the outside is rightfully suspect from the start. None of us is without sin, which is why casting aspersion stones willy nilly is such folly. Given the continuing tensions between various Muslim groups and Western political and cultural intrusion, the impact of Islam as played out in the current islams cannot be ignored. But the abstract "can we ever be objective" malaise is not conducive to those of us who think it worthwhile to attempt reducing tension and promoting tolerance of diverse worldviews. Advocates of the "clash of civilizations" thesis are equally unproductive, as long as the artificial division of the world into Cains and Abels satisfies the baser instincts of polemicists hellbent on clashing. In the final analysis, there is the less politically correct but more pragmatic matter of whether we really want to be objective in the tried and tired positivist sense. As long as influential people justify violence by Islam, it is worth studying how and why they do this. Caring about how religion seemingly informs destructive behavior is a moral imperative worth keeping. [...]

As an anthropologist primarily concerned with how Muslims act and view their world, I agree with Abdul Hamid el-Zein that a pregiven, ideal-typed and essentialized idea of Islam has little heuristic value as an anthropological concept. What does make analytical sense is considering how such notions and definitions influence behavior and flavor the full gamut of social interaction, institutions, and socially relevant discourses. I am perfectly satisfied to work from the indigenous notions of Muslims about the meaning of their own faith and to learn from alternative models proposed by Marxists, feminists, pragmatic political scientists, and even the occasional scholar claiming to be totally objective. Unfortunately, the definitions advocated consciously or in default by Geertz, Gellner, Mernissi, and Ahmed are not "anthropological" in the sense of applying across cultures to any "religion." They are all, as Talal Asad reminds us, influenced by "a certain narrative relation" that is ultimately either supportive or oppositional to how Muslims define themselves (Asad 1986: 17). Searching for the idea of an anthropology of Islam, I argue, should not lead us beyond ideology and theology but rather probe these very powerful discursive traditions through thick description of ethnographic contexts. Observing Muslims in particular "islams" is one of the few things that anthropologists have been able to contribute to the broader academic interest in how Islam is continually defined and redefined and, indeed, how religion itself is conceptualized. [...]

Muslims will continue to be Muslims and many new converts will be found despite any attempt by academic scholars to explain the process away. Many scholars have a tendency to reduce what Muslims see as a vibrant and revelatory faith to something not essentially religious at all. For example, Pierre Bourdieu in his influential studies on North African society writes as if Islam were primarily a mislabeling of the local *habitus.* "Islam" is absent from his *The Logic of Practice,* except for its ultimate appearance under the index entry for magic (Bourdieu 1980). In pointing out this kind of omission, Carol Delaney raises an important issue: "We must ask whether an approach to the study of human culture that is grounded on universalistic premises about work, the division of labor, and the transformation of society is appropriate for all cultures, including Muslim cultures" (Delaney 1991: 21).[33] Indeed we must, although it is hard to imagine an anthropological response that would not ultimately insist that what is true about Muslims must be potentially true in any other human context. Individual cultures must be appreciated for their individuality and not unduly typed into artificial and unproductive categories, but if anthropology is not about a panhuman, and at times pan-primate, sharing of something called "culture" as such, what do we as observers of human diversity have to contribute beyond encyclopedic data banking for the polemicists?

Defining Islam will not explain what Muslims do and why they do things differently over time and space. [...]The real issue is how Islam, however defined, is represented in native or indigenous views and by outsiders. The anthropologist has the opportunity to be ethnographically present to observe what Muslims do and say. "What is distinctive about modern anthropology," comments Talal Asad, "is the comparison of embedded concepts (representations) between societies differently located in time or space" (Asad 2003: 17). Anyone can compare concepts; anthropologists try to find out what people in various social contexts think and do with those concepts. Our best comparison is applied ethnography, which can be an important corrective to armchair philosophy.

I do not need or even desire an anthropological definition of Islam, especially an essentialized model that inevitably fudges the observable variations in Muslim behavior and thinking. It is enough to start from the definitions that are useful to understand human behavior as such. This is hardly a new idea. [...] Anthropology can only explore what it means to be Muslim against a shared humanity revealed by the always tentative, but not easily ignored, findings of modern science and challenging reflections of critical philosophy. Beyond that, in the realm where ideology and theology reign supreme, anthropology has little to contribute. Studying what Muslims believe or fail to believe may say something about human nature, but it offers no window into the truth of revelation. The anthropologist observes Muslims in order to represent their representations; only Muslims can observe Islam.

Notes

1 A similar sentiment can be found in Omid Safi's description of progressive Islam: "It cannot survive as a graft of Secular Humanism onto the tree of Islam, but must emerge from within that very entity" (Safi 2003: 8).

2 As Mark Woodward advises, non-Muslim scholars "can describe, but not define, Islam." If historical analysis is confused with the quest for religious truth, adds Woodward, "both endeavors are in peril" (Woodward 1996: 6).

3 It is relevant to note that Ahmed refers to Geertz and Gellner as "two of the most prominent Western anthropologists and both leading their distinct schools of anthropology on either side of the Atlantic..." (Ahmed 1986: 187–188). Raymond Firth adds: "Two thoughtful general studies of Islam, fairly sharply contrasted, are by Geertz 1968 and Gellner 1981" (Firth 1981: 597). Graham also quotes Geertz and Gellner in the same breath (Graham 1993: 504 n. 14).

4 This includes widely distributed public statements by Jerry Falwell and Franklin Graham. Symptomatic of the politicization of the debate is the attempt to stop the University of North Carolina in 2002 from using Michael Sells' acclaimed *Approaching the Qur'an* as summer reading for incoming freshman (Sells 1999). As Sells noted with irony, "In effect the plaintiffs are suing the Koran on behalf of the Bible" (Sells 2002). Unfortunately there appears to be no statute of limitations on religious intolerance.

5 Among anthropologists who criticize this approach are Talal Asad 1986: 15 and Nadia Abu-Zahra 1997: 37. As Gregory Starrett explains, "The persistent claim that Islam is a religion of

'orthopraxy,' concerned with correct performance of ritual, rather than of orthodoxy, concern for correct belief, has been used in part by Western scholars to distance out-directed Islam from inner-directed Christianity, the implication being that 'their' religion is empty while 'ours' has intellectual content" (Starrett 1995:15).

6 For a recent example, see Farid Esack 1999 or the older classic by Fazlur Rahman 1968.

7 Roy Ellen regards Snouck-Hurgronje as "an ethnographer in the grand manner; insightful and analytic as well as systematic and comprehensive" (Ellen 1983: 54). There is no denying the breadth of Snouck-Hurgronje's research, but it was still Orientalist or armchair in approach rather than based on participant observation or the critical use of social science methodology. Edward Westermarck (1862–1939) has been cited as a "pioneer of local anthropological fieldwork" (in Eickelman 2001: 43), even though he only visited Morocco intermittently over a number of years.

8 As a military officer during the war, the context is somewhat unusual. The focus of this text is on the social structure of the Bedouin tribes and the political role of the Sanusi religious order. Unfortunately, there is very little information about how Islam is practiced. Similarly, Emers Peters studies the Cyrenaican Bedouin after World War II, but ignores the role of religion as such. In a reflective article Peters later remarks on the failure of ethnographers to discuss ritual among Muslim pastoralists (Peters 1984).

9 Anthropological critiques of Wolf have been given by Lagace 1957 and Eickelman 1967; see also Asad 1980.

10 It is telling that Aswad's article appears in a volume of readings edited by an anthropologist in which the two major selections on Islam are by historians Anne Lambton and Bernard Lewis.

11 For his approach to Islamologie, see Chelhod 1969.

12 His *Recognizing Islam*, first published in 1982, is one of the best anthropological studies on the broad theme of Islam in practice.

13 The third edition of Coon's popular text was published in 1962.

14 Joseph Chelhod wrote on Arab tribal structure, primarily based however, on Arabic sources and the travel literature.

15 In this regard it is useful to observe that articles devoted to Islamic practice in ethnographic contexts were often published in non-anthropological journals before the mid-70s (e.g. Barclay 1963; Salzman 1975).

16 For pilgrimage, see Delaney 1990; Eickelman and Piscatori 1990; Fischer and Abedi 1990: 150–221; and Young 1993. For prayer, see Bowen 1989; and Mahmood 2001. For Egyptian *mawlid*, see Abu-Zahra 1997: 205–230; and for Turkish *mevlud*, see Tapper and Tapper 1987; and the critique of Abu-Zahra 1997: 41–49. Mortuary rituals in Egypt and Tunisia are discussed by Abu-Zahra 1997: 49–71. For sacrifice, see Bowen 1992; and Hammoudi 1993. Antoun 1968 discusses traditional Ramadān fasting, while Armbrust contextualizes a popular Ramadān television show in Egypt (Armbrust 2000). Hefner examines regional variations in the Javanese *slametan* ritual (Hefner 1985: 104–125).

17 See especially Banks 1990; Edwards 1996; Edwards 2002; el-Gundi 1982; Gladney 1999; Hefner 2000; Hirschkind 2001; Houston 2001; Munson 1987; Nagata 1982; Shahrani and Canfield 1984; Shamsul 1997; Tapper and Tapper 1987; and Toth 2003. For Iran, see Fischer 1980 and Swenson 1985. For Turkey, see White 2002. The American Anthropologist included a special section called "In Focus: September 11, 2001" with analysis of the "Islamic" dimensions of the terrorist issue by Andriolo 2002; Hefner 2002; Mamdani 2002 and Varisco 2002 among others.

18 Edwards 1995; Starrett 1995; Starrett 1998; see also Eickelman and Anderson 1997.

19 See Abu-Lughod 1993; Adra 1996; Armbrust 1996; Armbrust 2002; Gordon 1998; Murphy 2000; White 1999.

20 Anderson 1999; see also Varisco 2000; Varisco 2002.

21 Gilsenan remarks that his "own experience of Islam began with a surprised and uncomfortable recognition that things are not what they seem" (Gilsenan 1982: 9). This is not unique to anthropologists, by any means.

22 Arkoun provides a similar parody of book titles in which Christianity is applied as indiscriminately as Islam (Arkoun 1994: 16). Ironically, Joel Robbins has called for an anthropology Christianity given the "success" of the anthropology of Islam (Robbins 2003). However, Robbins' goal is not to invent a palatable concept for a Western audience, as has been the case in representing Islam, but to exorcise the spectre of the Christian heritage haunting Euro-American anthropologists.

23 Gellner taught most of his life in a sociology department. Gilsenan 1973 and Tapper 1984 routinely refer to the "sociology of Islam" as synonymous with anthropology. In a recent compendium

entitled *Islam: Critical Concepts in Sociology*, Turner includes a selection from Gellner, as well as excerpts from several American anthropologists (Turner 2003).

24 Anthropologists Fischer and Abedi likewise refer to the "sociological" texture of the Islamic culture of Iran (Fischer and Abedi 1990: xxi).

25 Bowen 1997: 159.

26 Consider, in this respect, the anecdote used by David Hume about Mustapha's spin on the trinity (Hume 1956: 56), or, to probe more deeply into the intellectual baggage of the Western study of religion, the canard about the Bororo parrot (Smith 1978).

27 Gellner, who makes light of his unfamiliarity with both Berber and Arabic (Gellner 1969: 205), at one point stating he stands by the sound of a name he heard, even though it is a phonetic impossibility (Gellner 1969: 306). No phonetic transcriptions are provided in his text, although he discusses several local legends.

28 Recently, several scholars have returned to el-Zein's point about multiple "islams" (Hussain 2003: 268, n. 14; Kassam 2003: 142, n. 3).

29 Asad, who, along with Eickelman, is interested in the institutional and discursive structures that produce social knowledge (Asad 1986: 2; Eickelman 2002: 245). For a nuanced critique of Asad, see Lukens-Bull (Lukens-Bull 1999).

30 This view of culture is not strictly Lévi-Straussian, as Asad implies but parallels the debate in linguistics at that time about the nature of language (Asad 1986: 2).

31 Regarding her fieldwork on Tunisian rain rituals, Nadia Abu-Zahra concludes: "The fieldwork data would have been incomprehensible had I not consulted the Qur'an and the Arabic works of the commentators on the prophet's traditions" (Abu-Zahra 1997: 4).

32 I say this not to avoid criticism, but to acknowledge that I personally cannot be an ethnographer without realizing what it means to be male, relatively well-off economically, formed in my formative years by a distinctive Christian upbringing and, like it or not, an American in a part of the world where America is more often reviled as the Great Satan rather than a promised land with streets paved of gold. For an example of how two anthropologist of Islamic Iran define post-modernity, see Fischer and Abedi 1990: XXXI–XXXII.

33 See Goodman 2003; Mahmood 2001; and Starrett 1995 for similar critiques of Bourdieu. In fairness to Bourdieu, his earlier published work on Algeria indicates a concern in demystifying the notion of Islam as a dogma that causes cultural phenomenon (Bourdieu 1962: 108).

References

Abu-Lughod, Lila (1993) "Finding a Place for Islam: Egyptian Television Serials and the National Interest " *Public Culture*, 5: 493–513.

Abu-Zahra, Nadia (1997) *The Pure and Powerful: Studies in Contemporary Muslim Society*, Reading: Ithaca Press.

Adra, Najwa (1996) "The 'Other' as Viewer: Reception of Western and Arab Televised Representations in Rural Yemen," in Peter I. Crawford and Sigurjon B. Hafsteinsson (eds) *Construction of the Viewer: Media Ethnography and the Anthropology of Audiences*, Højbjerg: Intervention Press.

Ahmed, Akbar S. (1980) *Pukhtun Economy and Society: Traditional Structure and Economic Development in a Tribal Society*, London: Routledge & Kegan Paul.

——— (1986) "Toward Islamic Anthropology," *American Journal of Islamic Social Sciences*, 3: 181–230.

——— (1988) *Discovering Islam: Making Sense of Muslim History and Society*, London: Routledge.

——— (1992) *Postmodernism and Islam: Predicament and Promise*, London and New York: Routledge.

Anderson, Jon W. (1999) "The Internet and Islam's New Interpreters," in Dale F. Eickelman and Jon W. Anderson (eds) *New Media in the Muslim World: The Emerging Public Sphere*, Bloomington, IN: Indiana University Press.

Andriolo, Karin (2002) "Murder by Suicide: Episodes from Muslim History," *American Anthropologist*, 104: 736–742.

Antoun, Richard T. (1968) "The Social Significance of Ramadan in an Arab Village," *Muslim World*, 58: 36–42, 95–104.

——— (1976) "Anthropology," in Leonard Binder (ed.) *The Study of the Middle East: Research and Scholarship in the Humanities and the Social Sciences A Project of the Research and Training Committee of the Middle East Studies Association*, New York: Wiley.

Arkoun, Mohammed (1994) *Rethinking Islam: Common Questions, Uncommon Answers*, Boulder, CO: Westview Press.

Armbrust, Walter (1996) *Mass Culture and Modernism in Egypt*, Cambridge and New York: Cambridge University Press.

——— (2000) "The Riddle of Ramadan: Media, Consumer Culture, and the Christmasization of a Muslim Holiday," in Donna L. Bowen and Evelyn A. Early (eds) *Everyday Life in the Muslim Middle East*, rev. edn, Bloomington, IN: Indiana University Press.

——— (2002) "Islamists in Egyptian Cinema," *American Anthropologist*, 104: 922–931.

Asad, Talal (1980) "Ideology, Class and the Origins of the Islamic State," *Economy and Society*, 9: 450–473.

——— (1986) *The Idea of an Anthropology of Islam*, Washington, DC: Georgetown University, Center for Contemporary Arab Studies.

——— (2003) *Formations of the Secular: Christianity, Islam, Modernity*, Stanford, CA: Stanford University Press.

Aswad, Barbara (1970) "Social and Ecological Aspects in the Formation of Islam," in Louise E. Sweet (ed.) *Peoples and Cultures of the Middle East: An Anthropological Reader*, Garden City, NY: Natural History Press.

Banks, David J. (1990) "Resurgent Islam and Malay Rural Culture: Malay Novelists and the Invention of Culture," *American Ethnologist*, 17: 531–548.

Barclay, Harold B. (1963) "Muslim Religious Practice in a Village Suburb of Khartoum," *Muslim World*, 53: 205–211.

Bourdieu, Pierre (1962) *The Algerians*, trans. Richard Nice, Boston, MA: Beacon Press.

——— (1980) *The Logic of Practice*, trans. Richard Nice, Stanford, CA: Stanford University Press.

Bowen, John R. (1989) "*Salāt* in Indonesia: The Social Meanings of an Islamic Ritual," *Man*, 24: 600–619.

——— (1992) "On Scriptural Essentialism and Ritual Variation: Muslim Sacrifice in Sumatra and Morocco," *American Ethnologist*, 19: 656–671.

——— (1997) "Modern Intentions: Reshaping Subjectivities in an Indonesian Muslim Society," in Robert W. Hefner and Patricia Horvatich (eds) *Islam in an Era of Nation-States: Politics and Religious Renewal in Muslim Southeast Asia*, Honolulu, HI: University of Hawai'i Press.

Bradburd, Daniel (1998) *Being There: The Necessity of Fieldwork*, Washington, DC: Smithsonian Press.

Burton, Richard F. (1855–1856) *Personal Narrative of a Pilgrimage to El-Medinah and Meccah*, 3 vols, London: Longmans.

Chelhod, Joseph (1969) "Ethnologie du monde Arabe et Islamologie," *L'Homme*, 9: 24–40.

Coon, Carleton S. (1951) *Caravan: The Story of the Middle East*, New York: Holt.

Crapanzano, Vincent (1973) *The Hamadsha: A Study in Moroccan Ethnopsychiatry*, Berkeley, CA: University of California Press.

Delaney, Carol L. (1990) "The *hajj*: Sacred and Secular," *American Ethnologist*, 17: 513–530.

——— (1991) *The Seed and the Soil: Gender and Cosmology in Turkish Village Society*, Berkeley, CA: University of California Press.

Digard, Jean-Pierre (1978) "Perspectives anthropologiques sur l'Islam," *Revue française de sociologie*, 19: 497–523.

Edwards, David B. (1995) "Print Islam: Media and Religious Revolution in Afghanistan," *Anthropological Quarterly*, 68: 171–184.

——— (1996) *Heroes of the Age: Moral Fault Lines on the Afghan Frontier*, Berkeley, CA: University of California Press.

——— (2002) *Before Taliban: Genealogies of the Afghan Jihad*, Berkeley. CA: University of California Press.

Eickelman, Dale F. (1967) "Musaylima: An Approach to the Social Anthropology of Seventh Century Arabia," *Journal of the Economic and Social History of the Orient*, 10: 17–52.

——— (1976) *Moroccan Islam: Tradition and Society in a Pilgrimage Center*, Austin, TX: University of Texas Press.

——— (2001) *The Middle East and Central Asia: An Anthropological Approach*, 4th edn, Upper Saddle River, NJ: Prentice Hall.

——— (2002) *The Middle East: An Anthropological Approach*, 4th edn, Englewood Cliffs, NJ: Prentice Hall.

Eickelman, Dale F., and Jon W. Anderson (1997) "Print, Islam, and the Prospects of Civic Pluralism: New Religious Writings and their Audiences," *Journal of Islamic Studies*, 8: 43–62.

——— (1999) "Redefining Muslim Publics," in Dale F. Eickelman and Jon W. Anderson (eds) *New Media in the Muslim World: The Emerging Public Sphere*, Bloomington, IN: Indiana University Press.

Eickelman, Dale F., and James P. Piscatori (1990) *Muslim Travellers: Pilgrimage, Migration, and the Religious Imagination*, Berkeley, CA: University of California Press.

El-Aswad, el-Sayed (2002) *Religion and Folk Cosmology: Scenarios of the Visible and Invisible in Rural Egypt*, Westport, CT: Praeger.

El Gundi, Fadwa (1982) "The Emerging Islmaic Order: The Case of Egypt's Contemporary Islamic Movement," *Journal of Arab Affairs*, 1: 245–261.

El-Zein, Abdul Hamid (1974) *The Sacred Meadows: A Structural Analysis of Religious Symbolism in an East African Town*, Evanston, IL: Northwestern University Press.

——— (1977) "Beyond Ideology and Theology: The Search for the Anthropology of Islam," *Annual Review of Anthropology*, 6: 227–254.

Ellen, Roy F. (1983) "Social Theory, Ethnography, and the Understanding of Practical Islam in South-East Asia," in Michael B. Hooker (ed.) *Islam in South-East Asia*, Leiden: Brill.

Esack, Farid (1999) *On Being a Muslim: Finding a Religious Path in the World Today*, Oxford: Oneworld.

Evans-Pritchard, Edward E. (1949) *The Sanusi of Cyrenaica*, Oxford: Clarendon Press.

Firth, Raymond (1981) "Spiritual Aroma: Religion and Politics," *American Anthropologist*, 83: 582–601.

Fischer, Michael M.J. (1980) *Iran: From Religious Dispute to Revolution*, Cambridge, MA: Harvard University Press.

Fischer, Michael M.J., and Mehdi Abedi (eds) (1990) *Debating Muslims: Cultural Dialogues in Postmodernity and Tradition*, Madison, WI: University of Wisconsin Press.

Geertz, Clifford (1968) *Islam Observed: Religious Development in Morocco and Indonesia*, New Haven, CT: Yale University Press.

Gellner, Ernest (1969) *Saints of the Atlas*, London: Weidenfeld & Nicolson.

——— (1972) "Doctor and Saint," in Nikki R. Keddie (ed.) *Scholars, Saints, and Sufis: Muslim Religious Institutions in the Middle East since 1500*, Berkeley, CA: University of California Press.

——— (1981) *Muslim Society*, Cambridge and New York: Cambridge University Press.

Gilsenan, Michael (1973) *Saint and Sufi in Modern Egypt: An Essay in the Sociology of Religion*, Oxford: Clarendon Press.

——— (1982) *Recognizing Islam: An Anthropologist's Introduction*, London: Croom Helm.

——— (1990) "Very Like a Camel: The Appearance of an Anthropologist's Middle East," in Richard Fardon (ed.) *Localizing Strategies: Regional Traditions of Ethnographic Writing*, Washington, DC: Smithsonian Institution Press.

Gladney, Dru C. (1999) "The Salafiyya Movement in Northwest China: Islamic Fundamentalism among the Muslim Chinese," in Leif O. Manger (ed.) *Muslim Diversity: Local Islam in Global Contexts*, Richmond, UK: Curzon.

Goodman, Jane E. (2003) "The Proverbial Bourdieu: Habitus and the Politics of Representation in the Ethnography of Kabylia," *American Anthropologist*, 105: 782–793.

Gordon, Joel (1998) "Becoming the Image: Words of Gold, Talk Television, and Ramadan Nights on the Little Screen," *Visual Anthropology*, 10: 247–264.

Graham, William A. (1993) "Traditionalism in Islam: An Essay in Interpretation," *Journal of Interdisciplinary History*, 23: 495–522.

Hammoudi, Abdellah (1993) *The Victim and its Masks: An Essay on Sacrifice and Masquerade in the Maghreb*, trans. Paula Wissing, Chicago, IL: University of Chicago Press.

Hefner, Robert W. (1985) *Hindu Javanese: Tengger Tradition and Islam*, Princeton, NJ: Princeton University Press.

——— (2000) *Civil Islam: Muslims and Democratization in Indonesia*, Princeton, NJ: Princeton University Press.

——— (2002) "Global Violence and Indonesian Muslim Politics," *American Anthropologist*, 104: 754–765.

Hirschkind, Charles (2001) "Civic Virtue and Religious Reason: An Islamic Counterpublic," *Cultural Anthropology*, 16: 3–34.

Holy, Ladislav (1991) *Religion and Custom in a Muslim Society: The Berti of Sudan*, Cambridge: Cambridge University Press.

Houston, Christopher (2001) "The Brewing of Islamist Modernity: Tea Gardens and Public Space in Istanbul," *Theory Culture Society*, 18: 77–97.

Hume, David (1956) *The Natural History of Religion*, Stanford, CA: Stanford University Press.

Hussain, Amir (2003) "Muslims, Pluralism, and Interfaith Dialogue," in Omid Safi (ed.) *Progressive Muslims: On Justice, Gender and Pluralism*, Oxford: Oneworld.

Kassam, Tazim R. (2003) "On Being a Scholar of Islam: Risks and Responsibilities," in Omid Safi (ed.) *Progressive Muslims: On Justice, Gender and Pluralism*, Oxford: Oneworld.

Kramer, Martin S. (2001) *Ivory Towers on Sand: The Failure of Middle Eastern Studies in America*, Washington, DC: Washington Institute for Near East Policy.

Lagace, Robert O. (1957) "The Formation of the Muslim State," *Anthropology Tomorrow*, 6: 141–155.

Lane, Edward W. (1973) *An Account of the Manners and Customs of the Modern Egyptians*, 5th edn, New York: Dover Publications.

Lewis, Ioan M. (1984) "Sufism in Somaliland: A Study in Tribal Islam," in Akbar S. Ahmed and David M. Hart (eds) *Islam in Tribal Societies: From the Atlas to the Indus*, London: Routledge & Kegan Paul.

Lewis, Bernard (2002) *What Went Wrong? Western Impact and Middle Eastern Response*, Oxford and New York: Oxford University Press.

Lukens-Bull, Ronald A. (1999) "Between Text and Practice: Considerations in the Anthropological Study of Islam," *Marburg Journal of Religion*, 4: 1–21.

Mahmood, Saba (2001) "Rehearsed Spontaneity and the Conventionality of Ritual: Disciplines of Salāt," *American Ethnologist*, 28: 827–853.

Mamdani, Mahmood (2002) "Good Muslim, Bad Muslim: A Political Perspective on Culture and Terrorism," *American Anthropologist*, 104: 766–775.

Mernissi, Fatima (1987) *Beyond the Veil: Male–Female Dynamics in Modern Muslim Society*, rev. edn, Bloomington, IN: Indiana University Press.

Messick, Brinkley M. (1993) *The Calligraphic State: Textual Domination and History in a Muslim Society*, Berkeley, CA: University of California Press.

Mosley, Charles W. (ed.) (1983) *The Travels of Sir John Mandeville*, Harmondsworth: Penguin Books.

Munson, Henry (1987) *Islam and Revolution in the Middle East*, New Haven, CT: Yale University Press.

Murphy, Richard N. (2000) "The Hairbrush and the Dagger: Mediating Modernity in Lahore," in Walter Armbrust (ed.) *Mass Mediations: New Approaches to Popular Culture in the Middle East and Beyond*, Berkeley, CA: University of California Press.

Nagata, Judith (1982) "Islamic Revival and the Problem of Legitimacy Among Rural Religious Elites in Malaysia," *Man*, 17: 42–57.

Peters, Emyrs (1984) "The Paucity of Ritual among Middle Eastern Pastoralists," in Akbar S. Ahmed and David M. Hart (eds) *Islam in Tribal Societies: From the Atlas to the Indus*, London: Routledge & Kegan Paul.

Rahman, Fazlur (1968) *Islam*, Garden City, NY: Doubleday Anchor Books.

Robbins, Joel (2003) "What is a Christian? Notes toward an Anthropology of Christianity: Introduction to the Symposium," *Religion*, 33: 191–199.

Rosen, Lawrence (2002) *The Culture of Islam: Changing Aspects of Contemporary Muslim Life*, Chicago, IL: University of Chicago Press.

Safi, Omid (2003) "Introduction: The Times They are A-Changin'—Muslim Quest for Justice, Gender, Equality and Pluralism," in Omid Safi (ed.) *Progressive Muslims: On Justice, Gender and Pluralism*, Oxford: Oneworld.

Said, Edward W. (1979) *Orientalism*, New York: Vintage Books.

——— (1981) *Covering Islam: How the Media and the Experts Determine How We See the Rest of the World*, New York: Pantheon Books.

Salzman, Philip (1975) "Islam and Authority in Tribal Iran: A Comparative Comment," *The Muslim World*, 65: 186–195.

Schimmel, Annemarie (1955) "Zur Anthropologie des Islam," in Claas J. Bleeker (ed.) *Studies in the History of Religions*, Leiden: Brill.

Sells, Michael A. (1999) *Approaching the Qur'an: The Early Revelations*, Ashland, OR: White Cloud Press.

——— (2002) "Understanding, Not Indoctrination," *The Washington Post*, August 8, 2002.

Shahrani, M. Nazif Mohib, and Robert L. Canfield (1984) *Revolutions & Rebellions in Afghanistan: Anthropological Perspectives*, Berkeley, CA: Institute of International Studies, University of California.

Shamsul, Amri B. (1997) "Identity Construction, Nation Formation, and Islamic Revivalism in Malaysia," in Robert W. Hefner and Patricia Horvatich (eds) *Islam in an Era of Nation-States: Politics and Religious Renewal in Muslim Southeast Asia*, Honolulu, HI: University of Hawai'i Press.

Smith, Wilfred Cantwell (1957) *Islam in Modern History*, Princeton, NJ: Princeton University Press.

Smith, Jonathan Z. (1978) *Map is not Territory: Studies in the History of Religions*, Leiden: Brill.

Starrett, Gregory (1995) "The Hexis of Interpretation: Islam and the Body in the Egyptian Popular School," *American Ethnologist*, 22: 953–969.

——— (1998) *Putting Islam to Work: Education, Politics, and Religious Transformation in Egypt*, Berkeley, CA: University of California Press.

Sweet, Louise E. (1970) *Peoples and Cultures of the Middle East: An Anthropological Reader*, 2 vols, Garden City, NY: Natural History Press.

Swenson, Jill D. (1985) "Martyrdom: Mytho-Cathexis and the Mobilization of the Masses in the Iranian Revolution," *Ethos*, 13: 121–149.

Tapper, Richard (1984) "Holier than Thou: Islam in Three Tribal Societies," in Akbar S. Ahmed and David M. Hart (eds) *Islam in Tribal Societies: From the Atlas to the Indus*, London: Routledge & Kegan Paul.

Tapper, Nancy, and Richard Tapper (1987) "The Birth of the Prophet: Ritual and Gender in Turkish Islam," *Man*, 22: 69–92.

Toth, James (2003) "Islamism in Southern Egypt: A Case Study of a Radical Religious Movement," *International Journal of Middle East Studies*, 35: 547–572.

Turner, Bryan S. (2003) *Islam: Critical Concepts in Sociology*, London and New York: Routledge.

van Lennep, Henry J. (1875) *Bible Lands: Their Modern Customs and Manners Illustrative of Scripture*, New York: Harper & Brothers.

Varisco, Daniel M. (1993) "The Agricultural Marker Stars in Yemeni Folklore," *Asian Folklore Studies*, 52: 119–142.

——— (1997) *Medieval Folk Astronomy and Agriculture in Arabia and the Yemen*, Aldershot: Ashgate Publishing Ltd.

——— (2000) "Slamming Islam: Participant Webservation with a Web of Meanings to Boot," *Working Papers of the MES*, Arlington, VA: American Anthropological Association.

——— (2002) "September 11: Participant Webservation of the "War on Terrorism"," *American Anthropologist*, 104: 934–938.

von Grunebaum, Gustave E. (1961) "An Analysis of Islamic Civilization and Cultural Anthropology," in *Actes du Colloque sur la Sociologie Musulmane*, Brussels: Centre pour l'Étude des Problèmes du Monde Musulman Contemporain.

Werbner, Pnina (1996) "Allegories of Sacred Imperfection: Magic, Hermeneutics, and Passion in The Satanic Verses," *Current Anthropology*, 37: S55–S86.

White, Jenny B. (1999) "Amplifying Trust: Community and Communication in Turkey," in Dale F. Eickelman and Jon W. Anderson (eds) *New Media in the Muslim World: The Emerging Public Sphere*, Bloomington, IN: Indiana University Press.

——— (2002) *Islamist Mobilization in Turkey: A Study in Vernacular Politics*, Seattle, WA: University of Washington Press.

Wolf, Eric R. (1951) "The Social Organization of Mecca and the Origins of Islam," *Southwestern Journal of Anthropology*, 7: 329–356.

Woodward, Mark R. (1996) "Introduction: Talking across Paradigms: Indonesia, Islam, and Orientalism," in Mark R. Woodward (ed.) *Toward a New Paradigm: Recent Developments in Indonesian Islamic Thought*, Tempe, AZ: Arizona State University, Program for Southeast Asian Studies.

Young, William C. (1993) "The Ka'ba, Gender, and the Rites of Pilgrimage," *International Journal of Middle East Studies*, 25: 285–300.

Glossary of anthropological terms

Jens Kreinath

This glossary is intended to be used as an analytical tool to enhance understanding of the terms used by the authors. The entries usually reflect the broader academic usage of the terms listed, but the attempt was made to always indicate the anthropological usage and relevance of these terms. This may imply that the actual terms provided here and the definitions given may differ from those employed or intended by authors. This difference in meaning, definition, and usage does not mean that one has to be preferred over the other, but should be seen rather as an editor's note indicating a difference in definition and understanding. This glossary is not only intended to clarify and sharpen the understanding of the terms but also as a means to compare the different theoretical approaches as employed by the authors. A further venue to achieve this goal is the listing and cross-referencing of alternative or related terms provided at the end of the main entry. Using this glossary as a toolbox for clustering anthropological concepts is finally intended to provide a multidimensional theoretical grid that allows to enhance the location and analysis of ethnographic data. For further readings on the definitions of anthropological terms see also: Alan Barnard and Jonathan Spencer (eds) (1998) *Encyclopedia of Social and Cultural Anthropology*. London and New York: Routledge; H. James Birx (2006) *Encyclopedia of Anthropology*, 5 vols., Thousand Oaks, CA: Sage; Tim Ingold (1994) *Companion Encyclopedia of Anthropology*, London and New York: Routledge.

a priori A philosophical concept used to refer to the possibility of universals in human knowledge not based on empirical data but prior to any form of experience. See also *epistemology*.

acculturation An anthropological concept to refer to forms of diffusion as part of cultural contact in the colonial encounter, in which the predominant culture forces subordinate groups to adopt its practices and traditions.

acquisition A concept widely used in numerous disciplines with differing definitions; in developmental psychology it is used to refer to the act of acquiring competence or gaining knowledge or mastery. In linguistics, it refers to the mastery of a language, its grammatical rules or elements. Anthropologists use this term to refer to the process of learning cultural features, habits or traditions.

aesthetics Generally used to pertain to processes of human perception as effected by physical stimuli upon the human body and its senses, more specifically in Western philosophical traditions also refers to the judgment of taste commonly classified as the sublime or beautiful. In anthropology, it is highly contested whether and how aesthetics can be employed as a cross-cultural category.

agency As a central anthropological term, it refers to the human ability to act on one's own behalf, but also to a person having the ability to be the subject of action. Agency suggests intentionality or consciousness in strategic actions, implying that the individual or group has the ability to perform actions that change social structure.

alienation Sociological term introduced by Karl Marx to refer to the economic and social state of the working class as being withdrawn, estranged, or isolated from the outcome of industrial processes of production. See also *capitalism* and *production*.

anthropology As a general term used in philosophical and theological discourses, it refers to the field of study dedicated to the human condition. As an academic discipline, it refers to the social, scientific and humanistic study of humankind in all its aspects and within a holistic perspective. Founded in the late nineteenth century as a comparative discipline with a predominantly evolutionary agenda in studying foreign societies and cultures, social and cultural anthropology in Europe and North America is transformed in the early twentieth century into a more descriptive and empirical discipline.

Arabist A scholar who specializes in the study of Arabic language, culture, and literature.

archaic This term used to classify a society, culture or religion as being in the earliest stages of human evolution. It also described societies that are seen as less advanced compared to modern civilizations; the paradigms of evolutionary models varied from advancements in technology, modes of production, forms of social organization, and features of religious beliefs among many others. In contrast to the notion of primitive, which refers to the degree of complexity, archaic rather employs a temporal point of reference. See also *primitive*.

area studies Anthropological approach to ethnological research intended to gather and relate data on various aspects of a geographical region and its inhabitants, such as: natural resources, history, language, religion, as well as the distribution of cultural and economic features. It is a field of study spanning from cultural diffusion to human ecology.

aristocracy A sociological and political term used to refer to a class or group of people which consider themselves as superior by holding exceptional rank and inherent privileges including the right to rule over the common people. The formation of aristocracy indicates a hierarchy in a society, although the opposite may not necessary be the case. See also *stratified society*.

armchair anthropologist A disparaging description, likely introduced by Bronislaw Malinowski, used to condemn anthropological research carried out by scholars in the Victorian era of the nineteenth century based solely on cross cultural comparison using non-anthropological sources like travelogues or missionary reports without ever having carried out original fieldwork.

asceticism A sociological term introduced by Max Weber to characterize a religious lifestyle in which a person attains spiritual and moral perfection through self-denial, self-mortification or similar practices.

assimilation A sociological and anthropological term used to refer to processes of socialization and enculturation that occurs when religious or ethnic minorities lose their religious and cultural features while adapting to the dominating society or culture by changing their native practices and discourses; partially due to the introduction of technology or new forms of political governance.

authority The persuasive force of a person, group or institution; often compared to the concept of power, used to refer to the attempt to determine control or command. The notion of authority as introduced by Max Weber; it implies the possibility of finding acceptance toward a command but is also used to refer to an accepted or contested source of information. See also *power*, *hegemony* and *dominance.*

autonomy Legal and political term to refer to the independence and freedom of will individuals are entitled to; also used to refer to a self-governing community and policy.

behavior As a generic term, it refers to any kind of observable activity, conduct or bodily carriage often patterned by social and cultural standards. As a psychological and sociological term, it is often used to imply the unconscious and habituated routines while de-emphasizing the intentionality of the human individual.

body technique As a technical term introduced by the French anthropologist and sociologist Marcel Mauss, it is used to analyze and describe the ways in which humans use and train their body to acquire cultural practices. Walking, dancing, and writing are examples for body techniques. See also *discipline*, *habitus*, and *mimesis.*

bourgeoisie A sociological term used to refer to the skilled middle classes that emerged in early modern times due to urbanization subsequent to the vanishing feudalistic systems and their systems of social and political organization; in Marxist theory also regarded as the promoters of capitalism, an economic system exploitative of the *proletariat* or working class. See also *capitalism.*

brotherhood Technical term used to refer to a more or less formally organized community of male members of a society, building a distinct social unit that is often engaged in a particular trade, profession or organization, sharing common ideological interests, and personal qualities. Often it refers to religious communities with tacit forms of hierarchy embedded in notions of egalitarianism.

bureaucracy A term referring to the formalized organization of political institutions with many administrative levels and responsibilities, in which tasks and authorities are delegated among individuals, offices, or departments, held together by a central body of administration. According to many sociologists, bureaucratic institutions are specific forms of political governance going along with the emergence of the concept of modern nation states. See also *institution.*

capital A major concept in the political economy, it refers to the assets held by an individual or incorporation that determines and controls access to resources of status, prestige, and power. It is not only an economic concept as introduced in the social and political theory of Karl Marx, but also has certain more immaterial ramifications as forms of symbolic or cultural capital with moral and religious implications as proposed by Pierre Bourdieu.

capitalism An economic system of production, distribution and consumption of material goods based simply on the desire to make and maintain profits, implying the justified exploitation of all human and natural resources available. Primarily the market and its supply-and-demand mechanism regulate the mode of production. See also *industrialism.*

caste A term most often used as a form of social stratification in which birth determines membership through a specific line of decent; where there is usually no mechanism for upward mobility to a higher social class. Predominantly found in India and South Asia. See also *hierarchy* and *stratified society.*

ceremony A term referring to the active bodily forms of worship, it was formerly reserved to denote to all forms of religious and ritual practice and behavior in the church service. Since the late nineteenth and early twentieth century, the term "ritual" almost fully replaced the usage of this term. See also *ritual.*

charisma This sociological concept usually refers to gifted persons possessing extraordinary talents in social and political theory. It is most commonly used to specify that form of authority based on the personal characteristics of the leader. A religious leader or prophet may obtain the legitimacy of charismatic authority through reference to non-human powers. Formerly proposed by the sociologist Max Weber, this term is often used to study revitalization movements. See also *authority*.

chiefdom Form of social and political organization in which a chief governs more than one tribe. In traditional societies, chiefs have a special social status or rank set apart from the rest of the members of the other tribes. Chiefs commonly rule together with family members and are in the position of power through lines of their clan descent or personal skills, often legitimized by reference to a divine institution of chiefdom. See also *stratified society* and *tribe*.

choreography As a theoretical term, it is used in the performing arts to refer to the study of dance and the performing of sequential body movements to refer to a specific arrangement of bodily actions.

civil society In sociology and politics it refers to the collective aggregate of non-governmental organizations and institutions that manifests the interests and will of citizens. In general, it also refers to all individuals and organizations in a society, which are independent of the government.

civilization It is used in anthropological theory to refer to stratified societies with complex forms of social and political organization, often characterized by reference to their modes of production such as irrigation and forms of intensive agriculture. It also refers to the use of writing and accounting techniques as well as the formation of a bureaucratic state apparatus.

clash of civilizations Proposed by political scientist Samuel P. Huntington as a theory of cultural conflict. It assumes that people's cultural and religious identities are the primary sources of conflict after the decline of the communist rule in 1980s. In the post-Cold War world, the key forces will not be societies or states but cultural entities (e.g., Western vs. Eastern cultures or Islam vs. Christianity).

class A sociological term commonly used in theories of political economy to describe the stratification of society, assuming that people with the same status share common political interests, as for example: the working class or the bourgeoisie. See also *hierarchy* and *stratified society*.

cleric A term often used in the sociology of religion to refer to a person taking a professional office in the Christian church. For example, a priest or monk is usually the leader of a religious community or order.

code Technical term used in linguistics, semiotics, and communication theory to indicate the mode by which a sender sequences and transmits information to a receiver, using discrete and unambiguously identifiable signals with a commonly agreed upon meaning. See also *communication*, *information*, and *semiotics*.

cognition As a technical term, it refers to the process of reasoning and knowing. In psychological anthropology, it also refers to any mental function, which deals with reasoning styles, causal inference, logic syllogisms, and methodical thinking. See also *epistemology*.

cognitive dissonance As technical term in social psychology, it is used to refer to conflicts and tensions in a society experienced and caused by its members' holding ideas contradictory or incompatible to their social environment.

collective memory A term used in the sociology of culture, introduced by Maurice Halbwachs, referring to the shared ways members of a society or culture remember the importance of significant events in their common past; also indicating the methods by which they achieve remembrance: rituals and festivals as religious and cultural events. See also *cultural memory* and *collective representation*.

collective representation A sociological term established by Émile Durkheim used to refer to shared and group-held representations of social reality, often expressing the foundational categories of a society or group that is important to the identity of the society or group itself, such as space, time, and causality. See also *production of knowledge.*

colonialism The term refers in political theory and history to the deliberate and strategic spread of political power and economic control over foreign territories by a sovereign state for the mere purpose of exploitation of natural and cultural resources. In the nineteenth century, it was one of the major means of European states to increase revenue and try to establish dominance over the rest of the world. See also *dominance* and *imperialism.*

communication In anthropology, it is the concept of conveying information from one to another. It is not limited to speech or writing but also uses art, music, and ritual, to set a precedent of shared understandings within a culture. Communication of this sort often takes an insider's perspective to decipher and as such is inherent only within the specific community. See also *code*, *conventionality*, *linguistics*, *semiotics*, and *symbol.*

constructivism A communication and system theory developed in the vein of cybernetics, based on the paradigm that people usually unconsciously construct ideas as well as categories and concepts (believed to be pre-existing) through forms of social interaction, including those such as gender and kinship. See also *production of knowledge.*

consumerism An economic term used in capitalist theories with the assumption that an increased consumption of goods and products is beneficial for the production and distribution of material objects. It also refers to the social and economic order based on the creation and fostering of a desire to purchase goods and materials in increasing amounts. See also *capitalism.*

contextualization As a general methodological term it indicates the mode of inquiry that considers a social or cultural event or a written or visual document in relation to the social, political, or historical context, in which it occurs, rather than as set apart from its specific setting.

conventionality A term used in linguistics and the semiotics of culture to refer to a certain degree of conformity and arbitrariness to a set of agreed upon or generally accepted rules and standards of social or linguistic norms or regulations. See also *symbol* and *linguistics.*

conversion Term commonly used in the sociology and psychology of religion to indicate the change of religion and religious aspirations of an individual based on spiritual or other events resulting in a comprehensive transformation of an individual's religious orientation.

cosmopolitanism Sociological term used to refer to the view or ideology held by the social and political elite of a society and based on the assumption that all kinds of human ethnic groups belong to a single community based on their shared morality. Being critical of ideas of patriotism and nationalism, it often objects communitarian and particularistic theories.

creolization Term used in linguistic anthropology to suggest a specific kind of language change based on continuing cultural contact, which also can imply the formation of a new language due to the extended contact between two linguistic communities. For example, whereas pidgin is a language emerging in situations of cultural contact with no native speaker of this language, creolé is a language with a community of native speakers. See also *diachronic analysis*, *heterogeneity*, and *syncretism.*

critical anthropology A specific approach in social and cultural anthropology, it fosters a critical stance in the analysis of social and cultural practices by employing sociological theories and theories of political economy. See also *critical theory.*

critical theory As a theory prevalent in cultural anthropology, it formerly only referred in the European context to the Frankfurt School and critical theory, a school of social theory and inquiry inspired by a refined concept of political economy by Karl Marx and applied to late-capitalist societies. More recently, critical anthropology in North America often follows, with inspiration from French structural and post-structural thought, raises objections to certain forms of objective knowledge as assumed in the Frankfurt School. See also *agency*, *discourse*, *deconstruction*, and *objectivism*.

cross cousin Anthropological term used to identify one's father's sister's children or to the mother's brother's children related through an opposite sex-sibling link.

cross cousin marriage The marriage of an individual to their parent's opposite-sex sibling's child, e.g., a son marrying his father's sister's daughter. See also *parallel cousin marriage*.

cross cultural analysis As a methodological procedure it refers to the examination of specific aspects or features of cultures found in more than one culture. It is usually the mode of comparing cultures by reference to ethnographic studies. See also *ethnology* and *typology*.

cult As a key term in the anthropology of religion, it is used with pejorative connotations to refer to deviant or heterodox and exclusive forms of worship, including rituals and ideologies, mostly seen as fixed to a specific set of beliefs and practices surrounding an individual with a charismatic authority. See also *revitalization* and *charisma*.

cultural memory A concept of cultural analysis introduced by Jan and Aleida Assmann to refer to those memories which a group or society shares and passes on through texts and images. This term indicates an emphasis on different modes of memory not as only an individual and private matter but a part of collective experience influenced by history and culture and the individual's placement in present time and place. See also *collective memory* and *collective representation*.

cultural relativism Fundamental assumption of modern approaches in cultural anthropology introduced by Franz Boas and based on the idea that one can understand cultural traits best when viewed within their respective cultural context. As a paradigm of cultural anthropology, it is the attempt to view and judge cultures only based on their value system and from the insider's perspective. See also *emic* and *ethnocentrism*.

cultural system A constructivist and system theoretical approach to the study of culture that views culture and the relation to its environment as linked through a number of systems in which change in one subsystem effects change in another subsystem.

culture In North American anthropology, it is taken as a core paradigm that everything that a human can learn is based on instruction, experimentation, or imitation and transmitted from one generation to the next shared among the members of a group of people. See also *anthropology*.

custom Even though a dated term, anthropologists use it to refer to persisting traditional patterns and often unconsciously transmitted practices, beliefs, and acts shared by a specific group as part of their culture and taken as the marker of ethnic identity. See also *behavior*.

deconstruction A theoretical program and literary method most eloquently proposed by the French philosopher Jacques Derrida. It is based on the idea that all meaning is created through ambivalent webs of signification that can be read in a multiplicity of ways to unravel and question unconsciously established meanings and to find hidden biases and subjective understandings. See also *production of knowledge*.

descent In general terms, it is in a literal and genetic connection through bloodline. In anthropology, it is characterized as a perceived connection to such lines that is not only personally but socially accepted (e.g., an emperors' descent from the gods, adoptive child as descendent, etc.).

description A term in general methodology that is used across academic disciplines to refer to the processes and methods of analyzing and organizing information in such a way that it serves to identify, locate, and envision specific phenomena in the natural and cultural worlds. See also *interpretation* and *explanation.*

determinism It is a worldview or philosophical theory positing that natural or cultural factors inevitably determine the human condition, often going along with denying the possibility of agency and free will. See also *essentialism* and *explanation.*

diachronic analysis As a methodological term it refers to the study of socio-cultural phenomena and empirical data based on a temporal framework, exploring these data through time rather than an analysis based exclusively on that single moment. See also *synchronic analysis.*

dialectics A philosophic concept coined in German idealism and refined in the dialectical materialism of Marxist and Neo-Marxist theories. It usually includes the steps of thesis and antithesis resulting in a synthesis of a higher order, often assuming a continuous progress and setting the stage for numerous evolutionary approaches to the study of society and culture, including long-term historical changes. In Neo-Marxist critical theory as proposed by Theodor Adorno, the term primarily refers the negative dialectics as a means to describe continuous differentiation between different social and political groups conceived as thesis and antithesis without a subsequent synthesis or necessary progress. See also *critical theory.*

dialogic anthropology A branch of cultural anthropology most prominently proposed by Dennis Tedlock and based on the idea that language and meaning are never fixed and only work in and through situations of dialogue; which are principally open-ended and contingent. See also *hermeneutics* and *interpretation.*

diaspora Sociological term formerly used to refer to the dispersion of Jews outside of Israel in times of late antiquity. Academically, it used to denote generally any form of migration or movement of a population away from their homeland, but also any community living away from their homeland.

dichotomy A philosophical term used to refer to often erratic categorical forms of classification of phenomena into two opposed but mutually exclusive and irreducible classes or subclasses. It is usually used pejoratively in order to call for overcoming erratic forms of classification in Western thinking, such as the mind-body dualism. See also *incommensurability.*

discipline As a generic term, it is often used to refer to coercive rules of conduct or rigid methods of practice imposed upon the human body. In the context of higher education it also refers to the different branches of knowledge and subdivisions in the fields of scholarly research within the university, such as academic disciplines.

discourse This term refers to an extended form or sequence of written or spoken communication or a chains of verbal expressions made in speech or writing about a specific topic often also in form of dialog and conversation. As an anthropological concept, employed in critical theory, it also describes thematic fields implying the idea that conflict and power are running though all forms of human spoken communication in their construction of reality. See also *critical theory.*

discursive tradition A term in the continental critical theory and coined by the French philosopher and intellectual Michel Foucault to conceptualize literary and academic traditions of classification and reasoning through discourse that shapes and is shaped by power and knowledge. See also *discourse*, *critical theory* and *tradition.*

disposition A term commonly used in social psychology to denote a person's habits, preparation or likelihood to act in specific and often predictable ways. See also *habitus.*

doctrine A generic term to refer to teachings and beliefs or systems of these commonly accepted as authoritative by and definitive for a particular group; not necessarily tied to specific ideological premises. See also *dogma.*

dogma A term usually confined to philosophy and theology used to refer to conventions or established beliefs people are forced to accept as being unquestionable and authoritative, often of ideological nature. See also *doctrine* and *ideology.*

dominance A sociological term used to refer to the state of being in which one group has power and authority over another, often seen as the coercive rule that delimits the agency of individuals. See also *hegemony* and *power.*

domination As a term on political and social theory, it refers to the use of power to dominate or defeat another group or individual. See also *dominance.*

economic anthropology As a branch of cultural anthropology, it studies modes of subsistence as well as systems of production, distribution, and consumption of material goods in relation to social organization by distinguishing between the modes and means of production as well as between the different forms of distribution and exchange. See also *political economy.*

efficacy A generic term used to refer to the ability to produce a desired effect or outcome, often used in the study of ritual and magic or other forms of symbolic acts to determine social and psychological effects. See also *ceremony* and *ritual.*

egalitarianism As a term in political theory, it refers to a system of political organization in which a society is classless and not stratified while all people are entitled to equal rights at birth. See also *hierarchy.*

elite A sociological term used to refer to a group of people who enjoy superior status through political, intellectual, social or economic means. See also *hierarchy* and *stratified society.*

embodiment As a technological term, it became an anthropological paradigm to study bodily and habituated forms of human cognition, emotion, and expression imbuing of culture in such forms as values, norms, identity, and physical forms; notably as inscribed in the human body as for example posture, gesture and mimic. See also *habitus* and *body technique.*

emic An anthropological term derived from linguistics (notably from the word "phonemics") introduced by Marvin Harris to refer to the insider's perspective, which is not necessarily identical with the "native's point of view". It serves as a heuristic concept in cultural anthropology to understand cultural traditions from the viewpoint of those who practice them by employing *interpretive* means of description. See also *etic, insider, interpretation,* and *hermeneutics.*

empiricism As a generic philosophical term, it was introduced in the nineteenth century to refer to a school of thought that holds the methodological position that human knowledge is and should be gained through observable and testable experience. See also *objectivism.*

Enlightenment A philosophical term used to refer to an era in Western philosophy, science, intellectual, and cultural life in the eighteenth century centered upon the assumption that intellectual and moral education of humankind through the arts and sciences is possible and advocating rationality as the major source of authority. See also *epistemology.*

epistemology Generic philosophical term used to refer to the study and theory of knowledge as an activity of the human mind by focusing on the understanding and reasoning of any given information.

essentialism Philosophical term that refers to the attempt to conclude from the constantly changing attributes of natural and cultural phenomena, an unchangeable and timeless essence. As a form of reductionism marked by suppression of temporality, it assumes primordial core of being to what are historically contingent products of human forms of agency. See also *determinism.*

ethics As a philosophical term, it refers to the moral study of human conduct that addresses accepted concepts of right and wrong as well as just and unjust within a society or culture. In its anthropological use, it is seen as a culturally specific lens on moral values in societies bounded in time and space.

ethnic group It is a group of people sharing numerous cultural features and identifying themselves, as distinct unit through their common heritage; which could include language, religion, folklore, and material culture.

ethnicity An anthropological concept used to describe a particular way of life by drawing boundaries between groups based on heritage and affiliation resulting from their ethnic kinship ties. See also *ethnic group* and *race.*

ethnocentrism Practice of viewing and judging another culture, including its values and traditions, in terms of the values of one's own culture and implying superiority of one's culture over the other culture. See also *cultural relativism.*

ethnography As a term in anthropological method, it refers to detailed and yet holistic description of a particular contemporary culture by means of an *interpretive* framework of analysis. It is based on direct contact with the people of the cultures studied referred to as fieldwork; it stands in clear contrast to any comparative account of other cultures. See also *anthropology* and *ethnology.*

ethnology This is a comparative and classificatory study of specific features of two or more cultures based on their respective differences and similarities. See also *anthropology* and *ethnography.*

ethos This term generally refers to customs and habits as the distinguishing characteristics or fundamental values of a person, society or culture. As a concept introduced by Gregory Bateson, it also refers to the attempt to study a person or culture as a means to capture the communality in the emotional tone and the tacit ambiance the members of a group share, as opposed to their cognitive and ideological communality. See also *behavior.*

etic It refers to the perspective or view of a cultural outsider, which cultural anthropologists may take in their attempt to theorize specific features in cross cultural comparison. This is in contrast with the insider's perspective. See also *emic* and *cross cultural analysis.*

etiquette Generic term used to refer to the proper codes and rules of conduct, which define and govern socially acceptable forms of human behavior and social interaction. See also *code* and *symbol.*

evolutionism As a general theoretical term, it refers to the nineteenth century school of thought in anthropology that explained variations in the cultures of the world by employing a single unilineal path of stages (savage, barbaric, civilized). The guiding theoretical models often associated with it (e.g., primitive or archaic) have been abandoned due to their ethnocentrism and underlying biases toward non-European people and cultures. See also *functionalism* and *structuralism.*

exegesis A theological term used to refer to the procedures of explanation and interpretation primarily of foundational religious or legal texts, usually resulting in the form of a commentary. See also *interpretation* and *hermeneutics.*

exoticizing A form of "*othering*" as commonly used in discourses on the "Orient" or other "non-Western" cultures by way of creating an idealized and essentializing image of the other culture as being an overtly exotic and strange people. See also *ethnocentrism, essentialism* and *orientalism.*

explanation As a generic term, it refers to the act of making something comprehensible, but when used as a methodological term in the social and natural sciences, it refers to the forms of scientific reasoning to decipher natural laws as a higher order of abstraction and generality in contrast to the description or interpretation of singular historical events. See also *interpretation* and *description.*

extremism As a political and sociological term, it refers to positions outside commonly accepted norms of a society, typically uncompromising in their policies, ideological doctrines and actions. See also *fundamentalism.*

feminism Generic term introduced in the 1960s to refer to doctrines and political or social movements, which advocate the economic, legal, and political emancipation of women and the protection of their equal rights. See also *gender* and *ideology.*

feminist anthropology Important approach in critical anthropology questioning tacit male biases in the study of societies and cultures. It focuses on women and gender, examining the differing understandings of roles, expectations, and inequalities based on differing conceptions of the different sexes. See also *critical anthropology.*

fieldwork As a hallmark method of modern social and cultural anthropology, it involves anthropologists living for an extended time with the people they study within their own culture in an attempt to gain an emic perspective or native's point of view through the method of anthropology. See also *ethnography* and *participant observation.*

folk culture This term generally refers to traditional and especially rural forms of culture, which often become markers of local cultural or ethnic identity, as, for example, in folklore, folktale, folk music, or folk classification.

formation As a technical term used in the context of critical theory, it refers to the act of arranging or making of a discourse, often implying that the genealogy reveals the processes and interests in the making of a discourse. See also *critical theory*, *genealogy,* and *production of knowledge.*

fragmentation A sociological term used to refer to the disintegration of social groups as well as their ethical norms and guidelines governing their behaviors, thoughts, and relationships. See also *alienation.*

framework As a theoretical term, it often refers to the model or underlying structure that is seen as determining a specific outcome. For example, religion can be a framework for social structure.

function This generic theoretical term usually employed in mathematical theory determines a specific relation in such a way that each element of a given set in a domain is associated with an element of another set as its scope or outcome. Also regarded as "something as being the purpose of something else". In anthropology it usually refers to the roles or responsibilities some person has or is expected to perform. See also *explanation.*

functionalism An anthropological approach to the study of society and culture that primarily searches for charters of social behavior and cultural practice and their functions in support of the fulfillment of individual needs for survival. The school of anthropological inquiry and analysis is uniquely attributed to the work of Bronislaw Malinowski. See also *structural functionalism.*

fundamentalism Sociological term used to denote any form of religious or ideological movements characterized by a return to foundational principles. It usually includes the objection of any form of compromise or deviation from an original doctrine or dogma often resulting in a resistance to the effects and threats of modernization and globalization with an emphasis on literal interpretation of the foundational scriptures. See also *extremism*.

gender A generic term used to mark the ways in which roles of the different sexes are culturally constructed and prescribed; including how members of the two sexes are expected to act according to these roles. See also *sexuality* and *feminism*.

genealogy In cultural anthropology generally used to refer to the successive generations of kins. In critical anthropology, it follows Michel Foucault in his philosophical usage as a historical technique that questions commonly held understandings of beliefs through tracing the development of people and society throughout history. See also *critical theory*.

gerontocracy A term in political anthropology used to refer to the formal or informal rule of elders with their authority usually attributed due to their age and experience.

gesture As a general term, it refers to any tacit bodily movement having a specific culturally agreed upon meaning. In the study of non-verbal communication, it often refers to bodily movements with symbolic significance as something done with an indication of intention.

globalization As a term of political theory and economy, it refers to the emergence of the world system and the growing interdependence of nations and people by world trade, transportation, media and technological innovations along with rapid changes in local economies. See also *colonialism*, *imperialism*, and *hegemony*.

government As a term of political sciences, it refers to a form of political organization in which an institution as the governing authority reigns over people as political unit. See also *bureaucracy* and *institution*.

great and little tradition Theoretical approach to the anthropological study of local traditions of the so-called world religions as proposed by Robert Redfield to distinguish between the regional variance in the local interpretations and practices of religious traditions arising from the differences between the texts, structures, and theologies of the respective religion in a global scale versus the lived reality of practitioners on a local level. See also *syncretism*, *heterogeneity*, and *hybridity*.

habit It refers to a pattern of behavior that is based on the routines and conventions as established through custom and repetition. See also *custom* and *habitus*.

habitus As a term of sociological and anthropological theory, it is widely used in conjunction with Pierre Bourdieu's theory of practice to denote the entire set of bodily, perceptual, emotional, and cognitive dispositions of humans, which shape and constrain their social practices as a totality of learned, bodily skills, including: habits, style, and taste. All aspects of culture are seen as embroidered and anchored by the techniques of the body. See also *embodiment*, *body techniques*, and *hexis*.

hegemony A term used in political theory and sociology coined by the Italian Marxist Antonio Gramsci to refer to the domination or power of one person or group over another, indicating that a diverse society can be ruled or dominated by one of its social classes through persuasive strategies. The specifics of hegemony versus other types of power are the normally unperceived force of constraint or expectations deemed natural, while preserving the privileged position of the ruler. See also *authority*, *domination*, and *power*.

heritage As a term in sociology of culture, it refers to practices handed down from generation to generation through tradition. See also *inheritance*.

hermeneutics As a philosophical and methodological term, it refers to the rules and codes of mutual understanding as well as to the study and interpretation of material expressions of human culture. This implies all techniques and methods that enhance the understanding one can gain from experiencing something, by way of reading, listening, or interacting, including questions of theory and practice alike. See also *interpretation*.

heterodoxy As term in the anthropology and sociology of religion, it is predominantly used to refer to positions, opinions or stances by a specific group of people that held additional or "other" doctrines, which a dominating community perceives as not correct and deviating from the official standards they define as acceptable. See also *othering* and *orthodoxy*.

heterogeneity Philosophical and theoretical term used to model and explain the origin of a similar set of phenomena by way of inferring from their recurrent features that they are the result or outcome of diverse sources and consist of multiple parts and variations. See also *diachronic analysis*, *explanation*, and *homogeneity*.

heuristics General methodological term referring to the procedures of scholarly problem solving techniques and strategies based on experience, often starting with tentative working definitions, assumptions or hypotheses based on general knowledge or common-sense, before analyzing and explaining the specific issues involved. See also *explanation*.

hexis Important aspect in anthropological theory by analyzing all forms of communication between people as taking place through fine-tuned body techniques, such as dynamics of movements and forms of bodily interaction usually studied on a microlevel. See also *habitus*.

hierarchy As a general term referring to any set or group which stands in asymmetrical relationship to another, in sociological terms referring to the social organization with the authority and power distributed to the higher ranks and statuses implying differences in access to wealth and prestige, found in all societies in which groups are distinguished by different strata and classes. See also *class*, *elite*, and *stratified societies*.

historiography Literally the writing of history; as a technical term in historical theory, it also refers to the study of literary genres and styles of historical documents and accounts. It also implies the methods of historical writing with an emphasis on the use of semiotics to understand and interpret how people and scholars transmit and appropriate their historical knowledge. See also *description* and *interpretation*.

holism As one of the major paradigms of anthropological research, it refers to study human societies and cultures as a systemic and integrated whole, which is more than the sum of its parts by taking all aspects of human activity, natural and cultural, into consideration. See also *anthropology*, *ethnography*, *fieldwork*, and *participant observation*.

homogeneity Philosophical and theoretical term used to explain the origin of a set of phenomena by way of inferring from their recurrent features that they are the result of the same or similar sources. See also *diachronic analysis*, *explanation*, and *heterogeneity*.

honor As a term in cultural anthropology, it refers to the virtue or respect of individuals one receives from their society due to their social and moral prestige. Also seen as a form of symbolic capital. See also *prestige*.

human rights Universally acclaimed concept of essential individual rights developed and refined in the West by the United Nations after World War II and in line with the philosophical ideals of Enlightenment considering the existence of basic rights and freedoms guaranteed to all humans, including: food, shelter, and education.

hybridity As a theoretical concept, used in anthropology to explain the assemblage or mixture of features from different cultures, languages, religions including all cultural practices, material goods, and customs. See also *diachronic analysis*, *heterogeneity*, and *syncretism*.

icon In its broadest sense, it is an image or any visual representation, which shows features that resemble the objects or events it captured; more specifically it is used as a semiotic term following the theoretical approach of Charles S. Peirce to refer to any set of signs of which physical or visual features resemble that which they signifies, including maps, statistical graphs and the like. See also *semiotics*, *index*, and *symbol*.

iconoclasm As a technical term, used to describe theological positions and proposals predominant in the history of monotheistic religions like Judaism, Christianity and Islam; the destruction of imagery as used in religious worship or institutions believed to be illegitimate representation of God. In general terms, it is also the privileging of the written word over visual imageries with the attempt to destroy them. See also *icon.*

ideal culture Anthropological term used to identify the statements people make about what their own culture is, usually based on prescribed values and ideals. This is used to distinguish them from their actual practices. See also *ethnocentrism*, *ideology*, and *real culture.*

ideal types As a technical term and analytical concept introduced by Max Weber to refer to a means of sociological reasoning used for methodological purposes to construct a pure category for types of action, which are utilized for classificatory and analytical reasons, but are rarely found in reality. See also *interpretation* and *heuristics.*

ideology This term literally means the study or doctrine of ideas; in modern sociological and political theory, it commonly refers to a set of propositions and beliefs of secular and political doctrines about governance and policy characteristic of the thinking of a religious group, political party, or nation state. As a worldview, it justifies the social arrangements under which people live. See also *critical theory* and *worldview.*

idiosyncrasy As a psychological and linguistic term, it refers to a temperament or behavior peculiar to a group or an individual and a peculiar way of speaking or writing not necessarily comprehensible to mainstream society or common sense. See also *linguistics.*

illuminationism Theological doctrine found in Islam and Christianity rooted in the Platonic theory of knowledge based on the assumption that human knowledge is enlightened, positing that God finally aids the human mind with what would be equivalent to the Platonic reign of ideas. See also *epistemology* and *idealism.*

imagined community A concept introduced by the political theorist Benedict Anderson to describe the formation of nation states and the sense of national identity and social belonging invoked by citizenship to a nation as a community that goes beyond the everyday contact with members of the local community.

imperialism Literally, the seeking of propagating of an empire, in historical terms it refers to the course and expansion of Western domination by way of political, military and economic means. It also implies a perceived moral right to subjugate the colony and in this respect is viewed as an extreme form of colonialism with the heightened exploitation of all human and material resources made available in the colonized areas. See also *colonialism*, *domination*, and *hegemony.*

incommensurability Methodological and theoretical term used to refer to the impossibility to compare or measure between two separate entities due to the lack of any common parameters, features, or factors that would allow a comparison between them. See also *dichotomy.*

index The recent use of this term can commonly be attributed to the semiotics of Charles S. Peirce , who introduced this concept to determine those classes of signs in which the relation between the sign and what it signifies is inferred by an interpretant as a causal relation. See also *semiotics*, *index*, and *symbol.*

indexical As a linguistic term, it is used to refer to any behavior or utterance, which is directly related to the "here" and "now" and "I;" it can only be fully understood within its respective context in which one uses these indexical terms. See also *linguistics* and *index.*

indigenous people As a generic term, used to refer to those people, who are considered upon first contact as the original or native inhabitants of a region. They usually wield little political power with regard to the dominance of colonial forces and whose culture or way of life the continuing processes of globalization and industrial development often threaten. See also *acculturation*, *colonialism*, and *imperialism*.

industrialism In modern economic theory, used to refer to the economic system and mode of engineered production based on serial reproduction of material goods and objects in fabrics of industrial production. See also *capitalism*.

industrialization As a term, used to demarcate the phase of a country's economic growth and development in which a significant shift in the mode of production from agriculture and manufacture to industrial production takes place. During this, industry grows at a fast pace, taking a lead in the modes of production, a development which is often confounded with notions of modernization. See also *industrialism* and *modernization*.

informant As a technical term in anthropological methods, used to refer a specific person of a local culture who is studied and who provides the ethnographer with necessary information about the local culture. See also *interlocutor*, *ethnography*, *fieldwork*, and *insider*.

information As a key term, it refers in semiotics and system theory to sequences of coded signals that represent and transmit knowledge, which one can acquire through feedback and instruction. See also *code*, *symbol*, *communication*, and *semiotics*.

infrastructure As a generic term, it literally refers to the organization of social relations through a network connecting the interrelationships. As a key term in Marxist economic and social theory, used to determine the forms of social organization based on the modes of production, which lead to the stratification of social and economic relations with different access to power and prestige, determining the superstructure, affecting political institutions, systems of classification, and enduring cultural practices. See also *production*, *political economy*, and *superstructure*.

inheritance In anthropological terms, it refers to the practice of passing on social class status, honorary title, political obligation as well as property after death. It is usually passed through kinship relations and lines of descent defining group affiliation. See also *kinship*, *heritage*, and *descent*.

insider In anthropological and sociological theory, it means to determine group membership by identifying the position of an individual in relation to a group. It also refers to the relationship of members within the group, having an impact on both the perspective and mode of communication an individual can have with or within a group. In ethnographic fieldwork, an insider often serves as an informant with whom the anthropologist works to gain the emic point of view. See also *emic*, *informant*, and *outsider*.

institution As anthropological and sociological term used to define rules and regulations in a society or structures and mechanisms of social order that governs the behavior of at least two parties and regulate their relationships to assure the endurance and continuation of the social structure as an element of social systems (e.g. marriage, bride wealth, family). Defining the roles and capacities in which persons interact in social situations, institutions lead to a stratification of societies, with a social purpose and permanence that goes beyond the agency of a single human individual. See also *bureaucracy* and *government*.

intentionality This philosophical term used in anthropology and social theory distinguishes action from behavior, taking human subjects as agents who make deliberate decisions based on the notion of free will in which they consciously perform for particular purposes or results. See also *agency*.

interaction Used as an anthropological and sociological concept to focus on sequences in the exchange of words and postures that go along with mimics, gestures, acts and bodily movements between two or more individuals or groups to study group and identity formation. See also *embodiment*, *communication*, and *habitus*.

interdisciplinary An approach to the academic study, which emerged in the late twentieth century and attempts to draw methods and information from multiple disciplines or schools of thought, usually based on the assumption that the boundaries of academic disciplines can also delimit the outcome of research. See also *discipline.*

interlocutor As an anthropological term, used in more recent ethnographic fieldwork approaches to indicate the mutual relationship and comradeship between the anthropologist and the people they work with and, nowadays, preferred over the term informant. See also *insider* and *informant.*

intermarriage As an anthropological term, used to refer to the marriage of a couple coming from kin groups with different social, economic, religious or ethnic status and background; in traditional societies also seen as a means to establish or foster relationship between the respective kin groups. See also *marriage.*

internal/external As a terminological distinction, often used in system theories or anthropological approaches in the study of social systems to determine conditioning factors in the relation between self and society, personality and culture and more generally referring to the determining features and factors stemming from the inside or outside of the respective systems of entities. See also *intrinsic/extrinsic.*

interpretation A methodological and meta-theoretical term used to refer to a procedure going beyond mere description. Emphasizing the significance and meaning of a set of data or specific elements within their respective contexts. Interpretation does not necessarily provide an explanation. See also *description* and *explanation.*

interpretive anthropology Theoretical approach in cultural anthropology used to emphasize the humanistic dimension in the study of societies and cultures, seen in contrast to a scientific approach that models its assumption according to the natural sciences. See also *dialogical anthropology* and *critical anthropology.*

intersubjectivity As a sociological and philosophical term, it is used to refer to the role of relationship between subjects in the formation of identity by de-emphasizing the self and subjectivity of the individual through making the communication of shared meanings key to the identity of groups and individuals. See also *interaction.*

intrinsic/extrinsic A theoretical distinction used in modes of causal explanation to identify the determining factors in the formation of identity in social and psychic systems, such as: disposition, motivation, or talent; more generally also referring to forms of determinism of factors situated inside or outside of the respective thing or action. See also *explanation, determinism, essentialism,* and *internal/external..*

jargon As a technical term in linguistics, refers to the highly elaborate language used by specific professions and academic disciplines, also referred to as technical language. See also *discipline* and *linguistics.*

kinship As an anthropological term, it refers to the web of social relationships found as an organizing principle in all societies based on the line of decent through relationships and established by links to the mother and/or father and marriage. Kinship is also established through other culturally significant links that would allow the establishment of kinship ties through imagined relatives, such as godparents. See also *descent* and *marriage.*

labor As an economic term, it refers to the means of production, but is manifest through social organization as a mode of production, implying forms of work in money economies and stratified societies usually done for wages. See also *production*, *alienation*, and *capitalism.*

law As a generic term, it refers to everything that follows or is enforced to follow prescribed rules. In legal theory, one distinguishes between natural and positive law by distinguishing between what is universal and particular for the human condition. In the natural sciences, law refers to the rule of nature. See also *legislation.*

legislation In modern political theory, used as a term to refer to the making and enactment of laws by the corporate political entity. See also *law.*

legitimacy As a juridical and political term, it refers to anything legal or lawful. See also *authority.*

legitimation In juridical contexts generally used to refer to the processes of making something legal or lawful. Also a sociological term, particularly employed by Max Weber to refer to justification of political power as reflected in different forms of authority. See also *authority* and *hegemony.*

lexicon As a linguistic term used to denote the comprehensive set of vocabulary of any given language; indicating its specific meaning and usage. See also *linguistics* and *semantics.*

liberalism Stance or position on social policy that emerged in the nineteenth century encouraging social progress through political and economic reform going along with belief in the self-regulation of the market as well as in individualism, liberty, and equal rights of all people. See also *agency*, *capitalism,* and *human rights.*

life history As a general term, referring to the sequence of significant events, stages, and circumstances of a person's life culminating in the biography of a person. In anthropology, it is taken as a means to study the social history of a specific group or culture through biographical interviews. See also *interpretive anthropology,* and *dialogical anthropology.*

life world A term introduced by phenomenological approaches in sociology and anthropology by Alfred Schütz to refer to the socially and culturally constructed worlds, which individuals or groups tacitly cope with and often take in their daily experiences as self-evident and for granted. See also *interpretive anthropology* and *phenomenology.*

liminality A concept in the study of rituals introduced by the French folklorist Arnold van Gennep and elaborated by the British social anthropologist Victor W. Turner to describe the state of ambiguity one undergoes in any form of initiation characterizing the transition phase of a rite of passage. See also *ritual* and *rites of passage.*

linguistics The study of spoken and written language in all its communicative aspects, including the study of sound patterns (*phonology*) and the smallest meaningful units in the formation of words (*morphology*), as well as the study of the meaning of words (*semantics*), the rules for building sentences (*syntax*), and the use of words in social situations (*pragmatics*). Linguistics also includes the study of writing systems as well as the history of language(s). See also *semiotics* and *lexicon*

locality As a general term, refers to a region surrounding or near a particular location. Introduced to anthropology by Arjun Appadurai to emphasize the social organization and distribution of local networks. See also *great and little tradition* and *globalization.*

longue dureé A term in historiography deriving from the French Annales School, namely Fernand Braudel , used to denote a specific approach to the study of enduring historical processes not necessarily confined to a specific people or culture and by giving priority of long-term historical structures over singular events. For example: the history of the Mediterranean Sea or trade routes like the Silk Road. See also *historiography.*

magic Concept in the anthropology of religion that is a system of beliefs and practices that invokes the manipulation of superhuman forces for intervening in a wide range of human activities and natural events. See also *agency*, *efficacy,* and *ritual.*

marginalization In sociological theory, used as a concept to describe the political processes that put people and predominantly minority groups at the margins or fringes of their society and culture with the attempt to make their concerns socially and politically irrelevant. See also *hierarchy*, *domination* and *stigma*.

market In the broadest sense, it refers to any commercial activity in which materials and services are bought and sold. As a term of economic theory it also refers to the supply and demand mechanism in the distribution and exchange of material goods and services. In capitalism, the market is the regulating principle for production and consumption. See also *consumerism* and *economic anthropology*.

marriage As a term in social and cultural anthropology, it refers to an institution that regulates the social relation and legal obligation between spouses by transforming the marital status of the participants and creating relationships between kin of the partners. Often symbolically marked in some way by a religious act and ceremony, it unites individuals and stipulates the degree of sexual access the partners have to perpetuate social patterns through the production or adoption of offspring. See also *polygamy* and *cross cousin marriage*, and *parallel cousin marriage*.

martyrdom It refers to the religious institution found particularly in Christianity and Islam that allows and celebrates the self-imposed death of a person to give witness and testimony of that person's religious belief and convictions. The killing and death of a person is imposed as a consequence because of the person's adherence to a religious faith or cause.

Marxism Social, political, economic, and literary theories following the main paradigms established through the works of Karl Marx by focusing on a critical analysis of the inequalities of access to resources and power. Its basic assumption is that any political process involves the struggle for power and going through phases of conflict. See also *critical theory*, *political economy*, *dialectics*, and *socialism*.

material culture All aspects of culture that involve the production, distribution, and consumption of material objects and services within the network of social relations, including technology and tools as well as clothing, art, and shelter. See also *production* and *market*.

materialism As a generic term it refers to the philosophical position emerging in the nineteenth century as an opposition to German idealism claiming, that nothing exists outside of the physical world and views material processes as a basis for human cognition and reasoning. See also *empiricism*, *positivism*, *critical theory*, *idealism*, and *Marxism*.

media As a key term in information and communication theory, it refers to those items and tools which are used to store and transmit information. In recent times, mass media, such as television, internet and other social networking tools are a common means to access, share, and distribute information. See *information* and *communication*.

mediation As a term in social and political theory, it refers to the processes of negotiation, intervention, and resolution in situations of conflicts which, in some way, brings about a settlement between the opposite claims of the conflicting parties. It is a common procedure, to institute a third and neutral party to mediate between two groups or parties in a conflict irresolvable by these parties themselves. See also *dialectics* and *negotiation*.

metaphor As a linguistic term used in literary theory as a figure of speech to refer to something which it does not literally denote, but connotes or alludes to by suggesting a similarity between the two things. See also *symbol* and *linguistics*.

metaphoric condensation As a technical term used in the study of ritual to refer to the feature of symbols which become present and efficacious in the performance of ritual action. See also *metaphor*, *ritual*, and *symbol*.

metaphysics As a term, used since the ancient Greek philosophers Plato and Aristotle to outline the foundational principles of reality going beyond any particular science or discipline; as a branch in philosophy and as a school of thought its studies are dedicated to cosmology, theology, and ontology. See also *essentialism* and *epistemology*.

meta-theory As a generic term, it refers to a theory about theory. Going beyond specific theories, meta-theory analyses not only how theories work but also how they are constructed and how they are situated in and applied to a particular field of research. More specifically, its aim is to define the framework within which scholars construct their theories to make the formation of theories possible. See also *critical theory*, *discourse*, *methodology*, and *semiotics*.

method As a meta-theoretical term, it refers to ordered sequences of steps and procedures that instruct about a series of acts or ways of doing something in a systematic manner, which accomplishes a particular result. See also *methodology*.

methodology It refers to the meta-theoretical reflection upon the methods used in a particular discipline and determines how the respective theories are only able to select and analyze a specific set of empirical data. See also *meta-theory* and *semiotics*.

milieu As a term in social theory and social anthropology, it is used to refer to the surrounding social environments of individuals and groups, including their social status indicating their belonging to a specific political and economic class. See also *class* and *social status*.

mimesis As generic term it indicates, across academic disciplines in the arts and sciences, embodied forms of imitation and representation. Also used as key concept in social and cultural theory to indicate processes of enculturation and socialization based on practice of imitation and the learning of body techniques, but in broader terms also referring to all forms of becoming similar or self-similar through bodily forms of representation established on similarity. See also *socialization*.

model As a generic term it is used to refer to any form of representation based on the principle of similarity, differing in size and materiality, but not necessarily in shape and proportion. Such a model can be seen as a "model of" or a "model for" reality as introduced by the cultural anthropologist Clifford Geertz. See also *representation*, *icon*, *prototype*, and *mimesis*.

modernism It denotes in the study of literature and the performing arts to the genre and style of writing and representation, which presents a clear break with the past as something being pre-modern and refers to a belief in progress and science. See also *modernity*.

modernity As a sociological and historical term, it refers to the state of being in and belonging to the modern era, which is the epoch since the times of the Enlightenment and the rise of colonialism. See also *enlightenment* and *colonialism*.

modernization It refers to the process and procedures of reform employed to the use of new techniques and technologies; making the transition from a "pre-modern" or "traditional" mode of production and social organization toward what is conceived as being modern and new. See also *industrialization*.

monograph As a generic term, it refers to any scholarly and comprehensive text dedicated to a single subject.

monotheism As a religious term, it is used in the anthropology and history of religion to refer to the belief in one God, usually confined to Zoroastrianism, Judaism, Christianity and Islam. In the study of religion, it is usually contrasted by the belief in many gods, also called polytheism.

moral economy As an anthropological term, it refers to forms of peasant economy, which are based on mutual institutions designed to insure against risk, rather than a principle of individual maximization. See also *reciprocity*, *capitalism*, and *political economy*.

morality As a term in anthropology and sociology, it is concerned with the ethics and morals of a community and defines and classifies certain acts and practices as good and evil or right and wrong according to their agreed upon rules of conduct. See also *ideal culture,* and *idealism.*

movement As a sociological term, it refers to a broader group of people with a common interest or ideology who attempt to achieve certain political, social or religious goals.

multiculturalism As a sociological term it usually refers to the doctrines and policies that assume several different cultures can coexist as equal and in harmony within a single country. In modern nation states, multiculturalism is questioned when a leading main stream culture is assumed and imposed. See also *cosmopolitanism*, *cultural relativism*, *clash of civilizations*, and *hybridity*.

multivocality As a technical term, it is used in linguistic and semiotic theories of meaning to refer to words or objects allowing the attribution of different interpretations, meanings, or values. Often used in theories of ritual to indicate the multiplicity of meanings attributed to ritual symbols and objects. See also *semantics*, *semiotics*, and *symbol.*

mystic As a term in the study of religion, it refers to an individual who is introverted and believes in an invisible realm and reality of enlightenment beyond human comprehension. Usually mystic treatises are speculative in nature and deal with metaphysical issues. See also *metaphysics*.

myth As a term in the study of religious oral traditions and written texts, it is used to refer to stories of religious significance, often concerning the creation of the existing cosmos and accepted as sacred history with supernatural agents as the main protagonists. They usually transfer culturally meaningful messages about the universe and locate the people's place within that universe. See also *narrative*, *ideology*, *worldview*, and *ritual.*

narrative As a term in literary theory, it is used to refer to any account of events told with a beginning, middle and end, building a dramatic unity, and usually with a climax in the ending. Narratives usually take human agents as protagonists and address their social and personal conflicts and concerns as the main point of departure. See also *myth.*

nation As a term in political theory, it refers to a specific group of people united by a single government and policy who share a real or imagined common past and history, culture or origin. See also *government* and *imagined community.*

nationalism As a political term, it refers to ideologies that enforce the belief that one's own national culture and its political and economic interests are superior to others. It also refers to political movements and their aspirations for national independence felt by people under foreign domination in times of colonialism. See also *colonialism*, *imperialism*, and *ethnocentrism* and *cosmopolitanism*.

native As an anthropological term, it usually refers to a person or a group inhabiting an area with long lasting historical ties to the region since time immemorial. In linguistics it is also used to refer to a person who grew up learning a language as mother tongue without receiving any formal instruction. See also *indigenous people* and *emic*.

negotiation In political theory and discourse analysis it is used as a term to refer to the processes of defining and redefining concepts, ideas, or solutions on issues of social and political relevance. See also *mediation* and *discourse*.

neocolonialism In political history and theory, used as a term to determine the continuing economic, political and military influence the former colonial powers in Europe and North America continue to have and exert over countries even after the period of colonization ended. See also *colonialism*, *imperialism*, *hegemony*, and *globalization.*

nepotism As a technical term it is used to refer to the forms of political governance using favoritism shown to relatives and close friends by individuals or groups holding power. In modern bureaucracy, it is a form of corruption. See also *dominance* and *hegemony*.

network A technical term used in sociological analysis to decipher webs of social relations that span over different degrees of relatedness through chains of relationships, like friends of friends. It also refers in modern social media to the communication in or between groups and its members indicating the interconnected systems and people. See also *social structure* and *infrastructure*.

nomadism As a key term in anthropology, it refers to a mode of subsistence, in which the whole group moves throughout the year with their animals. In general it refers to societies that subsist primarily by gathering and herding domesticated animals and migrating according to grazing patterns through the yearly cycle. Their social relations are considered as non-stratified and their mode of production is centered on the extended family. See also *egalitarianism*, *production,* and *subsistence*.

nominalism A philosophical term used since medieval times to refer to a system of beliefs which presupposes that universals do not exist and the terms used for objects or acts are only human representations similar to the objects represented in name or label. See also *realism*, *universalism*, *idealism*, and *metaphysics*.

non-governmental organization (NGO) As a technical and legal term for specific forms and organizations, it refers to a wide range of organizations that work in social welfare and development, spanning from grassroots cooperatives to multi-national charities. See also *civil society*.

norm As a sociological term, it refers to the standards or expectations of behaviors and rules of conduct.

normativity As a technical term it is used to determine the validity of norms; it gives the prescriptive or directive of what ought to be or how one ought to act. See also *ideal culture* and *ethnocentrism*.

objectification As a technical term in epistemology, it refers to the act of making an abstract idea, a person, group, or thing into a concrete object of study. See also *epistemology*, *essentialism* and *explanation*.

objectivism Any approach in the social sciences which regards its subject matter in some sense made up of objective data, which can be scientifically observed and studied as laws, rather than to be interpreted as subjects or individual agents with their own will and intentionality, which require some form of interpretation. See also *epistemology*, *empiricism*, *positivism*, and *production of knowledge*.

objectivity As a meta-theoretical and methodological term, it refers to any analysis and description made based on the premise that observable data can be represented in such a way that only their primary qualities are considered. Abstaining from their secondary qualities, such as color, smell and taste, observations become subject to emotions, judgments, or prejudices accounting for the researcher's perception and methods of analysis. See also *explanation*.

Occident As a generic and relational term, it refers to the West as opposed to the East. The usage of this term emerged in Europe and was used to distinguish Europe geographically and geo-politically from Asia. Since the discovery of the Americas and the expansion of European settlers, it usually refers to Europe and North America. See also *Orient*.

oral tradition It is used for literate as well as non-literate societies to refer to the body of myths and narratives, as those traditions pass down knowledge through spoken word.

Orient As a generic and relational term it literally means the East and is to be seen from the perspective of the West broadly referring to the Middle East and Central Asia. See also *Occident.*

orientalism A more or less ideological viewpoint held by anyone in the West who conceives Asia or specifically the Middle East as essentially exotic, mysterious, and irrational to impute a patronizing attitude. Although plainly referring to any knowledge of the Orient, Edward Said claimed that it represents a Western mode of colonial discourse with supporting institutions and scholarships along with a specific vocabulary, imagery, and doctrine.

orthodoxy As a generic term in the sociology of religion, it refers to the correct and approved doctrine as well as to the adherence to accepted and established traditions and beliefs in contrast to deviant forms of belief and practice. See also *heterodoxy.*

orthopraxy As a technical term, it refers to the correct and accepted practice and presupposes the prohibition of deviation from approved forms of ritual behavior. Practice or action which adheres to accepted and established traditions and beliefs. See also *orthodoxy.*

othering As a technical term in the anthropological discourse on cultures, it refers to the conceptualization of an outside group as overtly alien and different by further separating the "other" from the "self." See also *orientalism*, *essentialism*, and *ethnocentrism.*

paradigm An important concept in the history and methodology of science used to refer to the exemplary model or case study taken as an unquestioned doctrine to establish a theoretical framework for the formation of theoretical assumption of general relevance for the respective academic discipline as a whole. Also takes as a point of view or perspective of an individual or group at a particular point in time according to which empirical data are interpreted or explained. See also *methodology*, *framework*, *explanation*, and *interpretation.*

paradox As a philosophical term it is used to refer to any statement or relationship, in which the subject contradicts the predicate or one premise logically contradicts another premise in a syllogism by way of negation, e.g. "A" = "–A". See also *tautology.*

parallel cousin A cousin related through a same-sex sibling link, e.g., the relation of a daughter to her father's brother's son. See also *cross cousin.*

parallel cousin marriage As a technical term, it refers to the anthropological attempt to determine the marriage of an individual to their parent's same-sex sibling's child, e.g., a son marrying his father's brother's daughter. It contributes to keeping lineage resources from being transferred to other groups through marriage exchanges or inheritance. See *marriage*, *parallel cousin* and *cross cousin marriage.*

participant observation A research method in ethnographic fieldwork whereby the anthropologist is scholarly observing and at the same time engaged in the activities of the society under study with the aim of building a good rapport and gaining better understanding. See also *ethnography* and *fieldwork.*

pastoralism As a key term, used in anthropology to refer to food-gathering strategy based on animal husbandry found in arid areas and regions of the world where plant cultivation is impossible or limited. Where seasonal changes make migration necessary, herding of animals becomes the primary use of animals for food supply and the herding people must migrate with their animals to use the food available for them in different seasons at different place. See also *nomadism*, *egalitarianism*, *production*, and *subsistence.*

patriarchy As a term, it is used to refer to any political system in which men hold the power and distribute wealth, material goods, and prestige whereas women have limited access to social prestige and power. See also *hierarchy* and *domination.*

patrilineality As a central term in the anthropological study of kinship and lines of descent, it refers to a system of kinship classification which is marked by the identification of children, in particular of the sons, through the link of their father's and father's father lineage. See also *kinship*, *descent*, and *social organization*.

pattern of residence As a technical term, it is central to the cross cultural study of post-martial residence patterns. Based on forms of social organization and often tied to lines of descent, the pattern of residence is determined by such forces as subsistence strategy and post-marital residence rules. Anthropologists generally distinguish between matrilocality and patrilocality depending on whether the married couple moves to and lives with the bride's or groom's parents. See also *kinship* and *patrilineality*.

phenomenology As a philosophical term, it is often tied to a specific school of thought that emerged in the late nineteenth century in opposition to German idealism and scientific positivism with varying impact on related disciplines such as sociology, psychology, and anthropology. In the twentieth century, most commonly associated with the philosophy of Edmund Husserl and Martin Heidegger. In anthropology, it attempts to describe the life-world in its existential complexity in studying the ways in which people experience and understand everyday life. See also *hermeneutics*, *life world*, and *interpretation*.

pilgrimage As a term in the anthropology of religion, it refers to the religiously motivated travel to a sacred place. See also *ritual* and *rites of passage*.

political anthropology It refers to a sub-field in social and cultural anthropology studying the social organization and political stratification of society with a specific focus on the power relations and the establishment of institutions and hierarchies while employing an anthropological perspective. See also *critical anthropology*, *social organization*, *hierarchy* and *power*.

political economy Important field in political and economic anthropology formerly introduced by Karl Marx and referring to different, but related, approaches in studying the political pursuit of economic and political power to maintain a position of domination including all forms of social and political behavior. Anthropology considers political economy by studying the relationship between world capitalism and its impact on destroying local cultures. See also *political anthropology*.

politics It refers to the general interest of a community or society employing any strategic use of power in order to negotiate social relations and gain power and legitimize political authority. See also *political anthropology*.

polygamy As anthropological term, it refers to the form of marriage in which an individual can have multiple spouses, found in numerous traditional societies. It can be further divided into the marriage of a male with multiple wives (polygyny) and the marriage of a female with multiple husbands (polyandry). See also *marriage*.

positivism As a methodological term, it refers to a philosophical school of thought and scientific reasoning emerging in the eighteenth and nineteenth century that only presupposed given empirical facts, based its reasoning only on the observable, and the relationship of increasing complexity between one another. See also *empiricism*, *materialism*, and *objectivism*.

possession As a key term used in the anthropology of religion to refer to altered states of consciousness, in which people believe that the agency of a non-human agent or supernatural spirit takes over one's mind and body. See also *embodiment*.

postcolonialism As a historical term, it refers to the era of the formal political independence from a foreign formerly ruling country culminating in the 1960s. As a term in critical theory, it is used to the intellectual discourse in critical analysis of, and political reaction, to the cultural heritage of colonialism. See also *colonialism* and *hybridity*.

postmodernism As a generic term, it is used to refer to a philosophical school of thought that fundamentally questions the very possibility of objective knowledge and scientific reasoning. In this respect, knowledge is dependent on power relations. It questions cultural over-generalizations and laws in the study of society and culture as fundamentally flawed by privileging description and interpretation over explanation and scientific reasoning. See also *desconstuction* and *critical theory*.

poststructuralism A technical term used in literary analysis and critical theory to identify a position or doctrine, which rejects the structuralist claim of objectivity by placing the emphasis on the plurality and multiplicity of meaning based on the notion of paradox and metaphor in the play of signs. See also *structuralism* and *postmodernism*.

power As a term in social and political theory, it refers to the ability to influence others and to have a causal impact on the outcome of social and natural events. See also *agency*, *authority*, *domination*, *hegemony*, and *politics*.

practice As an important term in anthropological theory, it refers to any customary or learned mode of acting and behaving. Generally, it refers to anything people do while following their rules of conduct. See also *discourse*, *habitus*, and *mimesis*.

practitioner As a key term in theories of practice, it refers to any individual who engages in a sequence of customary or learned actions. See also *insider*.

pragmatics A sub-field of linguistics and semiotics, it focuses on the use of or the doing of language. One of the main insights of pragmatics is that the meaning of sentences and utterances has to be understood in their respective context of usage. See also *linguistics*, *semantics*, and *syntax*.

prestige As a term in social and cultural anthropology, it identifies those forms of status based on level of success through influence, wealth, and power. See also *honor*, *moral economy*, and *power*.

prestige system As a technical term in anthropology, it refers to symbol systems based on honor or respect within the society. See also *prestige*.

primitive As an anthropological term, it is no longer in use due to its inherent evolutionary connotations. Although a key term in evolutionary theories in the nineteenth century used in opposition to civilized, anthropologists commonly abandoned this term since the 1970s due to ambiguity and disqualifying bias in reference to the people studied by the anthropologist. See also *archaic* and *evolutionism*.

production As a key concept in the study of economic behavior, it refers in general to all acts or processes of creating something or more specifically to the transformation of natural raw materials into a form that is suitable for human use based on human labor. One commonly distinguishes between modes of production and means of production. The modes of production refer to the way the process of production is organized through a set of social relations, whereas the means of production refer to the factors that determine the production process, such as tools, skills, and technology. See also *economic anthropology*.

production of knowledge As a technical term used in anthropology to refer to the creation of culturally constructed and understood facts through forms of discourse and based on traditional forms of reasoning and power structures. See also *cognition*, *critical theory*, *discourse*, and *epistemology*.

prophet As a religious term, it is used to refer to an individual as a religious specialist who speaks with divine inspiration, often seen as divinely authoritative figure speaking and interpreting of the will of God.

prototype As a technical term, it refers to the standard or typical model according to which other types of the same kind are produced. See also *model*.

public event As a sociological and anthropological term, it refers to all kinds of happenings that take place in the open and in sight of others in the public sphere. See also *ritual*.

public sphere As a sociological term, it refers to the social and political distinction between public and private. This is the designation and separation of the political aspect of life from the private one.

puritanism As a general term, it can refer to the strictness and austerity in the conduct of a religion. More specifically in relation to Protestantism, it is often used to refer to a form of religious practice commonly found among the pilgrims and founding figures of North America.

race As a term used primarily in biological anthropology, it refers to culturally constructed sets of people who anthropologists grouped and classified based on believed biological traits usually only observable on one's phenotype. See also *racism.*

racism A technical term used for the discrimination, domination, and subjection of a group of people merely based on their physical appearance and the assumption of their racial inferiority. See also *race* and *ethnocentrism.*

rank As a sociological term, it is used to indicate one's position of power within the hierarchy of a stratified society or any web of asymmetrical social relations. See also *social status.*

rationality As a generic term, it usually refers in philosophical discourses to the modes of thinking as based on a consistency and logic as well as to modes of analyzing information which are systematically gathered through methodical observation. In anthropology, the work of Edward Evans-Pritchard is usually identified with the idea, denoting that even seemingly "primitive" modes of thinking are based on some kind of inherent rationality, which anthropology is charged with deciphering. See also *metaphysics* and *paradox.*

real culture It refers to the actual and observable actions and behaviors of people as they act out culture regardless of their own perception and description or their values and ideals. See also *ideal culture.*

rebellion As a political term it indicates the opposition to a ruling power, authority, code of conduct, or tradition, which can be organized, but does not necessarily lead to the coup of the ruling power. See also *revolt* and *revolution.*

reciprocity As a technical term commonly used in economic anthropology, it refers to a mode of distribution characterized by the mutual exchange of goods and services based on trust and which are of approximately equal value between parties. See also *economy* and *economic anthropology.*

redistribution A form of economic exchange in which goods and services are given by members of a group to a central authority then distributed back to the donors.

reductionism As a methodological term it refers to a method of scientific reasoning that aims at reducing the phenomena to constitutional elements and factors through analysis; it also refers to the totality of a complex phenomenon in its constitutive elements determining their main features and functions. See also *holism.*

reflexive anthropology As an approach in cultural anthropology, this term refers to the recognition by most ethnographers of the symbolic anthropology in North America that adequate anthropological accounts cannot be crafted without acknowledging the forces, epistemological and political, that condition and shape their research, writing, and thinking. See also *critical anthropology*, *discourse theory*, and *reflexivity.*

reflexivity As a technical term, it most commonly refers to the reflection of reflection, but more specifically it is used in the anthropological context to refer to the reflection upon how the researcher is perceived by the people whom he or she works with. See also *critical theory* and *reflexive anthropology.*

reform As a sociological and juridical term it refers to the making of changes within a social, legal, and political system with the attempt to improve some malfunctions of that system; often, it refers to changes made to eliminate abuses, corruption or injustice.

Reformation In the history of Christianity, this term specifically refers to the religious movement of the sixteenth century that began with Martin Luther as an attempt to reform the Roman Catholic church in light of its corruptions and resulted in the creation of numerous Protestant churches.

regime As a political term, it generally refers to the governing authority of a political unit. It is, in public discourse, also used to refer to those forms of political governance which are perceived as illegitimate. See also *power* and *authority*.

relativism As a term in the humanities and sciences, it refers to the theoretical stance that perceives all aspects of human experience and thinking as relative; assumes that human reality is a web of interrelatedness in which all aspects of culture and society are interdependent to different degrees and related to other aspects. See also *cultural relativism* and *holism*.

religiosity A technical term which encompasses all aspects of religious activity with an emphasis on individuals, including their practices and beliefs. See also *spirituality*.

Renaissance As a historical term it is used to refer to the area of European history at the closing of the Middle Ages and the rise of the modern world, which was literally perceived as a cultural "rebirth" of the ideals of Greek antiquity spanning from the fourteenth through the middle of the seventeenth centuries. As a term it also refers to a cultural concept that emphasizes the rebirth of former traditions. See also *revitalization*.

representation As a theoretical term used in linguistics and semiotics, it most generally refers to anything that stands for or takes the place of something else. In anthropological theory, it involves the attempt to represent the culture of other people and their way of life through writing. In the 1980s, the writing culture debate in American anthropology coined the term of the "crisis of representation," referring to the problem of writing about other cultures with the attempt to give an objective representation of it. See also *critical anthropology* and *discourse theory*.

revitalization As a term in cultural history and the study of religion, it refers to any social movement that attempts to enhance and revive the endangered cultural or religious identity of a group, designed to bring about a new way of life within a global society often by way of returning to the presumed origins of that culture or religion. See also *renaissance*.

revival As a term in the sociology of religion, it refers to the social movement intended to bring about a renewal or resurgence of a religious practice or cultural tradition. See also *renaissance* and *revitalization*.

revolt As a sociological and political term, it refers to the armed and organized opposition to a ruling authority or regime in the attempt of a coup. See also *rebellion* and *revolution*.

revolution As a generic term, it is generally used to refer to any drastic and far-reaching change in ways of thinking and acting. In social and political theory, it refers to the successful coup of a ruling regime. A key concept in Marxist political theory, which is based on the assumption that historical change can only take place through revolution.

rhetoric As a term in the theory of communication and public speech, it refers to the effective use of language through the choice of vocabulary, style and expression to please or persuade listeners. See also *metaphor* and *trope*.

rites of passage As a technical term introduced by Arnold van Gennep and refined by Victor Turner it is used to refer to ceremonies and rituals performed to mark and celebrate the transition in a person's life from one social status to another. For example: initiation or marriage. See also *ritual* and *ceremony*.

ritual As a key term in the anthropology of religion, it denotes the performance of a prescribed procedure for conducting religious ceremonies, which consists of acts and utterances held at particular times and places, often by ritual specialists or mediators such as priests or shamans. The expectations and results of ritual are based on its ritual efficacy. See also *ceremony* and *efficacy*.

ritualization A widely used term to refer to the making or creation of a ritual, but also used to refer to the formalization and routinization of social acts and utterances. See also *ritual*.

role A term in social theory used to refer the dynamic aspect of status an individual agent takes on in contexts of social relations and interactions. See also *social actor* and *social role*.

sacralization As a term in the anthropological approach to religion, it is used to refer to the practice of making an object or action sacred, often by way of dedicating or sanctifying it to God or a deity. See also *sacred and profane*.

sacred and profane As a foundational distinction in the anthropology and sociology of religion, it was introduced by Émile Durkheim to designate the categorical difference and separation of the worldly (profane) from the other-worldly (sacred). See also *religion*.

sacrifice As a key term in the anthropology of religion, it refers to the practice of making an offering to a god, which often consists of the ritual killing of animals and the offering of lives, food or objects to sanctify or worship as an exchange between the human and divine spheres. See also *sacralization*.

saint As a term in the sociology of religion, it is used to refer to a person of exceptional charismatic authority due to his or her way of life or state of holiness. See also *charisma* and *prophet*.

savage As a derogatory term it is no longer used in anthropology due to its evolutionary bias; it formerly referred to a group of people who were, due to their use of technology and mode of subsistence, considered members of an uncivilized society. See also *archaic*, *primitive*, and *evolutionism*.

scientism As a technical term in methodology and the philosophy of science, it refers to the positivistic stance that perceives only proven empirical data as valid sources of scientific knowledge. See also *objectivism*.

scriptualism As a technical term in the study of religious traditions, it refers to the strict and unquestioned compliance with literal interpretation of religious texts. It is often identified with a narrow view in the reading of religious scriptures which are taken as being the revealed word of God.

secularism As a sociological and political concept it is based on the assumption that religion and religious considerations are rejected, particularly in regard to government or other entities.

segmentary society Social system which is made up of many small sovereign groups that occasionally come together to form a larger group and may appear to be a single community.

semantics It is the branch of linguistics concerned with the study of the meaning of words, acts, and gestures; in linguistics it is usually concerned with the lexicon of words and often marks the bridge between language and culture as it indicates how languages conceptualize and classify reality. See also *linguistics*, *syntax*, and *pragmatics*.

semiology As a term for the study of linguistic signs, it was introduced by the Swiss general linguist Ferdinand de Saussure and is often identified with the French tradition of signification processes; it calls for the distinction between signifier and the signified. See also *semiotics* and *sign*.

semiotics The study of signs in all its aspects, including their nature and function in society and culture, as a modern philosophical school of thought founded by Charles S. Peirce. See also *semiology* and *sign*.

sexuality This is the culturally constructed way by which people conceptualize the sexes and choose partners for sexual intercourse. See also *gender*.

sign In semiology as the study of linguistic signs, signs are usually defined as consisting of signifier (sound pattern) and signified (mental image) as introduced by Ferdinand de Saussure. In semiotics as proposed by Charles S. Peirce, signs consist of a dynamic relation of three components, the interpretant, representamen (sign), and the dynamic object. Based on the nature of how the interpretant conceptualizes the relationship between representamen and dynamic object, Peirce classified the signs into index, icon and symbol. See also *semiology* and *semiotics*.

simulation A term used in social psychology and the study of symbolic interaction to determine the pretense and imitation of behavior or processes by something suitably analogous, including the purposes or study or training. See also *play*.

social action In sociological theories of action developed since Talcott Parsons, it is a key concept to refer to actions which consider the social impact both these actions and the reactions to them have on individuals within a society.

social actor As a sociological term, it is used in interaction and performance theory to determine the way an individual is engaged in social processes. It emphasizes the deliberate and strategic decisions individuals make in social settings as opposed to the hierarchical structures of social organization. See also *agency*, *interaction*, and *social organization*.

social distinction As a term in sociology and social anthropology, it denotes the subtle but important distinctions which are made by and between individuals to place varying value on their social status.

social identity As a term used in sociology and social psychology, it refers to those defining characteristics or features of a group of people, by which they develop an understanding of solidarity and group identity. See also *imagined community* and *solidarity*.

social organization As a term in sociology and social anthropology, it refers to the patterns by which a society is organized through specific institutions with the basis on different attributes such as kinship, modes of production, and social status. See also *hierarchy*, *institution*, and *social structure*.

social role A concept derived from social psychology referring to standardized expectations society has for individuals, as well as their own expectations of self and others, based on their gender, social status, and place within the social structure. See also *role* and *social status*.

social status As a technical term in sociology and anthropology, it refers to the place of an individual within the hierarchy of a given society, which defines the capacities in which the individual interacts with others. One often distinguishes between the achieved or ascribed status. An achieved social status one can acquire over the course of a lifetime, an ascribed status is given to an individual at birth. See also *prestige*, *inheritance*, and *social role*.

social structure As a key term in sociology, it refers to enduring relationships and bonds between groups and individuals, which are often asymmetric in nature and define the role and capacity in which individuals interact. See also *social organization*, *hierarchy*, *institution*, and *social status*.

socialism Political theory proposed by Karl Marx in the late nineteenth century advocating collective and state ownership of industry as well as administration of production and allocation of resources. Marx conceived the only means of reaching this form of social and political organization through revolution. See also *revolution* and *Marxism*.

society As a key term in sociology and social anthropology, it is used to refer to a group of people, who have structured and distinctive relationships among each other, including continuous processes of social and cultural interaction as well as economic and political exchange.

solidarity As a term in social theory it refers to the unity and integration of a group of people or society with their direct neighbors or neighboring groups. It became a central concept in the study of religion and society due to the work of Émile Durkheim.

sovereignty As a concept in political anthropology, it refers to the quality of people having independence and authority over a territory, their people and inheritance. See also *authority*, *power*, and *government*.

spirituality As a term used in the study of modern religiosity to denote human concern for things of the spiritual and immaterial world; it also refers to the appreciation for religious values and beliefs. See also *religiosity*.

spontaneity As a concept, used in social psychology to refer to the doing, thinking, or writing without any advance strategic planning or constraint. See also *convention* and *habitus*.

stereotype A term commonly used in the sociology and anthropology of culture to refer to popular and standardized, but not necessarily negative, perceptions of a minority group by a culturally dominant one. See also *ethnocentrism*.

stigma As a technical term it is used primarily in social psychology to refer to the negative reputation an individual or group receives as a means of exclusion usually based on a culturally understood breach of norms that are spread and reinforced through rumor. See *transgression*.

stratified society Anthropological term to classify societies based on the complexity of social organization. Stratified societies have a considerable degree of inequality among their members in their social rewards, including the unequal distribution of, and access to, resources of power and knowledge as well as wealth and prestige. See also *segmentary society*, *hierarchy*, and *social organization*.

structural functionalism A theoretical approach in social anthropology that sees society as a set of embedded systems related to each other, analogous to the systems of a biological organism, formerly introduced by the British anthropologist Alfred Radcliffe-Brown. See also *functionalism* and *structuralism*.

structuralism An anthropological school of thought founded by Claude Lévi-Strauss in the mid-twentieth century that searches for the universal cognitive deep structures of humankind and uses the semiological analysis of binary oppositions as a model of analysis. See also *structure, semiology*, *linguistics*, and *synchronic analysis*.

structure An organized whole that is based on asymmetrical relations between the elements it is composed of, it is often related to the enduring aspects of a society that surround and subsume an individual. See also *hierarchy* and *social structure*.

style As a general term, it refers to the defining features of form used in types of cultural expression. In anthropology, it also refers to the mode or way in which something is done or performed as a form of cultural practice. See also *discourse* and *rhetoric*.

subaltern studies Approach derived from the applied dimension of social and cultural anthropology on peasant societies concerned with the post-colonial and post-imperial societies of south Asia and the developing world. See also *postcolonialism* and *marginalization*.

subjectivism As a philosophical position it refers to the assumption that the human mind inherently creates and shapes perceptions of reality. It is also used in cognitive psychology to refer to knowledge and value as shaped by subjective experience. See also *constructivism* and *objectivism*.

subjectivity Used as a philosophical term to refer to an individual's perspective of opinions, beliefs, and feelings in contrast to knowledge and facts. In philosophical discourses, it is generally used to refer to the state of the human mind.

subsistence Technical term in economic anthropology used to mean any strategy of surviving by use of technology and forms of production, often at a minimal level including shelter and survival. See also *production* and *economic anthropology.*

sui generis Philosophical term used in classification theory to refer to any class of phenomena that stands on its own and that one cannot integrate into the system of classification based on a coherent set of criteria. See also *a priori* and *essentialism.*

superstition As a modern anachronistic and derogatory term referring to beliefs and practices which the observer perceives as being based neither on faith or belief nor on reason or knowledge; it usually refers to beliefs of people perceived as irrational. See also *survival* and *evolutionism.*

superstructure As a term in economic and social theory it refers to the institutions of a society emerging from, but set apart from, the infrastructure of the modes of production that is its economic base. The superstructure includes institutions such as laws, politics, religion, education, art, philosophy, and ethics and both expresses and determines the ideology of a society and culture. See also *ideology* and *institution.*

survivals It was particularly used in evolutionary theories which presupposed that the elements of archaic cultures survive and remain alive in higher stages of human evolution. Generally it refers to a cultural phenomenon that outlives the set of conditions under which they emerged, as a term; it is no longer used in anthropology due to its evolutionary overtones. See also *evolutionism*, *primitive*, and *diachronic analysis.*

symbol Widely used in cultural anthropology, it denotes anything verbal or non-verbal that stands for and refers to something else based on a culturally coded and agreed upon meaning. It is also a shared understanding about the meaning of certain words, attributes or objects. See also *code*, *information*, *representation*, and *semiotics.*

symbolic anthropology The school of thought in American cultural anthropology often associated with Clifford Geertz and Victor Turner, which posits that the main goal of anthropology is to explicate the meanings of communicative acts and items within which humans live, think, and act. See also *emic* and *interpretation.*

symbolic interactionism A sociological school of thought most prominent in North America as a reaction against behaviorism introduced by George Herbert Mead and based on the premise that meaning is imbued with a constant flux of exchanges in the process of human interaction, including the defining of social identities of others against the self and vice versa. See also *intersubjectivity*, *subjectivity*, *interaction*, and *symbol.*

synchronic analysis Method of analyzing cultural an empirical data collected at a single point in time without considering any historical or other data through time. As a form of anthropological inquiry, it is most prominent in functionalism and structuralism, it is a reaction against all sorts of evolutionary or developmental theories. See also *diachronic analysis*, *functionalism*, *structuralism*, and *structural functionalism.*

syncretism An anthropological term derived from the history of religion to determine the partial fusion of religious concepts, practices, and traditions from different cultural contexts in the formation of new religions and yet permitting the retention of the component traditions by not fully subsuming or molding the old forms into the new religion. See also *hybridity* and *heterogeneity.*

syntax Central term in linguistics used to refer to the formal rules of language that determine how phrases are combined in order to construct sentences and build meaningful and grammatically correct propositions. See also *semantics* and *semiotics.*

synthesis As a general term used in methodology, it refers to the procedure for the theoretical integration of a set of distinct and disparate elements, concepts, or propositions into an ordered and structured complex whole. In epistemological theories of judgments, it is often seen as the opposite to analysis. In German idealism, as opposed to materialism and its critique by Karl Marx, it is often used in reference to the higher level integration of thesis and antithesis. See also *dialectics, critical theory*, and *Marxism*.

tautology As a philosophical concept it is used in logic to refer to statements or formulas, which are considered to be true under any circumstances and in every interpretation. See also *paradox*.

taxonomy As a methodological term in the organization and categorization of empirical data, it is used to classify organisms or items into groups based on formal similarity or common origin. See also *typology*.

teleology As a philosophical concept it is used for the causal explanation of phenomena by determining its ends or purpose.

terrorism The calculated use of violence (or the threat of violence) against civilians in order to attain goals that are political, religious or ideological in nature; this is done through intimidation or coercion or instilling fear. See also *tyranny* and *rebellion*.

theoretical approach As a technical term, it refers to a particular perspective, which has been thoroughly tested and agreed upon, in order to explain reality. In contrast to theories, theoretical approaches use multiple concepts and methods resulting from theoretical propositions and hypotheses to organize a particular field of research by focusing on theoretical issues related to the empirical data under scrutiny.

thick description Method or technique of ethnographic description attributed to Clifford Geertz involving the layering levels of interpretation of all sorts within a reflexive framework, including those of the ethnographer, the informant and the people's interpretations of culture. See also *interpretation*, *description*, and *symbolic anthropology*.

tradition In the anthropological study of a society and culture, it refers to all elements that their members adhere to and are passed on between its generations. See also *transmission* and *discursive tradition*.

transformation In the anthropological study of cultural change, it refers to a quality of alteration, in which the defining conditions change radically, as it challenges the identity and can finally lead to a change of identity. See also *variation*.

transgression As a term in the anthropology of religion and law, it refers to the overstepping or violation of cultural boundary markers or moral principles. In the study of religion it is used to denote the religious concept of sin.

transmission A technical term in communication and information theory used to refer to the spread of messages or as a communication of information through different media such as: signs, traditions, or practices. See also *communication*, *information*, and *media*.

tribe Concept in political anthropology used to determine units of social and political organization in a segmentary society larger than a clan and smaller than chiefdom with kinship as the main principle for social and political organization. See also *chiefdom* and *social organization*.

trope Rhetorical figure of speech, also a concept used in linguistic anthropology to indicate the non-referential or creative aspects in the use of language. See also *rhetoric*, *metaphor*, and *historiography*.

typology A form of classification based on resemblance of types, used in cultural anthropology to discriminate variations empirical cultural phenomena and to determine cross cultural categories as points of comparison. See also *ideal types* and *ethnology*.

tyranny A term in political theory used to refer to the dominance of the ruling power over the people through threat of punishment and violence. See also *regime*.

unconscious A term introduced by the psychoanalysis of Sigmund Freud and used to refer to actions or thoughts that slip the direct awareness of the individual or are done without the consciousness of the actor. See also *custom*, *habit,* and *habitus*.

universalism As a religious, theological or philosophical term, it refers to a doctrine that assumes some foundational principles as universal to all people regardless of their social, political and cultural differences. See also *nominalism*, *realism*, and *relativism*.

universality As a term in cultural anthropology, it refers to those features or qualities of culture as a theoretical concept that apply or are common to all human societies or cultures. Universal features of culture are usually taken as points of comparison to determine the general, regional, and local differences between these societies and cultures. See also *cultural relativism*, and *ethnology*.

Utopia A social and political term to refer to an ideal and perfect but non-existent state of being, taken as a model for the governance of a society or community including all aspects of political, cultural, religious, and moral life.

validation A methodological term used to refer to the act of finding the evidence and testing the truth value of a scientific hypothesis, it also refers to the establishing of a proof for such an hypothesis. See also *explanation*, *essentialism*, and *scientism*.

variation As a term in cultural anthropology, it refers to changes or modifications in acts or states of being, which is slightly, but noticeably different from what is perceived as the norm or standard. See also *transformation*.

world-acculturative approach A theoretical model in cultural anthropology that views the transformations of the global world economy as a process that brings about systemic forms of inequalities on a global level. See also *acculturation*, *globalization*, and *political economy*.

worldview As a general term, it refers to the all-encompassing but often unconscious way in which a society and its members perceive and interpret the reality transcending their immediate surrounding environment, determining the place of humans within it, along with social and ethical obligations. See also *ideology*.

worship As a term in the anthropology of religion, it refers to acts of religious commitment, usually in veneration and reverence to a deity. See also *ceremony* and *ritual*.

Glossary of Islamic terms

Jens Kreinath

The transliterations for the Arabic language used in this glossary for preference follow the academic standards established by the *International Journal of Middle East Studies* (*IJMES*). In cases where the transliterations by the authors significantly differ from those listed here (due to other linguistic variants in Persian, Turkish, or Urdu or academic standards in use), special entries are provided to refer back to those entries used in the Arabic language. Alternative transliterations of the respective terms are given at the end of the main entries. For reasons of convenience, the entries follow the order of the English alphabet. The names of significant persons and places as well as movements and months are indicated through capital letters. This glossary not only aims to clarify the understanding of terms and names in their respective context, but also to serve as a tool to compare different data presented in this Reader by providing ample cross-references throughout the entries. Further alphabetically listed cross-references are provided at the end of each entry to assist and enhance a thorough understanding of the beliefs and practices as discussed in the contributions. For further definitions of these terms see also: H.A.R. Gibb and H. Kramers (1953) *Shorter Encyclopaedia of Islam*, Ithaca, NY: Cornell University Press; P.J. Bearman, Th. Bianquis, C.E. Bosworth, E. van Donzel, W.P. Heinrichs, and et al. under the patronage of the International Union of Academies (ed.) (1960–2005) *Encyclopædia of Islam*, 2nd edn, 12 vols. with indexes and etc. Leiden: E.J. Brill; and Glassé, Cyril (2008) *The New Encyclopedia of Islam*, 3rd edn, Lanham, MD: Rowman & Littlefield Publishers, Inc.

abangan (Ind.: "red" or "peasantry"). A population in Java practicing a syncretic form of Islām inclined to follow a local traditions (see *adat*) in contrast to the more orthodox group of Muslims (see *santri*), who follows a strict interpretation of Islām.

abdest (Turk., derived from Pers. compound: *ab*: "water" and *dast* "hand"). Practice of ritual cleaning and ablution; involves especially the washing of parts of the body with water before ritual prayer (see *namaz*), also performed before touching or reading the Qur'ān. See also *ṣalāt* and *wuḍū'*.

'Abduh, Muḥammad (1849–1905). Egyptian juridical and religious scholar educated at al-Azhar University in Cairo and among the first to favor nationalism in attempting to modernize religious institutions; founder of the late nineteenth century movement called Islamic Modernism (see *Salafiyya*).

adab (Arab.: "norm of conduct," "behavior," "courtesy," or "politeness"). Good manners and proper etiquette, concerning the behavior performed in accordance with the prescribed Islamic protocol (see *sunna*). In the contemporary Arab world, it furthermore refers to literature, but also to the humanities and social sciences as distinct from the natural sciences (see *"ilm*). See also *'aql* and *fiqh*.

ʻadhāb (Arab.: "torment" and "suffering"). Suffering inflicted by God (see *Allāh*) primarily due to unbelief and doubt in the message of his Prophet Muḥammad. The punishment in the afterlife begins with the "torments of the tomb" or "punishment of the grave" (*ʻadhāb al-qabr*). See also *yawm al-qiyāma*. (Other transliterations include *ʻathab* and *ʻazzab*.)

adhān (Arab.: "announcement"). Call to prayer, performed five times a day and recited by a person (see *mu'adhdhin*) responsible to perform the call for prayer from the minaret of the mosque. See also *"ilm al-tajwīd*, *La ilaha illā Allāh!*, and *ṣalāt*.

adhkār (Arab.: "remembrance"). Referred to as the repeating of Qur'anic and supplementary verses for ritual prayer (see *ṣalāt*). See also *dhikr*, *La ilaha illā Allāh!*, and *tesbihat*. (Other transliterations include *athkar* and *azkar*.)

ʻahd (Arab.: "command" or "covenant"). Sacred oath (see *shahāda*) or binding pledge enforcing an irrevocable and life-long commitment by becoming a Muslim or a member in a religious order (see *ṭarīqa*). At present, it is a common term for civil engagements, economic contracts, and political treaties, but also refers to the number 'one' or more specifically to the theological doctrine of the Oneness of God (see *Allāh*). See also *tawhīd*.

ahl al-bayt (Arab.: "the people of the house"). Generally the term refers to a noticable family. It particularly refers to the descendants of Muḥammad (see *sayyid*) through his dauther Fatimah and his brother's son and son-in-law 'Alī ibn Abī Ṭālib. Through Ḥasan and Ḥusayn, the people of the house of Muḥammad hold an honoray status in Muslim society (see *sharīf*). See also *Shīʻa*.

Ahmadiyya Religious movement founded by Mirzā Ghulām Aḥmad Kādiānī (1835–1908) in India at the end of the nineteenth century and, as a branch of Islām, it is based on the articles of faith held by most Muslims. Its differences concern the belief in the finality of prophethood. The Ahmadiyya hold the belief that Jesus did not die, but migrated to India after his crucifixion and resurrection. Their other difference concerns the notion of peace as the major means of the struggle against the unfaithful (see *jihād*). Whereas Pakistan is the country with the most Ahmadis, the African Republic of Ghana is the country with the largest percentage per capita population of Ahmadis.

akaid (Turk.: "dogma" or "doctrine"). Religious doctrine or dogma as being true without proof. See also *sharīʻa*. (Other spellings include *akait*.)

ʻAlawī (Arab.: "of ʻAlī"). Name of the royal family and reigning dynasty in Morocco. Throughout the Islamic world, this also refers to various religious groups called Alawites, Alawi or Alevi as different interpretations of Islām, which are followers of ʻAlī. See also *ahl al-bayt*, *'Alī ibn Abī Ṭālib*, and *Shīʻa*.

'Alī ibn Abī Ṭālib (598–661). As the son of Muḥammad brother Abū Ṭālib he became later also his son-in-law due to his marriage with Muḥammad's dauther Fatimah. He was one of the first converts to Islām and later became the fourth caliph (see *khalīfa*). His elder son Ḥasan succeeded his father as fifth caliph for a short period before he was poisoned. His second son Ḥusayn was also persecuted at the battle of Kerbala in 680. See also *ahl al-bayt*, *ʻAlawī*, *Ḥusayn*, *Muḥammad*, and *Shīʻa*.

ʻālim (Arab.: "one who is knowledgeable," pl. *ʻulamā'*). Scholar trained in any field of knowledge. See also *fiqh*, *ʻilm*, *mullah*, and *qāḍī*.

Allāh (Arab.: "God"). The term was used among Arabic speaking people before the Qur'ān was revealed to refer to the Name of God. The name of Allāh is not restricted to Islām, but used throughout the Arabic speaking world by Orthodox and Oriental Christians to call upon their God.

Allahü ekber! (Turk.: "God is Magnificent!"). Ubiquitous formula and religious exclamation, an essential part of the ritual prayer (see *namaz*) framing each of its cycles (see *rekât*). See also *basmala*, *rakʻa*, *ṣalāt*, and *tekbir*.

'amāl (Arab.: "performances" or "actions"). As a generic term, it refers to the practice of moral actions and good deeds closely connected to belief (see *īmān*) in practice, in contrast to mere knowledge (see *'ilm*). See also *'ibāda.*

Ansorisunna (Thai). First Islamic reform movement in Thailand established in the 1930s as an association with monthly periodicals. With its orientation toward a puritanical approach to Islamic reformism among the modernist Muslims in Thailand (see *Kaum Muda*), it had considerable impact on Muslim intellectuals based in Bangkok. See also *Salafiyya.*

'aqīqa (Arab.: "name"). Non-obligatory, traditional practice of a name giving ceremony performed in conjunction with sacrificing a ewe for the newborn baby in a Muslim family usually on the seventh, fourteenth, or twenty-first day after its birth. This practice can also include shaving the hair of the baby, the sacrifice of a sheep, followed by the distribution of the equivalent value of the hair's weight in silver to the poor and needy (see *masākīn*). See also *haqiqa*, *kikah*, and *ṣadaqa.*

'aql (Arab.: "intellect," "reason," or "thinking"). The rational interpretation of an authorized and written Islamic tradition (see *ḥadīth*) of the practice of the Prophet Muḥammad (see *sunna*) emphasizing the intellectual capacities of the educated individual Muslim; a central concept of the Islamic reform movement. See also *Salafiyya.*

'Arafāt A plain or mount east of Mecca outside of its sacred territory (see *ḥarām*), which is also site of one of the central ceremonies of the annual Muslim pilgrimage to Mecca (see *ḥajj*). On the 9th of *Dhū al-Ḥijja*, the Day of 'Arafāt, the pilgrims erect as the sixteenth step of their pilgrimage a camp to stay for a celebration of the festival assembly, which begins after their midday ritual prayer (see *al-ẓuhr*), continuing with the pilgrimage address (see *khuṭba*) and lasts until sunset. The pilgrims stay all night in their camp at the Mount 'Arafāt (see *wuqūf*).

arkān al-dīn (Arab.: "tenets of religion" or "adobe of faith"). Obligatory acts of worship as part of the ceremonial law (see *'ibāda*) indicating the submission to God (see *Islām*), formally accepted by all branches of Islām. These so-called five pillars are: 1.) the declaration of faith (see *shahāda*) affirming that "there is no god but God (see *Allāh*) and that Muḥammad is the Prophet of God," 2.) the performance of a ritual prayer five times a day (see *ṣalāt*), 3.) the giving of yearly alms to the poor and needy (see *zakāt*), 4.) the fasting in the month of Ramaḍān (see *ṣawm*), 5.) the performance of the pilgrimage to Mecca once in a lifetime (see *ḥajj*). According to the Islamic law (see *sharī'a*), all acts related to the five pillars are obligatory (see *wājib*).

'Ashūrā (Arab.: "tenth"). Name for a commendable and voluntary fast day observed by Sunnī Muslims on the 10th of *Muḥarram*, the first month of the Islamic year, followed with a festival after the breaking of the fast (*'īd al-fiṭr*). Some Sunnī Muslims celebrate this festival by eating and sharing special dishes with giving alms to the poor and needy (see *masākīn*) and sweet treats to the children. The traditions of celebrating this day can vary greatly according to the region. For the Shī'a, the tenth of *Muḥarram* is a time of mourning culminating in the anniversary of the martyrdom of Ḥusayn at Kerbala in 680 along with the performance of special passion plays (see *ta'ziyya*).

al-'aṣr (Arab.: "afternoon"). Late afternoon ritual prayer (*ṣalāh al-'aṣr*) consisting of four cycles (see *rak'a*, sing.). See also *ṣalāt.*

awqāf (Arab.: "endowment," sing. *waqf*). A religious endowment managed by a ministry or religious institution to collect alms (see *zakāt*). See also *waqf.*

āya (Arab.: "sign," "token," or "miracle," pl. *āyāt*). Verse of the Qur'ān and the smallest unit of the chapter (see *sūrah*).

al-Azhar Name of one of the principle mosques in present day Cairo, also the name of famous Islamic University in Cairo, which played an important role in the Islamic reform movement in the early twentieth century. See also *madrasa* and *Salafiyya.*

azza (Hausa: "grievance"). Type of religious mourning ceremony among Shīʿa Muslims in Africa, in particular rooted in the history of remembrance ceremonies for the martyrdom of Ḥusayn at the battle in Kerbala in 680. See also *ʿashūrā*, *Muḥarram*, and *ta'ziyyah*.

bait almal (Swahili: "house of wealth"). See *bayt al-māl*.

bakhsh (Urdu: "forgiveness"). Commonly used for forgiveness, especially when asking forgiveness from God or someone very higher in status.

bakra (Urdu: "sacrificed animal"). See *baqara*.

bakshish (Urdu: "reward," "tip," "gift" or "donation"). A reward to somebody for doing good deeds, for example a tip for a waiter, in a religious context this also refers to as reward or alms (see *zakāt*). See also *bakhsh*.

bala (Urdu: "calamity" or "distress"). Condition or bad omen that causes misfortune or affliction. See also *barkat*.

baqara (Arab.: "cow" or "sacrificial victim"). According to Islamic tradition, Muslims are expected to divide the sacrificed animal into three equal parts, distributed in thirds with one share for the sacrificing family, one for their relatives and friends, and one for the poor and needy (see *masākīn*). See also *baraka*, *qurbān*, and *zakāt*.

baraka (Arab.: "blessing"). Spiritual blessings or beneficent forces sent by God (see *Allāh*) and distributed to the believer, it also refers to any miraculous increase or incredible surplus in substance, quantity, or quality due to the Muslim's belief in God. The power God conveys and transmits to certain persons, objects, including the act of sacrifice (see *qurbān*) and the sacrificial animal (see *baqara*). As a source to receive blessings, also found in local traditions of Islām and specifically within the context of Sufi traditions (see *ṭarīqa*) and their worship of saints by visiting their tombs (see *ziyāra*).

baraza (Swahili: "council"). Type of meeting in combination with a festive meal held at a specific place. In Eastern Africa, it also refers to a public meeting or a place for a communal assembly.

barkat (Urdu: "blessing" or "prosperity"). As a theological concept it refers to the blessing going along with the enhancement in prosperity and good fortune. See also *baraka*.

basmala (Arab.: "In the name of God"). The abbreviated name for the recurring Islamic phrase: *Bi-ism Allāh al-raḥmān al-raḥīm* ("In the name of God, the Merciful, the Compassionate"). The invocation of the basmala at the beginning of every important religious act calls down the divine blessing (see *baraka*) to sanctify it. Muslims utter a mandatory basmala during the sacrifice before cutting the throat of the sacrificial animal (see *qurbān*). See also *ḥamdilla*, *ʿīd al-aḍḥā*, and *niyyah*.

bāṭil (Arab.: "falsehood"). As a common term, it refers to the qualities of vain and unreal or false and wrong, in religious contexts these qualities render a ritual null and void.

bayt al-māl (Arab.: "house of wealth"). It is the name for the financial institution of the fiscus or treasury of the Islamic state responsible for administrating the taxation and the distribution of alms (see *zakāt*). See also *jizya*, *kharāj*, *khums*, and *ʿushr*.

Bedouin (French, derived from Arab. *badawī*: "desert dweller"). People of the Arab tribes in the Middle East, dwelling mainly in the desert of Saudi Arabia but also found in Syria, Palestine, and Egypt, with pastoral nomadism as their main economic activity. The Bedouin are predominantly Sunnī Muslims following the Shāfiʿī school (see *madhhab*) of Islamic law (see *sharīʿa*).

Beduin See *Bedouin*.

Berber Name of a nomadic ethnic group widely spread all over North Africa West of the Nile Valley. In Morocco, Berber is a people with Berber as a distinct language living and moving between countries throughout northwestern Africa. They are Sunnī Muslims following the Mālikī school (see *madhhab*) of the Islamic law (see *sharī'a*) and place strong emphasis on the blessings (see *baraka*) of the descendants of Muḥammad for their religious leader (see *sharīf*).

Berti Ethnic group scattered around parts of Southwestern Ethiopia and Northern Darfur province in Southwestern Sudan, living in small sedentary villages with raising millet and herding cattle as their main economic activity. Nowadays Arabic speaking, the Berti are Sunnī Muslims and follow the Mālikī school of Islamic law (see *madhhab*) with an unorthodox interpretation of prescribed religious practices known for their local tradition of healing practice of drinking the Qur'ān.

bida (Ghana: "novelty"). See *bid'a.*

bid'a (Arab.: "innovation"). Modernization in religion particularly associated with new forms of worship, belief, or practice for which there is not precedent from the time of the Prophet Muḥammad and even in partial breach with the tradition of the Prophet (see *sunna*); pejoratively used and being categorically rejected by strict Islamists as deviation. See also *Salafiyya* and *Wahhābiyya.*

bikin suna (Hausa: "name giving"). Name giving ceremony in West Africa usually held when the parents publicly announce the name of their baby on the seventh day of the birth. See also *'aqīqa.*

Al-Bīrūnī, Abū al-Rayḥān Muḥammad ibn Aḥmad (973–1048). Important Islamic scholars in medieval Islām and the first Muslim knowlegeable in Sanskrit, recognized for travelling throught the Muslim world. He is most well-known for his most lucid account of the religions and people of South Asia in "Chronicles of India" (*Kitāb al Hind*).

Bismillah Allah Akbar! (Arab.: "In the name of God, God is Great!"). Islamic expression *Bi-ism Allāh Allāh akbar!* Is commonly used in the context of the ritual prayer (see *ṣalāt*). See also *basmala* and *euzü-besmele.*

Bori Name of a form of female spirit possession commonly known among Hausa Muslims throughout West Africa, particularly in Northern Nigeria. Supported by drumming on traditional musical instruments (*calabashes*), women perform the possession dances and enter trance for purposes of healing. See also *zar.*

Brahmo Samaj (Hindi: "society of God" or "community of men worshipping Brahman"). An influential religious movement in modern India and throughout Southeast Asia to promote a reformed monotheistic Hinduism with Islamic overtones, supporting equal rights of women and being opposed to forms of animal sacrifice.

al-Bukhārī, Muḥammad (810–870). Well-known compiler of the important and famous Islamic collection of the oral and written Islamic traditions (see *ḥadīth*, sing.) of the life and deeds of the Prophet Muḥammad (see *sunna*). Sunnī Muslims considers the *Saḥīḥ Bukhārī* to be the first of the six authentic books of its kind.

burnous (French, derived from Arab. *burnus* and Greek *birros*: "cloak"). Name for a long hooded traditional cloak of coarse woolen fabric woven in one piece, usually white in color worn by Berbers and Arabs in Morocco found throughout North Africa.

caliph (Engl., derived from Arab.: "successor"). See *khalīfa.*

caliphate (Engl., derived from Arab.: "succession"). See *khilāfa.*

cemaat (Turk.: "community" or "people"). As a generic term, it refers to a religious or ethnic community of any sort.

chuo (Swahili: "school"). As a term it is used to refer to a local elementary school.

couscous (French, derived from Arab. *kuskus*: "pasta"). Name of a traditional spicy dish in North Africa consisting of pasta of crushed semolina grains and steamed with a meat and vegetable stew. See also *Berber.*

dā'iyat (Arab.: "preacher"). Refers to a religious instructor at a mosque, also a job title of a person who travels to other countries to 'invite' people to Islām (see *da'wa*). See also *da'wa*, *imām*, *khuṭba*, and *mu'adhdhin*.

da-kpariba (Ghana, "mutual assistance"). Generic term that refers to as reciprocal support and help among neighbors and friends including financial aid. See also *zakāt*.

daku (Swahili: "breakfast"). See *saḥūr*.

daraja (Hausa: "value," "worth," "respect," "rank," or "position"). This term refers to social rank and respectability in contrast to forms of vulgar public display.

darasa (Swahili: "classroom"). See *dars*.

dars (Arab.: "lesson," pl. *durūs*). Lecture in a class setting. Also refers to a religious class.

ḍarūra (Arab.: "necessity"). As a theological term, it refers to the state of necessity in the Islamic legal system (see *fiqh*), but in social and economic terms it also refers to the necessities and demands of everyday life. See also *sharī'a*.

dawa (Arab.: "to invoke"). See *da'wa*.

da'wa (Arab.: "to call," "to invite," or "to invoke"). In the religious sense, call to believe in Islām as the true religion addressed to all humans by God (see *Allāh*) and the Prophet Muḥammad, also refers to the preaching of Islām or proselytizing. See also *dā'iya* and *khuṭba*.

dervish (Pers./Turk.: "the poor" or "mendicant friar"). Member of any of the various Muslim ascetic orders or brotherhoods (see *ṭarīqa*, sing.), known for their extreme poverty and austerity, also a religious mendicant or initiate of the Sufi path (see *ṭarīqa*) associated with a particular method of spiritual instruction, some of which perform ecstatic whirling dances and energetic chants as a form of spiritual devotion. See also *faqīr* and *masākīn*. (Other spelling and transliterations include *darvish*, *darwish*, and *derviş*.)

dhikr (Arab.: "remembrance" or "reminding" also "mention"). Act of reminding oneself by continuously and repeatedly invocating the name of God (see *Allāh*) performed in a litany as part of ritual worship (see *'ibāda*). In Sufism, the most common form of prayer is glorifying the name of God repeatedly sung in communal rituals under the guidance of a spiritual master (see *salaf*). As a method of concentration, this also goes along with bodily movements and breathing techniques. See also *khushū'* and *La ilaha illā Allāh!* (Other transliterations include *thikir*, *zikir*, and *zikr*.)

Dhu al-Hajj (Hausa: "month of pilgrimage"). See *Dhū al-Ḥijja*.

Dhū al-Ḥijja (Arab.: "month of pilgrimage"). The twelfth and last month of the Islamic calendar also called "the month of pilgrimage," during which Muslims perform their pilgrimage to Mecca (see *ḥajj*) and celebrate the feast of sacrifice (see *'īd al-aḍḥā*). (Other transliterations include *Dhū 'l-Hijjah*, *Dūu al-Hijja*, *Thu al-Hijja*, and *Zu al-Hijja*.)

dhunūb (Arab.: "faults" or "mishaps," sing. *dhanb*). Conceived as wrong doings and in general the violation of the Islamic moral code. Sometimes seen as minor sins, but not always identical with voluntary sinful transgressions (see *ithm*, sing.), also it refers to impurity without taking the ritual shower after sexual intercourse. (Other transliterations include *thunub* and *zinub*.)

dīn (Arab.: "judgment" and "custom" but also "religion" or "way of life"). Usually translated as "revealed religion," but more specifically referring to the worship of God (see *'ibāda*) and the way of life as based on Islamic principles of revelation and submission encompassing all beliefs and practices of Muslims. See also *sharī'a*.

dindar (Turk.: "religious" or "pious"). Adverb or adjective of *dīn*.

diyanet (Pers./Turk., derived from Arab. *diyāna*: "religion," "religiosity," or "piety"). As a generic term, it refers to the adopted religion of a community or the council of

Islamic scholars who interpret the Islamic law (see *sharīʿa*). In Turkey, it is the name of the Directorate of Religious Affairs. See also *dindar* and *muftī*.

dua (Turk.: "prayer"). See *duʿā'*.

duʿā' (Arab.: "appeal," "request," or "prayer"). Spontaneous and personal prayer that can go along with a petition for a blessing on behalf of oneself or somebody else or a cursing against someone; practitioners tend to add, after completing the canonical prayer (see *ṣalāt*), a more personalized wish without necessarily using prescribed formula.

dupatta (Urdu: "veil" or "scarf"). Name for the multi-purpose chiffon scarf worn by many South Asian women to cover their heads and the upper body fully, while they read the Qur'ān or during devotional prayer meetings.

durūs (Arab.: "lessons"). See *dars*.

eid zoha (Urdu: "feast of sacrifice"). As a religious feast of sacrifice performed on the tenth day of the month of pilgrimage (see *Dhū al-Ḥijja*) and an integral part of the pilgrimage to Mecca (see *ḥajj*), it is celebrated in the remembrance of Abraham's sacrifice (see *Ibrāhīm*). Also referred to as *korban* or *niaz* among Pakistani (see *qurban*). See also *ʿīd al-aḍḥā*. (Other transliterations include *eid ul azha* and *eid-e-zoha*.)

euzü-besmele (Turk.). Name of a prayer formula used during the ritual prayer (see *namaz*), which follows the *sübhaneke* and precedes the recitation of the opening chapter (see *sūrah*) of the Qur'ān (see *fātiḥa*). See also *basmala* and *tekbir*.

ezan (Turk.: "prayer announcement"). See *adhān*.

faḍā'il (Arab.: "excellence" or "merits"). Practice of virtues and good deeds, referring to a specific category of literature praising the excellence of places, things, and persons; also the name of a chapter of the written Islamic tradition (see *ḥadīth*): *Kitāb al-Faḍā'il* ("Book of Merits").

al-fajr (Arab.: "dawn"). The name of a voluntary silent ritual prayer (see *ṣalāt*) performed in two cycles (see *rakʿa*, sing.) after dawn and before sunrise. Muslims start their fast (see *ṣawm*) at sunrise. See also *al-ṣubḥ*.

faqīr (Arab.: "poor person," pl. *fuqarā'*). It means penniless or financially poor, also referred to as somebody who lives for God (see *Allāh*) alone and rejects any personal property in total resignation to the will of God. See also *dervish* and *masākīn*. (Other transliterations include *fakir*.)

farā'iḍ (Arab.: "appointed or obligatory portions in a property" or "inheritance"). Term for the fixed shares in an estate based on specific rules which are outstanding features of the Islamic law of inheritance, also name of a chapter on the written Islamic tradition (see *ḥadīth*): *Kitāb al-Farā'iḍ* ("Book of Inheritance"). See also *farḍ*.

farḍ (Arab.: "appointed" or "obligatory"). Acts of worship and duties made obligatory and incumbent upon Muslims by God (see *ʿibāda*). Religious duty or obligation, the omission of which will be punished and the fulfillment rewarded, as prescribed in the Islamic law (see *sharīʿa*), for example the ritual prayer (see *ṣalāt*) or almsgiving (see *zakāt*). See also *wājib*.

farz (Turk.: "obligatory"). See *farḍ*.

fātiḥa (Arab.: "opening"). The first and opening chapter (see *sūrah*) of the Qur'ān, which is the indispensable formula for the canonical prayer (see *ṣalāt*) as well as used to mark all other ritual occasions or festivals (see *ʿīd*, sing.). See also *Qur'ān*.

fatwā (Arab.: "opinion" or "decision"). Opinion on juridical matters by publishing a ruling or juridical order regarding a religious doctrine or law (see *sharīʿa*) by a recognized legal authority (see *muftī*). Although applying to all matters of civic and religious life, it is not legally binding, since it is an opinion, and the civic community can dismiss it when compared to the opinion of other legal scholars.

fiqh (Arab.: "understanding" or "knowledge," but also "jurisprudence"). As a generic term, it refers to the science of the practice of religion, including the proper understanding of the rituals and laws of Islām. Also term for the form of religious jurisprudence, which is in accordance with the principles of Islām and built around the religious doctrine or Islamic law (see *sharīʿa*) and based on custom and community practices (see *ʿurf*). It deals with laws regulating the observance of rituals (see *ʿibāda*) and matters of social and economic life (see *muʿāmalāt*) based on the foundational principles of Islām. One distinguishes between four Sunnī schools of jurisprudence, each with its different foundational articles of interpretation with specific prohibitions (see *madhhab*). See also *qāḍī*.

fitra (Arab.: "creation," "disposition," or "nature"). As a theological term, it refers the natural or God-given innate disposition of humans. See also *nafs*.

fungate (Swahili: "seven" or "seven day period"). Referring to ceremonies related to the honeymoon Muslims perform after wedding, lasting seven days, also used to denote the month of Ramaḍān.

fuqarā' (Arab.: "poor men"). See *faqīr*.

gallabiya (Arab.: "dress"). Name for the short hemmed and long loose gown worn by men and women in Egypt.

Gayo Language spoken among others in the central mountain region of the Aceh province in Northern Sumatra, also refers to the ethnic group of rice and coffee farming people with a distinct art and culture. The Gayo follow predominantly the Shāfiʿī school of Islamic law (see *madhhab*). Although the Gayo have been Muslim since the seventeenth century, modernist Muslims (see *Kaum Muda*) sought to purge improper elements in their most common ceremonial events of the ritual meal (see *kenduri*).

ghafla (Arab.: "carelessness"). As a theological term, it refers to negligence or indifference in religious matters. Also referring to the absent mindedness or forgetfulness in the performance of ritual practice as an involuntary act and weaknesses not be seen as a sin (see *ithm*). See also *dhunūb*.

gharib (Urdu: "poor"). In the Islamic tradition of Pakistan, the category of the poor and needy (see *masākīn*) can involve any person, even members of one's own family or community, including widows and orphans cutting across the categories of social groups.

gum'a (Arab.: "gathering"). See *jumʿa*.

Hadhramaut Historical name of a landscape with a broad valley (see *wādī*) in Southern part of today's Yemen, being the center for the origin of a number of Arab tribes with numerous sanctuary sites and cities. See also *Quraysh*.

ḥadīth (Arab.: "narrative" or "speech" also "report" and "tradition," pl. *aḥādīth*). Used for reports and recorded traditions that account for the Prophet Muḥammad's exemplary practice (see *sunna*), including his sayings and deeds as well as his judgments and approvals. These reports built a traditional source of knowledge second in authority to the Qur'ān. Transmitted through his first companions, it is one of the main resources for the foundation of Islām preceding and guiding later Muslim practice. They establish guidelines for education and learning (see *madrasa*) as much as for their religious identity, juridical practice and everyday way of life. As conceptual framework, it also served in the formation of Islamic law (see *sharīʿa*) and jurisdiction (see *fiqh*).

ḥāji (Arab.: "pilgrim"). See *ḥājji*.

ḥajj (Arab.: "greater pilgrimage"). The pilgrimage to Mecca is one of the five pillars of Islām (see *arkān al-dīn*) and is obligatory (see *wājib*) for all those who can afford it and are able to make their way to Mecca. The Qur'ān attributes in Sūrah 22 Abraham (see *Ibrāhīm*) as its founder and consists of a series of rituals lasting several days. Muslims are required to perform the rituals of pilgrimage at the Grand Mosque in Mecca and at surrounding sites of the city during the 8th and 13th of *Dhū al-Ḥijja*. The particular steps of the pilgrimage in Mecca and near by places are prescribed, including the circumambulation of the Ka'ba seven times (see *ṭawāf*), followed by personal prayers (see *du'ā'*), ritual prayers (see *ṣalāt*) as well as drinking of the water of Zamzam and the ritual walking (see *sa'y*) between the two hills of Ṣafā and Marwah seven times on the first day of the pilgrimage. The rituals are followed by a visit on Mount 'Arafāt at the 9th of *Dhū al-Ḥijja* and culminates in the feast of sacrifice (see *'īd al-aḍḥā*) in Minā on the 10th of *Dhū al-Ḥijja*. During the remaining days, Muslim pilgrims stay in Minā and upon leaving they are recommended to perform another circumambulation of the Ka'ba seven times (see *ṭawāf*) as a closure of their pilgrimage. Those who performed the pilgrimage are entitled to add a prefix to their name with the honorary title "pilgrim" (*al-ḥājj*). See also *'umra* and *ziyāra*. (Other transliterations include *hadj* and *haj*.)

ḥājja (Arab.: "pilgrim"). Honorary title for a woman after having performed her pilgrimage (*ḥajj*) to Mecca.

ḥājji (Arab.: "pilgrim"). Honorary title for male pilgrims. See *ḥājja*.

ḥājjiya (Hausa: "pilgrim"). See *ḥājja*.

ḥalāl (Arab.: "permitted" or "lawful"). Referring to all acts honorable, beneficial, permitted, and pure as prescribed in the Islamic law (see *sharī'a*). See also *ḥarām*.

Hamās (Arab. *ḥamās*: "zeal"). Acronym for the "Islamic Resistance Movement" (*Ḥarakat al-Muqāwama al-Islāmiya*), which grew out of the Palestinian resistance against the Israeli occupation in 1987 (*intifāḍa*) and was inspired by the Muslim Brotherhood (*al-Ikhwān al-Muslimun*) and the Hezbollah, a Shī'a organization with affinities to forms of militant resistance. Israel formerly supported Islamic movements like the Hamas to undermine the Palestine Liberation Organization (PLO).

Ḥamdillah (Arab.: "praise to God"). The prayer formula "*al-hamdu li-Llah*" is used as an interruption for suitable situations. It is uttered to mark the formal end of an activity and to terminate activities that begun with the *basmala*. See also *ṣalāt*.

Ḥāmidīya Shādhilīya Name of an important Islamic religious order (see *ṭarīqa*) founded by Shaykh Abū al-Ḥasan al-Shādhilī (1196–1258) in Cairo and later on reformed by Sidi Salāma al-Rāḍī (1867–1927). It is based on a corpus of Islamic laws (see *sharī'a*), which define a strict hierarchy of roles and functions among its members.

Hamidiya Shaziliya See *Ḥāmidīya Shādhilīya*.

Ḥanafī One of the four schools of Islamic law (see *madhhab*, sing.), founded by Abū Hanīfah an-Nu'man ibn Thābit (699–767). As the most prominent among the Sunnī legal schools (see *fiqh*), it is widely accepted by many adherents in the Muslim world predominantly in Central Asia, including Afghanistan, Pakistan, India, Bangladesh, Northern Egypt, Iraq, Turkey, and the Balkans. One of the main characteristics of the Ḥanafī school of law concerns the ritual prayer (see *ṣalāt*), which needs to be performed in its usual time with the exception of the times of pilgrimage (see *ḥajj*). Despite slight differences in prayer times, the hands are not raised during or after the ritual cycles (see *rak'a*, sing.). Furthermore, Ḥanafī requires a sixth prayer (see *witr*) after the night prayer (see *al-'ishā'*) and before the morning prayer at dawn (see *al-ṣubḥ*). See also *sharī'a*.

Ḥanbalī One of the four Sunnī schools of Islamic law (see *madhhab*, sing.). Founded by Imām Aḥmad ibn Ḥanbal (780–855) nowadays predominantly practiced among Muslims in Saudi Arabia and Qatar. Some main characteristics of Ḥanbalī concerns ritual pruity (see *wuḍū'*) and ritual prayer (see *ṣalāt*), as touching a woman nullifies ritual purification. Other minor differences relate to the position of the hands during the prayer. Ḥanbalī fold their hands during the standing position above the naval (*qayyam*) and raise their hands before entering and standing up for the two consecutively performed ritual cycles (see *rak'a*, sing.). Ḥanbalī recommends a sixth prayer (see *witr*) on a voluntary basis to be performed after the night prayer (see *al-'ishā'*) and before the morning prayer at dawn (see *al-ṣubḥ*). See also *sharī'a*.

haqiqa (Urdu: "name"). When a baby is born people give a charity or sacrifice a goat or lamb and distribute meat in the poor and needy (see *masākīn*), some organize a party to celebrate the birth of a child. See also *'aqīqa*.

ḥaraka (Arab.: "motion" or "movement"). As a term, it commonly refers to social or political movements.

ḥarām (Arab.: "forbidden"). Prohibited acts, Muslims are believed to receive reward (see *thawāb*) by keeping away from things or acts prohibited by the Islamic law (see *sharī'a*) out of obedience, also referring to the blood of a sacrificial victim. See also *ḥalāl*.

ḥasanāh (Arab.: "beneficence"). As an ethical term, it refers to kind acts or good deeds (*hasanat*, pl.).

Hausa Name of a language spoken across Northern Nigeria and Niger with numerous local dialects, but also used throughout West Africa as a *lingua franca*. Also used to refer to the largest ethnic group of native speaking Hausa people scattered across the savannah in Niger and Northern Nigeria with agriculture and trade as their main economic activities. The vast majority of the Hausa people practice Sunnī Islām and follow the Mālikī school of Islamic law (see *madhhab*) blended with local religious and Sufi traditions (see *ṭarīqa*).

henna (Engl., derived from Arab. *hinnā'*: "shrub"). Name for a brown-reddish dye made from the black powder of the dried leaves of the Henna shrub. Used for temporarily tattooing the skin and nails of especially women for ceremonial purposes, but also used to purify the animal selected for sacrifice transforming it from an ordinary animal into a sacrificially appropriate one. See also *'īd al-aḍḥā* and *qurbān*.

hijra (Arab.: "migration"). The migration of Muḥammad and his first followers from Mecca to Medina performed in 622 in order to avoid their persecution in Mecca. This migration also indicates the beginning of a new calendrical era. (Other transliterations include *hegira*.)

Ḥusayn (624–680). The second son of 'Alī ibn Abī Ṭālib and Fatimah and grandson of Muḥammad. The martyrdom of Ḥusayn at the battle at Kerbala in 680 is a central event for the formation of the Shī'a. His death is mourned by Shī'a Muslims on the tenth days of *Muḥarram* (see *'ashūrā*) through passion plays (see *ta'ziyyah*).

huwa (Arab.: "he"). Refers to "He" as one of the titles of God.

'ibāda (Arab.: "submission" or "worship"). Term referring to expressions of any servitude to God (see *Allāh*) defined as a religious duty that is left to the individual in particular in the Islamic law (see *sharī'a*) in regards to ceremonial law and more specifically to the obligatory acts of worship (see *arkān al-dīn*), like fasting (see *ṣawm*) or prayer (see *ṣalāt*). However, submission does not only relate to religious or ritual acts or matters of worship, it generally also includes the pursuit of knowledge as well as charity and modesty. See also *sharī'a*. (Other transliterations include *'ibādah*, *'ibādat*, and *ibadet*.)

ibadet (Turk.: "worship"). See *'ibāda*.

Ibn Baṭṭūṭa, Abū 'Abd Allāh Muḥammad (1304–1368). Moroccan Berber and Islamic scholar travelling in Northwest Africa, Southeast Europe and Central and Southeast Asia and known for the chronicles of his journeys called *Riḥla*.

Ibn Khaldūn, Abū Zayd 'Abd al-Raḥmān ibn Muḥammad (1332–1406). Important Muslim scholar born in Tunisia and trained in Fez. Later on he served as judge (see *qāḍī*) of the Mālikī school of law (see *madhhab*). Due to his talent of observing human culture and society, he is often conceived of as the father of historiography or social theory and a forerunner of numerous social scientific disciplines such as the science of civilization (see *"ilm al-'umrān*) including demography and economics. His most well known work is the "Book of Examples" (*Kitāb al-'Ibar*), describing the history and society of the Arabs and Berbers.

Ibrāhīm (Arab.: "Abraham"). In the Islamic tradition, Abraham is believed to have submitted himself fully (see *Islām*) to the belief in God (see *Allāh*) proven through his willingness to sacrifice his firstborn son Ismā'īl with his first wife Hagar. Muslims believe that he reinstalled the house of God (see *Ka'ba*) and established the pilgrimage to Mecca (see *ḥajj*) as revealed through the Prophet Muḥammad who himself is believed to be descended from Abraham through his son Ismā'īl. See also *Muḥammad.*

'īd (Arab.: "feast" or "festival"). Generic term referring to religious celebration, in particular referring to the feast of sacrifice (see *'īd al-aḍḥā*) and the feast of breaking fast (see *'īd al-fiṭr*). (Other transliterations include *eid.*)

'īd al-aḍḥā (Arab.: "the feast of sacrifice"). Annual feast of sacrifice beginning with a ritual sacrifice on the 10th of *Dhū al-Hijja* and an integral part of the pilgrimage to Mecca (see *ḥajj*) lasting four days during which the meat of the sacrificed animal (see *baqara*) is distributed to the family, neighbors and the poor and needy (see *masākīn*). This feast also commemorates the willingness of Abraham (see *Ibrāhīm*) to sacrifice his son at God's command originating in the Qur'ān (Sūrah 22:34–38; 108). See also *zakāt.*

'īd al-fiṭr (Arab.: "the feast of breaking of the fast"). Name of the religious festival marking the end of fasting (see *ṣawm*) performed in the nights throughout the month of Ramaḍān. (Other transliterations include *'īd 'l-fiṭr.*)

idul fitri (Ind., derived from Arab.: "feast of breaking of the fast"). See *'īd al-fiṭr.*

ifṭār (Arab.: "end or breaking of the fast"). Name for the end of the fast day, also name for the evening meal served subsequent to the evening prayer (see *al-maghrib*) after sunset to break the fast (see *ṣawm*) during the Islamic month of Ramaḍān, also a form of social festivity.

ihlâs (Turk.: "sincerity" or "faith"). See *ikhlāṣ.*

iḥrām (Arab.: "consecration"). State of ritual purity (see *wuḍū'*) signified through ritual prayer (see *ṣalāt*) and white dress, as with the special clothing pilgrims wear during their pilgrimage to Mecca (see *ḥajj*).

iḥtirām (Arab.: "respect" or "honor"). Form of respect particularly with regard to community and family members held in honor.

ihyā' (Arab.: "revival"or "return to life"). Practice of spending a night in worship and ritual prayer (see *al-tarāwīḥ*), preferably in the month of Ramaḍān, when the Qur'ān is be lieved to be revealed to the Prophet Muḥammad. See also *i'tikāf*, *laylat al-qadr*, and *ṣalāt.*

ijmā' (Arab.: "consensus"). The formal consensus of the Muslim community (see *umma*) or the scholars (see *ulamā'*), conceived along with the Qur'ān, the written Islamic tradition (see *ḥadīth*) and the analogy of reason (see *qiyās*) as one of the four essential bases of Islamic law (see *sharī'a*).

ijtihād (Arab.: "critical thinking"). The term refers to the rational and new interpretation of the Qur'ān and the written Islamic tradition (see *ḥadīth*) by individual Muslims, but it stands in clear contrast to the complete innovation (see *bid'a*) in the form of ritual worship (see *'ibāda*). The differences between the legal schools (see *madhhāb*) of Islamic law (see *sharī'a*) are believed to enforce and lead to critical thinking. Central concept widely used among members of Islamic reform movements (see *Salafiyya*) to allow variation letting individual Muslims make their own choices. Muḥammad ʿAbduh (1849–1905) and Rashid Rida (1865–1935) have claimed that each Muslim can interpret the Qur'ān and *ḥadīth* on his or her own. See also *al-Ṣaḥwa al-Islāmiyya.*

ikhlāṣ (Arab.: "purity" also "fidelity" or "sincerity"). It generally refers to the purity of faith and the sincerity of devotion. Al-Ikhlāṣ is also the name for Sūrah 112 of the Qur'ān consisting of four verses (see *āyā*, sing.) declaring God's absolute unity (see *tawḥīd*).

al-Ikhwān al-Muslimūn (Arab.: "Muslim Brotherhood"). Islamist transnational movement and largest political opposition in many Arab states, founded in 1929 in Egypt by Hassan al-Banna (1906–1949). It is the oldest and largest Islamic political group opposed to secular regime in Muslim countries and the world's most influential Islamist movement to establish Islamic states.

ʿilm (Arab.: "science" or "knowledge"). As a generic term, it refers to all forms of knowledge based on science and scientific reasoning, but also used to indicate any form of education, teaching, and learning in the principles and practices of Islām (see *madrasa*). See also *adab*, *ʿaql*, and *fiqh*

ʿilm al-tajwīd (Arab.: "science of adornment"). Science of the art of reciting or chanting the Qur'ān according to prescribed rules of pronunciation taught in mosques and traditional religious schools as well as in institutions of higher education (see *madrasa*). See also *tajwīd.*

ʿilm al-ʿumrān (Arab.: "science of civilization"). Science of social organization primarily developed by the medieval Islamic scholar Ibn Khaldūn within the framework of his social theory.

ilmihal (Turk.: "catechism"). Name for the collection of the most central tenets of Islām concerning the appropriate form and rules of how Muslims have to conduct their religious obligations (see *ʿibāda*) including the ritual prayer (see *ṣalāt*) comparable to the catechisms in Christianity. See also *talqīn.*

iltizām (Arab.: "commitment"). Any form of legal commitment (see *mu'amalāt*), e.g., to a contract, not necessarily an ideology or system of belief. It also refers to somebody who is committed (see *multazim*).

imām (Arab.: "leader"). As an honorary title, it refers to the head of a Sunnī or Shīʿa Muslim community and religious authority leading the mosque and ritual prayer (see *ṣalāt*). Among the Shīʿa, the leaders of the religious community, who are descendants of Muḥammad (see *sayyid*) with a proven blood lineage (see *ahl al-bayt*) are called Imāms who, for the Sunnī, in return represent the illicit institution of the succession of religious authority (see *khalīfa*).

īmān (Arab.: "faith" or "belief"). Personal belief or faith in God, which in principle implies the full obligation to Islamic law (see *sharīʿa*) as laid out in the Qur'ān and the tradition of the Prophet Muḥammad (see *sunna*). See also *ʿibāda*, *mu'min*, and *taqwa.*

imani (Swahili: "faith" or "belief"). See *īmān.*

Irshadi A political force and reform movement formerly founded in Indonesia in the early twentieth century, after the revolution of 1962 in Yemen, operating as opposition to the Alawi and politically active in the area of Hadhramaut.

al-ʿishā' (Arab.: "evening" or "night"). Name for the fifth canonical prayer (*ṣalāh al-ʿishā'*) performed at dusk after the onset of night and favorably before midnight but possible until dawn. Consisting of four cycles (see *rakʿa*, sing.), the first two are usually performed aloud and the second two silent. See also *ṣalāt.*

Islām (Arab.: "submission" or "obedience"). The literal meaning of this term is submission or total surrender to the will of God (see *Allāh*) as revealed to the Prophet Muḥammad through the archangel Gabriel (see *Jibrīl*) and transmitted on the Qur'ān. See also *arkān al-dīn* and *shahāda*.

İslam ahlakı (Turk.: "morals of Islām" or "ethics of Islām"). Name for the normative framework of proper religious behavior guiding the practice of Muslim virtuous morality, it also refers to pious subjectivity.

Ismā'īl (Arab.: "Ismael"). Name of the eldest son, Abraham (see *Ibrāhīm*) had with his first wife Hagar. The Islamic tradition considers Ismael and not Isaac as the first-born son who Abraham intended to sacrifice according to God's will, although even the Qur'ān does not specify whom Abraham was going to sacrifice. Muslims commemorate and celebrate this event, which testified Abraham's faith and his obedience, during the feast of sacrifice (see *'īd al-aḍḥā*) on the 10th of *Dhū al-Ḥijja*, when Muslims perform their pilgrimage to Mecca (see *ḥajj*). See also *Minā*.

isrāf (Arab.: "expenditure" or "extravagance"). Referred to as acts of wasteful expenditure and meaning excess and extremism, from which Muslims, according to the Islamic law (see *sharī'a*), are discouraged (see *makrūh*). See also *mu'amalāt* and *taslīya*.

ithm (Arab.: "transgression" or "sin"). Voluntary transgressions are believed to be the worst sins and most punishable in the afterlife (see *qiyāma*). See also *dhunūb*, *ghafla*, *ma'ṣiya*, and *zīna*.

i'tikāf (Arab.: "applying oneself to the service of God"). This term refers to a particularly recommended pious practice of spending a period of retreat in a mosque. Often involves spending all available time secluded in a mosque praying (see *al-tarāwīḥ*) and reciting the Qur'ān, particularly during the last ten nights of the month of Ramaḍān when the archangel Gabriel (see *Jibrīl*) is believed to have revealed the Qur'ān for the first time to the Prophet Muḥammad (see *laylat al-qadr*). See also *iḥyā'*.

Ja'farī Name of the major Shī'a school of Islamic law (see *madhhab*) in Iran as most common among the Twelve Imām Shī'a founded by Ja'far aṣ-Ṣadiq (699–765). Ja'far is the sixth imam and is as spiritual master (see *shaykh*) key for the development of the Twelve Imām Shī'a as a religious and political doctrine. He is believed to possess a book of secret knowledge (*Kitāb al-Jafr*), known exclusively by the family of Muḥammad (see *ahl al-bayt*). The Twelve Imām Shī'a holds the belief that the Prophet Muḥammad intended to have successors (see *khilāfa*) as mediators between God and men. These mediators (see *imam*) were the descendents of 'Alī ibn Abī Ṭālib (see *sayyid*). Through Ja'far's eldest son Ismā'īl, succeeding him as the seventh imam, the Seven Imām Shī'a (or Ismā'īlīs) trace the religious doctrines and practices. See also *madhhab*, and *Shī'a*.

Jandarma (Turk., derived from French: "gendarmerie"). Military police force in Turkey.

Javanese Language spoken in the provinces of East and Central Java by an ethnic group in Indonesia, living with fishing in the coastal areas and wet rice agriculture as a principal form of peasant economy and plantations established by the Dutch. Although virtually all Javanese are Muslim generally following the Shāfi'ī school of Islamic law (see *madhhab*), their religious practices are syncretic, with Islām layered over their indigenous forms of Hindu-Buddhist belief. See also *kenduri* and *slametan*.

Jibrīl (Arab.: "Gabriel"). The archangel Gabriel as God's Mighty One also known in the Jewish and Christian tradition as the Divine Messenger sent off to Daniel and Mary. In the Muslim tradition, Jibrīl is the Angel of Revelation appearing to all prophets beginning with Adam and ending with the Prophet Muḥammad as the seal of all prophets. The Qur'ān is believed to be the final Word of God (see *Allāh*) revealed in full to the Prophet Muḥammad as transmitted through Jibrīl in the last days of *Ramaḍān*. See also *laylat al-qadr*.

jihād (Arab.: "struggle" or "effort"). Serious determination to fight against wrong doings and struggle for the righteous way of Islām, including teachings and other duties to improve morality as believed to be a duty assigned by God. Although it generally means to enhance humanity and moral standards, it also refers to the institution of warfare to defend Islām from threats and extend Islām into non-Islamic territories.

jihadist (Engl.: "a person who takes place in the Islamic warfare"). This is the English derivative from *jihād*, but not an Arabic word (see *mujāhid*). Currently, used primarily by English speaking non-Muslims, it is a collective term for a member in social and religious movements that explicitly support warfare to defend Islām. See also *jihād*.

jizya (Arab.: "tax" or "tribute"). Generally, the name for the tax for civil protection and support of the military, but also a form of tribute indicated in the Qur'ān to be paid by non-Muslim male members living under Islamic rule in return for their protection by the state. See also *bayt al-māl* and *zakāt*.

al-jum'a (Arab.: "gathering" or "Friday"). Common abbreviation for the special Friday prayer (*ṣalāh al-jum'a*) performed only by men in a congregational meeting in the mosque subsequent to the delivery of the sermon (see *khuṭba*).

Jumūd (Thai: "decadence"). Islamic Reformists in Southeast Asia (see *Khana Mai*) condemn local customs and traditions of folk Islām (see *'urf*) among Muslim communities as sign of depravity or self-indulgence.

juta (Urdu: "leftover"). Commonly it is used for someone's left over meal. It can also be used to refer to the practice of giving away left overs of sacrificial meals (see *niaz*) to low caste people in India, partially comparable with the Islamic ideal of giving part of their sacrificial meal to poor and needy people (see *masākīn*). See also *bakra* and *zakāt*.

juz' (Arab.: "part"). One of thirty parts in which the Qur'ān is divided to be recited by individual practitioners during a night in a mosque (see *ihyā'*) so that all parts of the Qur'ān can be read during one month, most commonly during the month of Ramaḍān (see *laylat al-qadr*). Due to the descending length of the chapters of the Qur'ān (see *sūrah*), the first of these thirty parts (*juz'*) covers only the first chapter of the Qur'ān (see *fātiḥa*) and the first part of the second chapter (*sūrah*), whereas the last of these thirty parts (*juz'*) covers the 38 last chapters (*sūrah*) of the Qur'ān. See also *kara* and *spara*.

Ka'ba (Arab.: "cube house"). Black, cube-shaped tomb or building in Mecca, which is sacred for Muslims and toward which they direct their prayers (see *qibla*). The act of going around Ka'ba (see *ṭawāf*) is an important part of the pilgrimage to Mecca (see *ḥajj*). See also *'umra*. (Other transliterations include *Ka'bah*.)

kala sahib (Hindi: "black sahib"). As a derogatory term, it refers to as a common feature of the colonial administrators of the British Empire showing a considerable lack of sympathy with the colonized people in South Asia, also used to indict the arrogance of Indian intellectuals against their companions.

k'anzu (Swahili: "robe"). Name for a white or cream-colored ankle-length robe worn by men or boys in East African countries.

kara (Swahili: "part"). Subdivision of the thirtieth part of the Qur'ān (see *juz'*) recited by a person during a ceremonial event at night in a mosque (see *ihyā'*) during the month of Ramaḍān (see *laylat al-qadr*). See also *spara*.

kaum muda (Ind.: "young group" or "young community"). Name for the innovative Islamic reformist movement disseminated at the beginning of the twentieth century in Southeast Asia holding modernist ideals among educated segments of the Muslim population and in nationalist discussions. It stands against the traditionalist group (see *kaum tua*). See also *khana mai* (in Thailand) and *Muhammadiyah*.

kaum tua (Ind.: "old group" or "old community"). Name for the reactionary group of traditionalists opposing the Islamic reformist movement in Southeast Asia (see *kaum muda*). See also *khana kau* (in Thailand).

kenduri (Gayo/Ind.: "feast"). Name for a ritual meal in Indonesia blending the recitation of prayers with the burning of incense and the offering of foods usually held on Muslim calendar holidays such as Muḥammad's birthday (see *mawlid*) and or the feast of breaking fast (see *'id al-fitr*). Muslims also perform them for numerous purposes: to fulfill a promise, to request help for healing an ill person, or to ensure God's help in the afterlife (see *qiyamah*). See also *slametan* and *thambun*.

khalīfa (Arab.: "deputy" or "successor"). Title for the successor of the Prophet Muḥammad and the temporal ruler of an Islamic state, it is also the name for the representative of God (see *Allāh*) on earth and supreme head of the Muslim community (see *imām*). Sunnī and Shī'a have different of the role and institution of the succession amd split over the legitimacy of 'Alī ibn Abī Ṭālib (598–661) as the fourth caliph. See also *khilāfa*.

khana kau (Thai: "old traditionalist group"). Name for an important political force in Thailand, known for its conservative agenda. It stands in opposition to the Islamic reformist movement (see *khana mai*). See also *kaum tua* (in Indonesia).

khana mai (Thai: "new reformist group"). Group of reformist Muslims in Thailand that emphasizes the teaching of sophisticated techniques of ritual prayer (see *ṣalāt*), methods of chanting the Qur'ān (see *tajwid*), as well as the memorization Arabic verses from the Qur'ān and the study of Islamic jurisprudence (see *fiqh*). It builds the opposition to the traditionalists in Thailand (see *khana kau*). See also *kaum muda* (in Indonesia).

kharāj (Arab.: "tax"). Name for the tax on the property owned by non-Muslims. See also *bayt al-māl*, *jizya*, and *'ushr*.

khashya (Arab.: "virtuous fear" or "awe"). Fear associated with the intimate knowledge of God (see *Allāh*) as part of the ritual prayer (see *ṣalāt*). See also *taqwa*.

khatam qur'an (Urdu: "sealing of the Qur'ān"). The name for the complete recitation of Qur'ān with all chapters (see *sūrah*) on one occasion, but also a specific communal ritual of reading the whole Qur'ān, to solicit forgiveness (see *bakhsh*), thanksgiving (see *shukriya*), and blessing (see *baraka*). The complete recitation of the Qur'ān is a major accomplishment for Muslims.

khaṭīb (Arab.: "a person who delivers a sermon"). Honorary title for the preacher. See also *khuṭba*.

khatm (Urdu: "conclusion" or "seal"). Also used for the ritual of sealing the Qur'ān (see *khatam Qur'an*).

al-Khiḍr (Arab.: "the green one"). Spiritual figure that indicates the moment of Divine presence widely known throughout the Muslim world and commonly identified with the messenger mentioned in the Qur'ān (Sūrah 18:64). (Other transliterations include *Hıdır*, *Hızır*, *Khadir*, and *Khudr*.)

khilāfa (Arab.: "succession" or "system of governance"). This term is commonly translated as the status of vice-regency. Islamic political institution and system of governance that assures the succession in government of the Prophet Muḥammad, it also refers to the supreme head of the Muslim community. See also *khalīfa*.

khoms (Arab.: "the fifth part"). See *khums*.

Khuda (Pers./Urdu: "God"). Pakistani Muslims may tend to avoid the term God, because for them the word "*Allāh*" cannot be replaced by any other word. (Other transliterations include *Khudda*.)

Khudr (Arab.: "the green one"). See al-*Khiḍr*.

khums (Arab.: "the fifth part"). A fifth part in taxation as generally practiced among Muslims, but also a special religious tithe or charity tax among the Shī'a making a one-fifth charge annually on the net income and wealth and paid to Shī'a scholars (see *'ulamā'*) to enable them to stay autonomous from the influence of the state. See also *bayt al-māl*, *'ushr*, and *zakāt*.

khushū' (Arab.: "concentration during praying"). State of concentration, exclusively used in relation to prayer (see *ṣalāt*) as being in the presence of God (see *Allāh*) is one of the criteria of correctness (*waqt*) to make the prayer valid (see *ṣāliḥ*).

khuṭba (Arab.: "exhortation" or "narration" but also "sermon"). As a technical term, it is the congregational sermon having a fixed place and following a prescribed order during a congregational meeting directly before the special Friday prayer (see *al-jum'a*) in the mosque. This institution of the sermon on Friday—other than in all other Muslim ceremonies and services—preceding the special canonical prayer (see *ṣalāt*) derived from the practice of the Prophet Muḥammad (see *sunna*) who gave his sermons in Medina before the Friday prayer. The Friday prayer made by the imām or a preacher (see *khaṭīb*) opens with praise to God (see *ḥamdillah*), the blessings upon the Prophet Muḥammad (see *taslīm*) and the declaration of faith (see *shahāda*) followed by proclamation of the unity of God (see *tawḥīd*), which sets off the actual sermon and closes with a blessing upon the believers (see *baraka*). It also refers to the period of engagement before the consummation of a marriage.

kiamat (Ind.: "resurrection"). See *qiyāma*.

kijaji (Ind.: "scholar" or "teacher"). Honoray title used to address or refer to a respected scholar or teacher of Islām. (Other transliterations include *kiai*.)

kikah (Ind.: "name"). See *'aqīqa*.

kıyam (Turk.: "upright"). Name for the first part of the canonical prayer (see *namaz*) in which the practitioner recites sequences of fixed and variable prayer formulas or verses taken from the Qur'ān while standing in an upright position. See also *ṣalāt*.

kiyāma (Arab.: "resurrection"). See *qiyāma*.

kofia (Swahili: "hat" or "head covering"). Name for a brimless cylindrical cap with a flat crown, which men in East Africa traditionally wear, especially common among Swahili-speaking people.

Komachi Ethnic group in South-Central Iran making a living by nomadic pastoralism as their main form of economy and having unique ritual traditions and their own calendar and interpretation of Shī'a Islām. The commonly are identified with the Ja'farī school of Islamic law (see *madhhab*).

Koran (Turk./Pers.: "reading" or "recitation"). See also *Qur'ān*.

korbani (Urdu: "offering"). Sacrifice performed on the feast of sacrifice (see *eid zoha*). See also *'īd al-aḍḥā* and *qurbān*.

La ilaha illā Allāh! (Arab.: "There is no god but God!"). Sacred phrase used only twice in the Qur'ān (Sūrah 37:35 and 47:19). It is part of the basic Muslim statement of faith (see *shahāda*), which is also included in the call for prayer (see *adhan*) and echoed five times a day throughout the Muslim world. Furthermore, it is recurrently chanted as a central part of Sufi gatherings (see *dhikr*). See also *ihyā'*, *i'tikāf*, and *laylat al-qadr*.

La ilaha illā huwa! (Arab.: "There is no god but He!"). As sacred phrase frequently used in the Qur'ān and recurrently recited in Sufi forms of nightly prayer (see *dhikr*). See also *ihyā'*, *i'tikāf*, and *laylat al-qadr.*

laylat al-qadr (Arab.: "night of power" or "night of destiny"). Muslims commonly believe that the archangel Gabriel (see *Jibrīl*) first revealed the Qur'ān to the Prophet Muḥammad in the year 610 in one of the last ten nights of the month of Ramaḍān. Although the exact night is now unknown, it is commonly assumed that the revelation happened during one of the odd dates—i.e., the 23rd, 25th, 27th or 29th of Ramaḍān. Muslims therefore conceive these times as extraordinarily powerful times for blessing (see *baraka*) and often spend all their time secluded in the mosque (see *i'tikāf*) and believe that a ritual prayer (see *ṣalāt*) during this time is particularly worthwhile (see *al-tarāwīḥ*). See also *ihyā'*.

madhhab (Arab.: "school of thought," "direction," or "way to act"). Based on the codification of the Islamic law (see *sharīʿa*) and jurisdiction (see *fiqh*), the Sunnī distinguish broadly between four religious and juridical doctrines or recognized legal schools in Islām named after their founding jurists (*fuqahā'*, see *fiqh*, sing.). These schools of interpreting Islamic law are following the teaching of Mālik ibn Anas (see *Mālikī*), Abū Ḥanīfa (see *Ḥanafī*), Muḥammad al-Shāfiʿī (see *Shāfiʿī*), and Aḥmad ibn Ḥanbal (see *Ḥanbalī*). Sunnī Muslims also conceive the Shīʿa as a legal school in their own right following the doctrine of Ja'far al-Ṣādiq (see *Jaʿfarī*), which is in itself one of the major schools of law among the Twelve Imām Shīʿa. The differences between these schools Muslims become manifest in the performance of the ritual prayer (see *ṣalāt*) and are believed to enhance critical thinking (see *ijtihād*) to give them a moral choice. (Other transliterations include *mathhab* and *mazhab*.)

madhmūm (Arab.: "reprehensible" or "abominable"). Often related to an innovation (see *bid'a*) that is not directly part of the Qur'ān or tradition of the Prophet Muḥammad as opposed to those innovations that are praiseworthy (see *maḥmūd*), as a legal distinction introduce by the Shāfiʿī school of law (see *madhhab*). (Other transliterations include *mathmum*.)

madrasa (Arab.: "the place of study"). A traditional school of advanced study and higher education; students entering the university were presumed to have completed memorizing the Qur'ān to study primarily the liberal arts and among other subjects the calculation of prayer times, the interpretation (see *tafsīr*) of the Qur'ān, and Islamic law (see *sharīʿa*) and jurisdiction (see *fiqh*). In late medieval times, these Islamic schools of higher education became the model for European universities. See also *al-Azhar.*

Maghrib (Arab.: "the place of sunset"). As a term of spacial orientation, it refers to West of the Arab world including numerous countries in North Africa spanning from Libya to Morocco, also the classical Arab name for Morocco (see *al-Maghrib al-Aqṣā*).

al-maghrib (Arab.: "sunset"). Name for the evening ritual prayer at sunset (*ṣalāt al-maghrib*) consisting of three cycles (see *rakʿa*, sing.), the first two usually performed aloud and the last silent, performed any time after the sun sinks below the horizon and until the last glow can be seen in the sky. See also *ṣalāt.*

maḥmūd (Arab.: "approved" or "praiseworthy"). Often refers to an innovation (see *bid'a*) that conforms to the Qur'ān and the tradition of the Prophet Muḥammad (see *sunna*) as opposed to those innovations that are not praiseworthy (see *madhmūm*). The disctinction was introduced by the *Shāfiʿī* school of Islamic law (see *madhhab*).

al-maḥshar (Arab.: "plain" or "place of gathering"). Name for the place for the assembly of all creation at the Day of Judgment (see *yawm al-qiyāma*. This gathering takes place after the resurrection of the dead (see *qiyāma*) and before resurrected human creatures can cross the bridge (see *al-sarāt*), either leading to heaven or hell.

makaranta (Hausa: "school"). Prevalent name for Islamic school for Qur'ān lessons among the Hausa people. See also *madrasa.*

malaka (Arab.: "virtue"). As a technical term, it refers to as a certain state of mind or habit as based on the education of the intellect, also translated in Greek as *hexis.*

Mālikī Name of one of the four major legal schools of law (see *madhhab*) and jurisdiction (see *fiqh*) in Sunnī Islām as founded by Mālik ibn Anas (711–795) practice predominantly in the Arab West and North-West Africa. One of the major differences of the Mālikī school in contrast to the other schools concerns the ritual prayer (see *ṣalāt*) where the standing position in prayer (*qiyām*) is preferred and the dominant (*mashhūr*) position is to leave the hands to dangle at one's sides during the ritual prayer.

mallam (Hausa, derived from Arab. *mawlan*: "learned"). Title or form of address in West Africa for a learned man who is educated in the Qur'ān and received some higher education (see *madrasa*), also referred to a professional Muslim scholar (see *'ālim*) or a leader in the Islamic community or mosque (see *imām*).

al-Manār Name for the Islamic reform movement of the late nineteenth century originating in Cairo. It disseminated into South-East Asia, particularly to Thailand, Indonesia, and the Netherland East Indies. It is also the name of a journal published in the Arabic language and read throughout the Muslim world. See also *Kaum Muda* and *Khana Mai*.

mannat (Urdu: "vow" or "oath"). Promise to God that one will do something in the name of God (see *Allāh*) after bad times or troubles (see *musibat*) are gone, also refers to a conditional oath made by Muslims in times of suffering or bad omen (see *bala*). See also *ziyāra*.

maqbūl (Arab.: "acceptable"). Technical term used to describe the condition under which a prayer (see *ṣalāt*) is rendered satisfactory. If a prayer is performed the correct way (*waqt*) it becomes valid (see *ṣāliḥ*) and is acceptable by God. See also *khushū'*.

maqra (Swahili: "reading"). It refers to the practice of reading of a text as part of Islamic revival. It usually refers to the reading of the Qur'ān or the written Islamic tradition (see *ḥadīth*) on usually continuous days and is supervised by an Islamic scholar. See also *kara*.

marabout (French, derived from Arab. *marbūṭ*: "attached"). Title of a local Muslim hermit or saint (see *walī*) or any respected member of his family, who has spiritual influence or blessing (see *baraka*) even after his death, also refers to the tomb of this saint or hermit often visited by devout adherents in a devotional visit (see *ziyāra*).

maraboutism (French, derived from Arab. *marbūṭ*: "attached"). Term invented to refer to the spiritual practice of the adoration and veneration of local saints (see *walī*) in North and West Africa. See also *marabout*.

masākīn (Arab.: "poor" or "unlucky"). Term used to refer to extremely poor Muslims who are particularly entitled to receive alms (see *zakāt*). Also means someone who is poor because of some sort of a handicap. See also *dervish*, *gharib*, and *faqīr*.

ma'ṣiya (Arab.: "disobedience"). Refers to the explicit and complete rejection of the faith of Islām and most properly be seen as a form of atheism believed to be a great sin (see *ithm*).

al-Mas'ūdī, Abū al-Ḥasan 'Ali (896–956). Arab historian and geographer from Baghdad who travelled throughout the Islamic world and is well-known for his intimate knowledge of the scholars and intellectuals of his time as well as the history of Islām. He is best known for his *Muruj al-dhahab* ("The Book of Golden Meadows") and *Akhbār az-zamān* (*The History of Time*).

Mataram (Ind.). Name for a formerly important Islamic kingdom of Java, also called Mataram Islām, which controlled the interior regions until the seventeenth century, but lost its independence after it became part of the Dutch colonies.

mauhil (Arab.: "capable"). See *mu'ahhil*.

maulid (Hausa: "birthday"). See *mawlid*.

mawlāy (Arab.: "master"). Moroccan title used for a descendant (see *sharīf*) of Muḥammad. See also *'Alawī*. (Other transliterations include *mawlan*.)

mawlid (Arab.: "birthday" or "anniversary"). Observation of the anniversary of Muḥammad's birthday (*mawlid al-nabī*) as a holy day often celebrated throughout the Muslim world with a ceremony that gives reverence to him by reading respective parts from the Qur'ān. In particular, Sufis and numerous Muslims celebrate the birthday of saints by visiting and worshipping at their tombs (see *ziyāra*) to receive blessings (see *baraka*) as these days Muslims believe as being particularly powerful. See also *sīra*. (Other transliterations include *maulid*, *mevlüd* and *mulid*.)

Mecca Name of the city located in Western Saudi Arabia, which is, since ancient times, a holy place and spiritual center with the Ka'ba as sanctuary at its center. It is also the birthplace of Muḥammad and the holiest city for Muslims, to which they are required to make a pilgrimage once in their lifetime (see *ḥajj*) as part of the five pillars of Islām (see *arkān ad-dīn*).

Medina Name for a historically important sanctuary in Saudi Arabia laying in the middle of volcanic mounts surrounded by a small plain; after the migration of the Prophet Muḥammad with his first followers from Mecca (see *hijra*), also called 'the city of the Prophet' (see *madīnat al-nabī*). Although not official or required part of their pilgrimage (see *ḥajj*) to Mecca, Muslims often make visit to Medina to worship at the tomb of the Prophet Muḥammad.

mevlüd (Turk.: "birthday" or "anniversary"). Name for the unique tradition of celebrating Muḥammad's birthday in Turkey praising the miraculous birth, life and virtuous merits of the Prophet Muḥammad by a hymn specifically written by the Ottoman poet Süleyman Çelebi for that occasion. Embroidered with Arabic verses from the Qur'ān, the rhythmic recitals by one or more singers play a central role in Turkey and are performed at different social and religious occasions varying in length, structure and content, not specific to Muḥammad's birthday (see *mawlid*).

mfungo (Swahili: "release"). The name for the months following Ramaḍān, also the name for the charge made to the teacher of a Qur'ān school right before Ramaḍān on the 24th and 25th of *Sha'bān*. See also *muharama*.

Minā Name of a small town East of a rocky valley near Mecca. According to the Islamic tradition, the site where Abraham (see *Ibrāhīm*) sacrificed a sheep instead of his son Ismael (see *Ismā'īl*). Important place which Muslims visit and pray as part of their pilgrimage to Mecca (see *ḥajj*). In following the model of Abraham, Muslim pilgrims to Mecca also carry out their annual feast of sacrifice in the city of Minā (see *'īd al-aḍḥā*) on the tenth day of the month of pilgrimage (see *Dhū al-Ḥijja*).

minare (Turk., derived from Pers. *menaret* and Arab. *manāra*: "lighthouse" or "prayer tower"). High and often slim tower or turret attached to a mosque with one or more projecting balconies as an elevated place with a balcony from which the muezzin (see *mu'adhdhin*) performs his call for prayer (see *adhān*).

minhaj (Arab.: "way" or "path"). Way of life particularly being related to religion (see *dīn*) and the Islamic law (see *sharī'a*); also referred to as the "way of the Qur'ān" (*minhaj al-Qur'ān*).

mosque (Engl., derived from Arab. *masjid*, through French *mosquée*: "place of prostration" or "place of worship"). Muslim house of worship particularly named as "*masjid*" by learned and pious Muslims or in Arabic countries.

mu'adhdhin (Arab.: "proclaimer" or "crier"). This is the title for the official of a mosque leading the call for prayer (see *adhān*) and reciting parts from the Qur'ān on one of the mosque's minarets facing the direction (see *qibla*) of the Ka'ba in Mecca. As a person working at the mosque, the muezzin usually qualifies due to his noble character, excellent voice, and outstanding reading and recitation skills. See also *"ilm al-tajwīd* and *tajwīd*. (Other transliterations include *mu'athen* and *müezzin*.)

mu'ahhil (Arab.: "capable"). As a legal and economic term, it refers to capability or credential.

mu'āllim (Arab.: "teacher"). Teacher at a Qur'ān school including instructions in Arabic.

mu'amalāt (Arab.: "contracts" or "treatises," but also "transaction" or "procedure"). Matters of civil transactions and treaties of public utility the Islamic law (see *sharī'a*) for which the primary benefit lies in worldly welfare and delight of the here and now. Categorically distinguished from matters of religious observances (see *'ibāda*) of which the primary benefit lies in the afterlife (see *qiyāma*) made under the Islamic jurisprudence (see *fiqh*) and accepted in all four Sunnī legal schools. In religious contexts also referred to as the application of social duties.

muamelât (Turk.: "behavior," "contracts," or "treatises"). See *mu'amalāt.*

mubārak (Arab.: "blessed one" or "fortunate one"). Also used as a greeting formula, literally meaning to knee or prostrate oneself to receive blessing. See also *baraka.*

müezzin (Turk.: "proclaimer" or "crier"). See *mu'adhdhin.*

muftī (Arab.: "one who gives legal opinions"). Sunnī jurist or scholar of law (see *fiqh*) who interprets the Islamic law (see *sharī'a*) and is entitled to make legal decisions (see *fatwa*), of general religious significance and to function as a judge (see *qāḍī*) or his assistant.

Muḥammad (570–632). Prophet of Islām and messenger of God (see *Allāh*) and his Word (see *Qur'ān*), which was revealed to him through the archangel Gabriel (see *Jibrīl*). He is believed to be a descendent of Abraham (see *Ibrāhīm*) through his son Ismael (see *Ismā'īl*) and, according to the tradition, he is born 570 in Mecca into the Arab tribe of the *Quraysh.* Raised by his grandfather and working as a merchant, the Prophet Muḥammad received the first revelation of *Qur'ān* with the Sūrah 96 during the last ten days of Ramaḍān in 610 a cave of mount Hira. To avoid persecution in Mecca, the Prophet Muḥammad and his first followers (see *salaf*), including his first wife Khadījah and'Alī, the son of his brother Abū Ṭālib, migrated to Medina in 622 (see *hijra*), making the beginning of the Islamic calendar indicating the beginning of a new era. With Muslims believe that the Prophet Muḥammad possessed human nature in its perfection. His life and deeds are an example and model for human conduct (see *sunna*). The reports and recorded traditions of the Prophet Muḥammad's practice, including his words and deeds (see *ḥādīth*) built the main source of knowledge as transmitted through his first companions and first collected by Muḥammad al-Bukhārī (810–870). His birthday is celebrated throughout the Muslim world (see *mawlid*) with specific recitals readings at times also of his biography written by *al-Bukhārī* (see *sīra*).

Muhammadijah See Muhammadiyah.

Muhammadiyah Name for the Islamic reformist movement in Indonesia and throughout Southeast Asia with modernist and nationalist aspirations and the attempt to purify Islām by promoting and fostering primarily religious education by replicating the strategies of the colonizing powers, it spread mainly among middle-class Muslims. See also *Kaum Muda*, *Khana Mai*, and *Salafiyya.*

muharama (Swahili: "liability" or "charge"). Payment to Qur'ān school teachers made by their pupils on the 24th and 25th of Ramaḍān. See also *mfungo.*

Muḥarram (Arab.: "forbidden"). The first month of the Islamic calendar, of which the first day as the Islamic New Year Day is celebrated without special observances. The first ten days of Muḥarram are a period of mourning for Shī'a culminating on the tenth day (the day of *Ashūra*) in remembering the anniversary of the death or martyrdom of Ḥasan and Ḥusayn, the two grandsons of Muḥammad. Sunnīs also celebrate the 10th of Muḥarram as a day of beneficiary blessing. See also *'ashūrā.*

mujāhid (Arab.: "someone who struggles"). As a term it refers to someone who performs or takes part in a kind of holy war (see *jihād*).

mulay (Arab.: "prince"). Arabic title for the prince of the blood. See also *'Alawī* and *mawlay.*

Mulay Ismail (1675–1727). Powerful king of the dynasty of 'Alawites in Morocco consolidating their rule in the seventeenth century; notably one of the greatest figures in Moroccan history known for his persistent cruelty, often called "the Bloodthirsty."

mulid (Arab.: "birthday"). See *mawlid*.

mullah (Engl., derived from Arab. *mawlan*: "master"). Muslim trained in Islamic law (see *sharī'a*) and leading a Muslim community as the head of a mosque. In Iran and partially in Central Asia also used as a title of respect for religious scholars or notable persons. See also *muftī* and *qāḍī*.

multazim (Arab.: "committed" or "religious"). Term used to describe someone who is committed, not exclusively used with religious connotations. See also *iltizām*.

mu'min (Arab.: "faithful"). As a religious term, it refers to the faithful man who fully submitted his way of life (see *dīn*) to the will of God (see *Allāh*) and has established his faith (see *īmān*) firmly in his heart.

mu'mina (Arab.: "faithful"; female form of *mu'min*). Faithful women.

mümin (Turk.: "believer"). Term used to refer to someone who is a believer of Islām and practices accordingly. See *mu'min* and *mu'mina*. See also *īmān*.

musibat (Urdu: "trouble"). See *bala*.

mawsim al-'ibāda (Arab.: "season of worship"). Term used to refer to fasting month of Ramaḍān. See also *ihyā'* and *i'tikāf*.

mūsim al-'ībāda (Arab.: "season of worship"). See *mawsim al-'ibāda*.

Muslim (Arab.: "one who has surrendered to God," from the verb *aslama*: "to surrender," "to submit," or "to seek peace"). Adherent of Islām implying the complete submission and surrender to the will of God (see *Allāh*). To submit to God's will not only involves to be obedient to the guidance of God, but also the belief in being directed and acted upon by God. This also means that a Muslim in principle observes the foundational pillars of Islām (see *arkān al-dīn*), and follows for the course of life the Islamic law instituted upon Muslims (see *sharī'a*).

nafs (Arab.: "soul" or "spirit"). Term used to refer to the individual substance of a human being as living entity, meaning self, spirit, or soul. Among Muslims also used as pejorative term for fallen souls. See also *fitra*.

namaz (Pers./Turk.: "prayer"). The Persian word for the ritual prayer (see *ṣalāt*) replacing the Arabic word as primarily used in Central and South Asia spanning from Turkey to India. See also *abdest*, *basmala*, *tekbir*, and *Hanafī*.

Nasserism Name for an Arab nationalist political ideology based on the thinking of the former Egyptian President Gamal Abdel Nasser. As a form of nationalism, Nasserism replaced the ideology of the British colonial rule, having a major impact on pan-Arab politics in the 1950s and 1960s; and it became a model for other nationalist movements during the 1970s. Anwar El-Sadat, the third Egyptian President (1961–1970) abandoned the main tenets of Nasserism.

Nasserist Name for a member of the Arab Democratic Nasserist Party in Egypt, which conceives itself as the ideological successor of the Arab Socialist Union party formerly led by Gamal Abdel Nasser, who became the second president of Egypt (1954–1961).

niaz (Urdu: "sacrifice" or "offering"). Offering food in the name of God, it also refers to a communal meal following a reading of the Qur'ān, interchangeably used with sacrifice (see *korbani*). It is usually made after coming out of some misfortune or in the anticipation of coming out of misfortune. See also *mannat* and *qurbān*.

niṣāb (Arab.: "threshold" or "quota"). In political processes, this term is used to refer to the quota or majority one needs in a voting process. It also refers to the fixed amount or minimal amount of wealth, including savings and capital, a Muslim must have in order to be responsible or obliged to charity payments, in general, to the amount needed to support one's family for a year, but modern interpretations vary as to the exact threshold. Muslims below this threshold or quota do not have to pay taxes (see *zakāt*).

niya (Urdu: "intention"). See *niyyah.*

niyat (Urdu: "intentions"). See *niyyah.*

niyaz (Urdu: "desire," "poverty," or "need"). See *niaz.*

niyet (Turk.: "intention"). See *niyya.*

niyyah (Arab.: "purpose," "intention," or "will"). Acts of ceremonial law that require the performer precedes the performance of any ceremonial acts with the declaration or statement of intent in performing the respective acts. Intention of the heart (see *qibla*) or intentions brought into the person's heart distinguish between worship and habit or between different types of worship (see *'ibāda*). As an Islamic concept, it implies that performer invokes the intention by declaring in his or her heart to do such an act for the sake of God. Other transliteration include *niya*, *niyet*, and *niyyat.*).

nūr (Arab.: "light"). Often referred to as the essence of the Prophet Muḥammad as light who Muslims believe was created before the creation of the world with the Qur'ān, but always referring to the light of God (see *Allāh*) itself, as it is one of his 99 names as mentioned in Sūrah 24:35 (see *ṣifa*). See also *raḥma* and *ṣamād.*

pahla (Ind.: "merit" or "benefit"). Reward for moral conduct one receives from the performance of the sacrifice (see *kenduri*) and the distribution of food in ritual meals (see *ṣadaqa*), also refers to religious duties, which are likely to bring about blessings (see *baraka*) particularly for the life after the resurrection (see *qiyāma*). See also *baqara*, *pamrih* and *ṣawāb.* (Other transliterations include *pahala.*)

pamrih (Ind. "profit" or "self-interest"). Term used to refer to as the strategic interest to receive economic profit or social rewards in strong contrast to religious duties, which Muslims should perform without self-interest in receiving profit or reward in this world. See also *pahla* and *riba.*

p'ishi (Swahili). Name for rice as the food commonly consumed in Swahili-Land; also used as an equivalent for cash or a weight unit in East Africa. Muslims donate these as alms to poor and needy (see *masākīn*) at the last day of Ramaḍān to ensure that they do not go without food on the feast day (see *'īd al-fiṭr*). See also *zakāt* and *zakāt al-fiṭr.*

Pukhtun This is a name for an ethnic minority group speaking Pashto (a variant of Urdu) making a living in the mountain ranges of Southeastern Afghanistan and Northwestern Pakistan. Nomadism is their main economic activity. They are predominantly Sunnī Muslims following the Ḥanafī school of law (see *madhhab*), but also have a small community of the Twelve Imām Shī'a following the Ja'farī school of law. (Other transliterations include *Pakhtun*, *Pashtun*, and *Pushtun.*)

qāḍī (Arab.: "judge"). A judge of the Islamic law (see *sharī'a*) appointed by a government or sovereign due to his excellent knowledge in jurisdiction (see *fiqh*) who must be able to abstain from any personal judgment and remain free from any business interest that could interfere with his neutrality as functionary of the Muslim community (see *umma*). See also *muftī* and *mullah.*

Qadiriyya Name of one of the first and oldest Sufi order (see *ṭarīqa*) founded by Abd al-Qādir al-Jīlānī (1077–1166) in the twelfth century in the Middle East. Following the Ḥanbalī school of law (see *madhhab*), it was first established in Iran and Iraq. Following the Islamic law (see *sharī'a*) as the source for spiritual development and religious culture, the different groups within the Sufi order follow their own ritual practices and prayers. The tomb of Al-Jīlānī's in Baghdad is venerated as place of pilgrimage (see *ziyāra*) and annual festivals are held in honor of his founder on his birthday (see *mawlid*) accompanied by the continuous repetition of specific ritual prayers (see *dhikr*). See also *ṣūfī*.

qahar (Arab.: "fury" or "to defeat"). Usually referred to as God's fury to defeat and win over enemies.

qalb (Arab.: "heart"). The faith (see *īmān*) in the will of God is established firmly in the heart of the believer (see *mu'min*).

Qawigjiya-Shadhiliya See *Ḥāmidīya Shādhilīya*.

qibla (Arab.: "direction" or "orientation"). Direction of the ritual prayer (see *ṣalāt*) towards the Ka'ba in Mecca is one of the requirements for the prayer being valid (see *ṣāliḥ*).

qiyāma (Arab.: "resurrection" or "the end of time"). As theological term, it is a central element of Islamic eschatology concerning the resurrection of all human on the Day of Judgment (see *yawm ad-dīn*). The end of times is also the return of the dead at the Day of Resurrection (see *yawm al-qiāama*). The sequence of events of resurrection Muslims commonly believe as the annihilation of all creatures, resurrection of the body, and the judgment of all sentient creatures; it is also the name of Sūrah 75 of the Qur'ān. See also *al-maḥshar*, *al-sarāt*, and *yawm al-dīn*. (Other transliterations include *kiyama*.)

qiyās (Arab.: "analogy"). The analogy of reason is one of the four essential bases of Islamic law (see *sharī'a*).

qudra (Arab.: "omnipotence"). Muslims perceive omnipotence as one of the main characteristics of God. See also *raḥma*, *ṣamād*, and *tawḥīd*.

Qur'ān (Arab.: "reading" or "recitation"). The holy book for Muslims believed as being revealed by God (see *Allāh*) through archangel Gabriel (see *Jibrīl*) in the form of an elaborate poetic Arabic, beginning during the last ten days of Ramaḍān (see *laylat al-qadr*) in the month of Ramaḍān in 610 at the cave of Hira at the summit of the peak of mount Jabal Nur where the Prophet Muḥammad stayed for times of retreat. The first verses of revelation began with the Sūrah 96. The Qur'ān is divided in distinct chapters (see *sūrah*, sing.), which are arranged according to length and themselves consist of verses as their smallest units (see *āyā*, sing.). The Qur'ān is, as final revelation, the authoritative and unquestionable source for Muslims. Besides the written accounts of the Islamic traditions (see *ḥadīth*, sing.) on the practice of the Prophet Muḥammad (see *sunna*) it is the main basis for Islamic law (see *sharī'a*), but plays also a crucial role in guiding the ritual practice (see *'ibāda*). See also *"ilm al-tajwīd*, *tafsīr*, and *tajwīd*.

Quraysh Name of the Arab tribe in Mecca to which Muḥammad and his lineage belonged. It was a prominent tribe in Mecca before the birth of Muḥammad ruling the city. It is also the name of Sūrah 106. (Other transliterations include *Qrueish*, *Quresh*, and *Qureshi*.)

qurbān (Arab.: "victim" or "offering," from *qarraba*: "to bring near"). It means, in general, any practice that brings one near to God, but in particular refers to sacrifice (see *baqara*), especially of animals slaughtered and offered during the feast of sacrifice (see *'īd al-aḍḥā*) on the tenth day of the month of pilgrimage (see *Dhū al-Ḥijja*), which in Turkey is called *kurban bayramı*. See also *baraka*.

rabb (Arab.: "the Lord"). Divine title to describe one of the attributes of God. Also used as "my Lord" (*rabbī*).

Rabī' al-Awwal (Arab.). Name for the third month of the Islamic calendar also called "the First Spring," the month, during which some Muslims celebrate the birthday of Muḥammad (see *mawlid*).

al-Rāḍī, Sidi Salāma (1867–1927). Founder and leader (see *shaykh*) of the important Islamic brotherhood (see *ṭarīqa*) of the *Ḥāmidīya Shādhilīya* order in Cairo.

raghba (Arab.: "desire"). Generic term used to refer to as desirous, not exclusively used in religious contexts.

raḥma (Arab.: "kindness," "mercy," or "compassion"). As important theological term, it refers to as kindness, one of the attributes or qualities of God (see *ṣifa,* sing.) and is mentioned as one of the 99 names of God (see *Allāh*) in Sūrah 55:1. The terms also refers to the mercy received from God. See also *ṣamād.*

raj'a (Arab.: "hope"). Term used to refer to the hope in God. See also *ikhlāṣ* and *īmān.*

rak'a (Arab.: "bowing"). Complete cycle of prescribed words and movements to perform the ritual prayer (see *ṣalāt*) properly. Each of the cycles consecutively consists of a sequence of stations. A full cycle includes standing, bowing, prostration, and sitting. The performance of gestures and postures which may differ according to different schools of Islamic law (see *madhhab*). Each of the five ritual prayers (see *aṣ-ṣubḥ, al-ẓuhr, al-'aṣr, al-maghrib,* and *al-'ishā'*) consists of a varying number of these cycles, which are combined through the pronouncement of the formula *Allāh Akbar* (see *takbīr*).

Ramaḍān (Arab.: "a hot summer day" or "the month of the fast"). The ninth month of the Islamic calendar. Fasting during the month of Ramaḍān (see *ṣawm*) is one of the five pillars of Islām (see *arkān ad-dīn*). Alms (see *zakāt*) given during the month of Ramaḍān are believed by many Muslims as being more meritorious than at other times of the year (see *zakāt al-fitr*).

raza (Urdu: "will"). Will of God, but can also mean anybody's will when generally used.

rekât (Turk.: "bowing"). Prescribed sequences for each of the five daily ritual prayers (see *namaz*). Each of these prayers consists of a different number of cycles (*rekâts*), which in turn consist of a sequence of stations. See also *rak'a, rükû,* and *ṣalāt.*

reraya (Gayo: "holiday"). Gayo people refer to the big feast at the end of the fasting month of Ramaḍān (see *idul fitri*) generically as holiday. On the contrary, they refer to the feast of sacrifice (see *'īd al-aḍḥā*) specifically either being the holiday of sacrifice (see *reraya qurbën*) or simply the great holiday (see *reraya kul*). (Other transliterations include *hariraya.*)

reraya haji (Gayo: "holiday of pilgrimage"). As Muslims carry out their sacrifice in Minā on the tenth days of the month of pilgrimage (see *Dhū al-Ḥijja*), Gayo people refer to the local events of sacrifice also as the pilgrimage holiday (see *reraya*). See also *Dhū al-Ḥijja, 'īd al-aḍḥā,* and *ḥajj.*

reraya kul (Gayo: "great holiday"). See *'īd al-aḍḥā.*

reraya qurbën (Gayo: "holiday of sacrifice"). See *'īd al-aḍḥā.* See also *qurbān.*

riba (Arab.: "interest" or "increase"). Charging and paying of bank interest from the loan of money or goods as the opposition to alms (see *zakāt*) is prohibited (see *ḥarām*) at any scale according to the Islamic law (see *sharī'a*). (Other transliterations include *riba.*)

ribāṭ (Arab.: "hospice" or "hostel," but also "post" or "fort"). Small fortification built along a frontier of Islām during the first years of the Muslim conquest of North Africa to house military volunteers (*murābiṭūn*) who defended Islām as a pious duty. See also *jihād* and *mujāhid.*

Riḍā, Muḥammad Rashīd (1865–1935). One of the most influential reformist scholars and jurists of his time in Egypt, he taught at the Islamic University al-Azhar in Cairo and was a leading figure of the Islamic reform movement in the early twentieth century in the Middle East. His ideas had subsequently a considerable impact on the Islamic reform movement in Southeast Asia. See also *al-Azhar* and *Salafiyya.*

rijstaffel (Ind., derived from Dutch *rijstafel*: "rice meal"). Rice banquet commonly served at festivals and celebratory occasions in Indonesia. See also *kenduri* or *slametan.*

Riyaḍah Name of the main mosque in Lamu of Northern Swahili-Land.

rükû (Turk.: "bow" or "bowing position"). Second position of the ritual prayer (see *namaz*), during which the practitioner stands still but bows the upper body until it reaches a horizontal position. See also *rak'a*, *rekât*, and *ṣalāt*.

sādah (Arab.: "lords" or "masters," sing. *sayyid*). Name of an ethnic group in of Southern Arabia that claims to inherit the genealogical descent from Muḥammad and entitled to be the ruling religious elite. Claiming a correspondence between religious knowledge and the concept of privileged inheritance, their descent from Muḥammad gives them a superior knowledge with which they create the content of a system of religious symbols claiming to be the mediators between man and God (see *Allāh*) and the direct representation of the reality of God. Most of them subscribe to the less known Shī'a Zaydī school of law (see *madhhab*). (Other transliterations include *sādah.*)

ṣadaqa (Arab.: "righteousness," derived from the verb *ṣadaqa* means "to speak truth" or "to be true"). Voluntary charity or almsgiving to those who are in need or as personal sacrifice or voluntary almsgiving in general, also referred to as a specific portion of sacrificial food set aside for the poor and needy (see *masākīn*) which is not the sacrifice of an animal as a whole (see *qurbān*). It is distinct from the obligatory almsgiving (see *zakāt*) or the taxation of a fixed portion of one's wealth (see *'ushr*).

sadqa (Urdu: "righteousness"). Money given to poor in name of God. See also *ṣadaqa.*

saḥūr (Arab.: "breakfast"). Light meal eaten before dawn during the fasting (see *ṣawm*) in the month of Ramaḍān. Throughout the Muslim world, some people make rounds in the streets of cities and villages beating drums or calling out as a duty to wake their companions to participate at the meal. The breakfast is taken before the morning prayer at dawn (see *al-ṣubḥ*).

al-Ṣaḥwa al-Islāmiyya (Arab.: "Islamic awakening"). Name used to refer to the Muslim Brotherhood (see *al-Ikhwān al-Muslimūn*). Islamists in general often refer to their reform movement as al-Sahwa al-Islamiyya. See also *Salafiyya.*

salaf (Arab.: "predecessors" or "ancestors"). Generally referred to as the first three generations of Muslims as pious ancestors and for later generations conceived as authoritative source for Islamic practice and guidance elucidating questions not made explicit in the Qur'ān or the practice of the Prophet Muḥammad (see *sunna*); it also implies the sacred lineage among spiritual masters in Sufism (see *ṣūfī*). See also *ṭarīqa.*

Salafī See *Salafiyya.*

Salafiyya Name for a neo-orthodox branch of the Islamic reformist movement of the late nineteenth century in the times of weakened Ottoman Empire with its center in Egypt. As a 'return' to the tradition of Islām as represented by the first followers (see *salaf*), whose name it derives from the first generations of Muslims, the Salafiyya opposed Westernization as well as conservative clerics and jurists. Well-known leaders are Muḥammad 'Abduh (1849–1905) and Rashid Rida (1865–1935). See also *al-Ṣaḥwa al-Islāmiyya.*

ṣalāt (Arab.: "prayer," "worship," pl. *salawāt*). Ritual prayers, for the Sunnī Muslims, the second most important pillar of Islām (see *arkān ad-dīn*), which follows a prescribed liturgy performed five times a day oriented toward Mecca (see *qibla*) and can performed at any place which is ritually clean (see *wuḍū'*). The five ritual prayers each following a specific liturgy, consisting of a varying series of cycles (see *rak'a*) joint by the declaration of God's greatness (see *takbīr*) and concluded (see *taslīm*) by invocating God's blessing upon the Prophet Muḥammad followed a greeting (*tāḥiya*) and the declaration of faith (see *shahāda*). The five ritual prayer are: Morning prayer at dawn (see *aṣ-ṣubḥ*), the noon prayer (see *al-ẓuhr*), afternoon prayer (see *al-'aṣr*), evening prayer after dusk (see *al-maghrib*) and the prayer at night (see *al-'ishā'*). Besides there are numerous voluntary prayers (see *al-fajr* and *witr*) performed on a daily basis or on various occasions as for example the Friday prayer (see *al-jum'a*) in a congregational meeting in the mosque following the Friday sermon (see *khuṭba*) or special prayers during the feasts (*ṣalāh al-'īd*) as well as congregational supererogatory night prayers in the month of Ramaḍān (see *al-tarāwīh*) See also *namaz*.

sāliḥ (Arab.: "righteous" or "virtuous"). Term used to refer to the validity of the payer (see *ṣalāt*) accepted by God. In order to be valid (*ṣāliḥ*), the performance of the ritual prayer must fulfill the following criteria: The Muslim must perform the prayer at the right time and right order, with the chest facing in the direction (see *qibla*) of the Ka'ba in Mecca, he or she must fulfill the condition of ritual purity (see *wuḍū'*). It also refers to righteous and virtuous morals as well as to the sources, which transmit the traditions of the Prophet Muḥammad uncorrupted. See also *maqbūl*.

ṣamād (Arab.: "self-sustained," "eternal" or "absolute"). Referring to one of the 99 names of God (see *Allāh*) and the quality of God (see *ṣifa*, sing.) as being self-sustained and absolute as indicated in the Sūrah 112:2 of the Qur'ān. See also *raḥma*. (Other transliterations include *shamad*.)

samadiyah (Gayo/Ind.: "meditation" or "chanting"). Night-long liturgical chanting sessions with the recitation of the Sūrah 112 of the Qur'ān as a central part and led by a religious leader (see *teungku*, a Gayo term for *ulama*) with the male and female devotees swaying their bodies and clapping rhythmically, performed also at occasions of death and mourning. See also *ihyā'*, *i'tikāf*, *ṣamād*, *takbīr*, and *al-tarāwīḥ*.

santri (Java.: "student"). This term generally refers to as a student at a traditional Muslim school, but also a specific social class of rather urban dwellers within the Java society who practice a more orthodox version of Islām, being more oriented to the teaching and interpretation of the Qur'ān (see *tafsīr*) and the Islamic law (see *sharī'a*) and jurisdiction (see *fiqh*). The Santri are opposed and distinctively different from the abangan who have more of village background with their blending of both Hindu and Muslim traditions and forming a culture of folk Islām. See also *abangan* and *kaum muda*.

Sanūsiyya Name for a group of people named after the Muslim religious-political order in Libya and Sudan called with a partially military orientation founded by Sayyid Muḥammad 'Alī al-Sanūsī (1791–1859).

al-Sanūsī, Sayyid Muḥammad 'Alī (1791–1859). He is the founder of the *Sanūsiyya* order in Mecca after educating himself in Fez and performing his pilgrimage to Mecca (see *ḥajj*). He combined Sufi teachings with fundamental puritanical ideas of Wahhabism (see *Wahhābiyya*).

al-sarāt (Arab.: "the back" or "bridge"). In the Islamic doctrines of afterlife, the name of the legendary bridge all human beings are required to walk over in the Hereafter after their resurrection (see *qiyāma*), it is a central part of the end of time at the Day of Judgment (see *yawm ad-dīn*). If one is able to pass the bridge, one enters heaven; if not, one enters hell.

sarki (Hausa: "sovereign"). Name for the traditional ruler of the region of Maradi, a territory in the Hausa speaking area of Niger, which was an autonomous and bellicose kingdom prior to the introduction of colonialism.

sarong (Ind.: "kilt" or "skirt"). Name for a traditional long loose skirt consisting of brightly colored fabric wrapped around the body worn by both sexes particularly in South East Asia and the South Pacific. (Other transliterations include *sarung*.)

saum (Arab.: "fast"). See *ṣawm*.

ṣawāb (Urdu: "reward"). Reward or religious merit for a good deed that facilitate to one's entry into heaven at the Day of Judgement (see *yawm ad-dīn*). Religious merit also believed to occur when Muslims read or recite the Qur'ān in full on specific religious occasions (see *laylat al-qadr*), scoring merits for the afterlife (see *qiyāma*). (Other transliterations include *thawab.*)

ṣawm (Arab.: "fast" or "fasting"). The Prophet Muḥammad instituted fasting in the month of Ramaḍān from dawn to sunset as a spiritual practice and discipline and one of the five pillars of Islām (see *arkān al-dīn*). Following the model of the Prophet Muḥammad, Muslims conceive fasting as a spiritual discipline, observing the fast in the month of Ramaḍān from dawn to sunset. See also *ifṭār* and *saḥūr*. (Other transliterations include *saum.*)

sa'y (Arab.: "walking"). Ritual of walking between the hills of Ṣafā and Marwah repeated seven times during the pilgrimage (see *ḥajj*) to Mecca imitating Hagar searching for water. See also *'umra*.

sayyid (Arab.: "lord" or "master," pl. *sāda*). A direct descendant of Muḥammad through his daughter Fatimah and her husband 'Alī ibn Abī Ṭālib and through one of the Prophet's two grandsons, Ḥasan and Ḥusayn; it is also a title of respect for royal members. In some regions, a distinction exists between the descendants of Ḥusayn, called *sayyid*, and the descendants of Ḥasan, called *sharīf*.

şehadet (Turk.: "testimony"). See *shahāda*.

Sha'bān The eighth month of the Islamic calendar preceding the month of Ramaḍān.

al-Shādhilī, Shaykh Abū al-Ḥasan (1196–1258). Famous founder of the *Ḥāmidīya Shādhilīya* order as one of the most important Sufi brotherhoods (see *ṭarīqa*). After being trained by spiritual leaders (see *shaykh*, sing.) in Morocco, he went to Egypt and made it to the center of his teachings, which focused on the inward and intellectual nature of his spiritual path.

Shāfi'ī Name of one of the four legal schools of jurisdiction in Sunnī Islām founded by Muḥammad al-Shāfi'ī (767–820). His book *al-Risala* is considered as the founder of Islamic jurisprudence (see *fiqh*) in distinguishing between the four sources of Islamic law (see *sharī'a*). A further contribution of al-Shāfi'ī for the foundations of the Islamic law was his division of innovation (see *bid'a*) into good and bad and whatever innovation conforms to the Sunna is approved (see *maḥmūd*), and whatever opposes it is abominable (see *madhmūm*). The Shāfi'ī also fostered the congregational night prayers in the month of Ramaḍān (see *al-tarāwīḥ*). The Shāfi'ī school of law is predominantly practiced in Egyt, Somalia, and Yemen as well as in South East Asia, Indonesia, Malaysia, Philippines, Singapore, and Thailand.

shahāda (Arab.: "testimony" or "witness," from the verb *shahida*: "to testify" or "to witness"). Public affirmation and creed essential to Islām, specifically the verbal attestation given for the submission (see *Islām*) to the will of God (see *Allāh*) in the presence of at least two witnesses by stating the two testimonies, 1.) "I bear witness (*ashahadu*) that there is no god but God" and 2.) "I bear witness (*ashahadu*) that Muḥammad is the Prophet of God." The Sunnī conceive this as the first of the five foundations of their belief (see *arkān al-dīn*). (Other transliterations include *şehadet.*)

shamad (Ind.: "eternal" or "absolute"). See *ṣamād*.

sharī'a (Arab.: "way of life" or "religious law," derived from the verb *shara'a*: "to enact" or "to prescribe"). Islamic law or the ethical and moral code conceived by Muslims as based on the Qur'ān and its jurisdictional interpretation (see *fiqh*), the practice of the Prophet Muḥammad (see *sunna*) and its accounts in the written Islamic tradition (see *Ḥadīth*) as its scriptural sources and the consensus of the community (see *ijmā'*) and analogy of reason (see *qiyās*). The Islamic law is constitutive for practicing Islām, including all aspects of life. It is divided into issues dealing with ritual and worship (see *'ibāda*) and those related to social life as well as political and economic transactions (see *mu'amalāt*). Three principles constitutive for the Islamic law are necessity (see *darūra*), welfare (see *maslaḥa*) and justice (see *istiḥsān*). The Islamic law distinguishes all acts into the five categories, i.e. acts that are obligatory (see *wājib*), recommended (see *mandūb*), permitted (see *mubāḥ*), discouraged (see *makrūh*), and forbidden (see *ḥarām*). The interpretation of the Islamic law in Sunnī Islām is codified through the four schools of law (see *madhhab*, sing.). (Other transliterations include *shariah.*)

shariah (Arab.: "religious law"). See *sharī'a.*

Shari'ati, Al (1933–1977). Modernist political theoretician and activist from Iran, known for his ideas critical of, and in opposition to, Western capitalism to which he saw the solution by proposing the social doctrines of Islām. One of his most influential work is "The Pilgrimage" (Hajj), *On the Sociology of Islam: Lectures*, and *Marxism and Other Western Fallacies: An Islamic Critique.*

sharīf (Arab.: "noble" or "eminent"). A traditional Arab tribal title given to those who serve as the protector of the tribe and all tribal assets, as an adjective also meaning "noble" or "highborn." In specific terms, it also refers to the descendants of Muḥammad or "the people of the house" (see *ahl al-bayt*) traced through his daughter Fatima and her husband 'Alī ibn Abī Ṭālib as well as through one of the Prophet's two grandsons, Ḥasan and Ḥusayn. In some regions, there is a differentiation between the descendants of Ḥasan (called *sharīf*), and Ḥusayn (called *sayyid*). (Other transliterations include *sherif.*)

Shawwāl (Arab.: "to uplift"). Name for the tenth month of the Islamic calendar, following the month of *Ramaḍān.* Muslims believe that marriages made during the month of *Shawwāl* last longer.

shaykh (Arab.: "leader" or "respected elderly man"). As an honoray title, it refers to an older spiritual or religious leader and authoritative teacher commonly used for a man over fifty years old, whose hair has already gone white; also title of a judge (see *qāḍī*) in Islamic law (see *sharī'a*); in various mystical traditions of Sufism and Shi'ism used to refer to the spiritual leader or religious master. See also *Shī'a* and *ṣūfī.* (Other transliterations include *sheikh.*)

shayṭān (Arab.: "mischief" or "devil"). Satan as common in the Jewish and Christian tradition, in the Islamic tradition also known as *Iblīs.*

sheikh (Arab.: "leader"). See *shaykh.*

sherif (Arab.: "noble"). See *sharīf.*

Shī'a (Arab.: "fraction" or "party," from *Shī'at 'Ali*: "the party of Ali"). Any faction or supporter claiming that 'Alī ibn Abī Ṭālib as son-in-law of Muḥammad and the son of his brother Abū Ṭālib had the Divine rights to succeed (see *khilāfa*) the mediatory leadership as the fourth caliph (see *khalīfa*) after receiving a special mandate from him. See also *ahl al-bayt* and *Shi'ism.*

Shii See *Shī'a.*

Shi'ism Name for the religious and political doctrine of the Shī'a, an important branch of Islām consisting of approximately less than 10% of all Muslims. It has significantly different doctrines and practices other than the more orthodox majority of Sunnī Islām. In particular, the belief in the existence of divine or superhuman qualities of some selected members of the religious leaders (see *khilāfa* and *imām*), who derive their legitimacy from being members of the family of the Prophet Muhammad (see *ahl al-bayt*). As central role in the formation of Shi'ism plays 'Alī ibn Abī Ṭālib as the brother's son and son-in-law of Muḥammad and the fourth caliph (see *khalīfa* and *imām*). His eldest son Ḥasan (625–670) succeeded him and became fifth caliph for six months before being poisoned. The martyrdom of Ḥusayn (624–680) at Kerbala became an ever-present element in Shi'ism most detailed enacted in the yearly passion plays (see *ta'ziyyah*). One of the major groups in Shi'ism is the Twelve Imām Shī'a, which has also been the official religion in Iran for centuries. See also *Sunnī*.

Shi'ite (older term for Shī'a, as is the case for Sunnīte, which is no longer used). Adherent of Shī'a Islām. See also *Shī'a* and *Shi'ism*.

shirk (Arab.: "idolatry" or "polytheism"). Islamic concept for the sin (see *ithm*) of the attachment to forms of polytheism and related to the belief in and worship of any divinity except God (see *Allāh*) or visual representation; in a more general way refers to serving anything other than the One, also known as idolatrous act, which is the worst form of disbelief. See also *tawhīd*.

shukriya (Urdu: "Thanksgiving"). As a phrase, it refers to as a gesture of thanksgiving for God (see *Allāh*) in particular for the fulfillment of a promise (see *mannat*). See also *niaz*.

ṣifa (Arab.: "attribute," derived from the verb *wasafa*: "to describe"). Generally referred to as the attributes of objects, in a more specific sense, it refers to the attributes of God (see *Allāh*) as distinct from his essence (*adh-dhāt*) also referring to the 99 names of God as for example being compassionate (see *raḥma*), eternal (see *ṣamād*) and light (see *nūr*). See also *tesbih*.

sīra (Arab.: "biography"). Written account of the life of the Prophet Muḥammad, which is particularly read during the third month of the Islamic lunar calendar (see *Rabī' al-Awwal*), in which some Muslims celebrate the Prophet Muḥammad's birth (see *mawlid*).

slametan (Java.: "ceremonial meal"). Name for an important communal ritual feast in the religion of Java. It celebrates social unity and solidarity, similar to the traditional ritual feast in Indonesia (see *kenduri*). See also *thambun* and *'urf*.

spara (Urdu: "chapter"). It is used to refer to thirty units according to which the Qur'ān is divided up, and each of them may contain several chapters (see *sūrah*). See also *juz'*, *laylat al-qadr*, and *Ramaḍān*.

al-ṣubḥ (Arab.: "morning"). Name for the morning ritual prayer (*ṣalāh al-ṣubḥ*) consisting of two cycles performed aloud in the time between the moment of dawn with the first thread of light on the horizon until the actual rising of the sun. See also *al-fajr*.

sübhaneke (Turk.). Name of a prayer formula in the ritual prayer (see *namaz*), preceding the *euzü-besmele* and *fatiha*. See also *basmala* and *ṣalāt*.

ṣūfī (Arab., derived from the noun *ṣūf*: "wool"). Member of a Muslim order or brotherhood (see *ṭarīqa*) who follows the mystical and esoteric path of Islām. Although the doctrines and teachings of Sufism (Arab.: *al-taṣawwuf*) derive from the Qur'ān and the revelations of Islām, the formation and social organization of the Sufi orders is influenced by other continuous mystical teachings emphasizing the inner path or esoteric dimension of Islām and deemphasizing the literal interpretations and practices of orthodox Islām. *Ḥāmidīya Shādhilīya*, *Qadiriyya*, and *Tijāniyya*. See also *dervish*, *walī*, and *ziyāra*.

sunna (Arab.: "custom" or "practice"). Name for the practice of the Prophet Muḥammad including all aspects of his life, his sayings and deeds and being the model for all Muslims. Although the oral and written Islamic traditions (see *ḥadīth*, sing.) of the Prophet Muḥammad and his first companions are not part of the Qur'ān, these are the most important aspects shaping Muslim identity in practical and legal terms. Its records and elaborations built up a large number of texts, which became together with the Qur'ān the foundation for the Islamic law (see *sharī'a*) and jurisprudence (see *fiqh*).

sünnet (Turk.). Name for the recommended cycles for each of the ritual prayer (see *namaz*), also meaning the traditions of the Prophet Muḥammad (see *sunna*). See also *ṣalāt*.

Sunnī (Arab., derived from the adjective *sunna*: "custom [of the Prophet]"). The major branch of Islām, which strictly adheres to the practice of the Prophet Muḥammad (see *sunna*) often referred to as orthodox. The Sunnī are the largest group of Muslims emphasizing in the direct guidance of the individual believer through God (see *Allāh*) without any form of instituted central authority. The Sunnī are distinct due to their different legal schools of Islamic law (see *madhhab*). See also *Shī'a*. (Other transliterations include *Sunnīte*.)

sūrah (Arab.: "chapter"). The Sūrah is an independent and distinct unit or chapter of the Qur'ān, of which there are 114 in the Qur'ān arranged according to their length with the exception of the first Sūrah (see *fātiḥa*). Each of them has a name, which often derives from the theme or character mentioned or addressed. See also *juz'*.

Swahili (derived from Arab. *sawāhil*: "coastal people"). Ethno-linguistic group living at the narrow tip of the East African coastline along the Indian Ocean inhabiting areas spanning from northern Kenya and Tanzania to Mozambique with long distance commerce as their main form economy. The majority of Swahili people are Sunnī Muslims following the Shāfi'ī school of law (see *madhhab*) and practicing a rather strict and orthodox interpretation of Islām.

tafsīr (Arab.: "interpretation" or "eludication"). Any form of explanation, but in particular a literary genre not always restricted to the exegesis and commentary of the Qur'ān, giving more background information and elucidating judgments and opinions. It is an essential part of the higher education (see *madrasa*) in Islām, along with the study of the written accounts of the traditions of the sayings and deeds of the Prophet Muḥammad (see *ḥadīth*) and the jurisprudence (see *fiqh*).

tajwīd (Arab.: "embellishment"). Recital or chanting of the Qur'ān according to prescribed rules of smooth and balanced pronunciation and intonation making the revelations of the Qur'ān beautiful. See also *'ilm al-tajwīd*.

takbīr (Arab.: "declaring greatness"). The term generally used to pronounce the Arabic formula *Allāh Akbar* ("God is great!") at the beginning of the ritual prayer (see *ṣalāt*) as well as during it, combining each of the subsequent cycles (see *rak'a*, sing.). As formula, Muslims also repeatedly chant it in nightly prayer sessions in the mosque (see *ihyā'*) or during important religious festivals (see *laylat al-qadr*) dedicated to the proclamation of God's absolute superiority and greatness. Pious Muslims also use it in their daily life as a form of religious exclamation or invocation. (Other transliterations include *tekbir*.)

ṭālib (Arab.: "student"). This term refers to a student of Islām, in particular at a universities or Islamic institution of higher education (see *madrasa*).

talqīn (Arab.: "instruction" or "insinuation"). Spiritual teaching or religious instruction, often also referred to as catechism as comparable in Christianity; also a catechism read to a deceased after burial. See also *ilmihal*.

taqlīd (Arab.: "imitation" or "emulation" as well as "acceptance" or "tradition"). This term refers to the obedience of traditionally accepted values as the received way of doing things in human affairs and the willingness to follow the judgments of Islamic jurisprudence (see *fiqh*). It implies the public acceptance of traditional authorities as taught through religion, also used by members of Islamic reform movements as a pejorative for regress and retreat. It also refers to blind following. See also *ijtihād*.

taqwā (Arab.: "righteousness" or "piety"). As a theological term, it refers to piety originating in the awe and fear of God (see *Allāh*) due to his punishment for committing sins (see *ithm*). See also *īmān* and *khashya*.

tarawehe (Swahili: "rest"). See *al-tarāwīḥ*.

al-tarāwīḥ (Arab.: "rest"). Additional voluntary ritual prayer (see *ṣalāt*) consisting of twenty, thirty-two or forty cycles (see *rak'a*, sing.) at the end of the night before the morning ritual prayer (see *al-ṣubḥ*) and often performed only in the nights of the month of Ramaḍān (see *iḥyā'*) shortly after the completion of the fifth and last obligatory prayer (see *al-'ishā'*). See also *laylat al-qadr*, *ṣalāt* and *witr*.

targhīb (Arab.: "evocation"). Referred to as the evocation of desire for doing good things. In particular, it refers to the desire for the love for God (see *Allāh*) and the rewards (see *thawāb*) one will receive in heaven after resurrection (see *qiyāma*); it is also a means to make things desirable for the possible convert to Islām, e.g., that one will go to heaven and be with the Prophet Muḥammad. See also *mandūb* and *tarhīb*.

tarhīb (Arab.: "discouragement"). As theological term, it refers to the evocation of avoidance, e.g., creation of fear of being in hell at the Day of Judgment (see *yawm ad-dīn*), or the appeal to stay away from hell. See also *makrūh* and *targūb*.

tari (Ind.: "dance"). Name for traditional dances.

tari guël (Gayo: "groom dance"). Name for a traditional ritual dance among Gayo people performed once by a new groom.

ṭarīqa (Arab.: "way" or "path," but also "order" or "brotherhood"). Generic term to refer to the methods and doctrines of mystic union, in particular used to denote a Muslim religious order, usually of Sufi orders. In Sufism, it also refers to a form of mysticism indicating the way, which guides the pious Sufi from the manifest Islamic law (see *sharī'a*) to the Divine Reality (*haqīqa*), including the methods by which members of the Sufi order reach the state of ecstasy through the repetition of specific prayers (see *dhikr*). Well-known Sufi order are *Ḥāmidīya Shādhilīya*, *Qadiriyya*, and *Tijāniyya*. See also *'ahd*, *dervish*, *ṣūfī*, *tawhid*, and *walī*.

taslīm (Arab.: "submission"). The saying of the formula "Peace be upon you" (*al-salām 'alaykum*), refers to the invocation of God's blessing upon the Prophet Muḥammad and commonly used as name for the concluding section of the ritual prayer (see *ṣalāt*) following the greeting (*tāḥiya*) and the declaration of faith (see *shahāda*). See also *ḥamdillah* and *khuṭba*.

taslīya (Arab.: "amusement"). Things for pious Muslims to stay away from, as they are not perceived as proper for religious conduct, in the Islamic law (see *sharī'a*) also classified as those kinds of actions one is discouraged from (see *makrūh*). See also *isrāf*.

taṣarruf (Arab.: "behavior"). As generic term it is used to refer to behavior of doing something or to change one's behavior, not having necessarily religious connotations. See also *adab*.

tatsuniya (Hausa: "traditional tale"). Name for folktales identified by specific verbal markers by Hausa speaking people, which are in contradiction to more conservative understanding of proper Islamic practice. See also *'urf*.

ṭawāf (Arab.: "encircling"). The ritual of walking around of a sacred object, in particular also referring to the obligatory ritual (see *wājib*) of going around the Ka'ba during the pilgrimage to Mecca (see *ḥajj*) performed seven times during the *'umra* by encircling counterclockwise with the Ka'ba on the left hand side. This practice also applies to the circumambulation during devotional visits (see *ziyāra*) of the shrines of saints (see *walī*) as a means to perform prayers (see *du'ā'*) and receive blessings (see *baraka*).

tawḥīd (Arab.: "unity"). As a theological term, it refers to the unity of God (see *Allāh*) as a central doctrine of Islām, also central to the unity of humankind and the basis of salvation. Within Islām, interpreted in diametrical ways, the one excluding any analogy or similarity in creation that reflects or conveys God (see *Wahhābiyya*) while the other being all-inclusive, assuming that nothing is outside of God (see *ṣūfī*). See also *'ahd*, *ikhlāṣ*, *shahāda*, and *walī*.

ta'ziyyah (Arab.: "condolence," "comfort" or "solace"). Usually translated as a passion, play. Shī'a Muslims perform at the 10th of Muḥarram (see *'ashūrā*) specific passion dramas by carrying a representation of the tomb of Ḥusayn to commemorate and mourn his death at the battle of Kerbala in 680.

tekbir (Turk.: "greatness"). Declaring the greatness of God by uttering the formula *Allahü ekber* at the end of each cycle (see rekât) of the ritual prayer (see *namaz*). See *takbīr*.

tesbih (Turk.: "rosary" or "prayer chain," Arab.: *subḥa* or *misbaḥa*). Traditionally, a rosary in Islām consisting of a chain with 99 beads, most commonly subdivided into three sections of 33 beads each (representing the Divine Names of God, smaller versions of the rosary are with 33 beads); comparable to Christian rosary. See also *şifa*. (Other spellings include *tespih*.)

tesbihat (Turk.: "remembrance"). Contemplative repetition of certain formulas for the praise God (see *zikir*), in which the practitioner uses a chain of beads (see *tesbih*) to keep track of the number of recitations with specific formulas for the litanies (*awrad*) such as the repeated declaration of faith (see *şehadet*) or phrases of the Qur'ān as an essential means or method of concentration. See also *dervish* and *zikir*. (Other spellings include *tespihat*.)

thambun (Thai: "charity," "virtue," or "value"). Name for a communal feast celebrated among traditional Muslims (see *Kaum Tua*) throughout Thailand, repeatedly lead by those who completed their pilgrimage to Mecca (see *hajji*) and who also tend to head life-cycle ceremonies as well as other rituals. Due to their similarities to Buddhist practices, Islamic reformists (see *Khana Mai*) often consider these feasts as non-Islamic traditions (see *'urf*), See also *kenduri* and *slametan*.

thawāb (Arab.: "merit" or "reward"). As a theological term, it refers to religious merit that facilitates one's entry into heaven after resurrection (see *qiyāma*) at the Day of Judgment (see *yawm ad-dīn*). The reward for good deeds accounted for by God's forgiving of sins is allowance to enter the paradise in the afterlife (see *qiyāma*) and the passing of the bridge (see *al-sarāt*). Religious merit is also believed to occur when Muslims read or recite the Qur'ān in full on specific religious occasions, as for example the night of power (see *laylat al-qadr*), scoring merits for the afterlife. (Other transliterations include *sawab* and *ṣawāb*.)

ṭība (Arab.: "good nature"). As a generic term, it refers to as morally good character, not necessarily in a religious context. See also *fitra* and *nafs*.

al-Tijānī, Sidi Aḥmad (1737–1815). Muslim scholar born in Algeria and buried in Fez, who founded in the late eighteenth century the *Tijāniyya* order (see *ṭarīqa*) subsequently spreading among Muslims in North Africa.

Tijāniyya Name of the Sufi order (see *ṭarīqa*) founded by Sidi Aḥmad al-Tijānī (1737–1815) in Fez, which is well-known in Morocco and Algeria but also in parts of sub-Saharan Africa, as for example, in Ghana. It is popular among the poor due to its social agenda and its reaction against the conservative *Qadiriyya* order with its focus on social reform and Islamic revival, also called "Islam for the poor" (see *masākīn*). In their social and political orientation, the *Tijāniyya* order bears considerable resemblances with the *Sanūsiyya*. See also *ṣūfī*.

tindanas (Hausa: "land priests"). Priests existing in pre-Islamic Northern Ghanaian societies and operating as spiritual leaders, traditionally in charge of land properties by other ways of distributing the fruits of the harvest.

toba (Swahili, derived from Arab. *tawba*: "repentance" or "regret"). Term used to refer to the practice of penitence and sorrow.

tobarak (Urdu: "blessed food"). Food over which verses of the Qur'ān (see *āyā*, sing.) have been recited, also referring to additional portions of blessed food, often fruits, sent home with the guests that attended the feast of sacrifice (see *'īd al-aḍḥā*) inheriting power and blessings (see *baraka*). See also *qurbān* and *bakshīsh*.

tuqūs (Arab.: "rituals," sing: *taqs*).

turban (Pers.: "headgear" or "wrapper," Arab.: *'imāma*). Name for a traditional cloth tied on the head, a headdress common among Muslims in Central Asia and the Middle East (but also among other ethnic and religious groups in that area, for example by oriental Christians and Jews). Color, material and size as well as the style of wrapping often indicate distinction in the national, social or ethnic identity of a group. For example, the headdress of the Sikhs is also a turban.

'ulamā' (Arab.: "the learned," sing. *'ālim*). Body of scholars educated in the teachings of Islām in an institution of higher education (see *madrasa*) including the interpretation of Qur'ān (see *tafsīr*) and the written Islamic tradition (see *ḥadīth*) as well as Islamic law (see *sharī'a*) and jurisdiction (see *fiqh*); they are recognized as authorities of the religious sciences and leaders of the Muslim community, including teachers in religious faculties at universities, judges, and imāms of important mosques. See also *'ālim*, *'aql*, and *'ilm*. (Other transliterations include *ulema*.)

umm (Arab.: "mother"). Title of respect for women, like in English Ms. or Mrs.

umma (Arab.: "nation" or "community"). Muslim community, commonly used to refer to the broader community of all Muslims especially as a non-political expression even worldwide, transcending local ethnic, religious, and national boundaries and divisions, but it also refers to the immediate group of Muslims in a local community. For Sunnīs, the consensus (see *ijmā'*) of the Muslim community is central part for the legitimization in the interpretation of the Islamic law (see *sharī'a*). (Other transliterations include *ummah*.)

'umra (Arab.: "lesser pilgrimage" or "visitation"). Minor pilgrimage to Mecca and abbreviated version of the *ḥajj*, which Muslims can perform at any time outside of the month of pilgrimage (see *Dhū al-Ḥijja*). The lesser pilgrimage entails ceremonies only in the precincts of the Grand Mosque in Mecca, without all the other rituals and ceremonies as prescribed for the greater pilgrimage, in this context also used as visit (see *ziyāra*). The *'umra* is also part of the *ḥajj* when performed at the fixed dates between the 8th and 13th of *Dhū al-Ḥijja* entailing the ritual walk around the "House of God" (see *Ka'ba*) seven times (see *ṭawāf*), followed by a ritual prayer of two cycles (see *rak'a*, sing.), the drinking of the water of Zamzam, and ritual of walking between the hills of Ṣafā and Marwah seven times (see *sa'y*). See also *ḥajj* and *ziyāra*.

Urdu Hindustani language locally developed by Indian Muslims emerging from Hindi influenced by Persian, Turkish and Arabic; the national language of Pakistan also commonly spoken among Muslims and Muslim minorities in Central and South Asia.

'urf (Arab.: "custom"). Local or tribal customs or laws that exist beside the Islamic law (see *sharī'a*) which can always be put into question and subsequently rejected or agreed upon (see *ijmā'*), but they are neither derivations nor innovations (see *bid'a*). See also *'adāt* and *ziyāra*.

'ushr (Arab.: "a tenth part"). Tithe on the property owned by Muslims, as for example, one-tenth of the total amount of grain harvested and collected as a form of tax, opposed to the tax on property owned by non-Muslims (see *kharāj*). It has been regarded as a form of almsgiving, but not necessarily identical with obligatory almsgivings (see *zakāt*), frequently also used in the sense of voluntary alms (see *ṣadaqa*). See also *bayt al-māl* and *khums*.

Usman 'dan Fodio, Sheha (1754–1817). Islamic reformer and teacher of Islamic law in Niger, follower of the Mālikī school of law (see *madhhab*), member of the *Qadiriyya* order (see *ṭarīqa*) and founder of the Sokoto caliphate (see *khilāfa*) with influences upon the 'Yan Taru movement in Niger and Nigeria.

ustaz (Arab.: "teacher"). See *ustādh.*

ustādh (Arab.: "teacher"). Title of respect for a teacher.

wādī (Arab.: "valley"). Dry riverbed only irregularly containing water during times of heavy rain. See also *Hadhramaut.*

wafd (Arab.: "delegation"). Name for the nationalist and liberal political party in Egypt, known as the abbreviation for the New Delegation Party (*Hizb al-Wafd al-Jadīd*).

Wahāb, Ahmad Indonesian refugee exiled by the Dutch authorities in the early part of the twentieth century and later immigrated to Bangkok, who studied for a considerable time in the Middle East learning about the religious reform movement and introduced these ideas to Thailand indirectly through Dutch colonial policy in Indonesia. See also *Kaum Muda, Khana Mai,* and *Salafiyya.*

Wahhāb, Muḥammad ibn ʿAbd al-Wahhāb (1703–1787). Muslim scholar from Saudi Arabia and founder of the Islamic community Wahhābiyya. After being educated in Medina, he traveled throughout the Middle East and lived in Baghdad, Kurdistan, and Isfahān where he studied Sufi systems. Later on he became an strong advocate of the Ḥanbalī school of Islamic law (see *madhhab*) rejecting all forms of innovation (see *bid'a*). His main work is the "Book of Unity" (*Kitāb al-tawḥīd*).

Wahhābiyya Name for a religious movement within Sunnī Islām founded by Muḥammad ibn ʿAbd al Wahhāb (1703–1787) deriving from a radical interpretation of the Ḥanbalī school of law (see *madhhab*) with the attempt to eradicate all later impurities from the practice of Islām and cultivating a traditional and very strict interpretation of the Qur'ān and the practice of the Prophet Muḥammad (see *sunna*). Its members, the Wahhabi, consider themselves as not belonging to any of the legal schools of Islamic law (see *madhhab*) claiming to observe the earliest form of Islām and rejecting all kinds of innovations (see *bid'a*). The Wahhabi are predominant in Saudi Arabia with considerable influence throughout the Muslim world by funding mosques and religious schools.

wājib (Arab.: "obligatory" or "mandatory"). In particular, refers to obligatory religious duties (see *ʿibāda*) such as the five foundations or pillars of Islām (see *arkān al-dīn*) as specified by the Islamic law (see *sharīʿa*). See also *farḍ.*

wa'ka (Hausa: "song" or "poetry," pl. *wa'ko'ki*). Name for the genre of oral songs (*wa'kar baka*) as well as written poetry (*rubatuc ciyar wa'ka*) with specifically coded differences in the conventions and expectations of their performance. The Hausa particularly seem to appreciate the novelty of the oral song in contrast to the written poem to contradict conservative forms of orthodox Islamic practice.

walī (Arab.: "friend"). Saint referred to primarily in the Sufi context (see *ṣūfī*), also referred to as *marabout,* but as a term also mentioned in the Qur'ān as "friend of God" (*walī Allāh*). As a category for a saint, the Wahhabis (see *Wahhābiyya*) combat this practice as it infringes the category of the unity of God (see *tawhīd*).

waqf (Arab.: "standing" or "stopping," pl. *awqāf*). Donation or endowment of money or personal property to the Islamic state for religious purposes, also referred to as charitable trust. The yield usually serves the public welfare with specified purposes such as supporting the poor and needy (see *masākīn*) or the mosque. See also *zakāt.*

wa'y (Arab.: "awareness"). Refers to human consciousness and does not necessarily have a religious connotation. See also *khushū'.*

wiḥsha (Arab.: "bad"). As a generic term, it refers to bad rumors or accusations. (Other transliterations include *wihshaya.*)

wilayat-i-faqih (Pers.: "government of the jurisprudent"). Policy that Khoemeni first proposed in 1971 to legitimize the governing authority of jurists (see *mullah*). This was part of the main Shīʿa doctrine that religious leaders (see *ulamāʾ*) exercise the guardianship of the Imamate (see *khilāfa*) mandated by the Hidden Imām; after the Islamic Revolution in 1978 also used to refer to a doctrine in Iranian politics that defines the concept of nation and nation-state based on major Shīʿa doctrines and beliefs.

witr (Arab.: "odd number"). A ritual prayer with an odd number of prayer cycles (see *rakʿa*, sing.), which is performed after the ritual night prayer (see *al-ʿishāʾ*) and before the dawn prayer (see *al-ṣubḥ*). With the exception of the Ḥanafī school of law (see *madhhab*), this ritual prayer is voluntary. See also *ṣalāt* and *tarāwīḥ*.

wuḍūʾ (Arab.: "making clean"). Act of washing and purifying parts of the body using water. Muslims are required to be clean in preparation for ritual prayer (see *ṣalāt*), also refers to a clean place. See also *abdest* and *iḥrām*.

wuqūf (Arab.: "standing"). Ritual of the pilgrimage to Mecca (see *ḥajj*) describing a standing ceremony at Mount ʿArafāt performed on its 9th of *Dhū al-Ḥijja*, which the pilgrims visit after leaving Minā. This ritual near the hill from which the Prophet Muḥammad gave his last sermon, called the Hill of Forgiveness (*Jabal Al-Raḥma*), is considered one of the highlights where pilgrims spend the afternoon praying (see *al-ʿaṣr*), thanksgiving, and reciting parts of the Qur'ān until after sunset. Although no specific rituals or prayers are required during this stay, the pilgrimage to Mecca is incomplete or invalid without the afternoon on ʿArafāt.

ʿYan Taru (Hausa: "the collective" or "those who came together"). Name for an Islamic educational movement in the Sokoto caliphate (see *khilāfa*) in Nigeria, in which women played a significant role. See also *Usman ʿdan Fodio*.

yawm al-dīn (Arab.: "day of religion"). The Day of Judgment, also called the "Day of Resurrection" (see *yawm ad-qiyāma*), and is believed as having a specific apocalyptic imagery. See also *al-maḥshar* and *al-sarāt*.

zabaya (Hausa: "female singer"). As social term, it is used to refer to woman of a socially low status who makes a living by singing at religious occasions that mark major life cycle events. See also *wa'ka*.

zakāt (Arab.: "alms" or "tax" also "purification," from the verb *zaka*: "to thrive" or "to be pure"). Alms giving is one of the five pillars (see *arkān al-dīn*) and one of the major duties for Muslims, implying a form of taxation on one's personal property and giving up a portion of one's wealth (see *khums* and *ʿushr*). As a practice of charity, almsgiving is for Muslims as purification for the remaining property (see *farā'iḍ*). It can also refer to charitable giving or an endowment (see *awqāf*). Almsgiving as a religious duty is distinct from voluntarily alms (see *ṣadaqa*). See also *bayt al-māl*. (Other transliterations include *zakah*.)

zakāt al-fitr (Arab.: "almsgiving of fast breaking"). Name for the alms given on the breaking of the fast (see *iftar*) or payment to the needy at the feast of breaking the fast (see *ʿid al-fitr*) at the end of the fasting period during Ramaḍān (see *ṣawm*). See also *zakāt*.

zār Type of female spirit possession dance increasing the health and strength of its devotees through trance. Despite its supposedly pagan origins, Muslim women practice this form of spirit possession originating in central Ethiopia during the eighteenth century, later spreading throughout East and North Africa, particularly in Egypt and Sudan.

zikir (Turk.: "mention" or "remembrance"). See *dhikr*.

zikr (Arab.: "remembrance"). See *dhikr*.

zīna (Arab.: "adultery" or "extramarital sex"). Adultery and any extramarital sexual relation as one of the greatest sins (see *ithm*, sing.) in Islām is absolutely prohibited and considered an unlawful crime (see *mu'amalāt*) according to the Islamic law (see *sharīʿa*) with quite different measures of punishment. In addition to the punishments rendered before death, sinners receive severe punishment after death, unless purging their sins by appropriate punishments (see *yawm al-qiyāma*).

ziyāra (Arab.: "visit"). Visit of the tomb of Prophet Muḥammad and other mosques and holy places in Medina and referring to the visit to and worship at the tombs of Sufi saints (see *walī*) or Shī'a imāms (see *shaykh*). Used also in the context of the pilgrimage to the sites or tombs of Sufi saints often in conjunction with the practice of veneration and personal prayers (see *du'ā'*) in search of blessing (see *baraka*), particularly in times of festive ceremonies performed at the saint's anniversary (see *mawlid*). See also *ḥajj*, *ṣūfī*, *ṭawāf*, and *'umra*. (Other transliterations include *ziyaret*.)

al-zuhr (Arab.: "noon"). Noonday ritual prayer (*ṣalāh al-ẓuhr*) consisting of four cycles (see *rak'a*, sing.) performed in the midst of the day when the shadow of a stick vertical in the ground reaches its shortest length. See also *ṣalāt*.

Index

'ilm 59
'ilm al-'umran 300
'ilm al-tajwīd 115, 166
ilmihal 146, 152
iltizam 182
imām 196, 209, 248, 253, 333
īmān 124, 126, 144, 152–3, *see also* mu'min
īmāni 162, *see also* īmān
imperialism 52, 54, 59, 72, 286, 311–15, *see also* colonialism *and* hegemony
incommensurability 68, *see also* dichotomy
index 16, 112, *see also* indexical
indexical / indexicality 70, 152, 231, 240, *see also* linguistics *and* index
indigenous people 72, 99–100, 192–3, 201, 280, 298, 300–2, 332, 336–7
industrialism 70, 104, 106, 195, 202, 232–3, 319, *see also* capitalism
informant 3–4, 7–8, 94, 208, 236, 238, 247–51, 263, 271, 285, 312, 328, 333–4, *see also* interlocutor
infrastructure 147, 201, 208, *see also* production, political economy *and* superstructure
inheritance 51, 287, 298, *see also* descent
insider 4–5, 9, 14, 112, 269–70, 303–8, *see also* informant *and* interlocutor
institution 6, 14, 17, 43, 53–4, 67, 70, 78–9, 83, 90–1, 104, 123, 129, 142, 144–6, 154, 246–9, 252–3, 260, 270, 280–2, 284–5, 294, 312, 315, 320, 328, 336
intentionality 122–3, 127, 131–4, 136, 318
interaction 7, 11, 78, 84, 87, 112, 23, 280, 286, 289, 296, 320, 336
interlocutor 112, 143, 145–7, 152, 314, *see also* informant *and* insider
intermarriage 192, *see also* marriage
interpretation 3, 4, 6, 8, 10–12, 45, 52–4, 59, 66, 77–80, 82, 83, 85–9, 127, 128, 144, 151–4, 166, 179, 183, 193, 204, 216, 219, 226, 258–61, 270, 271, 284, 300, 310, 311, 314, 317–20, 332, 336
interpretive anthropology 65, 335
intersubjectivity 78–9, 81, *see also* interaction
intrinsic 69, 71–2, 96, 105–6, 151, 224–9, *see also* a priori *and* essentialism
Irshadi 59
Ismā'īl 15
isrāf 165

jargon 182, 288
Javanese 69, 73, 219, 226
Jibrīl 166
jihād 202, 260, 287
jihadist 202, *see also* jihād
jumūd 193
juta 238
juz' 166

k'anzu 161–2, 168
Kaba 200
Kang, Yu-Wei 54
kara 166, *see also* spara
kaum muda 192, 219, *see also* khana mai
kaum tua 219, *see also* khana kau
Keddie, Nikki 104
kenduri 220–3
Khaldun, Ibn 98, 279, 286, 300–1, 324, 334
khalīfa 61, *see also* caliph
khana kau 193–6, *see also* kaum tua
khana mai 193–5, *see also* maum muda
khashya 124, 132–3
khatam 234–6, 239–40
khatam quran / khatme quran 233–9
khatib 105
Al-Khayyat, Abdul-Aziz 260–2, 264
khilāfa 299, *see also* caliphate
Khomeini, Ayatollah 56, 294
Khuda 237
Khudr 60
khushū' 124, 133–4
khuṭba 262
kiamat 221
kijaji 73
kikah 221
kinship 2, 53, 200, 203, 205, 284, 297, 300, 303, 328, *see also* descent *and* marriage
kıyam 148
kiyāma 221
kofia 161
Komachi 331
Koran 68, 73, 166, 209, 233–9, 298, 300–1, 303–4, *see also* Qur'ān
korbani 239, *see also* qurbān
Kramer, Martin 324
Kuhn, Thomas 296
Kulsiriswasd, Direk 193

labor 8, 16, 114, 194, 207, 282, 337, *see also* production
Lach, Donald 310
Laidlaw, James 150–1
Lambek, Michael 144–5, 175, 328
lamma 175
Lane, Edward 331
Laroui, Abdallah 54, 57
Launay, Robert 328
law 51–2, 54–5, 59, 71, 97, 99, 103, 178, 215, 246, 248, 250, 252, 262, 281, 327, *see also* legislation
Lawrence, T.E. 283
laylat al-qadr 161, 176–7
legislation 194, *see also* law
legitimacy 54, 72, 83, 201, 205, 216, 226, *see also* authority
legitimation 44, 202, *see also* authority
Lévi-Strauss, Claude 285, 311, 335
Lewis, Bernard 96, 103, 324
Lewis, Ioan M. 327